PROPAGANDA IN AUTOCRACIES

A dictator's power is secure, the authors begin in this muscular, impressive study, only as long as citizens believe in it. When citizens suddenly believe otherwise, a dictator's power is anything but, as the Soviet Union's collapse revealed. This conviction – that power rests ultimately on citizens' beliefs – compels the world's autocrats to invest in sophisticated propaganda. This study draws on the first global data set of autocratic propaganda, encompassing nearly eight million newspaper articles from fifty-nine countries in six languages.

The authors document dramatic variation in propaganda across autocracies: in coverage of the regime and its opponents, in narratives about domestic and international life, in the threats of violence issued to citizens, and in the domestic events that shape it. The book explains why Russian President Vladimir Putin uses Donald Trump as a propaganda tool and why Chinese state propaganda is more effusive than any point since the Cultural Revolution.

Erin Baggott Carter is an assistant professor in the Department of Political Science and International Relations at the University of Southern California, a Hoover fellow at Stanford University's Hoover Institution, and a nonresident scholar at University of California San Diego's 21st Century China Center. Her work has been published in the *British Journal of Political Science*, *Journal of Conflict Resolution*, *Security Studies*, *Foreign Affairs*, and *International Interactions*, and has been featured in *The New York Times*, *Washington Post*, and the *Little Red Podcast*, among others.

Brett L. Carter is an assistant professor in the Department of Political Science and International Relations at the University of Southern California and a Hoover Fellow at Stanford University's Hoover Institution. His work has appeared in the *Journal of Politics*, *British Journal of Political Science*, *Journal of Conflict Resolution*, *Security Studies*, *Journal of Democracy*, and *Foreign Affairs*, and has been featured in *The New York Times* and NPR's *Radiolab*, among others.

T0370942

POLITICAL ECONOMY OF INSTITUTIONS AND DECISIONS

Series Editors

Jeffry Frieden, *Harvard University*
John Patty, *Emory University*
Elizabeth Maggie Penn, *Emory University*

Founding Editors

James E. Alt, *Harvard University*
Douglass C. North, *Washington University of St. Louis*

Other books in the series

Continued on page following index

PROPAGANDA IN AUTOCRACIES

Institutions, Information, and the Politics of Belief

ERIN BAGGOTT CARTER

University of Southern California
Hoover Institution, Stanford University

BRETT L. CARTER

University of Southern California
Hoover Institution, Stanford University

CAMBRIDGE
UNIVERSITY PRESS

Shaftesbury Road, Cambridge CB2 8EA, United Kingdom

One Liberty Plaza, 20th Floor, New York, NY 10006, USA

477 Williamstown Road, Port Melbourne, VIC 3207, Australia

314–321, 3rd Floor, Plot 3, Splendor Forum, Jasola District Centre, New Delhi – 110025, India

103 Penang Road, #05–06/07, Visioncrest Commercial, Singapore 238467

Cambridge University Press is part of Cambridge University Press & Assessment, a department of the University of Cambridge.

We share the University's mission to contribute to society through the pursuit of education, learning and research at the highest international levels of excellence.

www.cambridge.org
Information on this title: www.cambridge.org/9781009271240

DOI: 10.1017/9781009271226

First published 2023

A catalogue record for this publication is available from the British Library.

Library of Congress Cataloging-in-Publication Data
NAMES: Carter, Erin Baggott, 1986– author. | Carter, Brett L., 1979– author.
TITLE: Propaganda in autocracies : institutions, information, and the politics of belief / Erin Baggott Carter, Brett L. Carter.
DESCRIPTION: Cambridge ; New York, NY : Cambridge University Press, 2023. | Series: Political economy of institutions and decisions | Includes bibliographical references and index.
IDENTIFIERS: LCCN 2022028943 | ISBN 9781009271240 (hardback) | ISBN 9781009271226 (ebook)
SUBJECTS: LCSH: Propaganda | Dictatorship. | Press and propaganda | Press and politics
CLASSIFICATION: LCC JF1525.P8 C37 2023 |
DDC 303.3/75–dc23/eng/20221108
LC record available at https://lccn.loc.gov/2022028943

ISBN 978-1-009-27124-0 Hardback
ISBN 978-1-009-27123-3 Paperback

For Fiona.
We love you more than we can express.

Propaganda becomes ineffective the moment we are aware of it.

— Joseph Goebbels

The struggle of man against power is the struggle of memory against forgetting.

— Milan Kundera

Contents

ix

Contents

Contents

Figures

Tables

Acknowledgments

We are profoundly grateful to so many friends and colleagues and mentors. It is a pleasure to acknowledge them here.

This book began over a series of conversations at Stanford, when Erin was a predoctoral fellow at the Center for International Security and Cooperation (CISAC) and Brett was a postdoctoral fellow at the Center on Democracy, Development and the Rule of Law (CDDRL). For scholars working at the intersection of social science and public policy, there is no place quite like it. Our mentors and colleagues soon became friends, and our debts to them cannot possibly be overstated: Larry Diamond, Lynn Eden, Marcel Fafchamps, Jim Fearon, Frank Fukuyama, Erik Jensen, Mike McFaul, Scott Sagan, Steve Stedman, Kathryn Stoner, and Amy Zegart. We were also fortunate to meet and befriend so many extraordinary young scholars, who provided some combination of insightful comments and warm encouragement: Mike Albertus, Dan Altman, Katherine Bersch, Julia Choucair Vizoso, Kate Cronin-Furman, Shelby Grossman, Morgan Kaplan, Shiri Krebs, Didi Kuo, Melissa Lee, Dan Mattingly, Dinsha Mistree, Ken Opalo, Terry Peterson, Hesham Sallam, Nina Silove, Will Spaniel, Kharis Templeman, and Lauren Young.

Though begun at Stanford, this book was written at the University of Southern California (USC). We cannot imagine more supportive or helpful faculty mentors. Gerry Munck read the full manuscript on several occasions, and each time devoted hours to helping us improve it. His contributions appear throughout. Carol Wise was a constant source of encouragement, feedback, wise counsel, and close friendship. Our debts to them are enormous. So many other colleagues provided good cheer and helpful feedback, on this project and others: Pablo Barberá, Jeb Barnes, Laurie Brand, Ann Crigler, Rob English, Ben Graham, Christian Grose, Fayez Hammad, Allison Hartnett, Jacques Hymans,

Jane Junn, Dave Kang, Saori Katada, Steve Lamy, James Lo, Jonathan Markowitz, Alison Renteln, Stan Rosen, Bryn Rosenfeld, Wayne Sandholtz, Stephanie Schwartz, Jeff Sellers, Audrye Wong, and Sherry Zaks. Our thanks also to the administrative and support staff, who do so much for the community: Cathy Ballard, Cort Brinkerhoff, Chandra Caldwell, Yue Hou, Linda Cole, and Matt Stevens.

The Center for International Studies at USC hosted a manuscript review conference, at which Jim Fearon and Haifeng Huang gave generously of their scarce time and immense talent. On the morning after the conference, Jim spent several hours fielding our follow-up questions. The book is immeasurably better for their feedback.

We presented portions of this project at a number of venues: successive New Directions in Analyzing Text as Data conferences, the Southern California Methods Conference, the Politics and Computational Social Science Conference, mini-conferences on autocratic politics at the Western and Southern Political Science Association meetings, the European University Institute, Harvard University, New York University, Princeton University, Stanford University, the University of California at San Diego, and Yale University, surely among others. So many colleagues made this book better: Consuelo Amat, Quintin Beazer, Graeme Blair, Carles Boix, Sam Bonilla Bogaert, Gretchen Casper, Andrew Coe, Lei Guang, John Kennedy, Holger Kern, Nathalie Letsa, Alex Yu-Ting Lin, Anthony Little, Peter Lorentzen, Paasha Mahdvi, Anne Meng, Monika Nalepa, Rich Nielsen, Jack Paine, John Reuter, Molly Roberts, Michael Rochlitz, Arturas Rozenas, Victor Shih, Dave Siegel, David Szakonyi, Rory Truex, Josh Tucker, Anne Van Wijk, Josef Woldense, and Maiting Zhuang.

We finished the book as Hoover Fellows at Stanford's Hoover Institution, which has proven to be as idyllic as our time at CISAC and CDDRL. Our return to Stanford has been happy and rewarding, due, again, to colleagues and friends and mentors: Misha Auslin, Michael Bernstam, Peter Blair, Val Bolotnyy, Kathy Campitelli, Adi Dasgupta, Steve Davis, Joe Felter, Paul Gregory, Justin Grimmer, Anna Grzymala-Busse, Matt Loewenstein, Oriana Mastro, Jim Mattis, H. R. McMaster, Jean Oi, Rebecca Perlman, Allison Post, Condoleezza Rice, Jackie Schneider, Glenn Tiffert, Yiqing Xu, and Andrew Walder, in addition to those above.

This book was made possible by a small army of research assistants at USC's Lab on Non-Democratic Politics: Anbar Aizenman, Yining Bei, Kayla Caldwell, Connor Chapkis, Caroline Chen, Bryant Cong, Hanna Fasholtz, Nitika Johri, Yash Kamath, Brian Kerrigan, Young-Kyung

Kim, Megan Lee, Jeff Levine, Claire Liu, Katherine McDowell, Kathleen Morris, Mohini Narasimhan, Tolulope Ogunremi, Lisa de Rafols, Abhiram Reddy, Maryalice Rosa, Tarek Roshdy, Alanna Schenk, Sama Shah, Joshua Shaw, Ciara Taylor, Leia Wang, and Kathleen Xue. They read thousands of propaganda articles in various languages, investigated the media environments of countries around the world, and caught numerous errors of grammar and syntax. We owe special debts to Megan Angulo, Eva Isakovic, and Hector Reyes, who managed this team and so much else besides. They will all do extraordinary things.

This book was also made possible by generous financial support. For Erin: the Chiang Ching-Kuo Foundation, Harvard's Institute for Quantitative Social Science and Weatherhead Center for International Affairs, Smith Richardson Foundation, and USC Center for International Studies. For Brett: the Chiang Ching-Kuo Foundation, Guggenheim Foundation, Harvard Academy for International and Area Studies, Institute for Quantitative Social Science, National Science Foundation, Smith Richardson Foundation, Social Science Research Council, United States Institute of Peace, USC Center for International Studies, and Weatherhead Center for International Affairs.

Several scholars generously shared data they worked hard to collect: Manfred Elfstrom, Erica Frantz, King-wa Fu, Barbara Geddes, and Joseph Wright.

This book began after we left the Harvard Government Department, but the imprints of our dissertation advisors are everywhere. We hope it makes them proud. We cannot imagine more supportive or incisive dissertation committees. For Erin: Iain Johnston, Beth Simmons, and Arthur Spirling. For Brett: Bob Bates, Steve Levitsky, and Jim Robinson. They remain models for us in so many ways. We are equally grateful to mentors in the years before grad school. For Erin: Michael Kremer and Yu Feng. For Brett: Carles Boix, Jim Hentz, and Duncan Snidal.

It was a privilege to work with Robert Dreesen at Cambridge University Press: for his early belief in the project and his support throughout the review and publication process. The editors of the Political Economy of Institutions and Decisions series – Jeff Frieden, John Patty, and Maggie Penn – provided an exceptionally helpful review memo that focused our efforts for the final submission. Our thanks also to two anonymous reviewers, who sharpened the book in so many ways. Erika Walsh provided expert editorial assistance.

Acknowledgments

Our families have sacrificed so much for us. We are enormously grateful for their support throughout this process and in the many years before. Our daughter, Fiona, arrived just before the book was finished. This book is dedicated to her.

PART I

Foundations

I

Persuasion and Domination

1.1 STRATEGIES OF PROPAGANDA IN AUTOCRACIES

"As long as people think that the dictator's power is secure," Tullock (2001, 144) wrote, "it is secure." When citizens think otherwise, all at once, a dictator's power is anything but, as Kuran (1989, 1991, 1997) and Lohmann (1993) observed as the Soviet Union collapsed. This conviction – that power rests on citizens believing in it – has long compelled the world's autocrats to invest in sophisticated propaganda apparatuses. This book draws on the first global dataset of autocratic propaganda, encompassing over 8 million newspaper articles from fifty-nine countries in six languages. We document dramatic variation in propaganda across autocracies: in coverage of the regime and the opposition, in narratives about domestic and international life, in the threats of violence issued to citizens, and in the domestic events that shape it. We also show that propaganda discourages popular protests.

Why does propaganda vary so dramatically across autocracies? Our answer is that different autocrats employ propaganda to achieve different ends. Most autocrats now govern with nominally democratic institutions: regular elections, national parliaments, and opposition parties. Some autocrats are more constrained by these institutions than others, perhaps because their recourse to repression is limited by international pressure or because they confront domestic institutions or pressure groups that bind them. Where these electoral constraints are relatively binding, autocrats must curry some amount of popular support, and so they employ propaganda to persuade citizens of regime merits. To be persuasive, however, propaganda apparatuses must cultivate the appearance of neutrality, which requires conceding bad news and policy failures. Where electoral constraints are binding, we find, propaganda apparatuses cover the regime much like Fox News covers Republicans.

3

Where autocrats confront no electoral constraints – where autocrats can fully secure themselves with repression – propaganda serves not to persuade citizens but to dominate them. Propaganda derives its power from absurdity. By forcing citizens to consume content that everyone knows to be false, autocrats make their capacity for repression common knowledge. Propaganda apparatuses engage in effusive pro-regime coverage while pretending opposition does not exist. Narratives about a country's contemporary history are presented in absurd terms, since these absurdities give them power. Citizens are told that their countries are envied around the world, that "democracy" is alive and vibrant, and that the dictator is a champion of national sports. Propaganda apparatuses routinely and explicitly threaten citizens with repression.

Many scholars regard nominally democratic institutions as forces for stability and regime survival as secured through patronage and repression. Our approach is different. We view nominally democratic institutions as constraints that autocrats attempt to loosen and citizens' beliefs as the battlefield on which the struggle for political change is waged. Our focus on citizens' beliefs accords with how scholars understood autocratic survival for much of the twentieth century. Autocrats wage the battle for citizens' beliefs with a range of tools, propaganda chief among them. Most broadly, we show that even weak electoral constraints force autocrats to wage this battle from a position of weakness. To persuade citizens of regime merits, electorally constrained autocrats must acknowledge policy failures that risk affirming citizens' frustrations and facilitating collective action.

We draw from several disciplines to illustrate how this occurs. Our theory is informed by field research in China and Central Africa, and aided by the tools of game theory. We use computational tools to collect and measure propaganda, statistical and network techniques to analyze it, survey experiments to probe its effects on those who consume it, and case studies to bring it to life. Many of these case studies are of historical importance. We explain why Russian president Vladimir Putin's propaganda apparatus uses Donald Trump as a propaganda tool, why the Chinese Communist Party's (CCP) flagship propaganda newspaper is more effusive than at any point since the Cultural Revolution, why Tunisian president Zine El Abidine Ben Ali publicized his regime's failures before becoming the Arab Spring's first casualty, and why Cameroonian president Paul Biya produces different propaganda in English and French.

Two autocracies are emblematic of the propaganda strategies we document: the People's Republic of China and the Republic of Congo. China is among the few autocracies that does not organize national elections. Congo, though a leading oil exporter, is so afflicted with high-level corruption that it routinely seeks debt relief from Western creditors, which require regular elections in return. Their propaganda strategies, we learned during years of field research, look dramatically different to readers. The CCP aims to dominate citizens; Denis Sassou Nguesso, who has ruled Congo for all but five years since 1979, must persuade them.

1.1.1 Propaganda as Persuasion: The Republic of Congo

Sassou Nguesso is among the world's most corrupt autocrats. As of 2012, in France alone, Sassou Nguesso owned more than 30 properties, 112 bank accounts, and a fleet of luxury vehicles. In 2016, a Canadian court ruled that the Sassou Nguesso family was "a criminal organization." Sassou Nguesso has so badly mismanaged the economy that in 2017, just six years after it received debt relief from the IMF and World Bank, the government's debt/GDP ratio reached 130 percent.

Congolese citizens are aware of Sassou Nguesso's corruption, and many loathe him for it. Yet they also read his propaganda newspaper, *Les Dépêches de Brazzaville*, or "Dispatches from Brazzaville." To be sure, *Les Dépêches* is Congo's easiest newspaper to access. It is printed daily, subsidized by the government to keep its purchase price low, and printed in color. In each of these respects, *Les Dépêches* is more attractive than its competitors. *La Semaine Africaine* has long been regarded as Congo's *vieille dame*: its "gray lady," a reference to *The New York Times*. Founded as a church newsletter in the 1950s, *La Semaine Africaine* became Congo's newspaper of record during the democratic transition of the early 1990s. It now publishes twice weekly and, although its journalists self-censor, it remains independent. Many other independent newspapers dot newsstands, some more critical of the government and routinely punished for it.[1]

Why do citizens who loathe Sassou Nguesso consume his propaganda? The answer is not uncertainty about its ownership. Although *Les Dépêches* is neither state-run nor legally affiliated with Sassou Nguesso's *Parti Congolais du Travail* (PCT), there is no doubt it is Sassou Nguesso's mouthpiece. The answer is also not that citizens have no other

---

[1] Carter (2022).

options. Citizens are not forced to purchase *Les Dépêches* and boycott *La Semaine Africaine*. Having moderated its editorial line, *La Semaine Africaine* is now regarded as an "acceptable" independent newspaper. Perhaps as a result, it has also attracted enough consumers to remain in print.

The answer, many citizens say, is that *Les Dépêches* publishes a substantial amount of legitimate news, which they want to read. It is, indeed, a professionally run media organization. It recruits top students from Congo's flagship university, who are lured by salaries substantially higher than its competitors. It has foreign bureaus in Kinshasa and Paris. It prints a daily Kinshasa edition and is sold at several Paris newsstands. Its French editor, Jean-Paul Pigasse, was previously a senior figure at several widely respected French publications, including *Les Echos*, *L'Express*, and *Jeune Afrique*, before he was lured to Brazzaville. Pigasse is reportedly part of Sassou Nguesso's money laundering operation.[2]

The journalistic integrity of Sassou Nguesso's propaganda apparatus should not be overstated. It exists to advance Sassou Nguesso's interests. Its coverage is consistently if subtly skewed in his favor. Sassou Nguesso figures prominently in the account of Congo's history that *Les Dépêches* narrates for readers. The newspaper publishes roughly thirty-five articles per day, distributed across topics that readers of *The New York Times* would find familiar: current affairs, finance, sports, culture, and classified ads. Each day, Sassou Nguesso appears in about three of these articles, mostly in connection with the economy or foreign affairs. *Les Dépêches*, we show in Chapter 4, covers Sassou Nguesso about as positively as Fox News covers Republicans. His political rivals receive some coverage, but, upon reflection, a bit less. They are seldom criticized explicitly.

Citizens read Sassou Nguesso's propaganda by choice. It is skewed, but not so heavily that they refuse to consume it.

1.1.2 *Propaganda as Domination: The People's Republic of China*

Few Chinese citizens enjoy reading the *People's Daily*, although more than half report doing so regularly.[3] China's most disliked newspaper sits prominently on every newsstand. Persuaded that propaganda was "the most important job of the Red Army," Mao Zedong routinely

---

[2] Le Parisien (2002).
[3] See Chapter 4.

edited the *People's Daily* himself.[4] For citizens, reading it was "a political obligation."[5] Government offices were until recently required to subscribe. The *People's Daily* is the CCP's flagship newspaper and its content frequently appears in other platforms, since all Chinese media outlets are majority owned by the state. Journalists are required to pass ideological exams and, later, attend the Propaganda Department's "refresher courses."[6] Most journalists are Party members. Non-members are forbidden from covering politics.[7]

The *People's Daily* seeks not to persuade readers but to dominate them. Huang (2015*b*, 420) put it succinctly: "Such propaganda is not meant to 'brainwash' people with its specific content about how good the government is, but rather to forewarn the society about how strong it is via the act of propaganda itself." Its effusively pro-regime content, as well the threats it occasionally issues to citizens, make this clear. On April 26, 1989, the *People's Daily* published a now infamous editorial: "We Must Take a Clear-cut Stand against Disturbances." The editorial condemned the student protests in Tiananmen Square, and newspapers across the country were required to place it on their front pages. An "extremely small number of people with ulterior motives" had taken advantage of the students, who were engaged in a "conspiracy" to "plunge the whole country into chaos." It concluded with a warning:

If we are tolerant of or conniving with this disturbance and let it go unchecked, a seriously chaotic state will appear. ... Our country will have no peaceful days if this disturbance is not checked resolutely.'[8]

The massacre came on June 4, when the People's Liberation Army (PLA) killed roughly 2,000 citizens, with estimates ranging from several hundred to several thousand.[9] "Stability overrides everything," Deng Xiaoping announced in the massacre's aftermath and again, in a front page editorial, on its one year anniversary.[10] Several *People's Daily* reporters joined the Tiananmen protests, with signs that read: "We don't want to lie anymore." They were purged.[11] Although open discussion

[4] Mao Zedong (1929).
[5] Yu (1964, 97).
[6] Brady (2008, 81).
[7] Brady (2008, 116).
[8] English translation available at http://tsquare.tv/chronology/April26ed.html.
[9] Human Rights Watch (2010), Buckley (2019), Lusher (2017).
[10] People's Daily (1990).
[11] Bell (2014).

of Tiananmen is forbidden in the press, the CCP now reminds China's urban class each June 4 of its brutal campaign of repression against ethnic Uyghurs in Xinjiang region.[12]

The CCP is quite clear about its propaganda objectives. In 2013, journalist Gao Yu leaked an internal Party directive, known as Document 9, that described China's "ideological situation" as "a complicated, intense struggle." Media must be "infused" with the "spirit of the Party" and "promote the unification of thought." The Party must "allow absolutely no opportunity for incorrect thinking to spread."[13] Though Gao was sentenced to seven years in prison, CCP officials occasionally say the same thing. In 2009, Jiangxi party secretary Su Rong told journalists that "stability is our principle task." "Particularly in the case of sudden-breaking news and mass incidents" – protests, that is – "we must get in faster, forestalling our opponents by a show of strength."[14] In 2010, the Propaganda Department simply banned bad news from the front pages of newspapers.[15] Consequently, as exiled novelist Ma Jian put it, Chinese propaganda is "filled with absurdities."[16] In 2017, the *People's Daily* claimed that Xi Jinping's contributions to Chinese diplomacy had "transcended 300 years of Western theory on foreign affairs." Not to be outdone, one state-run television network ran a six episode series on Xi's "Major Country Diplomacy." "Wherever he goes," announced one episode, "Xi Jinping sets off a whirlwind of charisma!"[17]

The *People's Daily* does obvious violence to the truth and hence to the lived experiences of Chinese citizens. For this, many loathe it, as its various and vulgar sobriquets make clear.[18] The newspaper is routinely called *Riren Minbao*, or "Raping People Daily," a phonetic play on *Renmin Ribao*.[19] Journalism professor turned dissident Jiao Guobiao likened the propaganda apparatus to "a street bully that nobody dares to tell to

---

[12] See Chapter 9.
[13] ChinaFile (2013).
[14] Bandurski (2009).
[15] New York Times (2010).
[16] Ma (2018).
[17] Phillips (2017).
[18] See, for example, Abad-Santos (2013). One ditty goes: "All conferences solemnly started and ended with glory // All speeches are important and the applause is warm // All the work is finished with success and all the achievements are tremendous // All the effort is thorough and remarkable" (Miao 2011, 105–107).
[19] 人民日报 and 日人民报, respectively. See http://chinadigitaltimes.net/space/日人民报.

stop." Far from persuading, CCP propaganda is "the worst eroder of popular opinion about the government and the party."[20]

The CCP's flagship propaganda bears virtually no resemblance to Sassou Nguesso's: in its stridency, its use of absurd narratives, and the extent to which it threatens citizens.[21]

1.2 ANTECEDENTS, EMPIRICAL AND THEORETICAL

These two propaganda strategies – persuasion and domination – appear to be at odds. For one, propaganda is powerful when subtle: when citizens are largely unaware of how they are being manipulated. For the other, propaganda derives its power from absurdity: from forcing citizens to consume information they know to be false and to do so publicly. However inconsistent they are, these two propaganda strategies also have deep historical origins. Scholars and practitioners have long sought to understand the principles that make each strategy effective.

1.2.1 *Propaganda as Persuasion: Joseph Goebbels, Bayesian*

"Propaganda," Joseph Goebbels wrote, "becomes ineffective the moment we are aware of it."[22] This conviction permeated his work atop the Nazi propaganda apparatus.[23] Since broadcasting exclusively positive news would "fairly compel the German public to listen to foreign and enemy broadcasts," Goebbels instructed state media to report bad news and policy failures. Goebbels insisted on truth, "otherwise the enemy or the facts might expose falsehoods." He routinely employed "black propaganda": "word of mouth" campaigns waged by "faithful citizens, which were successful as long as the citizens targeted by these campaigns were unaware of them."[24] Harold Lasswell (1938, 110, 203), who pioneered

---

[20] Jiao (2004).

[21] As we discuss in Chapter 4, there is substantial evidence that the CCP government permits local newspapers to occasionally criticize local governments. Stockmann (2013); Lorentzen (2014), and Repnikova (2017b) suggest that this enables Beijing to monitor local officials or to otherwise gauge public opinion. We distinguish between local newspapers and the *People's Daily*, the CCP's flagship newspaper, which, our evidence suggests, serves to signal the CCP's strength rather than monitor local officials.

[22] Taylor (1998); Cunningham (2002).

[23] Longerich (2015).

[24] For a distillation of Goebbels' 6,800 page diary into nineteen core principles, see Doob (1950).

the study of propaganda in the American academy, endorsed a similar approach to wartime propaganda: "Reveal losses when they come. ... It is ridiculous to pretend that the enemy never wins a point."

Propagandists have long imputed Bayesian rationality to their audiences and tailored their propaganda accordingly.[25] To recruit soldiers for the First Crusade, in 1065 Pope Urban II implored Christians to "wrest that land from the wicked race, and subject it to yourselves." He planted individuals in the audience to cry out "God wills it!" during the speech.[26] Otto von Bismarck employed a dedicated propaganda secretary, whose work Bismarck reviewed to ensure its style and syntax would resonate with its intended audience.[27] To build support in London, Napoleon Bonaparte quietly founded the *Argus* newspaper, which was fronted by an Englishman but surreptitiously produced by the French Foreign Office. Erich Ludendorff, a German general during World War I, wrote that good propaganda must "mold public opinion without appearing to do so."[28] Ludendorff's foes across the English Channel agreed. According to one British propagandist: "The art of propaganda is not telling lies, but selecting the truth you require and giving it mixed up with some truths the audience wants to hear."[29] Scholars in the mid-twentieth century were so impressed by the ability of propagandists to strategize with the tools of Bayesian rationality that they sought to explain why their contemporaries were so susceptible to manipulation.[30]

Much contemporary scholarship on autocratic propaganda is motivated by Goebbels' core insight: To persuade citizens of the regime's merits, propaganda must occasionally concede the regime's failings. Formal theorists have led this research agenda.[31] By mixing factual reporting with useful fictions, propaganda apparatuses can acquire a

---

[25] We use the term "Bayesian rationality" to refer to the idea that citizens will discount positive propaganda or political communication by how credible they view the messenger and how consistent it is with their past experiences. More generally, social scientists regard citizens as Bayesian if they update their beliefs in response to the information they consume.

[26] Thomson (1999); Jowett and O'Donnell (2012).

[27] Lasswell (1938).

[28] Quoted in Lasswell (1938).

[29] Siebert, Peterson, and Schramm (1955, 83).

[30] Ellul (1973).

[31] For useful literature reviews, see Groeling (2013); Gentzkow, Shapiro, and Stone (2014); Strömberg (2015); and Prat (2015).

reputation for credibility, and hence the capacity to shape citizens' beliefs.[32] If citizens are not completely rational, the scope for propaganda to manipulate their beliefs is more profound. Citizens may underestimate the biases in media content,[33] be constrained by memory limitations,[34] or double count repeated information.[35]

It is unclear whether Jean-Paul Pigasse, the architect of Denis Sassou Nguesso's propaganda apparatus, has read Goebbels' diaries. He has probably not studied the formal models of modern political science. But their approaches to propaganda are identical.

1.2.2 Propaganda as Domination: Hannah Arendt goes to China

China's *People's Daily* would be puzzling to Goebbels, and it is puzzling in the context of formal theories of persuasion. However, it would be deeply familiar to students of totalitarianism. For Hannah Arendt, propaganda in totalitarian dictatorships served to force citizens to submit to the regime's historical narrative, despite what they knew to be true.[36] As Levy (2016) put it:

> The great analysts of truth and speech under totalitarianism – George Orwell, Hannah Arendt, Vaclav Havel – can help us recognize this kind of lie for what it is. ... Saying something obviously untrue, and making your subordinates repeat it with a straight face in their own voice, is a particularly startling display of power over them. It's something that was endemic to totalitarianism. ... Being made to repeat an obvious lie makes it clear that you're powerless; it also makes you complicit.

Authoritarian regimes display this form of power in a range of ways. In North Korea, households must keep radios tuned to the state-run radio station. They can be turned down, but never off.[37] Independent media were illegal in the Soviet Union, as in contemporary China. In the 1930s, all Soviet cities had loudspeakers on the streets, which broadcast propaganda. Every day started with the national anthem and ended with it. The Soviet government outlawed radios that could access independent

---

[32] Gentzkow and Shapiro (2006); Gehlbach and Sonin (2014); Yu (2021).
[33] Cain, Loewenstein, and Moore (2005); Eyster and Rabin (2010).
[34] Mullainathan, Schwartzstein, and Shleifer (2008).
[35] DeMarzo, Vayanos, and Zwiebel (2003).
[36] Arendt (1951).
[37] Chun (2008).

stations and photocopiers that could print anti-regime pamphlets.[38] This domination gave rise to some of the twentieth century's most enduring literature. The "struggle of man against power," Czech novelist Milan Kundera wrote, is "the struggle of memory against forgetting." For Kundera, resistance is the individual's effort to insist on what she knows to be true in the face of an informational environment that claims otherwise. As Václav Havel and Milan Kundera recede from the spotlight, a new generation of Chinese luminaries – Yan Lianke, Ma Jian, and Ai Weiwei chief among them – is reminding the world about the struggle of memory against forgetting.

Arendt's insights helped contemporary scholars make sense of the twentieth century's most repressive dictatorships. In Hafez al-Assad's Syria, Wedeen (1999, 73) writes, "power manifests itself in the regime's ability to impose its fictions upon the world. No one is deceived by the charade, but everyone ... is forced to participate in it." Syrian citizens were not required to believe the "mystifications" the regime put forth. Rather, they were required to act *as if* they did. In so doing, Wedeen quotes Václav Havel approvingly, they live "within the lie." They "confirm the system, fulfill the system, make the system, *are* the system."[39] Wedeen continues:

By [saying something manifestly spurious], each [citizen] demonstrates the regime's power to dominate him. The [citizen] comes to know about himself, and about others, that each can be made to subordinate to state authority not only his body, but also his imagination.

Wedeen's account of Assad's Syria echoes Richard Rorty's study of George Orwell's 1984: "The only point in making Winston believe that two and two equals five is to break him."[40]

Huang's (2015*b*; 2018) work on Chinese propaganda should be understood in this context. As in Arendt's Soviet Union, Kundera's Czechoslovakia, Orwell's 1984, and Wedeen's Syria, CCP propaganda is designed to signal to citizens, not persuade them:

By being able to afford significant resources to present a unified propaganda message and impose it on citizens, a government that has a strong capacity in maintaining social control and political order can send a credible signal about

---

[38] Soldatov and Borogan (2015, 11–12).
[39] Havel (1978).
[40] Orwell (1949); Rorty (1989).

this capacity and distinguish itself from a weak government, hence implicitly intimidating the masses who may otherwise contemplate regime change.[41]

Propaganda compels citizens to view the government as strong, Huang finds, not good. For this, as the *People's Daily*'s sobriquets make clear, many citizens loathe it. This is propaganda as domination.

1.3 OUR EXPLANATION

1.3.1 *Institutions and Uncertainty*

Why do different autocrats employ different propaganda strategies? Our theory, which we develop with the aid of a formal model in Chapter 2, rests on two foundations. First, life in autocracies is marked by widespread uncertainty. Autocratic governments disclose information selectively and restrict media freedom.[42] Journalists self-censor.[43] Citizens know that saying the wrong thing to the wrong person may lead to incarceration or worse.[44] In China, this is so common that citizens have euphemisms for it: to be "invited to tea" or to be "harmonized."[45] This fosters a culture of distrust among citizens.[46]

Second, most autocrats now govern with political institutions that look democratic from afar. There are regular elections, national parliaments, opposition parties, and a handful of independent newspapers. Figure 1.1 illustrates this.[47] Since the collapse of the Berlin Wall in 1989, given by the vertical line, roughly 80 percent of the world's autocrats have governed with nominally democratic institutions. These electoral institutions are more binding in some autocracies than others. Some autocrats can engineer so much fraud that elections are completely meaningless, as in Uzbekistan, whereas other autocrats can tilt the electoral playing field only to a degree. This variation may be driven by many factors. Some autocrats are more vulnerable to international pressure to

[41] Huang (2015*b*, 420); Shih (2008).
[42] Egorov, Guriev, and Sonin (2009); Stier (2014); Hollyer, Rosendorff, and Vreeland (2015); Whitten-Woodring and Van Belle (2015).
[43] Stier (2014); Sundaram (2016).
[44] Policzer (2009); Truex (2019); Lichter, Loëffler, and Siegloch (2021); Thomson (2022).
[45] Carter and Carter (2021*b*).
[46] Lichter, Loëffler, and Siegloch (2021).
[47] The data are drawn from Gandhi (2008) and Svolik (2012). The dashed line gives the share of all governments that are autocracies.

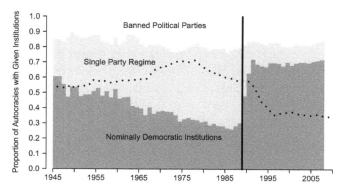

Figure 1.1 Political institutions in autocracies since 1945

respect citizens' basic rights.[48] Some autocrats may have less control over security forces[49] or key sectors of the economy.[50] Some autocrats may confront strong civil societies, which can credibly threaten protest.[51] The world's autocrats exist along a continuum, from totally unconstrained by electoral institutions, as in China or Uzbekistan, to potentially quite constrained.

1.3.2 Persuasion, Welfare, and Honest Propaganda

Our theory focuses on two sources of uncertainty. First, citizens are uncertain about the link between government policies and the outcomes around them.[52] They can observe the latter: whether incomes are rising, public schools are improving, or crime is under control. Citizens cannot, however, observe precisely what the autocrat did: whether he implemented sound policies or, instead, is incompetent or corrupt. As a result of this uncertainty, if living standards fail to improve, citizens are

[48] McFaul (2007); Levitsky and Way (2010); Hyde (2011); Donno (2013); Hyde and Marinov (2014); Escribà-Folch and Wright (2015); Carter (2016b); Carnegie and Marinov (2017); Carothers (2018).
[49] Levitsky and Way (2010); Schedler (2010b).
[50] Greene (2009, 2010); Seeberg (2017); Dasgupta (2018).
[51] Lehoucq and Molina (2002); McFaul (2002, 2005, 2007); Bunce and Wolchik (2006, 2010, 2011); Howard and Roessler (2006); Lindberg (2006); Beaulieu and Hyde (2009); Schedler (2009); Diamond (2010); Magaloni (2010); Schedler (2010a); Donno (2013); Beaulieu (2014); Hyde and Marinov (2014); Trejo (2014); Steinert-Threlkeld et al. (2015); Brancati (2016); Christensen and Garfias (2018).
[52] Egorov, Guriev, and Sonin (2009).

unsure precisely why. Although the regime may be incompetent or corrupt, it is also possible that its policies are sound, these issues are difficult and require time to resolve, and the government's policies will soon yield results. It is also possible that there was some exogenous shock, which was outside the government's control and prevented its otherwise sound policies from working.

If citizens are unhappy with the autocrat's performance, then, in the presence of regular elections, they can vote against him. This possibility leads to our theory's first use of propaganda. An autocrat can employ propaganda to persuade citizens that whatever frustrating outcomes they observe are not due to government failures and that the government is working to improve things. Here, the propaganda apparatus aims to cultivate genuine support, despite the frustrations citizens may have. To do so, however, the propaganda apparatus must have a reputation for credibility. For as long as the author of propaganda is also its chief beneficiary, citizens will be inclined to discount it, unless the propaganda apparatus has a history of providing some objective coverage. To persuade citizens of useful fictions, propaganda apparatuses must have a reputation for occasionally reporting damaging facts. This is Goebbels' core insight and a key result of formal theories of propaganda.[53] We refer to this reputation as *credibility capital* and the damaging facts required to build it as *honest propaganda*.

This is propaganda as persuasion. Denis Sassou Nguesso employs it when his propaganda apparatus covers a devastating fuel shortage, despite Congo's status as Africa's fourth leading oil producer. Russian president Vladimir Putin employs it when his television networks cover economic downturns.[54]

1.3.3 Domination, Common Knowledge, and Absurd Propaganda

Citizens may also attempt to remove an autocrat through mass protests. When autocrats can fully tilt the electoral playing field or simply refuse to hold elections, this is citizens' chief recourse. In deciding whether to protest, citizens consider a range of factors: the probability an alternative government implements better policies, the autocrat's capacity for

---

[53] Gentzkow and Shapiro (2006); Kamenica and Gentzkow (2011); Gehlbach and Sonin (2014); Yu (2021).
[54] Rozenas and Stukal (2018); Rosenfeld, Tertychnaya, and Watanabe (2018).

repression, and their compatriots' beliefs about all these.[55] Our theory focuses on the autocrat's capacity for repression. Citizens may have a sense for it, but they do not know it with certainty.[56] This constitutes citizens' second source of uncertainty.

Autocrats can signal their capacity for violence in a range of ways. They can incarcerate dissidents, block independent media, and flood the streets with police.[57] They can commit human rights abuses that the international community condemns, which broadcasts their capacity to withstand international pressure. These forms of repression aim not just to suppress dissent, but also to signal its consequences to citizens. Similarly, autocrats can employ *absurd propaganda*: content that everyone knows is false. Absurd propaganda is premised on *common knowledge of the possible*. Although citizens may not know the precise rate of economic growth or public health spending, there exist claims that citizens know are absurd, either because of direct observation or universally held conventional wisdom. This constitutes the second role of propaganda in our theory. By covering the regime in an absurdly positive way, the autocrat's propaganda apparatus signals that his capacity for violence is so unconstrained that he has no need for popular support. He has no need to persuade citizens of regime merits.

This is propaganda as domination, and its chief feature is absurdity. It was documented by Wedeen (1999) in Hafez al-Assad's Syria, by Arendt (1951) in the Soviet Union, and by Huang (2015*b*, 2018) in contemporary China. By broadcasting propaganda that everyone knows to be false, the autocrat makes his capacity for violence common knowledge.

1.3.4 *Why Electoral Constraints Matter*

This framework helps explain why different autocrats employ different propaganda strategies. Where an autocrat's limited capacity for fraud and repression constrain his ability to tilt the electoral playing field, the autocrat is forced to generate some amount of popular support to compensate. This has two effects. First, constrained autocrats must invest more in public policy. They must figure out which policies are best, invest in them, and monitor appointees who are charged with implementation. Second, constrained autocrats must persuade citizens of regime merits: in

---

[55] Little (2017).
[56] Edmond (2013); Huang (2015*b*).
[57] Truex (2019).

particular, that whatever policy failures citizens observe may not be the regime's fault. These two effects are complements. When the autocrat invests more in public policy, citizens are more willing to believe that bad news and policy failures are not the regime's doing. This requires a reputation for credibility, however. To acquire it, propaganda apparatuses must occasionally concede bad news and policy failures. Autocrats must employ a propaganda strategy that concedes damaging facts to persuade citizens of useful fictions. To be clear, these concessions are potentially costly. They help create common knowledge among citizens about the government's policy failures and may provide focal moments for unrest.[58] They also facilitate coups by regime insiders, who may decide their interests are better served by toppling the incumbent.[59]

When an autocrat's capacity for fraud and repression is so substantial that he can fully tilt the electoral playing field, his incentives are different in two ways. First, he wants citizens to know this, the better to deter protests because mass protests are always costly to repress. The violence required to suppress them may provide focal moments around which citizens can coordinate future protests.[60] The autocrat may also be prosecuted by the International Criminal Court or future governments for the atrocities his security forces commit.[61] This compels the autocrat to employ absurd propaganda as a signal: that the regime's hold on power rests not on their assent but on their submission, which is induced by the threat of violence. Second, since conceding regime failures is costly – doing so provides focal moments for coups by regime insiders and protests by frustrated citizens – the autocrat prefers not to do so. Since his electoral constraints are nonbinding, he has no incentive to concede the sorts of policy failures that are necessary to build a reputation for credibility.

Our theory generates several important comparative statics. It suggests that honest propaganda is more likely when autocrats preside over weak states, which make public goods provision relatively inefficient. It suggests that the effect of censorship on propaganda depends on the autocrat's repressive capacity. When repressive capacity is low, censorship lets the autocrat employ less honest propaganda. When repressive capacity is

[58] Egorov, Guriev, and Sonin (2009); Rozenas and Stukal (2018).
[59] Nordlinger (1977); Galetovic and Sanhueza (2000); Casper and Tyson (2014); Kim (2016).
[60] Carter and Carter (2020a).
[61] Simmons (2009); Simmons and Danner (2010); Bergsmo and Yan (2012); Meernik (2015); Jo and Simmons (2016); Dancy and Montal (2017); Jo, Radtke, and Simmons (2018).

high, censorship has no effect on propaganda, but lets the autocrat reduce public investment. It also suggests that when autocrats are vulnerable to elite threats, propaganda is more effusive.

At this book's core is a paradox. The autocrats who most need propaganda – who are forced to seek public support by the electoral institutions they confront – are most constrained in their ability to deploy it.

1.4 DATA, EMPIRICAL APPROACH, AND KEY FINDINGS

In Parts II and III of this book, we use our theory to explain the substance of propaganda across autocracies. In Part IV, we study the effect of propaganda on collective action. Table 1.1 presents a summary of our theory's observable implications by chapter. Our theory has implications for the nature of pro-regime propaganda, coverage of the regime's opponents, and the narratives that constitute the first draft of a country's history. It also has implications for what propaganda apparatuses tell citizens about the international community, the regime's engagement with it, the timing and substance of propaganda campaigns, and even coverage of ethnic minorities who want regime change.

1.4.1 A Global Dataset of Autocratic Propaganda

This book draws on the first global dataset of autocratic propaganda, which we introduce in Chapter 3. Our collection of state-run newspapers contains over 8 million articles from sixty-five newspapers in fifty-nine countries and six major languages: Arabic, Chinese, English, French, Russian, and Spanish. By population, our dataset encompasses a set of countries that represents 88 percent of all people who live under autocracy. As we discuss in Section 1.5, the early twenty-first century has changed autocratic politics in several ways, including one that made this book possible. Most autocrats make their propaganda newspapers freely available online, often with extensive historical archives. The digital analog to subsidized newsprint appears to be a freely available online archive. Propaganda, after all, is most useful when consumed.

After collecting this propaganda, we measured its content. We employed computational techniques to identify the topics of each article: the economy, public goods, electoral politics, foreign policy, international news, sports, and some two dozen others. We also measured the number of references in each article to the autocrat, ruling party, and

Table 1.1 *Our theory by chapter*

Unconstrained autocracies	Constrained autocracies
Chapter 4: The Politics of Pro-Regime Propaganda	
Absurdly positive.	Honest propaganda. Relatively neutral, concedes failures.
Chapter 5: Narrating the Domestic	
Absurdly positive economic coverage. Covers democracy as a principle. Neutral references to a general, unnamed opposition. Sports coverage includes absurd claims about regime engagement.	Concedes economic challenges but highlights efforts to address them. Covers electoral politics. Neutral references to specific opposition leaders. Sports coverage intended to attract readers.
Chapter 6: Narrating the World	
Critical coverage of comparison set countries, with sensitive topics selectively omitted. Advertises immunity from international pressure.	Critical coverage of comparison set countries, with sensitive topics selectively omitted. Partnership with international allies to advance the national interest.
Chapter 7: Threatening Citizens with Repression	
Occasional, especially around focal moments for popular protest.	Uncommon and reserved for profound crises.
Chapter 8: The Propagandist's Dilemma	
Propaganda spikes around the election, intended to discourage protest by intimidating.	Build credibility to manipulate citizen beliefs during election seasons.
Chapter 9: Memory and Forgetting	
Propaganda spikes around political focal moments, save those that recall regime crimes, which are targeted for censorship.	

political opposition. This required constructing day-level rosters for each country in our sample. For the opposition, these rosters include every candidate who competed in a national election, the senior leaders of every party that competed in a legislative election, political dissidents, political prisoners, and civil society activists. For the autocrat and ruling party, these rosters include an autocrat's various honorifics. In total, our rosters contain some 10,000 executive and opposition identifiers. Our computational techniques identified these references with accuracy rates of around 90 percent.

We measure the valence of propaganda with dictionary-based semantic analysis. The key idea is that some words have an intrinsic valence: some positive or negative sentiment. We use techniques from computational linguistics to measure the aggregate valence of each propaganda article, as well as the words immediately surrounding each reference to the autocrat, ruling party, and political opposition. The result is an article-level dataset that records the rate and valence of pro-regime coverage, the rate and valence of opposition coverage, the topics each article covers, and each article's aggregate valence. This conception of propaganda – as spin, not lies – accords with how scholars and practitioners have long understood it.[62] Since our dataset distinguishes between the frequency of regime coverage and its valence, we make no assumption that the frequency of regime coverage is a proxy for its valence, as do Qin, Strömberg, and Wu (2018). We regard this as a hypothesis to be tested, not assumed.

This dataset lets us test our theory with a range of statistical tools, but it also creates a dilemma. How can our measures of propaganda be intuitively scaled? We resolve this in two steps. As a baseline for comparison, our dataset includes state-affiliated newspapers from democracies. Many of these newspapers are holdovers from a previous autocratic regime and widely credited for their journalistic integrity. This lets us measure differences in bias: how much more effusive is pro-regime propaganda in some autocracy relative to a democratic baseline. We then situate these differences in bias in a context that many readers intuitively understand: how Fox News covers Republicans relative to Democrats. We measure the valence difference between these two quantities, and we refer to it as our Fox News index. This helps us overcome a problem that, Groeling (2013) observes, is intrinsic to empirical studies of propaganda: the "absence of suitable baselines against which to assess bias." This index also provides a measure of what amount of bias may be persuasive and what amount is so extreme that it invalidates itself. DellaVigna and Kaplan (2007) show that exposure to Fox News persuaded viewers to vote Republican in the 2000 presidential election, and Martin and Yurukoglu (2017) find its effect was even stronger in the 2008 presidential election. Ash and Galletta (2019) show that Fox News exposure leads to more conservative local policies, such as lower taxes and less redistribution. Fox News also persuaded viewers to be less cautious about the

---

[62] Doob (1935); Ellul (1973); Chomsky and Herman (1988); Bogart (1995); Jowett and O'Donnell (2012); Welch (2014); Stanley (2015); Van Herpen (2016).

COVID-19 pandemic.[63] By situating propaganda apparatuses in the context of Fox News, we distinguish content that aims to persuade from that which aims to dominate.

1.4.2 Pro-Regime Propaganda and Narrative Subtleties

In Chapter 4, we probe the politics of pro-regime propaganda. Using a series of statistical techniques, we show that pro-regime propaganda in electorally constrained autocracies is about as positive as Fox News's coverage of Republicans. By contrast, where autocrats are totally unconstrained, pro-regime propaganda is roughly four times more positive than Fox News is pro-Republican. To ensure these results are not driven by reverse causality or omitted variable bias, we exploit the propaganda records of two countries for which our dataset extends back decades: Gabon and China. When the Berlin Wall fell and the Third Wave of Democracy forced President Omar Bongo to concede a series of liberalizing reforms, his propaganda strategy changed as our theory predicts. We observe no such change in China, where the Third Wave of Democracy occasioned no such reforms. CCP propaganda, we show, is driven by politics, not economics or access to information. With Xi Jinping poised to rule indefinitely, its pro-regime coverage is now more effusive than at any point since the Cultural Revolution.

Our view of propaganda in constrained autocracies may be uncontroversial, as scholars typically view propaganda as intended to persuade.[64] This is consistent with quasi-experimental evidence that state television in Vladimir Putin's Russia – coded by Marshall and Jaggers (2005) as a constrained autocracy – is indeed persuasive.[65] Our view of propaganda in unconstrained autocracies may be more controversial, especially among scholars of Chinese politics. Many have suggested that CCP propaganda also aims to persuade citizens of regime merits, rather than,

---

[63] Bursztyn et al. (2020); Jamieson and Albarracin (2020); Simonov et al. (2020).

[64] McMillan and Zoido (2004); Lawson and McCann (2005); White, Oates, and McAllister (2005); Egorov, Guriev, and Sonin (2009); Enikolopov, Petrova, and Zhuravskaya (2011); Jowett and O'Donnell (2012); Gehlbach and Sonin (2014); Yanagizawa-Drott (2014); Adena et al. (2015); Guriev and Treisman (2015, 2018, 2022); Chen and Xu (2015); González and Prem (2018); Qin, Strömberg, and Wu (2018); Yu (2021).

[65] White, Oates, and McAllister (2005); Enikolopov, Petrova, and Zhuravskaya (2011). For more on the tactics employed by Putin's propaganda apparatus to persuade, see Gessen (2012, 2017); Judah (2013); Pomerantsev (2015b); Van Herpen (2016); Ostrovsky (2017).

as we and Huang (2015*b*, 2018) contend, intimidate them into submission.[66] In Chapter 4, we resolve this debate – and we confirm that our hypothesized mechanism is correct – with the first of this book's several survey experiments, which use quota sampling to construct a sample of respondents that reflects the demographic characteristics of China's population. We selected an article from the *People's Daily* in July 2020 that was characteristically effusive about Xi Jinping and the CCP. The article was appealing, in part, because it also appeared in several of the CCP's commercial newspapers, including the *Beijing News*. We find that this article – whether in the *People's Daily* or the *Beijing News* – made respondents less likely to protest against the government because they feared the consequences of doing so. Crucially, we employ list experiments to accommodate the possibility of preference falsification. This, we show, is widespread, roughly 2.5 times greater than Frye et al. (2017) estimate in Putin's Russia.[67] We also show that the CCP's commercialized local newspapers cover the regime just like the *People's Daily* flagship, although their non-regime coverage is more neutral.

Propaganda is more than just the rate and valence of regime coverage. It also entails *narratives*: the topics covered and omitted, and the account of current events that constitutes history's first draft. These narratives are the focus of Chapters 5 and 6. Five issue areas, we find, account for 80 percent of propaganda content: the economy and public goods provision; electoral politics, democracy, and the opposition; sports; international news; and international engagement. Chapter 5 focuses on the first three, all domestic. Chapter 6 focuses on the last two, both international. To capture the subtleties of propaganda narratives, we adapt a measure of semantic distinctiveness from computational linguistics. The key idea is that, across any two corpora of documents, words that are common to both are uninformative. These common words generally include conjugations of the verb "to be," question words like "who" and "where," and other building blocks of speech. Similarly, across any two corpora of documents, words that are uncommon to both are also uninformative. These words are peculiarities. Words that are common in one corpora but uncommon in another are *distinctive*. They convey something meaningful

---

[66] Brady (2002, 2006, 2008, 2012*b*); Stockmann (2010, 2013); Stockmann and Gallagher (2011); Esarey, Stockmann, and Zhang (2017); Stockmann, Esarey, and Zhang (2018); Roberts (2018); King, Pan, and Roberts (2017).

[67] For more evidence of preference falsification in China, see Jiang and Yang (2016) and Robinson and Tannenberg (2019).

about content in one corpora relative to another. Semantic distinctiveness is useful for capturing the subtleties embedded within millions of propaganda articles. It lets the data speak freely.

In Chapter 5, this empirical strategy yields novel insights. In the absence of electoral constraints, propaganda apparatuses trumpet the regime's democratic credentials, yet omit the stuff of democratic politics, like electoral campaigns and the opposition. Propaganda apparatuses cover a general, unnamed "opposition" rather than the actual opposition, since doing so would undermine absurd claims of universal support and potentially help citizens coordinate around particular protest leaders. They cast the autocrat as the champion of national sports teams. We observe none of these tactics where autocrats confront electoral constraints, but neither do they denigrate their opposition rivals. Doing so would undermine claims of credibility. Rather, electorally constrained autocrats acknowledge policy failures: fuel crises, vaccine shortages, and persistently high infant mortality rates. They acknowledge that the government has failed to invest adequately in the country's athletes.

Citizens generally know less about international conditions than domestic conditions. As a result, international news propaganda is analytically distinct from its domestic counterpart. First, recall that absurd propaganda requires common knowledge of the possible: a shared sense among citizens for what claims are absurd. This condition is easily satisfied for domestic affairs, but not for international news. Second, the constraints on honest propaganda are weaker, and so propaganda apparatuses can be more critical in their coverage about international news without undermining their reputations for credibility. Theoretically, these two forces render international news propaganda across autocracies more similar than domestic propaganda. Where electoral constraints are binding, propaganda apparatuses can be more critical without undermining their credibility. In the absence of electoral constraints, propaganda apparatuses have no access to absurd propaganda, for what constitutes absurdity is unclear. Chapter 6 documents two tactics in international news propaganda that are common across autocracies: selective coverage and comparison sets. The former entails omitting events that might inspire protests. The latter entails criticism of the countries against which citizens judge their own.

In Chapter 6, we expand our methodological approach to include tools from network analysis. We combine our global dataset with a paired comparison of Russia and China, the two most geopolitically important autocracies. Their international news coverage, we show, is dominated by the United States, and is critical but sophisticated. We record information about each international news article: the countries and international institutions that are referenced and the range of topics that are covered. We treat these entities as nodes in a network and the number of articles in which they co-occur as edges among them. The result is a set of weighted network graphs that visualize propaganda narratives. These network graphs yield several observations, including one of historical importance. The Russian propaganda apparatus uses Donald Trump as a tool to vindicate its longstanding international narrative: about the impending collapse of the European Union, the prevalence of terrorism, the political allegiances of Crimeans, the misadventures of America's foreign policy, and the shortcomings of American democracy. The Chinese propaganda apparatus is less enamored with Trump, but it covers the same issues: the corruption of American democracy by special interests, including the National Rifle Association, which, the CCP claims, is partly responsible for America's gun violence epidemic.

However similar international news narratives are, Chapter 6 finds striking differences in how propaganda apparatuses across autocracies cover their international engagements. We again combine cross-country regressions with a series of paired comparisons. The first pairs Russia and China, which lets us understand how propaganda narratives about international news are related to propaganda narratives about an autocrat's foreign policy. The second paired comparison focuses on Congo and Uzbekistan. Each government has a close relationship with the CCP and was recently visited by former congressman Dana Rohrabacher, who was suspected by his congressional allies of taking money from Vladimir Putin. Where electoral constraints are binding, we find, propaganda apparatuses emphasize the regime's pursuit of the national interest: their efforts to partner with the international community to advance living conditions or fight terrorism. By contrast, in the absence of electoral constraints, propaganda apparatuses emphasize the regime's immunity from international pressure, either because the world's Great Powers support the regime or because, as in China, the regime is so powerful that it is reshaping the international order. We show that CCP propaganda is narrating a new "hub and spoke" international order, with the CCP at its center and "national sovereignty" – rather than human rights – as its key principle.

Our theory regards absurd propaganda as implicitly threatening, intended to signal to citizens the regime's capacity for violence and to make this capacity common knowledge. Chapter 7 explores whether autocrats use their propaganda apparatuses to explicitly threaten repression. These threats, our field research in China and Congo taught us, are often issued via codewords that are sensitive in one country but innocuous elsewhere. These codewords trigger historical memories that recall the regime's capacity for violence. But they are costly as well. Threatening citizens with repression makes persuading them of regime merits more difficult and may endow certain moments or actions with even more popular salience. Using a series of paired comparisons, we show that propaganda-based threats of repression are more common in the absence of electoral constraints. Even as Zine El Abidine Ben Ali was losing power in Tunisia, for instance, his propaganda newspaper chose to concede citizen frustrations and emphasize the government's determination to do better rather than advertise the military's loyalty, training, and technological prowess, all routinely cited during the succession crisis in Uzbekistan. Cameroon's Paul Biya issues threats in English, but not in French; his political in-group is francophone, his out-group anglophone. The CCP is far more likely to explicitly threaten repression in the *Xinjiang Daily*, which targets the ethnic Uyghur out-group, and on the anniversaries of ethnic separatist movements.

1.4.3 Understanding Calendars of Propaganda

Chapters 4 through 7 document how propaganda apparatuses in constrained autocracies seek credibility. They do so to exploit it: to persuade citizens of useful fictions. Chapter 8 studies the propaganda campaigns that characterize their efforts to do so. Where autocrats confront at least somewhat binding electoral constraints, election seasons are critical to the autocrat's survival. They offer citizens an opportunity to vote against him and a focal moment to coordinate protests. These electoral propaganda campaigns are critical for regime survival, yet, precisely because they recur, they are easiest for citizens to discount. We refer to this tension as the *propagandist's dilemma*, and it is acute where autocrats confront relatively binding electoral constraints. To understand how autocrats manage the propagandist's dilemma, we combine our data with field research in Congo. These propaganda campaigns, we find, begin months before election day, slowly build, and attempt to simultaneously cast the electoral outcome as uncertain and yet prepare citizens to accept the autocrat's "legitimate" victory. Where autocrats confront no electoral constraints, by contrast, the propaganda spike occurs immediately before election day, and in some cases the post-election spike is even greater.

In the absence of electoral constraints, the chief moments of political tension are often the anniversaries of a regime's crimes against its citizens. In Chapter 9, we combine our data with field research in China to understand how propaganda apparatuses respond. Theoretically, we identify a trade-off. Propaganda spikes intended to threaten citizens are useful to deter protest but they also call attention to events or memories that the regime might prefer citizens forget. How do the most repressive governments resolve the tension between propaganda strategies that keep memories alive and censorship strategies that encourage forgetting? We emphasize three forces: whether some politically sensitive moment implicates the regime in historical crimes, whether the moment has any tangible present manifestation, and whether forgetting is actually possible. The first conditions the value of forgetting to the regime; the second and third condition its plausibility. The CCP, we find, goes to extraordinary lengths to scrub the anniversaries of failed pro-democracy movements from the public consciousness. Consequently, it reserves propaganda spikes and explicit threats of violence for major political events and the anniversaries of failed ethnic separatist movements.

There is one exception to this: one pro-democracy anniversary that is so powerful that the CCP knows citizens will not forget. On June 4, 1989, in Beijing's Tiananmen Square, the CCP massacred some 2,000 citizens, who had spent weeks demanding democratic reforms. Two decades later and thousands of miles away, the marginalized ethnic Uyghur community in Xinjiang staged a 10,000-person protest, now known as the Xinjiang Uprising of 2009. The CCP's subsequent crackdown killed hundreds, injured thousands, and culminated in a network of detention centers that now holds between 10 and 30 percent of China's 11 million Uyghurs. Since then, on each anniversary of the Tiananmen massacre, the CCP has used its propaganda apparatus to remind China's urban elite of its brutal campaign of repression against ethnic Uyghurs. Using another survey experiment, we show that this content has no effect on anti-Uyghur racism, the CCP's popularity, or citizens' views about which domestic issues are most pressing. Rather, this content makes politically engaged citizens less likely to engage in anti-regime protests due to fear of repression. Again, to mitigate the possibility of preference falsification, we employ list experiments. Most broadly, Chapter 9 suggests that the CCP's ethnic violence in Xinjiang has its origins, in part, in Beijing: in the CCP's incentives to ensure the urban elite does not again demand change.

1.4.4 *Propaganda and Protest*

The broader question, of course, is whether any of this matters. Does propaganda work? Using a range of natural experiments, scholars have found evidence that propaganda can shape citizens' beliefs about repressive governments.[68] Chapter 10 uses our measures of propaganda to understand its effect on protests across autocracies.

We first probe the effects of pro-regime propaganda. This is complicated by the fact that autocrats employ propaganda strategically. We confront two forms of selection bias. First, the regimes that employ more propaganda may be systematically different than others, and in ways that are correlated with protest. We refer to this as "unit selection bias," and it may occur for a variety of reasons. The regimes most likely to employ propaganda, for instance, may exert particularly strong control over their countries' media environments, and this degree of control could be associated with higher or lower levels of protest. Second, authoritarian regimes employ propaganda differently at different times of year, and these moments may be associated with protest. We refer to this as "temporal selection bias," and it too may emerge for a variety of reasons. The rate of propaganda may rise immediately before elections, when autocrats have a particularly strong incentive to manipulate the beliefs of their citizens. Additionally, autocratic propaganda apparatuses may provide more positive coverage when there is more genuinely good news: when the unemployment rate is lower or when the economy grows more quickly. If positive coverage indicates genuinely good news rather than pro-regime propaganda – and citizens are then less likely to protest – then an estimated relationship between propaganda and protest will be spurious.

To accommodate unit selection bias, we employ estimating equations with country-level fixed effects. In so doing, we ask how *changes* in the volume of propaganda on day $t - 1$ condition the rate of collective action on day t. To accommodate temporal selection bias, we control for a range of time-variant features that may condition whether autocrat i employs propaganda on a given day or during a given year. We find that

---

[68] Adena et al. (2015); Yanagizawa-Drott (2014); Enikolopov, Petrova, and Zhuravskaya (2011); White, Oates, and McAllister (2005); Huang (2015*b*, 2018); Boas and Hidalgo (2011); McMillan and Zoido (2004); Greene (2011); Lawson and McCann (2005); Gentzkow and Shapiro (2006); Gentzkow (2006); González and Prem (2018). On media effects in democracies, see Strömberg (2015); Hayes and Lawless (2015); Arceneaux et al. (2016); Wang (2020).

pro-regime propaganda is associated with a substantively meaningful reduction in the rate of popular protest. By increasing the level of pro-regime propaganda by one standard deviation, contemporary autocrats have reduced the odds of protest the following day by between 7 and 11 percent. This effect is relatively durable. Depending on the form of the decay function, the half-life of the effect is between two and five days. One month later, very little of the initial effect still persists. This temporal signature is consistent with political messaging in American politics.[69]

Chapter 10 then shifts attention to the effects of propaganda-based threats of repression. Again, we confront the possibility of selection bias. Repressive governments may be more likely to threaten citizens with repression during politically sensitive moments and in response to protests on day $t - 1$. This creates two competing effects on protests: a negative effect due to the threat and a positive effect due to tensions that compelled the threat. The calendar of popular protest in contemporary China, which we uncover in Chapter 7, suggests a novel identification strategy. We employ an instrumental variables estimator that rests on two features of China's political geography. First, propaganda in the *Workers' Daily* is set at the national level, but occasionally it responds to local conditions, which are salient in one province but unknown in other provinces. As a result, citizens in one province are occasionally "treated" with propaganda content that is intended for citizens in geographically and culturally distant provinces. Second, because China is ethnically diverse and geographically sprawling, the ethnic separatist anniversaries in Tibet and Xinjiang that drive propaganda-based threats are salient only in those regions and effectively unknown elsewhere. We argue that ethnic separatist anniversaries in Tibet and Xinjiang plausibly condition protest rates in *geographically and culturally distant provinces* only through the propaganda-based threats that the regime issues via the propaganda apparatus.

We present a range of evidence that this exclusion restriction is plausible: a nationally representative survey, an analysis of protest and repression by day and location, and a description of the language that protesters employ. As a further precaution, we exclude nine provinces where the exclusion restriction is most likely to be violated, which nonetheless yields a sample that includes 88.5 percent of Chinese citizens. We find that propaganda-based threats have a plausibly causal effect on protest levels outside the nine provinces we drop. We employ

---

[69] Hill et al. (2013).

Conley, Hansen, and Rossi's (2012) sensitivity analysis to show that these estimates are robust to non-trivial violations of the exclusion restriction.

1.5 BELIEFS, NOMINALLY DEMOCRATIC INSTITUTIONS, AND AUTOCRATIC POLITICS

This book is about autocratic propaganda. More broadly, however, it is about the struggle between citizens and repressive governments, the political institutions that mediate it, and how the international community can support citizens who wage it. Many scholars regard nominally democratic institutions as forces for autocratic stability and regime survival as being secured through patronage and repression. Our approach is different. The world's autocracies have experienced fundamental changes since the Berlin Wall fell. The rate of elite coups has declined, popular protests have emerged as the chief threat to autocratic survival, and, with 80 percent of the world's autocrats governing with nominally democratic institutions, there is now less institutional variation in the world's autocracies than perhaps ever before.

These changes inform our approach to autocratic politics. We view citizens' beliefs as the central battlefield on which the struggle for political change is waged and nominally democratic institutions as constraints that autocrats struggle to loosen. Autocrats wage this battle with a range of tools, propaganda chief among them, but their propaganda strategies are conditioned by the institutions they confront. In privileging citizens' beliefs as key to autocratic survival, we return to how scholars understood it for much of the twentieth century. In treating nominally democratic institutions as constraints that autocrats attempt to loosen, this book joins a growing literature that suggests these institutions are not as stabilizing as scholars once thought.[70] This is among this book's key arguments. Although nominally democratic institutions may yield some benefits to the world's autocrats, electoral constraints also force autocrats to wage the battle for their citizens' beliefs from a position of weakness.

1.5.1 *Autocracy, Its Problems, and How to Solve Them*

Scholars have long sought to understand the internal dynamics of the world's autocracies. Their conclusions often reflect prevailing

---

[70] Carothers (2018); Jang and Huang (2019); Reuter and Szakonyi (2019); Meng (2020).

geopolitical conditions. In the mid-twentieth century, with the United States locked in a Cold War against the Soviet Union, scholars probed how totalitarianism was distinctive. All autocracies were repressive, scholars observed, but totalitarianism assaulted citizens' beliefs with the tools of modern technology. Buchheim (1968, 14) described this assault with the same disturbing metaphor that Chinese citizens reserve for the *People's Daily*: "the creeping assault on man by the perversion of his thoughts." In the *Origins of Totalitarianism*, Arendt (1951, 383) wrote about the cognitive scars this assault leaves on citizens:

The result of a consistent and total substitution of lies for factual truth is not that the lie will now be accepted as truth and truth be defamed as a lie, but that the sense by which we take our bearings in the real world – and the category of truth versus falsehood is among the mental means to this end – is being destroyed.

This cognitive assault was enshrined in the era's literature. In *The Power of the Powerless*, Václav Havel (1978, 9) described "life in the system" as "permeated with hypocrisy and lies," where "banning independent thought becomes the most scientific of world views." In *Life Is Elsewhere*, Milan Kundera described the era as when "the poet reigned along with the executioner." Poet was Kundera's euphemism for propagandist.

Whether citizens' beliefs were actually reshaped was a matter of debate. Friedrich and Brzezinski (1956) registered their skepticism, as did Kirkpatrick (1981, 123):

Have they managed to reform human consciousness? Have they managed to educate Soviet citizens so that they would freely choose to live according to the norms of Soviet culture *if the constraints of coercion were removed*? The answer of course is that we do not know.

The Soviet Union's collapse effectively answered these questions. Scholars responded by treating autocratic politics as chiefly about repression. "What reproduces consent is the threat of force," Przeworski (1986, 51) observed, "and short of moments of true desperation this threat is sufficient." Quite appropriately, repression remains central to the study of autocracy. Scholars have sought to understand its effects on those who experience it,[71] how political institutions and modern communication

---

[71] Balcells (2012); Escribà-Folch (2013); Rozenas, Schutte, and Zhukov (2017); Simpser, Slater, and Wittenberg (2018); Bautista et al. (2021); Young (2018); Zhukov and Talibova (2018); Rozenas and Zhukov (2019); Amat (2019); Xue (2019); Desposato, Wang, and Wu (2021); Wang (2019).

technologies condition it,[72] whether the international community can prevent it,[73] and how bureaucracies are organized to wield it.[74] Dictators have accomplices, of course, and so scholars have also sought the non-coercive foundations of autocratic survival, patronage in particular.[75]

In the early 2000s, scholars advanced our understanding of autocratic politics in two ways. First, scholars more clearly defined the threats to autocratic survival. Autocrats, in Svolik's (2012) formulation, must secure the cooperation of a ruling elite and the acquiescence of citizens. These groups threaten autocrats in different ways: elites via coup, citizens via revolution. Tullock (1987) argued that elite coups were more threatening than popular revolutions, Geddes (2005) agreed, and Svolik (2009) demonstrated it empirically for the post–World War II period.[76] Second, scholars identified another tool that autocrats wield: institutions, especially robust political parties.[77] By providing an "institutional setting that generates political power and long-term security," Brownlee (2007, 33) writes, "ruling parties ... bridle elite ambitions and bind together otherwise fractious coalitions." Similarly, for Slater (2010, 51), ruling parties ... [prevent] elite defection" by creating a "political wilderness" with no "alternative routes to the political summit." These dominant parties emerge, Reuter (2017) finds, where autocrats and elites need each other to maintain power.[78]

Meanwhile, other scholars argued that nominally democratic institutions constitute forces for autocratic stability as well. These institutions, the arguments go, enable autocrats to credibly commit to revenue-sharing agreements with regime insiders or policy compromises

---

[72] Davenport (2007a,c,b); Bhasin and Gandhi (2013); Hill and Jones (2014); Frantz and Kendall-Taylor (2014); Christensen and Garfias (2018); Gohdes (2020).

[73] Escribà-Folch and Wright (2015); Carnegie and Marinov (2017); Carter (2016a).

[74] Policzer (2009); Sassoon (2012); Hassan (2016); Blaydes (2018); Geddes, Wright, and Frantz (2018); Shen-Bayh (2018); Thomson (2022).

[75] Wintrobe (1998); Bueno de Mesquita et al. (2003); Acemoglu, Robinson, and Verdier (2004); Padro i Miquel (2007); Arriola (2009); Albertus (2015); Roessler (2016); Albertus, Fenner, and Slater (2018).

[76] Relatedly, O'Donnell and Schmitter (1986, 19) traced successful revolutions to splits within the ruling regime: "There is no transition whose beginning is not a consequence – direct or indirect – of important divisions within the regime itself, principally along the fluctuating cleavage between hard-liners and soft-liners."

[77] Brownlee (2007); Slater (2010); Svolik (2012).

[78] Boix and Svolik (2013) make a related argument about power balances, but are more agnostic about the form that the resulting institutions take. Note that Meng (2019) provides evidence that strong ruling parties are much rarer than typically assumed, suggesting that some of the causal force attributed to them may be driven, in part, by Soviet support during the Cold War.

with other prominent figures.[79] Elections may enable autocrats to equitably distribute regime patronage,[80] locate pockets of popular discontent,[81] and identify effective party cadres.[82] In locating the origins of autocratic survival in nominally democratic institutions, scholars turned a longstanding assumption on its head. If nominally democratic institutions are actually forces for autocratic stability, then, by requiring them in exchange for development aid and debt relief, Western governments have rendered the world's autocrats more secure, not less. Lust-Okar (2006, 468) put it simply: "The logic of authoritarian elections should lead us to question the value of pressing for, and applauding, the introduction of elections in authoritarian regimes."[83]

1.5.2 Autocratic Politics in the Early Twenty First Century

In the early twenty first century, the relative salience of Svolik's (2012) two problems of autocratic rule changed, as did the relative accessibility of the tools with which autocrats solve them. These changes have made understanding autocratic propaganda more critical than at any point since the mid-twentieth century. The collapse of the Berlin Wall – and, with it, America's ascension to global hegemony – had three related consequences for the world's autocrats. First, most were forced to adopt nominally democratic institutions as a final effort to placate frustrated citizens, whose protests were driven by rising food prices, inspiration from revolutions abroad, and signals from Western democracies that development aid would be tied to democratic reforms. Since then, the international community has generally required nominally democratic institutions in exchange for development aid and debt relief.[84] With a few notable exceptions – China among them – autocrats no longer have easy access to the single-party regimes that helped stabilize their twentieth-century predecessors.

Second, the regular elections occasioned by nominally democratic institutions force autocrats to subject themselves to recurring opportunities

---

[79] Magaloni (2006, 2008); Gandhi and Przeworski (2007); Gandhi (2008); Wright (2008), and Geddes, Wright, and Frantz (2018).

[80] Lust-Okar (2006); Blaydes (2011).

[81] Ames (1970); Magaloni (2006); Brownlee (2007); Blaydes (2011); Cox (2009), and Geddes, Wright, and Frantz (2018).

[82] Birney (2007), and Blaydes (2011).

[83] For excellent overviews, see Gandhi and Lust-Okar (2009) and Pepinsky (2014).

[84] Bratton and van de Walle (1997); van de Walle (2001); Dunning (2004); Levitsky and Way (2010); Marinov and Goemans (2014).

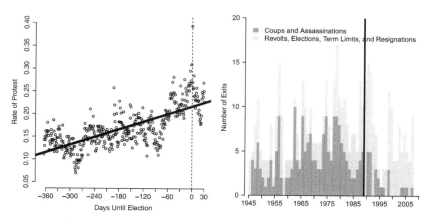

Figure 1.2 Dynamics of autocratic politics since the Berlin Wall fell

for collective action.[85] During election seasons, citizens are engaged in politics and aware of their neighbors' discontent.[86] Opposition leaders coordinate protests and alert citizens to electoral fraud.[87] By affirming the possibility of a post-regime future, elections decrease the costs to regime elites of defecting from the coalition and joining the opposition.[88] Hale (2005, 159) concludes that revolutions in Georgia, Kyrgyzstan, and Ukraine succeeded, in part, because security officials refused to suppress opposition leaders who "might be the authorities of the future." Elite defections helped end Senegalese president Abdoulaye Wade's ambitions for his son, catalyzed the Burkinabé Revolution of October 2014, and gave rise to Jean Ping's candidacy against Gabonese president Ali Ben Bongo in 2016. Consequently, from the left panel of Figure 1.2, the daily rate of protest across autocracies rises steadily as election day approaches, and on election day itself is nearly four times greater than on other days of the year.[89] These protests have consequences. In post–Cold

---

[85] Olson (1977); Granovetter (1978); DeNardo (1985); Tullock (1987); Przeworski (2006); Knutsen and Nygard (2015); Knutsen, Nygard, and Wig (2017).

[86] Kuran (1991); Tucker (2007); Hollyer, Rosendorff, and Vreeland (2015).

[87] Beissinger (2002); Javeline (2003); McFaul (2005); Radnitz (2010); Bunce and Wolchik (2011); Fearon (2011).

[88] Reuter and Szakonyi (2019).

[89] Note that we focus on the African continent, since daily records of protest are of particularly high quality; see Salehyan et al. (2012). For each election since 1990, we identify an election season that begins one year before election day and ends one month after, when the results have been announced and newly elected officials have assumed office. For each of 402 elections, we index each day within

War Africa, Aidt and Leon (2016) find, as the number of annual protests rises, so does the probability of democratic change.

Third, popular protests now constitute the chief threat to autocratic survival, as the right panel of Figure 1.2 makes clear.[90] Marinov and Goemans (2014) locate the decline of the coup in the same forces that compelled the rise of nominally democratic institutions. Pressured by Western donors to quickly transfer power to elected governments, would-be coup plotters view coups as less attractive than they once did. Western pressure appears to have amplified threats from the street by making repression costly. Carnegie and Marinov (2017), for instance, find that positive conditionality from the European Union has reduced human rights violations. Carter (2022) finds that Africa's autocrats were less likely to employ violence against citizens during debt relief negotiations with the Bretton Woods institutions, and, recognizing this, their citizens have been more likely to protest. A range of scholars have found that development aid and sustained international pressure can foster political liberalization.[91]

The threat of popular protest has been reinforced by modern communications technologies, which enable citizens to share information about regime crimes, organize mass protests, and ultimately topple governments. Just before the Arab Spring, Diamond (2010) dubbed them liberation technologies. Afterwards, Steinert-Threlkeld et al. (2015) and Howard and Hussain (2011, 2013) found that they were critical to its success. Manacorda and Tesei (2016) and Christensen and Garfias (2018) measured their effects around the world. In the most closed autocracies, protests are notoriously difficult for scholars to record for posterity. But, again, the available evidence suggests that the rate of protest is rising. The CCP records protests across China to locate pockets of discontent and identify local governments that fail to curb it. The government made these data public until 2005, when the protest rate rose so high that it made the depth of popular frustration common knowledge among citizens.

---

the season as $t \in \{-365, 30\}$, where day $t = -30$ denotes the 30th day until the election, day $t = 0$ gives election day, and day $t = 30$ is the 30th day after the election. We then compute the rate of protests for each day t. We draw regime type data from Svolik (2012).

[90] We draw data on autocratic exits from Svolik (2012).

[91] Dunning (2004); Brown (2005); Hafner-Burton (2008); Bearce and Tirone (2010); Kersting and Kelly (2014); Dietrich and Wright (2015); Gibson, Hoffman, and Jablonski (2015); Escribà-Folch and Wright (2015).

1.5.3 Propaganda, Institutions, and the Politics of Belief

As autocratic politics has changed, so too has how scholars study it. With popular protests increasingly the chief threat to autocratic survival,[92] scholars have sought to understand their dynamics: who protests,[93] when they protest,[94] how they organize,[95] which tactics they employ,[96] and which tactics are most effective.[97] Scholars have also sought to understand how the world's autocrats attempt to censor their citizens' informational environments,[98] deploy bots to shape social media conversations,[99] and block internet access altogether.[100] Still other scholars have sought to measure propaganda's effects. Just as political communication in democracies routinely shapes citizens' beliefs,[101] there is

---

[92] With political institutions increasingly fixed, a separate strand of scholarship has focused on how autocrats use non-institutional strategies to induce elite loyalty; see Arriola (2009); Francois, Rainer, and Trebbi (2014); Sudduth (2017), and Woldense (2018).

[93] Branch and Mampilly (2015); Brancati (2016); Rosenfeld (2017).

[94] Beissinger (2002, 2007); Tucker (2007); Fearon (2011); Beaulieu (2014); Trejo (2014); Brancati (2016); Carter and Carter (2020a).

[95] Diamond (2010); Tufekci and Wilson (2012); Howard and Hussain (2013); Steinert-Threlkeld et al. (2015); Manacorda and Tesei (2016); Christensen and Garfias (2018); Fu (2018).

[96] Chen (2012); Chenoweth and Ulfelder (2015).

[97] Chenoweth and Stephan (2011); Beber, Roessler, and Scacco (2014); Enos, Kaufman, and Sands (2019).

[98] King, Pan, and Roberts (2013); Guriev and Treisman (2015, 2018, 2022); Shadmehr and Bernhardt (2015); Qin, Strömberg, and Wu (2017); Gallagher and Miller (2019).

[99] King, Pan, and Roberts (2017); Munger et al. (2016).

[100] Atabong (2017); Rydzak (2019b).

[101] Zaller (1992); Jentleson (1992); Brody (1991); Zaller and Chiu (2000); Bennett, Lawrence, and Livingston (2006); Behr and Iyengar (1985); Cohen (1995); Entman (1993); Iyengar and Valentino (2000); Rahn (1993); Cohen (2003); Bullock (2011). Without elite cues, the relationship between ideological self identification and policy preferences is weak (Malka and Lelkes 2010; Popp and Rudolph 2011). Moreover, in the presence of media disagreement, citizens are more skeptical about leader statements (Iyengar and Kinder 1987; Krosnick and Kinder 1990; Larson 2000; Kuypers 1997; Graber 2002; Paletz 2002; Mueller 1973; Lee 1977; Brody 1991; Rahn 1993; Lupia and McCubbins 1998; Groeling and Baum 2008; Berinsky 2007). For a review, see Chong and Druckman (2007). The effects of persuasive communication quickly decay, which helps explain why political advertisements are most frequent in the weeks before an election (Cook and Flay 1978; Hill et al. 2013; Gerber et al. 2011). Research on the influence of casualty reports on war support reaches similar conclusions (Hayes and Myers 2009; Althaus, Bramlett, and Gimpel 2012; Sides and Vavreck 2013).

mounting evidence that autocratic propaganda can persuade citizens of regime merits.[102]

Common to much of this scholarship is a tacit conviction that citizens' beliefs are the central battlefield on which the struggle for political change is waged. This conviction – about the centrality of belief – is how scholars understood autocratic survival for much of the twentieth century, before the Soviet Union fell and the institutionalist approach to autocratic survival gained prominence. This conviction compelled the American government to drop "leaflet bombs" over Soviet territory during the Cold War, the African National Congress (ANC) to drop "ideological bombs" over South African townships during the struggle against apartheid, and a young Mao to describe propaganda as the "most important job" facing his insurgent movement. It animated the enduring prose of George Orwell, Václav Havel, Milan Kundera, Yan Lianke, and Ma Jian. It was central to Crassweller's (1966) remarkable account of Rafael Trujillo and Kapuscinski's (1989) equally remarkable account of Haile Selassie. It was even central to Wintrobe's (1998, 20) pathbreaking formal models of autocratic politics, before he chose to privilege patronage and repression rather than the power of citizens' beliefs. The "one thing even dictatorial powers cannot give," Wintrobe wrote, is "the *minds* of their subjects."[103] In turn, autocrats attempt to shape their citizens' beliefs. They do so with a range of modern technologies, as recent scholarship makes clear: sophisticated censorship operations, social media campaigns, and internet shutdowns.

Perhaps most importantly, however, autocrats employ propaganda. We trace the origins of divergent propaganda strategies across autocracies to differences in electoral constraints. In so doing, this book challenges how scholars understand the forces that condition media bias. Joseph Pulitzer located the origins of journalistic freedom in economics. "Advertising means money," he observed, "and money means independence."[104] Many scholars agree. As potential advertising revenues expand, the arguments go, media platforms have incentives to

---

[102] McMillan and Zoido (2004); Lawson and McCann (2005); White, Oates, and McAllister (2005); Greene (2011); Enikolopov, Petrova, and Zhuravskaya (2011); Adena et al. (2015); González and Prem (2018); Peisakhin and Rozenas (2018). On media effects in democracies, see Gerber, Karlan, and Bergan (2009); Boas and Hidalgo (2011); Da Silveira and De Mello (2011); Strömberg (2015); Hayes and Lawless (2015); Arceneaux et al. (2016); Durante, Pinotti, and Tesei (2019), and Wang (2020).

[103] Italics in the original.

[104] Starr (2004).

attract more readers, and do so by reporting objectively.[105] In nineteenth-century America, Petrova (2011) shows, areas with larger advertising markets had more politically independent newspapers, which emerged as government watchdogs.[106] Newspaper circulation is associated with better disaster relief in India,[107] more public goods in New Deal America,[108] and less public corruption in late-nineteenth-century America.[109] This was all anticipated by Thomas Jefferson, who wrote in 1781: "Were it left to me to decide whether we should have a government without newspapers or newspapers without a government, I should not hesitate a moment to prefer the latter."

Several scholars have extended this argument to China, where the commercially oriented, local media has expanded dramatically over the last forty years.[110] Over time, Qin, Strömberg, and Wu (2018, 2474) suggest, "economic development [will reduce] audience exposure to propaganda." Similarly, Guriev and Treisman (2018, 2) argue that "economic modernization, and in particular the spread of higher education," forces autocrats into a less biased propaganda strategy. If they are right, then the implications are profound, a modernization theory for the Information Age. As economies grow and citizens are better educated, repressive governments will confront powerful incentives to soften the biases in propaganda. With citizens better informed, political reform may well follow.[111] These arguments were anticipated by Inglehart and Welzel (2005, 22, 29, 46), who described "the causal primacy of socioeconomic development." "The evolution of mass media and modern information technology," they argue, "gives people easy access to knowledge, increasing their informational autonomy" and ultimately their capacity to force political change.[112]

---

[105] Besley and Prat (2006); McMillan and Zoido (2004); Corneo (2006); Gehlbach and Sonin (2014); Tella and Franceschelli (2011); Hamilton (2004); Gentzkow, Glaeser, and Goldin (2006); Petrova (2008, 2011, 2012). Relatedly, scholars have also attributed the growth of unbiased media to population growth. See, for example, Besley and Prat (2006); Ellman and Germano (2009), and Gentzkow, Glaeser, and Goldin (2006).

[106] For a formal treatment, see Besley and Prat (2006).

[107] Besley and Burgess (2002).

[108] Strömberg (2004).

[109] Gentzkow, Glaeser, and Goldin (2006).

[110] Lee (1990); Zhao (1998); Lynch (1999).

[111] Pei (1994); Hassid (2016).

[112] See also Inglehart (1997, 205–209); Inglehart and Welzel (2010, 561); Welzel and Inglehart (2009, 136–138); Welzel (2013, 38, 44, 268–269).

Our theory suggests otherwise, for ours is a *political* theory of autocratic propaganda.[113] The chief driver of variation in propaganda – both across countries and over time – is the set of electoral constraints that autocratic governments confront, not the access to information that citizens have. This book thus advances a different view of nominally democratic institutions in autocracies. We regard them not as forces of stability, but as constraints that autocrats aim to loosen. In 2016 alone, for instance, five of Africa's autocrats – Pierre Nkurunziza of Burundi, Idriss Déby of Chad, Paul Kagame of Rwanda, Denis Sassou Nguesso of Congo, Ali Bongo of Gabon, and Joseph Kabila of the Democratic Republic of Congo – either removed term limits or suspended elections altogether. To be sure, autocrats attempt to use these institutions to their advantage whenever possible. Autocrats "best respond" to their institutional constraints. But there is a profound difference between choosing nominally democratic institutions and making the best of them.

Nominally democratic institutions create new challenges for the world's autocrats. Regular elections constitute recurrent opportunities for collective action,[114] occasion elite defections from the ruling coalition,[115] and enable potential rivals to gain notoriety.[116] This book shows that even weak electoral institutions, such as those confronted by Denis Sassou Nguesso, force autocrats to wage the battle for their citizens' minds from a position of weakness. To persuade citizens of regime merits, electorally constrained autocrats must acknowledge policy failures, which occasionally are damning. As we show in Chapter 5, Denis Sassou Nguesso was forced to cover a catastrophic fuel shortage, despite presiding over Africa's fourth leading oil producer. His propaganda apparatus covers malnutrition, infant mortality, and vaccine shortages. These admissions risk confirming citizens' frustrations and coalescing this frustration into collective action. But his electoral constraints force him to do so.

---

[113] Munck (2018) describes Inglehart and Welzel as "[rejecting] the view that political institutions could themselves affect cultural change." His response, which privileges political institutions as causally primary, anticipates ours.

[114] See Figure 1.2.

[115] Reuter and Szakonyi (2019).

[116] Jang and Huang (2019).

2

A *Theory of Autocratic Propaganda*

2.1 BAYESIAN PERSUASION

For Joseph Goebbels and Denis Sassou Nguesso, propaganda draws strength from its plausibility, which gives it some capacity to manipulate citizens' beliefs. For Xi Jinping, George Orwell, and Hannah Arendt, propaganda is powerful because it forces citizens to consume information they know to be false, and to do so publicly. These two propaganda strategies – persuasion and domination – appear to be at odds. In one, propaganda is powerful when it is plausible. In the other, propaganda derives its power from absurdity.

Why do autocrats employ different propaganda strategies? Our answer is that they do so for different ends. When an autocrat's ability to tilt the electoral playing field is constrained by his limited capacity for fraud and repression, he is forced to generate some amount of popular support. In turn, he employs a propaganda strategy that concedes regime failures in order to persuade citizens of regime merits. When an autocrat's capacity for fraud and repression is so strong that he can fully tilt the electoral playing field, propaganda serves as a signal: that his repressive apparatus is sufficiently strong that his hold on power rests not on citizens' support, but on their acquiescence. Put simply, the electoral constraints an autocrat confronts determine the propaganda strategy he employs.

Our theory of autocratic propaganda rests on two foundations. First, for citizens who live under autocracy, uncertainty is pervasive. Citizens are uncertain about the link between policy and outcomes and hence the regime's performance.[1] Citizens are also uncertain about the regime's

---

[1] Egorov, Guriev, and Sonin (2009); Shadmehr and Bernhardt (2011); Gehlbach and Sonin (2014); Guriev and Treisman (2015, 2018, 2022); Chen and Xu (2015); Rozenas and Stukal (2018); Yu (2021).

capacity for repression.[2] Citizens may observe security forces in the streets and the weapons at their disposal, but they cannot observe the internal dynamics that determine whether the security forces will open fire on protesters or otherwise ensure that the regime survives a crisis.[3]

Second, the vast majority of the world's autocrats now organize regular elections. These elections provide information to citizens about the autocrat's ability to tilt the electoral playing field and hence his capacity for repression. Intuitively, citizens know how they feel about the autocrat and his opposition rivals. Consequently, if the autocrat claims electoral victory, citizens learn that his capacity for fraud is at least as great as the magnitude of their relative preference for the opposition. Since an autocrat's capacity for fraud is a function of his capacity for repression – a strong repressive apparatus lets the autocrat suppress opposition leaders and stuff ballot boxes – citizens can infer how likely some post-election revolt is to succeed.

If elections enable citizens to learn about the autocrat's capacity for fraud and repression, so too – in conjunction with the propaganda apparatus – do they enable the autocrat to signal. By using propaganda to broadcast claims that citizens know to be false, the autocrat can choose to leave citizens with a negative view of the regime. By securing electoral victory nonetheless, the autocrat signals that his capacity for fraud and repression is so substantial that he has no need for popular support. Crucially, this signal cannot be sent by an autocrat whose capacity for fraud and repression is low, since his limited ability to tilt the electoral playing field forces him to curry popular support to secure electoral victory. The constrained autocrat must use propaganda to persuade citizens of regime merits rather than intimidate them into submission.

We develop our theory of propaganda with the aid of a formal model. To illustrate its dynamics, we first analyze a model in which the autocrat uses propaganda to condition citizens' beliefs about regime merits and the probability a post-election revolt will succeed. Then, we give the autocrat a second tool with which to secure his political survival: investment in public policy, which informs citizens' prior beliefs about regime merits. Next, we extend this model by assuming the autocrat has access to censorship, which limits citizens' ability to detect when he underinvests in public policy. This environment yields several important comparative statics. Our theory suggests that honest propaganda is more likely when

---

[2] Edmond (2013); Huang (2015*b*).
[3] O'Donnell and Schmitter (1986); Dragu and Przeworski (2019).

autocrats preside over weak states, which make providing public goods relatively inefficient. Our theory suggests that the effect of censorship on propaganda depends on the autocrat's capacity for fraud and repression. When this capacity is low, censorship lets the autocrat employ less honest propaganda. When repressive capacity is high, censorship has no effect on propaganda, but lets the autocrat reduce public investment. In short, propaganda strategies are driven by politics, with informational forces secondary. Our theory also suggests that propaganda is higher when the autocrat is vulnerable to elite coups.

This chapter proceeds as follows. Section 2.2 presents our theoretical framework. After analyzing the model in Section 2.3, in Section 2.4 we characterize the baseline equilibria. Sections 2.5 and 2.6, respectively, extend the model to let the autocrat invest in public goods and censor citizens' informational environment. Sections 2.7 through 2.10 discuss other extensions to our theory.

2.2 ENVIRONMENT

2.2.1 *Citizens*

Most theories of propaganda begin with an autocrat, who employs some combination of repression, patronage, and propaganda to maintain power.[4] Citizens are generally uncertain about whether the autocrat implements sound policies,[5] or whether the autocrat has a substantial repressive apparatus.[6] Citizens may also be uncertain about whether their compatriots are prepared to revolt.[7] Propaganda is designed to manipulate these beliefs and ultimately discourage citizens from attempting to force the autocrat from power, either at the ballot box or via protests.

Our theory builds on this. We consider a society with an autocrat D and citizens O. For tractability, we treat citizens as homogenous. They derive utility from income y, which we take as fixed, and public policies implemented by the autocrat. We think of these policies broadly: infrastructure, schools, international diplomacy, or anything else that might advance society's welfare. Citizens' expected utility is given by

---

[4] Gehlbach, Svolik, and Sonin (2016).
[5] Egorov, Guriev, and Sonin (2009); Gehlbach and Sonin (2014); Guriev and Treisman (2015, 2018, 2022); Chen and Xu (2015); Yu (2021).
[6] Edmond (2013); Huang (2015*b*).
[7] Little (2017).

$$E\left[u_O\left(\theta_D\right)\right] = y + \delta\theta_D \tag{2.1}$$

The term $\theta_D \in \{0, 1\}$ is a random variable that indicates whether the autocrat's policies advance society's welfare. The value of θ_D is determined by Nature at the game's outset and is unknown to both citizens and the autocrat. We think of $\theta_D = 0$ as a shock that wipes out the returns from the autocrat's policies. This form of uncertainty for citizens is natural. It reflects the fact that their knowledge of policy is limited, that the returns from public investment may accrue only over time, or that the autocrat may be incompetent. This form of uncertainty is also natural for the autocrat. Like citizens, the autocrat may be uncertain about whether his investments will pay off, perhaps due to economic shocks or corruption by appointees charged with implementing his policies. The autocrat and citizens share a common prior μ_D^0 on the probability that $\theta_D = 1$.

The term $\delta \in [0, 1]$ measures how similar citizens' policy preferences are to those the autocrat implements. When their policy preferences converge, $\delta \to 1$. When their policy preferences diverge, $\delta \to 0$. We take these preferences as fixed, perhaps because the autocrat is committed to policies preferred by regime insiders.[8]

2.2.2 *Election and Revolution*

If citizens are unhappy with the autocrat's performance, they can vote against him in an upcoming election. This reflects the fact that most autocrats now organize regular elections.[9] Citizens make their electoral choice by weighing their expected utility from supporting the autocrat against their expected utility from the challenger, which is

$$E\left[u_O\left(\theta_O\right)\right] = y + \theta_O \tag{2.2}$$

Equations (2.1) and (2.2) differ in two ways. First, we assume that citizens and the challenger share the same policy preferences, so there is no term analogous to δ from equation (2.1). Second, the term $\theta_O \in \{0, 1\}$ is a random variable that indicates whether the challenger's public policies advance society's long-term welfare. Citizens have a prior belief μ_O^0 about

---

[8] Brownlee (2007); Magaloni (2008); Gandhi (2008); Slater (2010); Blaydes (2011); Gehlbach and Keefer (2011); Svolik (2012); Meng (2020); Yu (2021).

[9] In Section 2.9, we discuss how to interpret our model in the absence of regular elections.

the probability that $\theta_O = 1$. We think of $\mu_O^0 \to 1$, such that citizens are confident in the challenger.[10]

If the autocrat uses fraud to secure electoral victory, citizens can choose to revolt.[11] Here we draw on a large literature that suggests electoral protests are often driven by reports of fraud.[12] If citizens revolt, they induce a lottery over the future political regime. The lottery's outcome is determined by the strength of the autocrat's repressive apparatus, given by $\zeta \in [0, 1]$. As $\zeta \to 1$, the autocrat's repressive apparatus is sufficiently strong that he can effectively guarantee his survival. As $\zeta \to 0$, the autocrat is likely to be deposed by citizens.

For the autocrat, revolt is costly regardless of its outcome. If the autocrat survives, the violence required to suppress the revolt may provide focal moments around which citizens can coordinate future protests.[13] Alternatively, the autocrat could be prosecuted by the International Criminal Court for any atrocities his security forces commit.[14] If the autocrat does not survive, he may be prosecuted by a new government or the international community for human rights abuses that occurred during the revolution.[15] The term $-\gamma < 0$ reflects the autocrat's utility loss from a revolt.

For citizens, revolt is costly as well. If the revolt fails, their utility loss is commensurate with the strength of the autocrat's repressive apparatus. Citizens' payoff from a failed revolt is $-\psi\zeta$, where $\psi > 0$ reflects the ability of the autocrat's repressive apparatus to target dissidents. This represents one aspect of state capacity.[16] This may reflect the technological capabilities of the autocrat's intelligence apparatus or citizens' ability to evade the state. Where the autocrat's repressive apparatus is strong and can locate dissidents – such that $\zeta \to 1$ and ψ is high – citizens' punishment from a failed revolt is severe, perhaps incarceration or death.

---

[10] In particular, we assume $\delta\mu_D^0 < \mu_O^0$, so that, given their prior beliefs, citizens prefer the challenger by default.

[11] For simplicity, we abstract from issues of coordination and collective action. For more on how propaganda may impede collective action, see Little (2017).

[12] Tucker (2007); Fearon (2011); Kelley (2012); Daxecker (2012); Brancati (2016).

[13] Carter and Carter (2020a).

[14] Bergsmo and Yan (2012).

[15] Simmons (2009); Simmons and Danner (2010); Meernik (2015); Jo and Simmons (2016); Dancy and Montal (2017); Jo, Radtke, and Simmons (2018).

[16] Edin (2003); Lyall (2010); Blaydes (2018); Hassan (2020); Carter and Hassan (2021); Thomson (2022); Xu (2021).

Where the autocrat's repressive apparatus is weak – such that $\zeta \to 0$ or $\psi \to 0$ – citizens are more likely to emerge unpunished from a failed revolution.

2.2.3 *The Autocrat and the Electoral Playing Field*

The autocrat obtains utility from state revenue and other returns from power, which we denote as R and take as fixed. The autocrat has two tools with which to maintain power. First, the autocrat may be able to win the election by engaging in enough fraud to compensate for citizens' preference for the challenger. This captures the autocrat's ability to tilt the electoral playing field.[17] We think of electoral fraud broadly: vote rigging, banning or dispersing opposition rallies, incarcerating opponents, and other forms of coercion.

The extent to which autocrats are subject to electoral constraints varies tremendously. Some autocrats refuse to organize national elections, as in China and Eritrea. Some can marshal so much fraud and violence that elections are meaningless, as in Uzbekistan. Some, like Denis Sassou Nguesso, can tilt the electoral playing field only to a degree. Scholars have proposed a range of terms to describe these electoral constraints: pseudo-democracy,[18] quasi-democracy,[19] semi-democracy,[20] semi-authoritarianism,[21] electoral authoritarianism,[22] competitive authoritarianism,[23] single-party dominance,[24] and others.[25]

An autocrat's ability to tilt the electoral playing field may stem from multiple sources. Levitsky and Way (2010) aggregate these into three categories. First, state coercive capacity encompasses the "institutions – from security forces to local prefects to intelligence agencies – [that] furnish governments with tools to monitor, co-opt, intimidate, and repress potential opponents."[26] In post-Soviet Eastern Europe, Fortin-Rittberger

---

[17] Gyimay-Boadi (1999); Schedler (2002); Levitsky and Way (2010).
[18] Diamond, Linz, and Lipset (1995); Diamond (2002).
[19] Carothers (2018).
[20] Smith (2005).
[21] Ottaway (2003).
[22] Schedler (2002, 2006, 2009).
[23] Levitsky and Way (2002, 2010).
[24] Greene (2009, 2010); Reuter (2017).
[25] Collier and Levitsky (1997).
[26] Levitsky and Way (2010, 57). For more on state coercive capacity and regime transitions, see Skocpol (1979); Bellin (2004); Way (2005, 2015), and Slater (2010).

(2014, 20) finds, coercive capacity is associated with higher levels of "voter intimidation and election day cheating."[27] Variation in coercive capacity may itself be driven by a range of forces. Some autocrats may be vulnerable to international pressure, which reduces their capacity for fraud and repression.[28] Some autocrats may exert weaker control over the security apparatus, perhaps due to divisions within the elite or financial constraints that undermine incentives for loyalty.[29]

Levitsky and Way (2010, 63) also emphasize party strength: "Strong parties help win elections." Strong parties may distribute patronage to key allies,[30] reward loyalty with career opportunities,[31] mobilize local support,[32] augment security forces,[33] and help steal votes.[34] Party strength may also help the regime extend its authority across the country, which Seeberg (2020) finds is a key determinant of electoral fraud. Scholars have traced strong parties to elite conflict at their founding and a relatively even balance of power between autocrat and elite.[35]

Finally, control over a reasonably lucrative state apparatus "may enhance incumbents' capacity to preempt or thwart opposition challenges." Here, Levitsky and Way (2010, 66) build on Dahl (1971) and Greene (2009, 2010), who argue that control over the economy provides opportunities for patronage. This economic control may stem from partially reformed command economies or natural resource rents.[36] More recently, Seeberg (2017) argues that authoritarian elections are stabilizing only when the regime enjoys economic control. Dasgupta (2018) traces the decline of single-party dominance in India to the Green Revolution.

We model the autocrat's capacity for electoral fraud as $\beta\zeta$, where $\beta > 0$ reflects how his capacity for repression conditions his capacity for electoral fraud. The parameter β accommodates the possibility that the autocrat's capacity for electoral fraud may be driven by factors other than his capacity for repression, as the discussion above suggests.

---

[27] Simpser (2013); Seeberg (2014).

[28] McFaul (2007); Levitsky and Way (2010); Hyde (2011); Donno (2013); Hyde and Marinov (2014); Escribà-Folch and Wright (2015); Carter (2016b); Carnegie and Marinov (2017); Carothers (2018).

[29] Levitsky and Way (2010); Schedler (2010b).

[30] Geddes (1999); Brownlee (2007); Magaloni (2008).

[31] Geddes (1999); Brownlee (2007).

[32] Svolik (2012).

[33] Widner (1992).

[34] Levitsky and Way (2010).

[35] Slater (2010); Reuter (2017).

[36] Fish (2005); Ross (2001, 2012).

When the autocrat's capacity for fraud and repression is limited, such that $\beta\zeta \to 0$, the ruler is bound by the electoral results, as in democracy. When the autocrat's capacity for fraud and repression is substantial, such that $\beta\zeta$ is large, the election is effectively meaningless.

At the game's outset, the value of ζ is known only to the autocrat. Citizens may have an intuitive sense for the autocrat's capacity for violence, but they are unaware of the inner workings of his security apparatus or the loyalties of key regime insiders. Like Egorov, Guriev, and Sonin (2009), we regard electoral constraints as fixed in the short term. Autocrats may attempt to loosen these electoral constraints, but they take them as fixed when setting their propaganda strategy.

2.2.4 *Propaganda*

A key feature of our theory is that the autocrat can employ propaganda to shape citizens' beliefs about policy outcomes θ_D and his capacity for fraud and repression ζ. We discuss each in turn.

Honest Propaganda and Persuasion The first role of propaganda is to shape citizens' beliefs about regime performance. Here, propaganda aims to persuade citizens that whatever frustrating outcomes they observe are not due to government corruption or incompetence, and that the government is working to make things better. To persuade citizens of useful fictions, propaganda apparatuses must have a reputation for occasionally reporting information that is at least somewhat damaging. This information may take the form of bad news, policy failures, or legitimate government malfeasance, however it might be spun. We refer to this coverage as *honest propaganda*. By employing it, propaganda apparatuses build credibility, which enables them to manipulate citizens' beliefs: to persuade citizens to attribute the causes of bad news to something other than government corruption or incompetence. Honest propaganda helps propaganda apparatuses build *credibility capital*. This idea has a long theoretical and empirical history. It constituted Goebbels' core insight, is a key result of formal models of propaganda and censorship,[37] and builds on Iyengar's (1990) observation that framing can manipulate beliefs.

---

[37] Gentzkow and Shapiro (2006); Kamenica and Gentzkow (2011); Gehlbach and Sonin (2014); Shadmehr and Bernhardt (2015); Guriev and Treisman (2015, 2018, 2022); Yu (2021).

After consuming propaganda, citizens update their beliefs about θ_D with Bayes' Rule. As Kamenica and Gentzkow (2011) observe, Bayes' Rule restricts citizens' posterior beliefs, in expectation, to be equal to citizens' prior beliefs, but Bayes' Rule places no constraints on the distribution of citizens' beliefs about different outcomes. Therefore, the autocrat can benefit from persuasion when the propaganda apparatus disseminates pro-regime content that induces citizens' support with positive probability, but this is balanced with coverage of bad news and policy failures that sometimes strengthens citizens' impulse to vote against him. This is akin to assuming that, given their prior beliefs, citizens vote against the autocrat by default, which occurs when their policy preferences diverge from the autocrat's and their confidence in the challenger μ_O^0 is relatively high.

Following Kamenica and Gentzkow (2011) and Yu (2021), we let the autocrat choose a propaganda disclosure rule π at the game's outset, when the value of θ_D is unknown to both the autocrat and citizens. The propaganda disclosure rule governs how the propaganda apparatus reports on the value of θ_D once realized. The rule features four quantities. The first two quantities entail acknowledging the true state of the world: the probability of positive coverage s^+ when $\theta_D = 1$ and the probability of negative coverage s^- when $\theta_D = 0$. The other two quantities entail claiming the state of the world is contrary to the truth: the probability of positive coverage s^+ when $\theta_D = 0$ and the probability of negative coverage s^- when $\theta_D = 1$. This propaganda disclosure rule has an intuitive interpretation. The autocrat chooses a propaganda strategy, but delegates implementation to a bureaucracy, which oversees content production.[38]

We think of positive coverage s^+ when $\theta_D = 0$ as propaganda: as the propaganda apparatus claiming the autocrat's policies have advanced the public welfare when, in fact, they have not. We think of negative coverage s^- when $\theta_D = 0$ as honest propaganda: as the propaganda apparatus conceding bad news and policy failures. Honest propaganda may take many forms, as we document throughout this book. In Congo, Denis Sassou Nguesso's propaganda apparatus employs honest propaganda when it concedes vaccine and fuel shortages, despite the government's status as Africa's fourth leading oil producer. In Cameroon, Paul Biya's propaganda apparatus employs honest propaganda when it concedes

---

[38] Put differently, the autocrat is unable to "distort or conceal information" once he delegates implementation of the propaganda disclosure rule; see Kamenica and Gentzkow (2011, 2591) and Yu (2021).

persistently high maternal mortality, but also emphasizes his efforts with UNICEF to address it. In Russia, Vladimir Putin's propaganda apparatus employs honest propaganda when it concedes economic downturns.[39] To be sure, their propaganda apparatuses also craft plausible narratives alongside: that the origins of these failures are due mostly to exogenous shocks and their governments are working to surmount them.

Honest propaganda is not cheap talk. It has two costs. First, it helps create common knowledge among citizens about regime failures and provides focal moments for protest.[40] If Congolese citizens were not already aware of the vaccine and fuel shortages, for instance, Sassou Nguesso's propaganda apparatus ensured they were. Second, broadcasting policy failures facilitates coups by regime insiders.[41] Insofar as policy failures help citizens mobilize against the regime, insiders may decide their interests are better served by toppling the incumbent and installing someone more competent. As for citizens, so too for regime insiders. Policy failures provide focal moments for regime insiders to coordinate, enabling long-standing frustrations to coalesce into collective action. We model this by assuming that when the propaganda apparatus covers regime failures – again, by providing negative coverage s^- – the autocrat loses the election and is forced from power with probability $1 - \rho\zeta$. This reflects the fact that losing power is partly a function of the autocrat's repressive capacity ζ and his vulnerability to conspiracies by regime insiders ρ.

Absurd Propaganda and the Capacity for Violence Autocrats signal their capacity for repression in many ways. They incarcerate dissidents,[42] block independent media, and fill the streets with police. They commit human rights abuses that the international community condemns, which signals some capacity to withstand international pressure.[43] These forms of repression aim not just to suppress dissent, but also to signal its consequences to citizens. For these threats to shape citizen behavior, they must be received. This is the chief benefit of using propaganda to broadcast the regime's capacity for repression. Repressive governments can signal this capacity to many citizens simultaneously at relatively little cost.

[39] Rozenas and Stukal (2018).
[40] Egorov, Guriev, and Sonin (2009); Rozenas and Stukal (2018).
[41] Nordlinger (1977); Galetovic and Sanhueza (2000); Casper and Tyson (2014); Kim (2016).
[42] Truex (2019).
[43] Carter (2016a).

Autocrats signal the strength of their repressive apparatus by employing *absurd propaganda*: content that everyone knows is false and that everyone knows everyone knows is false. Our conception of absurd propaganda is premised on *common knowledge of the possible*.[44] Intuitively, although citizens may not know the rate of economic growth or maternal mortality, there are claims that citizens know are false, either because of direct observation or universally held conventional wisdom. Absurd propaganda may take a range of forms. Chinese citizens are told that Xi Jinping "sets off a whirlwind of charisma ... wherever he goes." Gambian citizens were told that ex-president Yahya Jammeh would turn their country into the "Silicon Valley" of Africa, despite a GDP per capita of $535 and virtually no investment in public goods. These claims violate common knowledge of the possible. Everyone knows they are false. We refer to them as absurd.

By covering the regime in an absurdly positive way, the propaganda apparatus signals the autocrat's ability to fully tilt the electoral playing field: that his capacity for fraud and violence are so great that he does not need popular support. Wedeen (1999, 73) described this in Hafez al-Assad's Syria: "Power manifests itself in the regime's ability to impose its fictions upon the world. No one is deceived by the charade, but everyone ... is forced to participate." This is how, for Havel (1978, 8), citizens who were oppressed by Czechoslovakia's Soviet government confirmed, fulfilled, made, and ultimately were the system. This is why survey evidence, which we present in Chapters 4 and 9, shows that Chinese citizens find CCP propaganda unpersuasive. It is intended to intimidate, not persuade.[45] As Little (2017) observes, this signal may shape a citizen's beliefs about the regime or her beliefs about her compatriots' beliefs about the regime.

This constitutes the second use of propaganda in our theory. As we show in Section 2.3, the election reveals information about ζ. Intuitively, citizens know their expected utility from both the autocrat and the challenger. Therefore, if the autocrat secures victory, citizens know that his capacity for electoral fraud is at least as great as their preference for the challenger. If, for instance, citizens prefer the autocrat's challenger by a wide margin and yet the autocrat still secures electoral victory, then

---

[44] Chwe (2001).

[45] Huang (2015*b*); Jin (2016). Note that Stockmann (2010) and others argue that Chinese citizens find the CCP's commercialized newspapers relatively persuasive. We address this in Chapter 4.

citizens learn that $\beta\zeta$ is substantial. For the autocrat, this is potentially useful. By using propaganda to signal the strength of his repressive apparatus, the autocrat can potentially discourage citizens from revolting.

2.2.5 Timing and Equilibrium Concept

The timing of the game is as follows:
1. The autocrat chooses a propaganda disclosure rule π.
2. Nature chooses $\theta_D \in \{0, 1\}$, which determines whether the autocrat's policies advance public welfare.
3. The propaganda apparatus issues positive coverage s^+ or negative coverage s^- based on the realization of θ_D and the propaganda disclosure rule π.
4. Citizens observe coverage and update their beliefs about $\Pr(\theta_D = 1)$ using Bayes' Rule.
5. The election occurs and citizens vote for either the autocrat or challenger.
    a. If the autocrat loses the election, the autocrat loses power with probability $1 - \rho\zeta$ and the game ends.
    b. If the autocrat wins the election without employing electoral fraud, he retains power and the game ends.
    c. If the autocrat wins the election and employs electoral fraud, citizens choose whether to revolt.
        i.   If citizens do not revolt, the autocrat retains power and the game ends.
        ii. If citizens revolt, the autocrat retains power with probability ζ and loses power with probability $1 - \zeta$.

We look for subgame perfect Bayesian equilibria. The solution profile consists of the autocrat's optimal propaganda disclosure rule π^* and citizens' decision to revolt after a fraudulent election.

2.3 ANALYSIS

We solve the game via backwards induction. All proofs appear in the Technical Appendix at the end of the chapter.

2.3.1 Citizens: Revolution and Voting

We first identify the conditions under which citizens revolt after a fraudulent election.

Lemma 1. *Citizens revolt after a fraudulent election when*

$$\widehat{\zeta} < \frac{\beta - \mu_O^0}{\psi} \tag{2.3}$$

where $\widehat{\zeta}$ is citizens' posterior belief about ζ after the election.

Lemma 1 implies that citizens revolt after a fraudulent election when they believe the autocrat's repressive capacity, denoted by $\widehat{\zeta}$, is relatively weak. Equation (2.3) suggests two important comparative statics. First, citizens are more likely to revolt when the autocrat's targeting capacity ψ is low, since the cost of a failed revolt is lower. Second, citizens are more likely to revolt when the mapping from repressive capacity to electoral fraud β is high. In this case, the autocrat's greater capacity for fraud enables him to secure electoral victory even when citizens are strongly opposed to the regime, which leaves revolution the only realistic opportunity for political change.

Next, we identify the conditions under which the autocrat secures electoral victory.

Lemma 2. *The autocrat secures electoral victory when*

$$\mu_D \geq \frac{\mu_O^0 - \beta\zeta}{\delta} \tag{2.4}$$

and loses the election otherwise. If the autocrat secures electoral victory, citizens learn that the autocrat's capacity for repression is at least

$$\underline{\zeta} \equiv \frac{\mu_O^0 - \delta\mu_D}{\beta} \tag{2.5}$$

For the autocrat to secure victory, Lemma 2 makes clear, his propaganda apparatus must induce in citizens a posterior belief μ_D about $\Pr(\theta_D = 1)$ that is at least $\frac{\mu_O^0 - \beta\zeta}{\delta}$. Define

$$\mu_V \equiv \frac{\mu_O^0 - \beta\zeta}{\delta} \tag{2.6}$$

as the posterior belief where the autocrat and the challenger have equal electoral support, inclusive of the autocrat's capacity for fraud. In this case, we assume the autocrat wins. We refer to μ_V as the posterior belief threshold for electoral victory. Equation (2.6) yields several comparative statics about how the belief threshold μ_V changes with the political environment. Most importantly, where the autocrat's capacity for fraud and repression ζ is high, the posterior belief threshold required for electoral victory μ_V is low. The autocrat's capacity for fraud and repression let him employ a propaganda strategy that requires less persuasion.

Lemma 2 has another implication. From equation (2.5), when the autocrat secures electoral victory, citizens learn that his repressive capacity ζ is at least $\underline{\zeta}$. The reason is that citizens know their posterior belief μ_D about $\Pr(\theta_D = 1)$, their beliefs about the challenger μ_O^0, the mapping from repression to fraud β, and their policy preference similarity δ. This lets citizens infer the autocrat's capacity for repression. If the propaganda apparatus concedes only enough bad news to secure a knife edge victory – which, as we discuss below, is what it does – then citizens learn the value of ζ.

Since μ_V is a probability, it is bound within the interval $[0, 1]$. When $\mu_O^0 < \beta\zeta$, the autocrat's capacity for fraud is so great that he can win the election even when citizens attach probability 0 to $\theta_D = 1$. In this case, we let $\mu_V = 0$. When $\mu_O^0 - \beta\zeta > \delta$, we let $\mu_V = 1$.

2.3.2 *The Autocrat: Propaganda*

Lemma 1 makes clear that citizens' beliefs about the autocrat's repressive capacity are critical to our theory's predictions. When citizens believe the autocrat's repressive capacity is weak – in particular, when $\zeta < \frac{\beta - \mu_O^0}{\psi}$ – they revolt after a fraudulent election. From Section 2.2.2, this has implications for the autocrat's payoffs. When citizens choose not to revolt after a fraudulent election, the autocrat retains power and receives amount R of state revenue. By contrast, when citizens revolt, the autocrat's expected utility from the revolution lottery is $\zeta R - \gamma$, or state revenue R weighted by his probability of survival ζ less the cost $-\gamma$.

We refer to autocrats for whom $\zeta \geq \frac{\beta - \mu_O^0}{\psi}$ as *unconstrained*. Their capacity for repression is sufficiently great that citizens prefer not to revolt after a fraudulent election. We refer to autocrats for whom $\zeta < \frac{\beta - \mu_O^0}{\psi}$ as *constrained*. Their capacity for repression is insufficient to deter a post-electoral revolt. The payoff differential we identified above gives constrained autocrats an incentive to act like unconstrained autocrats and unconstrained autocrats an incentive to ensure they avoid a post-electoral revolt. The constrained autocrat, however, is prevented from employing an absurdist propaganda strategy because he loses the election and political power with probability $1 - \rho\zeta$. The election effectively forces the constrained autocrat to employ a propaganda strategy that aims to persuade citizens of regime merits. In the Technical Appendix, we discuss this separating equilibrium in more detail.

For a given capacity for fraud and repression ζ and posterior belief μ_D, the autocrat confronts three possible outcomes:

$$
\hat{v}(\mu_D) = \begin{cases} \rho \zeta R & \text{if } \mu_D < \mu_V \\ \zeta R - \gamma & \text{if } \mu_D \geq \mu_V \text{ and } \zeta < \frac{\beta - \mu_O^0}{\psi} \\ R & \text{if } \mu_D \geq \mu_V \text{ and } \zeta \geq \frac{\beta - \mu_O^0}{\psi} \end{cases}
$$

The first, where $\mu_D < \mu_V$, entails losing the election and being forced from power with probability $1 - \rho \zeta$. The second and third correspond to electoral victory, with the outcome depending on whether ζ is greater or less than $\frac{\beta - \mu_O^0}{\psi}$.[46]

The autocrat chooses a propaganda disclosure rule π with two types of coverage, each leading to one of two possible outcomes for a given ζ. Negative coverage s^- leads to electoral defeat and hence survival with probability $\rho \zeta$. Positive coverage s^+ lets the autocrat secure electoral victory, at which point his expected payoff depends on ζ. The constrained autocrat survives a post-electoral revolt with probability ζ and incurs cost $-\gamma$. The unconstrained autocrat can deter a revolt by citizens, and so he survives with certainty. Denote the probability of positive coverage s^+ as α and the probability of negative coverage s^- as $1 - \alpha$. The optimization problem for the unconstrained autocrat is then

$$
\max_{\alpha} V(\pi) = \alpha \times R + (1 - \alpha) \times \rho \zeta R
$$
$$
\text{subject to } \mu_D^0 = \alpha \times \mu_V + (1 - \alpha) \times 0 \tag{2.7}
$$

The constrained autocrat's optimization problem is

$$
\max_{\alpha} V(\pi) = \alpha \times (\zeta R - \gamma) + (1 - \alpha) \times \rho \zeta R
$$
$$
\text{subject to } \mu_D^0 = \alpha \times \mu_V + (1 - \alpha) \times 0 \tag{2.8}
$$

We refer to equations (2.7) and (2.8) as Bayes plausibility constraints. These constraints require that, in expectation, citizens' posterior beliefs about θ_D equal their prior beliefs. The autocrat's propaganda apparatus can induce a change in the distribution of citizens' posterior beliefs, but the expected posterior probability must equal its prior probability.

The Bayes plausibility constraints imply that the autocrat's optimal distribution of beliefs is that with probability $\alpha^* = \frac{\mu_D^0}{\mu_V}$ the posterior

---

[46] We assume $\gamma < R\zeta (1 - \rho)$, so that conceding regime failures is always more costly than not.

belief is μ_V and that with probability $1 - \alpha^* = 1 - \frac{\mu_D^0}{\mu_V}$ the posterior belief is 0. We now solve for the autocrat's optimal propaganda disclosure rule π. Let $\pi_{\theta_D}^+ = \Pr\left(s^+ | \theta_D\right)$ denote the probability of positive coverage s^+ given θ_D.

Lemma 3. *The autocrat's optimal propaganda disclosure rule is*

$$
\pi_{\theta_D}^+ = \begin{cases} 1 & \text{if } \theta_D = 1 \\ \frac{\mu_D^0}{1 - \mu_D^0} \frac{1 - \mu_V}{\mu_V} & \text{if } \theta_D = 0 \end{cases}
$$

and $\pi_{\theta_D}^- = 1 - \pi_{\theta_D}^+$.

The key expression in Lemma 3 is $\frac{\mu_D^0}{1 - \mu_D^0} \frac{1 - \mu_V}{\mu_V}$, which gives the probability of positive coverage s^* when $\theta_D = 0$. Again, from Section 2.3.2, we refer to this as propaganda. This implies that the propaganda apparatus mixes positive and negative coverage when $\theta_D = 0$ so that citizens' posterior belief about θ_D given positive coverage s^+, denoted by $\Pr\left(\theta_D = 1 | s^+\right)$, is equal to μ_V, which is the threshold belief for securing electoral victory.

Lemma 3 yields two other insights. First, propaganda is constrained by the common prior μ_D^0. When citizens are less confident in the autocrat *ex ante*, the propaganda apparatus can provide only so much positive coverage without invalidating itself. Second, when the autocrat's capacity for fraud and repression ζ is so substantial that the posterior belief threshold μ_V is low, the propaganda apparatus employs more propaganda. This happens because, at lower values of μ_V, the autocrat's propaganda apparatus can afford to be less persuasive, and hence concedes regime failures less often.

2.4 PROPAGANDA STRATEGIES IN THE BASELINE MODEL

Figure 2.1 illustrates how the autocrat's electoral constraints determine his propaganda strategy. Where the autocrat's limited capacity for fraud and repression constrains his ability to tilt the electoral playing field, he must seek some amount of popular support. As a result, the autocrat employs propaganda to persuade citizens of regime merits, which requires occasionally conceding bad news and policy failures. By contrast, where autocrats can fully secure themselves with repression, propaganda serves not to persuade citizens, but to discourage revolt by signaling the regime's capacity for violence.

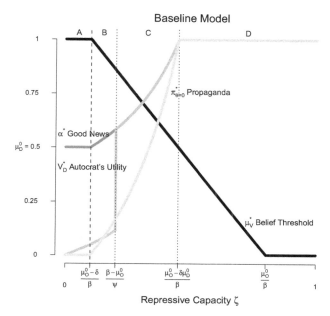

Figure 2.1 Theoretical predictions from the baseline model

We solve the model in terms of ζ. For values of ζ along the x-axis, Figure 2.1 features four curves that illustrate our theory's predictions: the posterior belief threshold for electoral victory μ_V^*, rates of positive coverage α^* and propaganda $\pi_{\theta_D=0}^{+*}$, and the autocrat's expected utility V_D^*.[47] For autocratic politics, Region A is less interesting. Here, the autocrat's capacity for fraud and repression is so weak relative to citizens' preference for the challenger that for the autocrat to survive the election, citizens must be certain that $\theta_D = 1$. As we discuss in Section 2.4.1, the autocrat is likely to prefer a "no fraud" equilibrium, which we think of as akin to democracy. In Regions B through D, the autocrat's capacity for fraud and repression lets him survive the election even when citizens are uncertain about θ_D. We discuss these equilibria in turn.

2.4.1 Region B: Binding Electoral Constraints, Honest Propaganda, and Revolt

We focus first on the constrained autocrat, depicted in Region B. Here, the autocrat's limited capacity for repression and fraud has two key

---

[47] For the simulations, we fix the following parameter values: $R = 1$, $\mu_D^0 = 0.5$, $\mu_O^0 = 0.8$, $R = 1$, $\delta = 0.7$, $\rho = 0$, and $\gamma = 0.01$.

implications. First, to survive the election, he must employ a propaganda strategy that leaves citizens relatively confident that the regime is advancing the public interest. Second, since the posterior belief threshold μ_V is relatively high, citizens infer that the autocrat's repressive capacity is limited, and so they revolt after a fraudulent election.

In Region B, there are two possible outcomes. In one, the autocrat prefers to forgo electoral fraud and compete in a free and fair election, which, again, we think of as democracy.

> **Proposition 1** (Propaganda in Democracies). *A constrained autocrat is more likely to forgo electoral fraud when his capacity for fraud and repression is low ($\zeta \to 0$), honest propaganda is costly ($\rho\zeta \to 0$), and the costs of a post-electoral revolt are high ($-\gamma \to -\infty$). Then the equilibrium is*
>
> - *The propaganda apparatus broadcasts positive coverage with probability $\alpha^* = \frac{\mu_D^0 \delta}{\mu_O^0}$, the rate of propaganda is $\pi_{\theta_D=0}^{+*} = \frac{\mu_D^0}{1-\mu_D^0}\left(\frac{\delta}{\mu_O^0}-1\right)$, and the rate of honest propaganda is $\pi_{\theta_D=0}^{-*} = 1 - \frac{\mu_D^0}{1-\mu_D^0}\left(\frac{\delta}{\mu_O^0}-1\right)$.*
> - *Citizens believe $\theta_D = 1$ with probability $\mu_V^* = \frac{\mu_O^0}{\delta}$ and do not revolt.*
> - *When the autocrat loses the election, he retains power with probability $\rho\zeta$. When the autocrat secures victory, he survives with certainty.*

The intuition for Proposition 1 is simple. Since citizens revolt after a fraudulent election, the autocrat expects the revolution lottery payoff $\zeta R - \gamma$. As $\zeta \to 0$ and the cost $-\gamma$ increases, the autocrat prefers to forgo electoral fraud, even if it means losing the election. When $\rho\zeta \to 0$, the autocrat is forced from power whenever the propaganda apparatus reports bad news, which occurs with probability $1 - \alpha^*$.

Next, we characterize the equilibrium outcome when the constrained autocrat employs electoral fraud despite the credible threat of revolt.

> **Proposition 2** (Propaganda in Constrained Autocracies). *When the autocrat's capacity for fraud and repression is $\zeta \in \left(\frac{\mu_O^0-\delta}{\beta}, \frac{\beta-\mu_O^0}{\psi}\right)$ and conditions for a "no fraud" equilibrium are not satisfied, the equilibrium is*

- The propaganda apparatus broadcasts positive coverage with probability $\alpha^* = \frac{\mu_D^0 \delta}{\mu_O^0 - \beta\zeta}$, the rate of propaganda is $\pi_{\theta_D=0}^{+*} = \frac{\mu_D^0}{1-\mu_D^0}\left(\frac{\delta}{\mu_O^0 - \beta\zeta} - 1\right)$, and the rate of honest propaganda is $\pi_{\theta_D=0}^{-*} = 1 - \frac{\mu_D^0}{1-\mu_D^0}\left(\frac{\delta}{\mu_O^0 - \beta\zeta} - 1\right)$.

- Citizens believe $\theta_D = 1$ with probability $\mu_V^* = \frac{\mu_O^0 - \beta\zeta}{\delta}$ and revolt after a fraudulent election.

- When the autocrat loses the election, he retains power with probability $\rho\zeta$. When the autocrat secures victory, the future political regime is determined by the revolution lottery, which the autocrat survives with probability ζ.

When his capacity for fraud and repression are limited, the autocrat is vulnerable. His propaganda apparatus cannot fundamentally change that. To survive the election, his propaganda apparatus must leave citizens relatively confident about regime merits, such that μ_V^* is relatively high. To do so, the autocrat can employ propaganda, but only in limited amounts. His use of propaganda is constrained by the common prior on θ_D, given by μ_D^0. Recall from Proposition 2 that the rates of propaganda and honest propaganda, respectively, are:[48]

$$\pi_{\theta_D=0}^{+*} = \frac{\mu_D^0}{1 - \mu_D^0}\left(\frac{\delta}{\mu_O^0 - \beta\zeta} - 1\right) \tag{2.9}$$

$$\pi_{\theta_D=0}^{-*} = 1 - \frac{\mu_D^0}{1 - \mu_D^0}\left(\frac{\delta}{\mu_O^0 - \beta\zeta} - 1\right) \tag{2.10}$$

When citizens are skeptical about θ_D, such that $\mu_D^0 \to 0$, the propaganda apparatus can persuade them that $\mu_D \geq \mu_V^*$, but only by employing a large amount of honest propaganda: by conceding bad news and policy failures. As a result, the autocrat's hold on power relies heavily on $\rho\zeta$ or on his ability to survive elite conspiracies occasioned by coverage of bad news and policy failures. When citizens are more inclined to believe $\theta_D = 1$, such that $\mu_D^0 \to 1$, then the propaganda apparatus can afford to reduce honest propaganda and still remain persuasive. Note also the effect of ζ. As the autocrat's capacity for fraud and repression increases,

---

[48] This is weakly positive, since $\mu_D^0 \geq 0$ and, for Proposition 2, $\delta > \mu_O^0 - \beta\zeta$.

he can secure electoral victory with a lower posterior belief threshold μ_V^*. Since the autocrat needs to generate less support, his propaganda apparatus can concede fewer regime failures.

The constrained autocrat must wage the battle for citizens' minds from a position of weakness. He must concede bad news and policy failures, despite the instability those admissions entail.

2.4.2 Region C: Intermediate Electoral Constraints, Propaganda, and Honest Propaganda

In Region C, the autocrat's capacity for fraud and repression is more substantial. This has implications for the autocrat's propaganda strategy and citizens' decision to revolt.

Proposition 3 (Propaganda in Semi-Constrained Autocracies). *When the autocrat's capacity for fraud and repression is* $\zeta \in \left[\frac{\beta - \mu_O^0}{\psi}, \frac{\mu_O^0 - \delta\mu_D^{0h*}}{\beta} \right)$, *the equilibrium is:*

- *The propaganda apparatus broadcasts positive coverage with probability* $\alpha^* = \frac{\mu_D^0 \delta}{\mu_O^0 - \beta\zeta}$, *the rate of propaganda is* $\pi_{\theta_D=0}^{+*} = \frac{\mu_D^0}{1 - \mu_D^0} \left(\frac{\delta}{\mu_O^0 - \beta\zeta} - 1 \right)$, *and the rate of honest propaganda is* $\pi_{\theta_D=0}^{-*} = 1 - \frac{\mu_D^0}{1 - \mu_D^0} \left(\frac{\delta}{\mu_O^0 - \beta\zeta} - 1 \right)$.
- *Citizens believe* $\theta_D = 1$ *with probability* $\mu_V^* = \frac{\mu_O^0 - \beta\zeta}{\delta}$ *and do not revolt after a fraudulent election.*
- *When the autocrat loses the election, he retains power with probability* $\rho\zeta$. *When the autocrat secures victory, he survives with certainty.*

When electoral constraints are only somewhat binding, the equilibria have three features. First, since the autocrat's capacity for fraud and repression is greater than in Region B, electoral victory is easier to secure. From Figure 2.1, the autocrat can claim electoral victory even when citizens are less confident about $\theta_D = 1$. Second, the propaganda apparatus can afford to be less persuasive. Relative to Region B, the autocrat employs more propaganda and less honest propaganda. This relative increase in propaganda informs citizens' decision about whether to revolt after a fraudulent election. In particular, they infer that the autocrat's repressive capacity is sufficiently strong that a revolt will likely fail.

For all these reasons, the autocrat's utility is greater in Region C than in Region B.

The distinctive feature of Region C is that substantial amounts of propaganda and honest propaganda are employed simultaneously. The propaganda apparatus can afford to be less persuasive, and hence signals to citizens that a post-election revolt is likely to fail.

2.4.3 Region D: Repression and Absurdity

In Region D, the autocrat's capacity for fraud and repression is high. This marks the transition to propaganda as domination. This strategy obtains only when the autocrat's capacity to tilt the electoral playing field is virtually unlimited.

Proposition 4 (Propaganda in Unconstrained Autocracies). *When the autocrat's capacity for fraud and repression is $\zeta \in \left[\frac{\beta - \mu_O^0}{\psi}, \frac{\mu_O^0 - \delta\mu_D^0}{\beta} \right)$, the equilibrium is*

- *The propaganda apparatus broadcasts positive coverage with probability $\alpha^* = 1$, the rate of propaganda is $\pi_{\theta_D=0}^{+*} = 1$, and the rate of honest propaganda is $\pi_{\theta_D=0}^{-*} = 0$.*

- *Citizens believe $\theta_D = 1$ with probability $\mu_V^* = \frac{\mu_O^0 - \beta\zeta}{\delta}$ and do not revolt after a fraudulent election.*

- *The autocrat retains power with certainty.*

When the autocrat's capacity for fraud and repression is $\zeta \geq \frac{\mu_O^0}{\beta}$, the equilibrium is unchanged, save that citizens believe $\theta_D = 1$ with probability $\mu_V^* = 0$.

When the autocrat is unconstrained, his propaganda strategy is much different. In Regions B and C, the autocrat was constrained to employ honest propaganda to persuade citizens of regime merits. In Region D, his capacity for fraud and repression is so great that the autocrat has no need for popular support. As a result, his propaganda apparatus broadcasts exclusively positive coverage: all propaganda, no honest propaganda. With no mention of bad news or policy failures, the propaganda apparatus loses its capacity to persuade citizens of regime merits. By making no attempt to do so, the propaganda apparatus signals to citizens that the autocrat's survival rests not on their approval but on his capacity for repression.

2.5 ENDOGENIZING PUBLIC POLICY

For simplicity, the baseline model treats the common prior μ_D^0 about $\Pr(\theta_D = 1)$ as exogenous. When citizens are skeptical about regime merits *ex ante*, such that $\mu_D^0 \to 0$, persuading them otherwise requires a relatively large amount of honest propaganda, which is destabilizing. Yet autocrats implement a range of public policies that inform citizens' assessment of regime performance. How does letting the autocrat choose these policies shape our theory's predictions?

When the autocrat chooses a propaganda disclosure rule π, we now also let him invest in public policy. We model this by letting the autocrat choose the common prior μ_D^0 about $\Pr(\theta_D = 1)$. This investment reflects the autocrat's various policy tools that strengthen public confidence in the regime. It may reflect the extent to which the autocrat monitors the appointees who implement his policies or the autocrat's efforts to learn which policies are most appropriate for the society. For the autocrat, investing in the common prior may be politically useful. When the common prior is relatively high, citizens are more inclined to believe that $\theta_D = 1$ and hence that the autocrat's policies advanced living standards. As we discussed in Section 2.4, a higher common prior makes persuading citizens of regime merits via propaganda more straightforward and electoral victory easier to secure.

Like any investment, manipulating μ_D^0 entails a cost, given by $\kappa \left(\mu_D^0\right)^2$, where $\kappa > 0$. The parameter κ measures the inefficiency of the autocrat's investment and hence reflects a second dimension of state capacity. The world's autocrats exhibit significant variation in their ability to monitor appointees and deliver public goods.[49] As κ increases, investment in the common prior becomes more costly for the autocrat. This captures the notion that, for some autocrats, public goods may be more costly to deliver and appointees more difficult to monitor.

Letting the autocrat invest optimally in the common prior reinforces our theory's key predictions and yields three additional insights. In the Technical Appendix, we characterize the full-equilibrium outcome. The first-order conditions imply that the autocrat's optimal investment in the common prior depends on his capacity for fraud and repression: in particular, on whether ζ is sufficient to deter a post-election revolt. Where the autocrat's repressive capacity is

---

[49] Edin (2003); Besley and Persson (2011); Dincecco (2017); Haggard (2018); Acemoglu and Robinson (2019).

insufficient to discourage a post-election revolt, such that $\zeta < \frac{\beta - \mu_O^0}{\psi}$, the first-order conditions imply the investment level

$$\mu_D^{0*}\left(\zeta^l\right) = \frac{\delta}{2\kappa} \frac{R\zeta(1-\rho) - \gamma}{\mu_O^0 - \beta\zeta} \qquad (2.11)$$

Where the autocrat's repressive capacity is sufficient to discourage a post-election revolt, such that $\zeta \geq \frac{\beta - \mu_O^0}{\psi}$, the first-order conditions imply the investment level

$$\mu_D^{0*}\left(\zeta^h\right) = \frac{\delta}{2\kappa} \frac{R(1-\rho\zeta)}{\mu_O^0 - \beta\zeta} \qquad (2.12)$$

The terms ζ^l and ζ^h refer to low and high repressive capacity, respectively.

Equations (2.11) and (2.12) have several important implications. First, where the repressive apparatus can deter a post-election revolt, the autocrat confronts neither the revolution lottery nor the cost $-\gamma$. At these higher ζ values, the autocrat's propaganda apparatus has less of a persuasive burden since the autocrat can claim electoral victory at lower posterior belief thresholds: $\mu_V^{h*} < \mu_V^{l*}$. The propaganda apparatus can afford to be less persuasive and hence broadcasts more propaganda and less honest propaganda. For both of these reasons, power is more valuable in the presence of a robust repressive apparatus, and hence optimal investment in the common prior is greater as well: $\mu_D^{0*}\left(\zeta^h\right) > \mu_D^{0*}\left(\zeta^l\right)$. Put differently, since power is more valuable, the autocrat invests more in the common prior to secure it. This is akin to Olson's (2000) "stationary bandit." An autocrat with a relatively long time horizon has an incentive to foster economic growth, which he can tax over time.

Figure 2.2 is analogous to Figure 2.1, but it presents the set of equilibrium outcomes when the autocrat can invest in the common prior.[50] Proposition 5 characterizes the autocrat's equilibrium investment in the common prior.

Proposition 5 (Endogenous Investment in Public Policy). *The autocrat's investment in the common prior depends on his capacity for repression ζ:*

---

[50] We fix the same parameter values as in Figure 2.1: $R = 1$, $\mu_O^0 = 0.8$, $R = 1$, $\delta = 0.7$, $\rho = 0$, and $\gamma = 0.01$.

$$
\mu_D^{0*} = \begin{cases}
0 & \text{if } \mu_0^*(\zeta) \leq 0 \text{ and } \alpha^* < 1 \\
\mu_D^{0*}(\zeta) & \text{if } \mu_0^*(\zeta) \in (0,1) \text{ and } \alpha^* < 1 \\
1 & \text{if } \mu_0^*(\zeta) \geq 1 \text{ and } \alpha^* < 1 \\
\mu_V^* & \text{if } \alpha^* = 1
\end{cases}
$$

where $\mu_D^{0*}(\zeta)$ depends on $\zeta \gtreqless \frac{\beta - \mu_O^0}{\psi}$ and is defined by equations (2.11) and (2.12).

The intuition behind Proposition 5 is straightforward. In Region B, where the autocrat's capacity for fraud and repression is limited, such that $\zeta < \frac{\beta - \mu_O^0}{\psi}$, his incentives to make costly investments in the common prior are weaker since political power is less valuable. With the common prior μ_D^{0*} relatively low, the rate of propaganda is lower – and the rate of honest propaganda higher – than in the baseline model. Recall from Figure 2.1 that we assumed the exogenous common prior was $\mu_D^0 = 0.5$. To an even greater extent than in the baseline model, the constrained autocrat is vulnerable, and his propaganda apparatus is unable to fundamentally change that.

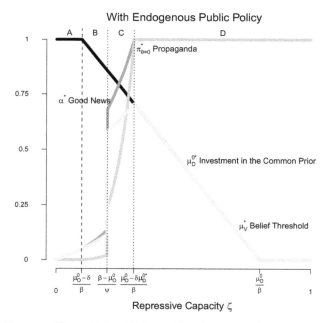

Figure 2.2 Theoretical predictions with endogenous policy investment

In Region C, the autocrat's repressive capacity is strong enough to discourage a post-election revolt, but it is still partially constrained. Consequently, he must continue to employ a mix of propaganda and honest propaganda, such that $\alpha^* < 1$. Since political power is more valuable in Region C than in Region B, the autocrat invests more in public policy to secure it. This yields the second key difference with the baseline model. Region C obtains for a smaller share of ζ values and Region D begins earlier. Intuitively, the Region C propaganda apparatus exploits the autocrat's additional investment in the common prior, which lets it support a higher rate of propaganda than in Region B. This lets the autocrat reduce honest propaganda and avoid the political instability it entails. In a sense, the credibility constraints on the propaganda apparatus are weaker, and so the propaganda apparatus can concede fewer regime failures. The Region C autocrat is investment-minded. His repressive apparatus is sufficiently strong that citizens do not revolt but not so strong that he can forgo investment in public policy. The autocrat employs investment and propaganda as complements. The aggregate amount of pro-regime content is high but so is its capacity to persuade.

Recall from Proposition 4 that Region D has two defining features. First, the autocrat's capacity for fraud and repression is substantial. Second, and as a result, the posterior belief threshold required for victory is very low. This lets the propaganda apparatus broadcast exclusively positive coverage, such that $\alpha^* = 1$. As ζ increases through Region D, the belief threshold μ_V^* decreases. As it does, the autocrat's ability to tilt the electoral playing field is even greater, and so the autocrat can reduce investment in the common prior to maintain the equality $\mu_D^{0*} = \mu_V^*$. This is because with $\alpha^* = 1$, the autocrat retains power with certainty and so has no incentive to invest further. At the highest values of ζ, propaganda content is distinguished by absurdity. The autocrat invests nothing in public policy, but the propaganda apparatus broadcasts exclusively positive coverage, which citizens know is false. This is the sense in which propaganda serves to signal the autocrat's capacity for repression, not persuade citizens of regime merits. By using the propaganda apparatus to set citizens' beliefs μ_V^* about $\theta_D = 1$ so low, the autocrat signals to citizens that his survival rests not on their approval, but on his capacity for repression. At the limit, there is only positive content, which citizens know is false. The propaganda apparatus has no capacity to persuade.

2.6 IMPLICATIONS OF CENSORSHIP AND INFORMATION ACCESS

Propaganda is but one component of an autocrat's informational strategy. Autocrats may also employ censorship. Scholars have suggested two broad targets of censorship: information about bad news and policy failures,[51] which may anger citizens and catalyze protests,[52] or information about dissidents and opposition leaders, who attempt to broadcast the regime's failures and mobilize citizens against it.[53] The inverse of censorship is information access. When autocrats are unable to censor, citizens can access alternative sources of information, such as independent newspapers and foreign news sources. As we discussed in Chapter 1, scholars and practitioners have suggested that this expanded access should moderate an autocrat's propaganda strategy.

We model censorship by assuming there is some lower bound of what citizens observe about the autocrat's policy investment. This lower bound is given by $\underline{\mu_D^0} > 0$. In Proposition 5, we effectively assumed there was no lower bound, such that $\underline{\mu_D^0} = 0$. This simply implies that citizens, in principle, could observe when the autocrat invested nothing in public policy. They could do so, presumably, by accessing alternative sources of information, such as independent newspapers and foreign news sources, which reveal the autocrat's underinvestment. Citizens could detect when he failed to invest in public goods, root out corruption, or monitor appointees who are charged with implementing policy.

Our theory suggests that censorship and information access are secondary drivers of propaganda strategies. Censorship tends to benefit autocrats at the extremes: in Region B, where capacity for fraud and repression is weak, and in Region D, where it is strong. At these two extremes, however, censorship has different implications for the autocrat's welfare and propaganda strategy. This is visualized in Figure 2.3, where we assume the autocrat can restrict citizens' informational environment such that they are unable to detect when investment in the common prior is below $\underline{\mu_D^0} = 0.3$.

In Region B, as we discussed in Section 2.5, the autocrat's capacity for fraud and repression is so limited that political power is less valuable

---

[51] King, Pan, and Roberts (2013); Chen, Zhang, and Wilson (2013); Lorentzen (2014); Roberts (2018).
[52] Shadmehr and Bernhardt (2015); Chen and Yang (2019); Carter and Carter (2020a).
[53] Pan and Siegel (2020); Gallagher and Miller (2019).

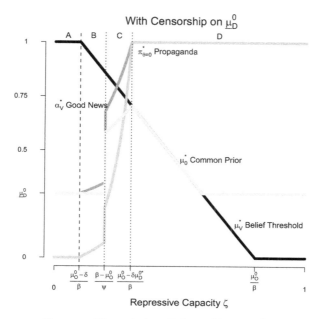

Figure 2.3 Theoretical predictions with censorship

than in Regions C and D. Therefore, the autocrat underinvests in public policy. A robust censorship apparatus shields that underinvestment from citizens.[54] In turn, the autocrat can exploit citizens' limited informational environment by increasing propaganda and decreasing honest propaganda. Comparing Region B in Figures 2.2 and 2.3 illustrates this; the rate of propaganda is substantially higher in Figure 2.3. This leaves the constrained autocrat better off.

In Region D, where the autocrat's capacity for fraud and repression is strongest, the effect of censorship is different. Note from Figures 2.2 and 2.3 that propaganda is unchanged. This is because the autocrat's capacity for fraud and repression is so substantial that propaganda is absurd; it serves to dominate, not persuade. Even as the autocrat's policy investment declines as ζ increases, the propaganda apparatus continues to broadcast exclusively positive coverage. At some point, however, the autocrat's optimal policy investment falls below the censorship level, such that $\mu_D^{0*}\left(\zeta^h\right) < \underline{\mu_D^0}$. When this happens, the autocrat reduces

---

[54] Formally, censorship shields underinvestment from citizens as long as $\mu_D^{0*}\left(\zeta^l\right) < \underline{\mu_D^0}$.

policy investment to 0. As a result, censorship advances the unconstrained autocrat's welfare by enabling him to further reduce policy investment.

Our theory's implication is clear. Access to information reduces propaganda only when the autocrat's capacity for fraud and repression is so limited that he underinvests in public policy. For understanding propaganda in autocracies, access to information is secondary to politics: to the electoral constraints an autocrat confronts.

2.7 IMPLICATIONS OF STATE CAPACITY

The world's autocrats vary dramatically in their capacity to enforce laws, provide services, and regulate economic activity.[55] It is increasingly clear that state capacity conditions politics in autocracies in important ways. State capacity may facilitate economic growth,[56] electoral fraud,[57] and intelligence gathering.[58] Acemoglu and Robinson (2012, 93–94) argue that the CCP government has generated growth, in part, by exploiting its ability to move surplus labor in agriculture into the more productive industrial sector.[59] Huang (2008) and Naughton (2018) think of this differently. Among the CCP's chief accomplishments, they argue, has been to regulate urban migration with its *hukou* system of registration permits to a pace it found manageable: around 2 million citizens moving from rural to urban areas per month. The CCP is also exporting its surveillance technologies to governments around the world, as we discuss in Chapter 11. By contrast, Africa's autocrats inherited weak states from colonial predecessors,[60] and many have since struggled to consolidate territorial control.[61]

---

[55] Scholars have linked variation in state capacity to many factors: geography and population density (Diamond 1997; Herbst 2000; Fukuyama 2011, 2014), the threat of interstate war (Hintze 1975; Brewer 1989; Tilly 1990; Besley and Persson 2011; Gennaioli and Voth 2015), the nature of economic activity (Mann 1993; Spruyt 1994; Acemoglu 2005; Besley and Persson 2011; Boix 2015), or the balance of power between civil society and political elites (Acemoglu and Robinson 2019).

[56] Knutsen (2013); Dincecco (2017); Haggard (2018); Acemoglu and Robinson (2019).

[57] Seeberg (2014, 2017, 2018, 2020); van Ham and Lindberg (2015).

[58] Edin (2003); Thomson (2022).

[59] Knutsen (2013); Fukuyama (2014); Rothstein (2015); Dincecco (2017, 26); Cheng and Gawande (2017).

[60] Young (1994); Acemoglu, Johnson, and Robinson (2001); Acemoglu and Robinson (2019).

[61] Herbst (2000).

The world's autocrats also vary in their capacity to detect dissenters. This variation may be driven by technology. The most sophisticated regimes employ a range of digital surveillance tools to monitor citizens, especially would-be dissidents.[62] Xu (2021) shows that these digital surveillance tools enable the CCP to target repression and decrease public goods. This variation may also be driven by the difficulties of governing societies divided by identity-based cleavages. Carter and Hassan (2021) show that autocrats routinely govern sub-national jurisdictions by appointing non-natives to key security posts, especially in opposition strongholds. This helps ensure that key security officials will repress opposition leaders and local activists, even though it limits local intelligence gathering capacity.[63]

How does state capacity condition propaganda in autocracies? Our theory incorporates state capacity in two ways. First, the parameter $\kappa > 0$ captures how costly it is for the autocrat to invest in the common prior μ_D^0. This may reflect how difficult it is to monitor local officials, who are charged with overseeing public goods projects. This may reflect how difficult it is to learn which public policies are most appropriate for the society. This may reflect other features of a society that make economic growth less likely, such as insecure property rights. Second, the parameter $\psi > 0$ reflects the ability of the autocrat's repressive apparatus to identify citizens who participated in a revolt that did not culminate in revolution. This may reflect the technological capabilities of the state's intelligence apparatus, which may limit citizens' ability to evade the repression. In societies divided by identity-based cleavages, this may also reflect the extent to which the state is forced to use non-native appointees to govern sub-national jurisdictions, which limits intelligence gathering.

These dimensions of state capacity have similar effects on propaganda in autocracies. Autocrats who govern with weak parties and preside over weak states are constrained in their ability to steal elections, provide public goods, and identify dissidents. These forces compel a propaganda strategy that must persuade citizens of regime merits, which requires conceding bad news and policy failures.

First, consider κ, which measures the relative inefficiency of the autocrat's policy investment. Increasing κ has two effects, one direct and

---

[62] Gunitsky (2015); Qin, Strömberg, and Wu (2017); Liu and Wang (2017); Gohdes (2020); Qiang (2019).

[63] Kalyvas (2006); Habyarimana et al. (2007); Lyall (2010); Carter and Hassan (2021); Hassan (2020); Carter (2022).

one indirect. The direct effect of weak state capacity is to reduce the autocrat's investment in the common prior μ_D^{0*} when $\mu_D^{0*}(\zeta) \in \left[\underline{\mu_D^0}, \overline{\mu_D^0}\right]$. This is intuitive. When investing in the common prior is relatively inefficient, the autocrat has a weaker incentive to do so. The indirect effect of weak state capacity is to shift the point $\frac{\mu_O^0 - \delta\mu_D^{0*}}{\beta}$, which is where the rate of positive coverage α^* reaches 1. As a result, the indirect effect of weak state capacity is to expand Region C at the expense of Region D. For a greater range of ζ values, the autocrat is semi-constrained (Region C) rather than unconstrained (Region D). Since the autocrat invests less in the common prior, his propaganda apparatus is forced to provide more honest propaganda to persuade citizens of the regime's merits. This has an important implication. Insofar as efficient investment ($\kappa \to 0$) fosters economic growth, our theory suggests κ-state capacity is associated with more effusive propaganda, rather than content that aims to persuade.

Now consider the effect of ψ. As ψ declines, autocrats lack the capacity to identify dissidents. As a result, citizens are willing to revolt after a fraudulent election for a greater range of ζ values. This effect is clear from Lemma 1. A decline in ψ shifts the revolt threshold $\frac{\beta - \mu_O^0}{\psi}$ toward the point $\frac{\mu_O^0 - \delta\mu_D^{0*}}{\beta}$, where the rate of positive coverage α^* reaches 1. Put differently, the principal effect of a reduction in ψ is to expand Region B at the expense of Region C. For ζ values within the expanded Region B, power is less valuable to the autocrat, and so he invests less in the common prior. Since the Region B propaganda apparatus must aim to persuade, it is constrained to retain credibility. It broadcasts less positive coverage and more honest propaganda. A more efficient security apparatus, our theory suggests, is associated with more propaganda and less honest propaganda.

2.8 IMPLICATIONS OF ELITE THREATS

Elite coups have long constituted a chief threat to autocratic survival.[64] Autocrats attempt to prevent them by building institutions that facilitate credible commitments with elites,[65] creating security forces with

---

[64] Tullock (1987); Geddes (2005); Svolik (2012).
[65] Brownlee (2007); Magaloni (2008); Gandhi (2008); Slater (2010); Svolik (2012); Meng (2020).

overlapping authorities,[66] and weakening their militaries.[67] Though coups are difficult to predict, scholars have also identified conditions that favor them: economic shocks,[68] income level and military spending,[69] popular protests and regime instability,[70] past coup attempts,[71] and others.[72] How does the credibility of elite coups condition propaganda?

Although our theory treats propaganda as primarily intended to condition citizens' beliefs about regime merits and repressive capacity, it has two implications for the nature of propaganda when elites can credibly threaten to remove the autocrat for policy failures. First, recall from Section 2.2.4 that when the propaganda apparatus broadcasts bad news and policy failures, regime insiders remove the autocrat with probability $1 - \rho\zeta$. When the autocrat's capacity for fraud and repression is limited ($\zeta < \frac{\mu_O^0 - \delta\mu_D^{0*}}{\beta}$, corresponding to Regions B and C), the threat of elite coups forces the autocrat to invest more in public policy. The autocrat does so to limit the policy failures that, if revealed by the propaganda apparatus, elites can use to coordinate coups. In turn, the propaganda apparatus exploits the autocrat's greater investment in public policy by broadcasting more positive coverage. The rate of propaganda rises and the rate of honest propaganda falls. Put simply, when the autocrat's capacity for fraud and repression is weak, the threat of a coup by regime insiders is associated with more propaganda and less honest propaganda.

By contrast, when the autocrat's capacity for fraud and repression is high ($\zeta \geq \frac{\mu_O^0 - \delta\mu_D^{0*}}{\beta}$, corresponding to Region D), our theory yields a different prediction. Here, the autocrat's strength vis-à-vis citizens effectively insulates him from elite threats. Intuitively, the autocrat's capacity for fraud and repression lets his propaganda apparatus avoid conceding bad news and policy failures, since he has no need for popular support. By broadcasting exclusively positive coverage, the autocrat's propaganda apparatus avoids having to expose him to the elite punishment that broadcasting policy failures may entail.

---

[66] First (1970); Quinlivan (1999); Powell (2012); Singh (2014); Geddes, Wright, and Frantz (2018).

[67] Reiter and Stam (1998); Quinlivan (1999); Pollack (2002); Belkin and Schofer (2003); Pilster and Böhmelt (2011).

[68] Nordlinger (1977); Galetovic and Sanhueza (2000); Kim (2016).

[69] Londregan and Poole (1990); Collier and Hoeffler (2007); Besley and Robinson (2010); Leon (2014).

[70] Finer (1976); Belkin and Schofer (2003); Powell (2012); Casper and Tyson (2014).

[71] Londregan and Poole (1990).

[72] See Jay Ulfelder's well-known annual forecasts: https://dartthrowingchimp .wordpress.com/.

2.9 IN THE ABSENCE OF ELECTIONS

The vast majority of the world's autocrats now organize regular elections, but not all. How does our theory apply to autocracies without regular elections? In our model, the election has two key features. First, from Lemma 2, the election provides citizens with information about the autocrat's capacity for fraud and repression ζ. This is driven by the fact that citizens know their posterior beliefs about θ_D, their utility from supporting the current regime, and their expected utility from some alternative. As a result, citizens can infer that the autocrat's capacity for fraud and repression is at least as great as $\underline{\zeta}$. Second, the election forces a separating equilibrium, since the constrained autocrat loses the election if he uses the propaganda apparatus to signal to citizens that his repressive apparatus is stronger than it actually is. This lets citizens distinguish between a constrained autocrat and an unconstrained autocrat. This also lets an unconstrained autocrat signal his repressive capacity to citizens in a way that the constrained autocrat cannot.

We regard autocrats who refuse to organize elections as, by definition, having very strong repressive apparatuses, such that $\zeta \rightarrow 1$. In this case, absurd propaganda remains useful as a reminder of the autocrat's capacity for repression in precisely the way that Wedeen (1999) described. Citizens can choose to engage in – or refrain from – a range of anti-regime activities. They can share information about government corruption with neighbors. They can engage in strikes. They can post anti-regime content on social media. When citizens observe each other choose to comply rather than dissent – despite a propaganda apparatus that broadcasts content that citizens know to be false – citizens signal to each other their *beliefs* about the autocrat's repressive apparatus. Intuitively, recall from Lemma 2 that, after the election, citizens learn that ζ is at least as great as the difference between citizens' utility from opposing the autocrat and supporting the autocrat. In the absence of an election, citizens still learn that their neighbors believe the autocrat's repressive capacity is at least as great as the difference between citizens' utility from dissenting and complying.

2.10 CHOOSING TO CONSUME PROPAGANDA, OR NOT

For propaganda to work, citizens must consume it.[73] Although our model abstracts from citizens' consumption decision, we suggest two

---

[73] Gehlbach and Sonin (2014); Yu (2021).

ways that an autocrat can induce citizens to consume propaganda. First, the autocrat can increase the share of factual news and entertainment content. As Goebbels suggested, citizens derive utility from genuine news and disutility from content they suspect is false. This is why, when Hugo Chavez forced Venezuelan TV to broadcast propaganda segments – known as *cadenas* – citizens simply changed the channel.[74] This is why state-owned television channels in Russia would gain some 20.3 percent more market share if they moderated their pro-regime bias.[75] This is why when Chinese citizens are provided with the tools to circumvent the Great Firewall, they do so.[76] Put simply, citizens are more likely to consume regime media if their utility from its factual news and entertainment content exceeds their disutility from what they suspect is fictitious. The autocrat can incentivize citizens to consume regime media accordingly.

Alternatively, some autocrats can force their citizens to consume propaganda. In Syria, Wedeen (1999) documents how al-Assad coerced citizens into reciting falsehoods in public. In North Korea, successive Kim regimes have required households to listen to state radio. Joseph Stalin, Mao Zedong, and Xi Jinping broadcast propaganda through village loudspeakers. Xi has pioneered new ways to force Chinese citizens to consume CCP propaganda, which are tailored to the Information Age. In 2017, at the CCP's 19th National Congress, Xi introduced a fourteen-point ideology, known as Xi Jinping Thought. The CCP then produced a smartphone app, "Study Strong Country," which aggregates propaganda content and awards users points for memorizing Xi's slogans. The app's name is itself a pun. In Chinese, the word for "study" is *xuexi*, and can be shortened to simply *xue*, omitting *xi*. The app is effectively named "Study *Xi* Strong Country," which explicitly underscores that CCP propaganda is intended to signal regime strength, not persuade citizens of regime merits. Since CCP members are required to download it, the regime can monitor who has memorized Xi's slogans and who has not. As of February 2019, it was China's most downloaded smartphone app.

Since, as Goebbels reminds us, citizens derive disutility from content they know is false, Chinese citizens resist CCP propaganda. The *New York Times* observed that online reviews for Xi Jinping's "Study Strong Country" app are "laced with dry sarcasm," similar to the dark humor that Czech novelist Milan Kundera described in *The Book of Laughter and Forgetting*. One reviewer, who awarded Xi's app a single star,

---

[74] Knight and Tribin (2019).
[75] Simonov and Rao (2022).
[76] Roberts (2018); Hobbs and Roberts (2018); Chen and Yang (2019).

wrote this: "Everybody is installing this app voluntarily. Nobody is forcing us." Another one-star review: "This software is great. I downloaded
it completely voluntarily. I like to study."[77] One dissident even launched
his own app, "Fuck Study Strong Country."[78] In 2009, when a building in the CCTV headquarters complex in Beijing burned down after
an illegal fireworks party held by CCP officials, citizens cheered. Said
one former *China Youth Daily* editor, Li Datong, who was fired for
criticizing the regime's censorship operation: "Many people were very
happy about the fire. Some said it's good that it burned." One popular
blogger, Zola, fielded a poll in which 30 percent of respondents agreed
with the statement "I hate CCTV. ... It's definitely good for it to be
self-immolated."[79]

That citizens can choose to consume propaganda has important implications for its content, which reinforces our theoretical expectations.
For propaganda to work, autocrats must induce citizens to consume it.
Where autocrats lack the repressive capacity to force consumption, they
must provide content that citizens want to consume. There are two ways
to do this. First, since citizens generally wish to avoid content they know
to be false, the propaganda apparatus can provide generally objective
news. Second, it is well established that citizens in democracies often prefer soft news to hard news.[80] This creates incentives to cover "topics
that appear exotic, cute and entertaining."[81] Accordingly, the autocrat
can induce citizens to consume propaganda by covering sports, entertainment, and other content that ostensibly has nothing to do with the
regime. This is why Denis Sassou Nguesso's *Les Dépêches de Brazzaville*
allocates a third of its daily content and its *entire* Saturday edition to
sports and culture.

2.11 CONCLUSION

The electoral constraints an autocrat confronts determine the propaganda strategy he employs. Where autocrats are limited in their ability
to tilt the electoral playing field, they must seek some amount of popular
support, and so they employ propaganda to persuade citizens of regime

---

[77] Zhong (2019).
[78] https://github.com/fuck-xuexiqiangguo/Fuck-XueXiQiangGuo.
[79] Spiegel (2009).
[80] Baum (2002, 2003); Hamilton (2004, 2010).
[81] Wu and Hamilton (2004, 527). As the market for advertising revenue has expanded, American newspaper editors have placed more value on audience interest
and cultural relevance; see Chang et al. (2012).

merits. To be persuasive, however, propaganda apparatuses must have some amount of credibility in the eyes of citizens. To acquire credibility, propaganda apparatuses must concede facts that are potentially damaging to the regime. They must cover economic crises, persistently high infant mortality rates, and breaches of public trust by government officials. These admissions foster frustration among citizens and facilitate collective action by elites. Still, conceding policy failures is an investment in the capacity to shape citizens' beliefs. Honest propaganda is an investment in making useful fictions credible.

Where autocrats confront no electoral constraints – where autocrats can fully secure themselves with repression – propaganda serves not to persuade citizens, but to intimidate them into submission. Propaganda derives its power from its absurdity. By broadcasting content that everyone knows to be false, propaganda serves to signal the regime's capacity for repression to citizens. Propaganda is a signal that the autocrat's hold on power rests not on their approval but on the regime's capacity for violence.

In Chapters 4 through 9, we show that this basic insight conditions the range of propaganda content that autocratic governments produce. It conditions how they cover economic performance, the political opposition, and the quality of their "democratic" governments. It conditions how they cover issue areas that ostensibly have little to do with domestic politics: sports, the domestic conditions of foreign countries, and the international order. It conditions how they cover election seasons and the anniversaries of failed pro-democracy movements, and whether they use the propaganda apparatus to threaten citizens with violence.

We begin, in Chapter 3, by introducing our dataset of autocratic propaganda.

2.12 TECHNICAL APPENDIX

2.12.1 *Proofs for Lemmas 1 and 2*

Lemma 2 summarizes when the autocrat secures electoral victory. This follows directly from citizens' expected utilities and the autocrat's capacity for electoral fraud:

$$y + \delta\mu_s + \beta\zeta \geq y + \mu_O^0$$

$$\mu_s \geq \frac{\mu_O^0 - \beta\zeta}{\delta}$$

Rearranging this yields the expression for $\underline{\zeta}$ in equation (2.5):

$$\underline{\zeta} \equiv \frac{\mu_O^0 - \delta\mu_s}{\beta} \tag{2.13}$$

Note that if the autocrat sets $\mu_V = \frac{\mu_O^0 - \beta\zeta}{\delta}$, then citizens learn the precise value of ζ. We discuss this in more detail below. This also implies that when $\mu_O^0 < \beta\zeta$, the autocrat's capacity for fraud is so great that he can win the election even when citizens attach probability 0 to $\theta_D = 1$.

Lemma 1 follows from citizens' expected utilities from revolting and from not revolting. Denote citizens' posterior value of ζ as $\widehat{\zeta}$. Then:

$$y + (1 - \zeta)\mu_O^0 + \widehat{\zeta} \times \left(-\psi\widehat{\zeta}\right) \geq y + \delta\mu_s$$

$$\frac{\beta - \mu_O^0}{\psi} \geq \widehat{\zeta}$$

2.12.2 *Proof for Lemma 3*

Recall from Section 2.3.2 that the autocrat's utility given posterior belief μ_D is given by $\hat{v}(\mu_D)$:

$$\hat{v}(\mu_D) = \begin{cases} \rho\zeta R & \text{if } \mu_D < \mu_V \\ \zeta R - \gamma & \text{if } \mu_D \geq \mu_V \text{ and } \zeta < \frac{\beta - \mu_O^0}{\psi} \\ R & \text{if } \mu_D \geq \mu_V \text{ and } \zeta \geq \frac{\beta - \mu_O^0}{\psi} \end{cases}$$

For a given ζ, the autocrat confronts two possible outcomes. The first, where $\mu_D < \mu_V$, entails losing the election and being forced from power with probability $1 - \rho\zeta$. The second two correspond to electoral victory, with the ultimate outcome depending on whether ζ is greater or less than $\frac{\beta - \mu_O^0}{\psi}$. Note that $\hat{v}(\mu_D)$ is a step function for a given belief μ_D.

To solve for the autocrat's optimal propaganda disclosure rule, we follow the concave-closure approach developed by Kamenica and Gentzkow (2011) and adapted by Yu (2021). Let V be the concave closure of $\hat{v}$:

$$V\left(\mu_D^0\right) \equiv \sup\{z| \left(\mu_D^0, z\right) \in co\left(\hat{v}\right)\}$$

where $co\left(\hat{v}\right)$ denotes the convex hull of the graph of $\hat{v}$. $V\left(\mu_D^0\right)$ is largest payoff the incumbent can achieve with any rule for propaganda disclosure when the prior is μ_D^0. Kamenica and Gentzkow (2011, 2596) show that if $\left(\mu_D', z\right) \in co\left(\hat{v}\right)$, then there exists a distribution of posteriors τ such that $E_\tau\mu_D = \mu_D'$ and $E_\tau\hat{v}(\mu_D) = z$. Thus, $co\left(\hat{v}\right)$ is the set of $\left(\mu_D^0, z\right)$

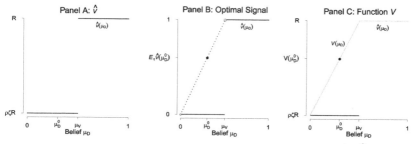

Figure 2.4 Illustrating the concave closure for $\alpha^* < 1$ and $\zeta \geq \frac{\beta - \mu_0^0}{\psi}$

such that if the prior is μ_D^0, there exists a rule for propaganda disclosure with value z. In turn, $V\left(\mu_D^0\right)$ is the largest payoff the autocrat can receive with any signal when the prior is μ_D^0.

Figure 2.4 shows the function $\hat{v}$, the optimal rule for propaganda disclosure, and the concave closure V when $\alpha^* < 1$ and $\zeta \geq \frac{\beta - \mu_0^0}{\psi}$. The parameter μ_D, which gives the posterior probability that $\theta_D = 1$, appears along the x-axes. From Panel A, $\hat{v}$ is a step function with respect to the posterior belief μ_D. When $\mu_D < \mu_V$, the autocrat's expected payoff is $\rho \zeta R$. When $\mu_D \geq \mu_V$, the autocrat's expected payoff is R. From Panel B, the optimal signal induces two posterior beliefs. When citizens consume bad news s^-, their posterior belief is $\mu_D = 0$ and $\hat{v}(0) = \rho \zeta R$. When citizens observe good news s^+, their posterior belief is $\mu_D = \mu_V$ and $\hat{v}(\mu_V) = R$.

Note that when $\alpha^* < 1$ and $\zeta < \frac{\beta - \mu_0^0}{\psi}$, the function $\hat{v}$ is as follows. When citizens consume bad news s^-, their posterior belief is $\mu_D = 0$ and $\hat{v}(0) = \rho \zeta R$. When citizens observe good news s^+, their posterior belief is $\mu_D = \mu_V$ and $\hat{v}(\mu_V) = \zeta R - \gamma$.

Let the probability that the realized signal induces belief μ_V be α. Since the distribution τ must be Bayes plausible, the Bayes plausibility constraints in equations (2.7) and (2.8) imply that $\alpha = \frac{\mu_D^0}{\mu_V}$. This implies that the optimal distribution of beliefs τ is that with probability $\alpha^* = \frac{\mu_D^0}{\mu_V}$ the posterior belief is μ_V and with probability $1 - \alpha^* = 1 - \frac{\mu_D^0}{\mu_V}$ the posterior belief is 0.

Lemma 3 characterizes the autocrat's propaganda disclosure rule, which represents the signal that induces the optimal distribution of beliefs τ. Let $\pi_{\theta_D}^+$ be the probability of positive coverage s^+ given θ_D and $\pi_{\theta_D}^-$ be the probability of negative coverage s^- given θ_D. When $\theta_D = 1$, the propaganda apparatus employs positive coverage s^+. When $\theta_D = 0$, the propaganda apparatus employs a mix of positive and negative coverage so that citizens' posterior belief given positive coverage s^+ is μ_V. From Bayes' Rule, this requires that

$$\Pr\left(\theta_D = 1|s^+\right) = \mu_V$$

$$\frac{\Pr\left(s^+|\theta_D = 1\right) \times \Pr\left(\theta_D = 1\right)}{\Pr\left(s^+|\theta_D = 1\right) \times \Pr\left(\theta_D = 1\right) + \Pr\left(s^+|\theta_D = 0\right) \times \Pr\left(\theta_D = 0\right)} = \mu_V$$

(2.14)

Note that $\Pr\left(s^+|\theta_D = 1\right) = 1$. This lets us solve for $\pi^+_{\theta_D=0}$, which, in equation (2.14), is given by $\Pr\left(s^+|\theta_D = 0\right)$. This yields

$$\frac{\mu_D^0}{1 - \mu_D^0} \times \frac{1 - \mu_V}{\mu_V} = \pi^+_{\theta_D=0}$$

This is the sense in which the signal $\pi^+_{\theta_D=0}$ induces the optimal τ. This lets us characterize the concave closure V, which appears in Panel C:

$$V\left(\mu_D\right) = R \times \mu_D \times 1 + \rho \zeta R \times (1 - \mu_D) \times \frac{\mu_D}{1 - \mu_D} \frac{1 - \mu_V}{\mu_V} \quad (2.15)$$

when $\mu_D < \mu_V$ and 1 when $\mu_D \geq \mu_V$. Note that (2.15) is simply the value of $\pi^+_{\theta_D}$, weighted by the probability μ_D that $\theta_D = 1$ and the probability $1 - \mu_D$ that $\theta_D = 0$.

2.12.3 *More on the Separating Equilibrium*

Regardless of ζ, the autocrat always prefers to set citizens' posterior beliefs μ_D at μ_V^*, which is the lowest posterior belief at which the autocrat can still secure electoral victory. Recall from the discussion around Lemma 3 that the autocrat mixes positive and negative coverage so that

$$\Pr\left(\theta_D = 1|s^+\right) = \mu_V$$

$$\frac{\Pr\left(s^+|\theta_D = 1\right) \times \Pr\left(\theta_D = 1\right)}{\Pr\left(s^+|\theta_D = 1\right) \times \Pr\left(\theta_D = 1\right) + \Pr\left(s^+|\theta_D = 0\right) \times \Pr\left(\theta_D = 0\right)} = \mu_V$$

Since $\Pr\left(s^+|\theta_D = 1\right) = 1$, setting some $\mu_D \geq \mu_V$ requires either increasing the prior $\Pr\left(\theta_D = 1\right)$ or reducing $\Pr\left(s^+|\theta_D = 0\right)$. Since the prior is fixed in the baseline model, setting some $\mu_D > \mu_V$ effectively requires setting $\Pr\left(s^+|\theta_D = 0\right) < \frac{\mu_D^0}{1 - \mu_D^0} \times \frac{1 - \mu_V}{\mu_V}$. This entails employing less positive coverage conditional on $\theta_D = 0$. Put differently, this entails employing less propaganda and more honest propaganda. Since, from Section 2.3.2, the autocrat loses power with probability $1 - \rho\zeta$ when the propaganda apparatus employs negative coverage s^-, employing more honest propaganda than is strictly optimal for the autocrat makes him more likely to lose power. As a result, the autocrat prefers to set $\mu_D = \mu_V$. This has an important implication. Recall from the discussion around Lemmas 1 and 2 that citizens learn the precise value of ζ after the election as long as $\mu_D = \mu_V$.

Now define the following posterior threshold beliefs:

$$\mu_V^{h*} = \frac{\mu_O^0 - \beta\zeta^h}{\delta}$$

$$\mu_V^{l*} = \frac{\mu_O^0 - \beta\zeta^l}{\delta}$$

where $\mu_V^{h*} < \mu_V^{l*}$, the superscript l denotes a constrained autocrat, and the superscript h denotes an unconstrained autocrat. A type ζ^l autocrat never prefers to set μ_V^{h*} rather than μ_V^{l*}, since this entails the type ζ^l autocrat losing the election. As a result, as long as $R\zeta\,(1 - \rho) > \gamma$ – or conceding regime failures is more costly than not – type ζ^l does not prefer to set μ_V^{h*}.

The type ζ^h autocrat also never prefers to set μ_V^{l*} rather than μ_V^{h*}. For a given μ_D^0, this follows from:

$$\frac{\mu_D^0}{\mu_V^{h*}}R > \frac{\mu_D^0}{\mu_V^{l*}}\left(R\zeta^h - \gamma\right)$$

$$\frac{R}{R\zeta^h - \gamma} > \frac{\mu_O^0 - \beta\zeta^h}{\mu_O^0 - \beta\zeta^l}$$

The inequality is strict, since $R > R\zeta^h - \gamma$ and $\mu_O^0 - \beta\zeta^h < \mu_O^0 - \beta\zeta^l$.

2.12.4 Proof for Proposition 2

For Proposition 2, which corresponds to Region B in Figure 2.1, the autocrat's capacity is $\zeta \in \left(\frac{\mu_O^0 - \delta}{\beta}, \frac{\beta - \mu_O^0}{\psi}\right)$. For these ζ values, from Lemma 2, the posterior belief threshold for victory is $\mu_V^* = \frac{\mu_O^0 - \beta\zeta}{\delta}$. Using the Bayes plausibility constraint in equation (2.8), the expression for μ_V^* implies $\alpha^* = \frac{\mu_D^0\delta}{\mu_O^0 - \beta\zeta}$. Using Lemma 3, the expression for μ_V^* also implies the rates of propaganda $\pi_{\theta_D=0}^{+*} = \frac{\mu_D^0}{1 - \mu_D^0}\left(\frac{\delta}{\mu_O^0 - \beta\zeta} - 1\right)$ and honest propaganda

$\pi_{\theta_D=0}^{-*} = 1 - \frac{\mu_D^0}{1-\mu_D^0}\left(\frac{\delta}{\mu_O^0 - \beta\zeta} - 1\right)$. From Lemma 1, since $\zeta < \frac{\beta - \mu_O^0}{\psi}$, citizens revolt after a fraudulent election. Note that the autocrat's expected utility is then

$$u_{Con}^* = \frac{\mu_D^0 \delta}{\mu_O^0 - \beta\zeta}(\zeta R - \gamma) + \left(1 - \frac{\mu_D^0 \delta}{\mu_O^0 - \beta\zeta}\right)\rho\zeta R$$

2.12.5 Proof for Proposition 1

There is a "democracy equilibrium" that may occur where $\zeta \leq \frac{\beta - \mu_O^0}{\psi}$. From Lemma 2, the posterior belief threshold for electoral victory when $\zeta = 0$ is

$$\mu_D^* = \frac{\mu_O^0}{\delta}$$

This defines α^* and, from Lemma 3, the propaganda disclosure rule $\pi_{\theta_D}^{+*}$. Then the autocrat's utility from democracy is

$$u_{Dem}^* = \frac{\mu_D^0 \delta}{\mu_O^0}R$$

Then the autocrat prefers to forgo electoral fraud when

$$\frac{\mu_D^0 \delta}{\mu_O^0}R > \frac{\mu_D^0 \delta}{\mu_O^0 - \beta\zeta}(\zeta R - \gamma) + \left(1 - \frac{\mu_D^0 \delta}{\mu_O^0 - \beta\zeta}\right)\rho\zeta R$$

These conditions are more likely to obtain when $\zeta, \rho \to 0$ and $-\gamma$ is substantially less than 0.

2.12.6 Proof for Proposition 3

Proposition 3 has the same structure as Proposition 2. However, since $\zeta \geq \frac{\beta - \mu_O^0}{\psi}$, citizens prefer not to revolt after a fraudulent election. The expressions for μ_V^*, α^*, $\pi_{\theta_D=0}^{+*}$, and $\pi_{\theta_D=0}^{-*}$ are identical.

2.12.7 Proof for Proposition 4

Proposition 4 obtains where $\alpha^* = 1$, which occurs when $\zeta \geq \frac{\mu_O^0 - \delta\mu_D^0}{\beta}$. This implies that the propaganda apparatus broadcasts exclusively positive coverage, which implies the rates of propaganda $\pi_{\theta_D=0}^{+*} = 1$ and honest propaganda $\pi_{\theta_D=0}^{-*} = 0$. Since $\zeta \geq \frac{\beta - \mu_O^0}{\psi}$, citizens prefer not to revolt after a fraudulent election. The posterior belief threshold μ_V^* depends on ζ. When $\zeta < \frac{\mu_O^0}{\beta}$, then $\mu_V^* = \frac{\mu_O^0 - \beta\zeta}{\delta}$. When $\zeta \geq \frac{\mu_O^0}{\beta}$, then $\mu_V^* = 0$.

2.12.8 Proof for Proposition 5

When the autocrat chooses μ_D^0 optimally, the set of possible outcomes is

$$\hat{v}(\mu_D) = \begin{cases} \rho\zeta R - \kappa\left(\mu_D^0\right)^2 & \text{if } \mu_D < \mu_V \\ \zeta R - \gamma - \kappa\left(\mu_D^0\right)^2 & \text{if } \mu_D \geq \mu_V \text{ and } \zeta < \frac{\beta - \mu_O^0}{\psi} \\ R - \kappa\left(\mu_D^0\right)^2 & \text{if } \mu_D \geq \mu_V \text{ and } \zeta \geq \frac{\beta - \mu_O^0}{\psi} \end{cases}$$

The optimization problem for the constrained autocrat is then

$$\max_{\alpha, \, \mu_D^0} V(\pi) = \alpha \times (\zeta R - \gamma) + (1 - \alpha) \times \rho\zeta R - \kappa\left(\mu_D^0\right)^2$$

subject to $\mu_D^0 = \alpha \times \mu_V + (1 - \alpha) \times 0$

The unconstrained autocrat's optimization problem is

$$\max_{\alpha, \, \mu_D^0} V(\pi) = \alpha \times R + (1 - \alpha) \times \rho\zeta R - \kappa\left(\mu_D^0\right)^2$$

subject to $\mu_D^0 = \alpha \times \mu_V + (1 - \alpha) \times 0$

Solving these for μ_D^0 yields

$$\mu_D^{0*}\left(\zeta^l\right) = \frac{\delta}{2\kappa}\frac{R\zeta(1 - \rho) - \gamma}{\mu_O^0 - \beta\zeta}$$

$$\mu_D^{0*}\left(\zeta^h\right) = \frac{\delta}{2\kappa}\frac{R(1 - \rho\zeta)}{\mu_O^0 - \beta\zeta}$$

which correspond to equations (2.11) and (2.12). These are positive as long as $\mu_O^0 > \beta\zeta$, which is also the condition for $\mu_V^* > 0$. When equations (2.11) and (2.12) are greater than 1, then $\mu_D^{0*} = 1$. Recall that the Bayes plausibility constraints imply that $\alpha^* = \frac{\mu_D^{0*}}{\mu_V^*}$. Since $\alpha^* \in [0, 1]$, the autocrat never prefers to set $\mu_D^{0*} > \mu_V^*$. Therefore, when $\alpha^* = 1$, then the autocrat sets $\mu_D^{0*} = \mu_V^*$. This yields the expressions for μ_D^{0*} in Proposition 5.

2.12.9 *Proof for Proposition 6*

The analysis in Section 2.6 is based on Proposition 6, which summarizes how access to some censorship technology shapes the autocrat's propaganda strategies.

Proposition 6 (Censorship and Information Access). *When the autocrat has access to some censorship technology that sets a lower bound $\underline{\mu}_D^0 > 0$, the autocrat's optimal investment in public policy is*

$$
\mu_D^{0*} = \begin{cases}
0 & \text{if } \mu_0^*(\zeta) < \underline{\mu}_D^0 \text{ and } \alpha^* < 1 \\
\mu_D^{0*}(\zeta) & \text{if } \mu_0^*(\zeta) \in \left[\underline{\mu}_D^0, 1\right] \text{ and } \alpha^* < 1 \\
1 & \text{if } \mu_0^*(\zeta) \geq 1 \text{ and } \alpha^* < 1 \\
\mu_V^* & \text{if } \mu_0^*(\zeta) > \underline{\mu}_D^0 \text{ and } \alpha^* = 1 \\
0 & \text{if } \mu_0^*(\zeta) < \underline{\mu}_D^0 \text{ and } \alpha^* = 1
\end{cases}
$$

Consider first the case where $\mu_0^*(\zeta^l) < \underline{\mu}_D^0$ and $\alpha^* < 1$, which is most likely to obtain in Region B. In this case, censorship technology increases the rate of positive coverage α^*, since

$$
\alpha^{C*} > \alpha^*
$$
$$
\frac{\underline{\mu}_D^0}{\mu_V^*} > \frac{\mu_0^*(\zeta^l)}{\mu_V^*}
$$

where the superscript C indicates censorship technology. The rate of propaganda increases as well, since

$$
\pi_{\theta_D=0}^{+C*} > \pi_{\theta_D=0}^{+*}
$$
$$
\frac{\underline{\mu}_D^0}{1 - \underline{\mu}_D^0} \left(\frac{\delta}{\mu_O^0 - \beta\zeta} - 1 \right) > \frac{\mu_0^*(\zeta^l)}{1 - \mu_0^*(\zeta^l)} \left(\frac{\delta}{\mu_O^0 - \beta\zeta} - 1 \right)
$$

Since $\alpha^{C*} > \alpha^*$, the censorship technology strictly increases the autocrat's probability of survival, which, in turn, strictly increases his expected utility.

Now consider the case where $\mu_0^*(\zeta^h) < \underline{\mu}_D^0$ and $\alpha^* = 1$, which only obtains in Region D. Since $\alpha^* = 1$, the rate of propaganda is $\pi_{\theta_D=0}^{+*} = 1$. As a result, the censorship technology has no effect on propaganda. However, censorship lets the autocrat reduce the policy investment by the amount

$$
\underline{\mu}_D^0 - \mu_0^*(\zeta^h)
$$

which leaves him strictly better off. Censorship advances the unconstrained autocrat's welfare by enabling him to reduce his investment in public policy.

2.12.10 Proof for Propositions 7 and 8

The analysis in Section 2.7 is based on Propositions 7 and 8, which summarize how state capacity shapes the autocrat's propaganda strategies.

Proposition 7 (Weak State Capacity via Investment Inefficiency). *As public policy grows more inefficient, such that κ increases, the autocrat's optimal investment in public policy decreases for $\mu_D^*(\zeta) \in \underline{\mu_D^0}, 1$ and $\alpha^* = 1$. As a result, the point $\frac{\mu_O^0 - \delta\mu_D^{0*}}{\beta}$, which is where the rate of positive coverage α^* reaches 1, also increases.*

Proposition 7 follows directly from comparative statics on $\mu_D^{0*}(\zeta)$, given by equations (2.11) and (2.12), and Proposition 5.

Proposition 8 (State Capacity via Targeted Repression). *Where the autocrat lacks the capacity to target repression, such that $\psi \to 0$, the revolt threshold $\frac{\beta - \mu_O^0}{\psi}$ increases toward the point $\frac{\mu_O^0 - \delta\mu_D^{0*}}{\beta}$, where the rate of positive coverage α^* reaches 1.*

Proposition 8 follows directly from comparative statics on the revolt threshold in equation (2.3).

2.12.11 Proof for Proposition 9

The analysis in Section 2.8 is based on Proposition 9, which summarizes how elite threats shape the autocrat's propaganda strategies.

Proposition 9 (Elite Threats). *As the threat of elite coups grows, such that $\rho \to 0$, the autocrat's propaganda strategy is unchanged where $\zeta \geq \frac{\mu_O^0 - \delta\mu_D^{0*}}{\beta}$ such that $\alpha^* = 1$. Where $\alpha^* < 1$ and $\mu_0^*(\zeta) > \mu_D^0$, the autocrat increases policy investment $\mu_0^*(\zeta)$ as $\rho \to 0$.*

Proposition 9 follows directly from comparative statics on $\mu_D^{0*}(\zeta)$, which appear in equations (2.11) and (2.12), and Proposition 5.

3

A Global Dataset of Autocratic Propaganda

3.1 INTRODUCTION

The two understandings of propaganda at this book's core – persuasion or domination – predate modern political science. Why have they not yet been joined in a unified theory of autocratic propaganda? The answer, we believe, was suggested by Warren (2014, 117): "The operations of soft power are inherently difficult to observe and quantify on a global basis." There is no central repository of autocratic propaganda, no archive to which the world's autocrats submit their content. Even if there was, it is unclear how propaganda would be measured. And without some form of measurement, it is unclear how propaganda across autocracies could be compared.

This book, to the best of our knowledge, draws on the largest collection of autocratic propaganda ever assembled. It is also the first to measure propaganda cross-nationally. Our dataset of state-run newspapers contains over 8 million unique articles from sixty-five newspapers in fifty-nine countries and six of the world's major languages. Although much of our propaganda collection dates from 2000, for several countries it extends back decades. This chapter introduces our dataset, our measures of propaganda, and the techniques we employed to create them.[1] Section 3.2 discusses how we assembled the collection. Section 3.3

---

[1] This book speaks to a large literature in computational linguistics that focuses on the role of framing, bias, and political content in text. See, for instance, Tsur, Calacci, and Lazer (2015); Baumer et al. (2015); Card et al. (2015, 2016); Boyd-stun, Ledgerwood, and Sparks (2017); Recasens, Danescu-Niculescu-Mizil, and Jurafsky (2013); Greene and Resnik (2009); Wiebe et al. (2004); Tan, Lee, and Pang (2014); Rao et al. (2010); Conover et al. (2011); Pla and Hurtado (2014); Bakliwal et al. (2013); Iyyer et al. (2014); Bammam and Smith (2015); Sim et al. (2013); Djemili et al. (2014); Nguyen et al. (2015); Johnson, Lee, and Goldwasser (2017); Morstatter et al. (2018); Tucker et al. (2018); Field et al. (2018).

provides an overview of dictionary-based semantic analysis, which constitutes the foundation for our measures of propaganda. Section 3.4 introduces our measures of pro-regime propaganda. One adopts a more restrictive view of who constitutes the regime; the other adopts a more expansive view. Crucially, these measures let us distinguish between the valence of pro-regime propaganda and its frequency. Section 3.4 also compares our measures of pro-regime propaganda to the one developed by Qin, Strömberg, and Wu (2018) in the context of China.

The world's autocrats employ propaganda to shape citizens' beliefs about many topics: the opposition, a country's contemporary history, the international community, and even the likelihood of violence in response to dissent. Our data reflect this. Section 3.5 discusses how we measure the rate and valence of opposition coverage. Section 3.6 discusses how we conceptualize and measure the narratives that propaganda apparatuses craft. Section 3.7 helps readers scale our measures of propaganda. We provide several examples from Rwanda, which has been ruled by President Paul Kagame since the 1994 genocide, and situate our measures of propaganda in a context with which many readers will be familiar: how Fox News covers Republicans relative to Democrats. Section 3.8 concludes by explaining why we focus on newspaper propaganda, rather than radio or television.

3.2 HOW TO BUILD A PROPAGANDA COLLECTION

3.2.1 *The Merits and Drawbacks of Online Propaganda Archives*

To create the dataset, we sought to identify the most widely distributed state-run newspapers for as many autocracies as possible across the world. We began by cataloging state-run newspapers. We consulted a variety of sources: Freedom House, *Press Reference*, the Knight Center for Journalism, and the Open Society Foundation, among others. Where a newspaper is owned by the state, like China's *People's Daily*, coding it as state-run was straightforward. In other cases, newspapers are owned by members of the ruling elite. Where these newspapers are regarded as government mouthpieces, we included them as well. Several of the state-run newspapers we identified were clearly intended for a foreign audience. Vietnam's *Le Courrier*, for instance, is published in French, rather than Vietnamese, and it circulates primarily among French expatriates in Southeast Asia. Although we regard outward-facing propaganda as theoretically interesting and substantively important – we discuss this in more detail in Chapter 11 – our focus is on inward-facing propaganda. Accordingly, we excluded from our sample state-run newspapers that are intended primarily for a foreign audience.

We restricted attention to languages for which quantitative text analysis methods are well developed: Arabic, Chinese, English, French, Russian, and Spanish. We further restricted attention to state-run newspapers with online archives. Although these two restrictions were critical for data collection and analysis, each entails a drawback. It is possible that state-run newspapers in major languages and with online archives are systematically different from their counterparts. Some autocrats may publish an English or a French newspaper for expatriates and a separate local language newspaper for citizens; the former may be more neutral and the latter more biased. Likewise, autocrats who finance online archives for their propaganda newspapers may do so because their populations enjoy better internet access. These autocrats may be constrained to employ more neutral coverage than those in less connected societies.

Although we cannot rule out either possibility, we believe neither is a major concern. First, many countries with a colonial history conduct official business not in local languages but in the language of the European colonizer. Their newspapers are often published in the language of the European colonizer as well. These newspapers target an overwhelmingly urban audience, usually in the national capital and a handful of regional capitals. Among these populations, English and French are widely spoken, and often at higher rates than local languages. The urban populations who consume these languages are also critical for the survival of autocrats. Because of their close geographic proximity to the national capital, protests by urbanites are far more threatening than by rural dwellers.[2]

Second, reflecting the growing prevalence of internet access across the world, we found that autocrats who govern the world's poorest countries are just as likely to maintain online archives as those from more affluent countries. Whether state-run newspapers maintain freely available online archives appears to be more a function of regime type than GDP. Most autocrats, we found, make their state-run newspapers available online, and accessible without restriction. Since propaganda is useful only when consumed, most autocrats maximize its distribution, and so seldom regard it as intellectual property. This is consistent with their approach

[2] Bates (1983).

to domestic distribution. Denis Sassou Nguesso is again instructive. *Les Dépêches de Brazzaville* remains Congo's only daily newspaper, printed in color on high-quality paper. At a market price of roughly $0.20, it is heavily subsidized by the state.[3] Its primary competitor is *La Semaine Africaine*, an independent newspaper that appears twice per week. Constrained by market forces, it sells for roughly $1.00, despite being printed in black ink on cheap paper. In democracies, we found that state-affiliated newspapers are more likely to operate as a business, with articles behind a paywall. The digital analog to subsidized newsprint is a freely available online archive.

Figure 3.1 reveals just how similar are autocrats who maintain online propaganda archives with those who do not. For several measures, we created density plots for autocracies in our sample and for some who are not. Sample autocracies include countries in our corpora with a Polity score less than 6. Other autocracies include countries in the same Polity range for which we do not have newspaper data. The dashed vertical lines give sample means. The distributions across the two groups are virtually identical. Autocrats who maintain propaganda archives are as affluent as those who do not. They govern societies with virtually identical rates of internet penetration and receive virtually identical Polity scores. There appears to be no clear selection bias that would undermine the external validity of the empirical results we present later.

3.2.2 *State-Affiliated Newspapers in Democracies as a Baseline*

Although ours is a theory of autocratic propaganda, we included state-affiliated newspapers from democracies as a baseline for comparison. These are generally holdovers from a previous autocratic regime. Many were reorganized during a democratic transition and thereafter subject to less political control than state-run newspapers in autocracies. In Senegal, for instance, *Le Soleil* was founded in May 1970 by President Leopold Sedar Senghor, who tightly circumscribed press freedom. Senegal transitioned to democracy in 2000, when Abdoulaye Wade defeated Senghor's successor, Abdou Diouf, in an election so lopsided that Diouf chose to step down after two decades rather than repress protesters. Two decades on, the Senegalese state remains *Le Soleil*'s chief shareholder.[4] While

---

[3] Interviews with anonymous journalists. Many claim that *Les Dépêches de Brazzaville* is subsidized by the state oil company.

[4] IREX (2014).

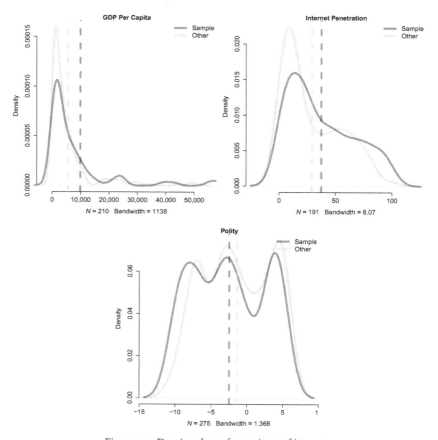

Figure 3.1 Density plots of covariates of interest

its editorial line remains somewhat pro-regime, it is regarded as far less biased than before the transition.

Mali's *L'Essor* has a similar history, and its reputation for journalistic integrity is relatively strong. First published in 1949, *L'Essor* became the organ of the military dictatorship following a 1968 coup. Until Mali's democratic transition in 1991, *L'Essor*'s coverage was limited to local news, government decrees and speeches, and articles from Soviet and Chinese wire services. After the democratic transition, *L'Essor* was transferred to a state-owned printing house managed by the Ministry of Communications. One of fifteen French daily newspapers, *L'Essor* confronts a competitive media market. The government fosters this competition by exempting all media organizations from taxes. Journalists generally agree: "There is, of course, no taboo subject."[5] Throughout the book, we occasionally distinguish between newspapers in autocracies and democracies; when we do, we refer to autocratic newspapers as "state-run" and democratic newspapers as "state-affiliated."

In Latin America, the newspapers that we coded as state-affiliated have different origins and are often owned by wealthy families that support certain politicians. We coded these according to the strength of their connection with the incumbent executive. For example, Argentina's *Pagina 12* was partly owned by Rudy Ulloa, a business partner of President Nestor Kirchner. It was widely considered friendly to the Kirchner government and benefited from a massive increase in government advertising revenue during Kirchner's time in office. In other cases, private newspapers were taken over by the state. Ecuador's *El Telegrafo* was founded in 1884 and remained private until the 2000s. Following owner Fernando Aspiazu Seminario's conviction for embezzlement and fraud, the state seized *El Telegrafo* in 2007. Since then, Ecuador's government has nationalized key parts of the media environment. After being elected in 2006, President Rafael Correa seized control of three television stations through a lawsuit and forced several private newspapers to close.

3.2.3 Pre-Processing

After we finalized our roster of newspapers, we either scraped their online archives with the Python programming language or manually downloaded all available articles from Lexis Nexis. In four countries – Congo, Gabon, Oman, and Togo – newspapers were archived as PDFs rather than text files. For these, we transformed PDFs into JPGs with the open-source command-line program imagemagick. This enabled us to optimize the quality of the resulting images, which is critical for text recognition. We then extracted text from JPGs with tesseract, an open-source optical character recognition program. These techniques are computationally demanding. Our collection of propaganda from Gabon alone included 127,000 PDF files between 1976 and 2018, totaling 71 gigabytes. On a single computer, this newspaper would have required several years to pre-process. For efficiency, we processed these files in parallel on a high-performance computing cluster. Since open-source optical character recognition programs sometimes have difficulty distinguishing article

---

[5] IREX (2008).

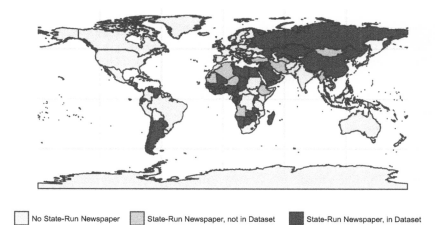

No State-Run Newspaper | State-Run Newspaper, not in Dataset | State-Run Newspaper, in Dataset

Figure 3.2 Global coverage of our propaganda dataset

boundaries in newspapers archived in PDF format,[6] for these countries we recorded data at the edition level rather than the article level.

3.2.4 Country Coverage

Figure 3.2 visualizes our dataset's country coverage. Countries for which we could not identify state-run or -affiliated newspapers appear in light gray. The fifty-nine countries in our dataset appear in black. The thirty-four countries that maintain state-run or -affiliated newspapers but were not in our dataset appear in dark gray.[7]

Our dataset included state-run newspapers from countries that cumulatively comprise 88 percent of the world's population that lives under autocracy. Of our sixty-five newspapers, thirty-seven were published under autocratic governments throughout the sample period, seventeen were published under democratic governments throughout the sample

---

[6] Commercial options, like ABBYY Finereader, do recognize article boundaries. However, they are very slow and cannot be run in parallel, making them unsuitable for large corpora.

[7] There are two sets of countries in this group. The first maintains state-run newspapers in a language outside our six major language groups, and in which one of those major languages is not widely spoken. These include countries like Kyrgyzstan, Tajikistan, Turkmenistan, Armenia, Cyprus, Cambodia, North Korea, Myanmar, Mongolia, Laos, Iran, Sri Lanka, and Vietnam. Computational methods are not as well developed for these languages. The second set maintains a state-run newspaper but with archives we were unable to access. Many of these are small island nations.

period, and eleven experienced one or more transitions between our four regime types. Fifteen experienced transitions on the more granular Polity scale.[8] Tables 3.6 and 3.7 identify the newspapers in our dataset, sample periods, and the number of articles from each. The Online Appendix includes more information about our coding decisions and a brief description of the environment in which each newspaper operates.

Asian countries are somewhat underrepresented in our sample for linguistic reasons. Local languages are more often the language of business and government in Asia than Africa. Most Asian countries have a bifurcated media environment, in which newspapers published in Vietnamese, Thai, Lao, Khmer, Korean, and Japanese target local audiences and newspapers published in English or French target expatriates. As a result, our sample includes Malaysia, Singapore, and China, the Asian autocracies in which English or Chinese is widely spoken.

3.2.5 Day-Level Missingness

Readers may wonder whether our propaganda collection is subject to another form of selection bias. Might autocrats who maintain online propaganda archives choose to omit newspaper issues that contain information that might damage regime interests? Might autocrats choose not to publish newspaper issues during periods of widespread protest and repression? If so, our propaganda collection may reflect a narrative that is unrepresentative of broader political or economic conditions.

To probe this, we created the variable $Missing_{it}$, which assumes value 1 if newspaper i in country j did not publish an issue on day t, as recorded by our dataset, and 0 otherwise. We included several day-level covariates. Since elections are often moments of tension, we recorded whether day t in country j occurred within fifteen days before an election, whether day t occurred on election day, and whether day t occurred within fifteen days after an election. Since autocrats may forgo publication during periods of state repression, we created the variable $Repression_{jt-1}$, which assumes value 1 if the Armed Conflict Event Location Dataset (ACLED) records whether the regime in country j employed repression on day $t - 1$. Likewise, the variable $Protest_{jt-1}$ assumes value 1 if ACLED records a popular protest in country j on day $t - 1$. We included country- and year-fixed effects, which accommodated unobserved

---

[8] We draw our regime classifications from Svolik (2012) and update them through 2019.

features that may condition how likely the government of country j is to publish a newspaper issue on day t.

Since the determinants of missingness may vary according to regime type, we estimated four regression models. We referred to countries with Polity scores between -10 and -6 as dictatorships, to countries with Polity scores between -5 and 0 as weakly constrained autocracies, to countries with Polity scores between 1 and 5 as constrained autocracies, and to countries with Polity scores between 6 and 10 as democracies. The results appear in Table 3.1, and they give us confidence that our corpus of propaganda is not subject to systematic, day-level missingness. State-affiliated newspapers in democracies appear to have less missingness just before elections, just after elections, and just after protests. They appear to have more missingness on election day, perhaps because

Table 3.1 *Determinants of day-level missingness*

	Dependent variable:			
	Missingness			
	Dictatorship	Weakly constrained autocracy	Constrained autocracy	Democracy
	polity -10 to -6 (1)	polity -5 to 0 (2)	polity 1 to 5 (3)	polity 6 to 10 (4)
Pre-election	0.181	0.184	−0.251	−0.308
	(0.146)	(0.238)	(0.178)	(0.205)
Election	0.420	1.217	0.804	1.321*
	(0.502)	(0.794)	(0.588)	(0.710)
Post-election	−0.007	0.300	−0.105	−0.550***
	(0.147)	(0.239)	(0.174)	(0.212)
Protests$_{t-1}$	0.069	0.012	−0.050	−0.383***
	(0.062)	(0.049)	(0.118)	(0.060)
Repression$_{t-1}$	−1.274***	0.158***	−0.017	−0.036
	(0.087)	(0.052)	(0.093)	(1.173)
Constant	−2.153	−0.662***	−1.009***	−12.566***
	(102.693)	(0.053)	(0.042)	(0.078)
Country-fixed effects	✓	✓	✓	✓
Language-fixed effects	✓	✓	✓	✓
Observations	38,268	18,221	12,294	37,509

Note: *p < 0.1; **p < 0.05; ***p < 0.01

elections are commonly scheduled for Sundays or declared national holidays. We found no evidence that state-run newspapers in autocracies were less likely to publish after periods of protest and repression, which suggests that our corpus of propaganda is not subject to day-level selection bias.

3.3 DICTIONARY-BASED SEMANTIC ANALYSIS

Our measures of propaganda employed dictionary-based semantic analysis, which is common in computer science and Silicon Valley. Sometimes referred to as opinion mining, the method begins with a text and a set of lexical dictionaries that group words by their broader meanings. It then infers the text's meaning by determining the frequency with which its constituent words appear in the lexical dictionaries specified by the analyst. Dictionary-based semantic analysis is routinely used to tailor advertising campaigns based on social media use, inform investment decisions based on financial tweets, and generate product feedback based on online reviews of consumer products.[9]

The key to dictionary-based semantic analysis is the quality of the lexical dictionaries employed by the analyst. We used the Harvard General Inquirer (2015), a set of dictionaries developed by linguists to measure different concepts in text.[10] Karadeniz and Dogdu (2018) describe the Harvard General Inquirer as a "clean and classical source of word and affect associations."[11] Computational linguists have used it for a range of applications, including studies of Twitter speech.[12] The Harvard General Inquirer features two main dictionaries. The first records 1,915 words that connote *positive* sentiment, and the other records 2,291 words that connote *negative* sentiment. It also features a series of dictionaries that capture more nuanced sentiments: strength, activity, power, failure, respect, overstatement, persistence, kinship, completion, effort, goals, authority, virtue, and work.

Dictionary-based semantic analysis has two drawbacks. First, some words may have multiple meanings. Words like "tax," "cost," and

---

[9] Ding, Liu, and Yu (2008); Taboada et al. (2011); Liu and Zhang (2012); Aggarwal and Zhai (2012); Feldman (2013); Anandarajan, Hill, and Nolan (2019).

[10] The original citation is Stone et al. (1966).

[11] Peslak (2017) confirms that the Harvard General Inquirer positive and negative lexicons perform similarly to other lexicons, including Affective Norms for English Words (ANEW) and Lexicoder Sentiment Dictionary.

[12] O'Connor et al. (2010); Vosoughi and Roy (2016); Chou and Roy (2017).

"crude" (oil), for instance, have negative lexical values in the Harvard General Inquirer, but, in the context of corporate earnings reports, may be positive.[13] To ensure that this form of measurement error was not substantial, we followed Grimmer and Stewart (2013) and O'Connor (2011), who advise extensive validation. We verified that the 100 most frequent words for each country that registered in our dictionaries were indeed consistent with their positive or negative lexical value. Crucially, these most frequent words seldom had multiple meanings. One notable exception was "opposition," an important term in politics and sports coverage that has negative valence in the Inquirer. In these cases, we dropped the offending word from the country's lexical dictionary. In the chapters that follow, we visualize word clouds of the most common words associated with a given sentiment. This allows us to show, for instance, exactly what the *People's Daily* is saying when it covers Chinese activity and strength in international affairs.

The second drawback is that dictionary-based semantic analysis has difficulty with negations, such as "this is not good." This phrase registers a positive lexical value for "good," rather than the negative lexical value that the bi-gram suggests. We addressed this problem in two ways. First, many of our analyses employed *n*-grams – phrases that consisted of multiple words – which implicitly accommodated negation. Second, as the size of a corpus increased, the negation problem tended to decrease and affect all countries equally. As a result, any measurement error from negation should be classical and hence attenuate statistical results to 0. For these reasons, we do not view negation as a major threat to inference.

3.4 MEASURING PRO-REGIME PROPAGANDA

In measuring pro-regime propaganda, we confronted a series of questions. Should pro-regime propaganda be defined as the rate of regime coverage or the valence of the words that describe the regime? If the latter, how should valence be measured? And who constitutes "the regime"? Surely the autocrat himself and likely the ruling party. Should a measure of propaganda also include government ministers and local appointees? If so, how can the range of appointees be captured across countries? We measure pro-regime propaganda in two ways.

---

[13] We draw this example from Loughran and McDonald (2011).

3.4.1 Measure 1: The Autocrat and the Ruling Party

Our first measure of pro-regime propaganda focused on the valence of the words immediately surrounding references to the regime. To construct it, we identified each instance that a newspaper from country j referenced the autocrat or his ruling party in article i.[14] The variable *References: Executive$_{ijt}$* counts these references. For each, we extracted the ten words before and after the identifier, a string known as a concordance segment. We then used the Harvard General Inquirer to measure the valence of these twenty words. The variable *Positive Coverage: Executive$_{ijt}$* measures the number of fulsome words, less critical words, from among the surrounding twenty, summed for article i. To measure the per reference rate of pro-regime propaganda, we standardize *Positive Coverage: Executive$_{ijt}$* by the total number of references to the autocrat or ruling party in article i:

$$
\text{Positive Coverage Standardized: Executive}_{ijt}
= \frac{\text{Positive Coverage: Executive}_{ijt}}{\text{References: Executive}_{ijt}} \quad (3.1)
$$

This constitutes our primary measure of pro-regime propaganda: how many positive less negative words were found among the surrounding twenty, on average, from every reference to the autocrat or ruling party in article i on day t.

This operationalization reflects our view that propaganda should be defined as coverage positivity, not as whether an assertion is strictly true or false. Our conception of propaganda – as spin, not lies – accords with how scholars and practitioners have long understood it. It was implicit in Plato's conception of rhetoric in *Gorgias*[15] and in Goebbels' work for Nazi Germany.[16] It was also implicit in the theories of propaganda that marked twentieth-century scholarship: those of Doob (1935); Ellul (1973), and Chomsky and Herman (1988). It is explicit in Van Herpen's (2016) account of Russian president Vladimir Putin's propaganda apparatus, Bogart's (1995) account of the U.S. Information Agency, Jowett and O'Donnell's (2012) justly famed textbook, and the epistemic

---

[14] We identified each incumbent's spell in office, to the day. Our list of executives and their parties appears in the Online Appendix. In machine learning parlance, this is a rule-based approach to named entity extraction. For more, see Jiang (2012).

[15] Stanley (2015).

[16] Welch (2014).

theory of propaganda in Stanley (2015). Welch (2014, 2) makes the point most sharply:

A basic misconception is the entirely erroneous conviction that propaganda consists only of lies and falsehood. In fact it operates with many different kinds of truths – from the outright lie, the half truth, to the truth out of context.

Our measure of propaganda registers spin by picking up the positive words that spin entails. We demonstrate how in Section 3.7.

This measure of propaganda is premised on our ability to identify references to the executive and ruling party in any article i. To maximize accuracy, we supplemented our roster of autocrats and ruling parties with country-specific honorifics. In English, these honorifics most often include "president," "head of state," or "prime minister." In monarchies and dictatorships, executive identifiers are more varied, such as "His Majesty" in Brunei or "The Leader" in Libya. These honorifics routinely constitute half of all references to the autocrat, and so accommodating them is critical. To minimize measurement error, we developed two filtering rules. First, we employed a *look-behind filter*. If multiple references occurred within the same twenty-word concordance segment, we counted the final reference only. This avoided double counting phrases like "President Sassou Nguesso." Second, we employed a *foreign executive filter*. If a foreign country was referenced five words before or after an executive identifier, we assumed that a foreign executive had been referenced and omitted it. In articles from Congo's *Les Dépêches de Brazzaville*, this avoids counting "Chinese President Xi Jinping" as a reference to Sassou Nguesso. Our complete list of executive identifiers, by country, appears in the Online Appendix.

To measure the accuracy of our reference counts, we randomly drew 300 articles from each language group. Then we instructed research assistants who were fluent in each language to record the number of true references to the executive and his or her ruling party in each document. We compared these true counts to the predicted counts from our algorithm. We employed two standards for accuracy. First, we coded our algorithm as accurate if the number of predicted references in article i was equal to the number of true references in article i. Second, and less restrictively, we coded our algorithm as accurate if it recorded a positive number of references in a document and our research assistants did the same. This captured the intuition that our algorithm was basically accurate if it recorded five references to Kagame when there were six.

Figure 3.3 presents a pair of heat maps, which report accuracy rates by language. The left panel corresponds to the more restrictive accuracy threshold; the right panel to the less restrictive threshold. Each cell corresponds to a language, with color shaded on a gradient between white, which represents lower accuracy, and black, which represents perfect accuracy. Numeric accuracy rates appear in gray. Our algorithm was quite accurate. Across language groups, it identified the precise number of references to country j's executive in article i with 82 percent accuracy, and it detected at least one reference to the domestic executive when he or she is actually referenced 86 percent of the time. Our algorithm was even more accurate at identifying references to foreign executives.

In a sense, these measures of positivity and negativity are aggregates. Many different sentiments can be associated with positivity, just as many different sentiments can be associated with negativity. The linguistic dictionaries that we employed enabled us to measure language with more precision. We identified ten sentiment dictionaries that enabled us to go beyond positivity and negativity: strength, power, activity, virtue, overstatement, respect, feeling, work, goal, try, completion, and failure. The respect dictionary, for instance, contained words like "admiration" and "status," whereas the failure dictionary contained words like "abandon." We then constructed measures of respect and failure exactly as we did our measure of pro-regime propaganda: by summing the number of words from the twenty surrounding each reference to the autocrat or ruling party that register in these more specific lexical dictionaries and then standardizing this sum by the number of references to the autocrat or ruling party in the article.

3.4.2 Measure 2: Coverage of Government Action

Our primary measure of pro-regime propaganda may be restrictive. Propaganda may reveal itself over the course of a newspaper article rather than in the twenty words surrounding references to the autocrat or ruling party. Perhaps a measure of pro-regime propaganda should include references to government ministers and local appointees, who are excluded from *Positive Coverage Standardized: Executive*$_{ijt}$. This is challenging in a cross-country setting, since it would be virtually impossible to identify all officials who might plausibly be included.

To accommodate these possibilities, we developed a second measure of pro-regime propaganda. Intuitively, words associated with government action – defined as engagement by government at any level – are

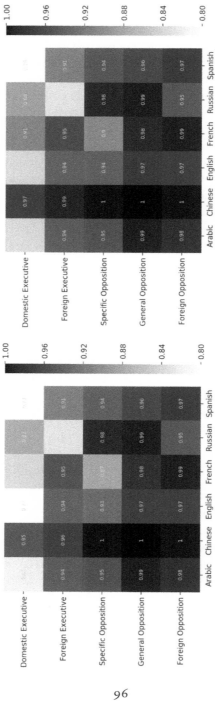

Figure 3.3 Validating executive and opposition identifiers

Table 3.2 *Coverage topics*

corruption	culture	democracy and human rights	economy
education	electoral politics	environment	**government action**
international cooperation	international news	law enforcement	legal system
media	military	nation	natural disaster
obituary	protest	public health	religion
science	social	sports	stability
terrorism	traffic	war	weather
youth			

different than words associated with sports or culture. We used machine learning techniques to train a computer to identify these words, as well as those associated with twenty-eight other coverage topics. This list, which we developed after reading several thousand articles, appears in Table 3.2. Next, we assigned topic labels to articles with a multi-label topic model, which accommodates the possibility that some articles cover multiple topics. Figure 3.3 reports the out-of-sample performance of our classifier. The *x*-axis gives language; the *y*-axis topic. Cells are shaded by accuracy, with numeric rates in gray. Across languages, our classifier's accuracy generally exceeds 90 percent. We discuss our validation procedures in greater detail below.

Next, we measured the aggregate valence of each article *i* in country *j* on day *t* by using the semantic dictionaries described above to identify its positive and negative words. We then computed the total number of positive less negative words and standardized it by the total number of dictionary hits:

$$\text{Article Valence: Regime}_{ijt} = \frac{\text{Positive Words}_{ijt} - \text{Negative Words}_{ijt}}{\text{Positive Words}_{ijt} + \text{Negative Words}_{ijt}}$$

$$(3.2)$$

By standardizing according to total dictionary hits, we accommodated the possibility that different language dictionaries are of different quality. If, for instance, the English language positive and negative valence dictionaries are simply more thorough than those in Arabic or Russian, standardizing by dictionary hits should correct this. This measure of aggregate article valence created a third axis of variation: how positive or negative a given article *i* was about a given topic *h*, which may or may not reference government action.

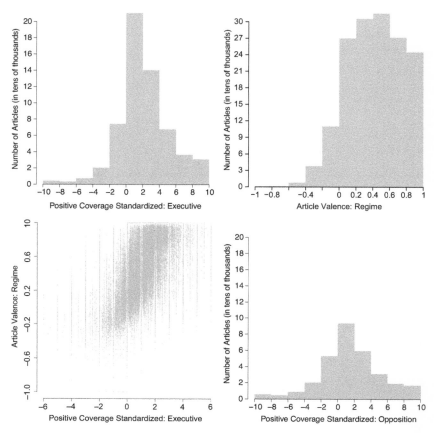

Figure 3.4 Descriptive statistics for regime and opposition coverage

The top panels of Figure 3.4 present the empirical distributions of our two measures of pro-regime propaganda. The *y*-axes measure the number of articles that contain the pro-regime propaganda levels, which are indicated along the *x*-axis. Although our first measure, *Positive Coverage Standardized: Executive$_{ijt}$*, technically spans the $[-20,20]$ interval, we display only the $[-10,10]$ interval, since the bulk of the distribution is centered between -2 and 2. The empirical distribution for our second measure, *Article Valence: Regime$_{ijt}$*, spans the $[-1,1]$ interval. The shapes of these distributions have a substantive implication. On average, much of the pro-regime propaganda we observe in our corpus is relatively neutral, although, perhaps unsurprisingly, the positive tails are substantially thicker than the negative tails. This suggests that, even though much pro-regime propaganda is neutral, very positive coverage is more common than very negative coverage.

Our two measures of pro-regime propaganda are correlated. The bottom left panel of Figure 3.4 presents a bivariate scatterplot, which, for every article in our corpus that contains an executive reference and is labeled government action, displays the value of *Positive Coverage Standardized: Executive*$_{ijt}$ along the x-axis and *Article Valence: Regime*$_{ijt}$ along the y-axis. The correlation coefficient is 0.485.

3.4.3 Is Pro-Regime Propaganda Valence or Reference Volume?

Qin, Strömberg, and Wu (2018) measure media bias in China partly by calculating how many times a given article references an official of the Chinese Communist Party. To do so, they assembled a roster of 2,111 CCP key officials. Of these, 108 hold central government appointments; 816 hold appointments at the provincial level; and 1,187 hold appointments at the prefecture level. Our measures of propaganda improve upon theirs in three ways.

First, our measures can be scaled to a global sample with relative ease. Although *Positive Coverage Standardized: Executive*$_{ijt}$, like Qin, Strömberg, and Wu's measure, is based on a roster of executives and ruling parties, *Article Valence: Regime*$_{ijt}$ uses machine learning techniques to identify all instances of government action. This enables us to distinguish propaganda content that references the autocrat from that which references lower-level officials, such as ministers or local appointees. This is potentially important, as propaganda apparatuses may blame government ministers or regional governors for the autocrat's policy failures. Second, *Positive Coverage Standardized: Executive*$_{ijt}$ also includes honorifics, which account for half of all executive references in our sample. Omitting these dramatically undercounts the volume of regime coverage. Finally, it is unclear whether the volume of regime coverage is a reasonable proxy for its valence. From Section 3.4.1, scholars and practitioners have long understood propaganda as the spin inherent in words themselves rather than simply how frequently the propagandist covers himself. These quantities may or may not be correlated. Put simply, the factors that drive references to the regime may be different from those that drive how positively the regime is covered. We treat this as a hypothesis to be tested, not assumed.

As a first cut, we compared our measures of pro-regime propaganda, *Positive Coverage Standardized: Executive*$_{ijt}$ and *Article Valence:*

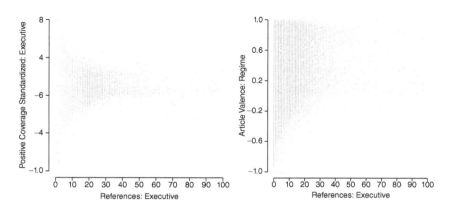

Figure 3.5 Volume and valence of pro-regime coverage

Regime$_{ijt}$, with our measure of coverage frequency, *References: Executive*$_{ijt}$. This let us probe whether a measure based on executive reference counts, such as Qin, Strömberg, and Wu's (2018), is a proxy for pro-regime propaganda across countries. We exploited the fact that our measures of pro-regime propaganda and executive references were measured at the article level. Figure 3.5 presents two bivariate scatterplots, which, for every article in our corpus, display the value of *References: Executive*$_{ijt}$ along the *x*-axis and our measures of pro-regime propaganda along the *y*-axis.

For both measures of pro-regime propaganda, there is no clear article-level relationship between the volume of regime coverage and its valence. As references to the executive and ruling party increase, we observe essentially no corresponding increase in the valence of pro-regime coverage. The determinants of coverage volume across countries and over time, this suggests, may be quite different than the determinants of pro-regime coverage. The *People's Daily*, for instance, may cover Xi Jinping frequently as a signal of regime strength, but the *New York Times* may cover Donald Trump frequently as part of its investigations into potential crimes and ethical failings. Contrary to Qin, Strömberg, and Wu (2018), our data suggest that executive reference counts are not a proxy for pro-regime propaganda. Reference counts are thus distinct from valence.

3.5 MEASURING COVERAGE OF THE OPPOSITION

In Chapter 5, we use our theory to explore how propaganda apparatuses cover the autocrat's rivals. Our conclusions are often surprising but consistent with our theory. Where autocrats confront no electoral constraints, propaganda apparatuses are conspicuous for not denigrating the opposition. They generally pretend there is none. Where electoral constraints are more binding, propaganda apparatuses are forced to cover the opposition with relative neutrality, which means reporting their claims of regime corruption and policy failures.

We measured the volume and valence of opposition coverage with the same techniques that we used to measure the volume and valence of regime coverage. We created an exhaustive list of opposition leaders and parties for each country in our sample. At a minimum, this entailed identifying every candidate that competed in a national election, as well as the senior leaders of every party that competed in a legislative election. We also included political dissidents, political prisoners, and civil society activists, who would likely emerge as prominent politicians if opposition were legal. Politics is fluid, and so we were attentive to the possibility that opposition leaders and parties are occasionally co-opted, and hence no longer members of the opposition. For all countries, we began identifying opposition leaders and parties at least five years before our sample period. The Online Appendix presents our full list of opposition identifiers. At a minimum, it includes several dozen for each country. In some cases, we counted several hundred.

Just as accurately counting executive references requires attending to honorifics, so too for the opposition. We created a list of *general* opposition terms for each of the six languages in our corpus. These appear in Table 3.3.[17] The distinction between general and specific opposition coverage is a focus of Chapter 5. Again, as critical as these honorifics are, they create the possibility of measurement error. Propaganda apparatuses routinely cover party competition elsewhere: for example, Sassou Nguesso's *Les Dépêches de Brazzaville* covers opposition to President Joseph Kabila in the Democratic Republic of Congo. To distinguish coverage of the domestic opposition from coverage of foreign opposition parties, we employed a *foreign opposition filter*. If a foreign country was mentioned in the first 100 words of an article or in the 20-word concordance segment centered on an opposition identifier, we designated that identifier as a reference to the *foreign* opposition and omitted it from our dataset. Otherwise, we designated it a *domestic* opposition reference. We

---

[17] We matched on substring tokens so that, for example, the token оппозицио counted references to оппозиционеры, оппозиционного, оппозиционерам, and оппозиционер.

Table 3.3 *General opposition identifiers*

English	French	Spanish	Arabic	Russian	Chinese
opposition	opposition	oposición	المعارضة	оппозиция оппозицио оппозиции	反对党 反对派

identified a second source of measurement error. Our general opposition identifiers in English and French are commonly used in sports coverage. As we show below, sports coverage accounts for roughly 30 percent of all propaganda content. To minimize this source of measurement error, we coded a random sample of 300 articles from each language group as "sports" or "not sports," and then omitted sports articles from our measures of opposition coverage.

We then created measures of the valence and frequency of opposition coverage. The variable *References: Opposition$_{ijt}$* counts references to country *j*'s political opposition in article *i* on day *t*. The variable *Positive Coverage: Opposition$_{ijt}$* measures the number of fulsome words, less critical words, from among the surrounding twenty, summed for article *i*. To measure the per reference valence of opposition coverage, we standardized *Positive Coverage: Opposition$_{ijt}$*:

$$\text{Positive Coverage Standardized: Opposition}_{ijt}$$
$$= \frac{\text{Positive Coverage: Opposition}_{ijt}}{\text{References: Opposition}_{ijt}} \quad (3.3)$$

These measures were analogous to our measures of pro-regime propaganda. We measured the accuracy of our opposition reference counts as we did for executive reference counts. After randomly drawing 300 articles from each language group, we instructed research assistants who were fluent in each language to record the number of true references to the opposition in each document. We compared these true counts to the predicted counts from our algorithm using the same two standards for accuracy that we describe above. The results appear in Figure 3.3. Again, across language groups, our algorithm is able to accurately identify both general and specific opposition references.

Figure 3.4 also includes the empirical distribution of our measure of opposition coverage. Again, the *y*-axis measures the number of articles that contain the levels of *Positive Coverage Standardized: Opposition$_{ijt}$* along the *x*-axis. For comparison, we maintain the same scale of the *y*-axis as for *Positive Coverage Standardized: Executive*$_{ijt}$. The shapes of these two distributions – which, to be clear, were calculated in analogous ways – have substantive implications as well. First, *Positive Coverage Standardized: Opposition*$_{ijt}$ is also centered around 0, suggesting that propaganda apparatuses do not systematically denigrate an autocrat's rivals. Second, the positive tail does not exhibit the same thickness as that for *Positive Coverage Standardized: Executive*$_{ijt}$, which suggests that opposition coverage does not reach the same heights as pro-regime coverage. Third, and perhaps most conspicuously, the counts along the *y*-axis for *Positive Coverage Standardized: Opposition*$_{ijt}$ are substantially lower than those for *Positive Coverage Standardized: Executive*$_{ijt}$. This will be a theme of Chapter 5. Many autocratic propaganda apparatuses are conspicuous not for denigrating the opposition but rather for pretending it does not exist.

3.6 MEASURING PROPAGANDA NARRATIVES

3.6.1 *Classifying Propaganda Content*

Propaganda is more than simply coverage of the regime and opposition. It also entails narratives about current history. These narratives are the focus of Chapters 5 and 6. To understand them, we drew on the computational techniques introduced in Section 3.4.2.

Intuitively, words associated with different coverage topics are distinctive. The words associated with economic coverage, for instance, are much different than those associated with electoral politics or international affairs, which themselves are distinct from the words associated with sports and crime. By employing machine learning techniques to classify propaganda content by topic, we can probe propaganda narratives. We can probe whether the nature of economic coverage varies according to whether an article references the autocrat, the ruling party, or some other part of the regime. We can probe what claims autocrats make about their own "democratic" politics. We can probe whether ostensibly non-political topics – like sports – are subject to the same political calculations as pro-regime propaganda. We can probe what autocrats tell their citizens about domestic conditions in foreign countries. Future scholars can study aspects of autocratic propaganda that we may have overlooked.

We trained a computer to identify the topics covered in a propaganda article based on the distinctive set of words associated with a given topic. We implemented the classifier in four steps. First, we sampled 500 articles from each of our six language groups. The sample was stratified, such that each country in a given language group contributed an equal number of articles to the language group's sample. We refer to these 500 articles as each language group's training set and the remaining articles as the test set. Second, we labeled each article in the training set with as many topics as applicable. Our universe of twenty-nine topics appears in Table 3.2. We developed this list inductively, after reading several thousand articles, with the intent of categorizing virtually all topics covered in newspapers.

Some labels are conceptually similar. Law enforcement and the legal system, for instance, both pertain to criminal justice. For our purposes, we define law enforcement as pertaining to the police, and the legal system to the courts. In practice, they frequently co-occur, and in the analysis that follows we aggregate them into a single "law/legal" tag. Education and public health are conceptually distinct but each is premised on the provision of public goods. Accordingly, we aggregate them into a single "public goods" tag. We define international cooperation as any reference to a bilateral diplomatic relationship or a multilateral institution, such as the World Bank or the IMF. By contrast, international news occurs only when one country's propaganda apparatus covers events in another country. Electoral politics and democracy/human rights may seem conceptually similar as well. In our scheme, electoral politics refers to party and candidate competition, while democracy/human rights refers to the principles of liberty, suffrage, and the like. Government action refers to any instance of agency by a government official.

Third, after coding a 500-article training set for each language group, we implemented a multi-label topic model on each state-run newspaper.[18] By permitting the classifier to assign multiple labels to a single article, we accommodated the possibility that narratives emerge partly according to which topics are covered together: whether, for instance, international news coverage selectively omits topics that might exacerbate citizens' domestic grievances.

Finally, we evaluated the performance of the classifier. We use two common metrics from computational social science: accuracy and precision-recall. Accuracy measures the number of correct classifications as a share of the total number of classifications performed. To assess our

---

[18] We used the `multilabel` package in Python's `sklearn` module to do so (scikit-learn developers 2018). The multi-label classifier employed a linear support vector classifier one-versus-rest model to assign as many topics as appropriate to the test set articles. Before classifying articles, we removed stop words from each language corpus, in addition to the other preprocessing techniques mentioned above.

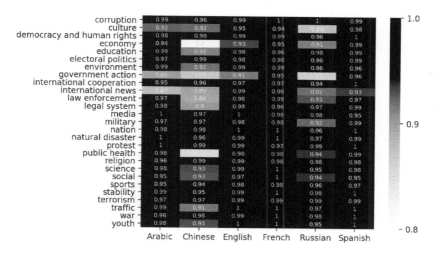

Figure 3.6 Validating topic classifications

classifier's accuracy, we instructed our team of research assistants to read a sample of 300 articles per language group, stratified by country, and record each topic in each article. We computed an overall accuracy rate for each topic through a series of binary classification decisions. For example, we recorded whether or not the economy was accurately predicted in each article, and then averaged the resulting set of 300 zeroes and ones to get our overall accuracy rate for economic coverage. Figure 3.6 reports our classifier's out-of-sample performance. The x-axis gives language; the y-axis gives topic category. Cells are shaded on a gradient between white, which reflects lower accuracy, and black, which represents perfect accuracy. Numeric accuracy rates appear in gray. Across languages, our classifier correctly identified the topic of coverage more than 90 percent of the time.

While accuracy is intuitive, it can be problematic when datasets are imbalanced, such that some labels are far more common than others. This was the case in ours, since most articles were coded 0 for most coverage topics. With this data structure, the accuracy metric can overstate the classifier's ability to correctly identify coverage topics that are not 0. To accommodate this, we employed the precision-recall metric. Precision measures the fraction of correct positives among the total predicted positives:

$$\text{Precision} = \frac{\text{True Positive}}{\text{True Positive} + \text{False Positive}}$$

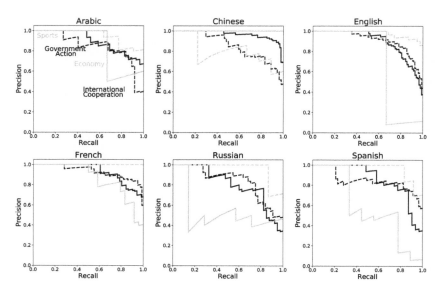

Figure 3.7 Precision-recall curves

Put differently, precision gives the accuracy rate of positive predictions. When precision is high, a classifier has a low false positive rate. Recall measures how many total positives are predicted correctly by the classifier:

$$\text{Recall} = \frac{\text{True Positive}}{\text{True Positive} + \text{False Negative}}$$

Recall gives the fraction of correct positives from among the total positives in the dataset. When recall is high, a classifier has a low false negative rate. A classifier performs well when both precision and recall are high, although in practice there is a trade-off between precision and recall. Figure 3.7 presents the precision-recall curves for our classifier by language group. These precision-recall curves give the relationship between precision and recall for every possible probability threshold for distinguishing positive predictions from negative predictions. The *x*-axes give the recall value for a given probability threshold; the *y*-axes give the precision value for a given probability threshold. We focus on the core topics that appear throughout this book: government action, the economy, international cooperation, and sports. The substantial area under each curve indicates that our classifier performs well for both precision and recall across language groups.

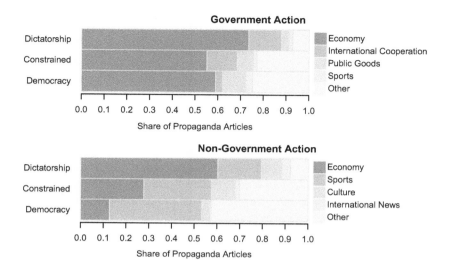

Figure 3.8 Leading coverage topics

3.6.2 *Coverage Topics by Regime Type and Government Action*

Figure 3.8 displays the most prominent propaganda topics across autocracies. The top panel focuses on articles about government action; the bottom panel focuses on articles not about government action. Within each panel, we further divide countries according to Polity's measure of regime type, which we discuss in more detail in Chapter 4. The top bar restricts attention to dictatorships, those with a Polity score between −10 and −6. The middle bar focuses on constrained autocracies, those with a Polity score between −5 and 5. The bottom bar focuses on democracies, those with a Polity score between 6 and 10. Just five topics – the economy, public goods, international cooperation, international news, and sports – constitute more than 80 percent of all propaganda content.

These descriptive statistics are noteworthy in several ways. First, coverage of electoral politics and democracy is most prevalent in democracies, accounting for 15 percent of content about government action and 10 percent of content that is not about government. In constrained autocracies, these shares fall to roughly 10 percent and 5 percent, respectively. In dictatorships, coverage of electoral politics and democracy is conspicuously absent. The incumbent government is virtually never portrayed as seeking the votes of citizens, and, as we show later, neither is the opposition. By contrast, propaganda apparatuses across autocracies allocate a disproportionate amount of coverage to the regime's international engagements. Sports coverage constitutes the first or second leading topic in articles that omit government action, accounting for roughly 30 percent of coverage. Economic coverage is salient across countries as well.

3.6.3 *Measuring Semantic Distinctiveness*

These computational techniques let us identify propaganda content along a range of dimensions – by whether it references the regime, the opposition, or any of the twenty-nine coverage topics in Table 3.2 – and measure its valence. Propaganda narratives are often subtle, however, and so we employed another technique to capture the subtleties in some 8 million propaganda articles.

This technique is known as *semantic distinctiveness*, and we use Kessler's (2017; 2018*b*) pioneering implementation.[19] The basic idea is that across any two corpora of documents, words common to both are generally uninformative. These common words are pronouns, conjugations of the verb "to be," question words like "who" and "where," other building blocks of speech, and generic words associated with a given topic (like "sports" for sports). Similarly, across any two corpora of documents, words uncommon to both are also uninformative. These words are peculiarities, low-frequency words in a given language. By contrast, words that are common in one corpus but uncommon in another are distinctive. They convey something meaningful about content in one corpus relative to another.

Kessler's algorithm positions words in two-dimensional space based on their frequency in two corpora, which we denote A and B. Figure 3.9 illustrates this. For each word across corpora A and B, the algorithm computed its coordinates in two-dimensional space as a function of its frequency in each corpora, standardized by the frequency of the most common word in each corpora. This yielded a measure of word frequency in each corpora on the $[0, 1]$ interval. Words at the bottom left of Figure 3.9 are uncommon to both corpora, whereas words at the top

---

[19] Monroe, Colaresi, and Quinn (2008) developed a distinctiveness model that yields a word score based on a log-odds ratio with an informative Dirichlet prior. Since software to implement that model with *n*-grams was not available at the time of writing, we elected for Kessler's implementation, which is otherwise quite similar. Benoit et al. (2018) provide a similar algorithm to measure semantic distinctiveness, known as the keyness statistic.

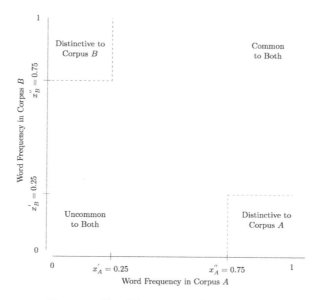

Figure 3.9 Visualizing semantic distinctiveness

right are common to both corpora. Words at the bottom right are distinctive to corpus A, whereas words at the top left are distinctive to corpus B. To compute our measure of semantic distinctiveness for words in corpus A, we restricted attention to words where $x''_A \geq 0.75$ and $x'_B \leq 0.25$. Then, for each of these words, we counted the number of references in corpus A, and then standardized this by the number of articles in corpus A. This yielded a measure of distinctiveness that incorporated not only a term's relative frequency to all others but also its relative frequency across articles. We computed an analogous measure for corpus B but with cutpoints $x''_B \geq 0.75$ and $x'_A \leq 0.25$.

As an example, Figure 3.10 visualizes the most distinctive terms associated with Fox News's coverage of Republicans and Democrats in the first year of the Trump presidency. To focus on specific discussions of Republican and Democrats rather than on discourse about politics more broadly, we extracted the ten words on either side of references to "Republican(s)" and "Democrat(s)." Larger terms are more distinctive. From the left panel, Fox News coverage of Republicans is distinctive in its focus on routine governance. The most distinctive terms are "govern," "republican lawmakers," and "unite." Also distinctive is Republicans' major policy goal: "repealing obamacare" and "replacing

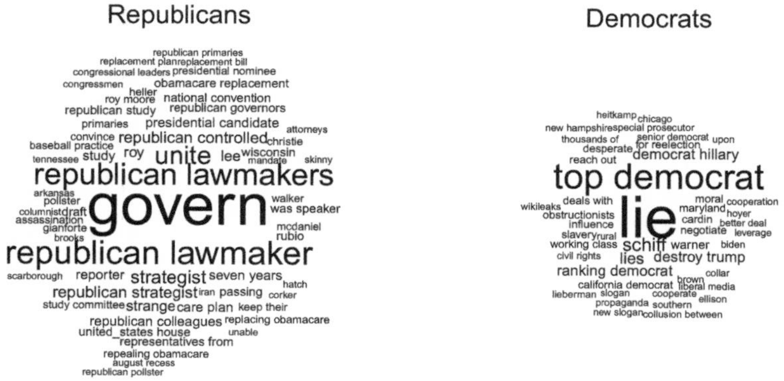

Republicans   Democrats

Figure 3.10 Semantic distinctiveness applied to Fox News

obamacare." From the right panel, Fox News coverage of Democrats is distinctive for its criticism, especially of Democratic "lies." Other distinctive terms include "obstructionists," the "liberal media," "propaganda," and the Democrats' "desperat[ion]" and apparent efforts to "destroy Trump." Fox News coverage of Democrats is also distinctive for its focus on alleged connections between Trump and Russia: "collusion"; "wikileaks"; and "fusion GPS," the private investigatory firm behind the Steele dossier. Semantic distinctiveness is a powerful tool to identify narrative subtleties.

3.6.4 Other Novel Measures

These computational techniques can be used to create other novel measures of propaganda. By identifying key words, we can study a range of potentially critical aspects of propaganda. In Chapter 6, we document what two of the most geopolitically important autocracies – China and Russia – tell their citizens about domestic conditions in the United States and the European Union. We also study what autocrats tell citizens about their bilateral relationships with the Chinese government. In Chapter 7, we exploit the fact that autocrats routinely threaten citizens with codewords, which recall historical episodes of violence and the regime's capacity for repression.[20] We then track these codewords to understand how repressive governments threaten citizens with repression and, in Chapter 10, measure how these threats condition the rate

---

[20] Huang (2015b); Young (2018); Carter and Carter (2021b).

of protest. In Chapter 9, we use several key words to document what the CCP tells readers about its ongoing campaign of repression against ethnic Uyghurs in Xinjiang.

3.7 OUR DATA IN CONTEXT

Our measures of propaganda are original, which is both a merit and a drawback. What does it mean for one additional word to be positive from among the twenty words surrounding the executive? Is this a meaningful difference? We help readers scale our measures of propaganda in two ways.

3.7.1 *Concordance Segments from Rwanda*

We focus first on Rwanda, where the *New Times* serves as President Paul Kagame's chief propaganda organ. Between April and July 1994, Rwanda's ethnic Hutus massacred approximately 800,000 Tutsis, goaded on by the state-run *Radio Télévision Libre des Mille Collines.*[21] After some semblance of stability was restored, the National Assembly elected Paul Kagame, a Tutsi and the leader of the Rwandan Patriotic Front (RPF), president under the transitional constitution. Notwithstanding his popularity among some Western donors, Kagame quietly assembled among the continent's worst human rights records. Among other violations, he routinely silences the political opposition by assassinating exiles. In 2014, Kagame addressed the murder of one, Patrick Karegeya:

Whoever betrays the country will pay the price. I assure you. Letting down a country, wishing harm on people, you end up suffering the negative consequences. Any person still alive who may be plotting against Rwanda, whoever they are, will pay the price.[22]

Table 3.4 displays concordance segments from Kagame's *New Times*. We **bold** references to the executive – for Rwanda, either "Kagame" or "RPF," his political party – and show the ten words on either side. Positive words are rendered in *italics*, whereas negative words are rendered in underline. The most flattering concordance, listed first, describes a speech in which Kagame thanks supporters for their "continued trust and

---

[21] Yanagizawa-Drott (2014) estimates that the radio station was responsible for 10 percent of violence.
[22] Human Rights Watch (2014).

Table 3.4 *Concordance segments from Rwanda by valence. For ease of interpretation, we did not preprocess concordance segments.*

Positive coverage	Concordance segment
5	2010 presidential candidate. In his *acceptance* speech, President Kagame *thanked* **RPF** members for their *continued trust* and *support* for him. He
4	focus on *education* as *well* as job creation. Murayire said **RPF**'s goal is to *enable* young people realise their *full* potential
3	about, among other factors, is rapid rural-to-urban migration; which the **RPF** *liberation* unleashed with the *freedoms accorded* the people to seek
2	to be. Our history has taught us the *right* choice. **RPF** made the choice to work <u>hard</u> to *achieve* the *dignity*
1	at the National University of Rwanda, said. Omar said the **RPF** electorate *appreciated* their MPs' previous performance basing on the infrastructure
0	Rwanda to *free* the people from <u>fear</u> caused by the **RPF** government. She made the statements during an interview at Voice
−1	Kayibanda before him. Yet, there was no *guarantee* that the **RPF** government would itself not <u>fall</u> in the same <u>trap</u> as
−2	ground in Rwanda. Trevidic's predecessor, Jean-Louis Bruguiere, previously <u>accused</u> the **RPF** of <u>shooting</u> down the plane, a move that led Rwanda
−3	a <u>different</u> story of the genocide in which he <u>blames</u> **RPF** for the <u>massacres</u> in 1994 that claimed over one million
−4	all <u>sorts</u> of <u>allegations</u> and <u>fabrications</u> aimed at <u>undermining</u> the **RPF** party and its <u>leadership</u>. In a lecture he held at
−5	<u>opponents</u> and <u>exiled</u> members of the genocidal machinery, Bruguiere <u>accused</u> **RPF** of carrying out the <u>deadly</u> April 6, 1994 <u>attack</u> that

support." This concordance contains five positive words surrounding our identifier, "Kagame," and zero negative words, so it registers a net positive coverage of 5. Concordance segments with scores of 2, 3, and 4 are also quite positive. They credit the RPF for promoting education, job creation, and urbanization. By contrast, negative concordances feature criticism of the ruling party, sometimes severe. The most critical among them acknowledges that some citizens believe the RPF participated in the 1994 genocide.

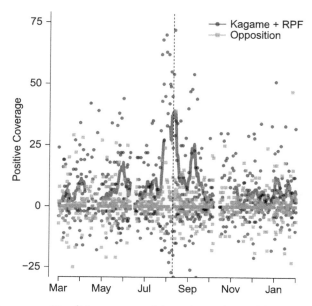

Figure 3.11 Visualizing coverage of the regime and opposition in Rwanda

Rwanda held a presidential election on August 9, 2010, when Kagame was reelected in an obviously fraudulent poll. Figure 3.11 depicts how the *New Times* covered Kagame and the Rwandan opposition during the year surrounding the election.[23] For each calendar day along the *x*-axis, the *y*-axis records our measures of *Positive Coverage: Executive*$_{ijt}$ and *Positive Coverage: Opposition*$_{ijt}$. These record the number of positive words less negative words among the twenty surrounding each class of identifier on day t. The solid lines give moving averages. When daily points cluster around 0, references to Kagame (or the political opposition) in the *New Times* on day t were neutral; when daily points are positive (negative), so too was coverage. The presidential election of August 9, 2010, is given by the dashed vertical line.

Save for the fortnight surrounding the election, the *New Times'* coverage of Kagame leaned positive, but it was occasionally critical. During

[23] The newspaper claims to be privately owned, but Human Rights Watch deems it state-owned and Kagame himself called it servile; see *The Economist* (2010). Many observers suspect the *New Times* is owned by Kagame himself.

election season, this changed. Although the *New Times* continued its relatively neutral coverage of the opposition, it endorsed Kagame without reservation, increasing its aggregate positive valence by a factor of 20. After the government declared victory and prepared for Kagame's inauguration, the *New Times* again registered its approval.

3.7.2 *Fox News, Democrats, and Republicans*

We intuitively scale our measures of propaganda in a second way: in the context of political coverage on Fox News. Notwithstanding its claims to fairness and balance, it is increasingly clear that Fox News has mobilized Republican support. Where broadcast, DellaVigna and Kaplan (2007) show that Fox News yielded an additional 0.6 percentage points for George W. Bush in the 2000 election. In the 2004 and 2008 elections, Martin and Yurukoglu (2017) show that Fox News generated an additional 3.59 and 6.34 percentage points, respectively, for the Republican candidate. Exposure to Fox News compels voters to support more traditionally Republican policy priorities, such as lower taxes and less redistribution.[24] Most recently, scholars have documented how Fox News persuaded viewers to take the COVID-19 pandemic less seriously.[25] Fox News is clearly biased in favor of the Republican Party, but it is also persuasive to viewers. Its support for Republicans is not so absurd that it loses its capacity to persuade.

We treated state-affiliated newspapers in democracies as a baseline against which we compared state-run newspapers in autocracies. Our general approach was to measure some difference between state-run newspapers in autocracies and state-affiliated newspapers in democracies, and then compare this difference to how Fox News covers Republicans relative to Democrats. To measure bias in Fox News, we used four identifiers – Republican, Republican Party, Democrat, and Democratic Party – and then computed our measures of propaganda by party. We focused on the period between June and October 2017.

The values appear in Figure 3.12. Groseclose and Milyo (2005) rate Fox News and the *Washington Times* as the two most right-leaning American media outlets based on the think tanks they reference. Our data are consistent with this. The mean value of *Positive Coverage Standardized$_{ijt}$* for Fox News coverage of Republicans is 0.44, whereas for

---

[24] Ash and Galletta (2019).
[25] Bursztyn et al. (2020); Jamieson and Albarracin (2020); Simonov et al. (2020).

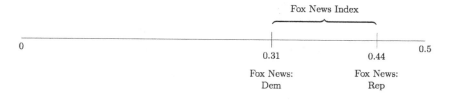

Figure 3.12 Visualizing the Fox News index

Democrats, its mean value of *Positive Coverage Standardized$_{ijt}$* is 0.31. The difference between them, 0.13, constitutes a single unit of our Fox News index. Throughout the book, we use this Fox News index to help readers intuitively scale the magnitude of our coefficient estimates.

3.8 WHY STATE-RUN NEWSPAPERS

State-run newspapers are not the only medium of government propaganda. Many governments operate television and radio stations, social media accounts, and other news platforms, which are clearly important. Venezuela's Hugo Chávez averaged forty hours per week of direct media time, including his own show, *Aló Presidente*, which ran for as long as he required every Sunday. International celebrities such as Naomi Campbell, Danny Glover, and Sean Penn appeared, "lending their star power to the Chávez brand of permanent socialist revolution."[26] Radio may be particularly critical in countries with lower literacy rates and in rural areas, where newspaper distribution is less certain.[27] We focused on newspaper propaganda partly for reasons of data availability. Archives are far more accessible for state-run newspapers than for other platforms. There are, however, other good reasons to privilege state-run newspapers.

First, autocratic governments treat newspaper propaganda as particularly critical. In 1901, Vladimir Lenin wrote in *Iskra*, a Bolshevik newspaper, that "a newspaper is not only a collective propagandist, it is also a collective organizer." In 1923, Stalin wrote the same in *Pravda*,

[26] Pomerantsev (2015a, 2).
[27] Bleck and Michelitch (2017).

in an article entitled "The Press as Collective Organizer."[28] The Soviet Union soon banned copy machines, which made distribution of anti-government pamphlets virtually impossible.[29] In 2014, the president of Venezuela's National Assembly said this:

> Having our own media is one of the goals for this year. God willing, in the following days we will have a newspaper, and we are doing everything we can to attain it.

President Nicolas Maduro created two state-run newspapers, purchased another, and closed the state-run paper importer, which undermined independent newspapers. Although the *Washington Post* reminds readers that "democracy dies in darkness," Venezuela's *Correo del Orinoco* casts itself as "the artillery of thought." In addition to subsidizing propaganda newspapers, autocrats carefully choreograph their content. When governments change, we find, the editorial lines of state-run newspapers change as well. Some propaganda newspapers even celebrate their journalistic integrity. In Uzbekistan, among the world's most repressive autocracies, the propaganda newspaper praises the government for its "consistent work to train highly professional journalists."[30]

Citizens routinely attach to propaganda newspapers the same importance as their repressive governments: as "symbols of the regimes" that oppress them.[31] Iraq's state-affiliated newspaper, *Al-Sabaah*, observed that Arab Spring protesters routinely selected two locations to ransack as repressive governments fell: the presidential palace and the propaganda building. In China during the 1989 pro-democracy movement, citizens protested outside the gates of the CCP's Propaganda Department.[32] In 2009, they celebrated when part of the CCTV headquarters in Beijing went up in flames. When citizens attempt to topple a government, they target its ability to control information. Afterwards, they celebrate its demise on the ashes of its propaganda apparatus.

Third, there is substantial evidence that state-run newspapers set the agenda for other state-run media platforms. "The 7pm news on China Central Television (CCTV)," Shirk (2011, 7–8) writes, "simply rehashed

---

[28] Soldatov and Borogan (2015, 11).
[29] Jowett and O'Donnell (2012).
[30] "The Role of the Internet Media Is Increasing," *Narodnoye Slovo*, May 4, 2015.
[31] Ahmed Mohamed Al Moussawi, "Arab Change Movement," *Al Sabaah*, April 25, 2011.
[32] Brady (2008, 1).

what had been in the *People's Daily*." In turn, local news stations are required to halt programming promptly at 7 p.m. to broadcast the CCTV's *Xinwen Lianbo*.[33] Brady (2008, 38) writes the same about local radio stations, which are required to "follow the lead" of *People's Daily* editorials.

Autocrats generally withhold consumption data for state-run newspapers, television, and radio. To understand how the rates and demographics of consumption may differ across propaganda platforms, we fielded a nationwide survey of over 4,000 Chinese citizens in late 2020 balanced on the most recent census. Although CCTV – and especially its evening news broadcast, *Xinwen Lianbo* – is the most widely consumed propaganda platform, the *People's Daily* is only slightly behind and well above the CCP's commercial, more market-driven newspapers, which we discuss in Chapter 4. Figure 3.13 visualizes this. Roughly 69 percent of Chinese citizens reported watching CCTV and *Xinwen Lianbo* in the past week, whereas 51 percent reported reading the *People's Daily*. By contrast, just 17 percent read their local provincial newspaper.

The average *People's Daily* reader is virtually identical to the average CCTV viewer. Table 3.5 documents this. For each demographic feature at left, the columns give the mean value for *People's Daily* readers, CCTV viewers, and all other respondents. *People's Daily* readers are as likely as CCTV viewers to be CCP members, ethnic Han, and religious. They have similar levels of educational attainment, income, and interest in domestic and international politics. As a measure of their urban or rural status, we mapped respondents' IP addresses onto night lights data for each of China's counties. This reveals that *People's Daily* readers and CCTV viewers live in similarly urban areas. Although *People's Daily* readers and CCTV viewers constitute a substantial majority of China's population, they are somewhat different from the broader population. They are more likely to be CCP members, ethnic Han, and male. They are more affluent, less religious, more interested in domestic and international affairs, more knowledgeable about domestic politics, and more likely to live in urban areas.

Our focus on state-run newspapers enables a vivid portrait of propaganda across autocracies. Our survey evidence from China suggests this focus entails no serious drawbacks.

---

[33] Miao (2011, 105–107).

Table 3.5 *Demographics of propaganda consumption in China*

	People's Daily readers	CCTV viewers	All other respondents	Scale & other notes
CCP member	0.197	0.182	0.139	Dichotomous: {0, 1}
Education	3.685	3.589	3.466	Categorical: 0 to 6
Income	2.211	2.194	1.635	Categorical: 0 to 5
Ethnic Han	0.939	0.920	0.917	Dichotomous: {0, 1}
Male	0.513	0.530	0.484	Dichotomous: {0, 1}
Age	37.505	39.166	34.864	Continuous
Religion	0.168	0.173	0.195	Dichotomous: {0, 1}
Night lights intensity	0.824	0.809	0.790	Continuous: [0, 1]
Interest in domestic politics	2.281	2.189	1.364	Categorical: 0 to 3
Interest in international politics	2.385	2.288	1.471	Categorical: 0 to 3
Political knowledge	2.485	2.487	2.037	Categorical: 0 to 3

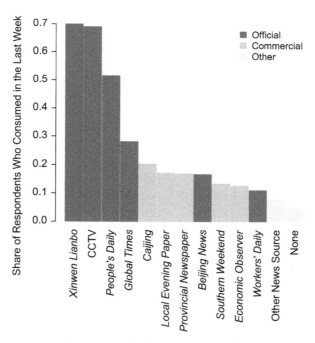

Figure 3.13 Media consumption in China

3.9 CONCLUSION

To the best of our knowledge, this dataset constitutes the most expansive collection of autocratic propaganda ever assembled and it is the first to measure propaganda across countries and language groups. Common in computer science and the private sector, the tools of dictionary-based semantic analysis let us measure the valence of the lexical content surrounding virtually any identifier of theoretical interest. We used them as the foundation of our measures of pro-regime propaganda and opposition coverage and adapted them to a range of other propaganda content.

Dictionary-based semantic analysis rests on our ability to identify each time that, in a mass of text, a propaganda apparatus references the autocrat, the ruling party, or the political opposition. This rests, in turn, not only on creating a roster of individuals but also on identifying the honorifics that propaganda apparatuses apply to them. The algorithms we developed to do so attained a striking level of accuracy. We supplemented them with supervised approaches to categorize the substantive topics discussed in each newspaper article. We hope they enable future scholars to extend our work.

Table 3.6 *Corpus of state-run newspapers. * Indicates editions or pages, rather than articles.*

Country	Language	Newspaper	Articles	Start date	End date
Argentina	Spanish	*Pagina 12*	3094	2016	2017
Bahrain	Arabic	*Akhbar al Khaleej*	212611	2012	2016
Belarus	Russian	*Belarus Segodnya*	168666	2013	2017
Belize	English	*Guardian*	12193	2009	2017
Benin	French	*La Nation*	4868	2013	2017
Bhutan	English	*Kuensel*	7383	2015	2017
Botswana	English	*Daily News*	3505	2012	2015
Brunei	English	*Borneo Bulletin*	97970	2014	2017
Burkina Faso	French	*Sidwaya*	23875	2010	2015
Cameroon	English	*Cameroon Tribune*	2718	2010	2017
Cameroon	French	*Cameroon Tribune*	21415	2010	2017
Chad	French	*Le Progrés*	729	2010	2016
Chile	Spanish	*La Nación*	1888	2017	2017
China	Chinese	*Beijing News*	238840	2012	2019
China	Chinese	*Caijing*	3608	2015	2019
China	Chinese	*Economic Observer*	57058	2006	2019
China	Chinese	*People's Daily*	1553456	1946	2017
China	Chinese	*Yangtse Evening Post*	189395	2012	2019
Congo – Brazzaville	French	*Les Dépêches*	1144	2013	2017
Congo – Brazzaville	French	*Vox*	914	2016	2017
Côte d'Ivoire	French	*Fraternité Matin*	6180	2012	2016
Cuba	Spanish	*Granma*	30062	2014	2016
Djibouti	French	*La Nation*	3402	2013	2015
Ecuador	Spanish	*El Telegrafo*	168984	2011	2017
Egypt	Arabic	*Al Ahram*	27515	2014	2017
El Salvador	Spanish	*Diario Co Latino*	31374	2013	2017
Eritrea	English	*Hadas Shabait*	8707	2010	2015
Gabon	French	*L'Union*	126596	1973	2015
Gambia	English	*Daily Observer*	36161	2007	2015
Ghana	English	*Ghanaian Times*	458	2013	2015
Guinea	French	*Aminata*	4871	2012	2015
Iraq	Arabic	*Al Sabaah*	5322	2011	2011
Jordan	Arabic	*Al Rai*	52881	2012	2017
Kazakhstan	Russian	*Kazakhstanskaya Pravda*	20479	2015	2017

Table 3.7 *Corpus of state-run newspapers (continued).* * *Indicates editions or pages, rather than articles.*

Country	Language	Newspaper	Articles	Start date	End date
Lesotho	English	*Lesotho Times*	7668	2008	2017
Liberia	English	*New Liberian*	1003	2007	2017
Libya	English	*JANA*	3291	2009	2015
Madagascar	French	*La Vérité*	1716	2012	2015
Malawi	English	*The Nation*	9391	2012	2015
Malaysia	English	*Star*	22517	2011	2015
Mali	French	*L'Essor*	775	1968	2016
Namibia	English	*New Era*	22702	2009	2015
Nepal	English	*Rising Nepal*	4001	2014	2015
Nicaragua	Spanish	*El Nuevo Diario*	40352	1998	2009
Nigeria	English	*Nigerian Observer*	11966	2014	2016
Paraguay	Spanish	*La Nación*	87365	2015	2017
Qatar	Arabic	*Al Rayah*	72907	2012	2016
Russia	Russian	*Rossiskaya Gazeta*	115478	2013	2017
Rwanda	English	*New Times*	40474	2010	2015
Saudi Arabia	Arabic	*Al Riyadh*	74878	2000	2005
Senegal	French	*Le Soleil*	30365	2010	2015
Seychelles	English	*Nation*	47824	2004	2017
Singapore	English	*Straits Times*	200851	2010	2015
Swaziland	English	*Swazi Observer*	838	2015	2015
Syria	Arabic	*Al Thawra*	19399	2005	2009
Taiwan	Chinese	*Liberty Times*	3616	2018	2018
Togo	French	*Togo Presse*	17	2017	2017
Tunisia	French	*La Presse*	53811	2010	2015
Uganda	English	*New Vision*	33013	2010	2013
United Arab Emirates	Arabic	*Al Ittihad*	117191	2012	2016
Uzbekistan	Russian	*Narodnoye Slovo*	6532	2014	2017
Venezuela	Spanish	*Diario Vea*	6585	2016	2017
Yemen	Arabic	*Al Thawra*	13989	2010	2017
Zambia	English	*Times of Zambia*	137486	2010	2015
Zimbabwe	English	*The Herald*	59718	2010	2015

PART II

The Political Origins of Propaganda Strategies

4

The Politics of Pro-regime Propaganda

4.1 EMPIRICAL STRATEGY

Our theory's key prediction is this: The electoral constraints an autocrat confronts determine the propaganda strategy he employs. When an autocrat's capacity for fraud and repression is so substantial that he can fully tilt the electoral playing field, pro-regime propaganda is absurdly positive. It makes claims about regime performance that citizens know are false. Where an autocrat's limited capacity for fraud and repression constrain his ability to tilt the electoral playing field, propaganda apparatuses must seek credibility. They must concede bad news and policy failures to acquire some capacity to persuade citizens of regime merits. They must admit damaging facts to persuade citizens of useful fictions.

This chapter tests this key prediction. Across estimation and measurement strategies, the results are consistent with our theory. Where autocrats are constrained to generate popular support, pro-regime propaganda is roughly as pro-regime as Fox News is pro-Republican. Where autocrats can fully secure themselves with repression, pro-regime propaganda is roughly four times more pro-regime than Fox News is pro-Republican. For two reasons, we treat these cross-country results with caution. First, they may be driven by reverse causality. If propaganda is successful, then propaganda may actually condition electoral constraints. Higher levels of pro-regime propaganda may diminish political competition or make a country's electoral institutions less binding. Second, the results may be driven by omitted variable bias. Although we control for many features that may be correlated with both changes in electoral constraints and changes in propaganda strategies, relevant features may remain unobserved. Changes in electoral constraints, for instance, may coincide with changes in political leadership, and this new political leadership may have different tastes for propaganda or less control over the propaganda apparatus.

To ensure that neither possibility is driving our results, we exploit a rapid, exogenous change in the electoral constraints confronted by many autocrats: the fall of the Berlin Wall on November 9, 1989. With the Cold War over, Africa's autocrats lost the ability to pit the United States against the Soviet Union. When Western governments attached genuine political conditions to development aid and debt relief, Africa's autocrats were largely forced to comply.[1] For two countries, we have propaganda data from before 1989: Gabon since 1974 and China since 1946. Using a regression discontinuity design, we show that the fall of the Berlin Wall had a plausibly causal effect on Gabonese president Omar Bongo's propaganda strategy. Using a Bayesian change point model, we show that the change occurred just before the first multi-party legislative election since 1967. We observe no such change in China, where the government was less exposed to the geopolitical shift. With no change to the government's capacity for repression – and no meaningful electoral constraints – its propaganda did not moderate. Quite the contrary. After the 1989 Tiananmen Square massacre, the CCP invested heavily in its repressive apparatus and its propaganda grew more effusive. Since ascending to power in 2012, Xi Jinping has penalized over four million CCP members under the guise of an anti-corruption campaign; placed over a million citizens in forced labor camps; and abolished the term limits that have bound paramount leaders since 1982.[2] He has consolidated personal authority to an extent that rivals only Mao Zedong. Pro-regime propaganda in the *People's Daily*, we find, has returned to Cultural Revolution levels.

These two cases also let us probe whether socio-economic changes condition propaganda in autocracies, as many scholars suggest. Although we control for these features in cross-country regressions, these trends are slow moving and may moderate propaganda only over time. If these theories are correct, we should observe a decline in the CCP's pro-regime propaganda. Since 1946, when our propaganda data begins, the Chinese economy has grown dramatically. The government has installed more broadband cable than anywhere in the world, part of an equally dramatic change in its informational environment. Consistent with our theory, however, we find that trends in the *People's Daily*, the CCP's flagship newspaper, have been driven by politics, not economic or social change. Some scholars have suggested these changes are apparent

---

[1] Bratton and van de Walle (1997); Dunning (2004); Levitsky and Way (2010).
[2] South China Morning Post Editorial Board (2022).

in China's commercial newspapers, which circulate widely in their respective provinces and aim, these scholars argue, to persuade rather than intimidate.[3] To test this, we collected several of the CCP's commercial newspapers, reproduced our measures of propaganda, and then compared them with the *People's Daily*. The CCP's commercial newspapers indeed cover non-regime content more neutrally than the *People's Daily*, but they cover the regime with precisely the same effusiveness. As in the *People's Daily*, this effusiveness has increased over time.

We conclude with a pair of survey experiments. To confirm that CCP propaganda – in the *People's Daily* and its commercial newspapers – serves to intimidate citizens rather than persuade them of regime merits, we fielded a survey in late 2020 that was balanced on China's most recent census. Since these topics are sensitive, respondents may misrepresent their true beliefs about the CCP. To accommodate this, we employ list experiments. We found the same effects for the CCP's commercial newspapers as we do for its flagship newspaper, the *People's Daily*. As our theory suggests, the CCP's pro-regime propaganda makes citizens less likely to protest due to fear. If anything, the CCP's pro-regime propaganda makes it less popular, not more.

This chapter proceeds as follows. Section 4.2 introduces our measures of electoral constraints and presents cross-country descriptive statistics. Section 4.3 probes the relationship between pro-regime propaganda and electoral constraints. Section 4.4 shows how the fall of the Berlin Wall had a plausibly causal effect on pro-regime propaganda in Gabon. Section 4.5 documents the history of Chinese propaganda in the *People's Daily* since 1946, analyzes the CCP's commercial newspapers, and presents the results of a survey experiment that verifies the cognitive mechanisms through which CCP propaganda conditions citizens' beliefs.

4.2 DESCRIPTIVE STATISTICS

4.2.1 *Measuring Electoral Constraints*

Our theory locates the origins of an autocrat's propaganda strategy in his capacity to tilt the electoral playing field via fraud and repression. Reflecting the breadth of these constraints, we use a series of variables as proxies.

---

[3] Brady (2002, 2006, 2008, 2012*b*); Stockmann (2010, 2013); Stockmann and Gallagher (2011); Esarey, Stockmann, and Zhang (2017); King, Pan, and Roberts (2017); Stockmann, Esarey, and Zhang (2018); Roberts (2018).

Our first two explanatory variables adopt a broad view of electoral constraints. Marshall and Jaggers (2005) describe the Polity score as capturing "a spectrum of governing authority that spans from fully institutionalized autocracies through mixed, or incoherent, authority regimes to fully institutionalized democracies." Gleditsch and Ward (1997) describe the Polity score as "fundamentally a reflection of decisional constraints on the chief executive."[4] The Varieties of Democracy (V-Dem) project's Polyarchy index is perhaps the leading alternative to the Polity score,[5] and measures the strength of electoral democracy: "the core value," as V-Dem puts it, "of making rulers responsive to citizens." The Polity index consists of whole numbers between -10 and 10, whereas the Polyarchy index is continuous on $[0,1]$. By employing both, we ensure that our results are robust to alternative measures of the same underlying concept. In our sample, the Polity and Polyarchy measures are tightly correlated, with a correlation coefficient of 0.93.

The V-Dem project also measures several subcomponents of electoral democracy. Our third and fourth explanatory variables, both drawn from V-Dem, focus on the autocrat's capacity for repression. V-Dem's physical integrity index measures "freedom from political killings and torture by the government." V-Dem's civil liberties index measures "the absence of physical violence committed by government agents and the absence of constraints of private liberties and political liberties by the government." These two variables, like the Polyarchy index, are continuous on $[0,1]$.

Our fifth and sixth explanatory variables provide more fine-grained measures of institutional constraints. V-Dem defines government accountability "as constraints on the government's use of political power through requirements for justification for its actions and potential sanctions." This measure encompasses citizens' ability "to hold its government accountable through elections," as well as "checks and balances between institutions." This includes, for instance, the ability of the legal system to bind the executive to electoral outcomes. V-Dem also measures legislative constraints on the executive, which it defines as the "extent [to which] the legislature and government agencies [are] capable of exercising oversight." This reflects the extent to which an autocrat is subject to constraints by other elected representatives. Each of these is tightly related to our theory's view of electoral constraints as the set of conditions

---

4 See also Jones (2019).
5 Coppedge et al. (2022).

that binds the autocrat to electoral outcomes. Again, these two variables are continuous on [0,1].

4.2.2 *Pro-Regime Propaganda*

For each country in our dataset, we compute the mean values of our two measures of pro-regime propaganda: *Positive Coverage Standardized: Executive$_{ijt}$* and *Article Valence: Regime$_{ijt}$*. We then compute each country's mean Polity score during our sample period. The associated bivariate scatterplots appear in Figure 4.1. For clarity, we overlay fitted ordinary least squares (OLS) regression lines. For scale, we plot the mean coverage valence for Democrats and Republicans in Fox News. The Online Appendix includes analogous bivariate scatterplots with V-Dem's Polyarchy index along the *x*-axis.

These descriptive statistics suggest two observations. First, there is a clear cross-country relationship between electoral constraints and pro-regime propaganda. Where electoral constraints are more binding, pro-regime coverage is less positive. Many of the most repressive countries – China, Uzbekistan, Eritrea, and The Gambia under Yahya Jammeh – report on incumbents four times as positively as Fox covers Republicans. Second, a range of autocracies in the middle of the Polity scale employ propaganda that covers their regimes much like Fox News covers Republicans. Perhaps most notably, this includes the Russian propaganda apparatus under Vladimir Putin. Many Americans acknowledge that Fox News is biased in favor of Republicans, as our

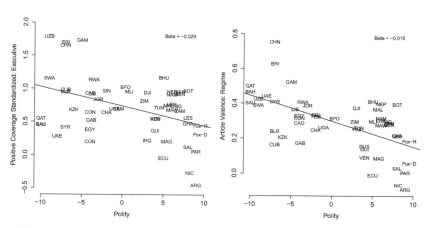

Figure 4.1 Descriptive statistics for electoral constraints and pro-regime propaganda

measure confirms, but this bias is not so great that it undermines its ability to persuade.[6] Similarly, a range of quasi-experimental research underscores the capacity of Russian state media to persuade citizens of Vladimir Putin's merits. Enikolopov, Petrova, and Zhuravskaya (2011) exploit random variation in the strength of independent TV station signals to show that state-run TV yielded an additional nine percentage points to Putin's United Russia in the 1999 legislative elections; White, Oates, and McAllister (2005) reach similar conclusions. This level of pro-regime propaganda is clearly persuasive across countries.

4.3 PRO-REGIME PROPAGANDA IN GLOBAL PERSPECTIVE

4.3.1 Country-Year Level Estimation

When a country's electoral institutions change, does the incumbent's propaganda strategy change as well? To answer this question, we estimated models of the form

$$Y_{js} = \alpha + \beta X_{js} + \phi W_{js} + \gamma_j + \epsilon \tag{4.1}$$

where j indexes country, s indexes year, X_{js} measures electoral constraints, and W_{js} is a vector of controls that may be correlated with changes in both electoral constraints and pro-regime propaganda. To accommodate unobserved, time-invariant differences across countries, we include country-fixed effects, given by γ_j. Since our measures of electoral constraints are observed annually, we compute country-year means for our outcome variables, *Positive Coverage Standardized: Executive$_{ijt}$* and *Article Valence: Regime$_{ijt}$*, which are measured at the article level. By using country-year averages, we ensure that our measures of electoral constraints and pro-regime propaganda are observed at the same time scale. Since these outcomes are continuous, we employ OLS with robust standard errors clustered by country.

We include a range of variables in the vector W_{js} that may be associated with changes in both electoral constraints and pro-regime propaganda. Economic growth may compel citizens to press for democratic reforms and generate more positive regime coverage. Therefore, we control for country j's GDP per capita in year s, as well as the

---

[6] DellaVigna and Kaplan (2007); Ash and Galletta (2019); Martin and Yurukoglu (2017); Bursztyn et al. (2020); Jamieson and Albarracin (2020); Simonov et al. (2020).

share of its GDP from trade. We control for the share of country j's GDP from natural resource revenue in year s, since increases in resource revenue could compel an autocratic government to consolidate more power and compel more pro-regime propaganda. We control for country j's informational environment, which may favor democratic reforms and constrain a government's ability to employ propaganda: in particular, the share of citizens who enjoy internet access in year s. We also control for whether country j witnessed civil wars or elections.

In addition to accommodating unobserved, time-invariant differences by country, country-fixed effects accommodate linguistic differences. Some languages express more sentiments per word or character than others. Our first measure of pro-regime propaganda, *Positive Coverage Standardized: Executive$_{ijt}$*, is sensitive to this. By extracting the same number of words surrounding each identifier across languages, our measure may overstate pro-regime propaganda in more expressive languages. We might observe systematic differences across languages for a second reason. Some linguistic dictionaries may simply recognize more words than others, and so they generate higher values of our propaganda measures. Country-fixed effects accommodate these linguistic differences.

4.3.2 Regime Transitions

Equation (4.1) imposes a linear relationship on changes in electoral constraints and changes in pro-regime propaganda. In so doing, it obscures the possibility that pro-regime propaganda in electorally constrained autocracies may more closely resemble state-affiliated newspapers in democracies than in dictatorships.

We adopted a more flexible estimation strategy by partitioning the Polity space. This partition appears in Table 4.1. Following Polity's standard partition, we label countries with Polity scores between -10 and -6 as dictatorships, which, in our theory, correspond to the set of autocracies where electoral constraints are non-binding. We label countries with Polity scores between 6 and 10 as democracies. Polity treats countries with scores between -5 and 5 as "anocracies," with elements of both dictatorship and democracy. To avoid aggregating countries with -5 and 5 Polity scores, we divide this category into two. We refer to Polity scores between -5 and 0 as weakly constrained autocracy and to Polity scores between 1 and 5 as constrained autocracy. We regard countries in this

Table 4.1 *Regime type codings*

Regime type	Polity score	Representative countries
Dictatorship	$[-10, -6]$	China, Uzbekistan
Weakly constrained autocracy	$[-5, 0]$	Congo, Tunisia under Ben Ali, Uganda
Constrained autocracy	$[1, 5]$	Russia, Zimbabwe
Democracy	$[6, 10]$	Argentina, Chile, Ghana, Senegal

range as akin to Levitsky and Way's (2010) competitive authoritarian regimes, where autocrats confront at least somewhat binding electoral constraints.[7]

4.3.3 Article-Level Estimation

We confirm that all country-year estimation results are consistent with trends at the article level. This offers several advantages. First, if electorally constrained autocracies are more likely to reference the political opposition – and that coverage is negative – then an observed decline in pro-regime propaganda may reflect opposition coverage rather than moderated pro-regime propaganda. To ensure this is not the case, we controlled for the number of opposition references in article i. Second, since we observed articles on specific days, we controlled for day-level factors that may compel autocrats to amplify pro-regime propaganda and that are associated with electoral constraints. We controlled for whether article i was published on an election day or within the 15 days before or after an election day, which we refer to as an election season. We also controlled for ongoing civil wars on day t.

Since our explanatory and outcome variables were measured at different intervals – the former at the year, the latter at the day – observations within country-years are no longer independent.[8] To account for this, we employed a full set of country-random effects. Like fixed-effects estimators, random-effects estimators let intercepts vary by unit, in this case, country. Unlike fixed-effects estimators, random-effects estimators

---

[7] Note that the statistical results in Section 4.3.4 are robust to defining full dictatorships and full democracies more narrowly, as follows: dictatorship (-10 to -7), weakly constrained autocracy (-6 to 0), constrained autocracy (1 to 6), and democracy (7 to 10). For more on Polity partitions, see Epstein et al. (2005).

[8] Gelman and Hill (2006).

assume that unit intercepts arise from a normal distribution with finite variance. Because these unit intercepts are estimated directly from the data, random-effects models can also estimate the effect of variables set at the unit level, such as political institutions. The random-effects estimator helps us avoid overstating confidence.

We included a full set of language-fixed effects as well. These language-fixed effects were unnecessary in the country-year models described above, since, by considering only within-country variation, the country-fixed effects implicitly accounted for language differences across countries. In a random-effects setting, we can directly estimate whether propaganda apparatuses in some languages are more positive or negative than others. We do so for two reasons. First, there may be systematic differences across language dictionaries; some may be more thorough than others. Second, there is variation across languages in the amount of meaning that can be conveyed in 20 words, which, from Chapter 3, is the length of the concordance segments we used to generate *Positive Coverage Standardized: Executive$_{ijt}$*. Language-fixed effects accommodate the possibility that 20 Chinese characters include more meaning than 20 words in English or French.

The baseline model is

$$Y_{ijt} = \alpha + \beta X_{is} + \kappa Z_{it} + \phi W_{is} + \gamma_k + \gamma_j + \epsilon \qquad (4.2)$$

where the vector Z_{it} gives the day-level control variables discussed above, the vector W_{is} gives the year-level control variables from equation (4.1), γ_k gives language-fixed effects, and γ_j gives country-random effects. For continuous outcome variables, we employed mixed effects linear models. For dichotomous outcome variables, we employ mixed-effects logit models.

4.3.4 Results

The results appear in Tables 4.2 through 4.5. Recall from Chapter 3 that the mean value of Fox News for *Positive Coverage Standardized: Republican* is 0.44 and for *Positive Coverage Standardized: Democrat* is 0.31. One unit of our Fox News index is thus 0.13. Likewise, the mean value of Fox News for *Article Valence: Republican* is 0.09, and for *Article Valence: Democrat* is 0.2. Here, one unit of our Fox News index is 0.11.

Table 4.2 presents the results for the Polity score and Polyarchy index, using the country-year and article as the units of analysis. Models 1

Table 4.2 *The politics of pro-regime propaganda, continuous*

	Dependent variable:							
Outcome variable	Positive coverage standardized		Article valence		Positive coverage standardized		Article valence	
Unit of analysis	Country-year	Article	Country-year	Article	Country-year	Article	Country-year	Article
Estimator	OLS	Mixed	OLS	Mixed	OLS	Mixed	OLS	Mixed
	(1)	(2)	(3)	(4)	(5)	(6)	(7)	(8)
Polity	−0.031	−0.075***	−0.016***	−0.014***				
	(0.045)	(0.003)	(0.004)	(0.0004)				
Polyarchy					−0.910	−1.623***	−0.276***	−0.282***
					(0.778)	(0.063)	(0.087)	(0.008)
Trade	0.0001	0.001***	−0.001*	−0.0001**	0.001	0.003***	−0.001**	−0.0002***
	(0.005)	(0.0003)	(0.001)	(0.00004)	(0.007)	(0.0004)	(0.001)	(0.00005)
Log GDP per capita	0.220	0.725***	−0.052	−0.002	0.294	0.708***	−0.012	−0.001
	(0.293)	(0.038)	(0.071)	(0.004)	(0.337)	(0.040)	(0.087)	(0.004)
Natural resources	−0.004	−0.002**	−0.0001	0.0005***	−0.004	−0.002**	0.0003	0.001***
	(0.005)	(0.001)	(0.0001)	(0.0001)	(0.006)	(0.001)	(0.002)	(0.0001)
Civil war	−0.159	0.012	−0.039	0.015***	−0.164	0.009	−0.046	0.013***
	(0.113)	(0.026)	(0.031)	(0.004)	(0.118)	(0.028)	(0.033)	(0.003)
Internet penetration	−0.00004	−0.00004***	−0.00003	−0.00001***	−0.00003	−0.00000	−0.00003	−0.00002***
	(0.0001)	(0.00001)	(0.00002)	(0.00000)	(0.0001)	(0.00001)	(0.00002)	(0.00000)
Election	−0.002		0.001		−0.002		−0.003	
	(0.057)		(0.009)		(0.054)		(0.008)	
Election season		−0.002		0.020***		0.013		0.021***
		(0.011)		(0.002)		(0.012)		(0.002)
Opposition references		−0.024***		−0.009***		−0.024***		−0.009***
		(0.0005)		(0.0001)		(0.0005)		(0.0001)
Constant	−1.900	−7.140***	0.648	0.370***	−2.267	−5.916***	0.332	0.478***
	(2.903)	(0.539)	(0.699)	(0.051)	(3.095)	(0.597)	(0.838)	(0.057)
Country effects	Fixed	Random	Fixed	Random	Fixed	Random	Fixed	Random
Language-fixed effects		✓		✓		✓		✓
Observations	190	335,583	188	892,257	190	335,583	188	892,257
R^2	0.775		0.828		0.782		0.834	

Note: *p < 0.1; **p < 0.05; ***p < 0.01
For OLS models, standard errors are cluster robust within countries.

through 4 focus on Polity, which spans $[-10, 10]$; Models 5 through 8 use Polyarchy, which spans $[0, 1]$. The Polity results suggest that, for every unit increase, the annual mean of *Positive Coverage Standardized: Executive$_{ijt}$* falls by -0.031 and the annual mean of *Article Valence: Regime$_{ijt}$* falls by -0.016. More intuitively, moving from -5 to 5 on the Polity scale is associated, respectively, with a reduction in pro-regime propaganda of $\frac{-0.031 \times 11}{0.13} = -2.62$ and $\frac{-0.016 \times 11}{0.11} = -1.6$ units of our Fox News index. These are large effects, and the results from the article-level models are substantively similar. The Polyarchy results are similar as well. Moving from 0.25 to 0.75 – an analogous distance to the Polity shift – is associated with a reduction in pro-regime propaganda of $\frac{-0.910 \times 0.5}{0.13} = -3.50$ and $\frac{-0.276 \times 0.5}{0.11} = -1.25$ units of our Fox News index, respectively.

Tables 4.3 and 4.4 present the results for the four V-Dem subcomponents. Again, across specifications, binding electoral constraints are associated with moderated pro-regime propaganda. Note that the two repression subcomponents in Table 4.3 have larger estimated effects than the institutional constraint subcomponents in Table 4.4. This has an important theoretical implication. Among the conditions that bind governments to electoral outcomes, the most important moderator of pro-regime propaganda is the government's capacity for violence and hence the extent to which it must seek popular support. For the physical integrity index, moving from 0.25 to 0.75 is associated with a reduction in pro-regime propaganda of $\frac{-1.661 \times 0.5}{0.13} = -6.39$ and $\frac{-0.319 \times 0.5}{0.11} = -1.45$ units of our Fox News index. For the civil liberties index, moving from 0.25 to 0.75 is associated with a reduction in pro-regime propaganda of $\frac{-1.513 \times 0.5}{0.13} = -5.82$ and $\frac{-0.353 \times 0.5}{0.11} = -1.60$ units of our Fox News index.

We relaxed the linearity assumption by using the Polity partition in Table 4.1. These results appear in Table 4.5. The *Positive Coverage Standardized: Executive$_{ijt}$* models suggest that propaganda apparatuses in dictatorships, on average, include between 0.9 and 1.25 more positive words from among the 20 surrounding each identifier. This is equivalent to between 6 and 9 units of our Fox News index. For the *Article Valence: Regime$_{ijt}$* models, the marginal effect in dictatorships is equivalent to between 3 and 4 units of our Fox News index. The article-level results are similar to the country-year results. Pro-regime propaganda in the absence of electoral constraints is effusive, as our theory suggests. By contrast, propaganda apparatuses in constrained autocracies cover the incumbent in a way that is not profoundly different from that of

Table 4.3 *The politics of pro-regime propaganda, repression*

	Dependent variable:							
Outcome variable	Positive coverage standardized		Article valence		Positive coverage standardized		Article valence	
Unit of analysis	Country-year	Article Mixed	Country-year	Article Mixed	Country-year	Article Mixed	Country-year	Article Mixed
Estimator	OLS	Mixed	OLS	Mixed	OLS	Mixed	OLS	Mixed
	(1)	(2)	(3)	(4)	(5)	(6)	(7)	(8)
Physical integrity	−1.661** (0.778)	−1.080*** (0.066)	−0.319*** (0.086)	−0.323*** (0.009)				
Civil liberties					−1.513*** (0.555)	−1.763*** (0.070)	−0.353*** (0.083)	−0.322*** (0.009)
Trade	0.001 (0.005)	0.001** (0.0003)	−0.0001 (0.001)	−0.0003*** (0.00004)	0.002 (0.006)	0.004*** (0.0004)	−0.0003 (0.001)	−0.0001* (0.00005)
Log GDP per capita	0.338 (0.314)	0.604*** (0.036)	0.025 (0.104)	−0.015*** (0.004)	0.291 (0.319)	0.602*** (0.039)	0.013 (0.107)	−0.021*** (0.004)
Natural resources	−0.003 (0.005)	−0.005*** (0.001)	−0.0003 (0.001)	−0.0001 (0.0001)	−0.003 (0.006)	−0.005*** (0.001)	0.0005 (0.001)	0.0004*** (0.0001)
Civil war	−0.187 (0.115)	−0.039 (0.026)	−0.049 (0.034)	0.007* (0.004)	−0.167 (0.122)	−0.015 (0.028)	−0.046 (0.033)	0.009** (0.003)
Internet penetration	−0.00003 (0.0001)	−0.00004*** (0.00001)	−0.00001 (0.00002)	−0.00001*** (0.00000)	−0.00003 (0.0001)	−0.00001 (0.00001)	−0.00002 (0.00002)	−0.00002*** (0.00000)
Election	−0.012 (0.051)		−0.011 (0.019)		−0.002 (0.054)		−0.010 (0.020)	
Election season		−0.011 (0.011)		0.019*** (0.002)		0.002 (0.012)		0.019*** (0.002)
Opposition references		−0.024*** (0.0005)		−0.009*** (0.0001)		−0.024*** (0.0005)		−0.009*** (0.0001)
Constant	−1.916 (3.250)	−4.911*** (0.462)	0.016 (0.998)	0.752*** (0.066)	−1.630 (3.181)	−4.554*** (0.554)	0.163 (1.024)	0.737*** (0.059)
Country effects	Fixed	Random	Fixed	Random	Fixed	Random	Fixed	Random
Language-fixed effects		✓		✓		✓		✓
Observations	200	400,332	198	984,999	190	335,583	188	892,257
R^2	0.797		0.833		0.781		0.831	

Note: $^*p < 0.1$; $^{**}p < 0.05$; $^{***}p < 0.01$
For OLS models, standard errors are cluster robust within countries.

Table 4.4 *The politics of pro-regime propaganda, institutions*

	Dependent variable:							
Outcome variable	Positive coverage standardized		Article valence		Positive coverage standardized		Article valence	
Unit of analysis	Country-year	Article	Country-year	Article	Country-year	Article	Country-year	Article
Estimator	OLS	Mixed	OLS	Mixed	OLS	Mixed	OLS	Mixed
	(1)	(2)	(3)	(4)	(5)	(6)	(7)	(8)
Legislative contraints	−0.629*	−0.952***	−0.170***	−0.170***				
	(0.367)	(0.039)	(0.038)	(0.004)				
Government accountability					−0.384***	−0.427***	−0.100***	−0.090***
					(0.090)	(0.016)	(0.031)	(0.002)
Trade	0.003	0.004***	−0.00004	−0.0001	0.001	0.004***	−0.0004	−0.0002***
	(0.007)	(0.0004)	(0.001)	(0.00005)	(0.006)	(0.0004)	(0.001)	(0.00005)
Log GDP per capita	0.297	0.583***	0.018	−0.016***	0.224	0.608***	−0.002	−0.012***
	(0.343)	(0.039)	(0.116)	(0.004)	(0.270)	(0.039)	(0.088)	(0.004)
Natural resources	−0.005	−0.003***	−0.0002	0.001***	−0.003	−0.002**	0.0003	0.001***
	(0.006)	(0.001)	(0.001)	(0.0001)	(0.006)	(0.001)	(0.001)	(0.0001)
Civil war	−0.160	−0.015	−0.044	0.009**	−0.128	0.012	−0.035	0.013***
	(0.130)	(0.028)	(0.036)	(0.003)	(0.108)	(0.028)	(0.027)	(0.003)
Internet penetration	−0.00002	0.00001	−0.00001	−0.00002***	−0.00002	0.00001	−0.00002	−0.00001***
	(0.0001)	(0.00001)	(0.00002)	(0.00000)	(0.0001)	(0.00001)	(0.00002)	(0.00000)
Election	−0.014		−0.013		0.007		−0.008	
	(0.058)		(0.020)		(0.054)		(0.020)	
Election season		−0.005		0.017***		0.009		0.020***
		(0.012)		(0.002)		(0.012)		(0.002)
Opposition references		−0.024***		−0.009***		−0.024***		−0.009***
		(0.0005)		(0.0001)		(0.0005)		(0.0001)
Constant	−2.468	−4.656***	−0.055	0.632***	−1.775	−5.418***	0.131	0.493***
	(3.275)	(0.576)	(1.138)	(0.056)	(2.593)	(0.569)	(0.849)	(0.057)
Country effects	Fixed	Random	Fixed	Random	Fixed	Random	Fixed	Random
Language-fixed effects		✓		✓		✓		✓
Observations	190	335,583	188	892,257	190	335,583	188	892,257
R^2	0.775		0.828		0.782		0.834	

Note: *p < 0.1; **p < 0.05; ***p < 0.01
For OLS models, standard errors are cluster robust within countries.

Table 4.5 *The politics of pro-regime propaganda, regime type*

	Dependent variable:							
Outcome variable	Positive coverage standardized				Article valence			
Unit of analysis	Country-year	Article	Country-year	Article	Country-year	Article	Country-year	Article
Estimator	OLS	Mixed	OLS	Mixed	OLS	Mixed	OLS	Mixed
	(1)	(2)	(3)	(4)	(5)	(6)	(7)	(8)
Dictatorship	0.903** (0.421)	1.065** (0.468)	1.253** (0.590)	1.069*** (0.137)	0.308*** (0.058)	0.301*** (0.070)	0.432*** (0.096)	0.350*** (0.024)
Weakly constrained autocracy	0.273 (0.421)	0.267 (0.438)	0.263 (0.444)	0.751*** (0.032)	0.115*** (0.058)	0.114* (0.061)	0.104 (0.065)	0.149*** (0.004)
Constrained autocracy	−0.292 (0.322)	−0.304 (0.330)	−0.302 (0.340)	−0.081*** (0.022)	−0.001 (0.020)	−0.004 (0.024)	−0.002 (0.021)	−0.011*** (0.003)
Trade		−0.001 (0.001)	0.0002 (0.005)	0.002*** (0.0003)		−0.00005 (0.0003)	−0.001* (0.001)	0.0001* (0.00004)
Log GDP per capita		0.025 (0.082)	−0.042 (0.361)	0.671*** (0.039)		0.016 (0.025)	−0.130* (0.067)	−0.020*** (0.004)
Natural resources		−0.004 (0.005)	−0.004 (0.005)	−0.002*** (0.001)		−0.001 (0.002)	0.0001 (0.001)	0.0003*** (0.0001)
Civil war		−0.127 (0.088)	−0.114 (0.099)	−0.004 (0.027)		−0.024 (0.029)	−0.018 (0.028)	0.018*** (0.004)
Internet penetration		−0.00002 (0.0001)	−0.00002 (0.0001)	−0.00003*** (0.00001)			−0.00002 (0.00002)	−0.00001*** (0.00000)
Election	0.012 (0.044)	0.009 (0.046)	0.008 (0.058)	−0.010 (0.011)	−0.006 (0.007)	−0.007 (0.007)	−0.003 (0.008)	
Election season				−0.024*** (0.0005)				0.018*** (0.002)
Opposition references								−0.009*** (0.0001)
Constant	−0.027*** (0.000)	−0.255 (0.822)	0.395 (3.497)	−7.046*** (0.537)	−0.053*** (0.000)	−0.204 (0.239)	1.277* (0.660)	0.398*** (0.057)
Country effects	Fixed	Random	Fixed	Random	Fixed	Random	Fixed	Random
Language-fixed effects				✓				✓
Observations	270	223	194	396,061	268	221	190	977,106
R²	0.862	0.838	0.794	0.537	0.965	0.945	0.954	0.398

Note: *p < 0.1; **p < 0.05; ***p < 0.01

For OLS models, standard errors are cluster-robust within countries

state-affiliated newspapers in democracies. The point estimates suggest that the difference between pro-regime coverage in constrained autocracies and democracies is equal to 1 or 2 units of our Fox News index: roughly the difference between how Fox News covers Republicans and how it covers Democrats. Constrained autocracies engage in pro-regime propaganda, for sure, but they do so in a way that is reminiscent of Fox News. These estimates were consistent across our measures of pro-regime propaganda.

Other coefficient estimates are equally noteworthy. We find little evidence that pro-regime propaganda changes with per capita GDP, trade openness, or internet penetration. These estimates are sensitive across models and not consistently significant. This suggests that pro-regime propaganda is driven by politics, not economics or access to information.

4.3.5 The Broader Informational Environment

The statistical models above accommodate citizens' access to information by controlling for internet penetration. Readers may be concerned that this measure is insufficient. Therefore, we control for a broader set of informational factors that may condition propaganda. The Freedom House Press Freedom Index combines a set of legal, political, and economic factors to measure how independent country j's media is in year s. Legal factors reflect law-based restrictions on the press. Political factors reflect whether the government exerts control over the media through intimidation, detention, jailing, assault, and other forms of intimidation. Economic factors reflect the structure of the media market: concentration, entry costs, transparency, government advertising, and bribery. For ease of interpretation, we transformed this variable so that a higher index value indicates more press freedom.

We draw other indicators from the V-Dem project. The Government Censorship Index measures the extent to which media outlets are censored by the government, both directly and indirectly via financial incentives and regulatory obstruction. The Critical Media Index records whether major media outlets represent a "wide range of political perspectives" compared to "only the government's perspective." The Diverse Perspectives Index measures whether media outlets represent a wide range of political perspectives. The Harassment of Journalists' Perspectives Index records whether individual journalists are threatened with libel, arrested, imprisoned, beaten, or killed while engaged in legitimate journalistic activities. The Media Corruption Index measures whether journalists, publishers, or broadcasters accept payments in exchange for altering news coverage. For ease of interpretation, we transformed these variables so that higher values indicate a higher level of the variable in question. Together, these variables paint a broad picture of the information environment: whether citizens can access non-government perspectives online, in print, on the radio, or on television.

The results appear in Table 4.6. Models 1 through 4 focus on *Positive Coverage Standardized: Executive*. Models 5 through 8 focus on *Article Valence: Regime*. We present country-year and article-level results. Odd-numbered models control for the Freedom House Press Freedom Index; even-numbered models control for the more fine-grained indicators from the V-Dem project. The results are substantively unchanged. In the Online Appendix, we show that our results are also robust to controlling for another well-known press freedom index from Reporters without Borders and a sophisticated new press freedom index developed by Solis and Waggoner (2020).

4.3.6 Electoral Constraints and the Geddes, Wright, and Frantz (2018) Typology

Geddes (1999) famously classified authoritarian regimes as monarchies, military-based, single parties, or personalist. This classification has been employed by Weeks (2008) to understand foreign policy in autocracies; by Escribà-Folch and Wright (2015) to understand when autocrats are vulnerable to international pressure; by Gandhi (2008) to understand how autocrats choose political institutions; and by Geddes, Wright, and Frantz (2018) to understand dynamics within ruling coalitions. Readers may wonder whether the effect of electoral constraints on pro-regime propaganda instead reflects some difference in autocratic regime type, as defined by Geddes, Wright, and Frantz (2018). Does the relationship between electoral constraints and pro-regime propaganda change when these regime typologies are accounted for?

We are unaware of a theory that would link variation in pro-regime propaganda to variation in the Geddes regime typology. Still, we re-estimated the models in Table 4.5 with controls for the Geddes, Wright, and Frantz (2018) typology. The results appear in the Online Appendix and are substantively unchanged. Across models, we consistently find that pro-regime propaganda is effusive where electoral constraints are non-binding. Geddes, Wright, and Frantz's (2018) regime type variables add relatively little explanatory power, save for single parties, which are

Table 4.6 The politics of pro-regime propaganda, information

	Dependent variable:							
Outcome variable	Positive coverage standardized				Article valence			
Unit of analysis	Country-year	Article	Country-year	Article	Country-year	Article	Country-year	Article
Estimator	OLS	Mixed	OLS	Mixed	OLS	Mixed	OLS	Mixed
	(1)	(2)	(3)	(4)	(5)	(6)	(7)	(8)
Dictatorship	0.695	1.470**	1.129***	0.717***	0.475***	0.595***	0.464***	0.463***
	(0.571)	(0.582)	(0.137)	(0.146)	(0.089)	(0.129)	(0.027)	(0.029)
Weakly constrained autocracy	0.056	0.129	0.788***	0.355***	0.067**	0.090*	0.216***	0.156***
	(0.344)	(0.223)	(0.032)	(0.049)	(0.034)	(0.048)	(0.006)	(0.010)
Constrained autocracy	−0.385	−0.318	−0.082***	−0.106***	−0.003	0.009	−0.020***	−0.014***
	(0.317)	(0.334)	(0.022)	(0.023)	(0.010)	(0.010)	(0.004)	(0.005)
Trade	−0.001	0.001	0.002***	−0.0001	−0.0004	−0.00002	0.0001	−0.0001
	(0.004)	(0.005)	(0.0003)	(0.0003)	(0.001)	(0.001)	(0.0001)	(0.0001)
Log GDP per capita	−0.082	0.053	0.700***	0.335***	−0.140*	−0.161*	0.060***	0.035***
	(0.354)	(0.385)	(0.040)	(0.041)	(0.077)	(0.089)	(0.008)	(0.008)
Natural resources	−0.002	−0.005	−0.004***	−0.003***	0.0001	−0.001	−0.0004**	−0.002***
	(0.004)	(0.005)	(0.001)	(0.001)	(0.001)	(0.001)	(0.0002)	(0.0002)
Civil war	−0.123	−0.124	−0.004	−0.025	−0.007	−0.003	0.018***	0.020***
	(0.089)	(0.113)	(0.027)	(0.027)	(0.020)	(0.022)	(0.005)	(0.005)
Internet penetration	−0.00002	0.00001	−0.00004***	−0.00001	−0.00001	0.00000	−0.00000	0.00000
	(0.0001)	(0.0001)	(0.00001)	(0.00001)	(0.00002)	(0.00002)	(0.00000)	(0.00000)
Election	0.027	0.016			−0.008	−0.009		
	(0.053)	(0.060)			(0.020)	(0.020)		
Election season			−0.016	−0.005			0.007***	0.004**
			(0.011)	(0.011)			(0.002)	(0.002)

(continued)

Table 4.6 (continued)

	Dependent variable:							
	Positive coverage standardized				Article valence			
Outcome variable	Country-year	Article	Country-year	Article	Country-year	Article	Country-year	Article
Unit of analysis	OLS	Mixed	OLS	Mixed	OLS	Mixed	OLS	Mixed
Estimator	(1)	(2)	(3)	(4)	(5)	(6)	(7)	(8)
Opposition references	0.382		−0.024***	−0.023***			−0.005***	−0.005***
	(0.310)		(0.0005)	(0.0005)			(0.0001)	(0.0001)
FH press freedom index			−0.042***		0.037**		0.013***	
			(0.007)		(0.018)		(0.001)	
Government censorship		0.259**		0.124***		0.043**		0.052***
		(0.105)		(0.010)		(0.020)		(0.002)
Critical media		−0.174*		−0.074***		−0.024		−0.019***
		(0.095)		(0.018)		(0.023)		(0.004)
Diverse perspectives		0.124*		0.012		−0.004		−0.005**
		(0.072)		(0.012)		(0.013)		(0.002)
Harassment of journalists		0.070		0.035***		−0.031*		−0.002
		(0.164)		(0.012)		(0.018)		(0.002)
Media corruption		−0.161		0.069***		−0.008		−0.009***
		(0.116)		(0.012)		(0.016)		(0.002)
Constant	1.590	−0.216	−7.412***	−3.055***	1.445*	1.489*	−0.492***	−0.201**
	(3.769)	(3.534)	(0.550)	(0.492)	(0.749)	(0.868)	(0.094)	(0.101)
Country effects	Fixed	Fixed	Random	Random	Fixed	Fixed	Random	Random
Language-fixed effects			✓	✓			✓	✓
Observations	194	194	396,061	396,061	192	192	394,631	394,631
R^2	0.810	0.817			0.838	0.840		

Note: *p < 0.1; **p < 0.05; ***p < 0.01
For OLS models, standard errors are cluster robust within countries.

142

associated with more effusive regime coverage. In our sample, this result is driven by the CCP's propaganda apparatus, which, as we discuss in Section 4.5, is among the most effusive in our sample.

4.3.7 Coverage Topics

Finally, we used the topic models introduced in Chapter 3 to identify the coverage topics with which pro-regime propaganda is associated. These associations are partly the subject of Chapters 5 and 6, which document propaganda narratives across autocracies. For now, Figure 4.2 displays three radar charts, with axes giving the share of articles *in which the autocrat is referenced* that cover the topics along the perimeter. The three panels visualize how coverage topics vary across regimes.

The topics associated with the executive and ruling party differ dramatically across autocracies, often in non-obvious ways. Broadly, propaganda apparatuses in constrained autocracies associate the regime with topics more similar to those in democracies than in dictatorships. In the absence of electoral constraints, roughly 5 percent of executive coverage is associated with sports and nearly 15 percent with the international community. Regime coverage in dictatorships is also notable for what it omits: in particular, electoral campaigns and regime opponents. This is consistent with a key result in Chapter 5. Where electoral constraints are non-binding, propaganda apparatuses are distinctive not for denigrating the opposition but for pretending it does not exist. By contrast, nearly 40 percent of regime coverage in constrained autocracies references the opposition and 10 percent features the regime engaging in electoral politics. Many topics constitute a relatively minor share of coverage: culture, nationalism, religion, military, and youth, among others.

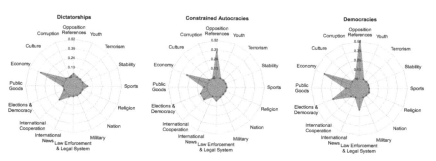

Figure 4.2 Topics associated with pro-regime propaganda

4.4 THE BERLIN WALL AS AN EXOGENOUS SHOCK: GABON

Where electoral constraints are binding, the results above suggest, autocrats are forced into a propaganda strategy that concedes bad news and policy failures. For two reasons, however, we treat these results with caution. First, they may be driven by reverse causality. If propaganda is successful, as scholars have found,[9] then it may actually loosen electoral constraints. Second, the results above may be driven by omitted variable bias. Although we control for a range of features that may be correlated with changes in both electoral constraints and pro-regime propaganda, some features may remain unobserved. Changes in electoral constraints, for instance, may coincide with changes in political leadership and with the fact that new leadership may have different tastes for propaganda or less control over the propaganda apparatus.

4.4.1 *The Berlin Wall*

To ensure that the results above are not driven by reverse causality or omitted variable bias, we exploit a rapid, exogenous change in the electoral constraints confronted by many autocrats: the fall of the Berlin Wall on November 9, 1989. The Berlin Wall's collapse marked a profound change for Africa's autocrats. During the Cold War, they could pit the United States and the Soviet Union against each other, and hence secure finance and weapons in exchange for membership in the Western or Eastern bloc. They lost this leverage when the Berlin Wall fell. When Western governments began to attach political conditions to development aid and debt relief, Africa's autocrats were largely forced to comply.[10]

In francophone Africa, this new world is associated with June 20, 1990, when French president François Mitterand announced in La Baule that France would henceforth tie foreign aid to democratic reforms:

Democracy is a universal principle.... When I say democracy, ... I naturally have a plan in mind: a representative system, free elections, multiparty politics, freedom of the press, independent judiciary, rejection of censorship. ... This is the direction that must be followed.

---

[9] Enikolopov, Petrova, and Zhuravskaya (2011); Yanagizawa-Drott (2014); Adena et al. (2015); Huang (2015*b*).
[10] Bratton and van de Walle (1997); Dunning (2004); Levitsky and Way (2010).

Mitterand's speech, delivered to African presidents, was widely covered in the press. The *New York Times* put his statement succinctly: "France Ties Africa Aid to Democracy."[11] In a sense, however, the real shift occurred several months earlier. In November 1989, citizens in Benin demanded the resignation of dictator Mathieu Kérékou, in power since 1972. Bankrupt and deprived of Soviet support, Kérékou's government conceded reforms to mollify protesters. Opposition parties, banned since 1975, proliferated, as did independent newspapers. Political prisoners were freed. A National Conference was convened in February 1990, where delegates declared themselves sovereign and effectively toppled Kérékou. The National Conference organized genuinely democratic elections in March 1991, which were won by Nicéphore Soglo.[12]

Benin's democratic transition was the first in a wave that swept the continent. Of the forty-two autocracies in Sub-Saharan Africa in 1988, sixteen held democratic elections by December 1994.[13] But even this understates the extent of political reform during the Third Wave of Democracy. Figure 4.3 displays two maps: one in 1985 and one in 1995. Democracies appear in white; autocracies that banned all political parties appear in light gray; autocracies with a single legal party appear in dark gray; and autocracies that governed with nominally democratic institutions appear in black. Prior to the Third Wave, less than a quarter of Africa's autocracies governed with nominally democratic institutions. After, less than a quarter did not. Of the thirty-seven constitutions in force by 1994, all but four featured presidential term limits. By the end of 1992, only two countries – Liberia and Sudan – had avoided meaningful reforms.

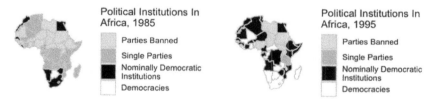

Figure 4.3 Evolution of political institutions in Africa

[11] Riding (1990).
[12] Heilbrunn (1993); Magnusson and Clark (2005).
[13] Bratton and van de Walle (1997).

The Berlin Wall's collapse predates much of our propaganda data. For two countries, however, our collection of extends further: Gabon to the 1970s and China to the 1940s.

4.4.2 *A Brief Introduction to Gabon*

These geopolitical changes were felt acutely in Gabon. Upon taking power in 1967, Omar Bongo, then thirty-one years old, outlawed opposition parties, save for his Gabonese Democratic Party (PDG). Bongo gave himself a handful of ministerial portfolios: Minister of Defense between 1968 and 1981, Minister of Information between 1967 and 1980, Minister of Planning between 1967 and 1977, Prime Minister between 1967 and 1975, and Minister of Interior between 1967 and 1970, among others. He ran unopposed in the 1973 elections, as did his handpicked deputies to the National Assembly; they were all "elected" with 99.56 percent of votes cast. He again ran unopposed in 1979, claiming 99.96 percent of the vote, and in 1986, with 99.97 percent.

Bongo earned a reputation for massive graft. French president Charles de Gaulle, faced with an economy that had been devastated by World War II, sought to rebuild France by rebuilding its energy industry. De Gaulle created two companies: Total, which focused on North Africa and the Middle East, and Elf, which focused on sub-Saharan Africa.[14] Elf's CEO described the company this way:

[Elf was] under full state control to support [de Gaulle's] African policies. Elf was ... a parallel diplomacy to control certain African states, above all at the key moment of decolonization. Opaque operations were organized to keep certain countries stable.[15]

Gabon was the system's centerpiece. In exchange for selling oil to Elf at below market value and financing Gaullist electoral campaigns in France, the French government made Bongo extraordinarily wealthy. For every barrel of crude oil that Gabon sold to Elf, the company received 57 percent of the proceeds, the Gabonese state treasury received 25 percent, and Bongo received 18 percent.[16] Bongo amassed a vast real estate portfolio in France. In 2008, *Le Monde* reported that French investigators

---

[14] Yates (1996); Shaxson (2007); Ghazvinian (2007); Heilbrunn (2014); Carter (2018).

[15] Le Floch-Prigent (2001).

[16] See the investigation by *Complement d'Enquête* at www.youtube.com/watch?v=YBlx6WSz5jg.

discovered thirty-three properties, including a mansion in the 8th arrondissement purchased in 2007 for nearly 19 million euros.[17] France guaranteed Bongo's personal security with a military installation that was connected by tunnel to the presidential palace.[18]

4.4.3 *Electoral Constraints Tighten*

French support was insufficient to insulate Bongo from the Third Wave of Democracy. Students at Omar Bongo University began protesting in January 1990, just two months after the Berlin Wall fell. Labor unions joined, launching a general strike that "shook the foundations" of the regime.[19] Like Kérékou in Benin, Bongo made concessions. He gave civil servants a raise and generous health benefits. He legalized political parties and independent newspapers. He no longer required citizens to possess an exit visa to travel abroad. He also convened a National Conference in April 1990, which imposed a limit of two presidential terms, reduced presidential terms from seven years to five, and created an independent judiciary. Presidential elections were scheduled for December 1993. These new electoral constraints were reinforced by Mitterrand's Socialist government in France, which promised transparency in its relationships with African governments and whose electoral campaigns Bongo had not yet funded. "The PDG controls the government," Bongo acknowledged, "but the opposition controls the streets."[20] Bongo also recognized the uprising's geopolitical origins. "The winds from the east," he observed at La Baule, "are shaking the coconut trees."[21]

Bongo confronted genuine electoral constraints as the 1993 elections approached. Opinion polls showed Bongo claiming only 40 percent of the vote, with the main opposition candidate, Rev. Paul Mba-Abessolé, slightly behind. He watched in March 1992 as his father-in-law, Denis Sassou Nguesso, was humiliated in Congo's post–Third Wave presidential election. The French government appeared poised to force Bongo to conduct a genuinely democratic election.[22] Bongo once relied on repression, but, as the election approached, he was forced to persuade citizens of the regime's merits.

[17] Bernard (2008).
[18] Heilbrunn (2014).
[19] Decalo (1998, 165–167).
[20] Gardinier (1997).
[21] Gardinier (1997).
[22] Gardinier (2000).

4.4.4 Electoral Constraints Loosen

Bongo narrowly survived, with just 51 percent of the vote. The outcome was fraudulent, and the French government was complicit. In 1993, when France joined the European Economic and Monetary Union, it was forced to meet a series of "convergence criteria," which limited annual budget deficits to 3 percent and debt/GDP ratios to 60 percent. As a result, the French government could no longer afford to finance budget deficits in its former African colonies, which employed a CFA currency that was tied to the franc. The French government settled on a 50 percent devaluation, which required the unanimous consent of African presidents. The French government believed Bongo would acquiesce; they doubted Mba-Abessolé would. On the eve of the election, Mitterrand dispatched electoral experts to help Bongo falsify election results in Haut-Ogooué, his native province. The final tally gave Bongo 40 percent more votes than the province's voting age population.[23]

The results elicited major protests, and the opposition demanded new democratic reforms. In response, the French government forced Bongo to concede an independent electoral commission and relinquish control of the Presidential Guard, once the primary instrument of state repression. He stalled in the implementation, however, and in May 1995 received a reprieve. Jacques Chirac, whose electoral campaign Bongo financed and who once called African democracy a "political error," was elected French president. Chirac effectively gave Bongo *carte blanche*. In July 1996, Chirac said this: "Gabon has been under the direction of President Bongo: under the best management possible."[24] The electoral constraints that Bongo confronted were gradually relaxed. In December 1998, Bongo claimed 67 percent of the vote, and in 2003, Bongo secured a change in the constitution that lengthened presidential terms to seven years, from five, and allowed him to seek re-election indefinitely. In November 2005, Bongo claimed 79 percent, giving him a seventh term in office. He died in 2009, at seventy-three years old, having spent 42 of those years as president.

Bongo confronted genuine electoral constraints only briefly: from the fall of the Berlin Wall through the late 1990s or early 2000s. Our theory suggests Bongo's propaganda strategy should have changed accordingly.

[23] Gardinier (2000).
[24] Gardinier (2000).

4.4.5 Descriptive Statistics and a Non-Parametric Smoother

Founded in 1973, *L'Union* newspaper was Bongo's chief propaganda outlet. We obtained its entire history: 125,797 pages published between 1973 and 2017, amounting to nearly 300,000 articles. Originally managed by a Frenchman, Fred Hidalgo, *L'Union* was first published weekly and, on December 30, 1975, began publishing daily. The left panel of Figure 4.4 presents *Positive Coverage Standardized: Executive$_{ijt}$*, averaged by month *m*, between 1974 and 2015. For clarity, we include two dashed vertical lines. The first indicates the fall of the Berlin Wall and the second Bongo's re-consolidation of power around 2000. The right panel of Figure 4.4 employs a regression discontinuity design, treating the fall of the Berlin Wall as a discontinuity. We fit a non-parametric regression to *Positive Coverage Standardized$_m$* on either side of the discontinuity, which rules out the possibility of some pre-existing trend in propaganda that simply coincided with the Berlin Wall's collapse. The shaded area represents a 95 percent confidence interval.

The results are consistent with our theory. Just before the Berlin Wall fell – as the winds from the east began to shake Libreville's coconut trees but before Mitterand delivered his La Baule speech – Bongo launched a propaganda campaign greater than any before. After the Berlin Wall fell, however, Bongo's propaganda apparatus moderated, as our theory predicts. When Bongo reconsolidated power in the late 1990s and early 2000s – as his electoral constraints loosened – his propaganda apparatus responded by gradually returning to levels of the single-party period.

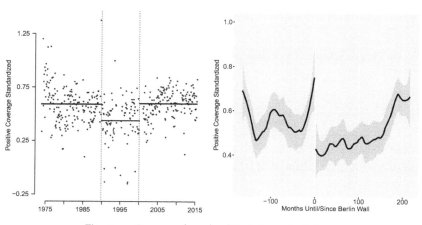

Figure 4.4 Propaganda and political change in Gabon

4.4.6 Regression

Next, we estimated models of the form

$$Y_t = \alpha + \beta \left(\text{Third Wave}_t\right) + \phi W_t + \epsilon \qquad (4.3)$$

where t indexes day, *Third Wave$_t$* is the explanatory variable of interest, and W_t is a vector of day-level controls. The explanatory variable of interest, X_t, assumes value 1 between November 9, 1989, and July 15, 1996, when Jacques Chirac, newly elected, announced his unequivocal support for Bongo during a visit to Libreville. We controlled for dates that could be associated with particularly elevated levels of pro-regime propaganda, including the six presidential elections between 1973 and 2017, as well as for the 15 days before and after each election, which we refer to as an election season.

The results appear in Table 4.7.[25] Again, Bongo's propaganda strategy changed after the Berlin Wall fell. Prior to November 9, 1989, the daily mean of *Positive Coverage Standardized$_{ijt}$* was 0.55. Between November 9, 1989, and Chirac's 1996 Libreville announcement, the daily mean

Table 4.7 *The politics of pro-regime propaganda in Gabon*

	Dependent variable:				
	Positive coverage standardized (1)	Positive coverage per day (2)	Executive references per day (3)	Executive references per page (4)	Positive coverage per page (5)
Third wave	−0.127***	−1.290***	−0.726**	−0.192***	−0.267***
	(0.017)	(0.221)	(0.311)	(0.032)	(0.026)
Post–third wave	0.010	3.423***	6.509***	−0.027	−0.059***
	(0.013)	(0.184)	(0.259)	(0.025)	(0.020)
Election	−0.277	4.034	18.876***	2.155***	0.495
	(0.308)	(4.138)	(5.820)	(0.573)	(0.471)
Election season	−0.044	6.647***	15.430***	0.916***	0.343***
	(0.050)	(0.763)	(1.072)	(0.092)	(0.076)
Constant	0.554***	4.008***	7.035***	1.271***	0.728***
	(0.009)	(0.120)	(0.168)	(0.017)	(0.014)
Observations	7,867	12,385	12,385	7,621	7,621
R^2	0.009	0.047	0.076	0.021	0.016

Note: *p < 0.1; **p < 0.05; ***p < 0.01

[25] Because we digitized this newspaper from historical archives, Models 4 and 5 estimate outcomes at page level rather than article level.

value of *Positive Coverage Standardized*$_t$ fell by nearly 25 percent. As expected, by the late 1990s, after his electoral constraints loosened, Bongo's propaganda strategy returned to its 1980s levels.

4.4.7 *Bayesian Change Point Models*

Finally, we probed when exactly Bongo's propaganda strategy changed. Did it occur in November 1989, when the Berlin Wall fell? In February 1990, when citizens in Benin toppled Kérékou? In June 1990, when Mitterand delivered the La Baule speech? Or did it occur at some other moment?

Intuitively, we treated the net positive words used to describe Bongo in the *L'Union* newspaper as driven by an underlying data generating process: the propaganda strategy. We employed a Bayesian change point model to identify the precise moment at which this underlying data-generating process changed. Poisson models require that the count being modeled be non-negative and whole. Since our chief measure of pro-regime propaganda, *Positive Coverage Standardized: Executive*$_m$, is neither, we rescaled it by shifting the entire set of values up by the absolute amount that the least value is negative, and then multiplying by 100, so that it is comprised exclusively of whole numbers. The model is

$$\text{Positive Coverage Standardized: Executive}_m \sim \text{Poisson}(\lambda_m) \quad (4.4)$$

$$\lambda_m = \exp(X_m \beta_{mn}) \quad (4.5)$$

where m indexes month and n indexes propaganda regime. This lets the covariates in vector W_m, which are identical to those in equation (4.3), condition propaganda differently according to the prevailing propaganda regime. We estimated the model via Markov chain Monte Carlo, with conjugate prior distribution Gamma for the rate parameter λ. We assigned an uninformative prior.

The results appear in Figure 4.5. For each month along the x-axis, the y-axis measures the probability that the propaganda strategy shift occurred then. The change point model assigns a 0.6 probability to the strategy shift occurring in September 1990, which coincides with the first multi-party legislative election since 1967. This election marked a profound shift in Gabon's political climate. Voting occurred in two rounds, with the first on September 16. As before, Bongo attempted to rig the election, though this time citizens responded with mass protests, ultimately forcing the annulment of results from more than 25 percent

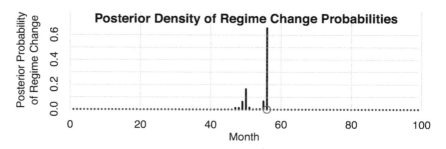

Figure 4.5 When Bongo's propaganda strategy changed

of electoral districts. The second round occurred on October 28, after which the government claimed 63 of the National Assembly's 120 seats. Although the results were almost certainly fraudulent, the election nonetheless marked the onset of genuine political competition. Figure 4.5 identifies a second candidate date for the propaganda strategy shift: March 1990, which coincides with two other critical events. The Benin National Conference concluded in late February, with Kérékou stripped of sovereignty and effectively toppled. In early March, Bongo announced that Gabon's National Conference would occur in April. Again, these two dates marked key changes in the electoral competition that Bongo confronted.

4.5 CAUSAL MECHANISMS, ALTERNATIVE EXPLANATIONS, AND SURVEY EXPERIMENTS: CHINA

Evidence from Gabon suggests that electoral constraints have a plausibly causal effect on pro-regime propaganda. Still, scholars have identified other factors that may condition propaganda in autocracies. If these alternative explanations are correlated with changes in electoral constraints and we have not adequately controlled for them, then these alternative explanations may drive the statistical results in Section 4.3. We turn, therefore, to China, since our collection of *People's Daily* propaganda dates from the 1940s. This temporal scope allows us to probe whether the CCP's pro-regime propaganda has moderated with China's extraordinary economic and social changes over the past seventy years. We find that it has not. The *People's Daily* under Xi Jinping is more effusively pro-regime than any point since the Cultural Revolution.

We turn to China for a second reason. In the absence of electoral constraints, our theory suggests, effusive propaganda serves to intimidate, not persuade citizens of regime merits. Yet many scholars suggest otherwise. Chinese citizens, the arguments generally go, are so inundated by CCP propaganda that they eventually accept its claims, a process described as "implicit persuasion" or "nondeliberative cognition."[26] To ascertain how CCP propaganda conditions citizens' beliefs, we conducted a survey experiment, which used quota sampling to balance the respondent pool on China's most recent census. To accommodate the possibility that citizens conceal their true feelings, we employed list experiments, which preserved respondents' anonymity. Pro-regime propaganda in the *People's Daily*, we find, deters citizens from protesting against the government because they fear the consequences, as our theory suggests. It has no effect on their support for the CCP.

Throughout, we distinguish between the *People's Daily*, which is the CCP's flagship newspaper, and China's commercial newspapers, which are majority owned by the government but receive fewer or no subsidies and are subject to less direct control. Though commercial newspapers may publish more engaging and relatively neutral coverage about a range of topics, as many scholars suggest, we show that pro-regime coverage in the CCP's commercial newspapers is nearly identical to that in the *People's Daily*. Our survey experiment reveals that political coverage in CCP commercial newspapers has the same effect as political coverage in the *People's Daily*.

4.5.1 *Alternative Explanations: Has CCP Propaganda Moderated over Time?*

Economic Development, Information Access, and Educational Attainment Scholars have proposed three primary alternative explanations for variation in pro-regime propaganda across autocracies. First, media bias may be constrained by market competition for advertising revenues. Where potential advertising revenues are higher, the logic goes, media platforms embrace relative objectivity to attract more readers and, in turn, more advertising revenue.[27] Scholars have extended these

---

[26] Kennedy (2009); Arceneaux and Truex (2020).

[27] McMillan and Zoido (2004); Corneo (2006); Gehlbach and Sonin (2014); Tella and Franceschelli (2011); Hamilton (2004); Petrova (2008, 2011, 2012). This view was articulated by Joseph Pulitzer, who said, "advertising means money, and money means independence." Scholars have also attributed the growth of unbiased media to population growth; see Besley and Prat (2006); Ellman and Germano (2009); Gentzkow, Glaeser, and Goldin (2006).

arguments to China: to explain the decline of media bias in the wake of Deng Xiaoping's 1980s reforms[28] and content in the CCP's local, commercial newspapers.[29] For many scholars, the market forces un- leashed by China's economic expansion will fundamentally reshape CCP propaganda. Over time, Qin, Strömberg, and Wu (2018) conclude, "eco- nomic development [will reduce] audience exposure to propaganda." Shambaugh (2007, 27) anticipated their argument a decade earlier: "The overall power and efficacy of China's propaganda state today has de- clined a great deal, and . . . commercialization has been one of the main factors in this declining capacity."

Lynch (1999) advanced a related argument: Economic growth would be accompanied by an expansion in internet access, which would force the CCP to moderate its propaganda. The availability of foreign news sources is partly why Goebbels routinely conceded bad news. Months before American president Bill Clinton quipped that censoring the In- ternet was "sort of like trying to nail Jello to the wall," Lynch (1999, 165) predicted that "eventually everyone with access to a telephone and more advanced technologies will be able to generate and circulate their own thought-work messages." This, Lynch argued, would amount to "pluralization in the extreme."[30]

Still other scholars have argued that the spread of education will force autocrats into a less biased propaganda strategy. Geddes and Zaller (1989, 320) suggest that the citizens most susceptible to autocratic pro- paganda are those who are "heavily exposed" to it but "not sophisticated enough to . . . resist."[31] Similarly, Guriev and Treisman (2018) write that "economic modernization, and in particular the spread of higher educa- tion," makes citizens more difficult to persuade. Insofar as propagandists are constrained by what citizens will believe, education will reduce the amount of propaganda to which citizens are exposed. Education may

---

[28] Lee (1990); Zhao (1998); Lynch (1999). For more on China's commercialized me- dia in the reform period, see Bishop (1989); Liu (1996); Hong (1998); Barmé (1998, 1999*a,b*); Lee (2000); Zhao (2000*a,b*); Fan (2001); Oksenberg (2001, 197); Li (2001, 2002); Donald, Keene, and Hong (2002); Jia, Xing, and Heisey (2002); Jirik (2004); Mengin (2004); Esarey (2006); Zhang and Cameron (2004); Brady (2008, 2012*b*); Bandurski and Hala (2010). For more on media "conglom- eration" or "convergence" in the 2000s, see Yin and Liu (2014); Shan and Liu (2017), and Xiong and Zhang (2018).

[29] Qin, Strömberg, and Wu (2018).

[30] For more on how media can facilitate regime change, see Pei (1994) and Hassid (2016).

[31] See also De Keersmaecker and Roets (2017, 108).

also induce a change in journalists. As they receive more formal training, Shirk (2011, 10) writes, journalists may "think of themselves as professionals instead of as agents of the government," and resist serving as propagandists.

What Mao Zedong and Xi Jinping Have in Common We first test these arguments in the context of the CCP's flagship newspaper, the *People's Daily*, which publishes editorials and commentaries that represent the definitive CCP line. The *People's Daily* targets CCP members, government bureaucrats, and China's urban elite, whose protests have long been regarded by the CCP as profoundly threatening. The *People's Daily* is also widely read; some 51 percent of Chinese citizens, we found, reported doing so within the past week. Its editorials and commentaries are routinely published under pseudonyms, including *Zhong Sheng*, which itself is threatening. A homophone for "Voice of China," its literal meaning is "bell tone," drawn from the saying "bell tone to warn the world."[32] During politically sensitive moments, other newspapers are required to reprint *People's Daily* content or follow its editorial line. After the Tiananmen Square massacre, the *People's Daily* was the platform through which Deng Xiaoping warned citizens that "stability overrides everything"; Deng's successor, Jiang Zemin, used the *People's Daily* to reiterate the warning.

We created an article-level dataset of the *People's Daily* that dated from May 1946. The dataset encompassed 1,572,726 articles from 24,659 days. Figure 4.6 visualizes the history of the *People's Daily*. The left panel displays *Positive Coverage Standardized: Executive$_{ijt}$*, averaged by month, since 1946. The right panel charts China's socio-economic change: in GDP per capita, trade intensity, urbanization rate, internet users per capita, and total newspaper copies published, which we interpret as a measure of media market size. Since all Chinese newspapers are government owned, these data have been recorded since the 1950s,[33] and so provide a unique opportunity to understand how propaganda has changed over the very long term as living standards rose and the media market expanded.

Again, we find, propaganda is driven by politics, with economic and informational trends either secondary or irrelevant. After founding the People's Republic of China in 1949, Mao spent the next decade

---

[32] The term is *jingshi zhongsheng*; see Bandurski (2018).
[33] We draw data from the China's National Bureau of Statistics.

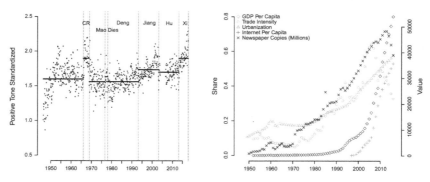

Figure 4.6 Propaganda and socio-economic change in China

consolidating power by expropriating the landed aristocracy and purging "counter-revolutionaries." As he did, pro-regime propaganda grew more effusive. These two trends climaxed with the high phase of the Cultural Revolution, between 1966 and 1969, when Mao had so consolidated power that he was able to send 17 million urban middle schoolers, generally the children of elites, to the countryside to learn communism from Chinese peasants. Among them: Xi Jinping, who was forced to do manual labor in Shaanxi for seven years. Xi, like others, lived in a cave.[34]

Mao's death in 1976 set off a power struggle. The ultra-leftist Gang of Four, led by his wife Jiang Qing, hoped to oust his designated successor and return China to a state of perpetual revolution. It looked like they might succeed, and so moderate elites compelled Mao's struggling successor, Hua Guofeng, to recall the popular Deng Xiaoping from exile. Within two years, Deng brought the Gang of Four to trial and sidelined Hua in a bloodless coup. This leadership struggle is evident in Figure 4.6. As soon as Mao died, propaganda skyrocketed, reflecting the Gang of Four's preference for repression and control of the Propaganda Department.[35] Once the Gang of Four was purged and Hua was sidelined, Deng proceeded with the moderate policies that made him popular. From 1978 onwards, he liberalized the economy and embraced collective decision-making among senior CCP officials. As he did, pro-regime propaganda declined.

The Tiananmen Square massacre in 1989 marked a fundamental shift. Before ordering the People's Liberation Army to clear the Square, Deng

[34] Connor (2015).
[35] Jiao (2004); MacFarquhar (2011).

predicted that 200 deaths would buy the CCP 20 years of stability.[36] Afterwards, he purged officials who sympathized with protesters. On the massacre's first anniversary, he reminded citizens on the front page of the *People's Daily* that "stability overrides everything." Pro-regime propaganda has risen steadily since. After assuming power in 1993, Jiang Zemin ordered newspapers to "guide public opinion" even more strictly. Hu Jintao's propaganda minister said that "one of the primary tasks of journalists is to make the people loyal to the Party."[37] The exception to this trend is the temporary reset that occurs when each new leader assumes power. Among their first priorities, Brady (2008, Ch. 3) observes, is to consolidate control of the Propaganda Department by appointing loyalists. Figure 4.6 reflects this. The effusiveness of pro-regime propaganda rises with each leader's time in office.

Xi Jinping took power in 2012 and quickly set about consolidating authority. He purged rivals with an "anti-corruption" campaign,[38] disappeared leaders of China's #MeToo movement, and sent over a million ethnic minorities to re-education camps.[39] In 2018, Xi abolished the term limits that ensured elite rotation atop the CCP, emerging as the most powerful leader since Mao. Xi's propaganda strategy changed accordingly. Hong Kong University's China Media Centre recently showed that Xi has appeared on more front pages of the *People's Daily* than anyone since Mao.[40] Our data yield the same conclusion. Under Xi, pro-regime propaganda has returned to its Cultural Revolution high point. The *People's Daily* is now more effusively pro-regime than at any point in the past 70 years.

Citizens have noticed and resisted. One online meme depicted the *People's Daily* front page as two words repeated over and over: "Xi Jinping." Use of virtual private networks (VPN) expanded, letting citizens circumvent the Great Firewall. In response, the CCP deployed software to monitor citizens' browsing habits; began enforcing prohibitions against VPN use; and built a "50 Cent Party," which floods social media with pro-regime content.[41] In 2016, the regime began installing loudspeakers

---

[36] Cheng (2016).
[37] Guangdong Provincial Propaganda Department (2006, 16), quoted in Brady and Wang (2009).
[38] Lorentzen and Lu (2018).
[39] Fincher (2018); Kinetz (2018); Duxfield and Burrows (2019).
[40] Gang (2014*b*).
[41] Gang (2013); Huang and Zhai (2013); King, Pan, and Roberts (2017).

in rural villages, forcing residents to consume CCP propaganda generally three times per day. Each broadcast begins: "The Party's good voice singing in the new countryside." The *Global Times*, a CCP newspaper, acknowledged that the loudspeakers sought to combat the "negative side effects" of smartphones, which "more and more villagers own." The loudspeakers, citizens are told, should "[evoke] nostalgic memories."[42] Village loudspeakers had not been used since the Mao era.

China's economic and informational landscape changed dramatically after 1949, particularly with Deng Xiaoping's reforms in 1978. Living standards rose, foreign trade grew, citizens moved to cities, the commercial newspaper market boomed, and the Internet spread. The alternative explanations above suggest that pro-regime propaganda in the *People's Daily* should have declined. This has not happened. Despite China's exponential growth, the *People's Daily* now covers the regime even more effusively than during Cultural Revolution. Xi has resurrected many slogans from the Mao era, perhaps none more telling than this: "East, west, south, north, and center; Party, government, military, society, and education; the Party rules them all."[43]

Estimation To probe the long-run relationship between propaganda and socio-economic change more systematically, we estimated models of the form

$$Y_s = \alpha + \beta X_s + \phi W_s + \epsilon \qquad (4.6)$$

where s indexes year, X_s gives China's Polity score, and W_s gives year-level variables that reflect alternative explanations. Since these are measured annually, our outcome variable is the mean annual value of *Positive Coverage Standardized: Executive*$_{ijt}$. The vector W_s includes GDP per capita, trade intensity, the urbanization rate, and several measures of media market size: the number of published newspaper copies, the number of newspapers and magazines published, the kinds of newspapers published, newspaper copies per capita, and internet users per capita.

The results appear in Table 4.8. As expected, China's Polity score is negatively associated with pro-regime propaganda. None of the economic or media market covariates has a consistent or substantively important effect. In Models 1 and 4, increases in GDP per capita are

---

[42] Chen (2019).
[43] For more on the rise of "gratitude education" under Hu Jintao and Xi Jinping, see Gang (2020).

Table 4.8 *The politics of pro-regime propaganda in China*

	Dependent variable:				
	Positive coverage standardized				
	(1)	(2)	(3)	(4)	(5)
Polity	−0.100**	−0.196***	−0.163***	−0.118***	
	(0.042)	(0.046)	(0.036)	(0.044)	
Log GDP per capita	0.190***	0.073	−0.013	0.139**	−0.696
	(0.056)	(0.056)	(0.063)	(0.053)	(0.630)
Trade	−0.239	−0.092	−0.333	0.071	−0.380
	(0.219)	(0.233)	(0.241)	(0.234)	(0.806)
Urbanization	−0.702	0.198	0.962	0.132	5.203*
	(0.592)	(0.679)	(0.691)	(0.576)	(2.656)
Log total copies	−0.130***				
	(0.040)				
Issues		0.00000			
		(0.00000)			
Kinds			0.0001**		
			(0.0001)		
Copies per capita				−0.016**	
				(0.007)	
Internet per capita					0.720
					(1.956)
Constant	2.793***	−0.410	0.187	−0.022	6.290
	(1.025)	(0.440)	(0.439)	(0.410)	(4.823)
Observations	62	62	62	62	18
R^2	0.614	0.544	0.586	0.583	0.486

Note: *$p < 0.1$; **$p < 0.05$; ***$p < 0.01$

associated with more propaganda, not less. Neither the number of newspapers and magazines published nor internet users per capita is associated with pro-regime propaganda.[44] Although Model 4 suggests that more newspaper copies per capita is associated with less pro-regime propaganda, the effect is substantively trivial. In 2016, China's National Bureau of Statistics reported that there were 28 newspaper copies per capita. It would require 100 additional copies per capita – an increase of some 350 percent – to reduce pro-regime propaganda by a single unit of

[44] Our measure of internet users per capita begins in 1996. Since China's Polity score has not changed since, it is omitted from Model 5.

our Fox News index. As China's economy expands and its media market grows, its local newspapers may indeed moderate, as Qin, Strömberg, and Wu (2018) suggest. But these dramatic changes have had no effect on the *People's Daily*, the CCP's flagship propaganda newspaper. Its content is driven by politics, not economics.

4.5.2 The Mechanisms of Belief Change: Intimidation, not Persuasion

Is CCP Propaganda Actually Persuasive? Huang's (2015b; 2018) understanding of CCP propaganda is consistent with ours: It serves to intimidate, not persuade. This suggests that many citizens express support for the CCP because they fear the consequences of dissent. This is known as preference falsification, and it is endemic in autocracies.[45] This, in our view, is why surveys routinely find that over 90 percent of Chinese citizens support the CCP.

Many scholars disagree. Chinese citizens, as Stockmann, Esarey, and Zhang (2018, 1) put it, do not "misrepresent political trust in surveys out of political fear."[46] In turn, many take the CCP's 90 percent approval ratings seriously,[47] and conclude that CCP propaganda must be persuasive.[48]

A Survey List Experiment To resolve this debate, we conducted a survey of over 4,000 Chinese citizens in late 2020.[49] To accommodate the possibility of preference falsification, we employed a list experiment. We gave survey respondents a list of statements and asked not which ones they agreed with but how many. The key is that Group A received one more statement – the sensitive statement – than Group B. The quantity of interest is the difference in means between the two groups.[50] List

---

[45] Kuran (1997); García-Ponce and Pasquale (2015); Jiang and Yang (2016); Tannenberg (2017); Li, Shi, and Zhu (2018); Robinson and Tannenberg (2019); Blair, Coppock, and Moor (2020).

[46] Truex (2017); Lei and Lu (2016); Birney, Landry, and Yan (2017).

[47] Chen, Zhong, and Hillard (1997); Zhong, Chen, and Scheb (1998); Shi (2000, 2001); Chen and Shi (2001); Chen (2004); Li (2004); Tang (2005); Wang (2005); Manion (2006); Chen and Dickson (2008); Kennedy (2009); Lewis-Beck, Tang, and Martini (2014); Dickson (2015); Guang et al. (2020).

[48] Truex (2017); Stockmann and Gallagher (2011); Cantoni et al. (2017).

[49] This survey was granted "exempt" status by the University of Southern California's Institutional Research Board.

[50] Similar list experiments have been used to estimate racism in the American south; see Kuklinski, Cobb, and Gilens (1997).

experiments have proven effective in China. Robinson and Tannenberg (2019) employed a list experiment with a non-representative, online sample of 1,953 Chinese citizens. Asked directly, they found, 91 percent of respondents said they supported the CCP. Asked in the form of a list experiment, CCP support was no higher than 66 percent. Consistent with our theory, this rate of self-censorship is 2.5 times greater than Frye et al. (2017) document in Putin's Russia.

We partnered with a professional survey company to conduct the experiment. We balanced survey respondents according to the most recent national census, in 2010.[51] We restricted attention to non-CCP members who passed a basic attention check embedded in the survey and finished the survey in between the 10th percentile and 90th percentile of completion times.[52] After asking several demographic questions,[53] we randomly assigned respondents to treatment and control groups. Respondents in the treatment group read an article that was published in the *People's Daily* on July 16, 2020.[54] For reference, the article appears in the Online Appendix. This article was first published in *Qiushi*, a CCP ideological magazine whose name means "Seeking Truth." It was then given front page placement in the *People's Daily* and widely distributed throughout the propaganda apparatus. Entitled "The Leadership of the Chinese Communist Party Is the Most Essential Characteristic of Socialism with Chinese Characteristics," it featured a list of eighteen Xi Jinping quotes. It underscored the CCP's control of the country and Xi's control of the CCP. It is emblematic of CCP propaganda. Our theory suggests that citizens interpret it as threatening, not persuasive.

Next, we asked respondents direct questions about their support for the CCP and their willingness to engage in anti-regime protests. These questions appear in Table 4.9. To facilitate comparison, several of these questions were drawn from previous surveys in China.[55] The CCP's reputation for online surveillance and repression creates incentives for citizens to conceal their dissent, so we expected Chinese citizens to answer direct questions as they believe the CCP would have them. To accommodate the possibility of preference falsification, we then asked

---

[51] Balance statistics appear in the Online Appendix.
[52] These are 5.4 and 24.7 minutes, respectively. The results are robust to other cutpoints.
[53] We drew many demographic questions from Johnston and Quek (2018) and Carter, Johnston, and Quek (2018).
[54] People's Daily (2020b).
[55] Jiang and Yang (2016); Huang (2018); Robinson and Tannenberg (2019).

Table 4.9 *Direct questions*

Regime support

    I support Comrade Xi Jinping's leadership.

    Overall, the government is working for the people and is responsive to the needs of the people.

    China's system of government is better than any other I can think of.

    I approve of government propaganda work.

    If given the opportunity, I would like to move abroad to study, live, or work.

Protest-related

    I would be willing to participate in a protest against the government.

    If No: Because I am afraid of the consequences.

        Because I support the government's policies.

---

respondents the same questions in the form of list experiments.[56] To implement the list experiments, within treatment and control groups, we randomized respondents into two subgroups. One subgroup received a set of three non-sensitive statements from which they were asked to indicate the number that applied to them. The other subgroup received the same three non-sensitive statements plus one sensitive statement from the direct questions in Table 4.9. They were then asked to indicate the number that applied to them. This let respondents express sensitive opinions without stating them directly. The list experiment prompts appear in Table 4.10.[57] To mitigate concerns about online surveillance, we made the non-sensitive items as non-verifiable as possible. For instance, rather than "I attend a sports match once a week," we used the more ambiguous "I consider myself a sports fan."

Although list experiments help elicit truthful responses to sensitive questions, they entail drawbacks. Ceiling effects may occur when respondents' true preferences are affirmative for all non-sensitive items and the sensitive item. Floor effects may occur when all uniformly negative responses are expected for all items. In each case, respondents in the treatment group may fear that answering the question truthfully would

---

[56] To facilitate comparison with the direct questions, we included two list experiments about protest preferences: "I would not be willing to participate in a protest against the government *because I am afraid of the consequences*" and "I would not be willing to participate in a protest against the government *because I support the government's policies*," respectively. There is no evidence that the ordering of direct and indirect questions affects results; see Frye et al. (2017).

[57] For ease of interpretation, the sensitive item appears in bold at the top of each list experiment; in reality its placement was randomized.

Table 4.10 *List experiments*

I support Comrade Xi Jinping's leadership.
I eat out everyday.
Being frugal is a virtue.
I love being close to nature.

**Overall, the government is working for the people and is responsive to the
needs of the people.**
Air pollution is one of the most important problems in our country.
Overall, the quality of life was better 30 years ago.
My family is better off now compared to five years ago.

China's system of government is better than any other I can think of.
It is important to follow religious norms and ceremonies.
Private ownership of businesses should be increased.
Women make equally good political leaders as men.

I approve of government propaganda work.
I am not particularly interested in local affairs.
I like to read the local newspaper.
I like to read the news online.

If given the opportunity, I would like to move abroad to study, live, or work.
I would like to go to a movie next week.
Saving money is really important to me right now.
I would like to buy a laptop.

**I would not participate in a protest or a collective walk against the
government because I am afraid.**
I would consider myself a sports fan.
I take vitamins every day.
Smoking sometimes is a great way to relax.

**I would not participate in a protest or a collective walk against the
government because I support government policies.**
I like Italian food.
Traditional norms and customs should be followed.
Marine ecosystems should be protected.

---

reveal their true (affirmative) preference for the sensitive item. These
effects generally understate the extent to which respondents prefer the
sensitive item.[58] To avoid ceiling and floor effects, we followed Glynn
(2013) by specifying nonsensitive items that were negatively correlated
with each other.

List experiments may also be subject to design effects, which occur
when preferences over non-sensitive items change with the addition of a

---

[58] Kuklinski, Cobb, and Gilens (1997); Kuklinski et al. (1997); Blair and Imai (2012).

sensitive item. Design effects may occur when respondents evaluate list items relative to one another. To avoid them, we chose non-sensitive items that were unambiguous and for which respondents likely had strong opinions.[59]

Perhaps the chief drawback of list experiments is precision. The standard errors around point estimates are much larger than under direct questioning.[60] We accommodated this by recruiting a large sample size.

Results: CCP Propaganda Threatens, Not Persuades The results for direct questions appear in Figure 4.7. The light-gray bars represent the control group, which read no article and hence represent the baseline views of Chinese citizens, subject to preference falsification. The black bars represent the treatment group, which read the *People's Daily* article. The dark-gray bars represent an extension discussed below: respondents who read the same article published in the *Beijing News*, a commercial newspaper.

Survey questions appear along the *x*-axis. The first five focus on explicit support for the regime; the next two focus on protest-related preferences. Of the seven, four implicate the CCP directly. For each, support for the regime hovers around 90 percent. Xi Jinping's approval rating is 95 percent; 95 percent of respondents say the government works

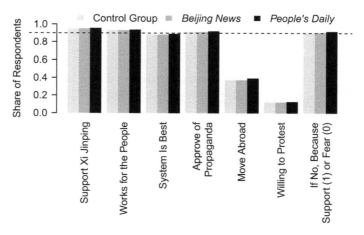

Figure 4.7 Effect of CCP propaganda, direct questioning

[59] Blair and Imai (2012).
[60] Corstange (2009).

for the people; 88 percent of respondents say China's system of government is best; and 90 percent approve of government propaganda. Just 40 percent of respondents said they wanted to move abroad. Only 10 percent of respondents said they would be willing to engage in anti-regime protests; of the 90 percent of respondents who answered no, 90 percent said this was because they supported the government. These results are consistent with the large literature that uses direct questions to probe the views of Chinese citizens.

The list experiment results confirm the prevalence of preference falsification. Figure 4.8 shows the views of respondents who read the *People's Daily* article compared to respondents who read no article. For each statement along the *x*-axis, the *y*-axis measures the estimated share of respondents in the treatment and control groups who agree, as well as the estimated difference between those two groups. When the confidence intervals of this estimated difference exclude 0, the treatment effect is statistically significant. CCP propaganda, we find, intimidates rather than persuades. The only effect of the *People's Daily* is to discourage citizens from protesting because they fear the consequences. To be clear, these estimates constitute ceilings for CCP support, since some respondents may still conceal dissent.

These results are robust to alternative specifications, which we discuss in the Online Appendix. We modified the completion time threshold. We checked for evidence of design effects, which occur when respondents' preferences over non-sensitive items change with the addition of a sensitive item. We employed statistical corrections to account for ceiling and floor effects. We dropped "satisficers," who expressed preferences over non-sensitive items in list experiments that were inconsistent with

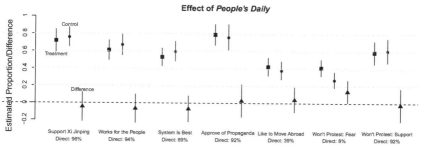

Figure 4.8 Effect of CCP propaganda, list experiments

their preferences in direct questioning.[61] These statistical corrections let us estimate several outcomes more precisely. Treated respondents support Xi Jinping less, are less likely to believe the government works for the people, and are less likely to believe China's system of government is best. Again, they are less likely to protest because they fear the consequences.

4.5.3 Are the CCP's Commercial Newspapers Different?

Investigative Journalism in a Dictatorship Pro-regime propaganda in the *People's Daily* is now more effusive than at any point since the Cultural Revolution, despite China's extraordinary socio-economic changes. Have these changes reshaped propaganda in the CCP's commercialized local newspapers and investigative television programs? Is the *People's Daily* anachronistic, unrepresentative of the propaganda that most Chinese citizens consume? Are citizens persuaded by pro-regime content in commercialized newspapers?

Commercial newspapers and investigative television programs emerged after the CCP cut subsidies to loss-making enterprises in the 1980s and 1990s. Newspapers were "cast to the sea" and forced to compete on the open market; investigative television programs quickly gained popularity. This, Gang and Bandurski (2011, 41) argue, marked a new era of accountability. *Focus*, a CCTV television channel supported by Ding Guangen, the CCP's top propaganda official, "routinely shed light on social and political problems," including corruption. These reports occasionally yielded reform. In 2003, coverage of the death of Sun Zhigang, a young migrant worker, led to the end of the detention and repatriation system. According to Repnikova (2017b, 84), investigative journalists are "permitted to investigate social justice issues within bounds set by the state."[62] These bounds are often strict. Repnikova (2017b, 84) quotes one investigative journalist:

---

[61] Satisficing occurs when respondents are overcome with the cognitive difficulty of counting items in a list experiment, and simply report a numerical value they think is reasonable. To check for satisficing, we follow Kramon and Weghorst (2012). We asked respondents three non-sensitive questions directly (whether respondents enjoy hiking, whether they enjoy travel, and whether they prefer urban life to rural life), and later asked respondents about these in a list experiment. When these responses are inconsistent, we define the respondent as a satisficer. Kramon and Weghorst (2012) found a satisficing rate of roughly 40 percent in Kenya. Ours is 52 percent.

[62] Hassid (2008); Tong (2011); Zhu (2014); Hassid (2016).

The most challenging part of my work is that I am often forced to give up on a story I would spend a long time working on because of an abrupt directive from the Central Propaganda Department. ...Half of the stories I investigate don't make it into print.

The commercial press is routinely sanctioned for offenses. Following coverage of Sun Zhigang's death in police custody in 2003, several editors were detained indefinitely or given decades-long prison sentences.[63] As a result of their occasional criticisms, China's commercial media appears to enjoy some credibility among readers.[64] They are, Brady (2008, 75) writes, "the newspapers people actually like to read."[65] Her account of the *Focus* investigative television show recalls our definition of honest propaganda: "The program has just the right sort of amount of critical material to provide a little cognitive dissonance aimed at strengthening support for the status quo."[66]

There is substantial evidence, however, that China's commercial newspapers and investigative television programs are also driven by politics rather than a changed economic or informational environment. Brady (2008, 110) argues that investigative journalism was primarily a tactic for political elites to wage power struggles, and it has been "severely restricted" to "low level officials and solvable problems."[67] Stockmann's (2013) interpretation of the CCP's local newspapers goes further. The Beijing government, she argues, permits local journalists to report wrongdoing by local officials in an attempt to gauge public opinion and monitor local governments.[68] Like us, Stockmann (2013) distinguishes commercial local newspapers from the CCP's "official" newspapers, chief among them the *People's Daily*.

Commercial Newspapers vs. the People's Daily The CCP's commercial newspapers emerged after 1978, rely on advertising revenue to survive, and are overseen by local governments. The *People's Daily*, by contrast,

---

[63] Brady (2008, 110).

[64] Steinhardt (2016); Repnikova (2017a, 2018, 2019); Hassid (2011); Polumbaum and Lei (2008); Zhao (2008); Repnikova and Fang (2019). For a somewhat different view related to Xi Jinping's increasing control of the media, see Tong (2019) and Wang and Sparks (2019).

[65] Shambaugh (2007); Brady (2012b).

[66] Brady (2008, 82).

[67] Relatedly, Shih (2008) finds that local officials use local newspapers to signal loyalty to senior officials.

[68] Lorentzen (2014); Edney (2014).

is subsidized by Beijing and supervised by the CCP Propaganda Department.[69] If the CCP's commercial newspapers have moderated in response to social and economic changes, we should find substantial differences between their content and the *People's Daily* flagship. We should also find that the CCP's commercial newspapers are more persuasive than intimidating.

To probe these alternative hypotheses, we collected the most historically expansive set of commercial newspapers that we could identify. Our corpus included *Caijing* (2015–2019), *Beijing News* (2012–2019), *Economic Observer* (2003–2019), and *Yangtse Evening Post* (2012–2019). These are among China's most widely read commercial newspapers, although their reach is far less than that of the *People's Daily*. Our survey evidence indicates that 20 percent of Chinese citizens read *Caijing*, 16 percent read the *Beijing News*, 12 percent read the *Economic Observer*, and 17 percent read local newspapers like the *Yangtse Evening Post*; 51 percent report reading the *People's Daily*. These are also regarded as among China's most liberal newspapers.[70] In total, our corpus included 433,570 articles from commercial newspapers, published on 2,709 days.

Figure 4.9 visualizes the history of China's commercialized newspapers compared to the *People's Daily*. In the top left panel, for each month along the *x*-axis, the *y*-axis records the mean value of *Positive Coverage Standardized: Executive*$_{ijt}$. In the top-right panel, the *y*-axis records the mean value of *References: Executive*$_{ijt}$. For clarity, we overlay a lowess smoother for each propaganda newspaper. This yields two insights. First, the valence of pro-regime coverage was nearly identical in commercial newspapers and the *People's Daily* between 2012 and 2019. Several of China's hardest hitting outlets – famous for their investigative reporting and whose editors were repeatedly sacked by the CCP – covered the regime as positively as the *People's Daily*. The major difference is the amount of regime coverage. By 2017, on average, the *People's Daily* referenced Xi Jinping and the CCP six times as often as commercial newspapers outlets per day.[71] The *People's Daily* covers the regime much more often than the commercial press, but the valence of coverage is now essentially identical.

---

[69] Piotroski, Wong, and Zhang (2017, 174–175).

[70] Other prominent liberal outlets do not maintain online archives, including *Southern Weekend*, read by 13 percent of our survey respondents.

[71] Gang (2014a) found that the *People's Daily* referenced Xi Jinping more often than other leaders save Mao Zedong and Hua Guofeng. In terms of reference counts,

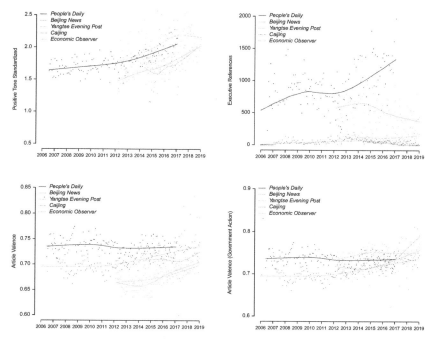

Figure 4.9 Official vs. commercial coverage in China

The bottom panels display trends in article valence. In the bottom-left panel, for each month along the *x*-axis, the *y*-axis records the mean value of *Article Valence$_{ijt}$* across all articles in a given propaganda newspaper. In the bottom-right panel, the *y*-axis records the mean value of *Article Valence: Regime$_{ijt}$*. We again overlay a lowess smoother for each propaganda newspaper. The aggregate valence of commercial newspapers is indeed lower than the *People's Daily*, which is perhaps why scholars regard these outlets as more credible. This difference, however, has diminished over time, and is now relatively small. Again, there is virtually no difference in *Article Valence: Regime$_{ijt}$* across commercial newspapers and the *People's Daily*.

The similarity of regime coverage across commercial newspapers and the CCP flagship should be unsurprising, both in light of our theory

---

Jaros and Pan (2017) suggest that provincial newspapers sit between official media and commercialized media. Between 2010 and 2014, Xi was mentioned with increasing frequency in provincial media.

and how the CCP's commercial newspapers source their regime content. During politically sensitive moments, the CCP requires propaganda newspapers – commercial and flagship – to publish content produced by Beijing's Propaganda Department.[72] Regime coverage is coordinated. Despite relying on advertising revenues, the CCP's commercial newspapers have grown more effusive over time, like the *People's Daily*. In their pro-regime content, they are virtually indistinguishable.

Another Survey List Experiment We conclude with a second survey experiment: to confirm that pro-regime content in the CCP's commercial newspapers has the same effect on consumers as pro-regime content in the *People's Daily*. If the CCP's commercial newspapers have a reputation for credibility, as some scholars suggest, then perhaps their pro-regime content – although virtually identical to the *People's Daily*'s – is persuasive. To test this, we exploit the fact that the treatment article from Section 4.5.1 appeared in many propaganda outlets: the Xinhua news agency; the CCTV evening news program *Xinwen Lianbo*; and provincial newspapers like *Heilongjiang Daily*, *Sichuan Daily*, and *Yunnan Daily*. It was also republished in major commercial outlets like *Beijing News* and *Yangtse Evening Post*, as well as metropolitan papers in Shanxi, Inner Mongolia, Xinjiang, Hangzhou, Zhejiang, Sichuan, and Jiangxi. For this survey experiment, respondents in the treatment group read the same article text but with a large *Beijing News* masthead and byline. The control group was the same as above.[73]

The results appear in Figure 4.10. For each statement along the *x*-axis, the *y*-axis measures the estimated share of respondents in the treatment and control groups who agree, as well as the estimated difference between those two groups. The results are identical to those in Figure 4.8. Pro-regime content in the *Beijing News* has the same effect as in the *People's Daily*: It makes citizens less likely to protest because they fear the consequences of dissent. In the Online Appendix, we reproduce Figure 4.10 with satisficers omitted and ceiling and floor effects corrected for. The results are unchanged, although these statistical corrections increase the precision of the estimates. As for the *People's Daily*, this increased precision suggests that treated respondents are less likely to support Xi Jinping, less likely to believe the government works for the

---

[72] Roberts (2018).
[73] To be clear, our total respondent pool was split equally across these three survey wings.

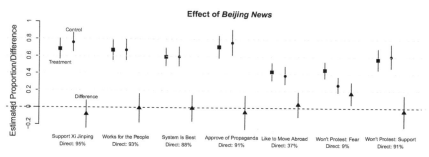

Figure 4.10 Effect of CCP commercial propaganda, list experiments

people, and less likely to think China's system of government is best. Of those who prefer not to protest, treated respondents are more likely to cite fear and less likely to cite CCP support.

4.6 CONCLUSION

Pro-regime propaganda exhibits dramatic variation across autocracies. This variation is driven by politics. Where autocrats confront no meaningful electoral constraints, pro-regime propaganda signals to citizens the consequences of dissent. Propaganda apparatuses describe the regime in terms everyone knows are absurd. These propaganda apparatuses, we show, are roughly four times more pro-regime than Fox News is pro-Republican. Where autocrats confront meaningful electoral constrains, pro-regime propaganda is strikingly neutral: roughly as pro-regime as Fox News is pro-Republican. It is biased, but not so egregiously that it loses its capacity to persuade.[74] These results are consistent across estimation strategies.

The case studies in Sections 4.4 and 4.5 are theoretically and historically important. The Third Wave of Democracy imposed relatively binding electoral constraints on Africa's autocrats. In Gabon, Omar Bongo responded as our theory predicts: by moderating pro-regime propaganda. This suggests that the cross-country evidence in Sections 4.2 and 4.3 is not driven by reverse causality. The year 1989 was pivotal in China as well but for different reasons. Although Chinese citizens also demanded change, the CCP was less exposed to the geopolitical

---

[74] DellaVigna and Kaplan (2007); Martin and Yurukoglu (2017); Ash and Galletta (2019); Bursztyn et al. (2020); Jamieson and Albarracin (2020); Simonov et al. (2020).

shift that rocked Eastern Europe and sub-Saharan Africa. The Tiananmen Square protests ended with a massacre on June 4, 1989, which killed some 2,000 citizens. As we show in Chapters 7 and 9, the CCP propaganda apparatus responded by threatening citizens with violence and, more recently, by reminding the urban elite of ongoing repression against ethnic Uyghurs in Xinjiang. Pro-regime propaganda in the CCP's flagship newspaper reflects prevailing political conditions, not long-term socio-economic change. These political conditions also shape coverage in the CCP's commercial newspapers, which, contrary to conventional wisdom, cover the regime as effusively as its flagship propaganda outlets. In the *People's Daily* and commercial newspapers, the CCP's pro-regime propaganda makes citizens less likely to protest due to fear. If anything, it makes the CCP less popular, not more.

Propaganda is more than pro-regime content. It is also the stories citizens are told: what is emphasized, what is omitted, and how details are spun. These narratives constitute the first draft of a country's history, written, in a sense, by its victor. These narratives are the focus of Chapters 5 and 6.

5

Narrating the Domestic

5.1 SOCRATES, PROPAGANDA NARRATIVES, AND A THEORY OF RHETORIC

The study of propaganda is as old as the Western intellectual tradition. In Plato's *Gorgias*, Socrates defines rhetoric as "the unreal image (counterfeit presentment) of a branch in Politics." Asked by Polus whether "it is a fine thing or a foul one," Socrates responds: "A foul one, for all bad things I call foul."[1] For Socrates, rhetoric is the tool through which individuals come to hold beliefs that are nonrational and contrary to their interests. Rhetoric is a form of propaganda.

The diversity of rhetorical devices at a propagandist's disposal compelled Socrates to view a theory of rhetoric as impossible.[2] Stanley (2015, 4) describes Socrates's thinking this way:

There are no general principles that one can convey to others which predict what one should do to successfully sway others nonrationally. . . . The manipulation of others depends upon particular facts about societies that are not part of a science of rhetoric.

The breadth of propaganda narratives documented by scholars seems to vindicate Socrates's skepticism. In Russia, Vladimir Putin is clothed in the presidency's "splendor" and promises "immediate, effective" action.[3] In Egypt, after the military deposed Mohamed Morsi, it claimed the mantle of the Arab Spring by emphasizing the "inseparability of the army and people throughout Egyptian history."[4] In Zimbabwe, after Robert Mugabe's ill-fated military campaign in the Democratic Republic of the Congo in 1998, the propaganda apparatus recalled his

[1] Plato (1864, 28).
[2] Plato (1864, 27).
[3] Liñán (2009, 147).
[4] van de Bildt (2015).

contributions to the liberation struggle and depicted independent news-papers – which reported military casualties and war profiteering by politicians – as instruments of Western governments. The Zimbabwe Broadcasting Corporation cut foreign programming to cover Mugabe's agrarian reforms.[5]

The Chinese government's propaganda narratives are well documented due largely to Anne-Marie Brady's pathbreaking work.[6] Since the 1989 Tiananmen massacre, the CCP has avoided bad news around politically sensitives dates, omitted problems that are not easily solved,[7] and celebrated economic performance. One leaked propaganda manual describes sports coverage as vital for "mass political thought work, particularly towards youth."[8] The propaganda apparatus tells ethnic minorities that "we are all part of the same family" and casts the military as a humanitarian organization, responding to floods and planting trees.[9] The goal, Brady (2002, 568) writes, is to create "popular acceptance of the inevitability of ... CCP rule."[10]

As we showed in Chapter 3, just five coverage topics constitute 80 percent of all propaganda: the economy and public goods, electoral politics, sports, international news, and foreign policy. This chapter focuses on the first three, all domestic; Chapter 6 focuses on the latter two, both international. In this chapter, we show that the political calculations that drive pro-regime propaganda also drive domestic propaganda narratives. In the absence of electoral constraints, propaganda apparatuses craft domestic narratives that are marked by absurdity. By narrating contemporary events with language everyone knows is false, the regime signals its power: It has no need to persuade citizens of regime merits. Where electoral constraints are binding, propaganda apparatuses employ honest propaganda. They concede damaging facts to persuade citizens of useful fictions.

---

[5] Bratton, Chikwana, and Sithole (2005, 81).

[6] Brady (2002, 2006, 2008, 2012*b,a*, 2015); Brady and Wang (2009); Brady and He (2012).

[7] Such as the income gap, the political influence of the wealthy, high-level corruption, financial instability, or blacklisted political activists.

[8] Chen Junhong (1999, 128).

[9] Brady (2012*a*).

[10] Wartime propaganda is also well documented. For more on Soviet propaganda during World War II, see Carmack (2014) and Hopf (2002). For more on British propaganda during World War II, see Siebert, Peterson, and Schramm (1955). For more on ISIS propaganda, see Cragin and Daly (2009); Dalton and Asal (2011); Halverson, Goodall Jr., and Corman (2011); Fox (2012); Mahood and Rane (2016); and Musial (2017).

How these principles are applied varies by topic. In the absence of electoral constraints, propaganda apparatuses trumpet the regime's economic achievements, great contributions to national athletics, and democratic credentials, all while omitting the actual stuff of democracy: electoral campaigns and the political opposition. They cover a general, unnamed "opposition" rather than the legitimate opposition, which would contradict absurd claims of universal support and help citizens coordinate around protest leaders. We observe none of these tactics where autocrats confront relatively binding electoral constraints. Neither do their propaganda apparatuses denigrate the opposition, since doing so would undermine credibility. Electorally constrained autocrats acknowledge policy failures: fuel crises, vaccine shortages, and persistently high infant mortality rates. These policy failures are routinely highlighted by the political opposition, which propaganda apparatuses cover as well. Sports coverage is subject to the same principles of honest propaganda. When the regime's investments in national athletics fail, those are reported too.

Extracting the narrative subtleties within millions of propaganda articles poses a methodological challenge. Our dataset records a range of information about each article in our propaganda collection: the valence and frequency of references to the regime and opposition, the topics each article covers, and its aggregate valence. This lets us capture the outlines of propaganda narratives. To capture narrative subtleties, we adapted Kessler's (2017; 2018b) measure of semantic distinctiveness. Intuitively, across any two corpora of documents, words common to both and uncommon to both are generally uninformative. The former consists of building blocks of speech; the latter consists of peculiarities. However, words common in one corpus but uncommon in another convey something meaningful about each. This lets propaganda convey its subtleties. This also lets us avoid simply looking for confirmatory evidence of narratives we postulate in advance.

This chapter proceeds as follows. Section 5.2 extends our theory from Chapter 2 to develop and test predictions about propaganda narratives for economic and public goods coverage. Section 5.3 illuminates these cross-country results by studying two potentially devastating economic crises: a fuel shortage in Congo and the 2008 financial crisis, which shook the Chinese economy. Section 5.4 turns to coverage of democracy, electoral politics, and the opposition. Again, it extends our theory and tests its predictions in a cross-country setting. Section 5.5 explores these propaganda narratives in two countries with a common language but different electoral constraints: Russia and Uzbekistan. Section 5.6 turns to propaganda narratives about sports, which Section 5.7 explores in two of Africa's anglophone autocracies: Uganda, where President Yoweri Museveni's *New Vision* newspaper was long overseen by a British citizen, and The Gambia, where Yahya Jammeh ruled until January 2017 as among Africa's most brutal dictators.

5.2 ECONOMIC PERFORMANCE AND PUBLIC GOODS: THEORY AND CROSS-COUNTRY EVIDENCE

5.2.1 *Theory*

In the absence of electoral constraints, propaganda apparatuses can make a range of absurd claims about economic performance and public goods provision. They can ignore economic crises. They can cover a global economic crisis but deny its effects on domestic welfare. They can make absurd claims about citizens' living standards. As we observed in Chapter 2, for instance, Yahya Jammeh's propaganda apparatus in The Gambia routinely told citizens that they lived in the Silicon Valley of Africa, despite a poverty rate approaching 40 percent. Jammeh's propaganda apparatus made equally absurd claims about public goods provision: "Since President Jammeh gave Gambian women free maternal health services, our maternal health sector has gradually been growing from strength to strength."[11] In reality, the World Health Organization judged The Gambia – with 3,120 and 5,490 neonatal and perinatal deaths per 100,000 live births, respectively – "very unlikely [to] attain the Millennium Development Goal target of below 262 deaths per 100,000 live births."[12] These claims generate common knowledge among citizens in the same way as absurdly positive pro-regime propaganda.

Where autocrats confront electoral constraints, propaganda apparatuses must build credibility by acknowledging economic crises and their occasionally devastating effects on citizens. Although doing so is costly, it provides opportunities beyond the credibility it fosters. First, by acknowledging economic crises and their devastating welfare effects, propaganda apparatuses can signal to citizens the regime's empathy. Second, acknowledging economic crises gives propaganda apparatuses an opportunity to spin them: to fashion a narrative that is useful to the

---

[11] "Forward with Health," *Daily Observer*, February 11, 2015.
[12] WHO (2018).

regime. The propaganda apparatus can highlight the regime's efforts to ameliorate the crisis, direct blame for the crisis on events outside the regime's control, and discuss the regime's successful efforts in other sectors. In Tunisia, Zine El Abidine Ben Ali's propaganda apparatus did both just before he became the Arab Spring's first casualty, as we show in Chapter 7.

Our theory contextualizes recent scholarship on the tactics of propaganda. Rozenas and Stukal (2018) show that Russian state television routinely reports bad economic news but attributes it to foreigners or global shocks. This bad economic news, Rosenfeld, Tertychnaya, and Watanabe (2018) show, is routinely covered with anodyne statistics, a stark contrast to the human interest angles that characterize its positive economic coverage, which are linked to government policy. These are forms of honest propaganda. Vladimir Putin's propaganda apparatus concedes bad news to build credibility and spins it to persuade citizens of useful fictions: that regime engagement has yielded policy successes or that exogenous forces have contributed to policy failures.

Hypothesis 5.1: *As electoral constraints grow more binding, the valence of economic and public goods coverage will decline, since propaganda apparatuses are forced to cover bad news and policy failures.*

5.2.2 Data and Estimation Strategy

To test Hypothesis 5.1, we measured the valence of economic coverage by drawing on our second measure of pro-regime propaganda, *Article Valence: Regime$_{ijt}$*. For each article about economics or public goods, we calculated its aggregate valence by measuring the total number of positive less negative words, standardized by the total number of dictionary hits. Again, this standardization accommodates the possibility that language dictionaries may vary in quality:

$$\text{Article Valence: Economy}_{ijt} = \frac{\text{Positive Words}_{ijt} - \text{Negative Words}_{ijt}}{\text{Positive Words}_{ijt} + \text{Negative Words}_{ijt}}$$

(5.1)

We computed two variants of *Article Valence: Economy$_{ijt}$*: one for articles that reference the executive and another for articles that do not. This let us measure whether economic coverage that implicates the autocrat is systematically more positive than economic coverage that does not. To measure the frequency of economic coverage, we create the variable

Table 5.1 *Representative words from the Harvard General Inquirer's "failure" dictionary*

abandon	incompet
bankrupt	laps
disappoint	lose
err	mishandl
fail	misunderstand
flaw	neglect
helpless	resign
imperfect	weaken

Economy$_{ijt}$, which assumes value 1 if article i is about the economy and 0 otherwise.

Our theory makes a specific prediction about the nature of economic coverage as electoral constraints grow more binding: Its valence should decline because the propaganda apparatus is forced to concede bad news and policy failures. To capture this nuance, we exploited the fact that the Harvard General Inquirer (2015) includes more fine-grained linguistic dictionaries, as we discussed in Chapter 3. Here, its "failure" dictionary is especially relevant. Table 5.1 features a representative sample of words that appear in it. We measured the extent to which country j's executive is associated with failure by first restricting attention to country j's economic coverage. Then, for each reference to country j's executive in article i, we extracted the ten words on either side and counted the number of these words that also appear in the "failure" dictionary. We standardized this count by the total number of executive references in article i. This yielded a per reference measure of whether the executive is associated with failure, which is analogous to *Positive Coverage Standardized: Executive*$_{ijt}$.

We employed the same estimation strategy as in Chapter 4. We estimated two models for each outcome of interest: one at the country-year level and another at the article level. For country-year models, since our measures of electoral constraints are observed annually, we computed country-year means for outcome variables, which were measured at the article or day level. The model is

$$Y_{js} = \alpha + \beta X_{js} + \phi W_{js} + \gamma_j + \epsilon \tag{5.2}$$

where j indexes country, s indexes year, X_{js} measures electoral constraints, and the vector W_{js} gives our standard set of control variables. The country-fixed effects, γ_j, accommodate systematic differences across languages and other unobserved characteristics by country. Since these outcomes are continuous, we employed OLS with robust standard errors clustered by country. For article-level models, we employed mixed-effects models to accommodate the fact that our outcome variables were measured at the article level, but our explanatory variables were measured annually. The model is

$$Y_{ijt} = \alpha + \beta X_{is} + \kappa Z_{it} + \phi W_{is} + \gamma_k + \gamma_j + \epsilon \qquad (5.3)$$

where the vectors Z_{it} and W_{is}, respectively, give day- and year-level controls; γ_k gives language-fixed effects; and γ_j gives country-random effects.

5.2.3 Results

The results for economic coverage appear in Table 5.2. From Models 1 and 2, the rate of economic coverage is somewhat higher in autocracies than democracies; this is consistent with the descriptive statistics in Chapter 3. From Models 3 and 4, where electoral constraints are weak, this coverage is far more likely to feature the autocrat and ruling party. Each five-point increase in the Polity score is associated with a reduction in the probability that economic coverage references the executive of between 9 percent and 13 percent. Propaganda apparatuses in the most repressive dictatorships are thus between 30 percent and 40 percent more likely to reference the executive in economic coverage than propaganda apparatuses in the most constrained autocracies.

From Models 5 and 6, this coverage is much more effusive. Each five-point increase in the Polity score is associated with a decrease in *Article Valence: Economy*$_{js}$ of nearly 0.7 unit of our Fox News index. This suggests that propaganda apparatuses in the most repressive dictatorships cover economics roughly two Fox News units more effusively than propaganda apparatuses where the Polity score hovers around 4 or 5. From Models 7 and 8, this effect remains consistent even when coverage does not directly reference the regime. The coefficients are very similar across estimation strategies. From Model 10, where electoral constraints are binding, propaganda apparatuses are substantially more likely to associate the regime with failure.

How meaningful is a marginal effect of two Fox News units? To illustrate this, we compare Senegal's *Le Soleil* and The Gambia's *Daily Observer*. *Le Soleil* is widely regarded as a legitimate newspaper. Its editorial line is mildly pro-government, but it is occasionally critical, as

Table 5.2 *The politics of economic propaganda narratives*

					Dependent variable:					
	Rate		Executive references		Article valence				Fail	
					Executive		Non-executive			
Outcome variable	Country-year OLS	Article Mixed	Country-year OLS	Article Mixed	Country-year OLS	Article Mixed	Country-year OLS	Article Mixed	Country-year OLS	Article Mixed
Unit of analysis Estimator	(1)	(2)	(3)	(4)	(5)	(6)	(7)	(8)	(9)	(10)
Polity	-0.004	-0.012***	-0.018***	-0.026***	-0.014***	-0.014***	-0.008**	-0.010***	-0.0001	0.002***
	(0.005)	(0.001)	(0.007)	(0.001)	(0.005)	(0.001)	(0.003)	(0.001)	(0.003)	(0.001)
Trade	0.002**	0.001***	-0.0003	-0.001***	-0.001**	0.001***	-0.001*	-0.001***	-0.0003	-0.0001
	(0.001)	(0.00004)	(0.001)	(0.0001)	(0.001)	(0.0001)	(0.001)	(0.00004)	(0.0004)	(0.0001)
Log GDP per capita	-0.001	-0.124***	0.024	0.092***	-0.089	0.090***	-0.088*	-0.028***	0.025	-0.003
	(0.054)	(0.006)	(0.078)	(0.007)	(0.065)	(0.009)	(0.040)	(0.005)	(0.045)	(0.004)
Natural resources	-0.001	-0.0001	-0.001	0.005***	-0.003**	-0.004***	0.001	0.002***	0.001	0.001***
	(0.002)	(0.0001)	(0.002)	(0.0002)	(0.001)	(0.0002)	(0.001)	(0.0002)	(0.001)	(0.0002)
Civil war	-0.039	0.031***	-0.036	-0.021***	0.013	0.031***	-0.029	0.008*	-0.030	0.001
	(0.030)	(0.004)	(0.040)	(0.006)	(0.027)	(0.008)	(0.022)	(0.005)	(0.019)	(0.007)
Internet penetration	0.00004*	0.00004***	-0.00001	-0.00003***	-0.00001	0.00001*	-0.00001	-0.00000***	-0.00001	-0.00000
	(0.00002)	(0.00000)	(0.00003)	(0.00000)	(0.00002)	(0.00000)	(0.00002)	(0.00000)	(0.00001)	(0.00000)
Election	-0.011		-0.044**		0.010		0.0004		-0.003	
	(0.012)		(0.021)		(0.018)		(0.011)		(0.012)	
Election season		-0.023***		0.053***		0.010***		0.004*		0.006**
		(0.002)		(0.003)		(0.003)		(0.002)		(0.003)
Constant	0.305	1.242***	0.615	-0.772***	0.959	-0.608***	0.988**	0.518***	-0.128	0.046
	(0.551)	(0.079)	(0.793)	(0.113)	(0.640)	(0.111)	(0.407)	(0.062)	(0.447)	(0.039)
Country effects	Fixed	Random	Fixed	Random	Fixed	Random	Fixed	Random	Fixed	Random
Language-fixed effects		✓		✓		✓		✓		✓
Observations	192	2,442,480	189	804,687	187	146,730	187	657,245	187	146,737
R^2	0.878		0.761		0.925		0.937		0.501	

Note: *p < 0.1; **p < 0.05; ***p < 0.01

when former president Abdoulaye Wade sought a third presidential term in 2012.[13] The mean valence of *Le Soleil*'s economic coverage is 0.32. The following article appeared in the *Daily Observer* in January 2012, and registers a valence of 0.56. The difference between them, 0.24, is roughly equal to two Fox News units:

Today by the grace of the Almighty Allah we will achieve the dreams of not only turning The Gambia into a Silicon Valley of Africa but an economic superpower in the world. I hereby give notice to countries that have triumphed in terms of socio-economic development such as Dubai and the United Arab Emirates, that in five years, no one will talk about them but The Gambia in terms of advancement. They have the tallest buildings in the world, but what we will have will be the highest standard of living, and the highest life expectancy in the world. In the next five years, we want to turn The Gambia into the most literate country in Africa and in the same period all Gambian children will go to school free of charge. Tomorrow's inauguration will therefore herald an era filled with great optimism and hope in the march towards greater development and advancement.[14]

In 2011, The Gambia's GDP per capita was $518, 40 percent of citizens lived in poverty, and life expectancy was just 58 years. President Yahya Jammeh allocated 2 percent of The Gambia's annual GDP to public health and 4 percent to education. Meanwhile, in twenty-two years atop The Gambia, Jammeh managed to steal $1 billion from the treasury, or nearly 6 percent of its total GDP.[15] The marginal effects of roughly two Fox News units are very substantial.

5.3 ECONOMIC CRISES IN CONGO AND CHINA

To probe narrative subtleties, we return to Congo and China, which experienced two of the most profound economic crises in our sample: a devastating fuel shortage in Congo and the 2008 global financial crisis, which, despite the Chinese government's ultimately successful policy response, initially posed a grave threat to the CCP. Their propaganda responses were dramatically different, as our theory predicts. Although Denis Sassou Nguesso's propaganda discussed the fuel shortage at length, CCP propaganda actually covered the Chinese economy more positively during the crisis.

---

[13] For more on Abdoulaye Wade's bid for a third presidential term in 2012 and the widespread opposition to it, see Jahateh (2012).

[14] Hatab Fadera, "Presidential Inauguration Is Tomorrow," *Daily Observer*, January 18, 2012.

[15] Sharife and Anderson (2019).

5.3.1 Congo: "Customers line up early in the morning"

Congo is among Africa's leading oil producers, but in 2017, citizens confronted a fuel shortage. CORAF, the state-owned oil refinery, can satisfy just 40 percent of domestic energy needs; the rest must be imported. The state-owned oil company, *Societe Nationale des Petroles du Congo* (SNPC), enjoys a monopoly on fuel imports and is controlled by Sassou Nguesso's son, Denis Christel. By early 2017, the SNPC was bankrupt, in default to a handful of oil traders, including Glencore and Trafigura.[16] As a result, the SNPC was unable to purchase fuel for import on the international market, and so Congolese citizens were unable to purchase fuel in Brazzaville and Pointe-Noire. Sassou Nguesso's monopoly on fuel imports – and hence the political origins of the fuel shortage – was not common knowledge among citizens.[17] Sassou Nguesso's propaganda apparatus had to cover the fuel shortage, explain its origins, and persuade citizens of Sassou Nguesso's efforts to resolve it. It had to employ honest propaganda: appear credible and spend its credibility on persuading citizens of useful fictions.

Vox Congo, an online counterpart to *Les Dépêches de Brazzaville*, first covered the fuel shortage on February 20, 2017, when it reported on price gouging in Brazzaville.[18] The article was frank about lines outside gas stations – "customers line up early in the morning" – but careful to distance the government.[19] Its next article was on April 3, 2017, when it announced that CORAF would cease production between April 1 and April 30. In one respect, it was candid. *Vox Congo* conceded the production stoppage would exacerbate the fuel shortage. In another respect, the article served the government's interests by reassuring readers that the production stoppage "is indeed normal."[20] The article also offered a plausible explanation for the shortage itself. Since the rail line between Pointe-Noire and Brazzaville was blocked, suppliers were unable to serve

---

[16] Interview with an anonymous high-level official in a multi-national oil company.

[17] Interview with anonymous opposition leader.

[18] *Vox Congo* was launched in late 2016 by Sassou Nguesso's son, Denis Christel, as a mouthpiece for his likely 2021 presidential campaign. We used *Vox Congo* rather than *Les Dépêches de Brazzaville* because the latter's PDF archiving prevented us from running a topic model that identified articles about the economy.

[19] "The Market for Gas in Brazzaville, a Veritable Yoyo," *Vox Congo*, February 20, 2017.

[20] "CORAF Stops Production for the Entire Month of April," *Vox Congo*, April 3, 2017.

the Brazzaville market. The rail line was indeed blocked, but, in reality, the blockage was unrelated to the shortage.

Vox Congo covered the shortage again on April 7, and it accused speculators of harming citizens: "At a time when the country is experiencing an arduous economic crisis, gas station owners appear to wish that the shortages would intensify, so that they can continue to earn substantial profits."[21] To underscore the logistical – rather than political – causes of the shortage, *Vox Congo* repeated its April 3 claim: "With fuel needs estimated around 1.2 million tons per year, the Congolese have only, thanks to CORAF, less than 800,000 tons. This represents just 45% of demand."

Vox Congo first implicated Sassou Nguesso in the fuel crisis on April 24, 2017, in an interview with Total Congo CEO Pierre Jessua. Jessua corroborated the government's explanation: "There are difficulties in the distribution of fuel, due to the difficulties of transport between Pointe-Noire, site of the refinery, and Brazzaville."[22] The article was headlined: "Total Invites Congo to Adapt to the Oil Crisis." In turn, this provided a foundation for how the propaganda apparatus conveyed Sassou Nguesso's policy response three days later: "A Pipeline to Resolve Fuel Shortages." The narrative was clear. Taking cues from international experts, the government would "adapt" to the "global" oil crisis by building a pipeline between Pointe-Noire and the rest of the country. "The pipeline will be of great interest to sub-regional partners. The Democratic Republic of Congo, Cameroon, Chad, and the Central African Republic will be major clients. Several partners have already expressed interest in the realization of the pipeline."[23] This article was the only to reference the government at length.

Vox Congo published 320 economic articles in the seven months before the crisis and 125 in the six months during the crisis. Figure 5.1 presents two word clouds that illustrate how economic coverage changed. To create it, we treated *Vox Congo*'s pre-crisis economic coverage as one corpora and its economic coverage during the crisis, defined as February through July 2017, as the other. We then computed our measure of semantic distinctiveness. Before the fuel crisis *Vox Congo*'s

---

[21] "The Repeated Shortage of Fuel Elicits Frustration of Motorists," *Vox Congo*, April 7, 2017.

[22] "Total Invites Congo to Adapt to the Oil Crisis," *Vox Congo*, April 24, 2017.

[23] "A Pipeline Between Pointe-Noire and Ouesso to Curb Fuel Shortages," *Vox Congo*, April 27, 2017.

Congo: Pre–Crisis Economic Coverage   Congo: Post–Crisis Distinctive Economic Coverage

Figure 5.1 Semantic distinctiveness in Congo's economic propaganda pre- and post-fuel crisis

economic coverage focused on standard topics: development projects, the government's efforts to finance them, vocational training programs, and new factory openings. During the crisis, coverage shifted: butane, fuel, oil, and even shortage appear prominently. It paired these concessions, however, with coverage of other public goods: water, schools, students, teachers, hospitals, and vaccines.

Our data let us measure how coverage of the fuel crisis impacted the aggregate valence of economic coverage. This is important: If coverage valence turned negative, then coverage of bad economic news may indeed be driving the results in Section 5.2. We estimated models of the form

$$Y_{it} = \alpha + \beta \left(\text{Crisis}_{it} \right) + \epsilon \tag{5.4}$$

where i indexes article, t indexes day, and Crisis_{it} assumes value 1 if day t occurred between February 1, 2017, and August 1, 2017, and value 0 if day t occurred between July 1, 2015, and February 1, 2017. The results appear in Table 5.3, and are again consistent with our theory. Before the crisis, *Vox Congo* referenced "shortage" in 0.6 percent of articles; during the crisis, 5.7 percent. Before the crisis, it referenced "gas" in 4.3 percent of articles; during the crisis, 21.0 percent. Before the crisis, it referenced "fuel" in 2.6 percent of articles; during the crisis, 7.6 percent. Reflecting this, the valence of economic coverage declined dramatically during the fuel crisis: from a daily average valence of 0.35 to 0.28, or nearly a single Fox News unit. Sassou Nguesso's propaganda apparatus made little effort to distance him from the crisis.

Table 5.3 *How Congolese propaganda changed during the fuel crisis*

	Dependent variable:				
	"Shortage" (1)	"Gas" (2)	"Fuel" (3)	"Business" (4)	"Development" (5)
Crisis	0.051***	0.167**	0.050	−0.115*	−0.120
	(0.018)	(0.084)	(0.049)	(0.061)	(0.086)
Constant	0.006	0.043	0.026	0.310***	0.658***
	(0.010)	(0.045)	(0.026)	(0.032)	(0.046)
Observations	917	917	917	917	917
R^2	0.009	0.004	0.001	0.004	0.002

	Dependent variable:				
	Economy (1)	Government action (2)	Executive references (3)	Positive coverage standardized (4)	Article valence (5)
Crisis	−0.019	−0.013	−0.099	0.283	−0.077***
	(0.037)	(0.044)	(0.147)	(0.346)	(0.021)
Constant	0.504***	0.773***	0.339***	0.440**	0.359***
	(0.020)	(0.023)	(0.077)	(0.202)	(0.011)
Observations	913	455	455	70	455
R^2	0.0003	0.0002	0.001	0.010	0.029

Note: $^*p < 0.1$; $^{**}p < 0.05$; $^{***}p < 0.01$

5.3.2 *China: "We are actively responding with solid work, ensuring growth and ensuring the stability of the central government"*

The CCP's propaganda response to the global financial crisis (GFC) was profoundly different. Since 1978, China's annual GDP growth has hovered around 10 percent. The GFC threatened this. Although China's banks were not exposed to mortgage-backed securities, its manufacturing sector was exposed to declines in Western demand and investment. During the first quarter of 2009, GDP growth fell to 6.1 percent, the lowest since the government began releasing quarterly statistics in 1992. Wallace (2014, 164–165) put it this way: "While China's subsequent economic recovery may give the impression that it sailed smoothly through the crisis, ... in November 2008 ... Chinese official economic data resembled nothing so much as an economy falling off a cliff." In the last quarter of 2008 and the first quarter of 2009, Chinese exports fell 40 percent. Globally, 40 percent of people who lost their jobs due to the crisis were Chinese. In September and October 2008, 117 factory bosses fled the city of Dongguan, Guangdong, abandoning 20,000 workers owed back pay. In the fourth quarter of 2008, in Guangdong alone 50,000 factories closed.[24] Some 20 million migrant workers lost their jobs.

The CCP, Wu (2010, 30) writes, "lived through 2009 in a panic of worrying about the next explosion of social instability." CCP leaders did not believe China could simply "decouple" from the United States by increasing intra-Asian trade and therefore "recognized that the country's high dependence on exports meant that it was acutely vulnerable to a global economic recession."[25] Said Yu Yongding, director-general of the Institute of World Economics and Politics at the Chinese Academy of Social Sciences: "The global economic crisis exposed the vulnerability of China's growth pattern."[26] Characterizing CCP leaders as "shocked," Naughton (2009, 8) writes that by the end of 2008 the government expected zero export growth for 2009. Some CCP leaders predicted the wave of migrant layoffs would culminate in a "February crisis" of social instability.[27] In response, the CCP reversed 2008's austerity measures in favor of a Keynesian monetary policy.[28] On November 5, 2008, it unveiled a $586 billion fiscal stimulus package to support strategic industries, create jobs, and hit the 8 percent GDP growth target for 2009. The CCP also ordered state-owned enterprises to buy up housing inventory to stave off panic in the housing market, where many feared a bubble.[29] The CCP combined these economic policies with repression. In early 2009, the government detained several dissidents, forced law firms to hire loyalists that would ensure "total coverage of the legal profession," invested in new crowd control technology, and launched "social discontent training programs" for local leaders.[30]

Despite historically low economic growth in the last quarter of 2008 and the first quarter of 2009, by the second quarter of 2009 it was clear that the economy was stabilizing, with growth back at 11.4 percent.[31]

---

[24] Wallace (2014, 166–168).

[25] Lardy (2012, 6).

[26] Yu (2010, 8).

[27] China News (2008). The CCP even sounded alarm bells that "foreign hostile forces" might organize these workers. This was a particular concern, given a number of sensitive political anniversaries that spring, as well as the publication of the Charter 08 pro-democracy manifesto signed by leading Chinese intellectuals in December.

[28] Naughton (2009, 1).

[29] Deng et al. (2011).

[30] Wu (2010, 32–33).

[31] Naughton (2016).

The CCP portrayed its response to the GFC as a signal of China's global stature, a narrative that Western observers largely accepted. Breslin (2012), for example, writes:

The crisis has shown the robustness of the Chinese economic system and the state's ability to mobilize resources to support national goals, has increased China's relative financial power, and has firmly established China at the center of global politics and as a key actor in any attempts to reform the structure of global governance.

We focus on the period between October 2008 and March 2009, when Chinese economic growth dropped to historic lows and CCP leaders were concerned about recession and widespread social upheaval. Rather than concede the economic contraction, the propaganda apparatus celebrated China's economic performance and the CCP's policy response, as our theory predicts. In December 2008, CCTV economic broadcasts featured a slogan alongside the anchor's head: "Face the challenge with unwavering confidence." Guo Zhenxi, head of the CCTV's economic channel, said this: "The main problem right now is a lack of confidence, so we must forcefully campaign to strengthen confidence."[32] The *Financial Times* noticed the obvious gap between economic reality and CCP propaganda:

With unprecedented frequency, CCTV's news and economic channels have invited economists on air to explain derivatives and foreign exchange reserves in an attempt to ward off potential panic. Faced with reports of a wave of bankruptcies and factory closures in the southern city of Dongguan, the broadcaster argued in one recent feature that the vast majority of companies were alive and well.[33]

Our data confirm this. The *People's Daily* initially ignored the global meltdown. In September 2008, when Lehman Brothers collapsed, just 1 percent of economic coverage referenced the "financial crisis." Coverage increased only in November 2008, after the CCP announced the stimulus. During the worst moments of the crisis, the *People's Daily* actually covered the Chinese economy *more positively*. Figure 5.2 visualizes this. From the left panel, economic coverage in 2007, well before the GFC, focused on standard topics: development, jobs, construction, enterprises, and rural development. From the right panel, during the last quarter of 2008 and the first quarter of 2009, it celebrated an economic "expansion," precisely the opposite of reality. One article from early

[32] Hille (2008).
[33] Hille (2008).

China: Pre–Crisis Economic Coverage

China: Distinctive Crisis Economic Coverage

Figure 5.2 Semantic distinctiveness in Chinese economic propaganda pre- and post-financial crisis

2009, which coincided with China's worst economic performance in 20 years, was entitled "Firm Confidence, Positive Response, Solid Work, and Good Signs for China's Economy":

China's economic activity is positive and strong. A series of macro-control measures to address the GFC have been effective and positive in all parts of the country. We are actively responding with solid work, ensuring growth, ensuring the stability of the people, and ensuring the stability of the central government.[34]

Later, the *People's Daily* claimed this:

Positive changes have taken place in China's economy this year. The warming trend is increasing. This reflects the hard work of all localities and departments to resolutely implement the directives of the Party Central Committee and the State Council. ... A series of policy measures for growth have been put into practice, turning pressure into motivation, turning challenges into opportunities, and actually ensuring growth.[35]

These obviously false pronouncements were routinely accompanied by codewords that the CCP uses to threaten citizens with violence: in particular, "stability" and the "Ministry of Public Security." We discuss these codewords in Chapters 7, 9, and 10. In March 2009, the National People's Congress discussed the GFC, and the *People's Daily*'s coverage concluded with a threat:

[34] Jingan Zhao, Furong Yue, Wangda Lu, Jie Chen, Shaozhong Zheng, Zhaonong Gu, Jiansheng Deng, Geping Pang, and Feng Tian, "Firm Confidence, Positive Response, Solid Work, and Good Signs for China's Economy," *People's Daily*, April 20, 2009.

[35] Shuyi Pi, Huimin Wang, Meng Yu, and Zhehan Qu. "Facing Difficulties and Maintaining Growth in Zhejiang: Overcoming Difficulties and Listening to Yue Songs." *People's Daily*, May 6, 2009.

Table 5.4 *How CCP propaganda changed during the global financial crisis*

	Dependent variable:				
	Positive coverage standardized: executive		Article valence		Economic share
	Aggregate (1)	Economic (2)	Aggregate (3)	Economic (4)	(5)
Crisis	0.132***	0.181***	0.012***	0.007**	0.142***
	(0.041)	(0.049)	(0.003)	(0.004)	(0.006)
Constant	1.652***	1.694***	0.739***	0.755***	0.473***
	(0.024)	(0.031)	(0.002)	(0.002)	(0.004)
Observations	3,743	2,208	25,205	13,799	26,650
R^2	0.003	0.006	0.001	0.0003	0.018

	Dependent variable: Positive coverage standardized				
	Economy (1)	Finance (2)	Financial crisis (3)	Anti-corruption efforts (4)	Serve the people (5)
Crisis	0.142***	0.331***	0.349***	0.390**	0.936**
	(0.035)	(0.091)	(0.010)	(0.162)	(0.369)
Constant	2.967***	1.997***	0.003	2.328***	2.004***
	(0.022)	(0.066)	(0.006)	(0.100)	(0.198)
Observations	7,084	1,203	26,650	282	87
R^2	0.002	0.011	0.043	0.020	0.070

Note: $^*p < 0.1$; $^{**}p < 0.05$; $^{***}p < 0.01$

Maintaining social stability is a difficult task with serious implications for public order during this time of economic challenges. Increasing social stability is even more challenging. President Hu Jintao emphasizes this issue every time he participates in deliberations and discussions.[36]

We estimated a series of regressions to explore how CCP propaganda changed during the GFC. We focused on the *People's Daily* during the last quarter of 2008 and the first quarter of 2009 and compared this to coverage in the year before the crisis struck, spanning the third quarter of 2007 through the third quarter of 2008. The results appear in Table 5.4.

[36] Chengbin Sun and Hongguang Lan. "Work Together to Overcome Difficulties and Promote Development: General Secretary Hu Jintao Discusses the State with NPC Deputies and CPPCC Members." *People's Dailly*, March 13, 2009.

From Models 1 and 2 in the top panel, the *People's Daily* covered Hu Jintao more positively, both in the aggregate and in economic coverage. From Models 3 and 4, the valence of aggregate and economic coverage became more positive as well. From Model 5, economic coverage occupied a larger share of total coverage. From the bottom panel, a series of codewords were covered more positively: "economy," "finance," "financial crisis," "anti-corruption efforts," and "serving the people."[37] This last term, in fact, is profoundly threatening. The *People's Daily* routinely advertised CCP efforts to "serve the people" during the Cultural Revolution, when millions died, and during the Great Leap Forward, when between 15 and 30 million starved to death due to Mao's economic mismanagement.[38]

The CCP responded to the most serious economic crisis since 1978 by celebrating an economic "expansion" and threatening citizens. Profoundly different than Sassou Nguesso's, the CCP's propaganda response illustrates the distinction between propaganda as persuasion and domination.[39] It recalls Jiao Guobiao, the journalism professor turned dissident from Chapter 4: "The Central Propaganda Department has the right to say black is white and white is black."[40]

5.4 POLITICS: THEORY AND CROSS-COUNTRY EVIDENCE

5.4.1 *Theory*

As in economics, so too in politics. In the absence of electoral constraints, propaganda apparatuses can signal a regime's repressive capacity by making a range of absurd claims about domestic politics. Havel (1978, 9) described these in Soviet Czechoslovakia:

The lack of free expression becomes the highest form of freedom; farcical elections become the highest form of democracy; banning independent thought becomes the most scientific of world views. ... [The regime] pretends to respect human rights. It pretends to persecute no one.

---

[37] These terms are 经济, 金融, 金融危机, 反腐倡廉, 反腐, and 服务群众.
[38] Yong (2000); Stern and O'Brien (2012).
[39] For more on the CCP's response to the global financial crisis, see Brady and He (2012). As our theory suggests, they find that the CCP's economic coverage is driven chiefly by politics, not economic realities.
[40] Jiao (2004).

Perhaps the most obvious absurdity is that a profoundly repressive regime is committed to respecting citizens' basic rights and their ability to choose their government. These claims are central to the CCP's political narrative. During his speech at the 2017 Party Congress – the CCP's equivalent of a quinquennial State of the Union address – President Xi Jinping referenced China's "democracy" or "democratic" system fifty-three times. Among his claims:

We have actively developed socialist democracy. ... Steady progress has been made in enhancing socialist democracy; intraparty democracy has been expanded, and socialist consultative democracy is flourishing.[41]

Hu Jintao's speech from a decade earlier referenced "democracy" sixty times.[42] For reference, in his 2016 State of the Union address, Barack Obama mentioned "democracy" or "democratic" eight times.[43]

Where autocrats confront electoral constraints, propaganda apparatuses can cover electoral politics in ways that build trust in the electoral process. In Chapter 8, we detail how Denis Sassou Nguesso's propaganda apparatus covered the 2016 presidential election, the most sensitive – for reasons we discuss there – since his return to power in 1997. His propaganda campaign was intricate, designed to make his victory appear uncertain initially – citizens had not yet voted – and more likely as the campaign unfolded and citizens expressed their enthusiasm for the candidates before them. We show that Sassou Nguesso's propaganda apparatus sought credibility among readers even during the election campaign: by covering rising food prices in Brazzaville and Pointe-Noire, stagnation in the banking sector, and the government's failure "to diversify the national economy."

Sassou Nguesso's propaganda apparatus also covered the opposition leveling all the same criticisms. His propaganda apparatus even covered allegations of electoral fraud. Three weeks before election day, opposition leader Charles Zacharie Bowao denounced the electoral commission as "illegitimate" and claimed an "inalienable right" to "civil and civic-minded disobedience."[44] *Les Dépêches* covered Bowao's allegations at length, as it did those of the European Union, which, almost

---

[41] "Full Text of Xi Jinping's Report at 19th CPC National Congress," *China Daily*, October 18, 2017.
[42] Brown (2017).
[43] Obama (2016).
[44] "The Opposition Declares the CNEI Illegitimate," *Les Dépêches de Brazzaville*, February 22, 2016.

simultaneously, announced its refusal to send an election observation mission given widespread allegations of fraud.[45] As we discussed in Chapter 2, these admissions are costly. Regular elections catalyze anti-regime protests in autocracies for a variety of reasons, among them that opposition leaders and international observers alert citizens to fraud, which serves as a coordinating device for collective action.[46] These admissions also broadcast the regime's policy failures to elites, who may exploit popular frustration by attempting to depose the autocrat.[47]

> **Hypothesis 5.2:** *As electoral constraints grow more binding, the share of political coverage allocated to actual electoral politics should rise and the share of coverage allocated to abstract principles of democracy and human rights should fall.*

> **Hypothesis 5.3:** *The valence of political coverage should be higher in unconstrained autocracies than constrained autocracies, reflecting the former's tendency to celebrate democracy itself and the latter's coverage of criticism by opposition leaders and the international community.*

In Chapter 2, we abstracted from how citizens organize protests. Protests may emerge spontaneously in response to egregious human rights violations by the regime. Protests may emerge as a result of initiatives by activists or opposition leaders, to whom citizens look for direction.[48] This possibility – that protests emerge at the initiative of activists and opposition leaders – suggests a role for propaganda. In environments where discussing anti-regime activities is profoundly dangerous, how do frustrated citizens know which opposition leaders and activists are most admired *by other citizens*? How do frustrated citizens know which opposition leaders hold views that are most closely aligned with their own, and for whom they would be willing to sacrifice?

The propaganda apparatus provides a potentially useful signal. By denigrating specific opposition leaders, propaganda apparatuses signal to citizens which individuals the regime regards as its chief opponents. Put differently, "going negative" signals to citizens that the regime is

---

[45] "The EU Excludes Itself from the Electoral Process," *Les Dépêches de Brazzaville*, February 23, 2016.

[46] Tucker (2007); Fearon (2011); Kelley (2012); Daxecker (2012); Brancati (2016).

[47] Nordlinger (1977); Galetovic and Sanhueza (2000); Casper and Tyson (2014); Kim (2016).

[48] Olson (1977); Tullock (1987).

sufficiently concerned about certain opposition leaders that it publicly denigrates them. This is why China's Propaganda Department maintains a blacklist of individuals whose names cannot be mentioned in the media. This blacklist include dissidents like Jiao Guobiao, the journalism professor turned dissident who gained notoriety in 2004 for denouncing the Propaganda Department.[49] This is also why the CCP's censorship operation targets specific dissidents more than specific content.[50]

In the absence of electoral constraints, autocrats have no need to cultivate the appearance of neutrality. In turn, they can avoid referencing opposition leaders altogether. Propaganda apparatuses in unconstrained autocracies can cover a "general" opposition rather than specific opposition leaders. When propaganda apparatuses do reference specific opposition leaders, they can also be selective: by covering only those "opposition" leaders who are financed by the regime or avoid impugning it. This lets propaganda apparatuses make absurd claims of universal support: that even the opposition supports it. In China, for instance, the *People's Daily* devotes high praise to China's "eight democratic parties," which enable the CCP to celebrate its "multi-party," "democratic" system, even though the other parties support the CCP. In Uzbekistan, the regime finances several "opposition parties" that routinely endorse the regime's candidates over their own.

By contrast, where electoral constraints are binding, propaganda apparatuses are forced to cover newsworthy events and individuals. Our theory suggests that the composition of opposition coverage should shift: from some unspecified "opposition" to the most relevant opposition leaders. Propaganda apparatuses in constrained autocracies, that is, are forced to cover the autocrat's rivals. Our theory suggests that this coverage should be relatively neutral. Propaganda apparatuses also avoid criticizing the opposition, but for a different reason than their unconstrained counterparts. Doing so would damage their reputation for neutrality. To be sure, propaganda apparatuses in constrained autocracies may also cover "opposition" leaders who are financed by the regime. This was key to Denis Sassou Nguesso's propaganda strategy during his 2016 election campaign, as we show in Chapter 8. But the need to build credibility forces propaganda apparatuses in constrained autocracies to cover legitimate opposition leaders with relative neutrality. Our theory,

---

[49] Brady (2008, 97).
[50] Gallagher and Miller (2019).

therefore, suggests no clear relationship between electoral constraints and the valence of opposition coverage.

Hypothesis 5.4: *As electoral constraints grow more binding, the share of total opposition coverage allocated to a "general" opposition should fall and the share allocated to specific opposition leaders should rise.*

Hypothesis 5.5: *There should be essentially no relationship between electoral constraints and the valence of opposition coverage.*

To summarize, our theory's key predictions for political coverage are these. In the absence of electoral constraints, we expect propaganda apparatuses to make absurd claims about their "democratic" politics, even though the substance of democratic politics is almost completely omitted. Where electoral constraints are binding, propaganda apparatuses are forced to cover the autocrat's opposition rivals and to avoid denigrating them.

5.4.2 Data and Estimation Strategy

To measure the valence of political coverage, we restricted attention to articles that our classifier labeled as electoral politics and democracy. Then, for each article i, we computed its aggregate valence in the same way that we computed *Article Valence: Regime*$_{ijt}$ and *Article Valence: Economy*$_{ijt}$. We defined aggregate valence as the total number of positive less negative words, standardized by the total number of dictionary hits:

$$\text{Article Valence: Elections \& Democracy}_{ijt}$$
$$= \frac{\text{Positive Words}_{ijt} - \text{Negative Words}_{ijt}}{\text{Positive Words}_{ijt} + \text{Negative Words}_{ijt}} \quad (5.5)$$

Next, we measured the composition of political coverage: whether it was biased towards the principles of democracy at the expense of electoral politics. We summed the number of articles about democracy in country j on day t, and then we divided it by the number of articles about either electoral politics or democracy:

$$\text{Democracy Bias}_{jt} = \frac{\text{Democracy}_{jt}}{\text{Electoral Politics}_{jt} + \text{Democracy}_{jt}} \quad (5.6)$$

This gave the share of political content in country j on day t that focused on democratic principles rather than the stuff of democratic politics.

To probe opposition coverage, we drew on measures we introduced in Chapter 3. *References: Opposition$_{ijt}$* counts references to country j's opposition in article i on day t. *Positive Coverage: Opposition$_{ijt}$* counts the number of fulsome words, less critical words, from among the surrounding twenty, summed for article i. We then standardized *Positive Coverage: Opposition$_{ijt}$* by the number of opposition references in article i, which yielded *Positive Coverage Standardized: Opposition$_{ijt}$*. These variables are analogous to our measures of regime coverage in Chapter 4. To accommodate the possibility that propaganda apparatuses treat an unnamed, general opposition differently than specific opposition leaders, we created variants of these three variables for both our general opposition identifiers and specific opposition identifiers. We also used these variables to measure the share of country j's opposition coverage in article i that focused on some unnamed, general opposition rather than on actual opposition leaders. This yielded a measure of general opposition coverage bias:

$$\text{General Opposition Bias}_{ijt}$$
$$= \frac{\text{References: General Opposition}_{ijt}}{\text{References: General Opposition}_{ijt} + \text{References: Specific Opposition}_{ijt}}$$
$$(5.7)$$

We also used these variables to measure coverage bias in favor of the regime:

$$\text{Regime Bias}_{ijt} = \frac{\text{References: Executive}_{ijt}}{\text{References: Executive}_{ijt} + \text{References: Opposition}_{ijt}}$$
$$(5.8)$$

This gave the share of all political content in article i in country j on day t that focused on the regime rather than the opposition.

We employed the same estimation strategy as in Chapter 4. For country-year models, since our measures of electoral constraints are observed annually, we computed country-year means for outcome variables. The baseline model is

$$Y_{js} = \alpha + \beta X_{js} + \phi W_{js} + \gamma_j + \epsilon \tag{5.9}$$

where j indexes country, s indexes year, and X_{js} measures electoral constraints. The vector W_{js} gives our standard set of year-level controls. To accommodate unobserved differences by country, we include country-fixed effects, γ_j, which again accommodate systematic differences across languages. Since these outcomes are continuous, we employed OLS with robust standard errors clustered by country. For article-level models, we employed mixed-effects models to accommodate the annually measured explanatory variables, and our article measured outcome variables. The model is

$$Y_{ijt} = \alpha + \beta X_{is} + \kappa Z_{it} + \phi W_{is} + \gamma_k + \gamma_j + \epsilon \qquad (5.10)$$

where the vectors Z_{it} and W_{is} give day- and year-level controls, respectively; γ_k gives language-fixed effects; and γ_j gives country-random effects.

5.4.3 Results

The results appear in Table 5.5. From Models 1 and 2, the rate of political coverage is slightly higher where electoral constraints are more binding. Models 3 through 12 reveal that the nature and composition of political coverage varies dramatically, as our theory suggests. In the absence of electoral constraints, Models 7 and 8 confirm, propaganda apparatuses cover the principles of democracy rather than its actual practice. From Models 3 and 4, this coverage is effusive, roughly on par with the valence of economic coverage from Table 5.2. Propaganda apparatuses celebrate the extent to which their regimes embody democratic principles while omitting the electoral competition that democracy entails. In the absence of electoral constraints, democracy itself is celebrated.

What does celebrating democracy entail? We discuss this in Section 5.5.2, but an excerpt from The Gambia makes it clear. The *Daily Observer* claimed the 2012 presidential election "was highly credited as free, fair, transparent and peaceful by observers from international bodies such as the Commonwealth, the African Union, and the Organisation of the Islamic Conference, among others." It marked the "culmination" of "a democratic process characterized by the highest manifestation of political maturity."[51] In reality, the Economic Community of West African States (ECOWAS) refused to send election observers because of "an opposition and electorate cowed by repression and intimidation."[52] In February 2015, the *Daily Observer* published this article, headlined "Jammeh Awarded for Championing African Democracy":

---

[51] Hatab Fadera, "Presidential Inauguration Is Tomorrow," *Daily Observer*, January 18, 2012.
[52] Al Jazeera (2011).

Table 5.5 Narratives about democracy, electoral politics, and the opposition

Dependent variable:

Outcome variable	Rate		Article valence		Regime bias		Democracy bias		General opposition bias		Opposition coverage standardized	
Unit of analysis / Estimator	Country-year OLS	Article Mixed	Country-year OLS	Article Mixed	Country-year OLS	Article Mixed	Country-year OLS	Article Mixed	Country-year OLS	Article Mixed	Country-year OLS	Article Mixed
	(1)	(2)	(3)	(4)	(5)	(6)	(7)	(8)	(9)	(10)	(11)	(12)
Polity	0.004	0.008***	-0.016**	-0.012***	-0.045***	-0.016***	-0.026**	-0.036***	-0.041**	-0.010***	-0.052	-0.023**
	(0.005)	(0.0002)	(0.007)	(0.001)	(0.015)	(0.003)	(0.011)	(0.002)	(0.016)	(0.003)	(0.080)	(0.010)
Trade	0.0005	-0.001***	0.0004	0.001***	-0.001	0.002***	0.001	0.0002	0.001	0.0005**	0.005	0.003***
	(0.001)	(0.00002)	(0.001)	(0.0001)	(0.002)	(0.0002)	(0.002)	(0.0002)	(0.002)	(0.0002)	(0.007)	(0.001)
Log GDP per capita	-0.079	-0.139***	-0.020	0.082***	-0.005	0.341***	0.494***	0.216***	-0.148	-0.067**	0.464	-0.059
	(0.052)	(0.002)	(0.086)	(0.018)	(0.217)	(0.033)	(0.135)	(0.022)	(0.272)	(0.027)	(0.926)	(0.066)
Natural resources	0.001	0.002***	0.001	0.002***	-0.005	-0.003***	0.004	0.005***	-0.004	0.002**	0.005	0.019***
	(0.002)	(0.0001)	(0.003)	(0.0004)	(0.005)	(0.001)	(0.004)	(0.0005)	(0.005)	(0.001)	(0.021)	(0.002)
Civil war	-0.016	-0.007***	0.018	0.038***	-0.020	0.028	-0.127*	0.036**	-0.060	0.065***	0.351	0.342***
	(0.028)	(0.002)	(0.044)	(0.013)	(0.088)	(0.024)	(0.069)	(0.015)	(0.110)	(0.022)	(0.352)	(0.095)
Internet penetration	0.00001	-0.00000**	-0.00001	-0.00000	0.00003	-0.00003**	-0.00001	-0.00002***	-0.00004	-0.0001***	0.0002	0.0001***
	(0.00002)	(0.00000)	(0.00004)	(0.00000)	(0.0001)	(0.00001)	(0.0001)	(0.00000)	(0.0001)	(0.00001)	(0.0002)	(0.00004)
Election	0.019*		0.032		0.083*		-0.031		-0.111**		0.001	
	(0.012)		(0.023)		(0.045)		(0.037)		(0.050)		(0.162)	
Election season		0.071***		0.028***		0.010**		-0.057***		-0.046***		0.065***
		(0.001)		(0.003)		(0.005)		(0.003)		(0.004)		(0.018)
Constant	0.746	1.503***	0.231	-0.774***	0.463	-3.321***	-4.686***	-2.207***	1.842	0.842***	-5.002	-0.001
	(0.524)	(0.081)	(0.867)	(0.196)	(2.138)	(0.408)	(1.367)	(0.262)	(2.681)	(0.294)	(9.021)	(0.701)
Country effects	Fixed	Random	Fixed	Random	Fixed	Random	Fixed	Random	Fixed	Random	Fixed	Random
Language-fixed effects		✓		✓		✓		✓		✓		✓
Observations	192	2,442,480	183	95,347	180	76,951	183	95,355	165	67,028	156	62,274
R^2	0.673		0.788		0.653		0.758		0.666		0.333	

Note: * p < 0.1; ** p < 0.05; *** p < 0.01

197

The President of the Republic, His Excellency Sheikh Professor Alhaji Dr. Yahya A.J.J. Jammeh has been awarded the Apex Merit Award as The Pride and Champion of African Democracy, by the Ecumenical Merit Award Commission International Inc.-USA. A media release from the Office of the President reveals that this honour was in recognition of various attributes and achievements that His Excellency, the President has established over a period of 20 years, namely: Effective Infrastructural Development, Agricultural Mobilization, Decentralisation with meaningful advancement within the territories of The Gambia, Excellency in Leadership and Improvement of the livelihood of the Citizens, Sustaining and Maintaining Peace, Tolerance and Free Movement of People, and Leading the Excellent Democratic and Good Example in Africa.[53]

This is what celebrating democracy entails. It is done only by propaganda apparatuses in the most repressive autocracies.

The results for opposition coverage are equally striking. From Models 5 and 6, as a share of all political references, propaganda apparatuses in the most repressive dictatorships display an overwhelming bias in favor of the regime and against the opposition. Each five-point increase in the Polity score is associated with a bias decrease of between 8 percent and 22.5 percent. In the most repressive dictatorships, the share of all political references to the regime is between 25 percent and 68 percent greater than where the Polity score hovers around 4 or 5. The magnitude of the general opposition bias is similar. From Models 9 and 10, as a share of all opposition references, propaganda apparatuses in the most repressive dictatorships cover the general opposition rather than specific opposition leaders between 15 percent and 62 percent more than where the Polity score hovers around 4 or 5. They cover the "opposition," not the opposition. From Models 11 and 12, we find no evidence that propaganda apparatuses across autocracies "go negative" on the opposition. If anything, opposition coverage is slightly more positive where electoral constraints are non-binding.

Figure 5.3 presents descriptive statistics for opposition coverage. The top-left panel presents a bivariate scatterplot for *Positive Coverage Standardized: Opposition*$_{ijt}$ by Polity score. The top-right panel presents the analogous bivariate scatterplot for *References: Opposition*$_{ijt}$. The bottom panel presents three radar charts that give the share of opposition coverage focusing on the topics around the perimeter. The conspicuous feature

---

[53] "Jammeh Awarded for Championing African Democracy," *Daily Observer,* February 13, 2015.

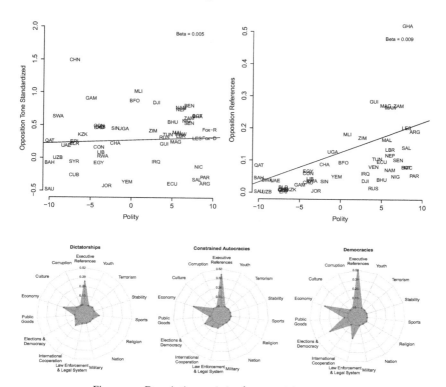

Figure 5.3 Descriptive statistics for opposition coverage

is the extent to which, in the absence of electoral constraints, the opposition is simply omitted from propaganda narratives about democracy and electoral politics. Where electoral constraints are binding, the topics with which the opposition is associated are similar to those in democracies: the economy, electoral politics, and alongside coverage of the regime itself.

5.5 DEMOCRACY AND ELECTORAL POLITICS IN RUSSIA AND UZBEKISTAN

The results above are consistent with our theory. In the absence of electoral constraints, propaganda apparatuses craft political narratives that are absurd, and that everyone knows are absurd. They celebrate the quality of democracy in terms that Havel (1978) would recognize, yet omit the actual practice of democratic politics. They cover an unnamed "opposition," rather than actual opposition leaders. They do so quite positively, the better to maintain the absurdity of universal support for the regime and to avoid identifying the potential protest leaders the regime most fears. We find none of this where autocrats confront binding electoral constraints. To cultivate the appearance of neutrality, propaganda apparatuses are forced to cover the autocrat's opposition rivals and the accusations they level against the regime, but without being overly critical.

To study these narratives in more detail, we focus on Russia and Uzbekistan, our two most extensive propaganda collections in Russian. We focus on autocracies with a common language to ensure that differences in propaganda content are not driven by differences in language. During our sample period, the Russian and Uzbek regimes confronted different electoral constraints. Uzbekistan's government is among the world's most repressive. The world's fifth leading cotton exporter, each fall the government conscripts roughly 1 million citizens for harvest, which cripples the health and education sectors. Government officials are effectively exempt.[54] Since cotton exports generate 25 percent of government revenue, the industry is organized to maximize proceeds. Farmers are forced to satisfy government-mandated production quotas, purchase inputs from state-owned enterprises, and sell to the state marketing board. Export profits are deposited into an account only accessible to senior officials.[55] Vladimir Putin's government is far from democratic – as its war in Ukraine rages, it is becoming even less so – but its Polity score has remained at 4 since 2006. Uzbekistan's Polity score has remained at −9 since it claimed independence from the Soviet Union in 1991.

We computed our measure of semantic distinctiveness for democracy coverage in Russia's *Rossiyskaya Gazeta* and Uzbekistan's *Narodnoye Slovo*. Distinctive words for *Rossiyskaya Gazeta* appear on the left of Figure 5.4 and for *Narodnoye Slovo* on the right. The most distinctive word for Russia and Uzbekistan refers to their national parliaments: Duma for Russia, Oliy Majlis for Uzbekistan. From there, however, the differences are stark, as our theory predicts.

5.5.1 Russia: Ella Pamfilova and the Electoral Commission

The second most distinctive word in Russia's political coverage is "Ella Pamfilova," who, in 2016, was appointed chair of the Central Election Commission, the body charged with ensuring the integrity of elections.

---

[54] Khan (2016).
[55] Cotton Campaign (2017).

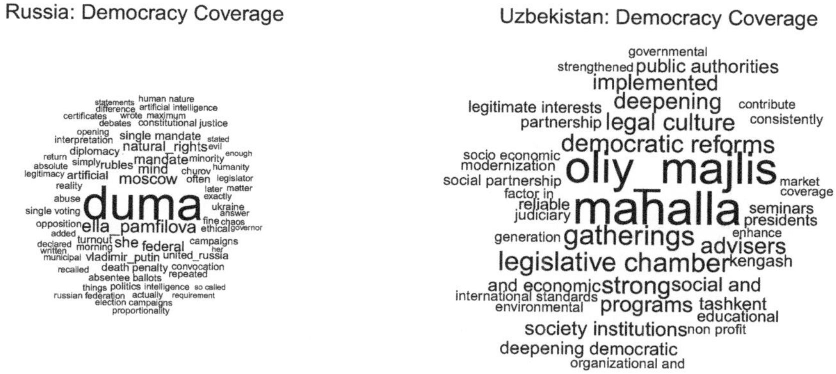

Russia: Democracy Coverage   Uzbekistan: Democracy Coverage

Figure 5.4 Semantic distinctiveness in political propaganda in Russia and Uzbekistan

To be clear, the second most distinctive word in the Russian government's political propaganda reflects its efforts to persuade citizens of the integrity of Russian elections. Pamfilova has a fascinating story, common in the world's electorally constrained autocracies. She served as a minister in President Boris Yeltsin's democratically elected government, ran against then-acting president Vladimir Putin in 2000, and was appointed human rights commissioner by Putin in 2014. The *Washington Post* welcomed her appointment as chair of the Electoral Commission in 2016:

From the fringes of power, Ella Pamfilova has spent decades fighting against the odds. As Russia's first female candidate for president, she ran against Vladimir Putin in 2000, earning just 1% of the vote. As Russia's human rights ombudsman, she sought compromise between harried advocates and hidebound officials.

But as the head of Russia's Central Elections Commission, she faces an even more improbable task: ensuring that Russia's parliamentary elections are free and fair....

The difference now, Pamfilova said, is that Putin has given a mandate for clean elections. She says she is the proof.

"If there were not a political desire for normal, fair and open elections, then they would never choose a person like me, someone hard to work with who won't play the subordinate," she said, adding that she thinks Putin respects her forthrightness. "I never brought Putin pleasant questions. He knows my difficult character."...

"Let them fear Pamfilova," she said with relish, describing her handling of a recent wage dispute for election workers in Rybinsk. In her telling, the main villains are local and regional officials seeking to massage the vote, not the Kremlin....

She has repeatedly resigned her posts in protest, first as social minister under Yeltsin, and then as the chairwoman of the Kremlin's commission on human rights in 2010.

"If I see that my work begins to contradict my personal principles and is not effective, I don't remain in my position."[56]

Pamfilova's appointment was welcomed even by Human Rights Watch:

Tanya Lokshina, head of Human Rights Watch Russia and a longtime colleague, said that she trusts Pamfilova's intentions but doubts her potential impact.

"Perhaps ... she can achieve small victories, make a difference where she's able to make a difference," Lokshina said. "She is doomed in terms of ensuring free and fair elections in Russia, at least this time around. But it won't be for lack of goodwill."[57]

Pamfilova has demonstrated some willingness to challenge the regime, or at least to go along with its propaganda strategy. In September 2018, she alleged that Putin's United Russia party had rigged a gubernatorial election in the Far East and recommended a revote.[58] After Pamfilova's announcement, a Kremlin spokesperson declared that the "priority of clean and fair elections" was more important than United Russia's victory. Of course, upon Putin's April 2018 reelection, Pamfilova congratulated him on a "convincing and clean victory."[59]

Putin's propaganda apparatus routinely concedes fraud in local and regional elections, and then uses any acquired credibility to validate his electoral performance. Table 5.6 displays a series of representative sentences that use the distinctive words from the left panel of Figure 5.5. *Rossiyskaya Gazeta* quotes Pamfilova discussing the Commission's efforts to ensure electoral integrity: The Commission, she said, "does everything possible to increase voter turnout," which "not only increases the legitimacy of the vote but reduces the space for abuse of ballots."[60] Elsewhere, *Rossiyskaya Gazeta* covered her efforts to "[organize] rapid response groups to combat electoral irregularities." *Rossiyskaya Gazeta* also covers allegations of electoral fraud:

The results of the elections to the State Duma were canceled at nine polling stations. "Improvements in the level of transparency" were noted by international

---

[56] Roth (2016).
[57] Roth (2016).
[58] Nikolskaya (2018).
[59] Radio Free Europe/Radio Liberty (2018).
[60] Alexandra Beluza, "On September 18, Russians will Elect the Seventh State Duma," *Rossiskaya Gazeta*, September 15, 2016.

Table 5.6 *Extracts from Russia's political propaganda*

Term	Representative extract
Ella Pamfilova	today at the meeting the chairman of the electoral commission **Ella Pamfilova** reported that she is negotiating with other departments on the organization of rapid response groups to combat electoral irregularities
Duma	State **Duma** deputy Boris Reznik won third place in the Khabarovsk single mandate electoral district
Federal	the Communist Party and its anti-crisis plan yesterday was approved at an extended meeting of the **federal** organizing committee of the party on the primaries
Mandate	Ella Pamfilova also said that the electoral commission received complaints from candidates in single **mandate** districts who were refused registration
Turnout	Pamfilova emphasized that the electoral commission does everything possible to increase voter **turnout**, this not only raises the legitimacy of the vote but reduces the space for abuse of ballots
Absentee ballots	the State Duma introduced a package of bills allowing the postponement of presidential elections in Russia to March suggesting the abolition of **absentee ballots** for these elections
United Russia	Dmitri Medvedev warned that he believes that the reasons for **United Russia's** losses in some regions are rooted in basic non-observance of party discipline because of the weakness of the regional offices' positions
Rubles	perhaps the most ambitious bold promise of the Russian Communists is to establish in January a minimum wage of thousands of **rubles**
Vladimir Putin	**Vladimir Putin** was the center of press attention due to the Russian military operation in Syria and allegations that Russian hackers were allegedly involved in hacking the US Democratic Party's national committee servers
Death penalty	recently in the lower house of the Russian parliament, deputies of the Fair Russia party have introduced a bill to return the **death penalty** for crimes of terrorism
Constitutional justice	a referendum embodies the direct will of all people that is the overwhelming majority even before any parliament and it is important to note the metapolitical fact that **constitutional justice** through legitimate interpretation of meanings can not only select the will of the majority but smooth out indignations brought about by a political minority
Churov	on the topic of cyclists over millions of voters in the state duma elections were joined by Vladimir **Churov** and the senator's critics of the OSCE ODIHR proposing that this organization be independent by the end of this year

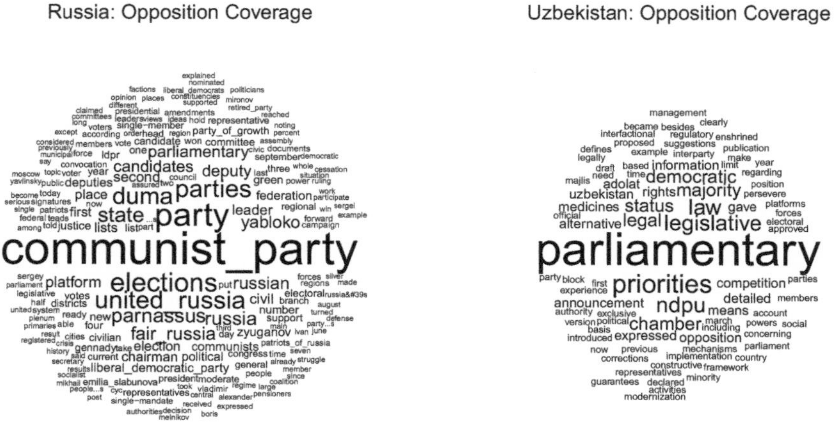

Russia: Opposition Coverage   Uzbekistan: Opposition Coverage

Figure 5.5 Common words in opposition coverage in Russia and Uzbekistan

observers from the OSCE. However, they drew attention to a number of legislative restrictions, stressing that "there are opportunities for improvement in terms of monitoring citizens, registering candidates, and organizing rallies." The main result – the legitimacy of the elections to the 2016 State Duma – is not subject to massive doubt. This is the key difference from the 2011 elections, when gross violations created public outcry on the streets. United Russia performed much better than in 2011, but there are no "angry citizens" this time. The "cushion of transparency" has made the new State Duma legitimate.[61]

Although *Rossiyskaya Gazeta* contends that "the main result … is not subject to massive doubt," it explicitly concedes irregularities to cultivate the appearance of neutrality.

Where electoral constraints are binding, propaganda apparatuses are forced to concede human rights violations alongside the regime's efforts to rectify them. On May 16, 2012, *Rossiyskaya Gazeta* published an interview with Tatyana Moskalkova, Pamfilova's successor as human rights commissioner, after she submitted her annual report to Putin. In 2016 alone, it reported, Pamfilova received 42,000 applications for human rights protection:

Meeting with the president is always an opportunity. It is extremely important to take advantage of it. There is no sense in sugar coating things. My task was to convey to the president a real picture of human rights, focusing on systemic issues and on people who were the victims of blatant injustice. Some situations cannot be solved without the head of state's intervention. Probably, this is wrong

---

[61] Alexandra Beluza, "United Russia Will Take More than 75% of Seats in the New State Duma," *Rossiskaya Gazeta*, September 21, 2016.

from the point of view of a systematic approach to the matter, but to me, as the Commissioner for Human Rights, it is important, as they say, "not to miss the moment." If there is an opportunity to save someone's life, to restore justice, then all means are good.[62]

Though the interview concedes human rights violations, it insists on the government's efforts to do better: "The topic of human rights is often politicized, but in fact it is outside politics." The final question that *Rossiskaya Gazeta* asks her is how Russia's international dialogue on human rights issues has evolved. She responds by citing the international community's apparent approval of the Putin government's human rights commission:

The effectiveness of the institution of the Commissioner for Human Rights in the Russian Federation has been recognized by the international community. We have the highest accreditation status: "A." Last year, a new phase began: joining the European Network of the Global Alliance of National Human Rights Institutions (HANRI). It is an international independent association that provides participants with a unique negotiating platform, indispensable in cases when it becomes necessary to protect the rights of their citizens.[63]

Our measure of semantic distinctiveness lets Russian propaganda speak for itself. Where electoral constraints are at least somewhat binding, propaganda apparatuses are constrained to employ a propaganda strategy that aims for credibility. It does so by conceding bad news and policy failures, which, it reassures readers, the government is doing its best to resolve.

5.5.2 *Uzbekistan: "Deepening democratic reforms"*

Where electoral constraints are non-binding, political coverage is profoundly different. Uzbekistan claimed independence from the Soviet Union on September 1, 1991, and Islam Karimov, President of the Uzbek Soviet Socialist Republic since March 1990, became its first president. His sudden death on September 2, 2016, which we discuss in Chapter 7, plunged the country into crisis. Shavkat Mirziyoyev, Karimov's longtime prime minister, was named interim president on September 8 and "elected" on December 16.

Distinctive words for Uzbekistan's political propaganda appear on the right of Figure 5.5. Table 5.7 displays a series of representative sentences that contain these distinctive terms. The second and fourth

---

[62] "Interview with Tatyana Nikolaevna," *Rossiskaya Gazeta*, May 16, 2012.
[63] "Interview with Tatyana Nikolaevna," *Rossiskaya Gazeta*, May 16, 2012.

Table 5.7 *Extracts from Uzbekistan's political propaganda*

Term	Representative extract
Mahalla	the unbeatable force of the **Mahalla** from time immemorial is a hotbed of national values
Gatherings	currently the country has about ten thousand citizens **gatherings** effectively solving many regional social and economic development issues
Democratic reforms	the constitutional law on strengthening the role of political parties of the state updates the country's modernization and democratization and has become a solid legal basis for increasing social and political citizens activity in developing a true multiparty system and deepening **democratic reforms.**
Strong	the Uzbek model of legal reform is crucial for the further implementation of the fundamental principle of development for our country, from a **strong** state to **strong** civil society to the formation of political guarantees for the reliable protection of human rights and other generally accepted values of democratic norms laid down by the country's constitution
Legal culture	karimov emphasized that we all need to recognize that one of the most important conditions for fully ensuring a rule of law society is educating people to respect the law and awareness of **legal culture** in Uzbekistan's educational system in the field of human rights
Advisers	in villages a law has been adopted for electing the chairman of a group of citizen **advisers** who regulate election procedures. The most important principle of this important event is equal suffrage
Deepening	president Islam Karimov put forward the concept of further **deepening** democratization. On the basis of this policy document a number of laws have been enacted that supplemented the legal framework to protect human rights
Programs	television and radio channels are preparing a series of **programs** that cover an electoral law aimed at increasing women's social and political activity in the upcoming elections
Society	further deepening democratic reforms and building open civil **society** elections are at the center of the international community's media attention
Institutions	citizens' rights to be elected as public authorities also strengthens the guarantees of the right to freedom of speech, as was noted by the results of monitoring studies that show the ever-increasing role of civil society **institutions** of democratic modernization in the country an essential condition for the formation of a strong civil society

most distinctive words, "Oliy Majlis" and "legislative chamber," refer to Uzbekistan's parliament. These references are standard, as we discussed above. Our measure of distinctiveness is otherwise revealing. The first and third most distinctive words, "Mahalla" and "gatherings," refer to the neighborhood councils that are central to the regime's surveillance operation. Human Rights Watch (2003) describes the Mahalla surveillance system this way:

[Mahalla committees] are the key government actors in repressing individuals and families whom the state deems suspect. They cooperate with law enforcement and other authorities to gather personal information on the population. . . . They keep files on those considered suspicious, including "scandalous families" with disobedient children, and pass this information onto the police and executive authorities.

The Uzbek propaganda apparatus routinely tells citizens that Mahalla committees fully penetrate society and are backed by the international community. One article from June 13, 2014, covered a Mahalla Institute presentation in the United States, ostensibly organized by the Ministry of Foreign Affairs and the University of Washington. Mahalla committees, it suggested, are admired by Western scholars and even the U.S. government:

. . . As Congressman Dana Rohrabacher said, the Mahalla is a social institution of self-government, which plays an important role in the everyday life of the population. In this regard, the effective use of the potential of the Mahalla Institute is one of the main factors for ensuring harmony in the country.

"The Mahalla is a unique institution, adapted to modern realities and combining both traditional values and elements of modern civil society," said Deputy Assistant Secretary of State Leslie Viguerie. The American side considers the institutions of local self-government as designed to serve the interests and rights of citizens on the ground. Professor of the State University of New York, Parviz Morvij, noted that the Uzbek Mahalla is a special case, since it integrates individuals, families, communities, and people into society. Mahalla is a link between individuals, society, and the state, and it is an instrument of their solidarity. This is the ideal concept of democracy.

. . . The Mahallas allow Uzbekistan to preserve and develop its unique heritage, which today is the main factor in national unity and social stability. . . . The Mahalla is a "bridge" between citizens and authorities that turns into a "vehicle" of protection.[64]

We were unable to locate a Parviz Morvij at the State University of New York.

Alongside Mahalla committees, the Uzbek propaganda apparatus routinely references "democratic reforms" and "legal culture." These are

---

[64] "Presentation of the Mahalla Institute in the USA," *Narodnoye Slovo*, November 30, 2016.

codewords, as Table 5.7 makes clear. Democratic reforms are typically discussed in the context of "strengthening the role of political parties" and "developing a true multiparty system." Of course, the government bans opposition parties save for those financed by the state and which routinely endorse the regime's candidates rather than its own. Similarly, "legal culture" is often discussed in terms of rule *by* law instead *of* rule of law, a distinction that students of China have identified as profoundly important in sustaining authoritarian rule.[65] From Table 5.7, Karimov calls for "educating people to respect the law and to be aware of legal culture" in order to "ensure a rule of law society." The implication is that citizens must submit. As in China, the regime dispenses laws rather than being bound by them.

The next most distinctive term in Uzbekistan's coverage of democracy and electoral politics is "strong." From Table 5.7, this is used to describe democratization, human rights, and the "Uzbek model of legal reform." Between February 1, 2014, and April 17, 2017, the term "Uzbek model" appeared once every seven publication days, always in quotation marks. From August 13, 2015:

It was noted that since independence, Uzbekistan has defined human rights, freedoms and interests as the highest value. This most important democratic principle is laid in the basis of the "Uzbek model" of development, which has provided the people of Uzbekistan with a confident progress towards the construction of a democratic legal state, a socially oriented market economy, and the formation of a strong civil society.[66]

The "Uzbek model" of development is described as "universally acclaimed," and the propaganda apparatus routinely has foreign observers praising it. One article, from August 31, 2016, is entitled "Clear Goals, Significant Achievements" and describes the "incomparable successes and milestones achieved on the basis of the 'Uzbek model' developed by the President of the country," which "cause admiration of foreign specialists."[67] The other terms in Table 5.7 – "advisers," "deepening," "programs," "society," and "institutions" – are similar. They describe the surveillance apparatus and make absurd claims about the status of human rights in Uzbekistan. Its coverage of democratic politics is effusive and threatening, often simultaneously.

---

[65] Perry (2008); Li (2010).
[66] "Raising the Legal Culture in Society – The Basis of Reforms," *Narodnoye Slovo*, August 13, 2015.
[67] "Clear Goals, Significant Achievements," *Narodnoye Slovo*, August 31, 2016.

5.5.3 Covering the "Opposition" and the Opposition

Where electoral constraints are non-binding, the statistical results suggest, propaganda apparatuses reference an unnamed, general opposition rather than specific opposition leaders. To understand what this entails in the context of Russia and Uzbekistan, we identified each reference to a general or specific opposition identifier and then extracted the twenty surrounding words. Figure 5.5 presents a pair of word clouds that display the most common words.

Our corpus of Uzbek propaganda spans 2014 to 2017 and encompasses two presidential elections: one in 2015 and another in 2016, after Karimov's sudden death. Not once did *Narodnoye Slovo* reference a genuine opposition leader. To be sure, it referenced the "opposition" parties financed by the regime, which routinely endorse its candidates and hence allow it to absurdly claim universal support. Two of these quasi-opposition parties – the National Revival Democratic Party (NDPU) and Justice Social Democratic Party (Adolat) – appear on the right of Figure 5.5. Freedom House (2017) described their activities during the 2016 electoral campaign:

There were no debates among the candidates during the campaign. The election programs did not differ significantly among the candidates, and none criticized the current government or Mirziyoyev. When the RFE/RL Uzbek Service asked the NDPU about this, they openly said that the party did not oppose the government. In some regions, members of all three parties were reportedly instructed to campaign for Mirziyoyev, not their own party's candidate.

Wilson (2005) charts the history of these fake opposition parties. Adolat "appropriated the name of a real opposition party set up by former vice-president (and for a time President Islam Karimov's only serious opponent) Shukrulla Mirsaidov."[68] The government next launched Milliy Tiklanish, a "faux-intelligentsia party." Karimov also created "fake NGOs [that] parallel groups critical of the autocracy." One of these, the Committee for the Protection of the Rights of the Individual, "regularly concluded that its work was barely necessary."[69]

Narodnoye Slovo referenced an unnamed, general opposition thirteen times during our four-year sample. Each of these references told citizens that the regime had undertaken "democratizing reforms" – again, see Table 5.7 – to foster a political opposition, although none was ever

---

[68] Wilson (2005, 149).
[69] Wilson (2005, 149–150).

specified. One article from January 25, 2015, asserted that a 2007 law, "On Strengthening the Role of Political Parties and Further Democratizing the Public Administration and Modernization of the Country," guaranteed the political opposition "exclusive rights and guarantees of effective activity." The law "had a huge impact on the development and strengthening of a real multiparty system in the country."[70] Another article, from November 29, 2016, claimed that the United Nations praised "inter-party competition and pluralism of opinions in Uzbekistan," as well as its "open and free elections."[71] These articles are why the word cloud in Figure 5.5 features words like "democratic," "legal," "status," "rights," "law," and "gave."

In Russia, by contrast, the word cloud reflects genuine electoral competition, with six opposition parties that routinely criticize the Putin government: the Communist Party, Parnassus, the Liberal Democratic Party, Yabloko, Fair Russia, and the Party of Growth. Some of these parties are more legitimate than others. The Communist Party, led by Gennady Zyuganov since 1993, is regarded by some as the perennial runner-up that validates the electoral charade.[72] It is also, however, occasionally quite critical. In September 2011, the Russian propaganda apparatus covered Zyuganov's speech at the Party Congress:

The Communists have pledged to beat the ruling party at the parliamentary elections, saying United Russia has brought the country to a deadlock.

"It will not be just the elections of State Duma or president, it will be a choice of the course after a 20-year experiment," the Communist leader Gennady Zyuganov told the delegates and guests of the Congress. "A gang of folks who cannot do anything in life has humiliated the country," he said, referring to the current government. . . .

Meanwhile, the party's leader commented on news coming from the United Russia Congress, held on the same day. The decision of the ruling tandem of the president and the prime minister "will not change the situation in Russia," he said. Nothing essential has been done in Russia during the last four years, and the government is still "unqualified and unprofessional," he stressed.[73]

---

[70] "Report of President Islam Karimov to the Joint Meeting of the Legislative Chamber of the Senate of the Oliy Majlis of the Republic of Uzbekistan," *Narodnoye Slovo*, January 25, 2015.

[71] "Inter-Party Competition and Pluralism of Opinions in Uzbekistan Is the Focus of the UN," *Narodnoye Slovo*, November 29, 2016.

[72] Pertsev (2018).

[73] "Communists Pledge to Stop 'Dollar-Lovers' Experiment on Russia," RT, September 24, 2011.

One key feature of constrained autocracies is that elections are stage-managed *until they are not*: until a co-opted opposition party generates enough popular support to challenge the regime.[74] There were some signs of this in Russia, at least before Putin's invasion of Ukraine ushered in a dramatic increase in domestic repression. In July 2016, *Newsweek* asked whether "Russia's Resurgent Communist Party" constituted "Vladimir Putin's Red Scare":

> Last September, in a result that shocked Russia's carefully controlled political system, the Communist Party's Sergei Levchenko was elected governor of east Siberia's Irkutsk region, defeating his rival from the ruling United Russia party. Levchenko's win marked the first time a Putin-supported candidate had been defeated since the Kremlin reintroduced direct elections for regional governors in 2012. Local Communist Party activists say their true margin of victory was so great that Kremlin-friendly election officials were unable to rig the vote in favor of the candidate from the ruling party. ...
>
> Recently, the Communist Party's rhetoric has become sharper, especially when it comes to state corruption. By the Kremlin's admission, corruption costs Russia some $30 billion a year. The Communists haven't directly accused Putin of involvement, but senior party members have lashed out at members of his inner circle.[75]

In January 2018, the *Washington Post* described the surprise Communist Party candidate in the presidential election, Pavel Grudinin:

> There's a Russian candidate for president who is wildly popular on YouTube, where he slams the policies of President Vladimir Putin. He has a nationwide political machine and a constituency of millions who are fed up with the current Kremlin occupant and his oligarch friends.[76]

This is what our theory predicts. Where electoral constraints are binding, propaganda apparatuses must cover the opposition to build credibility, which entails covering its occasional allegations of corruption and policy failures. This is absent where electoral constraints are non-binding.

5.5.4 *The Buzzwords of Democracy and Human Rights*

To explore how much more often unconstrained autocracies celebrate the ideals of democracy and human rights, we estimated the relative

---

[74] Schedler (2010a); Carothers (2018).
[75] Bennetts (2016).
[76] Filipov (2018).

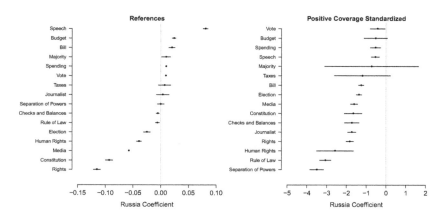

Figure 5.6 Coverage of democracy buzzwords in Russia and Uzbekistan

frequency of buzzwords: "rights," "human rights," "constitution," "media," "rule of law," "separation of powers," and "checks and balances," among others. As placebos, we also estimated the frequency of words that reflect the procedures of governing and the stuff of campaigning. Next, for every article i from Russia and Uzbekistan, we counted the number of references to these words. For each, we computed the number of positive words, less negative words, from among the surrounding twenty, standardized by the number of references per article. This yielded a measure of valence that was analogous to our primary measure of pro-regime propaganda, *Positive Coverage Standardized: Executive$_{ijt}$*. We estimated models of the form

$$Y_{ijt} = \alpha + \beta \left(\text{Russia}_{ijt}\right) + \epsilon \qquad (5.11)$$

where i indexes article, j indexes country, t indexes day, and *Russia$_{ij}$* assumes value 1 for Russia and 0 for Uzbekistan.

The results appear in Figure 5.6. The left panel reports the reference results; the right panel reports the valence results. The x-axes report the coefficient β. For the left panel, β measures how much more likely the words along the y-axis are to appear in Russian political propaganda. For the right panel, β measures how many more words from among the surrounding twenty are positive in Russian political propaganda. The buzzwords associated with the abstract principles of democracy – rights, human rights, constitution, media – are between 5 percent and 12 percent more likely to appear in Uzbek propaganda than Russian propaganda. These words are also covered far more positively in Uzbek propaganda.

When those words are mentioned, they are surrounded by between two and four more positive words from among the surrounding twenty. These are enormous effects, as our Fox News index makes clear. Recall from Chapter 3 that a single unit of our Fox News index is just 0.13. These effects amount to between 15 and 30 Fox News units.

Autocrats who most routinely and brutally violate their citizens' basic rights are far most likely to celebrate how democratic their politics are.

5.6 SPORTS: THEORY AND CROSS-COUNTRY EVIDENCE

5.6.1 *Theory*

We consider a final narrative topic: sports, which constitute some 20 percent of propaganda content across autocracies. Scholars increasingly recognize the power of sports to shape politics, often in surprising ways. American citizens are more likely to vote for incumbents when their favorite college football teams win on the Saturday before election day.[77] Countries that qualify for the World Cup soccer tournament are more likely to initiate militarized disputes afterwards, due perhaps to a rush of nationalism.[78] Other ostensibly non-political content apparently shapes citizens' political beliefs as well. Simply watching television dramas about crime increases the salience of criminal justice issues and makes viewers more critical of the president.[79] Voters, Achen and Bartels (2004) put it, "regularly punish governments for acts of God," which apparently include droughts, floods, and shark attacks.[80]

If sports so powerfully shape politics, we should expect autocrats to harness them. The Astana Professional Cycling Team, Koch (2012) observes, is routinely employed as an object of nation-building in Kazakhstan.[81] Brady (2008, 28) observes a similar situation in China. The CCP's Propaganda Department, she writes, regards sports as an "important means of engaging in mass political thought work, particularly towards youth."

---

[77] Healy, Malhotra, and Mo (2010).
[78] Bertoli (2017).
[79] Holbrook and Hill (2005).
[80] For more on shark attacks, see Fowler and Hall (2018).
[81] As Passi (1996, 98–99) put it: "Owing to its emotional expressions and nationalistic symbolism, sport should have a key place in general research into nationalism and national culture."

Our theory suggests that the core function of propaganda in the absence of electoral constraints is not to curry nationalism but to signal the regime's capacity for repression. How might this be accomplished in sports coverage? What does absurd propaganda look like in the realm of sports? There are at least two ways to make claims that everyone knows to be absurd. First, propaganda apparatuses can claim absurd successes for the country's sports teams. This may be useful, but national teams play rarely, and so opportunities for absurd coverage may be scarce. Alternatively, propaganda apparatuses can claim for the executive a level of engagement with – and support for – domestic sports teams that is obviously absurd.

Where autocrats confront electoral constraints, we expect sports coverage to serve different objectives. First, from Chapter 2, autocrats have to induce citizens to consume propaganda. This impulse, we argued, is especially strong where autocrats confront electoral constraints. By supplying sports content that citizens genuinely want to consume, propaganda apparatuses can attract readers, who are then exposed to their other content as well. Second, objective sports coverage offers propaganda apparatuses the opportunity to build credibility with readers, which may be useful for manipulating their beliefs about other topics. Insofar as sports coverage can help foster nationalism,[82] we should also expect propaganda apparatuses in constrained autocracies to cover the regime positively, though not as positively as in the most repressive dictatorships.

Hypothesis 5.6: *As electoral constraints grow more binding, sports coverage should be more credible, especially with respect to the executive.*

5.6.2 Data and Estimation Strategy

We created several variables to test these hypotheses. The variable *Article Valence: Sports$_{ijt}$* measures the valence of sports coverage in article i in country j on day t. We created it as we did its analogs above. We restricted attention to sports articles and, for each article i, we computed the total number of positive less negative words standardized by the total number of dictionary hits. We created variants for articles that reference the regime and for those that do not. To measure the frequency of

[82] Koch (2012).

sports coverage, we created the variable *Sports$_{ijt}$*, which assumes value 1 if article i is about sports and value 0 otherwise. Our estimation strategy again follows Chapter 4. For each outcome of interest, we estimated both country-year and article-level models. For country-year models, we computed country-year means for our measures of propaganda. The baseline model is

$$Y_{js} = \alpha + \beta X_{js} + \phi W_{js} + \gamma_j + \epsilon \qquad (5.12)$$

where j indexes country, s indexes year, X_{js} measures electoral constraints, and the vector W_{js} gives year-level controls. We included country-fixed effects, γ_j, which again accommodate unobserved differences across countries and systematic differences across languages. Since these outcomes are continuous, we employed OLS with robust standard errors clustered by country. For article-level models, we employed mixed effects estimators to accommodate the annually measured explanatory variables and our article measured outcome variables. The model is

$$Y_{ijt} = \alpha + \beta X_{is} + \kappa Z_{it} + \phi W_{is} + \gamma_k + \gamma_j + \epsilon \qquad (5.13)$$

where the vectors Z_{it} and W_{is} give day- and year-level controls, respectively; γ_k gives language-fixed effects; and γ_j country-random effects.

5.6.3 Results

The results appear in Table 5.8. From Models 1 and 2, we find no evidence that the rate of sports coverage differs substantially across regimes. From Models 3 and 4, we also find no evidence that the rate at which the regime is covered alongside sports differs across regimes. From Models 7 and 8, we even find no meaningful difference in the valence of sports coverage that is unrelated to the regime. In all these dimensions, sports coverage looks similar across the most repressive dictatorships, constrained autocracies, and democracies.

Models 5 and 6 reveal dramatic differences in the valence of sports coverage where the regime is implicated. Each five-point increase in the Polity score is associated with a decrease in *Article Valence: Economy$_{js}$* of nearly -1.25 units of our Fox News index. In the most repressive dictatorships, this coverage is nearly 3.7 Fox News units more effusive than in propaganda apparatuses where the Polity score hovers around 4 or 5. This is a large effect, on par with differences in pro-regime coverage documented in Chapter 4. These results suggest sports coverage is

Table 5.8 *The politics of sports propaganda narratives*

	Dependent variable:							
Outcome variable	Rate		Executive references		Article valence			
					Executive		Non-executive	
Unit of analysis Estimator	Country-year OLS (1)	Article Mixed (2)	Country-year OLS (3)	Article Mixed (4)	Country-year OLS (5)	Article Mixed (6)	Country-year OLS (7)	Article Mixed (8)
Polity	−0.001	−0.004***	−0.001	−0.001	−0.027***	−0.023***	−0.004	−0.003***
	(0.004)	(0.0004)	(0.008)	(0.001)	(0.006)	(0.003)	(0.006)	(0.001)
Trade	0.001	0.001***	−0.001	−0.001***	−0.002**	−0.001***	−0.001	−0.0002**
	(0.001)	(0.00003)	(0.001)	(0.0001)	(0.001)	(0.0002)	(0.001)	(0.0001)
Log GDP per capita	0.089**	0.142***	−0.190*	−0.046***	0.025	0.027	−0.002	0.012
	(0.040)	(0.004)	(0.106)	(0.010)	(0.084)	(0.019)	(0.085)	(0.008)
Natural resources	−0.002*	−0.008***	−0.007***	0.003***	0.002	0.001*	0.004*	−0.0004
	(0.001)	(0.0001)	(0.002)	(0.0002)	(0.002)	(0.001)	(0.002)	(0.0002)
Civil war	0.00000	0.022***	−0.059	−0.030***	−0.017	0.068**	0.064*	0.001
	(0.00000)	(0.003)	(0.046)	(0.008)	(0.039)	(0.027)	(0.036)	(0.008)
Internet penetration	0.00002	−0.00000***	−0.00003	−0.00002***	−0.0001**	−0.00003**	−0.00002	−0.00001***
	(0.00002)	(0.00000)	(0.00003)	(0.00000)	(0.00003)	(0.00001)	(0.00003)	(0.00000)
Election	−0.004		−0.008		0.027		−0.010	
	(0.009)		(0.026)		(0.027)		(0.020)	
Election season		−0.011***		0.003		−0.004		−0.016***
		(0.001)		(0.003)		(0.009)		(0.003)
Constant	−0.888**	−1.259***	2.953***	0.714***	0.160	0.115	0.330	0.237***
	(0.408)	(0.089)	(1.039)	(0.122)	(0.832)	(0.193)	(0.962)	(0.084)
Country effects	Fixed	Random	Fixed	Random	Fixed	Random	Fixed	Random
Language-fixed effects		✓		✓		✓		✓
Observations	192	2,442,480	170	304,429	150	25,617	168	278,488
R^2	0.702		0.744		0.936		0.901	

Note: *p < 0.1; **p < 0.05; ***p < 0.01

deeply political but subject to the same forces that drive pro-regime content and propaganda narratives in other issue areas. In the absence of electoral constraints, the valence of sports coverage that implicates the regime is characteristically effusive. Where autocrats confront binding electoral constraints, sports coverage is relatively neutral. This is consistent with the possibility that constrained autocrats use sports coverage to attract readers and that it is subject to the same principles of honest propaganda.

5.7 NATIONAL ATHLETICS IN UGANDA AND THE GAMBIA

To explore these differences, we focus on two of Africa's anglophone autocracies: The Gambia and Uganda. As in Section 5.5, their common language ensures that observed differences in propaganda content are not driven by differences in language of publication. Neither is an athletic powerhouse. Africa's most important sporting event is the African Cup of Nations, played every four years in the run-up to the World Cup. Neither has ever qualified for the World Cup, and neither has fared particularly well in the African Cup of Nations. Uganda last advanced to the final in 1978, which it lost to Ghana, and last advanced to the third-place match in 1962, which it lost to Tunisia. The Gambia has advanced to neither, but its under-17 men's team has recently fared quite well. It won the Africa U-17 Cup of Nations in 2005 and 2009, and in 2005 beat Brazil in the U-17 World Cup. Accordingly, any differences in the valence of sports coverage are unlikely to be driven by their respective national accolades.

The Gambia was ruled by President Yahya Jammeh between his 1994 coup and his decision to flee in 2017; he was widely regarded as among the continent's most repressive dictators. President Yoweri Museveni has ruled Uganda since 1986 and has much in common with Denis Sassou Nguesso. Each has held power for more than three decades, has organized a handful of presidential elections during the twenty-first century, usually claims between 60 percent and 70 percent of the vote, and is positioning his eldest son to succeed him. Each also attempts to avoid outright repression in the hopes of attracting financial support from Western governments. Museveni's propaganda apparatus, our theory suggests, should employ honest propaganda, like Sassou Nguesso's.

The Gambian and Ugandan propaganda apparatuses are profoundly different. One Gambian journalist described Jammeh's media environment this way: "A cloud of fear hovers over the country. Citizens express their true opinions only in safe corners."[83] Another Gambian journalist said:

Journalists in the state-run media and the pro-government private media are notorious for their lack of objectivity and ethical standards, but they are never sanctioned or punished for being [biased]. They are not punished simply because they are vilifying others in the name of and on behalf of the party in government whose [interests] they are promoting.[84]

By contrast, Museveni's *New Vision* is strikingly professional. It was founded in 1955 by the British colonial government and has served as each government's propaganda newspaper since. Its name has evolved. First, it was the *Uganda Argus*; then the *Voice of Uganda*; then the *Uganda Times*; and, since Museveni took power in 1986, *New Vision*. Its parent company, the Vision Group, owns a series of media platforms, is traded publicly on the Uganda Securities Exchange, and releases annual reports to investors that advertise its "vision" and "mission." It aspires to be "a globally respected African media powerhouse" that is "market-focused," "performance-driven," and "managed on global standards of operational and financial efficiency."[85] The Ugandan government is majority shareholder.

New Vision's leadership reflects the intrinsic tension between a legitimate newspaper and a government mouthpiece. William Pike, a British citizen, was editor-in-chief between 1986 and October 2006,[86] and his approach was that of Goebbels:

I always believed that a government newspaper should be like BBC, which broadcasts the negative as well as the positive things about British government, not like Radio Moscow or Voice of America that only reports positive things . . . .

By the time I left, Museveni thought that *New Vision* had become too negative about Uganda. . . . I would argue with Museveni, or the ministers of information, or the chairman of the board, that when you put the negative things in, then the people believe the positive things. If you just put in positive things, people won't take it seriously. . . . Museveni felt that it was time for change.[87]

The government appointed its spokesman, Robert Kabushenga, as CEO, and then lured a Belgian journalist, Els de Temmerman, to become

---

[83] IREX (2014).
[84] IREX (2014).
[85] Vision Group (2017).
[86] Mutegeki (2017).
[87] Opala (2013).

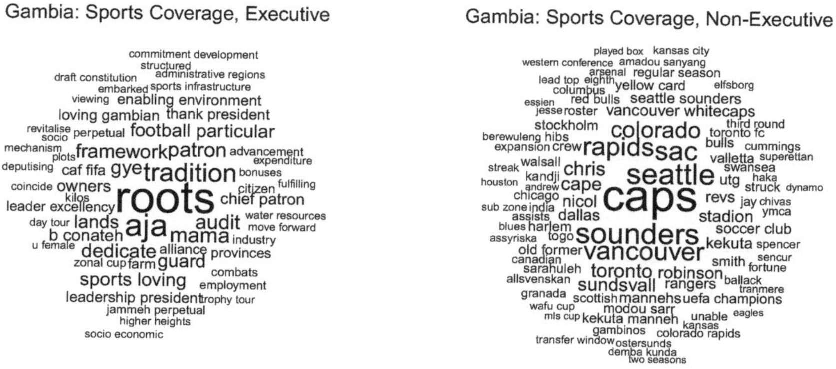

Gambia: Sports Coverage, Executive

Gambia: Sports Coverage, Non-Executive

Figure 5.7 Semantic distinctiveness in sports propaganda in The Gambia

editor-in-chief with written guarantees of independence.[88] De Temmerman resigned in protest in October 2008, returned in February 2009, and resigned again in April 2010.[89] A Ugandan, Barbara Kaija, has been editor-in-chief since.[90]

5.7.1 *The Gambia: "Professor Jammeh as her personal mentor and hero"*

The *Daily Observer* introduces Jammeh as "The President of the Republic, His Excellency Sheikh Professor Alhaji Dr. Yahya A.J.J. Jammeh." We first divide The Gambia's sports propaganda into two categories: articles where *References: Executive$_{ijt}$* ≥ 1 and articles where *References: Executive$_{ijt}$* $= 0$. There were 727 and 3,487 of these documents, respectively. Then we implement our measure of semantic distinctiveness across these two corpora. The results appear in Figure 5.7. The left panel presents distinctive words from sports coverage that references the executive; the right panel presents distinctive words from sports coverage that does not.[91]

Jammeh's propaganda apparatus casts him as the "chief patron" of Gambian sports. He is "sports loving," and his "dedication" has created an "enabling environment" that leads the country's athletics to "higher

[88] de Temmerman (2006).

[89] Njoroge (2010).

[90] Vasher (2015).

[91] We removed executive identifiers from these word clouds, so they contain executive descriptors only.

heights" and merits "thanks." Jammeh gives "bonuses" to athletes who win the "zonal cup" and accompanies them on a "trophy tour" across the country. By contrast, the right panel features words that are more about sports abroad than domestically. It includes references to "Los Angeles," the "Seattle Sounders," "yellow card," "Arsenal," "Kansas City," and "Toronto."

References to Jammeh are clearly absurd. In 2015, a Gambian citizen, Papa Bakary Gassama, was named African Referee of the Year by the Confederation of African Football. In recognition, the *Daily Observer* printed an article more about Jammeh than the awardee:

The 2014 World Cup referee eulogised President Jammeh for the support and encouragement saying the President's advice for him to remain honest and sincere as a referee has always been a motivation.

Papa dedicated the award to the Gambian leader and Gambians as well for obvious reasons. "When I am inside that field, I am not representing myself but my country and I know they are always there for me. Again I would say thank you my father [the President].

Addressing the gathering, the minister of Youth and Sports, Alieu Kebba Jammeh said: "On behalf of His Excellency the President, who you all know is the number one fan and biggest patron of football and sports in general, I take this opportunity to bring you sincere greetings, well wishes and congratulations to Mr. Bakary Papa Gassama. Mr. Gassama has made the entire country proud, but most importantly he has made the President happy and prouder than anybody."

Minister Jammeh added that the President is very passionate, and interested in the development of sports and sportsmen and women of The Gambia. Papa said that before he departed for the World Cup in Brazil last year, the President prayed for him and wished him well and that had very huge positive impact on him. It is my strong belief that any time he sets his feet on that pitch and recalling the words of wisdom from the President, it gives him more courage and determination. So we want to thank the President for being there for us.

The GFF president congratulated Papa Gassama on making The Gambia proud and assured that the Federation is committed to producing more Bakary Papa Gassamas. He urged youths to make best use of the environment created by President Jammeh.[92]

In 2014, the *Daily Observer* ran an article about the newly founded President Yahya Jammeh Football Academy. It celebrated Jammeh's contributions to both Gambian youth and sports:

The founder of President Yahya Jammeh Football Academy has called for concerted efforts in support of grassroots football so as to produce substantial

---

[92] Baboucarr Camara and Alieu Ceesay, "Gambia Celebrates Papa Gassama's CAF Award," *Daily Observer*, February 16, 2015.

amount of young talents that would go on to represent the country at future continental and other international tournaments.

Mariama Njie, who goes by her sobriquet, the girl who loves football, was speaking in an exclusive interview with *Observer Sports* Wednesday morning. Njie who gave an overview of the rationale behind setting up such a vibrant football academy, which she decided to name after the Gambian leader, described Professor Jammeh as her personal mentor and hero. According to her, President Jammeh himself is a sport lover and that it would be only ideal to name a football academy after him.[93]

These articles are typical.

5.7.2 Uganda: "Kipsiro attributed his double-gold winning achievement at the Commonwealth Games to the stability marriage has given him"

As above, we divided Uganda's sports propaganda into two categories: articles where *References: Executive*$_{ijt} \geq 1$ and articles where *References: Executive*$_{ijt} = 0$. Of the 4,460 sports articles in our collection of *New Vision* propaganda, just 105 referenced Museveni or his National Resistance Movement (NRM). That is, while 21 percent of Gambian sports propaganda implicates the regime, just 2.4 percent of Ugandan sports propaganda does. Next, we measured which words are distinctive. The left panel of Figure 5.8 presents distinctive words from sports coverage that references the executive; the right panel presents distinctive words from sports coverage that does not.[94]

To be sure, the two panels reflect important differences. Regime content is more likely to reference the "NRM," "State House," and "excellency," all shorthand for the regime; "ultra modern," which generally refers to construction projects for Ugandan athletics; and "preside," which refers to Museveni or his ministers attending a sporting event. These references are often critical. On October 28, 2010, *New Vision* reported that Museveni "is set to sink the first basket to inaugurate the official opening of the refurbished Lugogo Indoor stadium."[95] In November, *New Vision* published an update: "Barely a month after the renovated Lugogo Indoor stadium was opened by President Yoweri

---

[93] Bekai Njie, "Football Academy Founder Calls for Concerted Efforts," *Daily Observer*, June 12, 2014.

[94] Again, we removed executive identifiers from these word clouds so that they contained executive descriptors only.

[95] Norman Katende, "Museveni to Sink the First Basket at New Stadium," *New Vision*, October 28, 2010.

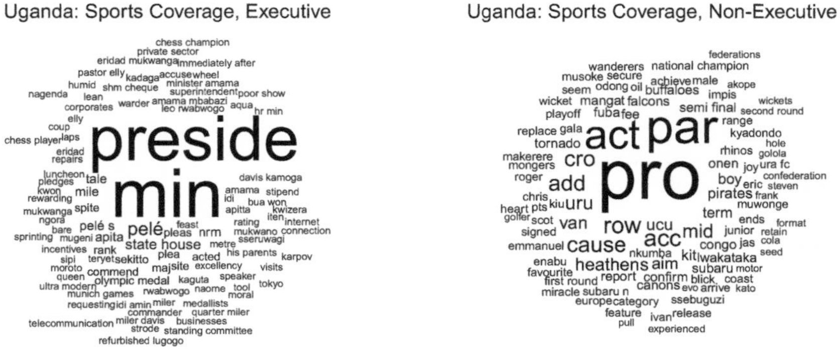

Uganda: Sports Coverage, Executive

Uganda: Sports Coverage, Non-Executive

Figure 5.8 Semantic distinctiveness in sports propaganda in Uganda

Museveni, the floor needs urgent repairs. ... The ultra-modern facility was opened by President Museveni in October but the floor has now developed defects."[96] In February, after the repairs were finished, the newspaper described the "premature opening" of the facility as "one of the biggest blunders." It reported that the chairman of the building committee "conceded that they were pressured into opening the hall. Someone in the sports circles apparently wanted political capital from the grand opening."[97] In short, Museveni's propaganda apparatus linked him to a defective construction project, traced these defects to its premature inauguration, and accused the government of interference.

In contrast to Jammeh's "patronage," *New Vision* covers the government's efforts to encourage private sector investment in Ugandan athletics. Speaking at an event "where he represented President Yoweri Museveni," the housing and urban development minister said this:

Some companies have been sponsoring sports in Uganda but this has been more in a comical way, goat and dog races. For sports to succeed let us not leave it to government and the national budget alone. There is need for more private sector support.[98]

Some articles even feature sports fans making political demands of Museveni. Outraged by their team's exclusion from the Professional Uganda Super League, citizens said this:

---

[96] Usher Komugisha, "Refurbished Lugogo Floor in Sorry State," *New Vision*, November 30, 2010.

[97] James Bakama, "Lugogo Repairs Are a Big Boost," *New Vision*, February 6, 2011.

[98] James Bakama, "Let's Invest in Sports: Atubo," *New Vision*, May 8, 2010.

Football fans in the north have openly told His Excellency Yoweri Kaguta Museveni that "No Boroboro FC in the super league, no votes" in next year's presidential elections.

The locals were telling the president "use your authority to get Boroboro FC back into the league and we use our voting power to get you back into office."

If this were a movie, the title would be "Indecent Proposal." For [Museveni] to get votes, he has to grant the northern club league status but if the unthinkable happens, FIFA will immediately ban Uganda indefinitely for political interference.

If any action has ever really defined what FIFA calls "political" interference, this is it.[99]

Like Jammeh's *Daily Observer*, Museveni's *New Vision* associates him with Uganda's national teams. Again, however, these associations are more distant and conspicuously neutral. Several months before the Lugogo stadium incident, *New Vision* covered the national soccer team's departure for the Commonwealth Games:

The country's Commonwealth Games team will be paraded at the Cranes-Angola match at Namboole [Stadium] in a bid to drum support for the New Dehli bound contingent.

The Games team will walk onto the field and wave to the 40,000 spectators expected for the match. The Cranes face Angola on September 4 in their opening match for the 2012 Nations Cup qualifier. Uganda Olympic Committee vice president Wilson Tumwine said yesterday the team show is aimed at bringing it closer to Ugandans.

President Museveni is expected to flag off the team two weeks before the Games start in New Delhi, India, on October 3. Tumwine said that the contingent will for a fortnight before the Games acclimatize in the Indian capital.[100]

New Vision's subsequent coverage of the Cranes-Angola soccer match is again instructive: "The Cranes and Angola clashed in chaotic style at Mandela National Stadium yesterday and both the performance and overall result must have pleased the almost capacity crowd that included President Yoweri Museveni."[101] The remainder of the article discussed "a series of nervous moments" in the game, a "rescue" staged by goalkeeper Denis Onyango, and the "deserving" win by the Cranes. It otherwise said nothing about Museveni.

---

[99] Aldrine Nsubuga, "Bakkabulindi Is Just Fighting for His Job," *New Vision*, November 13, 2010.

[100] Swalley Kenyi and James Bakama, "Club Games Team to Grace Angola Match," *New Vision*, August 24, 2010.

[101] Fred Kaweesi, "Cranes Humiliates Angola in 3-0 Win," *New Vision*, September 4, 2010.

The Commonwealth Games concluded on October 14, and Moses Kipsiro, a long-distance runner who nearly medaled in the 2008 Olympics, emerged as Uganda's national hero. *New Vision* covered his homecoming:

Kipsiro is set to be welcomed back today by a mammoth crowd at Entebbe Airport. He will then head to State House, where he is expected to meet President Yoweri Kaguta Museveni before attending a welcome cocktail party for the entire delegation at Lugogo.

It will be a rewarding return for the soft-speaking athlete, who confessed that his marriage to wife Benna Chebet had been the turning point to all his recent achievements.

Kipsiro has attributed his double-gold winning achievement at the Commonwealth Games to the stability marriage to his childhood sweetheart has given him.[102]

The Gambian propaganda apparatus casts its sports heroes as attributing their success to Jammeh. Museveni's *New Vision* casts Uganda's heroes as attributing their success to their families.

Kipsiro met with Museveni, as expected, and afterwards *New Vision* published an op-ed that criticized Museveni's sycophants and his willingness to surround himself with them:

After Melbourne 2006 [Commonwealth Games], we were invited for a state dinner at Nakasero. The visit left the impression that politicians have to lie to get their way.

The President's invitation was a good gesture, but as usual, politicking took over and speakers took centre stage to peddle lies.

One high-profile person started off by telling the President that his good governance and immunisation policy had kicked polio out of Uganda and as such, medals have started trickling in. How I wish this person had talked about a sports policy.

The President went to greet Boniface Kiprop and Dorcus Inzikuru, the 2006 gold medallists, and asked them when they were born. They were all outside the time bracket of the said immunisation policy.

I believe the President, who seems willing to do something about sports, usually gets people who hoodwink him into politics, causing him to miss important information about problems on the ground.

Our stars of 2006 are in oblivion. Let the President know that the money was swindled and we had to beg for support from the Indian community.[103]

---

[102] Norman Katende, "Moses Kipsiro Attributes Glory to Marriage," *New Vision*, October 16, 2010.

[103] James William Mugeni, "Sports Fraternity Want to Meet President Museveni," *New Vision*, October 16, 2010.

New Vision covers Museveni's financial gifts to Ugandan athletes. Again, however, this coverage is occasionally critical. Museveni gave a reward of about $5,500 to Kipsiro following the Commonwealth Games, and suggested that other "outstanding sportsmen" be offered stipends and government employment. *New Vision* then criticized Museveni for not giving enough: "There are reports that some of the best Kenya athletes are actually Ugandans who chose to cross the border because of better rewards."[104] In 2012, *New Vision* reported, "President Yoweri Museveni concedes that not much has been invested in the sports sector. ... Experts believe that what sports needs is not only a more serious policy but more investment. The [$900,000] that is allocated to sports annually is peanuts."[105]

5.7.3 Comparing Sentiments in Executive Coverage

The propaganda excerpts above suggest our data should register a difference in the sentiments associated with Yoweri Museveni and Yahya Jammeh in their respective propaganda apparatuses. To probe this, we restricted attention to sports content and then extracted the twenty words surrounding each reference to Museveni or Jammeh. Next, we used the Harvard General Inquirer (2015) linguistic dictionary to capture the sentiments of these twenty words. We estimated models of the form

$$Y_{ij} = \alpha + \beta X_{ij} + \epsilon \qquad (5.14)$$

where i indexes article, j indexes country, and X_{ij} is an indicator that assumes value 1 was published by the Ugandan propaganda apparatus and value 0 otherwise. The outcome variable Y_{ij} measures the number of words associated with each of our sentiment dictionaries in article ij, standardized by the number of executive references in the same article. This yielded a per reference rate of sentiment association.

The results appear at the top of Figure 5.9. Sentiments associated with Yahya Jammeh have negative coefficients, whereas sentiments associated with Yoweri Museveni have positive coefficients. The results are consistent with our theory and the propaganda above. The *Daily Observer* is distinctive for the extent to which it casts Jammeh as virtuous,

---

[104] James Bakama, "Gov't to Takeover Cranes Coach Welfare," *New Vision*, November 12, 2011.

[105] James Bakama, "Uganda Sports Excellence, Failure over Past 50 Years," *New Vision*, October 9, 2012.

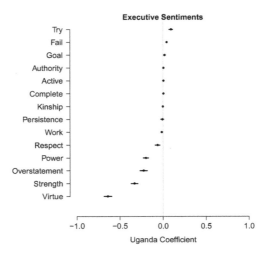

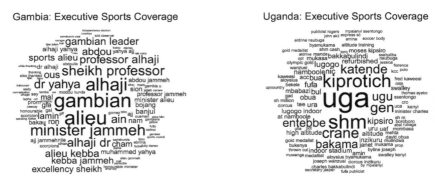

Figure 5.9 Regime coverage in sports propaganda in Uganda and The Gambia

strong, and powerful. On average, each reference to Jammeh has 0.5 more words that reflect those three sentiments than each reference to Museveni. The bottom-left and -right panels, respectively, display distinctive words from the concordance segments surrounding executive identifiers in The Gambia and Uganda. These distinctive words reflect the regression results. Distinctive words surrounding references to Museveni are overwhelmingly about legitimate sports content: the names of teams, athletes, and the like. Distinctive words surrounding references to Jammeh are either honorifics or absurd expressions of gratitude from citizens.

5.8 CONCLUSION

Some 20 percent of propaganda content makes no reference to the autocrat or ruling party, and about 50 percent makes no reference to the regime. Autocrats *pay* to produce content that seldom covers them, their regimes, or their opposition rivals. To capture the narrative subtleties embedded within millions of propaganda articles, we paired our global data with Kessler's (2017; 2018*b*) work on semantic distinctiveness. We found dramatic variation in propaganda narratives across autocracies. In the absence of electoral constraints, narratives are absurd. Citizens are routinely told that their economies are growing rapidly, despite global financial crises, and that their repressive governments are global icons of democracy. These propaganda apparatuses omit the actual stuff of democracy: electoral campaigns, political parties, and opposition leaders. The dictator is cast as a champion of the country's athletes, whose achievements are due to his patronage.

Where binding electoral constraints force propaganda apparatuses to seek credibility, narratives are profoundly different. Propaganda apparatuses cover devastating fuel crises, persistently high mortality rates, vaccine shortages, and the government's failure to diversify the economy. The valence bias of economic coverage in constrained autocracies is roughly equal to the valence bias in pro-regime coverage: comparable to a single unit of our Fox News index. Electoral campaigns are covered extensively and depict the autocrat asking for citizens' trust and opposition leaders alleging widespread corruption. Sports are covered with relative neutrality as a way to induce readers to consume propaganda otherwise meant to persuade them of useful fictions.

In Chapter 6, we shift attention to propaganda narratives about international affairs.

6

Narrating the World

6.1 WHERE PROPAGANDA STRATEGIES CONVERGE

American citizens know surprisingly little about the world beyond their borders. In July 2017, just 60 percent of Americans knew that the United Kingdom had voted to leave the European Union, and just 37 percent knew that Emmanuel Macron was the president of France.[1] In 2011, nearly a quarter of American citizens were unaware that the United States claimed independence from Great Britain. *Forbes* called the American public "indifferent";[2] the Cato Institute diagnosed an "attention deficit."[3] *Foreign Policy* once published a story with this headline: "8 Crazy Things Americans Believe about Foreign Policy."[4] In this, Americans are not unique. Citizens around the world simply know less about life abroad.[5]

This uncertainty about life abroad has two theoretical implications for propaganda in autocracies. First, absurd propaganda requires common knowledge of the possible: a shared sense among citizens for what claims are absurd. This condition is more easily satisfied for domestic affairs than international affairs. Chinese citizens have a shared sense for domestic unemployment but not the depth of racial tensions in the United States or the flaws of American democracy. Second, the constraints on honest propaganda are weaker, and so propaganda apparatuses can be more critical in their coverage about international news without undermining their reputations for credibility. Theoretically, these two forces render

---

[1] Pew Research Center (2015).
[2] Friedman (2014).
[3] Thrall (2018).
[4] Friedman (2012).
[5] Pew Research Center (2013); Huang (2015a, 2020).

international news propaganda across autocracies more similar than domestic propaganda. Where electoral constraints are binding, propaganda apparatuses can be more critical without undermining their credibility. Where electoral constraints are non-binding, propaganda apparatuses have less access to absurd propaganda since what constitutes absurdity is unclear.

What autocrats tell their citizens about the international community – and their engagement with it – remains largely undocumented,[6] despite constituting 20 percent of all propaganda content. We distinguish two types of international propaganda. *International news* focuses on domestic conditions in foreign countries or their foreign policies. *International cooperation* focuses on a regime's engagement with the international community: its foreign policy, relationships with international allies, and partnerships with international institutions.

This chapter documents two tactics that mark international news propaganda across autocracies: *comparison sets* and *selective coverage*. The former entails critical coverage of the foreign countries against which citizens judge their own; the latter entails omitting events abroad that might exacerbate citizens' grievances or inspire protests. Empirically, we supplement our global dataset with a comparison of propaganda apparatuses in Russia and China, the world's most geopolitically important autocracies. We focus on the period between 2016 and 2017, which encompasses terrorist attacks across Europe, the Brexit referendum in the United Kingdom, and the rise of far-right politicians across Western democracies, several of whom seemed strikingly uncommitted to democracy itself. To the best of our knowledge, this constitutes the first account of what the Russian propaganda apparatus told citizens about Donald Trump's campaign for the American presidency. Trump, we show, is effectively a tool of Russian propaganda, quoted as saying precisely what it has long reported. Using tools from network analysis, we show that Trump occupies the central node in Vladimir Putin's international news narrative. The *People's Daily* is less enamored with Trump, but its coverage of Western democracies is similarly critical. The CCP routinely suggests American democracy has been corrupted by special interests, including the National Rifle Association, which it partly blames for America's gun violence epidemic.

---

[6] For notable exceptions, see Brady (2002, 2008); Rozenas and Stukal (2018), and Field et al. (2018).

For a regime's international engagements, common knowledge of the possible is more likely to obtain and the constraints on honest propaganda are again more binding. Accordingly, propaganda narratives about international cooperation resemble domestic propaganda narratives. Where electoral constraints are binding, propaganda apparatuses can cover the regime's pursuit of the national interest: their efforts to partner with the international community to advance domestic welfare or combat terrorism. To be credible, this coverage must be paired with policy failures or bad news: persistent shortcomings in domestic health care or persistent frustrations of ethnic minorities who occasionally use violence to compel policy change. Where electoral constraints are non-binding, propaganda apparatuses again signal the regime's capacity for violence. They do so partly by broadcasting the regime's international standing and hence their immunity from international sanctions. If citizens protest, the propaganda apparatus implicitly argues, the international community will not intervene to protect them. The nature of these signals varies according to a regime's international position. In lower-income autocracies, propaganda apparatuses publish letters (ostensibly) from Xi Jinping, Vladimir Putin, and Barack Obama, which convey their great personal esteem. The CCP's propaganda apparatus has no need to publish these letters, since it can highlight its creation of a new international order that privileges "non-intervention" and "sovereignty," rather than universal human rights norms.

Empirically, we supplement our global dataset with two paired comparisons: one for high-income autocracies and another for low-income autocracies. The first paired comparison again focuses on Russia and China, which reveals that what autocrats tell their citizens about the world is related to what they tell citizens about their engagement with it. The CCP's propaganda apparatus casts it as the central node in a refashioned international order. The second paired comparison focuses on Congo and Uzbekistan. Each has sought a closer relationship with the CCP, and each was visited by Republican Dana Rohrabacher, regarded as "Putin's best friend" in the American Congress until his November 2018 defeat.

This chapter proceeds as follows. Sections 6.2 and 6.3 probe the politics of international news propaganda: the former with our global dataset, and the latter with a paired comparison of Russia and China. Sections 6.4 through 6.6 turn to foreign policy narratives. Section 6.4 does so with our global dataset; Section 6.5 returns to Russia and China; and Section 6.6 returns to Congo and Uzbekistan.

6.2 INTERNATIONAL NEWS: THEORY AND CROSS-COUNTRY EVIDENCE

6.2.1 Theory

Recall from Chapter 2 that citizens update their beliefs about the regime's performance θ_D by using Bayes' Rule. Citizens have some prior belief μ_D^0 about θ_D, and they update it based on the content of the autocrat's propaganda and the credibility they attach to it. Citizens may use other sources of information to update their beliefs. They may have access to independent newspapers, which offer a competing narrative of the country's history and domestic conditions. They may have access to information about foreign countries, which, if better off, may cast the regime in a poor light.[7]

This is why autocrats censor independent news sources and content from abroad.[8] It is also why autocrats use propaganda to shape citizens' beliefs about the domestic conditions of foreign countries. Autocrats do so with two tactics. The first is *comparison sets*. To determine whether economic stagnation is driven by regime failures or an exogenous shock, citizens may look to comparable countries, such as regional neighbors.[9] In Central Africa, Rwandan president Paul Kagame is widely esteemed for having engineered an economic miracle after the 1994 genocide.[10] Citizens across the region see powerful images of Kigali's clean streets and towering skyline, and judge their own governments worse by comparison.[11] Comparison sets may comprise geopolitical rivals or countries with similar histories. Russian citizens may compare their domestic conditions to those in the United States or in Western Europe. Chinese citizens may look to post-communist countries in Eastern Europe for cues about life after communist governments fall.[12] Brady (2002, 568)

---

[7] Besley and Case (1995); Easterlin (1995); Duch and Stevenson (2008); Kayser and Peress (2012); Huang (2015a).

[8] King, Pan, and Roberts (2013); Shadmehr and Bernhardt (2015); Huang (2015a); Huang and Yeh (2016); Qin, Strömberg, and Wu (2017); Roberts (2018); Gallagher and Miller (2019).

[9] Kayser and Peress (2012).

[10] Rwanda's GDP statistics appear to have been fabricated since 2005; see Anonymous (2017, 2019).

[11] Interview with anonymous opposition activist, Brazzaville, Congo.

[12] Przeworski (1986); Shi, Lu, and Aldrich (2011); Huang (2015a); Robertson (2017).

observes that the CCP propaganda apparatus covers "chaos" in Eastern Europe, which "is deliberately contrasted with an incessant barrage of positive stories on China's 'economic prosperity and 'ethnic harmony.'"[13] This is one reason why the CCP releases an annual report on human rights in the United States. Its epigraph in 2020: "I can't breathe," a reference to George Floyd's plea to Minneapolis police before his murder.[14]

The second tactic is *selective coverage*. When covering foreign countries, propaganda apparatuses may omit events that exacerbate citizens' grievances or compel them to engage in anti-regime behavior. Propaganda apparatuses may omit coverage of electoral politics in foreign countries, perhaps to avoid reminding citizens of past electoral fraud or related grievances. Propaganda apparatuses may also omit coverage of foreign citizens attempting to overthrow their own governments, perhaps via mass protests or other forms of violence. Note that this form of selective coverage may be in tension with the comparison set tactic described above. The CCP propaganda apparatus, for instance, has an interest in portraying democracies as plagued by corruption and injustice, as evidenced by Black Lives Matter protests in the United States or anti-corruption protests in South Korea. Our theory suggests an important distinction: between instability abroad that aims to topple governments and instability abroad that reflects the failures of democracies, which may constitute an autocratic regime's comparison set.

Our theory traces variation in propaganda strategies across autocracies to differences in electoral constraints. As we discussed in Section 6.1, however, citizens generally know less about international affairs than domestic conditions.[15] This is why the Russian government's outward-facing propaganda – lead by RT, the outlet formerly known as *Russia Today*, which in 2017 had a budget of $327 million[16] – has a stronger effect on Americans' opinions about foreign policy than domestic conditions.[17] This uncertainty about conditions abroad makes propaganda narratives about international news analytically distinct from propaganda narratives about domestic conditions. Where electoral constraints are binding, propaganda apparatuses are able to "get away" with more

---

[13] Note that Stockmann (2013) attributes negative coverage of the United States in CCP propaganda to its citizens' preferences, not the CCP's political strategy.

[14] The State Council Information Office of the People's Republic China (2021, 1).

[15] Druckman and Leeper (2012); Huang (2015a); Huang and Yeh (2016).

[16] Erlanger (2017). We discuss RT in more detail in Chapter 11.

[17] Carter and Carter (2021a).

negative coverage about international affairs without undermining their claims to neutrality. Where electoral constraints are non-binding, absurd propaganda is more difficult to employ, since citizens lack a shared sense of what claims are absurd. For these two reasons, our theory suggests propaganda narratives about international news should be more similar across autocracies than propaganda narratives about domestic conditions.

The two tactics above – comparison sets and selective coverage – are useful to autocrats regardless of the electoral institutions they confront. Insofar as citizens are willing to incur the risks of protest in proportion to the likelihood of better living standards under democracy, autocrats have powerful incentives to shape citizens' beliefs about democracies: whether by omitting coverage of topics that might aggravate their citizens' grievances or by allocating more attention to political corruption in Western democracies.[18] For unconstrained autocracies, however, this poses a challenge. The reason is that claims about comparison set countries – which are useful for citizens to believe – sit alongside claims about domestic conditions that citizens know are false. This juxtaposition requires that propaganda apparatuses in unconstrained autocracies somehow provide citizens with evidence that comparison set claims are credible, even while claims about domestic conditions are not. Again, the CCP's annual report on human rights in the United States is instructive. It substantiated its claims about the Trump administration's failures by citing a list of verifiable statistics about its response to the COVID-19 pandemic. These verifiable statistics appeared on the report's very first page, just below its allusions to George Floyd's death at the knee of a Minneapolis police officer:

The epidemic went out of control and turned into a human tragedy due to the government's reckless response. By the end of February 2021, the United States, home to less than 5 percent of the world's population, accounted for more than a quarter of the world's confirmed COVID-19 cases and nearly one-fifth of the global deaths from the disease. More than 500,000 Americans lost their lives due to the virus.[19]

As our theory suggests and our survey experiment in Chapter 4 documented, Chinese citizens find the CCP's pro-regime propaganda threatening, not persuasive. That is why the CCP must substantiate its claims about comparison set countries.

---

[18] Diamond (2015); Huang (2015a).
[19] The State Council Information Office of the People's Republic of China (2021, 1).

Hypothesis 6.1: *Propaganda apparatuses across autocracies should attempt to manipulate their citizens' beliefs about living standards in comparison set countries by covering them more negatively and make these claims credible.*

Hypothesis 6.2: *Propaganda apparatuses across autocracies should engage in selective coverage of foreign affairs by omitting topics that exacerbate citizens' grievances and encourage protests.*

6.2.2 Data and Estimation Strategy

Knowing which countries constitute a comparison set for country j is difficult. Comparison sets may differ dramatically across countries and change over time. Therefore, to test Hypothesis 6.1, we restricted attention to all international news articles published by country j's propaganda apparatus, as identified by the multi-label classifier we described in Chapter 3. Then, for each international news article i, we computed the total number of positive less negative words, standardized by the total number of dictionary hits:

$$\text{Article Valence: International News}_{ijt}$$
$$= \frac{\text{Positive Words}_{ijt} - \text{Negative Words}_{ijt}}{\text{Positive Words}_{ijt} + \text{Negative Words}_{ijt}} \quad (6.1)$$

This variable is analogous to our second measure of pro-regime propaganda, *Article Valence: Regime*$_{ijt}$, and the measures of aggregate article valence we employed in Chapter 5. It gives the aggregate valence of all international news coverage, by article, published by the state-run or state-affiliated newspaper in country j.

To test Hypothesis 6.2, we again restricted attention to international news articles and then recorded whether those articles also focus on topics that might exacerbate citizens' grievances or embolden protests. We focused on two topics. First, propaganda apparatuses may avoid covering electoral politics abroad, since citizens lack the ability to choose their leaders through free and fair elections. The variable *International News: Elections & Democracy*$_{ijt}$ assumes value 1 if article i reports on electoral politics abroad and 0 otherwise. Second, propaganda apparatuses may omit coverage of civil disobedience abroad to prevent the demonstration effects that accompanied the fall of the Soviet Union and the Arab

Spring.[20] To capture this, we created *International News: Protests$_{ijt}$*, which assumes value 1 if article i covered anti-regime protests in foreign countries and 0 otherwise.

We employed the same estimating strategy as in Chapters 4 and 5. We estimate country-year and article-level models for each outcome of interest. For the country-year models, since measures of electoral constraints are observed by year, we computed country-year means for our propaganda variables, which were measured at the article or day level. The model is

$$Y_{js} = \alpha + \beta X_{js} + \phi W_{js} + \gamma_j + \epsilon \tag{6.2}$$

where j indexes country, s indexes year, X_{js} measures electoral constraints, and the vector W_{js} gives our standard set of controls. Country-fixed effects, γ_j, accommodate systematic differences across languages and unobserved differences across countries. Since these outcomes are continuous, we employed OLS with robust standard errors clustered by country. For article-level models, we employed mixed effects estimators to accommodate our article-level propaganda variables and country-year–level explanatory variables. The model is

$$Y_{ijt} = \alpha + \beta X_{is} + \kappa Z_{it} + \phi W_{is} + \gamma_k + \gamma_j + \epsilon \tag{6.3}$$

where the vectors Z_{it} and W_{is}, respectively, give day- and year-level controls; γ_k gives language-fixed effects; and γ_j country-random effects.

6.2.3 Results

The results appear in Table 6.1. From Models 1 and 2, we find no difference in the rate of international news coverage across state-run newspapers in autocracies and state-affiliated newspapers in democracies. Rather, the best predictor of international news coverage is the size of a country's economy. For each country in our dataset, the top panel of Figure 6.1 presents mean GDP per capita during the sample period along the x-axis and the rate of international news coverage along the y-axis. For clarity, we overlay a fitted OLS regression line. International news propaganda is almost entirely the province of high-income countries. This makes sense. International news requires foreign

---

[20] Beissinger (2002); Steinert-Threlkeld et al. (2015).

Table 6.1 The politics of international news propaganda narratives

	Dependent variable:							
Outcome variable	Rate		Article valence		Elections & Democracy		Protest	
Unit of analysis Estimator	Country-year OLS	Article Mixed	Country-year OLS	Article Mixed	Country-year OLS	Article Mixed	Country-year OLS	Article Mixed
	(1)	(2)	(3)	(4)	(5)	(6)	(7)	(8)
Polity	-0.00005 (0.001)	-0.0001 (0.0001)	0.060*** (0.020)	0.022*** (0.008)	-0.014 (0.048)	0.011*** (0.004)	0.057** (0.029)	0.001 (0.001)
Trade	-0.0002* (0.0001)	-0.0001*** (0.00001)	-0.001 (0.002)	-0.001*** (0.0002)	0.0005 (0.004)	-0.001*** (0.0002)	-0.001 (0.002)	0.00002 (0.00004)
Log GDP per capita	-0.004 (0.007)	-0.001 (0.001)	0.118 (0.133)	0.027 (0.033)	0.414 (0.317)	0.070*** (0.021)	0.242 (0.190)	0.002 (0.004)
Natural resources	0.001*** (0.0002)	0.0003*** (0.00003)	0.004 (0.004)	-0.001 (0.001)	-0.008 (0.010)	-0.003*** (0.001)	0.004 (0.006)	-0.0001 (0.0001)
Civil war	-0.00004 (0.004)	-0.002** (0.001)	-0.003 (0.072)	-0.009 (0.024)	0.430** (0.172)	-0.002 (0.028)	-0.065 (0.103)	-0.001 (0.006)
Internet penetration	-0.00000 (0.00000)	-0.00000*** (0.00000)	-0.00001 (0.0001)	-0.00004 (0.00002)	-0.0001 (0.0002)	0.0001** (0.00003)	0.00001 (0.0001)	-0.00001 (0.00001)
Election	0.0005 (0.002)		-0.039 (0.048)		0.014 (0.115)		0.015 (0.069)	
Election season		-0.001** (0.0004)		0.005 (0.011)		0.005 (0.014)		0.003 (0.003)
Constant	0.061 (0.069)	0.034*** (0.011)	-1.638 (1.444)	-0.048 (0.338)	-3.883 (3.459)	-0.482** (0.208)	-2.883 (2.072)	-0.015 (0.038)
Country effects	Fixed	Random	Fixed	Random	Fixed	Random	Fixed	Random
Language-fixed effects		✓		✓		✓		✓
Observations	192	2,442,480	80	21,193	80	21,203	80	21,203
R²	0.823		0.938		0.606		0.282	

Note: *p < 0.1; **p < 0.05; ***p < 0.01

236

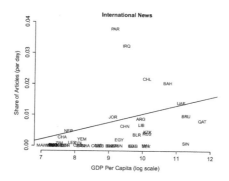

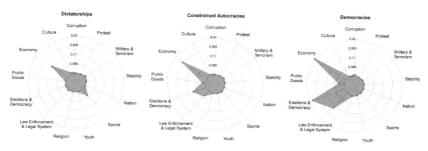

Figure 6.1 Descriptive statistics for international news propaganda

correspondents, subscriptions to wire services, and other costly investments, which may be beyond the means of propaganda apparatuses in
low-income countries.

The relative lack of international news coverage in low-income countries reduces our sample size in Models 3, 5, and 7. Still, the results
across models are consistent with our theory. Models 3 and 4 confirm the
salience of comparison sets. Propaganda apparatuses in autocracies cover
foreign countries with a negativity unmatched in democracies. The effect
is large. Each five-point increase in the Polity score is associated with a
decrease in *Article Valence: International News$_{js}$* of between 1.0 and 2.7
units of our Fox News index. In the most repressive dictatorships, this
coverage is between three and eight Fox News units more critical than
that in more constrained autocracies.

Models 5 through 8 confirm the salience of selective coverage. Although Model 5 is indistinguishable from 0, Model 6 suggests that
propaganda apparatuses are more likely to cover democratic politics
abroad where electoral constraints are more binding. Each five-point increase in the Polity score is associated with a 6 percent increase in the

likelihood a given article *i* about international news focuses on democratic politics abroad. Model 7 suggests that propaganda apparatuses are more likely to cover foreign protests where electoral constraints are more binding as well. Here, each five-point increase in the Polity score is associated with a nearly 30 percent increase in the share of international news coverage about foreign protests.

These differences appear in the raw data. The left panel of Figure 6.1 presents a radar chart that gives the share of international news articles that focus on the topics around the perimeter. In democracies, roughly 20 percent of international news coverage focuses on democratic politics abroad. In unconstrained autocracies, this figure is just 2 percent. In democracies, roughly 1 percent of international news coverage focuses on protests abroad. In unconstrained autocracies, this figure is just 0.5 percent. In each case, constrained autocracies constitute a midpoint.

6.3 THE FLAWS OF WESTERN DEMOCRACIES, AS TOLD BY RUSSIA AND CHINA

What do these two tactics – comparison sets and selective coverage – look like in practice? To document this, we focus on the world's most geopolitically important autocracies: China and Russia. We do so for two reasons. First, notwithstanding the different electoral constraints their respective governments confront, they occupy similar positions in the international system. They have nuclear weapons. They are permanent members of the United Nations Security Council. They are both rivals to the United States for global leadership. Second, given their geopolitical relevance, what their propaganda apparatuses tell citizens about conditions abroad – especially in the United States and Western Europe – is of intrinsic interest.

We read hundreds of international news articles from the Chinese and Russian propaganda apparatuses. In so doing, we identified a set of topics that were salient in each. The most common appear at the top of Figure 6.2 as a share of all international news topics. The bottom panel displays the most commonly covered countries as a share of all foreign references.[21]

---

[21] To make the top panel, we randomly sampled a 300 document training set of Russian international news articles. We machine translated these into English, inductively applied as many topic labels as appropriate, and classified the remaining international news articles with our standard multi-label classifier. We repeated this process for China's international news coverage. To make the bottom panel,

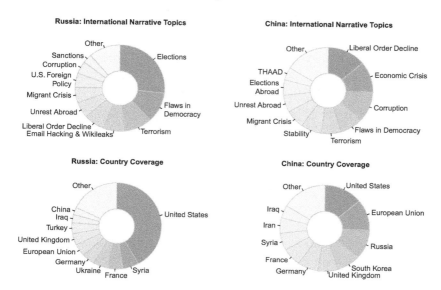

Figure 6.2 International news propaganda in Russia and China

The conspicuous feature is their similarity. Both countries cover the corruption of American democracy, the crises tearing at the EU, the Western foreign policy errors that destabilize the international system, and the decline of the liberal international order. Here, their propaganda narratives diverge in ways that anticipate the divergent foreign policy narratives we discuss in Section 6.5. *Rossiskaya Gazeta* celebrates the liberal order's decline, as the dissolution of NATO and the EU will give way to a multipolar world in which Western governments will no longer "impose" their "ideological values" on Russia. The *People's Daily* is less sanguine, since the CCP aims to revise the international order, not dismantle it: to maintain the trading system that underpins China's economic growth but replace universal human rights norms with a commitment to national sovereignty.[22]

The topics and countries in Figure 6.2 are routinely linked, and these links reveal narrative subtleties. To capture linkages, we treated international news propaganda as a weighted network, with nodes given by topics, countries, and international institutions. Edges between nodes

we translated the Correlates of War list of country names into Russian, counted the number of times each country name was referenced in Russia's international news coverage, and then repeated the process for China.

[22] Piccone (2018).

represent the number of articles in which two nodes co-occur. We restricted attention to 2016 and 2017, encompassing a series of elections and terrorist attacks across Western democracies.[23] Throughout, we refer to Figures 6.4 and 6.6, which use our measure of semantic distinctiveness to identify the distinctive words in Russia's international news propaganda relative to China's. The left panels focus on aggregate coverage; the right panels focus on coverage of the United States.

6.3.1 *Russia: Donald Trump, Russian Propaganda Tool*

Figure 6.3 visualizes the network for *Rossiskaya Gazeta*. Its central node is Donald Trump, featured in 80 percent of its coverage. For Russian propaganda, as we discuss below, Donald Trump is profoundly vindicating. We focus on three aspects of this narrative: decay within Western democracies, their foreign policy failures, and the liberal international order's decline.

The European Union as a "House of Cards" Rossiskaya Gazeta casts European integration as an elite-led project, which forced on Europeans a "neoliberal ideology" that is incompatible with the "traditional values" of "European civilization." In foreign policy, Europe's elite subordinated themselves to the United States at the expense of ordinary citizens. This narrative was captured in an interview with Alexei Pushkov, chairman of the Duma Committee on International Affairs between 2011 and 2016:

> Until recently, Europe had two sacred cows: its commitment to globalization and its neoliberal ideology. But it turns out that both contradict democracy and European identity. Europeans' resistance to globalization is so great that it had to be imposed on them through deception. .... Five years ago, there were two visions of the European Union. One was a Europe of nations. The other was a United States of Europe .... This United States of Europe has effectively been rejected by modern history.[24]

To substantiate its rejection, *Rossiskaya Gazeta* focuses on four related topics. The migrant crisis accounts for 40 percent of European coverage, and it contributed to a spike in domestic terrorism, featured in 25 percent

---

[23] For clarity, we omitted nodes that were referenced in fewer than 1 percent of articles.

[24] Ariadna Rokossovskaya, "Brussels Deadlock," *Rossiskaya Gazeta*, May 24, 2016.

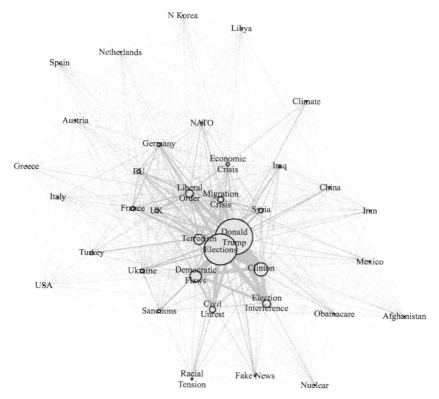

Figure 6.3 International news propaganda in Russia as a weighted network

of European coverage. The left panel of Figure 6.4 reflects this: "terrorist act," "tragedy," "explosion," "bomb," "were injured," "IGIL," and "banned." The latter two are tightly linked, for *Rossiskaya Gazeta*'s references to the Islamic State are generally followed by "(banned in Russia)." This excerpt followed the July 2016 attack in Nice, France, which claimed eighty-six lives:

President François Hollande called this terrorist attack an act of absolute cruelty. ... According to Hollande, the attack was obviously an act of terrorism. ... France decided to extend the state of emergency for another three months. It was introduced in November last year after the terrorist attack in Paris.[25]

---

[25] Nadezhda Yermolaeva, "Death Toll from Terrorist Attack in Nice Increases to 84 People," *Rossiskaya Gazeta*, July 15, 2016.

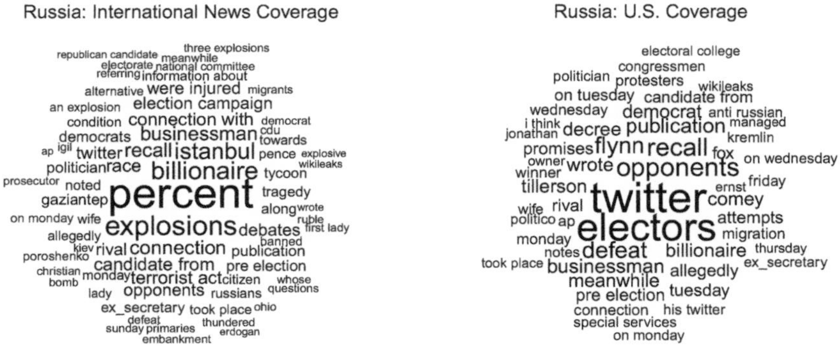

Figure 6.4 Semantic distinctiveness in Russia's international news propaganda

It later inflated the death toll: "More than a hundred people were killed."[26]

Coverage of foreign terrorism spikes during domestic crises. In April 2012, after a citizen of Kyrgyz extraction detonated a bomb in St. Petersburg, *Rossiskaya Gazeta* recalled attacks in Sweden, Egypt, Turkey, and Germany. "A series of terrorist attacks has swept the world. . . . It seems there are no safe places on the planet."[27] *Rossiskaya Gazeta* often cites ostensibly objective international experts to substantiate its claims, as Lasswell (1938, 88–92) instructed. After the Nice bombing, it quoted Tom Fuentes, a former FBI official and member of Interpol's executive board: "Homebred terrorism is a serious problem in Europe."[28]

The third key topic is the European elite's failure to abide citizens' preferences, which implicitly underscores the shortcomings of European democracy. Europe's leaders are unwilling, for instance, to acknowledge that their immigration policies contribute to domestic terrorism:

German authorities were in no hurry to recognize the tragedy in the square as a terrorist act, although the parallels with the attack in Nice that claimed the lives of many people were obvious: the same method, the same blind violence, the same hatred.[29]

---

[26] Nadezhda Yermolaeva, "Police Detain One during Nice Search," *Rossiskaya Gazeta*, July 15, 2016.

[27] "Explosion in the Metro in St. Petersburg," *Rossiskaya Gazeta*, April 13, 2012.

[28] "Terrorist Attack in Nice," *Rossiskaya Gazeta*, July 15, 2016.

[29] Ekaterina Zabrodina, Anna Rose, "Terrorist Attack before Christmas," *Rossiskaya Gazeta*, December 20, 2016. The article goes on to cite other terrorist plots, each linked to an immigrant or refugee.

Europe's leaders also forced on citizens "a notorious political correctness" that is inconsistent with the "traditional values" of "European civilization":

America's globalist project implies new values that all European societies must joyfully embrace. In France, the Hollande administration took advantage of its majority in parliament to legalize same-sex marriage, ... even though most citizens were against it. This led to massive demonstrations and clashes with the riot police.[30]

The economic policies favored by the European elite have proven equally damaging, the article continued:

The French have rejected the political program to which François Hollande adhered, as well as the leadership of many European countries. [The EU] has a socio-economic policy that prevented France from emerging from the long economic downturn, which naturally led to social discontent.

Angela Merkel is among *Rossiskaya Gazeta*'s common targets. This is why her Christian Democratic Union (CDU) appears on the left of Figure 6.4:

[A German newspaper] asked readers to vote for the least honest politician. The list included dozens of candidates from around the world. More than 3,000 people voted. ...The most deceitful politician, according to the poll: Chancellor Angela Merkel.[31]

To underscore the EU's flaws, *Rossiskaya Gazeta* allocates 12 percent of its European coverage to Greece, always for the migrant crisis or the financial crisis that nearly culminated in Grexit.[32]

The heroes in the struggle for Europe's soul are its far-right, Euroskeptic parties. Their ascension is partly why 90 percent of *Rossiskaya Gazeta*'s European coverage focuses on electoral politics. Austria, Europe's twelfth largest economy, is covered as often as Italy, and often features Norbert Hofer, leader of the Freedom Party: "Hofer warned his fellow citizens against the loss of their Austrian values due to

---

[30] Ariadna Rokossovskaya, "Alexey Pushkov: When the Dominant Trend in the United States Changes, European Politics Inevitably Adapts to It," *Rossiskaya Gazeta*, December 20, 2016.

[31] Anna Fedyakina, "Readers of the German Media Have Chosen 'Liars of the Year' among Politicians," *Rossiskaya Gazeta*, December 13, 2015.

[32] Maxim Makarychev, "Bloomberg Predicted the Presidency of Le Pen and the Withdrawal of France from the European Union," *Rossiskaya Gazeta*, December 7, 2016.

new migration."[33] Austria is part of "a clear trend ... challenging the dictatorship of liberal democracy."[34] In The Netherlands, "Gert Wilders hopes to save his compatriots from Brussels."[35] In Hungary, where Putin ally Viktor Orbán holds power, "not by chance, ... marriage is defined as a union between a man and a woman."[36] These parties represent a silent majority across Europe:

Poland declared that it would not let the EU play dictator on [the migration] issue. The Czech Republic supports Poland. Slovakia, Hungary, and a number of countries quietly share the same views. The Austrians simply closed the borders to limit new refugees.[37]

Rossiskaya Gazeta notes that these parties favor closer relations with Moscow. Of Austria's Hofer: "In the event of his victory, one of his first foreign visits will be to Russia."[38] Of Marine Le Pen:

Bloomberg predicts victory for Marine Le Pen in the French presidential elections. According to analysts, this will lead to a referendum on the withdrawal of France from the European Union, similar to Brexit. According to Bloomberg, Frexit will be a triumph for Euroskeptics and European politicians who favor closer relations with Russia.[39]

Of the Alternative for Germany (AfD), following the September 2016 elections:

Given the helplessness of the authorities in the face of over one million refugees, the Alternative for Germany is a real threat to the traditional parties, particularly in economically depressed areas."[40]

---

[33] Evgeny Shestakov, "How to Save the 'House of Cards' of the EU," *Rossiskaya Gazeta*, November 28, 2016.

[34] Rodion Mikhailov, "Conservative March," *Rossiskaya Gazeta*, November 17, 2016.

[35] Evgeny Shestakov, "Kiev Decided to Shoot," *Rossiskaya Gazeta*, November 27, 2016.

[36] Ariadna Rokossovskaya, "Alexey Pushkov: When the Dominant Trend in the United States Changes, European Politics Inevitably Adapts to It," *Rossiskaya Gazeta*, December 20, 2016.

[37] Ariadna Rokossovskaya, "Brussels Deadlock," *Rossiskaya Gazeta*, May 24, 2016.

[38] Evgeny Shestakov, "Kiev Decided to Shoot," *Rossiskaya Gazeta*, November 27, 2016.

[39] Maxim Makarychev, "Bloomberg Predicted the Presidency of Le Pen and the Withdrawal of France from the European Union," *Rossiskaya Gazeta*, December 7, 2016.

[40] Konstantin Volkov, "Alternative for Germany Threatens Merkel's Party," *Rossiskaya Gazeta*, September 4, 2016.

Together, these crises are causing the EU's collapse. "Slowly but surely," *Rossiskaya Gazeta* wrote in November 2016, "the European Union is transformed into a 'house of cards'." As usual, it let a European politician – Joachim Gauck, the German president – speak for it:

"Not all citizens could or wanted to follow us. ... Not everyone feels like a citizen of the world." People need a home, a homeland, they want to feel they belong to something. Is Brussels ready for the implementation of Gauck's proposed pause in the further integration of countries within the European Union? It remains unclear.[41]

The failure of the European project, according to *Rossiskaya Gazeta*, has been driven by the failures of European democracy. The European elite has consistently failed to abide the obvious preferences of their citizens.

Trans-Atlantic Foreign Policy as a "Largely Discredited ... Doctrine of Regime Change" *Rossiskaya Gazeta* traces the origins of Europe's migrant crisis to NATO's misadventures in the Middle East. This is why Afghanistan, Iraq, Libya, and Syria appear in Figure 6.3. Western interventionism is driven by "ideological purposes, the promotion of democracy, regime change, and so on."[42] This represents an American bid for ideological hegemony, reminiscent of the Cold War:

The European Union supports the USA in Syria because their shared global project implies external intervention and regime change for the sake of the triumph of the liberal model and hegemony of the American globalist project.[43]

Again, *Rossiskaya Gazeta* prefers to quote Americans. Among its favorites is Glenn Greenwald, who collaborated with Edward Snowden to reveal the American government's domestic surveillance program:

"The American elite always want to believe that the US bombs other countries again and again not because of aggression or desire to dominate," writes the well-known journalist Glenn Greenwald for *The Intercept*.

---

[41] Evgeny Shestakov, "How to Save the 'House of Cards' of the EU," *Rossiskaya Gazeta*, November 28, 2016.

[42] Fyodor Lukyanov, "And What if Trump," *Rossiskaya Gazeta*, September 13, 2016.

[43] Ariadna Rokossovskaya, "Alexey Pushkov: When the Dominant Trend in the United States Changes, European Politics Inevitably Adapts to It," *Rossiskaya Gazeta*, December 20, 2016.

"...We all want to believe that this time our bombs are full of love and freedom."[44]

These interventions destabilized the Middle East, and so have "largely discredited" the "doctrine of regime change."[45] The "military campaigns in Afghanistan and Iraq" were "protracted and almost fruitless."[46] "The American missile strike on Syria ...made the situation in the Middle East even more unpredictable."[47] *Rossiskaya Gazeta* reminds readers of America's intelligence failures: "The CIA dragged the world community along by convincing it that the former head of Iraq, Saddam Hussein, had nuclear weapons that, in the end, were never found."[48] It wrote the same of ISIS: "With a multi-billion dollar budget and the latest technology, the Americans were unable to prevent or predict one of the greatest crises of recent years."[49]

Part of Europe's awakening is its realization that America's foreign policy has damaged Europe's interests. Again, *Rossiskaya Gazeta* quoted Alexei Pushkov: "If the United States takes a certain position on Syria, then Europeans need to support it and they end up, as a result, with a huge flow of Syrian refugees."[50] In turn, Europeans increasingly reject the trans-Atlantic alliance:

Thousands of people took to the streets of Hanover to protest Barack Obama's visit to Germany. Europe is just now starting to shed its dependence on the United States. Europe supported the United States in Libya and Syria, and most European states participated in the war in Iraq. Now they are paying the price, as the wave of refugees covers them, not the United States. Europe loses from the

---

[44] Igor Dunaevsky, "Obama Jealous of Republicans, Putin," *Rossiskaya Gazeta*, September 14, 2016; Igor Dunaevsky, "Aggression: Seven Reasons for Alarm after US Strikes on Syria," *Rossiskaya Gazeta*, April 8, 2017. The original article can be found at Greenwald (2017).

[45] Ariadna Rokossovskaya, "Alexey Pushkov: When the Dominant Trend in the United States Changes, European Politics Inevitably Adapts to It," *Rossiskaya Gazeta*, December 20, 2016.

[46] "Clinton Has Promised to Respond to Threats from the Russian Federation and China," *Rossiskaya Gazeta*, September 1, 2016.

[47] Galina Mislivskaya, "Trump 100 Days," *Rossiskaya Gazeta*, April 28, 2017.

[48] Evgeny Shestakov, "Who Are the US Intelligence Services?" *Rossiskaya Gazeta*, December 13, 2016.

[49] Evgeny Shestakov, "Who Are the US Intelligence Services?" *Rossiskaya Gazeta*, December 13, 2016.

[50] Ariadna Rokossovskaya, "Alexey Pushkov: When the Dominant Trend in the United States Changes, European Politics Inevitably Adapts to It," *Rossiskaya Gazeta*, December 20, 2016.

Trans-Atlantic partnership. . . . To save itself, Europe needs to revise its subordination to the United States.[51]

This failed foreign policy includes the sanctions that Western governments imposed following Russia's invasion of Crimea. These sanctions, *Rossiskaya Gazeta* writes, hurt European citizens:

In Italy, they told me that one region was losing one million euros per year due to sanctions. . . . Many understand that the sanctions were imposed under pressure from the United States.[52]

"Trumpism" and the "Crisis of the Liberal Democratic Model" Donald Trump figures so prominently in Figure 6.4 – "billionaire," "businessman," "tycoon," "twitter" – and is central to Figure 6.3 because he validates the Putin government's propaganda narrative:

Trumpism is the most vivid manifestation of the profound crisis of the liberal democratic model of the West. . . . The Trump phenomenon should not be viewed as purely American, although it has a number of national characteristics. In Europe, Trumpism already has a wide following. Until recently, liberal democracy was regarded as the highest and universal point of human development: the end of history. In Europe, the contradictions that led Donald Trump to the Presidency of the United States have long existed, and are due to the radical transformation of the value structure of Western society in its departure from the origins of European civilization. . . . Trumpism is not a one-time event, but part of the rise of parties in the West that are challenging the dictatorship of liberal democracy.[53]

Rossiskaya Gazeta quotes Trump saying precisely what it has long reported. On the European Union: "Donald Trump predicted the collapse of the European Union if the migration problem is not resolved."[54] On Brexit: "People are fed up here in Great Britain and you'll see other countries follow this example."[55] On Paris:

Trump referred to his very dear friend Jim, who always loved Paris and visited with his family every summer. However, not long ago, Donald Trump asked Jim how things were in the city. He replied that he no longer goes there because Paris

---

[51] Ariadna Rokossovskaya, "Brussels Deadlock," *Rossiskaya Gazeta*, May 24, 2016.
[52] Ariadna Rokossovskaya, "Brussels Deadlock," *Rossiskaya Gazeta*, May 24, 2016.
[53] Rodion Mikhailov, "Conservative March," *Rossiskaya Gazeta*, November 17, 2016.
[54] "Donald Trump: Immigration Will Soon Destroy the EU," *Rossiskaya Gazeta*, June 27, 2016.
[55] "Donald Trump: Immigration Will Soon Destroy the EU," *Rossiskaya Gazeta*, June 27, 2016.

is no longer the same. . . . Trump wrote on Twitter that France was again on the verge of implosion.[56]

On Crimea, after Western governments imposed sanctions: "The inhabitants of Crimea would prefer to be with Russia and not where they were. Trump explained that Ukraine is in chaos, which, in his opinion, is the result of the [Obama] administration's misguided policies."[57] On American democracy promotion: "The United States should concentrate on combating terrorism and solving its own problems and not pouring military and financial resources to promote their values abroad. Precisely this position has been advocated by Trump."[58] On NATO: "He called [it] an outdated organization."[59] On American elections: "I'm afraid everything will be rigged."[60] Again, in October 2016: "Donald Trump refused to guarantee that he will recognize the election results."[61]

Though Trump is vindicating, he is also evidence of America's decline. "During the election campaign," *Rossiskaya Gazeta* reported on November 10, "headlines about the 'Divided States of America' were not uncommon in [American] media." It then cited *Atlantic* columnist Ron Brownstein: "Elections have almost become a cultural civil war between the two Americas."[62] Brownstein's quote appeared again on November 11.[63] On November 12, it reported "large-scale riots and clashes with the police," with "several hundred people detained." "Protesters painted walls with cans of paint, including slogans like 'Kill Trump!'" *Rossiskaya Gazeta* later covered a petition, signed by three million people, that called on the Electoral College to make Hillary Clinton president:

Americans who exported democracy to other regions of the world now face a "Maidan" at home. It is possible that the forces behind Hillary Clinton still hope to change the situation in their favor.

[56] Vyacheslav Prokofiev, "No to Paris," *Rossiskaya Gazeta*, February 25, 2017.

[57] "Trump Criticizes Kyiv," *Rossiskaya Gazeta*, August 1, 2016.

[58] Alexander Bratersky and Igor Kryuchkov, "Trump Came with a Revolution," *Rossiskaya Gazeta*, November 10, 2016.

[59] Anna Fedyakina, "Trump Is Entangled in the EU Structure," *Rossiskaya Gazeta*, January 16, 2017.

[60] Anna Fedyakina, "Trump Did Not Rule out the Possibility of Losing the US Presidential Election," *Rossiskaya Gazeta*, August 11, 2016.

[61] Igor Dunaevsky, "Victory Could Be Stolen," *Rossiskaya Gazeta*, October 18, 2016.

[62] Igor Dunaevsky, "White House Is Waiting for Repair," *Rossiskaya Gazeta*, November 10, 2016.

[63] Alexander Bratersky and Igor Kryuchkov, "Trump Came with a Revolution," *Rossiskaya Gazeta*, November 10, 2016.

Racial tensions feature prominently in the narrative of America's decline. Trump's approval ratings are "catastrophic among African-Americans, …no more than 1.5%." "In Ohio and Pennsylvania, his level of support is completely zero."[64] At times, *Rossiskaya Gazeta* seems to approve: "Trump understands this perfectly and does not burn with a desire to persuade African-Americans. His electorate is 'middle America,' shaken by crises, having lost their calm and their confidence in the future."[65] At other times, *Rossiskaya Gazeta* suggests his supporters are racist: "Unpleasant images of Trump fans gathered at the Republican Party convention, who give xenophobia, etc., solid black marks to the candidate."[66] In August 2016, *Rossiskaya Gazeta* linked Trump to anti-Semitism:

The billionaire has been called anti-Semitic several times, including after the image of Hillary Clinton appeared on one of his campaign posters against a backdrop of money, with the star of David next to her and the slogan "the most corrupt candidate in history." Trump denied these accusations, pointing out that his daughter turned to the Jewish faith and married a Jew.[67]

Rossiskaya Gazeta often reports Trump's ethical failings. In August 2016, while covering allegations that Melania Trump was a prostitute in the 1990s, it noted the age gap between "70-year-old Donald and 46-year-old Melania Trump."[68] In October 2016, it covered the St. Louis presidential debate, including "the main topic of the past few days":

Trump's scandalous statements about women ten years ago. The magnate discussed with his acquaintances his claims regarding a certain married woman, details of his intimate life with his wife Melania, and the size of his daughter Ivanka's bust.[69]

Rossiskaya Gazeta also noted that "[Steve] Bannon was accused of anti-Semitism and domestic violence."[70]

---

[64] Maxim Makarychevachalo, "Hillary's Cold Calculation," *Rossiskaya Gazeta*, July 26, 2016

[65] "The Democratic Party Congress Begins," *Rossiskaya Gazeta*, July 26, 2016.

[66] "Donald Trump the Official Candidate for the Republican Party in the US Election," *Rossiskaya Gazeta*, July 26, 2016.

[67] "Donald Trump Accused of Anti-Semitism and Domestic Violence," *Rossiskaya Gazeta*, August 29, 2016.

[68] "Melania Trump," *Rossiskaya Gazeta*, August 8, 2016.

[69] "The US Presidential Election Debate," *Rossiskaya Gazeta*, October 10, 2016.

[70] "Donald Trump Accused of Anti-Semitism and Domestic Violence," *Rossiskaya Gazeta*, August 29, 2016.

Trump's election, *Rossiskaya Gazeta* writes, is "a victory" for Moscow. But it denies that Moscow intervened on his behalf since doing so would undermine its vindication by American voters:

His election is a psychological victory for the Kremlin. Not in the sense that Moscow influenced the outcome. That is nonsense. But in the sense that Putin has once again shown he knows how to wait. As the ancient Chinese proverb holds: Do nothing and everything will be done by itself.[71]

Rossiskaya Gazeta later explains why Trump's victory is equally a victory for Moscow:

With Trump's rise to power, Western pressure on Russia has significantly weakened, and the United States and the West as a whole have stopped imposing their values on Russia.[72]

On November 9, following Trump's election, *Rossiskaya Gazeta* predicted warm relations to come: "Trump hopes to meet with Russian President Vladimir Putin and use his charm and negotiating skills to build a more cooperative relationship."[73]

Rossiskaya Gazeta's international news propaganda is an exercise in comparison sets. Against American decay and the EU's collapse – each substantiated with legitimate coverage of ongoing events – the Putin government may look reasonably competent by comparison.

6.3.2 *China: The Causes and Consequences of Democratic Corruption*

The *People's Daily* employs similar comparison sets. Western democracy has been corrupted by special interests, their economies have stagnated, and the international order is under stress. Figure 6.5 visualizes China's international news propaganda as a network. Figure 6.6 shows the distinctive words in China's international news propaganda relative to Russia's.

American Democracy as a Contest in Money Burning The "chaos of the [2016] US presidential election," the *People's Daily* observes, has "seriously affected the image of the United States." The "defect in the

---

[71] Leonid Radzikhovsky, "Concentration," *Rossiskaya Gazeta*, November 14, 2016.

[72] Evgeny Shestakov, "How to Save the 'House of Cards' of the EU," *Rossiskaya Gazeta*, November 28, 2016.

[73] "Elections in the USA," *Rossiskaya Gazeta*, November 9, 2016.

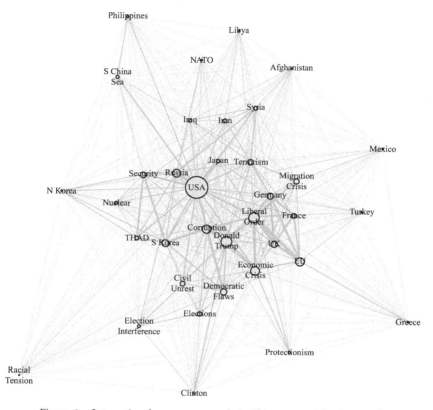

Figure 6.5 International news propaganda in China as a weighted network

China: International News Coverage

unemployment rate discrimination
lisbon international community
united nations financial crisis
enrichment abe solve asian greek exports
six party fiscal promote iaea
sade insurance natural gas u s polish
cut indian summit wang wei
poor rok iranian nuclear xian bill
resolve status human rights deficit
tehran wen liu two sides technology
member states afghan prisons
resolution uranium us dollars debt crisis
homeless palestinian euro zone
nuclear power climate
pyongyang soldiers

China: U.S. Coverage

korean peninsula
international atomic
analysts believe reduction newspaper
energy agency international community
financial crisis sade natural gas
pakistani south korean atomic energy
liu poverty pakistan atomic
asian brazil
see note india wang us dollar
zhang nuclear issue census
u s prisons
xian south korea gun
iranian nuclear wen resolve
increased by two sides li uranium
nearly anti missile missile system
fiscal prisoners comprehensive
exports party talks six party
manufacturing released by homeless
uzbekistan enrichment
uranium enrichment
unemployment rate

Figure 6.6 Semantic distinctiveness in China's international news propaganda

[American] electoral system" is the role of money in politics. Its account is sophisticated:

Politics has become a money game for American society. Before, American democracy was wary of erosion through money. Precautions included the Tillman Act, which prohibited companies from donating directly to political campaigns, and the Hatch Act, which restricted electoral spending. ... But the [Supreme Court] ruling that American companies can make unrestricted campaign donations opens Pandora's box. ... American scholar Lawrence Lessig commented on this in *Lost Republic*. The political system is in a serious crisis. Electoral democracy in the United States has become a money-burning contest between candidates, each of whom cater to the financial elite.[74]

Since Democrats and Republicans now rely on the same financial interests, "campaign platforms are gradually becoming similar."[75] As a result, "public opinion has little effect on government policy."[76] With few policy differences, "more time is spent on personal attacks than policy debates."[77] The 2016 vice presidential debate, for instance, was a "quarrel rather than an inspiring point of view."[78] "The third and final presidential debate should have been about the economic issues that voters are concerned about. Instead, Hillary Clinton and Donald Trump again launched personal attacks."[79]

The *People's Daily* covers America's other domestic ills, especially when the State Department issues its annual human rights report. "The US government, which casts itself as a world human rights judge, has once again criticized the human rights situation in nearly 200 countries. ...In fact, human rights in the United States continue to deteriorate." It then catalogues legitimate failings: violent crime, domestic surveillance, solitary confinement, homelessness, unemployment, gender and racial

---

[74] Xu Chongwen, "Money Politics Is a Chronic Illness in American Society," *People's Daily*, February 5, 2017.

[75] Zhang Ruizhuang, "Observations from a City in the Mountains," *People's Daily*, October 16, 2016.

[76] Xu Chongwen, "Money Politics Is a Chronic Illness in American Society," *People's Daily*, February 5 2017; Lin Hongyu, "Elections Are a Farce at the Mercy of Others," *People's Daily*, February 2, 2017.

[77] Xu Chongwen, "Money Politics Is a Chronic Illness in American Society," *People's Daily*, February 5 2017; Lin Hongyu, "Elections Are a Farce at the Mercy of Others," *People's Daily*, February 2, 2017.

[78] Xu Chongwen, "Money Politics Is a Chronic Illness in American Society," *People's Daily*, February 5 2017; Lin Hongyu, "Elections Are a Farce at the Mercy of Others," *People's Daily*, February 2, 2017.

[79] Zhang Penghui, "Mutual Attacks, Resentment, and Disappointment," *People's Daily*, October 21, 2016.

discrimination, and child labor. Many of these words appear on the right of Figure 6.6: "prisoners," "homeless," "poverty," and "unemployment rate."

Although *Rossiskaya Gazeta* pairs coverage of America's flawed democracy with Europe's, the *People's Daily* targets South Korea: "South Korea's domestic politics is a mess."[80] In 2016 and 2017, its coverage focused on two topics: the impeachment of President Park Geun-hye for corruption and the THAAD missile defense system. For the *People's Daily*, the THAAD system is evidence that South Korea's democracy is as unresponsive to citizens as America's. The government "turned a deaf ear to public opinion," revealed by anti-THAAD protests across Korea.[81] This appears prominently in the right of Figure 6.6: "South Korean," "THAAD," "missile system," and "anti missile."

Like *Rossiskaya Gazeta*, the *People's Daily* lets others speak for it. In July 2015, it published an article by Boris Guslevov of the Russian Academy of Sciences. Its headline: "American Democracy Encounters Difficulties: Internal and External Double Standards, Inequality Continues to Grow."[82] "The international academic community," Guslevov writes, "has many different definitions of democracy," but they share four principles: "people's sovereignty, majority rule, political equality, and political participation." Guslevov omitted voting.

The United States has monopolized the right to define democracy and human rights, and accuses other countries of violating them. But trying to tell other countries how to build democracy and protect human rights violates international law, which holds that countries must not interfere in each other's internal affairs. At the same time, the United States has clearly violated universal democratic principles: growing social inequality; racial, ethnic, and religious discrimination; restricting fair elections; monitoring dissidents; transnational application of US law; improper use of violence against peaceful demonstrators; indefinite imprisonment; torture; and extrajudicial executions.

Money has always played an important role in US elections. Elections are a costly activity, so the source of campaign funding is critical. Political scientists

---

[80] Zhong Sheng, "Harming Other Countries' Security Endangers the Aggressor," *People's Daily*, March 3, 2017.

[81] Zhong Sheng, "Harming Other Countries' Security Endangers the Aggressor," *People's Daily*, March 3, 2017; Chen Shangwen, "Korean People Protesting THAAD Threaten Regional Peace," *People's Daily*, February 5, 2017.

[82] Boris Guslevov translated by Zhou Xiaolin, "American Democracy Encounters Difficulties: Internal and External Double Standards, Inequality Continues to Grow," *People's Daily*, July 26, 2015.

have always believed that campaign funds should come from social organizations rather than business organizations to avoid their inappropriate influence on politics. The total amount of funds for US presidential campaigns has reached a record $5.3 billion. As a result, the general electorate is increasingly excluded from the decision-making process, and the more powerful class effectively runs the government.

American democracy is no model.

Guslevov then argues that China's democracy is superior:

Western politicians and scholars accuse China of not complying with democratic principles, but the opposite is true. China has demonstrated its determination to increase people's rights through ongoing reforms. These aim to improve the welfare of the overwhelming majority of the population, reduce social inequality, and lift more people out of poverty. In the political arena, we observe the orderly change of government officials at all levels, from rural to national. Representatives of democratic parties and non-partisan people participate in the administration and play an important role. ... This is not to say that China has solved all problems. Its political, social, and economic models are far from perfect, as Chinese leaders recognize. The new generation of Chinese leaders does not conceal these difficulties, but publicly commits to resolving them.

Social Decay and the Consequences of Corruption in America The corruption of American democracy has many consequences. Among these is gun violence, referenced in 5 percent of international news propaganda. It attributes this to the political influence of the National Rifle Association:

The root of the difficulty in passing gun control legislation is money in politics. ... The National Rifle Association announced that it will spend tens of thousands of dollars on advertising to support gun rights and the Republican presidential candidate Trump.[83]

Another article describes the "gun control debate in Congress" as "still fruitless," even though Americans favor it.[84] "The U.S. government has not done anything to control guns and other issues, which

---

[83] Zhong Sheng, "The Root of the Gun Control Problem Is Money Politics," *People's Daily*, September 25, 2016. Note that Zhong Sheng is "a pen name used in the paper since November 2008 for important pieces on international affairs on which the leadership wishes to register its view" (Bandurski 2018).

[84] Chen Lidan, Zhang Penghui, and Gao Shi, "Members Are Busy with Fundraising, and the Party Is Fighting for Nothing," *People's Daily*, September 18, 2016.

exposes the deep-seated malpractices of American politics."[85] "Gun" appears prominently in Figure 6.6, referenced in 20 percent of U.S. coverage.

America's gun violence epidemic has fueled racial tensions. "Racial discrimination is tearing the United States apart":[86]

Citizens in Dallas, Texas, held a parade to protest the shooting of African Americans in Louisiana and Minnesota. ... On duty police officers were suddenly attacked by an unidentified gunman, causing at least one police officer to be killed. ... Demonstrations in protest of police violence have also broken out in Washington, New York, Atlanta, and Philadelphia. ... On the other hand, the police are also worried about their own safety in a country with more than 100 million guns.[87]

The corruption of American democracy has led to economic stagnation as well: "The root cause of the current economic crisis in the United States lies in the structure of its political economy."[88] In exchange for "financial contributions from oil and energy companies," Republican presidents "eliminated oil and gas price controls." The *People's Daily* is bipartisan in its criticism: "Barack Obama protected the financial industry after the international financial crisis,"[89] which itself revealed the depth of America's corruption:

The greed and corruption of financial executives was exposed by the financial crisis, and the failure of the US government to hold these financial giants responsible shocked ordinary Americans, and filled them with despair and anger. Occupy Wall Street Movement is one manifestation of this. It quickly spread to other countries, and caused global challenges to the US economic system.[90]

America's economic crisis will soon come for the elderly:

The two pillars of the US welfare system for senior citizens, Social Security and Medicare, will be exhausted by 2037 and 2017, respectively. This is the third time in 15 years that the ability to pay for the two major US welfare systems has

[85] Zhong Sheng, "The Root of the Gun Control Problem Is Money Politics," *People's Daily*, September 25, 2016.
[86] Zhang Penghui, "Racial Discrimination Tearing America Apart," *People's Daily*, July 10, 2016.
[87] Zhang Niansheng and Zhang Penghui, "US Dallas Policeman Shot," *People's Daily*, July 9, 2016.
[88] Song Guoyou, "Trade Protectionism Cannot Solve US Problems," *People's Daily*, February 26, 2017.
[89] Xu Chongwen, "Money Politics Is a Chronic Illness in American Society," *People's Daily*, February 5 2017.
[90] Zhang Ruizhuang, "Observations from a City in the Mountains," *People's Daily*, October 16, 2016.

been cast into doubt. If it is not fundamentally reformed, Americans will face a trillion-dollar welfare crisis.[91]

Though Trump is less central to the narrative, the *People's Daily* quotes him frequently. Of his inaugural address: "He said that the American people have not benefited from economic development for a long time."[92] Again, economic crisis is prominent in the right of Figure 6.6: "financial crisis" appears in 23 percent of U.S. coverage and "unemployment rate" in 17 percent.

America's economic mismanagement jeopardizes global stability. "US government debts are high," which "hinders US economic growth and threatens the world's economic security":

US government debt is equivalent to each American owing tens of thousands of dollars. This year, treasury bonds will break through the trillion-dollar mark. ...High debts have highlighted the weakness of the US system. This not only restricts US economic growth but also adversely affects the world economy.[93]

The *People's Daily* later quoted the *British Times*: "The gap between the American Dream and the American reality is growing."[94]

The Liberal Order, "Self-Interested Values," and "Hegemonic Anxiety Disorder" Given China's position as a net exporter, the *People's Daily* treats international trade as "an important driver of world economic growth" and "employment."[95] Accordingly, while *Rossiskaya Gazeta* celebrates the liberal international order's decline, the *People's Daily* has a more complicated relationship with it.

The *People's Daily* criticizes the American government for failing to abide the rules of global trade. Nearly 70 percent of its coverage of Donald Trump focuses on his plan to stimulate economic growth via protectionism. This is the first of two critical foreign policy errors the *People's Daily* documents. Trump's protectionism is "very irrational":[96]

[91] Ma Xiaoning, "US Welfare System in the Red," *People's Daily*, May 17, 2009.
[92] Zhang Niansheng, Zhang Penghui, and Chen Lidan, "Trump Sworn in as US President," *People's Daily*, January 21, 2017.
[93] Zhou Qi and Fu Suixin, "US Government Debt," *People's Daily*, December 11, 2016.
[94] Zhong Sheng, "American Election Chaos Highlights the System's Drawbacks," *People's Daily*, October 8, 2016.
[95] Song Guoyou, "Trade Protectionism Cannot Solve US Problems," *People's Daily*, February 26, 2017.
[96] Zhou Shizhen, "Trade Protectionism Harms Others and Oneself: Win-Win Cooperation Is the Right Way for Everyone," *People's Daily*, February 26, 2017.

The root cause of the US economic dilemma lies in the imbalance of economic and political society. Trade protectionism cannot solve these problems. ... The Trump administration has announced its withdrawal from the Trans-Pacific Partnership Agreement and asked to revisit the North American Free Trade Agreement. The rise of US trade protectionism is clearly becoming the latest uncertainty affecting the global economy. For the United States, trade protectionism cannot solve its problems. On the contrary, it will cause greater losses.

"Trade protectionism harms others" and "reflects self-interested values."[97] In this respect, the United States is damaging the international order it created:

[Trump's] protection of domestic industries has triggered a trade war that has intensified economic depression in the US and the world. Engaging in trade protectionism will inevitably lead to retaliation across the world.[98]

America's second great foreign policy error is its penchant for intervening in the domestic affairs of sovereign countries. The *People's Daily* dubs this "hegemonic anxiety disorder":

At the end of the Cold War, the United States was at the peak of its power. However, in recent years, due to the decline in its economic strength, its ability to mobilize resources to serve its political and diplomatic goals has been limited. As a result, the United States has shifted from its former "positive hegemony" to "negative hegemony." ... Incapable of maintaining its leadership, it has sought to maintain its status by disrupting the world order.

The *People's Daily* then cataloged America's global misadventures:

The United States launched the Iraq war, causing the country to fall into long-term turmoil. The Western countries, headed by the United States, have violently interfered in the internal affairs of Libya and Syria, causing the two countries to remain in civil war. The US-led NATO expansion has worsened Russia's relations with Ukraine and the European Union. Since the implementation of the "Asia-Pacific rebalancing strategy," tensions on the Korean Peninsula have intensified. ... US warships illegally entered waters adjacent to the Nansha Island reef in China, which has led to unrelenting setbacks and tension in the security situation in this region.[99]

---

[97] Zhou Shizhen, "Trade Protectionism Harms Others and Oneself: Global Trade Environment Faces Short-Term Risk," *People's Daily*, February 26, 2017.

[98] Zhou Shizhen, "Trade Protectionism Harms Others and Oneself: Win-Win Cooperation Is the Right Way for Everyone," *People's Daily*, February 26, 2017.

[99] Li Wen, "Why Is the United States the Source of Global Turmoil? An International Strategy of Self Interest," *People's Daily*, September 19, 2016.

America's interference in the affairs of sovereign countries is "most destructive," both for the international order and for America's international standing. "International law, based on the UN Charter signed after World War II, has been trampled."[100]

The *People's Daily*'s international news propaganda, like *Rossiskaya Gazeta*'s, is an exercise in comparison sets. It also strives for credibility in ways its domestic coverage often does not. Its coverage of money in American politics is sophisticated, starting with the Tillman and Hatch Acts of 1907 and 1939, respectively, and concluding with a logically coherent argument for why "similar campaign platforms" have yielded presidential debates that feature "personal attacks" rather than "the economic issues that voters are concerned about." The *People's Daily*'s accounts of racial tension, poverty, police violence, and economic mismanagement are generally factual and often substantiated with statistics. This is not the sort of absurd propaganda that marks its pro-regime and domestic content.

Our theory makes sense of this. When what constitutes absurdity is unclear, propaganda apparatuses lack their usual tool to signal the regime's capacity for violence. However, the force that makes absurd propaganda relatively inaccessible – citizens' uncertainty about living conditions abroad – also makes critical coverage more plausible. The constraints on honest propaganda are weaker. This critical coverage is potentially valuable, insofar as it undermines the appeal of an alternative, more democratic government.

6.4 INTERNATIONAL COOPERATION: THEORY AND CROSS-COUNTRY EVIDENCE

6.4.1 Theory

We turn now to the second topic of international propaganda: international cooperation, which focuses on a regime's engagement with the international community. Although international news propaganda is almost entirely the province of high-income autocracies, international cooperation propaganda is salient across the income distribution.

Its composition, however, differs dramatically. Figure 6.7 illustrates this. For each country in our dataset, the x-axes give mean GDP per

---

[100] Zhang Ruizhuang, "Observations from a City in the Mountains," *People's Daily*, October 16, 2016.

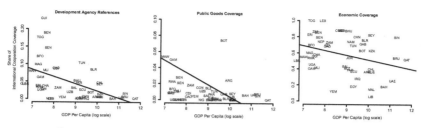

Figure 6.7 International cooperation propaganda by GDP per capita

capita during the sample period. The left graphic displays the share of all foreign references in international cooperation coverage accounted for by development institutions. The center graphic displays the share that focuses on public goods. The right graphic displays the share that focuses on the economy. For clarity, we overlay fitted OLS regression lines. Propaganda apparatuses in low-income countries allocate far more coverage to development institutions, economic performance, and public goods. Put differently, in lower-income countries, international cooperation coverage focuses on how the regime engages with the international community to foster economic growth and provide public goods. This difference in the composition of international cooperation propaganda across the global income distribution has theoretical implications.

Where electoral constraints bind, our theory suggests, propaganda apparatuses should cast the autocrat as pursuing the national interest, broadly construed. This national interest should exhibit substantial variation. In low-income countries, autocrats can cast themselves as partnering with the international community to advance domestic welfare. They can highlight development projects that aim to vaccinate citizens, combat poverty, improve schools, and create jobs. To be credible, propaganda apparatuses must also acknowledge the challenges that their societies confront. They must acknowledge persistently high infant mortality, malnutrition, illiteracy, and the poor condition of domestic infrastructure. In high-income countries, the national interest is different. As a permanent member of the UN Security Council, Russian foreign policy centers on global governance rather than development aid. Nonetheless, Vladimir Putin's propaganda apparatuses should have some conception of the national interest and emphasize his efforts to pursue it.

In the absence of electoral constraints, international cooperation coverage is useful for a novel reason. Recall that when choosing whether to protest, citizens consider the likelihood of repression. If citizens believe the international community will sanction their governments for employing violence against them,[101] they may believe their governments are constrained and so be more willing to protest.[102] This gives repressive governments an incentive to signal information to citizens about their standing in the international community. That is, if they can persuade citizens that they are regarded by the international community as key partners, then citizens may view sanctions from the international community as less likely.[103] This is why President Paul Biya of Cameroon broadcast his government's military partnerships with Western governments during the Anglophone Crisis, which has raged since October 2016 and we discuss in Chapter 7. This is why President Aleksandr Lukashenko of Belarus had his state news agency report that Putin pledged "comprehensive assistance will be provided to ensure the security of the Republic of Belarus" in the face of widespread protests in August 2020.[104] This is also why the Uzbekistan government routinely prints lengthy – and possibly fabricated – statements of support from the governments of Great Powers.

Xi Jinping has no need to tell citizens that the CCP is supported by the international community's Great Powers; China is a Great Power. But Xi Jinping can use international cooperation coverage to signal his strength in other ways. His propaganda apparatus can cover his ongoing efforts to remake the international system in the CCP's image: from one premised on human rights norms to one that privileges sovereignty and non-interference. If the CCP is sufficiently strong to remake the international order in its image, it will not be constrained by it. To be sure, this partly reflects the CCP's foreign policy. In 2021, *the New York Times* described China's "alliance of autocracies" as a "bid to lead a new world order."[105] But our theory suggests it has a domestic component as well: to frame its foreign policy in a way that signals to citizens the regime's strength.

For propaganda apparatuses in unconstrained autocracies, the key challenge is that endorsements from the international community – or,

---

[101] McFaul (2007); Levitsky and Way (2010); Hyde (2011); Donno (2013); Hyde and Marinov (2014); Escribà-Folch and Wright (2015); Carnegie and Marinov (2017); Carothers (2018); Carter (2022).
[102] Carter (2022).
[103] Nielsen (2013).
[104] Higgins and Nechepurenko (2020).
[105] Myers (2021).

in Xi's case, his reshaping of the international order – sit alongside domestic propaganda that citizens know is false. That is, international cooperation coverage that is useful for citizens to believe sits alongside domestic claims that are obviously absurd. This juxtaposition requires that propaganda apparatuses in unconstrained autocracies provide citizens with evidence that the international community's praise is authentic, even as claims about domestic economic and political conditions are not. We expect propaganda apparatuses in unconstrained autocracies to rest their claims of international support on two sources. First, propaganda apparatuses can reference support from members of the international community who are unconcerned about human rights violations, who espouse "sovereignty" and "non-interference" over basic human rights. Second, propaganda apparatuses can publish apparently authentic statements of support. They can publish interviews with international leaders and letters from heads of state. They can trumpet state visits and other summits. They should substantiate their claims of support.

Hypothesis 6.3: *As electoral constraints grow more binding, the valence of international cooperation coverage should decline. Where electoral constraints are non-binding, propaganda apparatuses should broadcast the regime's international prominence. Where electoral constraints are binding, propaganda apparatuses should cover the regime's efforts to pursue the national interest, which entails honest propaganda.*

6.4.2 Data and Estimation Strategy

To some extent, these hypotheses are difficult to test in a cross-country regression framework. It is unclear, for instance, how to measure the pursuit of the national interest across countries. Still, we created several variables to probe whether global trends are consistent with our theoretical expectations. First, we measured the valence of international cooperation propaganda by calculating the total number of positive less negative words, standardized by the total number of dictionary hits, which yields the variable *Article Valence: International Cooperation*$_{ijt}$. We calculated this for articles that reference the executive and for those that do not. Second, we recorded whether article i about international cooperation references country j's executive. Third, for each of these references, we computed our primary measure of pro-regime coverage, *Positive Coverage Standardized: Executive$_{ijt}$*. We also created variables that indicate which *other topics* international cooperation coverage touches on.

We estimated country-year and article-level models for each outcome of interest. For the country-year models, since measures of electoral constraints are observed by year, we computed country-year means for our propaganda variables, which were measured at the article or day level. The model is

$$Y_{js} = \alpha + \beta X_{js} + \phi W_{js} + \gamma_j + \epsilon \qquad (6.4)$$

where j indexes country, s indexes year, X_{js} measures electoral constraints, and the vector W_{js} gives control variables. Country-fixed effects, given by γ_j, accommodate systematic differences across languages and unobserved differences across countries. Since these outcomes are continuous, we employed OLS with robust standard errors clustered by country. For article-level models, we employed mixed-effects estimators to accommodate country-year–level explanatory variables and article level propaganda variables. The model is

$$Y_{ijt} = \alpha + \beta X_{is} + \kappa Z_{it} + \phi W_{is} + \gamma_k + \gamma_j + \epsilon \qquad (6.5)$$

where the vectors Z_{it} and W_{is}, respectively, give day- and year-level controls; γ_k gives language-fixed effects; and γ_j country-random effects.

6.4.3 Results

The results appear in Table 6.2. From Models 1 and 2, each five-point increase in the Polity score is associated with a 3 percent decrease in the rate at which propaganda apparatuses cover the regime's international engagements. In the most repressive dictatorships, the probability that article i focuses on the regime's international engagements is nearly 10 percent greater than in propaganda apparatuses where the Polity score hovers around 4 or 5. From Models 7 and 8, much of this international cooperation coverage implicates the autocrat and ruling party. Here, each five-point Polity increase is associated with a 12 percent reduction in executive references. This implies that propaganda apparatuses in the most repressive dictatorships are roughly 35 percent more likely to explicitly link the autocrat to international engagement than where the Polity score hovers around 4 or 5.

Table 6.2 The politics of international cooperation propaganda narratives

Outcome variable	Dependent variable:									
	Rate		Article valence				Executive references		Positive coverage standardized	
			Executive		Non-executive					
Unit of analysis	Country-year	Article	Country-year	Article	Country-year	Article	Country-year	Article	Country-year	Article
Estimator	OLS	Mixed	OLS	Mixed	OLS	Mixed	OLS	Mixed	OLS	Mixed
	(1)	(2)	(3)	(4)	(5)	(6)	(7)	(8)	(9)	(10)
Polity	-0.006**	-0.006***	-0.017***	-0.016***	-0.005	-0.009***	-0.023*	-0.024***	-0.062*	-0.053***
	(0.003)	(0.0002)	(0.005)	(0.001)	(0.006)	(0.001)	(0.013)	(0.002)	(0.036)	(0.006)
Trade	0.0004	-0.00003*	0.00001	0.001***	-0.001	0.001***	-0.002	0.001***	0.00005	0.002**
	(0.0004)	(0.00001)	(0.001)	(0.0002)	(0.001)	(0.0002)	(0.002)	(0.0003)	(0.006)	(0.001)
Log GDP per capita	0.026	-0.003	0.030	-0.010	-0.035	-0.038***	-0.087	0.275***	0.374	-0.137**
	(0.030)	(0.002)	(0.063)	(0.014)	(0.074)	(0.014)	(0.154)	(0.030)	(0.449)	(0.061)
Natural resources	0.0001	-0.0001	-0.004**	-0.004***	-0.0005	-0.004***	-0.008	-0.008***	0.009	-0.010***
	(0.001)	(0.00005)	(0.002)	(0.001)	(0.002)	(0.001)	(0.005)	(0.001)	(0.014)	(0.003)
Civil war	-0.039**	0.001	-0.089**	0.004	-0.151***	-0.026**	-0.173**	-0.017	0.048	0.0001
	(0.016)	(0.001)	(0.037)	(0.016)	(0.042)	(0.013)	(0.083)	(0.020)	(0.265)	(0.078)
Internet penetration	0.00001	0.00000**	-0.00000	0.00001	-0.0001**	-0.0001***	0.00004	-0.0001***	-0.0002	-0.00000
	(0.00001)	(0.00000)	(0.00003)	(0.00002)	(0.00003)	(0.00002)	(0.0001)	(0.00003)	(0.0002)	(0.0001)
Election	0.001		0.006	0.001	0.032		-0.039		-0.034	
	(0.007)		(0.034)	(0.010)	(0.039)		(0.070)		(0.246)	
Election season		-0.007***				-0.008		-0.034***		-0.040
		(0.001)				(0.008)		(0.012)		(0.049)
Constant	-0.201	0.043	0.039	0.465***	0.522	0.732***	1.085	-2.348***	-3.986	1.826***
	(0.300)	(0.035)	(0.702)	(0.146)	(0.742)	(0.144)	(1.546)	(0.345)	(5.024)	(0.628)
Country effects	Fixed	Random	Fixed	Random	Fixed	Random	Fixed	Random	Fixed	Random
Language-fixed effects		✓		✓		✓		✓		✓
Observations	192	2,442,480	158	20,175	159	28,819	164	49,044	158	20,189
R^2	0.884		0.914		0.891		0.645		0.707	

Note: * $p < 0.1$; ** $p < 0.05$; *** $p < 0.01$

Figure 6.8 Coverage topics associated with international cooperation narratives

From Models 3, 4, 9, and 10, international cooperation propaganda that directly implicates the autocrat is consistent with our theoretical expectations: effusive in the most repressive dictatorships and modest where electoral constraints are binding. From Models 3 and 4, in the most repressive dictatorships, international cooperation coverage that explicitly references the autocrat is nearly 2.5 Fox News units more positive than that where the Polity score is 4 or 5. From Models 9 and 10, in the most repressive dictatorships, pro-regime coverage is between six and seven Fox News units more positive than that where the Polity score is 4 or 5.

Figure 6.8 presents three radar charts that give the share of international cooperation propaganda that focuses on the topics around the perimeter. Two features are noteworthy. As electoral constraints grow more binding, so too does the probability that international cooperation coverage focuses on the economy and electoral democracy. This makes theoretical sense. Constrained autocrats have powerful incentives to persuade citizens that their foreign policies foster growth and that their regular elections are regarded by the international community as free and fair.

These cross-country results leave unanswered what sorts of claims drive the effusive valence of pro-regime coverage in the absence of electoral constraints, and how propaganda apparatuses in constrained autocracies emphasize the regime's pursuit of the legitimate national interest. To understand these subtleties, we employed two sets of paired comparisons. At the upper end of the global income distribution, we return to Russia and China, which lets us explore how international news and international cooperation narratives are related. At the lower end of the global income distribution, we focus on Congo and Uzbekistan, which have sought close relationships with the CCP and were visited by the same Republican Congressman, Dana Rohrabacher, during our sample period.

Section 6.3 revealed important differences in how the Russian and Chinese propaganda apparatuses cover the international order. What governments tell their citizens about the world is closely related to what they write about their engagement with it.

Rossiskaya Gazeta is modest about the Kremlin's foreign policy. Putin is cast as advocating for a multipolar world and a Europe of conservative values. The *People's Daily* is immodest. It emphasizes Xi Jinping's transformation of the international order: from one based on human rights norms to one privileging national sovereignty. It depicts an alliance system with the CCP at the center of a reimagined international community. This, our theory suggests, is an implicit signal to citizens. A government that can reshape the international order can also compel their acquiescence.

Again, the Russian and Chinese propaganda apparatuses make an appealing comparison. First, both governments routinely acknowledge their goal of a multipolar international order. Sergey Lavrov, Russia's foreign minister, put it sharply in 2018: The "post-West world order" would mark a new "historical epoch" in which "five or so centuries of domination of the collective West" give way to "other powerhouses."[106] Xi Jinping put it only slightly differently in 2017: "The overall direction of multipolarization of the world ... and the democratization of international relations has not changed. ... We must maintain our strategic steadiness, strategic confidence and strategic patience."[107] Second, both governments have built coalitions for their global leadership bids. As we discuss in Section 6.5.2, the CCP's efforts have centered on cultivating client governments by providing military and financial support. The CCP has employed multiple channels: the Shanghai Cooperation Organization, Belt and Road Initiative, and other forms of

[106] Gehrke (2018).
[107] "Xi Calls for Global Vision in China's National Security Work," CGTN, February 18, 2017.

Military Firepower Ranking	2005	2006	2007	2010	2011	2012	2014	2015	2016	2017	2018	2019	2020
	USA	USA	USA	USA	USA	USA	USA	USA	USA	USA	USA	USA	USA
	China	China	Russia	China	Russia	Russia	Russia	Russia	Russia	Russia	Russia	Russia	Russia
	Russia	Russia	China	Russia	China	China	China	China	China	China	China	China	China
	Pakistan	India	India	India	India	India	India	India	India	India	India	India	India
	India	Pakistan	Germany	UK	UK	UK	UK	UK	France	France	France	France	Japan

Figure 6.9 Global Firepower's military capability ranking

development and military aid. The Putin government has cultivated client governments more directly: by manipulating electoral outcomes across Western democracies and elsewhere.[108] Third, their military capabilities are similar. Figure 6.9 presents the five countries with the strongest military capabilities, according to Global Firepower, since 2005.[109] The Global Firepower ranking incorporates military size, industrial production, access to energy resources, and economic output, among other factors.[110] Notwithstanding claims about China's rise, Global Firepower puts Russia's military capacity only slightly above China's. Put simply, the CCP and Putin governments have similar ambitions for the international order and similar military capabilities with which to actualize them.[111]

We treated international cooperation coverage as a weighted network, with nodes given by topics, countries, and international institutions. Edges between nodes were sized according to the number of articles in which nodes co-occur. To facilitate comparison, we again restricted attention to 2016 and 2017. Figure 6.11, to which we refer throughout the section, displays the distinctive words that characterize Russian and Chinese foreign policy narratives. In Section 6.5.3, we use the linguistic dictionaries from Chapter 3 to measure how much more effusively the CCP's propaganda apparatus describe Xi Jinping's global leadership relative to its Russian counterpart.

---

[108] Bessi and Ferrara (2016); Kollanyi, Howard, and Woolley (2016); Van Herpen (2016); Howard and Kollanyi (2016); Ferrara (2020); Morgan and Shaffer (2017); Howard et al. (2018); Benkler et al. (2018); Woolley and Guilbeault (2018); Badawy, Ferrara, and Lerman (2018); Stewart, Arif, and Starbird (2018); Woolley and Guilbeault (2018); Linvill et al. (2019); Bastos and Farkas (2019); Woolley and Howard (2018); Schwirtz and Borgia (2019); Golovchenko et al. (2020).

[109] Global Firepower did not release an update for 2008, 2009, or 2013.

[110] For more, see www.globalfirepower.com.

[111] Friedberg (2017); Stent (2020).

6.5.1 *Russia: The Conscience of Conservative Europe and a Champion of Multipolarity*

With a disintegrating European Union and a United States committed to the "doctrine of regime change," *Rossiskaya Gazeta* casts Putin as standing up to the "globalist project of the West," a defender of "traditional values" despite pressures for "notorious political correctness." Putin is the embattled conscience of conservative Europe: After casting Trump's victory in November 2016 as a "psychological victory for the Kremlin," *Rossiskaya Gazeta* went on:

> Long ago Putin made an ideological bet against the globalization of political correctness and in favor of Euroskepticism and the traditional values of conservatism. In the West these views were marginalized. ... Putin was one of the first to invest in a new conservative startup. Since then, the ideological capitalization of this startup has increased tenfold.[112]

Putin is equally cast as a champion of a multipolar world in the face of Western expansion. *Rossiskaya Gazeta* printed this excerpt from Putin's speech at the UN General Assembly in September 2015:

> Unfortunately, bloc thinking from the Cold War still dominates. NATO not only remains, but is expanding, and this creates for post-Soviet countries a false choice: be with the West or the East.[113]

The eradication of regional blocs – in particular, a return to a "Europe of nations" – is a key part of the multipolar world that Putin advocates:

> Foreign Minister Sergey Lavrov told conference participants that northern Europe does not need dividing lines or artificial tensions. ... Russia has consistently advocated the preservation of northern Europe as a space for good-neighborliness, partnership, and mutually beneficial cooperation. "We are convinced that our common interests will help us overcome various challenges, uphold international law, and ensure the principle of equal and indivisible security." ... Lavrov expressed hope that "the conference will make a useful contribution to the maintenance of trust and mutual understanding between Russia and the Nordic countries and will contribute to the development of international humanitarian cooperation."

This multipolar world, which will emerge in the wake of America's "globalist project," will privilege "humility" and "sustainable development":

---

[112] Leonid Radzikhovsky, "Concentration," *Rossiskaya Gazeta*, November 14, 2016.
[113] "Vladimir Putin Takes Part in the 70th Session of the UN General Assembly," *Rossiskaya Gazeta*, September 28, 2015.

At the [UN Development] Summit, Lavrov stressed that Moscow … does not ask for anything from the world community. On the contrary, it is ready to help achieve the goals of global development. "We are not trying to teach partners how to live their own lives." Unlike some countries, Moscow does not "impose political models and values on anyone." Lavrov described the elimination of poverty as the chief goal of Russia's development assistance. Moscow, according to the minister, considers development assistance as an investment in global stability. Lavrov called on all countries to act "based on universally recognized norms of international law" and seek collective decision-making.[114]

Rossiskaya Gazeta explicitly rejects the notion of Russia as a global superpower. In January 2016, responding to Barack Obama's description of Russia as a "regional power," *Rossiskaya Gazeta* quotes Putin:

Russia does not pretend to be a superpower, but it cannot be called a regional one. … If threatened, the Russian Federation will defend its security with all available means. … [Obama's statement was] his opinion, just as I know he believes the United States is exceptional. I do not agree with either.[115]

Russia, Putin explained, has no pretensions to superpower status: "It is very expensive, and for nothing." But neither will Putin abide Obama's apparent insult. "If we talk about Russia as a regional power," Putin is quoted as saying, "we first need to decide which region we are talking about."

These rejoinders to the West are common, as is how *Rossiskaya Gazeta* casts the Kremlin as a defender of the national interest. For however modest it is about Moscow's global leadership, *Rossiskaya Gazeta* is equally clear that the regime will not let Russia be bullied. In March 2016, it reported that Russia had withdrawn from an upcoming Nuclear Security Summit in Washington because the United States was not serious about disarmament. Though nuclear safety is "very relevant," Putin's spokesman is reported as saying:

Moscow believes that the development of issues related to nuclear safety requires common and joint efforts and mutual consideration of interests and positions in the course of preliminary work. … We experienced a certain lack of interaction during the preliminary study of the issues and topics of the summit, so in this case the participation of the Russian side will not take place.[116]

---

[114] "The Historical Past and Prospects for the Future of Russia and the Nordic Countries," *Rossiskaya Gazeta*, September 27, 2015.
[115] "Russian President Vladimir Putin Gave an Interview to the German Publication Bild," *Rossiskaya Gazeta*, January 12, 2016.
[116] "Nuclear Security Summit will be held in Washington on March 31-April 1," *Rossiskaya Gazeta*, March 30, 2016.

NATO is Russia's chief antagonist, and its policy failures have made citizens around the world less secure. In May 2017, *Rossiskaya Gazeta* asked: "Are there any joint projects with NATO to combat terrorism and neutralize radical extremists? Does Moscow now cooperate with NATO in any areas? Maybe it's worth stopping relations with the Alliance if in Brussels they demonstrate a frank desire to provoke Russia and humiliate it?" The article reported that NATO had suspended all joint projects across a number of areas: counterterrorism, Afghanistan, and piracy. These, *Rossiskaya Gazeta* reported, had previously enjoyed success:

We jointly trained Afghan technicians to service Russian-made helicopters, anti-drug personnel for Afghanistan, Pakistan and Central Asian countries, and worked on the STANDEKS joint system for the remote detection of explosives. The initiative on cooperation in airspace allowed in real time to exchange information about aircraft suspected of being captured by terrorists.

Rossiskaya Gazeta observed that, until 2014, the Russia-NATO Council met on a regular basis and "really improved the security of Russian and NATO citizens." Unfortunately, it concluded, Russia has seen "no signs" of NATO's willingness to resume cooperation.[117]

Rossiskaya Gazeta accuses Western governments of attempting to shape global opinion against Russia, a tactic anticipated by Lasswell (1938), who described it as "of particular importance" in wartime: "The enemy [should be cast as conducting] a lying propaganda." In October 2015, *Rossiskaya Gazeta* quoted one military general as arguing that the West used a "large-scale information campaign to widely disseminate misinformation" about Russia's intervention in Ukraine. *Rossiskaya Gazeta* then suggested that Western propaganda campaigns against Russia have a long history. Between 1979 and 1989, the general observed, Western governments accused "Soviet troops" of "genocide against the Afghan people." More recently, Western propaganda campaigns "demonize the government of Bashar al-Assad and represent him as a dictator." These propaganda campaigns aim to "remove the regimes that do not fit into the political conception of world order developed by the American ruling circles."[118]

---

[117] "Are There Any Joint Projects with NATO to Combat Terrorism and Neutralize the Activities of Radical Extremists?," *Rossiskaya Gazeta*, May 22, 2017.
[118] "Adopted in the US, Bill Allowed Arms Supplies to Ukraine," *Rossiskaya Gazeta*, October 8, 2015.

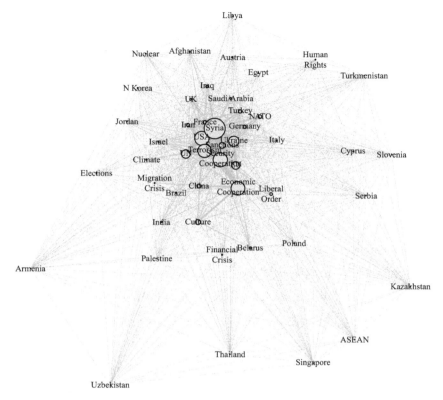

Figure 6.10 International cooperation propaganda in Russia as a weighted network

These excerpts, readers may notice, cover Putin only occasionally. Whereas 75 percent of the *People's Daily*'s international cooperation coverage references Xi Jinping or the CCP, just 35 percent of *Rossiskaya Gazeta*'s coverage features Putin or United Russia. Rather, as Figure 6.10 suggests, *Rossiskaya Gazeta* privileges the government's efforts to engage the international community to solve problems. Chief among these is terrorism, which accounts for 33 percent of coverage. After the "monstrous attack" in Nice, *Rossiskaya Gazeta* covered Moscow's efforts to partner with the European Union:

Russia's Permanent Representative to the EU Vladimir Chizhov expressed the hope that after the tragedy in Nice, the West will resume contacts with Moscow to combat terrorism, which were suspended after the leaders of Russia's anti-terrorist security structures were blacklisted in the European Union. "Yes, now, within the framework of the political dialogue, we have resumed consultations

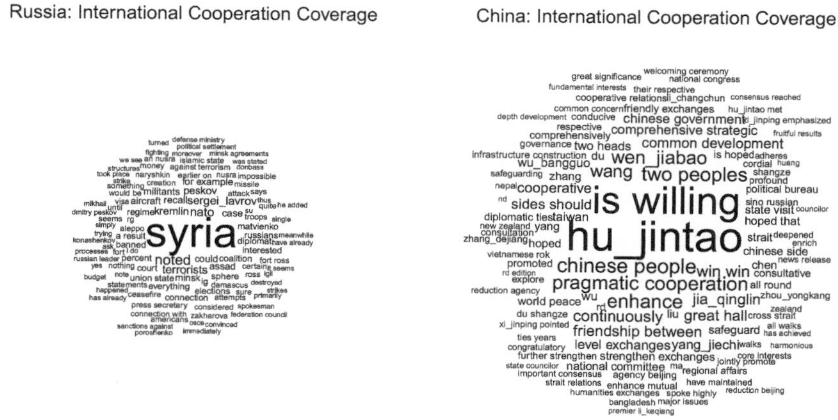

Russia: International Cooperation Coverage   China: International Cooperation Coverage

Figure 6.11 Semantic distinctiveness in international cooperation coverage for Russia and China

on the methods of combating terrorism, but this does not replace practical cooperation between relevant services, which is not yet available."[119]

Later, *Rossiskaya Gazeta* quoted UN Secretary General Antonio Guterres: "The fight against terrorism is impossible without Russia's participation."[120] This is how *Rossiskaya Gazeta* explains Moscow's engagement in Syria, which constitutes 40 percent of coverage. Another article quoted Deputy Foreign Minister Alexei Meshkov:

We have never denied that Russia is providing military assistance to Syria. [This engagement] is happening within the framework of international law. ... We do so with the consent of the Iraqi government and through it. ... Everyone who is fighting terrorism must work together.[121]

This is why the term "against terrorism" appears in 15 percent of *Rossiskaya Gazeta*'s international cooperation articles, and is prominent in the left panel of Figure 6.11. The Putin government pursues Russia's legitimate national interest.

---

[119] "Terrorist Attack in Nice," *Rossiskaya Gazeta*, July 15, 2016.
[120] Maria Golubkova, "The Head of the UN Called the Lack of Trust the Main Problem of Our Time," *Rossiskaya Gazeta*, June 1, 2017.
[121] "Russia Does Not Supply Syrian Kurds with Weapons," *Rossiskaya Gazeta*, October 15, 2015.

6.5.2 China: Remaking the International Order

The *People's Daily* displays none of *Rossiskaya Gazeta*'s modesty. From Section 6.2, the *People's Daily* suggests the United States has abdicated its traditional leadership role. The CCP is moving to fill it and ultimately to refashion the international order in its image. This new order will maintain the principles of free trade but be premised on sovereignty and non-intervention.[122] Wu Xinbo, a professor at Fudan University, describes the new order this way:

> We see a liberal, hegemonic order created by the United States and giving you dominant power and the ability to ignore international institutions when they don't suit your needs, such as when you waged war on Iraq. So the international order today is good, but we see too much US dominance and too little respect for the sovereignty of smaller states. From the Chinese perspective the current international order needs improvement.[123]

The CCP's refashioned international order will dispense with the traditional conception of human rights and redefine it to include economic prosperity. In so doing, Piccone (2018) writes, the CCP will cast itself as a leading human rights defender. Human Rights Watch puts it simply: "China is trying to get rid of human rights at the UN, one post at a time."[124]

Although *Rossiskaya Gazeta* observes that "Russia does not pretend to be a superpower," the *People's Daily* casts Xi Jinping's transformation of the international order as being met with widespread approval. From its coverage of Xi's speech at the 2017 World Economic Forum:

> In the face of the sluggish world economy and the turbulent international situation, President Xi Jinping attended the Davos forum, telling the story of China, proposing China's ideas, and contributing Chinese wisdom.
>
> During the four-day period, President Xi Jinping was speaking, day and night, and moved to Zurich, Bern, Davos, Lausanne, and Geneva. He concentrated on dozens of double-multilateral activities, extensively contacted leaders of various countries and people from all walks of life, and announced policies. This led to cooperation, fruitful results, and far-reaching impact.

---

[122] There is substantial evidence that China erects barriers around its domestic market; see Dooley, Folkerts-Landau, and Garber (2004); Godement (2010); Beeson (2009); Yu (2017); and Nager (2016). For counterarguments, see Prasad and Wei (2005); Goldstein and Lardy (2005).

[123] Kitfield (2018).

[124] Wainer (2019).

...This visit is a successful roadshow of China's governance experience, development achievements, and institutional model. As the world is rethinking the concept of national and global governance, China's development and role are constantly attracting international attention. President Xi Jinping's trip to Switzerland shows international sentiment and great power influence. In the historical process of the evolution of international relations, he has engraved the deep imprint of great power diplomacy with Chinese characteristics.

Chairman Xi Jinping's vivid elaboration and profound explanations deepened the world's thinking on the nature of globalization, clarified people's understandings of its effects, strengthened the world's confidence in it, and effectively pointed the way toward its proper governance.

President Xi Jinping's speech won the applause of the participants. All parties highly valued the important and positive message that President Xi Jinping conveyed to the world and believed that President Xi Jinping's "historic" speech was timed just right, bringing sunshine to Davos in the winter and adding confidence to all walks of life. The Chinese Dream and the world dream have become increasingly connected.[125]

This "new type of great power relations" is the premise of Xi Jinping's official foreign policy platform.

Figure 6.12 visualizes the *People's Daily's* international cooperation coverage. It is profoundly different than Russia's. Whereas *Rossiskaya Gazeta's* network reflects a multilateral foreign policy, the *People's Daily's* network is dominated by small nodes connected only to the CCP government. This represents a "hub-and-spoke" alliance system, with bilateral relationships arrayed around the hegemon, rather than a network of interconnected relationships embedded in multilateral institutions.[126] Figure 6.13 illustrates this. For each node in Figures 6.10 and 6.12, we computed the eigenvector centrality score, which measures node centrality based on the centrality of other nodes with which it is connected. Intuitively, nodes with high eigenvector centrality scores are connected with other nodes that have high eigenvector centrality scores. The y-axis measures the frequency of the eigenvector centrality scores along the x-axis. The dashed vertical lines give mean eigenvector centrality scores.

The *People's Daily* covers the CCP's bilateral relationships from across Africa, Latin America, the Middle East, Asia, and North America. Figure 6.11 visualizes the nature of this coverage. For Russia, the distinctive words reflect its foreign policy priorities: NATO, Syria, terrorism,

---

[125] "The Chaotic Cloud Is Still Calm: Foreign Minister Wang Yi Talks about President Xi Jinping's Visit to Switzerland," *People's Daily*, January 20, 2017.
[126] Ikenberry (2014); Lee (2015).

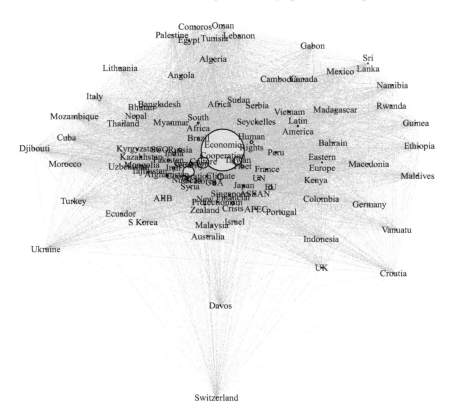

Figure 6.12 International cooperation propaganda in China as a weighted network

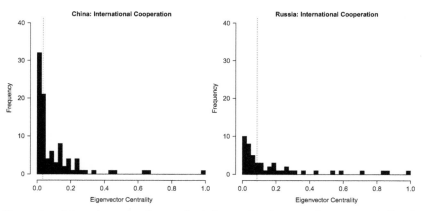

Figure 6.13 Measuring network centrality in international cooperation coverage in Russia and China

and a handful of others. For China, the distinctive words capture how the *People's Daily* describes the regime's bilateral relationships: "pragmatic cooperation," "two peoples," "win-win," "friendship between," "common development," "strengthen exchanges," and "world peace." The *People's Daily* tells readers that the CCP government is building a constituency for a transformed international order, with the CCP at its center.

The institutional centerpiece of this transformed international order is the Shanghai Cooperation Organization (SCO), which the *People's Daily* references as often as the UN. The SCO has the highest eigenvector centrality score of any international institution. When the *People's Daily* covers the CCP's multilateral relationships, it most commonly references the SCO. The *People's Daily* describes it this way:

With the aim of the people's hearts and minds, with the expansion of foreign exchanges and cooperation as the driving force, we will fully promote the development of the Shanghai Cooperation Organization in the direction of more comprehensive cooperation and more openness to the outside world.[127]

The article goes on to emphasize China's leadership: "to expand the final size of the China-Eurasia Economic Cooperation Fund to US$5 billion," to provide 2,000 personnel to member governments over the next two years, and to invite "50 young leaders" in SCO countries to study in China. To underscore the CCP's ambitions, the article notes that countries far beyond the SCO's Asian core are welcome to join. The only condition is that members must "adhere to the 'Shanghai spirit' of mutual trust, mutual benefit, equality, consultation, and respect for diverse civilizations," and thus implement "the common and cooperative Asian security concept." Member countries, that is, must subscribe to China's vision of non-interventionism.

The *People's Daily* treats the Asian Infrastructure Investment Bank (AIIB) and the Belt and Road Initiative (BRI) as substitutes for the World Bank and IMF. Again, the conspicuous feature of these institutions is their geographic ambition:

More than 100 countries and international organizations have actively responded to the opportunity for support, and more than 40 countries and international organizations have signed cooperation agreements with China. The "friend circle"

---

[127] Du Shangze, Huang Wendi, Li Tao, and Qi Peng, "Xi Jinping Attends the Dushanbe Summit of the Shanghai Cooperation Organization and Delivers an Important Speech," *People's Daily*, September 13, 2014.

is constantly expanding rapidly. The "Belt and Road Initiative" initiative comes from China, but the results benefit the world.[128]

The *People's Daily* reports later: "Germany, France, the United Kingdom, and other countries have joined the AIIB." "From the beginning," China has "[welcomed] the United States to participate."[129]

6.5.3 Comparing Sentiments in Executive Coverage

Rossiskaya Gazeta casts the Kremlin's foreign policy objectives as modest: defending multilateralism in the face of Western "bloc thinking" from the Cold War. The *People's Daily* celebrates Xi Jinping's efforts to transform the international order in the CCP's image, with new institutions that require member-states to embrace the CCP's vision of sovereignty and non-intervention. Our data should register a difference in the sentiments associated with Vladimir Putin and Xi Jinping in their respective propaganda apparatuses. To probe this, we restricted attention to international cooperation articles, and then extracted the twenty words surrounding each reference to Putin or Xi. Next, we used the semantic dictionaries from Chapter 3 to capture the sentiments of these twenty words. Finally, we estimated models of the form

$$Y_{ij} = \alpha + \beta X_{ij} + \epsilon \tag{6.6}$$

where i indexes article, j indexes country, and X_{ij} is an indicator that assumes value 1 if article ij was published by the Russian propaganda apparatus and value 0 otherwise. The outcome variable Y_{ij} measures the number of words associated with each of our sentiment dictionaries in article ij, standardized by the number of executive references in the same article. The result is a per reference rate of sentiment association.

The results appear in Figure 6.14. Sentiments associated with Xi Jinping have negative coefficients; sentiments associated with Vladimir Putin have positive coefficients. The results are consistent with our theory and the propaganda content above. The *People's Daily*'s international cooperation coverage is distinctive for casting Xi Jinping's international engagements as marked by strength, power, activity, and virtue. On average, each reference to Xi Jinping in the *People's Daily* has between 0.5

---

[128] "The Chaotic Cloud Is Still Calm: Foreign Minister Wang Yi Talks about President Xi Jinping's Visit to Switzerland," *People's Daily*, January 20, 2017.

[129] Zhong Sheng, "The Root of the Gun Control Problem Is Money Politics," *People's Daily*, September 25, 2016.

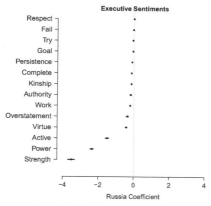

Figure 6.14 Sentiments associated with regime coverage in Russian and Chinese international cooperation propaganda

and 2 more words that reflect those four sentiments than each reference to Vladimir Putin in *Rossiskaya Gazeta*. These effects are large and reflect how the *People's Daily*'s celebrates Xi Jinping's transformation of the international order.

6.6 ENGAGING WITH XI JINPING AND DANA ROHRABACHER IN CONGO AND UZBEKISTAN

How Vladimir Putin is cast as pursuing the legitimate national interest and Xi Jinping is cast as internationally powerful are clearly conditioned by their positions at the core of the international system. In lower-income autocracies, we should observe propaganda narratives that reflect their different international positions.

We focus on two countries, which featured in Chapter 5: Congo and Uzbekistan. Here, they make an appealing comparison. Their levels of GDP per capita and development aid are similar. Each experienced periods of sustained growth in the early 2000s. The poverty rate declined somewhat more in Uzbekistan than Congo, but Uzbekistan also conscripts citizens for several weeks each fall. They were also visited by the same ethically compromised American politician during our sample period, and each propaganda apparatus covered the visit extensively.

Each government has also sought a close relationship with China. In 2016, as part of China's Belt and Road Initiative, Xi Jinping and Islam Karimov inaugurated a new railroad connecting the Ferghana Valley and

277

Tashkent, Uzbekistan's capital. According to China's Ministry of Commerce, China is now Uzbekistan's second-largest trade partner and its largest single investor. Likewise, Sassou Nguesso has emerged as among China's key African partners. The centerpiece of Sassou Nguesso's economic diversification plan is his Special Economic Zone (SEZ) initiative. Modeled on Shenzhen, China, Sassou Nguesso hopes to attract multinational firms to four SEZs by offering public goods and favorable tax rates. These relationships also entail a security component. Although the Sassou Nguesso government refuses to discuss this publicly, Western diplomats note an increase in the number of Chinese nationals employed at the Chinese embassy, which they attribute to expanded support for Sassou Nguesso's digital surveillance apparatus.[130] The Uzbekistan government's police force is trained by the CCP.[131]

Their respective propaganda apparatuses have a common set of international engagements from which to draw. Still, how these common international engagements are covered is dramatically different and in ways that are consistent with our theory. Sassou Nguesso is cast as pursuing the legitimate national interest: by working with international partners to foster growth and provide public goods, which, his propaganda apparatus acknowledges, are desperately needed by citizens. By contrast, successive Uzbek regimes have emphasized their widespread international support – especially in the security sector – and hence their immunity from international sanction.

Figure 6.15 reflects these differences. To capture these narrative subtleties, we restricted attention to international cooperation coverage, and then we translated both corpora into English. The set of distinctive words appears in the top two panels of Figure 6.15. The middle and bottom panels, respectively, do the same for their bilateral relationships with China and the United States.

6.6.1 Congo: "A pilot country for economic cooperation in Central Africa"

These word clouds illustrate how honest propaganda permeates Sassou Nguesso's international cooperation coverage. In February 2017, at precisely the moment of the fuel shortage we discussed in Chapter 5, Congo also confronted a vaccine shortage. These shortages had the same cause:

---

[130] Interview with anonymous senior Western diplomat, November 2012.
[131] Hashimova (2018).

Congo: International Cooperation Coverage

Uzbekistan: International Cooperation Coverage

Congo: China Coverage

Uzbekistan: China Coverage

Congo: USA Coverage

Uzbekistan: USA Coverage

Figure 6.15 Semantic distinctiveness for international cooperation propaganda in Congo and Uzbekistan

a bankrupt government, despite its oil wealth. During the sample period, "vaccine" appears in 9 percent of articles and "immunization" appears in 8 percent. Sassou Nguesso's propaganda apparatus also covered his efforts to address persistent food insecurity. "Malnutrition" appears in 15 percent of international cooperation coverage; "UNICEF," the government's partner in food security programs, appears in 13 percent; and "nutrition" appears in 8 percent. The propaganda apparatus covered this debt crisis frequently, with "debt" appearing in 23 percent of articles. These are substantial coverage rates. By comparison, references to "Sassou Nguesso" appear in 55 percent of articles. These articles, moreover, are forthright about domestic challenges. In November 2016, *Vox* published an article with this headline: "Approximately 175,000 Congolese Children of 0–5 Years of Age Malnourished." It quoted this statistic from a UNICEF official, Dr. Aloys Kamuragive, who also cited a chronic malnutrition rate of 24.4 percent. To be sure, *Vox* concluded the article by noting the government's efforts to address them. The UNICEF meeting had been hosted by the government and yielded new donor commitments.[132]

Sassou Nguesso aspires to be Central Africa's elder statesman, and so persuaded the African Union to appoint him chief mediator for the Libyan crisis. As a result, "African Union" and "Libyan crisis" figure prominently in the top left panel of Figure 6.15. Sassou Nguesso also brands himself a leader in the fight against climate change. In March 2017, Sassou Nguesso convened a regional summit to discuss the Congo Basin, which is the world's second leading carbon reservoir. Words associated with this project – "Blue Funds," "Congo Basin," "forest," and "climate change" – each appear in roughly 10 percent of international cooperation content.

The centerpiece of Sassou Nguesso's economic policy is the Special Economic Zone (SEZ) initiative, which he claims will diversify the economy away from oil. SEZs are planned for Brazzaville and Pointe-Noire, Congo's two largest cities, and Oyo, a remote village in northern Congo with 5,000 residents, including Sassou Nguesso. Some 12 percent of all international cooperation articles reference these SEZs, and, in the China subset, these SEZs are referenced more than once per article. "Special economic zone" appears 50 percent more often than "Sassou Nguesso." These articles emphasize the benefits of Chinese investment to Congolese

---

[132] "Approximately 175,000 Congolese Children of 0–5 Years of Age Malnourished," *Vox Congo*, November 3, 2016.

citizens. On January 20, 2017, days after the Chinese foreign minister visited Brazzaville, Sassou Nguesso's propaganda apparatus ran this headline: "The Pointe-Noire Economic Zone Will Create Nearly 40,000 Direct Jobs." Later in the article, a government minister claimed the project would generate another 50,000 indirect jobs and a $2 billion increase in GDP. Congo, the article advertised, is "a pilot country for [Chinese] economic cooperation in Central Africa."[133]

The propaganda apparatus routinely covers the financial investments these projects require. "CFA francs" appears in some 25 percent of articles, "funding" appears in 18 percent, "yuan" in 10 percent, "euros" in 8 percent, and "bond" in 9 percent.

6.6.2 Uzbekistan: "As a scientist, I am very interested in the special model of civil society development implemented in your country"

The word clouds for Uzbekistan reveal a different narrative. While Sassou Nguesso attempts to persuade citizens of his commitment to domestic welfare, Uzbek propaganda is conspicuous for these phrases, which appear in between 12 percent and 40 percent of content: "your country," "mutually beneficial," "between our," "further development," "strategic partnership," "beneficial cooperation," "dynamically," "consistently developing," "further strengthening," "highly appreciated," and "great importance."

These phrases convey absurd claims about Uzbekistan's domestic conditions and the regime's powerful foreign backers. Table 6.3 documents this. *Narodnoye Slovo* routinely publishes interviews with foreigners, who lavish praise on the government: "As a scientist, I am very interested in the special model of civil society development implemented in your country. It needs to be studied."[134] These articles occasionally reference specific areas of bilateral cooperation, especially criminal justice: "Cooperation with China is gradually expanding in many areas, including in the legal sphere. Expansion of the contractual and legal bases of mutually beneficial cooperation serves the consistent development of cooperation between the prosecutor general's offices of our countries."[135]

---

[133] "The Pointe-Noire Economic Zone Will Create Nearly 40,000 Direct Jobs," *Vox Congo*, January 20, 2017.

[134] "Eckhard Priller: 'Uzbekistan is an Intensively Developing Country,'" *Narodnoye Slovo*, August 4, 2015.

[135] Babur Abidov, "Meeting in the Prosecutor General's Office," *Narodnoye Slovo*, October 8, 2014.

Table 6.3 *Extracts from Uzbekistan's international cooperation propaganda*

Term	Representative extract
Your country	As a scientist I am very interested in the special model of civil society development implemented in **your country**. it needs to be studied. Uzbekistan is famous for its history, original and rich culture.
Between our	Zhang Gaoli stressed that due to the invaluable merits of Islam Karimov in June this year, the interlinkages **between our** states were raised to the level of a comprehensive strategic partnership, that China is ready for the consistent development of
Further development	the judicial and legal system of the country. "Successful reform of Uzbekistan's judicial and legal system creates great opportunities for **further development** of cooperation between the prosecutor general's offices of our countries," said Vietnam's Attorney General
Strategic partnership	carrying out my diplomatic mission, I will put all my strength and knowledge to achieve this goal. The development of **strategic partnership** with Uzbekistan is a priority for Chinese diplomacy. Your country is on the way to expanding cooperation with the world
Mutually beneficial	China is gradually expanding in many areas, including in the legal sphere. Expansion of the contractual and legal bases of **mutually beneficial** cooperation serves the consistent development of cooperation between the prosecutor general's offices of our countries.
Dynamically	The experience of Uzbekistan is in demand by the world community. Today, Uzbekistan is a **dynamically** developing state and a full member of the world community, which plays an important role in the international system
Consistently developing	the implementation of joint programs and projects." Becoming a sovereign state, Uzbekistan began to establish independent cooperation with foreign countries, **consistently developing** relations based on mutual trust and interest. One of the most important partners of our country is China.
Further strengthening	For a historically short period, the republic has made tremendous progress in all spheres of life, in particular, in **further strengthening** state sovereignty, ensuring security and stability, a gradual transition from a planned economy to a market economy, raising the level
Highly appreciated	basis of the "Uzbek model" of development, democratic processes, and the formation of civil society in the country. The guests **highly appreciated** the peaceful policy of Uzbekistan, its efforts and actions aimed at ensuring security and stability in the region
Great importance	Since the first days of independence, Uzbekistan, moving steadily forward, has achieved great success. Your state attaches **great importance** to the preservation of peace, security and stability in the region, thereby making a great contribution to peace.

The regime's propaganda apparatus occasionally tells citizens that the Chinese government is investing in its ability to prosecute them.

The distinctive words for general and China-specific international cooperation coverage are notable for their similarities. The Shanghai Cooperation Organization (SCO) figures centrally. We discussed the CCP's ambitions for the SCO in Section 6.5, especially its principle of non-intervention in the internal affairs of member-states. Uzbekistan's word clouds privilege security and sovereignty as well, implicit references to the government's capacity to suppress dissent. "Security" and "independence" appear, on average, more than once per article in Uzbekistan's China coverage, roughly on par with "special economic zones" in Congo and, again, 50 percent more often than "Sassou Nguesso." The terms "great" and "high" appear 1.7 and 1.4 times per article, respectively, and generally reference the CCP's support for President Karimov, who is referenced 1.6 times per article, or more than twice as often as Sassou Nguesso is mentioned in *Les Dépêches*. The first genuinely economic terms – "investment" and "industry" – appear 0.8 time per article, roughly the rate of another security term, "stability."

Uzbekistan's propaganda apparatus is so committed to broadcasting foreign support that some letters may be fabricated. For its independence holiday in 2016, *Narodnoye Slovo* published expressions of international support for nearly a week. These articles, remarkable for their length, catalog the diplomatic congratulations received by the government, each listing between a dozen and three dozen apparent international allies. Of these congratulatory letters, *Narodnoye Slovo* published three in full: from Barack Obama, Xi Jinping, and Vladimir Putin. Two of these three diplomatic messages conclude with the same salutation: "Yours faithfully," world leaders tell Karimov.

My sincere congratulations

August 31, 2016

His Excellency Mr. Islam Karimov, President of the Republic of Uzbekistan

Dear Mr. President!

On behalf of the people of the United States of America, I send to you and the people of Uzbekistan heartfelt congratulations on the occasion of the 25th anniversary of Uzbekistan's independence, celebrated on September 1.

While Uzbekistan celebrates this historic achievement, we remain committed to supporting its independence, sovereignty and territorial integrity. I look forward to continued cooperation between our countries for many years on the road to a safer, prosperous and democratic future.

The people of the United States of America congratulate you on this important milestone.

Yours faithfully,

Barack Obama, President of the United States of America

The Chairman of the People's Republic of China, Xi Jinping, sent the following message:

His Excellency Mr. Islam Karimov, President of the Republic of Uzbekistan

Dear Mr. President!

On the occasion of the 25th anniversary of the independence of the Republic of Uzbekistan on behalf of the Chinese people and on my own behalf, I express to you and the friendly people of Uzbekistan sincere congratulations and heartfelt wishes.

Over the 25 years of independence, under the firm leadership of the President, Uzbekistan has maintained political stability, dynamic economic development, international prestige has increased significantly and bright progress in building the state has been achieved. Practice proves that the Uzbek model, initiated by the President, corresponds to the realities of the country and has a great vitality.

In recent years, Sino-Uzbek relations have reached a new strategic level. I greatly value the sincere friendship between us. I am ready together with you to make efforts for the promotion of Chinese-Uzbek relations, a comprehensive strategic partnership in order to achieve great results and for the benefit of the peoples of the two countries.

I wish your country prosperity and power, and the people - happiness and prosperity.

I wish the President good health and success!

Xi Jinping, Chairman of the People's Republic of China

The letter of support from Vladimir Putin was published the next day, with the same headline.

My sincere congratulations

September 1, 2016

His Excellency Mr. Islam Karimov, President of the Republic of Uzbekistan,

I heartily congratulate you on the 25th anniversary of the proclamation of the independence of the Republic of Uzbekistan.

Your country has made significant progress in socio-economic, scientific, technical, humanitarian and other fields. Uzbekistan's authority on the world arena is very high.

Relations between our states, based on the good traditions of friendship and mutual respect, are actively developing in the spirit of strategic partnership and alliance. I am convinced that we will continue to strengthen mutually beneficial bilateral cooperation in all areas, to effectively coordinate efforts in resolving pressing issues on the international agenda. This meets the fundamental interests of the peoples of Russia and Uzbekistan, is in the line of ensuring regional stability and security.

I sincerely wish you, dear Islam Abduganievich, good health, prosperity and success, and to all citizens of Uzbekistan - happiness and prosperity.

Yours faithfully,

Vladimir Putin, President of Russian Federation

In our view, the strikingly similar salutations cast doubt on the messages' veracity. Each of these articles concluded with this: "Congratulatory telegrams continue to arrive."

6.6.3 *When Dana Rohrabacher Visits: Covering the United States of America*

In Congo, where Sassou Nguesso is constrained to seek some public support, coverage of international cooperation – both aggregate and China-specific – is overwhelmingly about Sassou Nguesso's efforts to attract foreign investment and diversify the economy. In Uzbekistan, coverage of Chinese engagement focuses on security and expressions of unbridled support. These differences even appear in coverage of their bilateral relationships with the United States. The same ethically compromised American congressional representative visited both countries during our sample period: Dana Rohrabacher, a Republican from California, whom Republican leaders suspect of accepting money from Russian president Vladimir Putin.

The word clouds for American coverage appear in the bottom panel of Figure 6.15. Although Uzbekistan's coverage of the United States focuses less on security cooperation than in its coverage of China, it still emphasizes the American government's backing. The second most distinctive word is "I," which reflects its penchant for first-person expressions of support. *Narodnoye Slovo* covered Rohrabacher's visit this way:

July 26, 2016

High assessment of the success of independent Uzbekistan

Chairman of the Subcommittee on Europe, Eurasia and Emerging Threats of the US House of Representatives, Congressman from the State of California Dana Rohrabacher: "Over the years, Uzbekistan has become a stable and prosperous state, the development model of which can serve as a vivid example for many countries. Thanks to the wise leadership of President Islam Karimov, the republic took a worthy place in the international arena. Uzbekistan is one of the key partners of the United States in the region, and I hope that our countries continue to develop close friendly relations. As chairman of the subcommittee, I intend to contribute to the creation of a Central Asian caucus in the House of Representatives. The delegation of congressmen intends to again visit Uzbekistan to discuss the prospects for expanding inter-parliamentary ties and cooperation in other areas. I count on further deepening relations with the republic for the benefit of our peoples."

By contrast, Sassou Nguesso's coverage of the United States again focuses on economic cooperation; "youth" and "employment" are prominent. This difference is even evident in how his propaganda apparatus covered his meeting with Rohrabacher. On December 26, 2017, Sassou Nguesso departed Brazzaville for Miami, Florida, where disgraced American lobbyist Jack Abramoff had arranged for Sassou Nguesso to meet President-Elect Donald Trump. The meeting, ostensibly about the Libya crisis, would have been Trump's first with an African president. Sassou Nguesso's propaganda apparatus broadcasted it widely and even distributed a picture of Trump and Sassou Nguesso embracing *before the meeting had happened*; Sassou Nguesso's head was photoshopped atop Mitt Romney's body, which gave the impression that Sassou Nguesso was slightly taller than Trump. The meeting was canceled once the American press caught wind, and so Sassou Nguesso was left in a Miami hotel between December 27 and December 30, waiting for a meeting that never happened. The snub was humiliating. One Burkina Faso newspaper mocked him: "What does [Sassou Nguesso] think he can teach the new American president about Libya?" One commentator suggested that Sassou Nguesso "stage a sit-in at Trump Tower." Paul Marie Mpouélé, a Brazzaville activist, called it "a national shame."[136]

Rohrabacher's visit to Brazzaville in February 2017 – leading a ten-person congressional delegation, on their way to a meeting with Putin in Moscow – constituted Sassou Nguesso's attempt to save face.[137]

---

[136] Carter (2017).
[137] Interview with a senior regime official, date withheld to preserve anonymity.

Sassou Nguesso's propaganda apparatus covered Rohrabacher's visit this way:

February 13, 2017

United States Inclined to Strengthen Relations with Congo

The delegation of American lawmakers, led by Dana Rohrabacher, was received on February 10 by President of the Republic, Denis Sassou Nguesso, in his residence. Upon leaving the interview, the head of the delegation expressed his country's will to consolidate its relations with Congo, at this moment in which American institutions have been renewed with the arrival of a new administration: "President Denis Sassou Nguesso was very pleased with our visit. A new page has turned in the United States, and the President of Congo understands the importance of the friendship between our two countries and our two peoples. He is committed to the well-being of Congolese youth. Together we will work on the development of the economy. In the field of potash for example, there are many opportunities to exploit.

Our theory makes sense of these differences. Given the absurdity of Uzbek propaganda, its claims of international support rest on first-person testimonials from the Great Powers. In Congo, testimonials from foreign officials emphasize Sassou Nguesso's efforts to advance domestic living standards.

6.7 CONCLUSION

Citizens around the world generally know little about life abroad.[138] This has two theoretical implications, which render international and domestic propaganda narratives analytically different. First, without some shared sense of what constitutes absurdity – without, that is, common knowledge of the possible – autocrats are less able to employ absurd propaganda as a signal of their capacity for repression. Second, in constrained autocracies, propaganda apparatuses are able to "get away" with more negative coverage without undermining claims to neutrality. These two forces render international propaganda narratives more similar across autocracies than propaganda narratives about domestic conditions.

This chapter documented two common tactics in international news propaganda: comparison sets and selective coverage. These tactics are

---

[138] Friedman (2012); Pew Research Center (2013, 2015); Friedman (2014); Huang (2015*a*, 2020); Thrall (2018).

useful regardless of the electoral constraints an autocrat confronts. If citizens are willing to engage in anti-regime protests in proportion to the likelihood of better living standards under democracy, autocrats have powerful incentives to shape citizens' beliefs accordingly: by omitting topics that aggravate citizens' grievances and documenting corruption in Western democracies.

The Russian and Chinese propaganda apparatuses are different in a range of ways, but their coverage of Western democracies is similar. *Rosiyskaya Gazeta* essentially lets Donald Trump speak for it, as vindicating its longstanding claims: about the impending collapse of the European Union, the prevalence of terrorism, the political allegiances of Crimeans, the misadventures of America's foreign policy, and the shortcomings of American democracy. Although less enthusiastic about Trump, the CCP's propaganda apparatus covers similar issues, often in a sophisticated way: the corruption of American democracy by monied interests and the gun violence epidemic currently gripping America.

However similar these international news narratives are, this chapter documents differences in coverage of international cooperation. Propaganda apparatuses in constrained autocracies emphasize their pursuit of the national interest: their efforts to partner with the international community to advance living conditions or, in some cases, in the fight against terrorism. Where electoral constraints are non-binding, propaganda apparatuses emphasize the regime's immunity from international pressure: either because the world's Great Powers hold the regime in high esteem or because, as in China, the regime is so powerful that it is bending the international order to its will.

Our theory treats effusive propaganda as implicitly threatening: a signal that repressive governments send to citizens about the consequences of dissent. Do propaganda apparatuses ever make these implicit threats explicit? If so, when? These questions motivate Chapter 7.

7

Threatening Citizens with Repression

7.1 THREATS OF REPRESSION AS POLITICAL COMMUNICATION

Repression is a defining feature of autocracy, yet scholars know little about when autocrats threaten citizens with violence. "An unwritten division of labor appears to exist," Davenport (2007a, 9) observes. "Scholars concerned with civil liberties, protest policing, human rights violations, and genocide/politicide focus on repression, while scholars interested in rhetoric, communication, and propaganda focus on persuasion." This was not always so. Scholars have documented how Joseph Stalin threatened Soviet elites in *Pravda*,[1] how Rafael Trujillo threatened Dominican elites in *El Caribe*,[2] and how the CCP warned Tiananmen protesters to disperse in the *People's Daily* before the massacre.[3]

In this chapter, we combine our theory of propaganda with insights from experimental psychology to understand which autocrats employ propaganda-based threats of repression, when, and against whom. Using propaganda to threaten citizens is potentially useful. By reminding citizens of the consequences of dissent,[4] threats of repression may deter anti-regime behavior. Explicit threats of repression are also costly. For propaganda apparatuses that aim to persuade citizens of regime merits, threats of repression undermine costly investments in credibility. For propaganda apparatuses that signal the regime's repressive capacity, the

---

[1] Montefiore (2004), Overy (2004), Service (2004).

[2] Crassweller (1966), Vargas Llosa (2000). *El Caribe* published a daily section, "Foro Público," that publicly disparaged Trujillo's political opponents; thanks to Samuel Bonilla Bogaert for this observation.

[3] Buckley (2014).

[4] Young (2018); Aldama, Vásquez-Cortés, and Young (2019). Fear may also cue risk aversion; see Johnson and Tversky (1983); Lerner and Keltner (2000, 2001); Lerner et al. (2003); Druckman and McDermott (2008); Guiso, Sapienza, and Zingales (2013); Cohn et al. (2015).

force of a threat may diminish how often it is issued. Threats of repression may also give special salience to moments that are already politically sensitive or recall the regime's historical crimes. For these reasons, our theory suggests, propaganda-based threats of repression should be used sparingly, when the regime is most concerned about mass protests. Our theory also suggests that explicit threats of repression should more commonly target political out-groups and be especially uncommon where electoral constraints are binding, since publishing threats of repression undermines investments in credibility.

Studying propaganda-based threats of repression across countries is difficult because threats are contextual, often premised on histories of violence and persecution. Language that citizens in one country interpret as threatening may be innocuous elsewhere. In Rwanda, Kagame's occasional appeals to the 1994 genocide are understood as evidence of his willingness to use violence in the future.[5] In Uzbekistan, President Islam Karimov's largely Muslim government has sought to suppress Christianity: by closing churches, harassing Christians, and banning Christian literature. On December 25, 2015, his propaganda apparatus published an article ostensibly about Uzbekistan's modern rail service, which citizens use to visit friends and family for the holiday. The article warned: "Cabins are equipped with modern instruments, such as video surveillance devices."

To accommodate this, we focus on four case studies. The first two let us probe whether the same propaganda apparatus treats a political in-group differently than an out-group. In the context of our theory, an autocrat confronts more binding electoral constraints from the in-group and weaker electoral constraints from the out-group. We focus first on Cameroon, a country of 20 million in Central Africa. Cameroon is linguistically divided: 20 percent of citizens speak English, 80 percent speak French. These linguistic divisions are political. Since independence in 1960, Cameroon has had just two presidents: Ahmadou Ahidjo, between 1960 and 1982, and Paul Biya since. Both have been francophone, governed with a francophone elite, and privileged the interests of francophone constituents. Biya's propaganda newspaper, the *Cameroon Tribune*, publishes articles in English and French, and so it can target Biya's francophone in-group and anglophone out-group with different propaganda. As our theory predicts, Biya attempts to persuade

[5] Sundaram (2016).

francophone readers of regime merits while threatening anglophone readers with repression.

Next, we return to China, where propaganda-based threats are widely associated with codewords, like "social stability" and "harmony," as well as allusions to the repressive apparatus.[6] Propaganda-based threats, we show, are occasioned primarily by anniversaries of ethnic separatist movements in Tibet and Xinjiang and secondarily by major political anniversaries. The CCP disproportionately targets identity groups that are excluded from the CCP's core, ethnic Han constituency. Threats of repression are between three and six times more likely in the *Xinjiang Daily*, a regional newspaper that targets ethnic Uyghurs, than in the *People's Daily* and *Workers' Daily*, which target the Han in-group. Threats of repression are correlated with spikes in pro-regime propaganda, which, as we documented in Chapter 4, are regarded by citizens as implicitly threatening.

Our final two case studies consider moments of crisis, when threats of repression are most valuable. Are constrained autocrats less likely to threaten citizens with repression even then? We study the two most profound crises in our sample: the unexpected death of Uzbek president Islam Karimov in September 2016 and the Tunisian Revolution that toppled President Zine El Abidine Ben Ali in January 2011. Again, we find that propaganda-based threats are more common where electoral constraints are non-binding. Amidst a succession crisis in Uzbekistan, the propaganda apparatus published articles that are among the most threatening in our collection. One advertised the "loyalty" of security forces, who "are harsh people" and whose families are "fully cared for by the President of the country." In Tunisia, even as Ben Ali was losing power, his propaganda apparatus sought to persuade citizens of regime merits: by conceding the government's failures to create jobs and highlighting new efforts to do so.

This chapter proceeds as follows. Section 7.2 develops a series of hypotheses about propaganda-based threats of repression in autocracies. Sections 7.3 and 7.4 test our theory in the context of Cameroon and China, respectively. Section 7.5 explores how propaganda apparatuses in Tunisia and Uzbekistan responded to crises.

---

[6] Brady (2008), Sandby-Thomas (2011), Yue (2012), Huang (2015*b*), Wang and Minzner (2015), Benney (2016), Steinhardt (2016), Yang (2017). Huang (2018) shows that after reading a newspaper article about "social stability" in an online survey experiment, Chinese citizens reported more negative views of the government, more willingness to move abroad, and less willingness to protest.

7.2 THEORY

7.2.1 Why Propaganda-Based Threats Are Useful

We define a threat as a commonly understood claim by the government that anti-regime behavior will be repressed. It is distinct from the sort of absurd pro-regime propaganda that serves to dominate. Repressive governments can threaten citizens in a range of ways. They can dispatch security forces to protest locations. They can employ repression against some citizens to discourage protests by others. They can use codewords that remind citizens of past repression or make clear that the government will employ repression in response to certain behaviors. For these threats to shape citizen behavior, they must be received. This is the chief benefit of broadcasting threats via propaganda. Repressive governments can threaten many citizens simultaneously at relatively little cost.

Threats of repression may deter protests in several ways. Threats of repression may signal to citizens the consequences of a certain form of dissent or the consequences of dissent at a given moment. Alternatively, threats of repression may induce fear. In Zimbabwe, Young (2018) finds that cueing fears of political repression among opposition sympathizers reduces their willingness to dissent, even without new information about the government's capacity for repression or willingness to employ it. Fear, political psychologists find, fosters pessimism and risk aversion, which deters public opposition.[7] By deterring protest, threats of repression enable the autocrat to forgo the costs associated with employing it. These costs can be substantial, since repression can give citizens focal moments around which to mobilize in the future.[8]

7.2.2 Why Propaganda-Based Threats Are Costly

Threats of repression are costly regardless of whether autocrats employ propaganda to persuade citizens or to dominate them.

Mechanism 1: Source Derogation (Propaganda as Persuasion) Source derogation occurs when individuals evaluate the source of a message

---

[7] Johnson and Tversky (1983); Lerner and Keltner (2001); Lerner et al. (2003); Druckman and McDermott (2008); Guiso, Sapienza, and Zingales (2013); Cohn et al. (2015).

[8] Opp and Roehl (1990), Goldstone and Tilly (2009), Lawrence (2017), Carter and Carter (2020a).

as "less objective and less trustworthy."[9] This mechanism is consistent with both Bayesian updating and experimental psychology. From a Bayesian perspective, publishing threats alongside content designed to persuade citizens should invalidate the persuasive content. If citizens are rational, propaganda-based threats make them update their beliefs about the regime's commitment to public welfare. From a non-Bayesian perspective, psychologists have long explored why individuals resist persuasion.[10] Individuals, many scholars contend, have an intrinsic desire for autonomy. When autonomy is threatened, individuals are compelled to maintain the opinion or behavior that elicited the threat.[11] Psychologists refer to these as "threats to freedom."[12] Messages that constitute threats to freedom compel individuals to contest their source.[13]

Where autocrats must persuade citizens of regime merits, the *source derogation* mechanism makes propaganda-based threats of repression costly. Building credibility with readers requires conceding policy failures, which is costly. These admissions help citizens coordinate protests and regime insiders coordinate coups. Source derogation undermines costly investments in credibility. Where propaganda apparatuses aim to persuade citizens of regime merits, propaganda-based threats of repression should be rare.

Mechanism 2: Boomerang Effect (Propaganda as Persuasion or Domination) Messages that challenge individual autonomy may also elicit a *boomerang effect*, in which individuals contest the message's content. Individuals do so by engaging in less (more) of the encouraged (discouraged) behavior,[14] leading to the opposite of the desired result.[15] If citizens perceive the threat as a warning against mass protests in response to an event or grievance, then the boomerang effect suggests that the threat itself could endow that event or grievance with special salience. In turn, the threat may help catalyze the collective action that it sought to discourage. The boomerang effect can also be placed in a Bayesian context. By issuing a threat prior to some event, a regime may signal to citizens that it regards that event as a focal moment for protests: that the regime

[9] Smith (1977).
[10] Cialdini (2006).
[11] Brehm and Brehm (1981), Burgoon et al. (2002), Rains (2013).
[12] Kronrod, Grinstein, and Wathieu (2012).
[13] Smith (1977).
[14] Baek, Yoon, and Kim (2015).
[15] Clee and Wicklund (1980), Ringold (2002).

believes other citizens will engage in collective action around a specific day.

The boomerang effect has been well documented in China. On April 26, 1989, the *People's Daily* published a profoundly threatening editorial. There would be "no peace," it warned, if student protesters in Tiananmen Square failed to disband. The editorial elicited a boomerang effect: Tens of thousands of citizens joined the students the next day. The boomerang effect should deter propaganda-based threats of repression in both contexts: where autocrats employ propaganda to persuade and to dominate.

Mechanism 3: Desensitization (Propaganda as Domination) Even if absurd propaganda makes the regime's repressive capacity common knowledge among citizens, its force may diminish over time. If so, threats of repression may provide a vivid reminder of the regime's capacity for repression. Psychologists refer to this as *desensitization*: "a reduction in emotion-related physiological reactivity to real violence."[16]

Desensitization has been widely documented. The canonical experiment entails exposing treatment and control groups to violence and then measuring their physiological responses. Psychologists have varied the medium of exposure, the kind of violence, and how the physiological response is measured. Across variants, past exposure to violence makes individuals less sensitive to violence in the future.[17] The link between exposure and desensitization is so accepted that it is part of military training.[18] Scholars of terrorism have documented the same effects. In response to sustained terrorist attacks during the Palestinian Intifada, Waxman (2011) argues, Israeli citizens "became accustomed to terrorism and adapted accordingly. ... The effects of ongoing, chronic terrorism may significantly differ from the effects of a one-off terrorist attack." By contrast, American citizens were so affected by the September 11, 2001, attacks precisely because they had no precedence.[19]

---

[16] Carnagey, Anderson, and Bushman (2007).
[17] Linz, Donnerstein, and Adams (1989); Bartholow, Bushman, and Sestir (2006); Carnagey, Anderson, and Bushman (2007).
[18] Grossman and Degaetano (1999).
[19] In one survey conducted six weeks after the attacks of September 11, 2001, Huddy et al. (2002) found that some 52 percent of respondents in the New York metropolitan area "had found it somewhat or very difficult to concentrate on their job or normal activities." Huddy, Khatib, and Capelos (2002) found that 71 percent of Americans reported depression; of those, 42 percent reported insomnia.

7.2.3 Hypotheses

This chapter's first hypothesis focuses on temporal variation in when propaganda-based threats of repression are employed. Because threats are costly, our theory suggests, they should be reserved for when autocrats need them most.

Hypothesis 7.1: *Propaganda-based threats of repression should be reserved for moments when collective action is most likely.*

The second hypothesis focuses on variation across regimes. The source derogation mechanism suggests that propaganda-based threats should be most costly where propaganda aims to persuade citizens of regime merits, since threats undermine investments in credibility. As a result, threats of repression should be more common where propaganda signals the regime's capacity to dominate citizens.

Hypothesis 7.2: *Propaganda-based threats of repression should be more likely where autocrats employ propaganda to intimidate rather than persuade.*

Hypothesis 7.2 provides a foundation for understanding which political groups are most often targeted. Many theories of autocratic politics feature an in-group whose support the autocrat must retain and an out-group that is marginalized and subjected to violence.[20] This group distinction may be based on ethnicity; religion; language; or simply political privilege, as in Bueno de Mesquita et al.'s (2003) theory of the selectorate. Insofar as the autocrat's hold on power rests on satisfying in-group demands, the propaganda strategy should vary accordingly: more persuasive propaganda for the in-group and more threatening propaganda for the out-group. This is not to suggest that in-groups are never threatened. Rather, our theory suggests out-groups should be threatened with repression most often.

Hypothesis 7.3: *Propaganda-based threats of repression should more often target a political out-group than a political in-group.*

---

[20] Bueno de Mesquita et al. (2003); Acemoglu, Robinson, and Verdier (2004); Padro i Miquel (2007); Carter and Hassan (2021).

7.3 CAMEROON, ANGLOPHONE AND FRANCOPHONE

We focus first on Hypotheses 7.2 and 7.3, which suggest, respectively, that propaganda-based threats should be more common where electoral constraints are non-binding and should disproportionately target political out-groups. Cameroon, a country of 20 million in West Africa, offers an unusual opportunity to test this.

Autocracies may be different in a range of ways that render propaganda-based threats more common in one than another. To rule out the possibility that these unobserved differences drive variation in propaganda-based threats, we focus on Cameroon, where roughly 20 percent of citizens speak English and 80 percent speak French. Cameroon has had just two presidents since 1960: Ahmadou Ahidjo and Paul Biya. Both have been francophone, governed with a francophone elite, and privileged francophone constituents. The *Cameroon Tribune*, Biya's propaganda newspaper, publishes articles in English and French, and so can target Biya's francophone in-group and anglophone out-group with different messages.

Our theory suggests that Biya varies his propaganda by language: to persuade the francophone in-group of regime merits and to threaten the anglophone out-group into submission.

7.3.1 *Language, Politics, and the Anglophone Crisis*

Cameroon's linguistic cleavage is a legacy of European colonialism. Germany claimed modern Cameroon at the Berlin Conference of 1884, where European leaders divided up a continent few had visited. After World War I, Germany was forced to cede its colonies to the victors. Today's Northwest and Southwest regions went to Britain; France received the East. Francophone Cameroon claimed independence in 1960. The British colonial administration organized a plebiscite for its territories in 1961. Given the choice of joining Nigeria or the newly independent *La République du Cameroun* – independence was not an option – the Northwest and Southwest regions opted for the latter. Though the newly unified Cameroon was governed from francophone Yaoundé, its federal constitution granted substantial autonomy to regional governments. English and French were made twin official languages.

The anglophone population has been marginalized since. At just 20 percent of the population, it is also electorally irrelevant. Cameroon's first president, Ahmadou Ahidjo, was francophone, and governed by maintaining an ethnic balance in his cabinet and civil service. In 1966, Ahidjo banned political parties, save for his Cameroon National Union. Ill, Ahidjo resigned in 1982 and ceded power to Biya, his prime minister. Biya's preference for his Beti co-ethnics was obvious by 1991:

> Opposition newspaper *Le Messager* found that 37 of 47 senior [regional governors], three-quarters of directors and general managers of parastatal corporations, and 22 of 38 high-ranking bureaucrats in the newly-created office of the Prime Minister were from the president's clan.[21]

Over time, Albaugh (2011) writes, Biya's Beti ethnic group expanded, as membership in it became politically useful:

> Previously distinct [ethnic] groups ... are now amalgamated into a widening category of "Beti," and the reach of this grouping stretches across a remarkable span of Cameroon's central and southern territory.[22]

As it did, Cameroon's anglophone population was further marginalized, and so the original linguistic cleavage became thoroughly political. This cleavage is also the foundation for widespread unrest, which the U.S. CIA anticipated in 1986:

> Although they currently lack the leadership and unity to effectively challenge Biya's rule, we believe the anglophone minority is a potential time bomb, and should the central government fail to respect their cultural and linguistic traditions, the 2 million strong community may view armed confrontation as their only alternative.[23]

The Anglophone Uprising began on October 11, 2016, when lawyers in Bamenda, capital of Northwest region, went on strike to protest Biya's long record of linguistic discrimination.[24] Their strike inspired others. On November 22, the Cameroon Teachers' Trade Union (CATTU) staged a sit-in across the Northwest and Southwest. By "trying to wipe out our system of education," CATTU's secretary general, Wilfred Tassang, proclaimed, the Biya government is "wiping out our cultural heritage."[25] These protests paralyzed the educational and legal systems throughout the Northwest and Southwest.

Biya responded violently. On November 22, his security apparatus killed four protesters and dispersed others with tear gas. By November

---

[21] Albaugh (2011, 391).
[22] Albaugh (2011, 392).
[23] Central Intelligence Agency (1986).
[24] Gaffey (2017); BBC (2016).
[25] Iaccino and Palumbo (2016).

23, more than 100 citizens had been arrested.[26] The protests continued throughout December, but the most significant occurred on December 8, in Bamenda, when a dozen anglophone citizens were killed by security forces.[27] On January 16, 2017, the government warned citizens of "criminal penalties" if they disseminated information on social media that they were "unable to prove." These warnings continued for weeks, routinely sent as mass text messages.[28] On January 17, the government shut down Internet in the Northwest and Southwest regions, depriving some 2 million citizens of access. It outlawed two prominent anglophone civil society groups, the Southern Cameroons National Council and the Anglophone Civil Society Consortium, and arrested two of the Consortium's leaders, lawyer Felix Agbor Balla and professor Fontem Neba.[29] Wilfred Tassang, CATTU secretary general, fled into exile.

The Anglophone Crisis poses two related challenges to Biya's hold on power. First, state repression transformed calls for reform into a struggle for secession. Second, although Biya's elite is overwhelmingly francophone, successive economic crises have caused Biya's popularity among francophone youth to plummet. If anglophone demands for reform spread to francophone youth – or if Biya's inability to contain anglophone unrest causes his francophone elite to defect – Biya would confront the most serious threat to his hold on power since the early 1990s. Accordingly, Biya's hold on power is now threatened by both anglophone and francophone unrest.

Biya's electoral constraints differ by linguistic group. Since he relies on francophone support, he is forced to persuade them of regime merits. Vis-à-vis francophones, his electoral constraints are at least somewhat binding. Meanwhile, anglophones constitute just 20 percent of the electorate, and so their votes are irrelevant, even in a fair election. Since Biya's elite is overwhelmingly francophone, repressing anglophones has little effect on elite support. Biya has also exploited the presence of Boko Haram, a terrorist group in northern Cameroon and eastern Nigeria, to secure immunity from international sanctions. To avoid "putting boots on the ground," the U.S. government effectively broke the Leahy Law – which prohibits support for foreign militaries that brutalize their citizens – to arm and train Biya's military.[30]

---

[26] Gaffey (2016); BBC (2016).
[27] Al Jazeera (2016).
[28] Gaffey (2017).
[29] Atabong (2017).
[30] Thompson (2016), Page (2017).

7.3.2 Data and Estimation Strategy

To probe whether Biya's *Cameroon Tribune* issues propaganda-based threats more often to anglophone readers, we identified three coverage areas that are widely considered threatening: explicit military coverage; coverage of Biya's international support; and expressions of national unity, which anglophones understood as refusing reforms that would provide regional autonomy. Next, we employed a topic model that classified articles accordingly. We coded a training set of 300 articles and then used a classifier to code the rest.

The two articles below are representative of those we coded as threatening.[31] The first announces the "perfect synergy" between the "army [and] nation." Although the article ostensibly covers the military's efforts against Boko Haram in the Far North region, its message to anglophones is clear: "Thanks to the perfect symbiosis between the nation and its army, no millimetre of the national territory has been lost to the terrorists." Biya's *Cameroon Tribune* also highlighted the role of local informants in facilitating the military's efficacy: "The strength of the population thus far has been their know-how of the terrain which they use to outmaneuver the terrorists."

Army – Nation – Perfect Synergy!

February 03, 2017

The two are constantly federating efforts and means to elbow out a common enemy - terrorism.

As the nation today pays homage to fallen soldiers following a helicopter crash in Bogo, Far North Region on January 22, 2017, the solemn ceremony at the Yaounde Military Headquarters will once again serve as an opportunity to showcase the near perfect symbioses existing between the nation and her defence forces. ... Although some of them, like the four senior military officials being bade farewell today, have paid with their precious lives, the synergy showcased thus far between the nation and the army remains historic. Thanks to the perfect symbiosis between the nation and its army, no millimetre of the national territory has been lost to the terrorists.

In a veritable show of gratitude to the relentless efforts of the country's defence forces and as a mark of contribution to the battle against the common enemy,

---

[31] Our coding decisions are based on a series of interviews with anglophone Cameroonians in late 2016, as the Anglophone Crisis was intensifying. We withhold their identities for confidentiality reasons.

the population – notably of the war-affected areas in the Far North Region – had constituted themselves into vigilante groups. . . .

Added to these salutary performances by the population through the vigilante groups are their spontaneous contributions in cash and kind to keep the security men highly spirited and combat-ready. When the wave of contributions started blowing, all and sundry never wanted to be left behind. Big and small groups, individuals and Cameroonians in the Diaspora, generously donated in cash and in kind to support and boost soldiers' morale. Thanks to these and coupled with the bravery and patriotism of Cameroon's military who are showing heightened resilience in the face of the enemy, the country continually scores points in the unwavering struggle to completely halt Boko Haram from wreaking havoc.

We also coded as threatening articles that advertise promises of support from the international community. The article below is again representative. It advertises the UN Security Council's "promises [of] continued support" to the Biya government. "We had a full cordial discussion with President Paul Biya and we pledged our continued support to him, his government and to the people of Cameroon." Again, the article is ostensibly about Boko Haram. But Biya's propaganda apparatus uses it to signal the depth of its international support.

UN Security Council Promises Continued Support

March 06, 2017

Growing humanitarian crisis in the Lake Chad Basin masterminded by activities of the nebulous terrorist group, Boko Haram, may receive special attention from the UN Security Council, donors and other international bodies. A 15-man visiting delegation of the UN Security Council, the first of its kind since the dreaded group started wreaking havoc in Cameroon and other neighbouring countries, has pledged to step up support and advocacy.

"We had a full cordial discussion with President Paul Biya and we pledged our continued support to him, his government and to the people of Cameroon for the interconnected challenges that they are facing. What we can do is to encourage the whole international community to step up support," the UK Ambassador to the UN Security Council and current President said. The working session saw a discussion between Cameroon and the visiting UN Security Council delegation. President Paul Biya was assisted by Ministers Joseph Beti Assomo, Rene Emmanuel Sadi and Minister Delegate Joseph Dion Nguti. Meanwhile, the visiting 14 UN Security Council Members from Bolivia, China, Egypt, Ethiopia, France, Italy, Japan, Kazakhstan, Senegal, Sweden, Ukraine, United Kingdom, United States of America and Uruguay all answered present. The Ambassador of the Russian Federation in Cameroon, H.E. Nikolay Ratsiborinskiy represented his country to bring the number to 15. The outgoing UN System Resident Coordinator in Cameroon, Najat Rochdi was also in attendance. President Biya showcased

Cameroon's legendary hospitality and generosity to the delegation when he personally shook hands with each of the members before the working session as well as handed to each of them Cameroon's 50th Anniversary Medals after the in-camera discussions.

This article may be less explicitly threatening than coverage of the military's prowess, but it celebrates just how thoroughly the international community supports the regime.

We created three outcome variables. The first, *Threats*$_{it}$, counts the number of threatening articles published in language i on day t. The second, *Threats*$_{it}^{S}$, gives the share of all articles published in language i on day t that constitute threats of repression. We also estimated the probability that *Threats*$_{it}$ is positive in language i on day t. Our baseline model is

$$Y_{it} = \alpha + \beta \left(\text{French}_{it}\right) + \delta \left(\text{Crisis}_{it}\right) + \phi \left(\text{French}_{it} \times \text{Crisis}_{it}\right) + \kappa X_{it} + \epsilon \quad (7.1)$$

where i indexes language and t indexes day. The interaction term ϕ lets Biya's threat strategy be a function of language and whether day t occurs after the Anglophone Crisis began on October 1, 2016. The interaction term ϕ accommodates the possibility that Biya's *Cameroon Tribune* responded to the Anglophone Crisis differently across language groups.

7.3.3 Results

The results appear in Table 7.1, and they demonstrate that Biya issues propaganda-based threats to anglophones far more often than to francophones. Model 4 is perhaps most intuitive. Even before the Anglophone Crisis began, the daily probability that Biya's *Cameroon Tribune* published a threat article in English was nearly 17 percent, or roughly once every business week. By contrast, the probability it published a threat article in French was just 7 percent, or less than half. The results from Model 2 are similar. In English, Biya's *Cameroon Tribune* prints nearly 0.20 threat article per day, or roughly one per business week. In French, it prints just 0.05 threat article per day, or one per month.

The Anglophone Crisis induced two changes in Biya's propaganda strategy. From Model 1, the number of threat articles increased sharply, by nearly 0.2 across language groups. From Model 7, it also reduced the aggregate number of English articles by roughly one per day. As a result, from Model 3, the share of threat articles in English spiked. This is also the key message of Figure 7.1, which measures the share of threat articles by language group, given by *Threats*$_{it}^{S}$. The dashed vertical lines around

Table 7.1 *How Cameroonian propaganda is different in English and French*

				Dependent variable:			
	Threats OLS (1)	Threats NB (2)	Threats^S OLS (3)	Threats≥ 1 OLS (4)	Executive references OLS (5)	Positive coverage standardized OLS (6)	Articles OLS (7)
Post-crisis	0.180***	0.778***	0.051***	0.058	0.107	−0.180	−1.027*
	(0.052)	(0.244)	(0.010)	(0.037)	(0.177)	(0.153)	(0.543)
French	−0.209***	−1.639***	−0.026***	−0.098***	−0.332***	−0.382***	3.995***
	(0.017)	(0.136)	(0.003)	(0.011)	(0.053)	(0.041)	(0.172)
Election season	−0.105*	−1.223**	−0.017*	−0.065	0.421**	−0.037	0.153
	(0.057)	(0.547)	(0.010)	(0.040)	(0.187)	(0.140)	(0.570)
Articles	0.014***	0.099***					
	(0.001)	(0.009)					
Post-crisis × French	−0.042	0.259	−0.042***	0.066	0.098	0.181	3.520***
	(0.068)	(0.351)	(0.012)	(0.048)	(0.230)	(0.184)	(0.768)
Constant	0.127***	−2.257***	0.034***	0.163***	1.073***	1.309***	3.233***
	(0.014)	(0.091)	(0.002)	(0.008)	(0.039)	(0.032)	(0.122)
Observations	3,358	3,358	3,339	3,358	3,339	2,539	5,444
R²	0.061		0.040	0.029	0.021	0.034	0.109

Note: *p < 0.1; **p < 0.05; ***p < 0.01

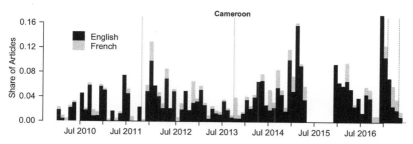

Figure 7.1 Threatening content in Cameroonian propaganda in English and French

October 2011 and September 2013 give legislative and presidential elections, respectively. The dashed vertical lines in late 2016 and early 2017 give important dates in the Anglophone Crisis. The first, December 8, 2016, is when four citizens were killed by Biya's security services in Bamenda; the second is the start of the internet shutdown; the third gives the conclusion of the internet shutdown. By December 2016, on average, threat articles constituted nearly 20 percent of total English language coverage. There was no similar change in French.[32]

Cameroon's linguistic divide offers another opportunity to confirm this book's central hypothesis, which was the focus of Chapter 4. Biya's power rests on some amount of support from francophones. They constitute his electoral constituency, a disproportionate share of his government ministers, and the core of his military. Anglophones, meanwhile, are the targets of sustained repression. Our theory suggests that Biya's pro-regime propaganda – not simply his threat strategy – should be different across language groups. He should employ honest propaganda in French and absurd propaganda in English. Models 5 and 6 confirm this. Even before the Anglophone Crisis began, the *Cameroon Tribune*'s English content featured, on average, nearly 0.4 more net positive words from among the 20 surrounding each executive identifier, or roughly three Fox News units. This magnitude is strikingly similar to a core result in Chapter 4.

Biya's propaganda apparatus offers an unusual opportunity to test Hypotheses 7.2 and 7.3. Since the *Cameroon Tribune* publishes different content in English and French, we can probe whether the same propaganda apparatus treats an in-group – on whose support his power relies –

---

[32] The *Cameroon Tribune*'s online archives exclude the period between June and November 2015; it is unclear why.

differently than an out-group. The results are consistent with our theory. For anglophone citizens, Biya's *Cameroon Tribune* engages in absurdly positive pro-regime propaganda and is far more likely to advertise the prowess of his military and the esteem in which the international community holds him. These differences obtained before the Anglophone Crisis began and have intensified since.

7.4 "OVERALL SOCIAL STABILITY IS ALWAYS GOOD" IN CHINA

Next, we return to China. The duration of the CCP's hold on power and the temporal scope of our propaganda data let us probe whether propaganda-based threats are associated with moments of political tension, as Hypothesis 7.1 suggests. The CCP also governs with an in-group and an out-group, which lets us again test Hypothesis 7.3. The Han majority, representing 90 percent of Chinese citizens, is the CCP's in-group. Though the government recognizes fifty-six ethnic minority groups, the Uyghurs are the most vilified. They practice Islam, speak a Turkic language, and live in far western China.

We focus on two newspapers. The *People's Daily* is the CCP's flagship and primarily targets the urban elite. From Chapter 3, over half of citizens read it. The *Workers' Daily* is also regarded as an official newspaper, in contrast to the more commercialized newspapers discussed in Chapter 4. The *Workers' Daily* was established by Mao Zedong in 1949, just months after the PRC's founding. It initially targeted Chinese workers, who were central to CCP legitimacy. Its language was colloquial. It routinely replaced "politicized" content from the *People's Daily* with labor issues of genuine interest to readers. On the eve of the Cultural Revolution, the *Workers' Daily* had a daily circulation of 400,000. It has since expanded its target audience to include migrant workers, intellectuals, and civil servants. It now reports a daily circulation of 960,000, nearly twice the weekday circulation of *the New York Times*. Roughly 12 percent of citizens read it.[33] Befitting its target audience, the average

---

[33] The difference between daily circulation rates and readership is explained by two factors. First, the *Workers' Daily* is routinely posted in factories and public spaces. In 2016, for instance, officials in Gansu province mandated that "factories, departments, and labor unions should subscribe to the *Workers' Daily*" (Gansu Province Trade Union Federation 2016). In 2017 and 2018, government documents in Guangxi province instructed that "newspapers like the *Workers' Daily*

Workers' Daily reader is slightly less affluent than the average *People's Daily* reader and less likely to claim CCP membership.

7.4.1 Measuring Propaganda-Based Threats

To measure threats of repression, we exploited the fact that the CCP uses codewords. The term "social stability maintenance," Huang (2015b, 426) writes, "is broadly understood as a codeword for maintaining the stability of the existing regime."[34] Three months after the 1989 Tiananmen Square massacre, Deng Xiaoping announced "stability overrides everything."[35] He continued:

> Our gravest failure has been in [political] education. We did not provide enough education to young people, including students. For many of those who participated in the demonstrations and hunger strikes it will take years of education, not just a few months, to change their thinking.[36]

Deng charged the education system and propaganda apparatus with emphasizing the CCP's commitment to social stability rather than the "peace and unity" of the Mao era.[37]

To mark the massacre's first anniversary, the *People's Daily* published an editorial that described "quelling the counter-revolutionary rebellion" as an "act of great significance." Its title was familiar: "Stability Overrides Everything."

and *Guangxi Workers' News* should be posted in the bulletin board of towns and communities, so that citizens can read them easily" (Liuzhou Trade Union Federation 2016; Wuming District Trade Union Federation 2018). These directives aimed to expand its readership: "Grassroots units must subscribe to the 'two newspapers' in the worker bookstore, the worker activity room, and the reading room, so that the voices of the CCP and trade union organizations can reach the broad masses of workers." Second, since 41.6 percent of migrant workers access the Internet via mobile phone (China Internet Network Information Center 2012), the *Workers' Daily* is active on social media, with 2.3 million followers on Weibo.

[34] Manion (1990), Shue (2004), Shirk (2008), Sandby-Thomas (2011), Yue (2012), Chen (2013), Stockmann (2013), Wang and Minzner (2015), Steinhardt (2016), Benney (2016), Yang (2017).

[35] 稳定压倒一切. Deng (1993, 331).

[36] Brady (2008, 45–46). Similarly, Jiang Zemin criticized the *People's Daily* and CCTV for "not transmitting the correct voice of the Central Committee" during the pro-democracy movement.

[37] Sandby-Thomas (2008).

Looking at today's situation and thinking about last year's events, people will more profoundly understand that the central authorities' strategic decision to resolutely quell the rebellion was entirely correct and necessary. . . . Hostile forces, at home and abroad, manufactured this disturbance in order to overthrow the CCP and make China dependent on capitalist developed countries. At this critical life or death moment, the Party and government had no choice but to resolutely quell the rebellion.[38]

The *People's Daily* then warned citizens that future dissent would be met with repression:

Party committees and governments at all levels, and all related departments, must regard safeguarding stability as the most important task and pay adequate attention to all aspects of this task. . . . Stability prevails over everything. We must preserve the country's stability as we would safeguard our own lives.[39]

Sandby-Thomas (2008, 207) documents how quick the CCP is to employ these codewords. In 1999, two days after a 10,000-strong Falun Gong protest, the *People's Daily* wrote this:

We must safeguard the hard-won situation of stability and unity as we would safeguard our own eyes. . . . The consensus of the whole party and all ethnic groups of China is that stability prevails over everything.

In 2005, after anti-Japanese protests threatened to become anti-CCP protests, the *People's Daily* responded with a new editorial, entitled "Keep in Mind Everything We Cannot Accomplish without Stability." It referenced stability thirty-two times. Two other articles published that week were entitled "Actively Produce Things in Favor of Social Stability" and "From a Harmonious Society See Stability." Each mentioned stability over twenty-five times.[40]

We identify propaganda-based threats by measuring frequency counts for "stability" and "harmony," which eclipsed "stability" in frequency after 2000. "Harmony" is so widely identified as a threat that it has entered colloquial speech. The phrase "being harmonized" is a euphemism for being detained, arrested, or censored.[41] The word "harmony" is also a homophone for "river crab." When the CCP scheduled dissident artist Ai Weiwei's Shanghai studio for demolition in 2010, hundreds of citizens

---

[38] Sandby-Thomas (2008, 158).
[39] Sandby-Thomas (2008, 162–164).
[40] Sandby-Thomas (2008, 256–257).
[41] China Digital Times (2019).

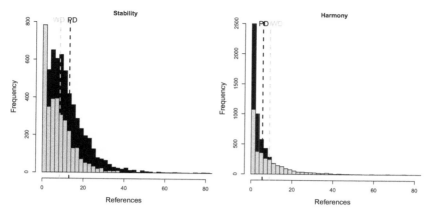

Figure 7.2 Histogram of word frequency counts

attended a "crab feast" in his studio to protest.[42] Under house arrest in Beijing, Ai said this:

Many had been warned by local police not to come. . . .I never encouraged them to go because I didn't want them to get hurt. But they felt that was their responsibility. It was very touching to see such solidarity. I'm surprised the police didn't do anything.[43]

These word frequency counts are attractive for measurement purposes. Our word frequency counts are continuous: combined, ranging from 0 to 348 per day with a mean of 19 in the *People's Daily*, and from 0 to 188 per day with a mean of 17 in the *Workers' Daily*. Accordingly, they let us measure how threatening Chinese propaganda content was on day t. Figure 7.2 presents histograms of "stability" and "harmony" references for the *People's Daily* in black and for the *Workers' Daily* in gray. The left panel gives the distribution of "stability" references per day. The right panel gives the distribution of "harmony" references per day. Mean values are given with vertical lines.

7.4.2 *The Calendar of Propaganda-Based Threats*

We worked with a team of Chinese citizens and consulted existing literature to categorize politically sensitive moments by how powerfully they should constitute focal moments for protest. We identified

[42] CNN (2010).
[43] Branigan (2010).

roughly twenty recurring dates and aggregated them into four categories: anniversaries of ethnic separatist movements, anniversaries of failed pro-democracy movements, major political events, and cultural anniversaries.

Anniversaries of Ethnic Separatist Movements Modern China has experienced two major separatist movements: one in Tibet and one in Xinjiang. These separatist movements have yielded four anniversaries that are now focal moments for protest and repression in Tibet and Xinjiang.[44] These anniversaries are summarized in Table 7.2.

Pro-Democracy Anniversaries Since seizing power in 1949, the CCP has repressed a series of pro-democracy movements. These are associated with anniversaries, which constitute focal moments for collective action. These anniversaries remind citizens that anti-regime sentiment is long-standing and that their compatriots mobilized against the regime in the past. They are temporally precise. Committed activists may use them to ensure other citizens do not forget.[45] In Carter and Carter (2020*a*,*b*), we show that the anniversaries of China's failed pro-democracy movements experience nearly 30 percent more protests than the typical day. The odds that a protest emerges are between 27 percent and 38 percent greater, and the probability of a two standard deviation protest spike nearly doubles. Protesters during pro-democracy anniversaries are far more likely to embrace "rights consciousness," which many scholars argue is code for democratic resistance.[46] The CCP knows that anniversaries of failed pro-democracy movements are profoundly sensitive. Focal moment protests are twice as likely to be repressed by security forces. We identified six pro-democracy movements in modern Chinese history: the Tiananmen Square protests, Democracy Wall, the National Peoples' Congress (NPC)

---

[44] Hillman and Tuttle (2016).

[45] There is a large literature on how governments and societies commemorate atrocities after war and dictatorship. Often referred to as transitional justice or memory studies, it tends to focus on efforts to remember that take place after a repressive regime has fallen. Scholars have explored the role of museums and truth and reconciliation commissions in many contexts; see de Brito, Gonzaléz-Enríquez, and Aguilar (2001); Gibson (2004); Davis (2005); Passerini, Crownshaw, and Leydesdorff (2005); Barak (2007); Laplante (2007); Hackett and Rolston (2009); Höhn (2010); Stern (2010); Manning (2011); Kent (2011); Collins, Hite, and Joignant (2013); Balcells, Palanza, and Voytas (Forthcoming).

[46] Bernstein and Lü (2003), Goldman (2005), Li (2010), Pei (2010), Wong (2011), Chen (2013).

Table 7.2 *Ethnic separatist anniversaries*

Date	Anniversary	Description
May 23	Tibetan "Liberation"	After founding the PRC in 1949, Mao reasserted state authority in Tibet, which enjoyed de facto autonomy in the nineteenth and early twentieth centuries due to the collapse of the Qing Dynasty. Mao launched a military intervention and on May 23, 1951, forced Tibetan leaders to sign the Seventeen Point Agreement, which stated that Tibet was part of China.
March 10	Tibetan Rebellion	On March 10, 1959, the Tibetan Rebellion began in Lhasa, the capital. The PLA suppressed the rebellion on March 20, and the Dalai Lama fled to India. That spring, 7,000 Tibetan refugees followed him. The exile community celebrates the day as Tibetan Uprising Day. The anniversary has occasioned Tibetan protests since, as well as increased repression in Tibet.
March 28	Serf Emancipation Day	The CCP commemorates the crushing of the Tibetan Rebellion as Serf Emancipation Day. On March 28, 1959, Premier Zhou Enlai dissolved the Tibetan government and assigned policy authority to the Preparatory Committee of the Tibet Autonomous Region.
July 5	Xinjiang Uprising	Following news of a factory altercation between Uyghur and Han workers in Guangdong, on July 5, 2009, protests broke out in Urumqi, the capital of Xinjiang. Officially, 197 were killed and 1,721 injured. Unofficial tolls are much higher. Over 1,000 Uyghurs were arrested, 30 of whom received death sentences.

Direct Election Movement, Constitution Day, Charter 08, and the Jasmine Movement. We employed two criteria for coding. First, these citizen movements must make explicit calls for democratic reforms. Movements such as the 1976 Qing Ming Movement, which called on the CCP to make internal reforms and fight corruption, are not sufficient. Second, we coded a single date for each movement as the focal moment: the date on which the movement reached its peak or was violently repressed by the CCP government. This final criterion ensures that we do not select on the dependent variable. These pro-democracy movements are summarized in Table 7.3.

Political Events and Anniversaries Existing literature also treats major political events as sensitive, since they foster a heightened awareness of politics and potentially the CCP's policy failures. In Carter and Carter (2020a), we argue that political events and anniversaries are analytically distinct from pro-democracy anniversaries because they are not associated with a regime's historical crimes. Although still sensitive, they exhibit weaker focal properties than pro-democracy anniversaries. Our list of political events and anniversaries includes the CCP's quinquennial Party Congress, which unveils economic plans and senior leadership decisions, and the annual meeting of the National People's Congress, often dubbed China's rubber stamp parliament. Our list also includes the CCP's two leading regime celebrations: the founding of the CCP itself and of the People's Liberation Army. These are summarized in Table 7.4.

Other Dates of Importance: Nationalist and Cultural Anniversaries Nationalist anniversaries may be politically sensitive as well. We identified four dates, all of profound historical significance. Youth Day, sometimes called the May Fourth Movement, witnessed the birth of modern Chinese nationalism after the Treaty of Versailles gave the German-occupied Chinese province of Shandong to Japan. National Day commemorates the founding of the People's Republic, when Mao famously declared that Chinese people had "stood up." The Mukden Incident and the Anti-Japanese War recall China's invasion by Japan.[47] These events are political and the regime has attempted to co-opt them,[48] but they are associated more with national pride than with the regime. As a result,

---

[47] Wasserstrom (2019). National sovereignty is an important issue for Chinese citizens; see Carter, Johnston, and Quek (2018).
[48] Buckley and Qin (2019).

Table 7.3 *Pro-democracy anniversaries*

Date	Name	Description
June 4	Tiananmen Square	In April 1989, following the death of a prominent liberal leader, thousands of students protested in Beijing's Tiananmen Square. Following an April 26 editorial in the *People's Daily*, which accused the students of being manipulated by foreign agents, over 100,000 citizens joined the protest. The People's Liberation Army cleared the square on June 4, murdering several thousand citizens.
November 27	Democracy Wall	In November 1978, citizens in Beijing's Xidan neighborhood hung pro-democracy posters. Activists formed a Democratic Assembly Group and, on November 27, led a 10,000-person march from "Democracy Wall" to Tiananmen Square. Protest leader Wei Jingsheng demanded the government adopt democracy as its "fifth modernization," a rejoinder to Deng Xiaoping's four modernizations. The CCP arrested participants, including Wei, who spent eighteen years in prison and was later exiled. After demolishing Democracy Wall in December 1979, Deng called for revoking the constitutional right to hang posters.
December 4	Constitution Day	On December 4, 1982, the CCP adopted a constitution that grants citizens freedom of speech and assembly, equality before the law, and the right to vote and stand for election. In 2014, the CCP moved to buttress its legitimacy by creating Constitution Day, celebrated on December 4. The proclamation sparked a backlash. On December 4, nearly 1,000 citizens protested outside the CCTV building in Beijing, and dozens of prominent lawyers signed an open letter demanding that the CCP respect the rights enshrined in the 1982 constitution.

(continued)

Table 7.3 (continued)

Date	Name	Description
December 10	Charter 08	On December 10, 2008, 303 civil society leaders signed a manifesto that demanded independent courts, respect for human rights, and an end to one-party rule. Entitled "Charter 08," it was inspired by the "Charter 77" pro-democracy manifesto released by Czech dissidents in 1977. The document collected 10,000 additional signatures from prominent citizens, compelling the government to forbid discussion of Charter 08 in the media. Citizens distributed the document on Beijing streets, but the movement did not culminate in major protests.
December 19	NPC Direct Election Movement	In 1986, public intellectual Fang Lizhi called on the government to respect freedom of expression. Constitutional rights, he declared, should be treated as "actual rights." On December 5, students at Hefei University of Science and Technology demanded the right to elect representatives to the National People's Congress. Protests spread to 150 universities. On December 19, Shanghai authorities forcibly dispersed protesters. In response, students in Hefei staged a sit-in at government offices on December 23. Fang brokered a compromise between the students and the Hefei government, after which the students called off protests. The government later abandoned the reforms.
February 20	Jasmine Movement	Styled after Egypt's Tahrir uprising, it began with an anonymous post on a U.S.-based online message board, which called for citizens to "stroll" in major cities every Sunday, holding jasmine. We code the Jasmine Movement's anniversary as February 20, 2011, the date of the first protest stroll. Our results are identical if we specify the second stroll as the candidate focal moment.

Table 7.4 *Political anniversaries in China*

Date	Name	Description
Mid-March	National People's Congress	Every March, the 3,000-member National People's Congress meets for two weeks. Though a rubber stamp parliament, the meeting is still widely televised across China.
July 1	CCP founding	On this day in 1921, the CCP was founded in Shanghai.
October–November	Party Congress	Every five years, the CCP holds its major political meeting.
August 1	Founding of PLA	On August 1, 1933, the CCP founded the People's Liberation Army.

Table 7.5 *Nationalist anniversaries in China*

May 4	Youth day	On May 4, 1919, young people in Beijing launched a movement against imperialism. In particular, they were angry that the Treaty of Versailles required China to cede Shandong province to Japan. This movement is often seen as the birth of modern popular nationalism in China.
July 7	Start of the Anti-Japanese War	On July 7, 1937, Japanese and Chinese troops were involved in an incident that escalated into a battle. So began the Second Sino-Japanese War, which would not end until after the conclusion of World War II.
October 1	National Day	On this day in 1949, the PRC was founded and Mao Zedong declared the Chinese people had stood up.
September 18	Mukden Incident	On this day in 1931, Japan invaded China.

they are distinct from the political anniversaries above. These nationalist anniversaries are summarized in Table 7.5.

Many of China's major cultural holidays have rich histories and occur on dates specified by the lunar calendar: the Lunar New Year, Tomb

Sweeping Festival, Lantern Festival, Dragon Boat Festival, Ghost Festival, Mid-Autumn Festival, Double Seventh holiday, and Double Ninth holiday. For these, we converted lunar dates into their Gregorian equivalents for each year in our sample. We also included cultural holidays of more recent vintage, such as Singles' Day.

7.4.3 Estimation Strategy

To probe the timing of propaganda-based threats, we estimated models of the form

$$Y_{nt} = \alpha + \beta \left(\text{Separatist Anniversary Window}_t\right) + \phi X_t + \gamma_n + \gamma_s + \epsilon \quad (7.2)$$

where n indexes newspaper, s indexes year, and t indexes day. Our two outcome variables give the number of times newspaper n published either "stability" or "harmony" on day t. Since these outcomes are counts, we estimated (7.2) with negative binomial models. Our primary explanatory variable is *Separatist Anniversary Window*$_t$. Although we expected threats to cluster around these anniversaries, we accommodated the possibility that the regime issues threats several days before or after. We did so by constructing anniversary *windows*, ranging from the anniversary plus/minus zero days to the anniversary plus/minus five days.

The vector X_t includes a series of day-level controls. It includes dichotomous indicators for the anniversaries of failed pro-democracy movements, political anniversaries, and cultural anniversaries. As for *Separatist Anniversary Window*$_t$, we constructed anniversary *windows*, ranging from the anniversary plus/minus zero days to the anniversary plus/minus five days. We are unaware of any features that may be correlated with these anniversary windows and propaganda-based threats, save one. We included in X_t a measure of underlying political instability. The variable *Protests*$_{t-1}$ counts the number of protests that occurred nationwide on day $t - 1$.[49] Year-fixed effects, given by γ_s, accommodate unobserved annual features, such as changes in economic conditions, the data-generating process, and the government's political strategy. Newspaper-fixed effects, given by γ_n, accommodate unobserved, newspaper-level features.

---

[49] The results were substantively unchanged when we controlled for the number of protests that occurred nationwide over the preceding week.

7.4.4 Results

The results appear in Table 7.6. Models 1 through 6 use "stability" references as the outcome of interest; Models 7 through 12 use "harmony" references. The results are consistent with Hypotheses 7.1 and 7.3. The CCP is far more likely to issue propaganda-based threats around the anniversaries of ethnic separatist movements. Each day within an ethnic separatist anniversary window experiences between 14 percent and 26 percent more mentions of "stability" and "harmony." The only other sensitive moments around which the CCP issues propaganda-based threats of repression are major political anniversaries, which underscore popular frustration with the regime. We find that references to "stability" are roughly 8 percent more likely during the three and four days surrounding major political anniversaries; references to "harmony" are between 15 percent and 46 percent more likely around major political anniversaries. Table 7.6 also suggests that protests on day $t - 1$ compel the government to issue propaganda-based threats on day t, consistent with Hypothesis 7.1.

These results are noteworthy in three other ways. First, they are consistent with the CCP's political strategy in Tibet and Xinjiang. The government routinely conducts military patrols, imposes curfews along with Internet and cellular shutdowns, and incarcerates Tibetans and Uyghurs *en masse*. In Xinjiang, the government banned the Quran, the name "Mohammed," and "unreasonably long" beards. At least 1 million and perhaps 3 million Uyghurs are held in re-education camps.[50] The CCP, we find, also issues propaganda-based threats of repression around the anniversaries of ethnic separatist movements, which are profoundly salient for Tibetans and Uyghurs. Second, Truex (2019) shows that the CCP begins incarcerating dissidents several days before politically sensitive moments, not just the sensitive day itself. We found the same pattern as that with propaganda-based threats. The CCP begins issuing propaganda-based threats several days before ethnic separatist anniversaries and continues several days after. Third, we find no evidence that the CCP issues propaganda-based threats of repression around the anniversaries of failed pro-democracy movements, even though these are the most politically sensitive dates of the year. This null effect is a focus of Chapter 9.

Since seizing power in 1945, the CCP has committed a range of human rights abuses: against pro-democracy activists, ethnic minorities,

[50] Stewart (2019).

Table 7.6 *When the CCP issues propaganda-based threats of repression*

	Dependent variable:											
	Stability						Harmony					
	0 day (1)	1 day (2)	2 day (3)	3 day (4)	4 day (5)	5 day (6)	0 day (7)	1 day (8)	2 day (9)	3 day (10)	4 day (11)	5 day (12)
Separatist anniversary	0.264*** (0.098)	0.135** (0.057)	0.121*** (0.045)	0.142*** (0.039)	0.246*** (0.034)	0.325*** (0.031)	0.129 (0.122)	0.034 (0.072)	0.058 (0.056)	0.078 (0.048)	0.139*** (0.043)	0.160*** (0.040)
Democratic anniversary	−0.113 (0.099)	−0.074 (0.058)	−0.063 (0.045)	−0.065* (0.039)	−0.041 (0.035)	0.002 (0.033)	−0.208* (0.124)	−0.122* (0.072)	−0.056 (0.056)	−0.065 (0.048)	−0.040 (0.044)	−0.037 (0.041)
Political anniversary	0.142** (0.057)	0.010 (0.034)	0.059** (0.028)	0.085*** (0.025)	0.069*** (0.023)	0.060*** (0.022)	0.376*** (0.069)	0.215*** (0.042)	0.213*** (0.034)	0.201*** (0.031)	0.201*** (0.029)	0.178*** (0.028)
Cultural anniversary	−0.147** (0.064)	−0.159*** (0.038)	−0.119*** (0.030)	−0.087*** (0.027)	−0.081*** (0.024)	−0.060*** (0.023)	−0.133* (0.079)	−0.140*** (0.047)	−0.122*** (0.038)	−0.085** (0.033)	−0.056* (0.031)	−0.058** (0.029)
Protests$_{t-1}$	0.116*** (0.026)	0.114*** (0.026)	0.113*** (0.026)	0.120*** (0.026)	0.125*** (0.025)	0.125*** (0.025)	0.117*** (0.032)	0.113*** (0.032)	0.112*** (0.032)	0.114*** (0.032)	0.121*** (0.032)	0.124*** (0.032)
Constant	2.921*** (0.032)	2.933*** (0.033)	2.928*** (0.033)	2.914*** (0.033)	2.896*** (0.034)	2.863*** (0.034)	2.114*** (0.040)	2.114*** (0.040)	2.105*** (0.041)	2.091*** (0.041)	2.063*** (0.042)	2.056*** (0.042)
Year-fixed effects	✓	✓	✓	✓	✓	✓	✓	✓	✓	✓	✓	✓
Newspaper-fixed effects	✓	✓	✓	✓	✓	✓	✓	✓	✓	✓	✓	✓
Observations	6,542	6,542	6,542	6,542	6,542	6,542	6,542	6,542	6,542	6,542	6,542	6,542

Note: *p < 0.1; **p < 0.05; ***p < 0.01
N Day column names give +/−N size of anniversary windows.

and ordinary citizens. The anniversaries of these human rights abuses now constitute focal moments for anti-regime protests. This lengthy record lets us probe whether propaganda-based threats are associated with moments of political tension, as Hypothesis 7.1 suggests, and disproportionately target the CCP's political out-groups, as Hypothesis 7.3 suggests. This is exactly what we find.

7.4.5 *Pro-Regime Propaganda and Propaganda-Based Threats of Repression*

Among our theory's central implications is that, in the absence of electoral constraints, autocrats employ absurd propaganda as a signal: that the government's capacity for repression is so substantial that it can compel citizens to consume content that everyone knows is false. Pro-regime propaganda, our theory suggests, is implicitly threatening. Are spikes in pro-regime propaganda correlated with propaganda-based threats of repression?

To answer this question, we defined a "high propaganda day" as that when the observed level of *Positive Coverage: Executive*$_{nt}$ in newspaper n is greater than or equal to the sample mean plus κ standard deviations. We let κ range from 0.25 to 2.0. We estimated the model

$$Y_{nt} = \alpha + \beta \left(\text{High Propaganda Day}_t\right) + \gamma_n + \epsilon \qquad (7.3)$$

where n indexes newspaper and t indexes day. We estimated (7.3) with OLS. The results appear in Table 7.7. Across outcome variables and κ thresholds, the CCP employs pro-regime propaganda and threats of repression at roughly the same moments. High propaganda days are associated with roughly four additional references to "stability" and six additional references to "harmony." Threats of repression and effusive pro-regime propaganda, this suggests, are complements, with threats most common during moments of profound political tension.

7.4.6 *Threats of Repression in the Xinjiang Daily*

In Section 7.3, we documented how Paul Biya's *Cameroon Tribune* issues propaganda-based threats more often to the anglophone out-group than the francophone in-group. Now, we exploit the fact that the CCP maintains provincial newspapers, which tailor content to local audiences. We obtained every issue of the *Xinjiang Daily* between 2018 and 2020. As for Cameroon, Hypothesis 7.3 predicts that the CCP should

Table 7.7 Threats of repression and pro-regime propaganda in China

Dependent variable: "Stability"

	$\kappa = 0.25$	$\kappa = 0.5$	$\kappa = 0.75$	$\kappa = 1.0$	$\kappa = 1.25$	$\kappa = 1.5$	$\kappa = 1.75$	$\kappa = 2.0$
High propaganda day	6.602***	6.874***	6.483***	6.284***	6.600***	6.196***	6.028***	6.296***
	(0.259)	(0.309)	(0.360)	(0.426)	(0.493)	(0.564)	(0.653)	(0.769)
Constant	12.074***	12.493***	12.738***	12.872***	12.941***	12.986***	13.014***	13.034***
	(0.135)	(0.133)	(0.133)	(0.133)	(0.133)	(0.134)	(0.134)	(0.134)
Newspaper-fixed effects	✓	✓	✓	✓	✓	✓	✓	✓
Observations	8,865	8,865	8,865	8,865	8,865	8,865	8,865	8,865
R^2	0.111	0.097	0.080	0.069	0.065	0.059	0.055	0.053

Dependent variable: "Harmony"

	$\kappa = 0.25$	$\kappa = 0.5$	$\kappa = 0.75$	$\kappa = 1.0$	$\kappa = 1.25$	$\kappa = 1.5$	$\kappa = 1.75$	$\kappa = 2.0$
High propaganda day	4.157***	4.606***	4.302***	5.124***	5.643***	6.856***	6.319***	6.970***
	(0.261)	(0.310)	(0.360)	(0.423)	(0.489)	(0.557)	(0.645)	(0.761)
Constant	4.911***	5.152***	5.318***	5.379***	5.430***	5.450***	5.484***	5.504***
	(0.137)	(0.134)	(0.133)	(0.132)	(0.132)	(0.132)	(0.132)	(0.132)
Newspaper-fixed effects	✓	✓	✓	✓	✓	✓	✓	✓
Observations	8,865	8,865	8,865	8,865	8,865	8,865	8,865	8,865
R^2	0.053	0.050	0.042	0.042	0.041	0.043	0.037	0.035

Note: $^{*}p < 0.1$; $^{**}p < 0.05$; $^{***}p < 0.01$

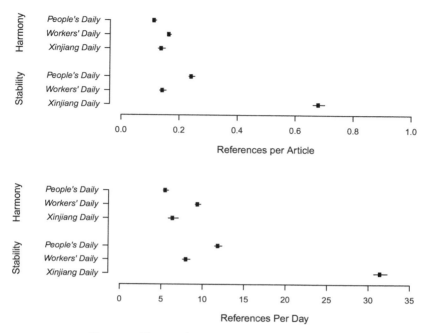

Figure 7.3 Threats of repression in the *Xinjiang Daily*

employ more propaganda-based threats in the *Xinjiang Daily*, read by the Uyghur out-group, than the *People's Daily* or *Workers' Daily*, which primarily target the Han in-group.[51] To probe this, we estimated models of the form

$$Y_{nt} = \alpha + \beta \left(\text{Newspaper}_n\right) + \gamma_s + \epsilon \qquad (7.4)$$

where n indexes newspaper, t indexes day, and s indexes year. We specified several outcome variables. The variable *Stability*$_{nt}$ measures the number of references to "stability" in newspaper n on day t. The variable *Harmony*$_{nt}$ measures the number of references to "harmony" in newspaper n on day t. We also standardized these variables by the number of articles in newspaper n on day t, which ensured that variation in *Stability*$_{nt}$ or *Harmony*$_{nt}$ was not simply driven by the volume of articles published. This yielded four regression models.

The results appear in Figure 7.3. In the top panel, for each threat codeword and each newspaper along the y-axis, the x-axis measures the

---

[51] For more on provincial newspapers, see Shih (2008), Jaros and Pan (2017), and Chen and Hong (2020).

number of codeword references per article. In the bottom panel, the
x-axis measures the number of references per day. As our theory predicts, the CCP issues far more propaganda-based threats in the pages
of the *Xinjiang Daily* than in either the *People's Daily* or *Workers' Daily*.
The difference is substantial and driven by stability rather than harmony.
The *Xinjiang Daily* references social stability between three and four
times more often than either the *People's Daily* or *Workers' Daily* does.
This effect persists regardless of whether we measure stability references
by day or by article.

As in Cameroon, the CCP's propaganda apparatus is far more likely
to threaten the Uyghur out-group than the Han in-group.

7.5 MOMENTS OF CRISIS IN UZBEKISTAN AND TUNISIA

Sections 7.3 and 7.4 featured two key results. First, propaganda-based
threats of repression are disproportionately targeted at political out-
groups. The division between in-group and out-group is especially stark
in Cameroon, where Biya relies exclusively on francophone support.
Biya's French language content features strikingly little threatening content. Second, propaganda-based threats emerge during moments of crisis,
when protests or other forms of collective action threaten the regime's
political survival. In China, these are the anniversaries of ethnic separatist movements and, secondarily, major political events. In Chapter 9,
we explain why China's pro-democracy anniversaries are conspicuously
absent.

Next, we study how propaganda apparatuses respond to profound
crises. When confronting crises that imperil the regime, do constrained
autocrats still employ propaganda-based threats of repression substantially less often than unconstrained autocrats? We focus on the two
most profound crises in our dataset: the unexpected death of Uzbek
president Islam Karimov in September 2016 and the Tunisian Revolution that toppled President Zine El Abidine Ben Ali in January 2011.
The Uzbek regime is among the most repressive in our dataset; Ben
Ali's regime earned a −4 Polity score during the sample period, precisely the same as Paul Biya's in Cameroon and Denis Sassou Nguesso's
in Congo.

The Uzbek propaganda apparatus responded to the succession crisis
by threatening citizens. Ben Ali, though ultimately forced to flee Tunisia,
responded by employing honest propaganda: conceding policy failures
and emphasizing the government's efforts to resolve them.

7.5.1 The Crises

Uzbekistan: Presidential Succession, August–September 2016   Islam Karimov's death on September 2, 2016 "plunged the country into uncertainty."[52] The crisis began on August 26, when Karimov suffered a sudden brain hemorrhage. Like many dictators, Karimov did not anoint a successor. As a result, his brain hemorrhage created a crisis for the ruling elite, who needed to agree on a successor and ensure that citizens would acquiesce. There were two choices: Shavkat Mirziyoyev, Karimov's longtime prime minister, and Rustam Azimov, who served as deputy prime minister and finance minister. *The Guardian* speculated that Mirziyoyev was the choice of Karimov's intelligence chief, Rustam Inoyatov, who, according to a classified diplomatic cable, had "sufficient compromising information on Mirziyoyev to ensure his own interests [would be] protected."[53] The government remained silent until the evening of September 2, when it announced Karimov's death on state television. Mirziyoyev was given responsibility for Karimov's funeral, named interim president on September 8, and "elected" on December 4.

Ensuring that citizens would acquiesce was non-trivial. Despite the government's reputation for brutality, Uzbek citizens have revolted in the past. On June 23, 2004, twenty-three businessmen in Andijan were arrested and charged with membership in Akromiya, an opposition organization that Karimov branded as terrorist and made illegal. They faced trial in early 2005, and some 4,000 citizens gathered at the Andijan courthouse on May 11 to hear the guilty verdict. On the night of May 12, armed citizens stormed the prison where the convicted businessmen were incarcerated, freed them and hundreds of others, and occupied the regional administration building. Inspired by the prison break, citizens gathered in Andijan's central square on May 13 to demand change. As the crowd grew, Karimov's security forces prevented citizens from departing the square. Without warning, security forces "opened fire on everyone indiscriminately, including women and children," as Bukharbaeva (2005) recounted. The government conceded that nine peopled were killed, all "extremists" and "terrorists." In 2008, a government defector estimated that 1,500 citizens were killed. Despite the massacre, on May 14 several thousand more citizens resumed the protest, denouncing Karimov's security services as "killers" and "murderers." Other citizens

---

[52] Walker and Harding (2016).
[53] Walker and Harding (2016).

opted to flee Uzbekistan altogether, burning police offices and cars in the border town of Qorasuv, fifty kilometers from Andijan. The government responded by killing hundreds more.

Uzbekistan emerged as a key ally in George W. Bush's "war on terror," serving as a transit route for military supplies destined for Afghanistan. This, along with its substantial natural gas and cotton production, gave the Karimov government effective immunity from international criticism. The Andijan massacre was so brazen, however, that the international community was forced to impose military sanctions, to which Karimov responded by expelling the American military from the Karshi-Khanabad Military Base. Given Uzbekistan's geostrategic importance, these sanctions were short-lived, and by 2008 had been largely repealed.

Between August 26 and September 2, 2016, the regime's central challenge was to ensure that citizens did not exploit political uncertainty among elites to engineer a revolution, as they nearly did in Andijan in 2005. Our theory suggests that the propaganda apparatus should have responded by threatening citizens.

Tunisia: The Arab Spring, December 2010–January 2011 President Zine El Abidine Ben Ali seized power in 1987 and fled on January 14, 2011, the Arab Spring's first casualty. The origins of the Tunisian Revolution are well known. Mohamed Bouazizi worked as a street vendor in rural Sidi Bouzid, despite his university education. On December 16, 2010, he contracted a $200 debt for produce, which he planned to sell on December 17. That morning, Bouazizi was harassed by local police for not having a permit, though none was required. Since Bouazizi lacked cash for a bribe, the police expropriated his wares, leaving him unable to repay the $200 debt. His family claims he was physically assaulted as well. Bouazizi appealed to the governor's office but was denied a hearing. He exited, stopped traffic, doused himself with paint thinner, and set himself aflame. He died on January 4, 2011, eighteen days later.

In a sense, the Tunisian Revolution began weeks earlier. On November 28, Wikileaks and five of the world's prominent newspapers posted the first of nearly 300,000 leaked documents that detailed massive corruption within the Ben Ali family.[54] Sidi Bouzid youth began protesting outside regional government headquarters on December 18. Over the next week two more protesters, Lahseen Naji and Ramzi Al-Abboudi,

---

[54] Freeman (2011).

committed suicide. On December 24, another protester, Mohamed Ammari, was killed by police. Protests spread to Tunis, the capital, on December 27. The Tunis protests quickly expanded to include urban professionals. The December 27 protests were called by the Federation of Labour Unions and quickly joined by the National Lawyers Order. By January 6, virtually all of Tunisia's 8,000 lawyers were on strike, bringing the legal system to a standstill. Ben Ali's *La Presse* newspaper went silent on January 4.

This represents a "hard case" for our theory, the only crisis in our dataset that ended with the regime's collapse. As it spun out of control, Ben Ali's incentives to threaten citizens should have been powerful. Ben Ali, however, confronted a different institutional landscape than in Uzbekistan. While he trusted the loyalty of the police, he was uncertain whether the military would fire on protesters. Since he took power in the 1980s, the military had become increasingly professionalized and less subject to his personal control. This became a matter of tension in 2002, when a helicopter carrying thirteen military officers crashed. The military suspected that Ben Ali had engineered the crash to eliminate opposition, especially from Brigadier General Abdelaziz Skik, who was then army chief of staff and on board.[55] Ben Ali's response to the protests that emerged in 2011 was shaped by his relatively limited capacity for repression.

7.5.2 The Propaganda Responses

Uzbekistan: "Oath of loyalty to the motherland" Although Karimov died on September 2, 2016, the crisis began with his massive brain hemorrhage on August 26 or early August 27. The propaganda apparatus responded quickly. On August 27, *Narodnoye Slovo* published two articles that are among the most threatening in our corpus. The first features testimony from a "senior operative" in Tashkent's Criminal Investment Department, who tells readers that Uzbekistan's police are "fully cared for by the President of the country":

Ensuring Law and Order Is an Honorable Mission

August 27, 2016

It is pleasant to realize that those who ensure peace and order are fully cared for by the President of the country. It manifests itself in improving the living

---

[55] Signé and Smida (2014, 7–8).

conditions of law enforcement personnel, which gives energy and strength in official duties.

Since independence, our country has carried out major reforms to the law enforcement agencies, which are an important in ensuring stability.

The Ministry of Internal Affairs is provided with modern motor transport, computer and other equipment for conducting various complex studies, and communication facilities. There is close cooperation and interaction of preventive inspectors with the public and Mahalla activists. An effective search system has been created that provides ample opportunities for rapid detection of crimes, ensuring the inevitability of punishment. Particular attention is paid to the protection of young people from the negative influence of various currents.

It is well known that peace and tranquility are the basis of prosperity. Like my colleagues, I clearly understand how important our work is in these times, when dark forces are opposed to progress around the world.

According to many, our officers are harsh people, but we are touched by the sincere concern of the state about law enforcement officers and their families. We will selflessly safeguard tranquility and confidence. In this we see our main task.

Kamoliddin ABIDZHANOV,
Commander of the Order of Mardlik.

The second article focuses on the military, deemed "A Reliable Guarantor of Peace and Stability." The article describes the military's extensive training regimen, which renders it "always ready to eliminate any threats [and] repulse any aggression." Soldiers, according to *Narodnoye Slovo*, are indoctrinated with "a vital motto": "This is my dear Homeland, I will cherish it as the apple of my eye and remain ready to sacrifice my life for its sake."

Armed Forces of Uzbekistan: A Reliable Guarantor of Peace and Stability

August 27, 2016

To protect this right – and therefore independence, by being always ready to eliminate any threats – it was necessary to have a powerful national army.

A radical reform of military education was launched. A number of higher educational establishments were opened, and training of highly qualified military personnel began, for which the words "This is my dear Homeland, I will cherish it as the apple of my eye and remain ready to sacrifice my life for its sake" became a vital motto.

The Academy of the Armed Forces, established in 1995 on the initiative of President Islam Karimov, opened a new chapter in the history of the formation of the national army. The Academy has an educational and technical base that meets modern requirements. Experimental officers conduct studies on the theory and practice of military art in its walls, together with leading scientists and experts of national universities and research institutions. Along with raising the theoretical knowledge of students in the Academy of the Armed Forces, much attention is paid to their practical skills.

Uzbekistan celebrated its twenty-fifth Independence Day on August 31, with Karimov comatose in the hospital, unbeknownst to citizens. *Narodnoye Slovo* printed "messages of congratulations" from nearly seventy-five world leaders. Of these, *Narodnoye Slovo* printed three messages in full: from Barack Obamba, Xi Jinping, and Vladimir Putin. These letters broadcast the regime's international support to citizens, which, presumably, would inoculate it against sanctions for human rights violations. On September 2, hours before Karimov's death was announced, *Narodnoye Slovo* published the article below, which reiterated the government's indoctrination of young soldiers.

Oath of Loyalty to the Motherland

September 2, 2016

An event that will forever be remembered by future officers was held at the Tashkent Higher All-Arms Command School.

As its participants noted, since independence, our country has created mobile, well-equipped Armed Forces capable of rebuffing any aggressor and ensuring peace and tranquility. Major work on improving the training system for military specialists is carried out continuously. To date, all higher educational institutions of the Ministry of Defense have been transferred to a multidisciplinary officer training system.

The National Anthem sounds, and then the team proceeds to the Military Oath. Students solemnly pronounce the oath of allegiance to the Motherland. Now, in bright, well-equipped classrooms and training centers, they are waiting for experienced officer-mentors who will help them become high-level specialists.

At the end of the celebrations, the relatives and friends came hurrying to the students in uniform. A sea of flowers, smiles, joyful exclamations alternating with tears of joy. A truly remarkable day in the life of young children who have chosen the honorable profession of defenders of the Motherland....

Figure 7.4 visualizes how *Narodnoye Slovo* responded to Karimov's death. For each month along the *x*-axis, the *y*-axis records the average daily share of articles that reference the internal security apparatus. These references generally emphasize its loyalty to the regime and its efficiency against threats. Threats spike at very predictable moments: the anniversary of the Andijan massacre, presidential elections, and the succession

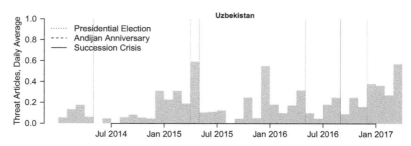

Figure 7.4 Threats in Uzbek propaganda between 2013 and 2017

crisis of September 2016. To confirm that the threat spike between Karimov's brain hemorrhage on August 27 and his death on September 2 was not due to random chance, we estimated models of the form

$$Y_t = \alpha + \beta \left(\text{Karimov Death}_t \right) + \delta \left(\text{Post--Karimov Death}_t \right) + \kappa\, W_t + \epsilon \quad (7.5)$$

where t indexes day, *Karimov Death$_t$* is a dichotomous indicator that assumes value 1 between August 27 and September 2, *Post–Karimov Death$_t$* is a dichotomous indicator that assumes value 1 between September 3 and September 9, and W_t is a vector of day-level control variables. We controlled for election seasons, independence day, the number of articles published on day t, and the anniversary of the Andijan massacre. We specified several outcomes of interest: the number of threat articles per day *Threat$_t$*, the share of articles per day that constituted a threat *Threat$_t^S$*, and whether the number of threat articles per day was positive.

The results appear in Table 7.8 and are consistent with the descriptive statistics in Figure 7.4. The rate of threatening articles to total articles increased between Karimov's brain hemorrhage and subsequent death, as did the absolute number of threatening articles. After Karimov's death was announced on September 2, the propaganda apparatus shifted: from publishing threats to absurd celebrations of Karimov. From Model 5, the daily number of references to the late Karimov increased from 0.3 to nearly 12, or a factor of 40. As a result, from Model 7, positive coverage of Karimov spiked as well. Across models, we again find evidence that the Uzbekistan propaganda apparatus routinely threatens citizens around the anniversary of the Andijan massacre, as our theory predicts.

Tunisia: "Together we meet challenges" Ben Ali attempted to respond to the 2011 protests as he did in 2008, when a food crisis prompted riots in the Gafsa Mining Basin. In 2008, protesters denounced corruption and

Table 7.8 How Uzbek propaganda changed around Karimov's death

	Threats OLS (1)	Threats NB (2)	Threats^S OLS (3)	Threats ≥ 1 OLS (4)	Executive references OLS (5)	Tone standardized OLS (6)	Executive tone OLS (7)
				Dependent variable:			
Andijan anniversary	0.460***	1.258***	0.051***	0.128	−1.589	0.539	−2.192
	(0.127)	(0.420)	(0.018)	(0.098)	(1.553)	(0.462)	(2.992)
Karimov death	0.563***	1.464**	0.056*	0.403***	−2.356	0.392	−4.661
	(0.201)	(0.646)	(0.029)	(0.155)	(2.461)	(0.768)	(4.741)
Post–Karimov death	−0.194	−20.660	−0.018	−0.165	11.739***	0.359	26.179***
	(0.179)	(15,967.930)	(0.026)	(0.138)	(2.190)	(0.463)	(4.219)
Independence day	−0.458	−21.399	−0.055	−0.355	2.016	−0.355	3.234
	(0.348)	(28,637.880)	(0.050)	(0.268)	(4.250)	(0.940)	(8.187)
Election season	−0.066	−0.471	−0.011	−0.044	3.475***	−0.187	5.399***
	(0.059)	(0.384)	(0.008)	(0.045)	(0.719)	(0.176)	(1.384)
Articles	0.007	0.039	−0.004***	0.004	0.383***	0.056**	0.718***
	(0.008)	(0.048)	(0.001)	(0.006)	(0.103)	(0.028)	(0.197)
Constant	0.121	−2.034***	0.054***	0.121**	0.293	1.304***	0.208
	(0.074)	(0.429)	(0.011)	(0.057)	(0.906)	(0.248)	(1.744)
Observations	772	772	772	772	772	561	772
R^2	0.032		0.029	0.015	0.079	0.016	0.081

Note: *p < 0.1; **p < 0.05; ***p < 0.01

Ben Ali's inadequate response to unemployment. When police were unable to contain the protests, Ben Ali called on the army. Military officials then faced a choice. Although few supported the regime – it murdered thirteen senior officers, they believed – they were forced to contemplate what would happen if they supported a revolution that failed. They decided that the Gafsa protests, because they were in the countryside and far from the capital, were unlikely to topple the regime. Accordingly, they assented to Ben Ali's order and put down the rebellion.[56] In 2011, the military's calculus was different. Protests had spread to other urban centers, and so the military's defection could prove decisive. Ben Ali's ability to employ violence was constrained by a military that might refuse to fire on citizens.

Ben Ali's propaganda apparatus responded to the Arab Spring much differently than Uzbekistan's propaganda apparatus responded to Karimov's death. *La Presse*, Ben Ali's propaganda newspaper, printed no articles that discussed police or military preparedness; there was only one that referenced "stability." It appears in Table 7.9 and is profoundly unthreatening. The article was occasioned by Ben Ali's speech to the nation on December 29, 2010, during which he addressed the crisis. The speech was printed in full, as were the responses of various regime allies. "The speech delivered Tuesday evening by President Zine El Abidine Ben Ali to the Tunisian people expressed, sincerely, the concerns of citizens and reflect the profound understanding of the country's leadership of the imperative of . . . resolving them." The article referenced "stability" only at the end:

The secretary general of the UDU [political party] reaffirmed his attachment to the climate of stability that reigns in the country, as it represents the only way to build a prosperous future and resolve all current and future problems, through dialogue, in the service of the people and the fatherland.

Ben Ali's propaganda apparatus amplified his message of empathy and commitment. Figure 7.5 visualizes this. For each day along the *x*-axis, the *y*-axis measures the number of articles about a given topic. The points in black give the total number of articles published. The vertical line marks December 17, 2010, when Mohamed Bouazizi set himself aflame. In the two months before the crisis, *La Presse* increased its publication rate, from roughly twenty articles per day to thirty. Its coverage focused on the regime's efforts to grow the economy, often

---

[56] Signé and Smida (2014).

Table 7.9 *How Tunisian propaganda changed during the Arab Spring*

	Dependent variable:							
	Articles	Executive references	Positive coverage standardized	International cooperation	Economy	Education health	Sports	Government action
	OLS	OLS	OLS	NB	NB	NB	NB	NB
	(1)	(2)	(3)	(4)	(5)	(6)	(7)	(8)
Arab spring	5.706**	5.013	0.103	−0.447	0.411***	0.311	0.085	0.315***
	(2.331)	(3.768)	(0.121)	(0.284)	(0.129)	(0.255)	(0.125)	(0.094)
Articles		1.021***	−0.003	0.072***	0.041***	0.040***	0.024***	0.042***
		(0.102)	(0.003)	(0.008)	(0.004)	(0.008)	(0.004)	(0.003)
Constant	23.794***	−0.024	1.525***	−1.596***	−0.048	−1.281***	1.441***	0.627***
	(0.630)	(2.633)	(0.087)	(0.227)	(0.123)	(0.235)	(0.095)	(0.088)
Observations	246	246	244	246	246	246	246	246
R^2	0.024	0.308	0.005					

	Dependent variable:							
	Completion	Work	Goal	Persistence	Failure	Respect	Strength	Virtue
	NB	NB	NB	NB	NB	NB	NB	NB
	(1)	(2)	(3)	(4)	(5)	(6)	(7)	(8)
Arab spring	0.429**	0.328*	0.313	0.477**	0.574**	−0.029	0.200	−0.103
	(0.181)	(0.173)	(0.196)	(0.193)	(0.278)	(0.092)	(0.165)	(0.136)
Articles	0.040***	0.041***	0.044***	0.045***	0.045***	0.008***	0.045***	0.027***
	(0.005)	(0.005)	(0.006)	(0.006)	(0.009)	(0.003)	(0.005)	(0.004)
Constant	0.912***	1.637***	0.342**	−0.051	−1.240***	1.775***	3.167***	2.253***
	(0.139)	(0.127)	(0.155)	(0.163)	(0.254)	(0.066)	(0.117)	(0.097)
Observations	246	246	246	246	246	246	246	246

Note: * p < 0.1; ** p < 0.05; *** p < 0.01

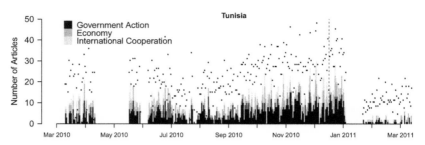

Figure 7.5 Evolution of Tunisian propaganda between March 2010 and March 2011

with international partners. This trend intensified between December 18 and January 2, *La Presse*'s last publication date before Ben Ali fell. During those two weeks, *La Presse* printed as many articles per day about public goods provision as it did *total articles per day* between March and October.

We confirmed these shifts statistically by estimating models of the form

$$Y_t = \alpha + \beta \left(\text{Arab Spring}_t \right) + \kappa\, W_t + \epsilon \qquad (7.6)$$

where t indexes day; T_t is a dichotomous indicator that assumes value 1 between December 18, 2010, and January 3, 2011; and W_t gives the number of articles published per day. We include several outcomes of interest: our standard measures of pro-regime coverage; the number of articles published on day t about some issue area h; and the number of words associated with a series of eight sentiment dictionaries, which helped us understand more about how the substance of Ben Ali coverage changed. For these, we took the total number of words from the twenty surrounding each identifier.

The results appear in Table 7.9 and are visualized in Figure 7.6. Strikingly, the only issue areas that became more prominent during the Arab Spring were the chief demands of protesters: the economy and the government's efforts to improve it. Coverage of Ben Ali himself shifted as well, as the article below demonstrates.

A First Batch of Development Projects in Sidi Bouzid – Approval of 3 Integrated Development Projects

December 24, 2010

The new presidential decisions aimed at consolidating development and employment in inland regions, in particular in the governorate of Sidi Bouzid, were at

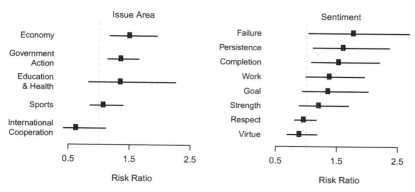

Figure 7.6 How coverage of the Ben Ali regime changed during the Arab Spring

the center of the special session of the of the governorate, held on Thursday at the governorate's headquarters, under the President of Mr Mohamed Nouri Jouini, Minister for Development and international cooperation in the presence of the Governor, deputies, senators and executives in the region.

Since the change, said the governor, the amount of investments in the region reached 2350 million dinars, which illustrates the the Head of State's continued interest in regional development, especially in the interior and its commitment to guaranteeing a decent life to all citizens.

Mr. Jouini affirmed that this session was vital for monitoring the implementation of the Presidential program "Together We Meet Challenges." He highlighted the achievements made since the change in the governorate of Sidi Bouzid, reflecting the challenges facing the country, especially employment.

Mr. Jouini also reviewed the various components of the strategy ordered by the Head of State on 15 December 2010 by means of investments on the order of 6500 million dinars. These investments are aimed at creating jobs, improving the quality of life, developing areas at urban peripheries. They stressed the value of creating a university in the region, as well as a dairy and meat plant, the development of road network to facilitate connections with neighboring governorates.

At the end of the session, the participants highlighted the concern shown for the region, expressing their full support for the policy and President Ben Ali as well as their attachment to him as Leader of the country.

Some 306 BTS project financing agreements have been distributed, as a first installment, to benefit many young people.

Before the Arab Spring, *La Presse* depicted Ben Ali as virtuous and worthy of respect, and as someone whose leadership had earned him the respect of the international community. Between December 18 and

January 3, *La Presse*'s coverage of Ben Ali shifted dramatically. It routinely and explicitly acknowledged that citizens endured hardships that the regime had failed to resolve. Failure, indeed, was the sentiment that *La Presse* emphasized the most, in relative terms, once the Arab Spring protests had begun. It emphasized Ben Ali's sensitivity to these hardships, his efforts to address them, and his determination to see government action to fruition. *La Presse* routinely spoke directly to urban youth, and even once to citizens in Sidi Bouzid, where Mohamed Bouazizi set himself aflame in front of the governor's office.

Ben Ali responded to the Arab Spring not by threatening his citizens, but by employing honest propaganda. He conceded the difficulties that his citizens endured and attempted to persuade them of his efforts to address them, including by firing the regional governor.

7.6 CONCLUSION

Autocrats routinely employ propaganda to threaten citizens with repression. To understand how, we combined our theory of propaganda with insights from experimental psychology. Using propaganda-based threats, we argue, is appealing to repressive governments. It reminds citizens of the consequences of anti-regime behavior and cues fear, which renders them more risk averse and hence less likely to challenge the regime. Using propaganda-based threats is also costly. It undermines efforts to persuade citizens of regime merits and renders sensitive dates even more so. For these reasons, our theory suggests, propaganda-based threats of repression should be relatively uncommon, especially where autocrats confront electoral constraints, and should be reserved for moments of crisis.

To measure threats of repression, we exploited the fact that autocrats use codewords. Since these codewords differ across countries – products of their unique histories and cultural contexts – we employed a series of case studies. We focused first on Cameroon, where, due to a colonial legacy, the chief cleavage between the political in-group and out-group is linguistic. Since Paul Biya's propaganda newspaper, the *Cameroon Tribune*, publishes in English and French, it can target the in-group and out-group with different messages. Biya's *Cameroon Tribune*, we show, was far more likely to threaten anglophone readers with repression, even before the secession crisis began in late 2016. Its pro-regime coverage is also more effusive.

Next, we returned to China, where the codewords employed by the Chinese government are well documented: "stability," "stability maintenance," and "harmony." These codewords are so common that citizens use them euphemistically. Being repressed is to be "harmonized." We find that propaganda-based threats are occasioned chiefly by anniversaries of ethnic separatist movements in the Tibet and Xinjiang regions and secondarily by major political anniversaries. The CCP disproportionately targets identity groups that are excluded from the CCP's core constituency, but it threatens the ethnic Han population as well, especially around major political events. Threats of repression are correlated with spikes in pro-regime propaganda, which, as we showed in Chapter 4, are regarded by citizens as implicitly threatening.

Our final paired comparison suggests that electoral constraints condition propaganda-based threats even during moments of crisis. When Islam Karimov's death plunged Uzbekistan into crisis in September 2016, the propaganda apparatus responded by announcing its military was well armed and had taken "an oath of loyalty to the motherland." As President Zine El Abidine Ben Ali was losing power in January 2011, his propaganda apparatus sought to persuade citizens of regime merits: by conceding the government's failures to foster economic growth and highlighting new efforts to do so.

Propaganda in autocracies also exhibits dramatic temporal variation. Chapters 8 and 9, which together constitute Part III, explore the calendar of propaganda in more detail.

The Propaganda Calendar

8

The Propagandist's Dilemma

8.1 THE PROPAGANDIST'S DILEMMA

Chapters 4 through 6 document how propaganda apparatuses in constrained autocracies seek credibility. Their pro-regime coverage resembles Fox News's coverage of Republicans. They report economic crises, allegations of corruption, irregularities in the electoral process, and failed efforts to diversify economies away from natural resources. Propaganda apparatuses are forced to cover allegations leveled by the autocrat's rivals and avoid denigrating these rivals too stridently. Propaganda apparatuses observe that the regime has not adequately invested in the nation's athletes. They cover persistently high unemployment and infant mortality rates, which the regime partners with international donors to ameliorate. Chapter 7 shows how propaganda apparatuses in electorally constrained autocracies generally forgo explicit threats of repression, which would undermine costly investments in credibility.

Where electoral constraints are binding, how do propaganda apparatuses use the credibility they acquire? In this chapter, we identify two non-mutually exclusive strategies. In one, the *steady exposure* model, autocrats employ a steady stream of plausibly favorable coverage, which aims for a reasonably high baseline level of popularity that insulates the autocrat from negative shocks. In the other, the *propaganda campaign* model, autocrats spend credibility capital during moments of crisis and political tension. Whatever its benefits, the propaganda campaign model entails a drawback. If propaganda campaigns recur at predictable moments, citizens should be keenly aware, at which point, Goebbels observed, propaganda loses its power to persuade. We refer to this as the propagandist's dilemma. The most important propaganda campaigns are driven by temporal incentives that are obvious to citizens.

337

In this chapter, we make two theoretical arguments. First, where electoral constraints are binding, we expect the propaganda calendar to be driven by moments of crisis and political tension. Notwithstanding the propagandist's dilemma, at these moments the value of persuasion is high. Second, these propaganda campaigns should be tightly choreographed: designed to persuade citizens of regime merits despite obvious temporal incentives to do so. Empirically, this chapter combines our dataset with two case studies. Across autocracies, we show, propaganda campaigns are relatively rare. Where autocrats confront electoral constraints, spikes occur overwhelmingly around elections. Propaganda campaigns begin well before election day and increase gradually. This makes sense. The regular elections occasioned by nominally democratic institutions constitute recurring opportunities for collective action. They can also be lost.

To understand the sophistication with which electoral propaganda campaigns are crafted, we return to Congo for the March 2016 presidential election, which was the most politically sensitive since Denis Sassou Nguesso returned to power in 1997. His propaganda campaign, we show, was intricate, designed to make his victory appear uncertain initially – citizens had not yet voted, after all – and more likely as the campaign unfolded and citizens expressed their enthusiasm for the candidates before them. Sassou Nguesso's propaganda campaign recalls Lasswell's (1927, 628) key insight: "The most subtle propaganda closely resembles disinterested deliberation." Sassou Nguesso's propaganda apparatus sought credibility even during the election campaign: by covering rising food prices, stagnation in the banking sector, and the government's failure "to diversify the national economy." Sassou Nguesso's propaganda apparatus covered the opposition leveling all the same criticisms. It is unclear what share of the Congolese electorate was swayed. But this choreography is consistent with evidence from Russia, the United States, and elsewhere that sophisticated electoral propaganda campaigns routinely generate legitimate electoral support.[1]

Where electoral constraints are non-binding, autocrats confront different strategic calculations. Since absurd propaganda serves to create common knowledge about the regime's capacity for violence, it aims not to persuade, but to intimidate. In turn, propaganda campaigns during

---

[1] Enikolopov, Petrova, and Zhuravskaya (2011); Adena et al. (2015); DellaVigna and Kaplan (2007); Martin and Yurukoglu (2017); Ash and Galletta (2019).

election seasons are different. With no need to persuade, propaganda apparatuses have no need to build and spend credibility. Propaganda spikes, we show, occur only around election day, when unrest is most likely. Propaganda often spikes after election day, which is not as counterintuitive as it might seem. Citizens must be compelled to accept obviously fraudulent results when they are announced. In Uzbekistan, the post-election propaganda spike is driven by congratulatory letters from the Great Powers, which advertise the regime's foreign backers to citizens.

This chapter proceeds as follows. Section 8.2 extends our theory to explore how constrained autocrats spend the credibility they acquire. Section 8.3 uses data from Congo to account for the frequency and timing of propaganda spikes where electoral constraints are binding. Section 8.4 documents the timing of electoral propaganda campaigns across autocracies. Section 8.5 studies how propaganda apparatuses in constrained autocracies resolve the propagandist's dilemma, focusing on Congo's March 2016 presidential election. Section 8.6 studies electoral propaganda campaigns in unconstrained autocracies, focusing on the March 2015 and December 2016 presidential elections in Uzbekistan.

8.2 THEORY

8.2.1 *Spending Credibility*

How do propaganda apparatuses in electorally constrained autocracies use credibility to persuade citizens of regime merits? We identify two broad models.

First, autocrats can spend credibility capital steadily over time, part of an effort to maintain some reasonably high baseline support. We refer to this as *steady exposure*, and it entails a steady stream of plausibly favorable content. In Congo, this includes coverage of Sassou Nguesso's various efforts to mediate conflicts across Africa – in Cote d'Ivoire, Democratic Republic of Congo, Libya, Sudan, and Zambia, among others – and partnerships with development institutions to improve public goods provision. It also includes coverage of the various charities founded by the Sassou Nguesso family and senior regime officials, which distribute goods to supporters: mosquito nets to prevent malaria, desks for schools, notebooks for school children, and others. On June 21, 2017, a date with no special political value, *Les Dépêches* announced this on its front page: "China Brings Its Support to the Actions of the FPA," a reference to *Fondation Perspectives de l'Avenir*, the "NGO" founded by son Denis Christel in 2012. The gift from the Chinese embassy "consisted of laptop and desktop computers, tablet computers, insecticide-treated mosquito nets, footballs, basketballs, volleyballs, solar flashlights and swimsuits."[2]

Of course, given the electoral constraints he confronts, Sassou Nguesso's propaganda apparatus also covers the occasional criticisms of his family's "charity" organizations, as well the defenses of these charities by the family's allies. On August 3, 2018, during a National Assembly debate, opposition leader Pascal Tsaty Mabiala asked this: "Where does Denis Christel Sassou Nguesso obtain his [financial] resources to do all that he does across the country? ... He is not Bill Gates. ... This is what causes corruption in this country, because we all know that he does all this because he wants to run for president [in 2021]."[3] In response, on August 14, *Vox Congo* covered one of Denis Christel's allies:

This morning's rally is a scathing denial of all the attacks, slander, wickedness of politicians from all sides who, instead of encouraging positive initiatives, see only "playing politics"[4] in all these humanitarian actions.[5]

As several recent books have documented, Vladimir Putin's propaganda apparatus employs the steady exposure model as well.[6]

The steady exposure model has its foundations in behavioral psychology. Jowett and O'Donnell (2012, 163) call this the "theory of exposure learning," and it dates at least to Zajonc's (1968) pathbreaking work. Using a series of experiments, Zajonc (1968) showed that individuals who were exposed to stimuli more often liked them better, regardless of whether those stimuli were meaningful. Later, Zajonc (1980) suggested that individuals find comfort in familiarity. More recently, Pennycook, Cannon, and Rand (2017, 1865) documented this effect in "fake news" during the 2016 American presidential election campaign. "Even a single exposure," they write, "increases subsequent perceptions of accuracy, both within the same session and after a week." This effect persists "even when the stories are labeled as contested by fact-checkers or are inconsistent with the reader's political ideology." Lamberova and Treisman

---

[2] "China Brings Its Support to the Actions of the FPA," *Les Dépêches de Brazzaville*, June 21, 2017.

[3] Jean-Claude Beri, "TSATY MABIALA, Has He Rediscovered the Path of Righteousness and Truth? *Les Dépêches de Brazzaville*, August 4, 2018.

[4] The original is *"la politique politicienne."*

[5] Pepy-Alchie Koussoukama, "A New Platform Launches for the Development of Congo," *Vox Congo*, August 14, 2018.

[6] Gessen (2012, 2017), Pomerantsev (2015*b*), Soldatov and Borogan (2015), Van Herpen (2016), Ostrovsky (2017).

(2020) argue that steady exposure helps autocrats achieve more baseline support, which helps them weather crises. This, we believe, is why the CCP's educational reforms between 2004 and 2010 have had lasting effects on students' views about CCP governance, democracy, and free markets.[7]

Second, autocrats can spend credibility capital during moments of crisis, when popular frustration threatens to coalesce into mass protest. We refer to these bursts as *propaganda campaigns*. The crises that motivate these campaigns often have economic origins.[8] During economic downturns, Russian state television balances admissions of bad news with suggestions that exogenous international forces are to blame.[9] Coverage of America's moral failures spikes as well, which we interpret, from Chapter 6, as a comparison set frame. In Chapter 5, we documented how Denis Sassou Nguesso's propaganda apparatus conceded a devastating fuel crisis and blamed it on logistical challenges, which the government promised to resolve. This timing makes sense. Economic crises provide focal moments around which citizens can organize[10] and reduce resources available to the autocrat to purchase support and finance the repressive apparatus.[11] Food price shocks may be especially threatening.[12] Food price shocks helped trigger the French Revolution of 1789,[13] the European revolutions of 1848,[14] the Soviet Union's collapse,[15] Suharto's demise in Indonesia,[16] the Syrian Civil War of 2011,[17] and the Arab Spring of 2010.[18]

For constrained autocrats, as we discussed in Chapter 1, the regular elections occasioned by nominally democratic institutions are perhaps even more threatening than economic downturns. Elections can be lost if autocrats are excessively confident or if fraud is costly. But even when

---

[7] Cantoni et al. (2017).

[8] Haggard and Kaufman (1997), Brancati (2016), Shih (2020).

[9] Rozenas and Stukal (2018).

[10] Acemoglu and Robinson (2005).

[11] Bueno de Mesquita et al. (2003).

[12] Arezki and Bruckner (2011), Brinkman and Hendrix (2011), Smith (2014), Bellemare (2015), Hendrix and Haggard (2015).

[13] Civitello (2003), Neely (2007).

[14] Berger and Spoerer (2001).

[15] Moskoff (1992).

[16] Mukherjee and Koren (2019).

[17] Gleick (2014); Breisinger, Ecker, and Trinh Tan (2015).

[18] Johnstone and Mazo (2011), Sternberg (2012), Hendrix and Haggard (2015).

autocrats can guarantee electoral victory with fraud, election seasons enable citizens to overcome collective action problems. Citizens are engaged in politics and aware of their neighbors' discontent.[19] Opposition leaders coordinate protests and alert citizens to fraud.[20] By affirming the possibility of a post-regime future, elections decrease the costs to regime elites of defecting from the coalition and joining the opposition.[21] As a result, the daily rate of protest across autocracies rises steadily as election day approaches, and on election day itself, it is three times greater than any other day of the year. "The probability of regime failure," Knutsen, Nygard, and Wig (2017, 117) write, "is seven times higher during election years than in nonelection years."[22]

8.2.2 Hypotheses

As a result, constrained autocrats should employ sustained propaganda campaigns in the run-up to election day and in its immediate aftermath, when evidence of fraud emerges and the autocrat's inauguration provides a final focal moment for mass protests. Where autocrats are constrained in their ability to tilt the electoral playing field, regular elections are uniquely threatening. There is perhaps no other moment when the capacity to manipulate citizens' beliefs is more valuable.

The drawback of spending credibility capital at recurring, predictable moments is that citizens will recognize the strategy, at which point, Goebbels observes, "propaganda becomes ineffective." This is the propagandist's dilemma, and it is acute where electoral constraints are binding. When the chief threats to an autocrat's survival are temporally determined, propaganda apparatuses must attempt to manipulate citizens' beliefs, even though citizens are aware of the temporal incentives to do so.

Hypothesis 8.1: *Where electoral constraints are binding, election seasons should constitute a disproportionate share of propaganda campaigns.*

---

[19] Kuran (1991); Tucker (2007); Hollyer, Rosendorff, and Vreeland (2015).
[20] Beissinger (2002), Javeline (2003), McFaul (2005), Radnitz (2010), Bunce and Wolchik (2011), Fearon (2011).
[21] Hale (2005), Reuter and Szakonyi (2019).
[22] Lindberg (2006), Bunce and Wolchik (2010), Hadenius and Teorell (2007), Seeberg (2014, 2020).

Hypothesis 8.2: *Propaganda campaigns during election seasons should be tightly choreographed to make the election seem fair and the autocrat's victory seem legitimate.*

Where electoral constraints are non-binding, the electoral calendar should still condition the propaganda calendar, since elections remain focal moments for protests. These propaganda campaigns should look fundamentally different from those in constrained autocracies. Their objective is not to persuade citizens of regime merits but to discourage electoral protests by creating common knowledge about the regime's capacity for violence. Electoral propaganda in the most repressive dictatorships should serve to intimidate by employing absurd propaganda and by emphasizing the regime's foreign backing.

Hypothesis 8.3: *Where autocrats do not confront binding electoral constraints, propaganda apparatuses employ electoral propaganda that aims to deter citizens from mass protests via intimidation.*

8.3 ACCOUNTING FOR PROPAGANDA CAMPAIGNS

To determine what share of propaganda campaigns in constrained autocracies are driven by election seasons, we return to Congo. Figure 8.1 visualizes pro-regime propaganda in Congo between 2013 and 2017. For each day along the x-axis, the y-axis gives the aggregate volume of pro-regime coverage, *Positive Coverage: Executive$_t$*, on day t. The horizontal line gives the threshold for a propaganda spike, defined as the mean value of *Positive Coverage: Executive$_t$* plus two standard deviations. Between April 2013 and March 2017, there have been just forty-two propaganda spikes, accounting for 3.6 percent of publication days.

For each propaganda spike, we consulted the relevant issue of *Les Dépêches de Brazzaville* to identify the topic that drove it. Propaganda spikes, we find, cluster at recurring, predictable moments. We identified the five leading categories; a sixth, "Unclear," denotes propaganda spikes not associated with an obvious event; a seventh, "Other," denotes propaganda spikes that were driven by other events. Then we calculated the share of propaganda spikes associated with each of these seven categories. The results appear in the bottom panel of Figure 8.1. Just 8 percent of propaganda spikes are unaccounted for. Propaganda spikes are easy to predict.

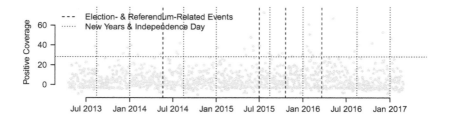

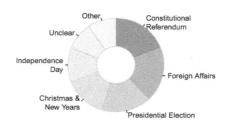

Figure 8.1 Pro-regime propaganda spikes in Congo

Our sample includes two primary election-related events: the constitutional referendum of October 2015, which provided legal cover for
Sassou Nguesso to run for a third presidential term since reclaiming
power in 1997, and the March 2016 presidential election, which gave
him the third term. Sassou Nguesso's propaganda strategy during these
two campaigns is the subject of Section 8.5. These two episodes account for nearly 40 percent of all propaganda spikes between April 2013
and March 2017. Two other election-related events account for another
5 percent of propaganda spikes: Sassou Nguesso's PCT party congress
in early 2016 and the local elections of 2014. These appear in the
"Other" category. The remaining propaganda spikes occurred when Sassou Nguesso was particularly active. His public speeches each New Years
and Independence Day account for 20 percent of propaganda spikes, and
foreign affairs – generally Sassou Nguesso's travels abroad or receptions
in Brazzaville – account for another 20 percent of propaganda spikes.
A final category encompasses moments when the government itself was
particularly active: the African Games, which were held in Brazzaville in
September 2015, and announcements of new governments.

Propaganda spikes are not random. In Congo, roughly half are tied to
elections.

8.4 PROPAGANDA AND ELECTION SEASONS IN GLOBAL PERSPECTIVE

The descriptive statistics above are consistent with our theory. Where electoral constraints are binding, the autocrat's incentives to manipulate citizens' beliefs are strongest at precisely the moment when citizens are most aware of them. This is the propagandist's dilemma. In response, our theory predicts carefully orchestrated electoral propaganda campaigns, which aim to minimize the volume of fraud required to secure victory and the probability of mass unrest. These electoral campaigns should aim to make the election seem fair and the autocrat's victory seem legitimate.

8.4.1 Data and Estimation Strategy

To explore the timing of electoral propaganda campaigns, we identified each election for which we had propaganda data, amounting to 102 elections across thirty-eight countries. Since executive elections are central to the regime's hold on power, we restricted attention to them, yielding a sample of forty-six elections across twenty-nine countries. For each executive election in our dataset, we focused on the year before election day and the year after. Then we indexed each day within this two-year period as $t \in [-365, 365]$, where day $t = -30$ denotes the thirtieth day until the election, day $t = 0$ denotes election day itself, and day $t=30$ denotes the thirtieth day after the election. For each day t, we compute several quantities of interest for the executive and opposition alike: the mean number of references per article; the mean per reference rate of positive coverage; the mean per article volume of positive coverage; and the mean share of articles about a range of coverage topics, discussed in Chapters 5 and 6. We compute these values for dictatorships, with a Polity score between -10 and -6; constrained autocracies, with a Polity score between -5 and 5; and democracies, with a Polity score between 6 and 10. This empirical approach lets us avoid imposing functional form assumptions about how electoral propaganda evolves as election day approaches. The results appear in Figure 8.2, with three-day moving averages in bold. The x-axes give days until or since election day, which is indexed as 0.

We paired these descriptive statistics with a regression framework. Building on the indexing described above, we created variables that record the proximity of day t to an executive election. The variable *Election Season:* 5_{jt} assumes value 1 if day t in country j is between one and five days from an executive election. The variable *Election Season:* 15_{jt} assumes value 1 if day t in country j is between fifteen and six days from

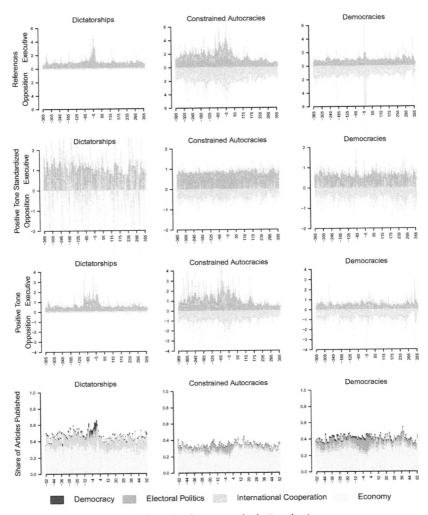

Figure 8.2 Life cycle of propaganda during election seasons

an executive election. The variable *Election Season: 30$_{jt}$* assumes value 1 if day t in country j is between thirty and sixteen days from an executive election. We also recorded election day itself. The baseline model is

$$Y_{jt} = \alpha + \beta X_{jt} + \eta \left(X_{jt} \times \text{Election Day}_{jt} \right) + \zeta \left(X_{jt} \times \text{Election Season: } 5_{jt} \right)$$
$$+ \psi \left(X_{jt} \times \text{Election Season: } 15_{jt} \right) + \delta \left(X_{jt} \times \text{Election Season: } 30_{jt} \right)$$
$$+ \kappa Z_{jt} + \phi W_{js} + \gamma_j + \epsilon \tag{8.1}$$

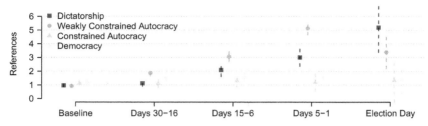

Figure 8.3 Predicted regime coverage during election seasons

where γ_j gives country-fixed effects, the variable X_{jt} gives country j's regime coding on day t, the vector Z_{jt} gives the base election season indicators, and W_{js} gives a year-level vector of controls. The results appear in Figure 8.3. Since, in practice, equation (8.1) entails twelve interaction terms, we present the results as predicted values by regime type and the proximity of day t to election day rather than as a standard regression table.

8.4.2 Where Electoral Constraints Are Binding

Propaganda apparatuses in constrained autocracies must accomplish two objectives – which are in tension – during election seasons: amplify pro-regime coverage to manipulate citizens' beliefs and avoid undermining their credibility. The results in Figures 8.2 and 8.3 are consistent with this. Outside of election seasons, we find relatively little difference in the average number of executive references per article across propaganda apparatuses. This begins to change a month before election day. The per-reference valence of pro-regime coverage, *Positive Coverage Standardized: Executive*$_{ijt}$, is mostly constant, but the frequency of regime coverage increases very gradually. Between 30 and 16 days out, we observe an increase of roughly two executive references *per article*. Between 15 and six days from election day, we observe an increase of just greater than three executive references per article. These propaganda campaigns reach their peak in the five days before election day, when the mean number of executive references per article increases by an additional five executive references. Since the per reference valence of regime coverage is constant, the aggregate amount of positive coverage tracks the rate of executive references. This sort of gradually intensifying propaganda campaign is unique to the world's constrained autocracies, as we discuss in Section 8.4.3.

In Chapter 5, we showed that constrained autocracies allocate a substantial amount of coverage to the opposition. Figure 8.2 confirms that this extends even to election seasons. The total volume of coverage allocated to the opposition is roughly equal to that of the autocrat. Since constrained autocracies generally feature a handful of major opposition leaders, this also implies that any single opposition leader is covered substantially less often than the autocrat. This is why, in democracies, the volume of opposition coverage in state-affiliated newspapers actually exceeds the volume of coverage of the incumbent. Again, there is no evidence that propaganda apparatuses in constrained autocracies "go negative" on the opposition.

The bottom panel of Figure 8.2 documents the topics on which electoral propaganda campaigns focus. Propaganda apparatuses in constrained autocracies cover not the abstract principles of democracy and human rights but rather electoral campaigns themselves. In actual democracies, coverage of the political horse race increases from 8 percent to 22 percent, whereas in constrained autocracies it increases from 5 percent to 15 percent. In democracies and constrained autocracies, less than 1 percent of coverage focuses on the principles of democracy. The rate of international cooperation coverage is effectively unchanged in both constrained autocracies and democracies, at roughly 5 percent of total coverage.

8.4.3 *Where Electoral Constraints Are Non-Binding*

Many regimes classified as dictatorships under the standard Polity partition – with Polity scores between −10 and −6 – routinely organize parliamentary and presidential elections, however fraudulent. In our dataset, these include Bahrain, Belarus, Gabon, Kazakhstan, Syria, the United Arab Emirates, and Uzbekistan. In the absence of electoral constraints, electoral propaganda is distinctive in three ways. First, there is no gradual build-up. The mean rate of executive references per article is constant until roughly one week from election day, oscillating between one and two. The per-article executive reference rate spikes only during the five days before, when it reaches between three and six. Since the per-reference rate of propaganda is generally constant over time, from the panels in the second row, the spike in positive coverage at the article level – from the third row of Figure 8.2 – tracks the rate of executive references. Where electoral constraints are non-binding, electoral propaganda campaigns are conspicuous for their absence.

Recall from Chapter 5 that opposition coverage in the most repressive dictatorships is distinctive largely because of the extent to which it is neglected. Figure 8.2 underscores this. The regime's chief critics are neglected not just during the calendar year but even as election day approaches. This constitutes the second way that electoral propaganda campaigns in the most repressive dictatorships are distinctive. The opposition is effectively omitted.

Finally, coverage topics evolve in conspicuous ways as election day approaches. Articles about international cooperation spike, from about 15 percent per day to 25 percent in the week surrounding election day. This makes sense in the context of Chapter 6. Propaganda apparatuses routinely tell citizens how esteemed the regime is by the international community and how prominent are its foreign backers. Although we observe some coverage of electoral politics, the much larger increase is in the principles of democracy and human rights. During election seasons, fully 10 percent of all articles that are published cover democracy and human rights. Virtually none focus on the political horse race.

8.5 MANAGING THE PROPAGANDIST'S DILEMMA: CONGO

The results above underscore the propagandist's dilemma. Where electoral constraints are binding, electoral propaganda campaigns must somehow manipulate citizens' beliefs despite obvious temporal incentives to do so. To understand how propaganda apparatuses resolve this dilemma, we return to Congo and again focus on the presidential election of March 20, 2016. *Les Dépêches de Brazzaville* engineered a propaganda campaign that featured four components: coverage of election monitors, Sassou Nguesso himself, the opposition, and its ongoing efforts to seek credibility. We discuss each in turn.

8.5.1 *Building Credibility in Advance: Electoral Fraud, Election Monitors, and International Cooperation*

Sassou Nguesso announced his reelection bid on January 25. Congolese law stipulates a two-week election campaign, which in this case spanned March 4 through March 18. For the four weeks preceding election day, the top panel of Figure 8.4 presents the number of articles that focused on either election observers or the *Commission nationale électorale indépendante* (CNEI). *Les Dépêches*'s efforts to persuade readers of the election's credibility began early and steadily intensified. Between February 22 and February 26, *Les Dépêches* ran three articles on the

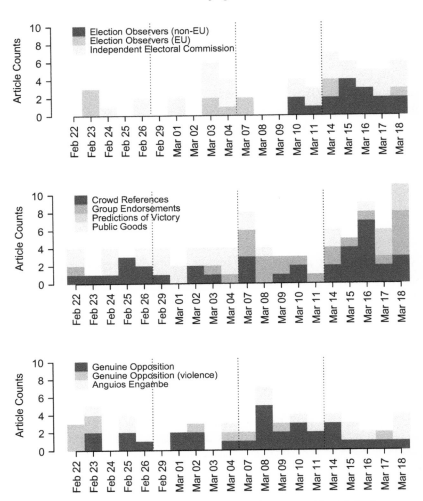

Figure 8.4 Propaganda during Congo's March 2016 presidential election

CNEI, one of which announced its members. This weekly total increased gradually until, during the campaign's final week, coverage of the CNEI and election observers nearly equaled coverage of Sassou Nguesso.

Inevitably, this coverage was not all flattering. On February 22, *Les Dépêches* published opposition leader Charles Zacharie Bowao's scathing criticisms on page 2. Headlined "The Opposition Declares the CNEI Illegitimate," the article quoted Bowao at length:

The members of CONEL have been purely and simply reappointed to the same roles in the CNEI. Almost all are members of the PCT or presidential allies, including the representatives of civil society and the moderate opposition. [We reserve] our right for civil and civic-minded disobedience.[23]

Almost simultaneously, the European Union refused to send election monitors. "Changes to the electoral law," the EU's press release announced, "are not sufficient to ensure the democratic, inclusive, or transparent character of the presidential election."[24] *Les Dépêches* covered this too: on its February 23 front page and all of its second page. The government spokesperson, Thierry Moungalla, claimed for the government the voice of reason: "To certify or to refuse to certify an election that has not yet occurred seems rather curious."[25] The page 2 editorial made the same point: "This attitude does little to improve citizens' opinions of the European machine."[26] *Les Dépêches* then called on citizens to claim the moral high ground:

Beyond the frustrations it rightly provokes for some, [the EU's decision] must compel the authorities of the Republic and civil society to redouble their efforts, so that the vote of March 20 unfolds in the best possible conditions to prove that Brussels' criticisms are unfounded, and that citizens are able to express themselves on election day without any constraints, freely. This constitutes the best response we can offer to those from abroad who attempt to disrupt the electoral process.

Les Dépêches also covered the government's apparent attempts to persuade the European Union to send observers after all, which created the impression the government welcomed scrutiny. The government's efforts even included dispatching the foreign minister to Brussels, which *Les Dépêches* covered in two separate articles on March 3 and with this front page headline on March 7: "A Compromise between Congo and the EU."[27] The European Union's decision not to send "an army of experts to Brazzaville," the article suggested, was driven by "very complex" budgetary disagreements among "the 28 member-states." The "best experts," it noted, were "already on the ground." In fact, neither the European Union nor the United States retracted their refusal to send election monitors. Congolese citizens, however, did not know this, and

---

[23] Jean Jacques Koubemba, "The Opposition Declares the CNEI Illegitimate," *Les Dépêches de Brazzaville*, February 22, 2016.

[24] Union Européenne (2016).

[25] "The EU Excludes Itself from the Electoral Process in Congo," *Les Dépêches de Brazzaville*, February 23, 2016.

[26] "To Observe," *Les Dépêches de Brazzaville*, February 23, 2016.

[27] Patrick Ndungidi, "A Compromise between Congo and the EU," *Les Dépêches de Brazzaville*, March 7, 2016.

so *Les Dépêches* spun things to suggest they had. On March 14, *Les Dépêches* reported the CNEI director's claim that the European Union and the United States were effectively sending monitors:

The ambassadors accredited to Congo, who are deploying across the country, constitute an observation mission. So, whether they actually come from France, from the Netherlands, from Germany, or from America is effectively irrelevant. This is an observation mission.[28]

As it covered the government's efforts in Brussels to secure monitors, *Les Dépêches* continued its quiet campaign to discredit Europe. On March 7, below the article that announced the government's "compromise" with the EU, *Les Dépêches* ran this "reflection," penned by Jean-Paul Pigasse, the French architect of Sassou Nguesso's propaganda:

Is Europe on the threshold of a major crisis?
    Each passing day increases the uncertainties that make Old Europe one of the most unstable and unpredictable [regions] in the world. Perceived throughout the last 50 years by the Great Powers and emerging countries as a reliable partner, which its prosperity protected from the crises that shake other parts of the world, it behaves today as a community of nations that no longer knows where it is going, that is torn by profound internal controversies, which may, if not careful, reopen the wounds of the tragic past, which have been so difficult to heal.[29]

The article was ostensibly about Europe's migration crisis. Still, it underscored an irony: Sassou Nguesso desperately wanted Europe to validate the election, but he also sought to persuade readers that the European Union was "imploding" under the weight of its policy errors.

8.5.2 *Covering Sassou Nguesso*

Les Dépêches equally sought to persuade readers of the objectivity of its campaign coverage. It cast Sassou Nguesso's campaign events and endorsements as legitimately newsworthy and then used them to update its predictions about his electoral prospects. This campaign had several phases.

First, although no campaigning was permitted until March 4, Sassou Nguesso undertook a "working trip" across the country between February 22 and March 3. He surveyed recently completed infrastructure

---

[28] "The European Union and the USA Will Content Themselves With Their Diplomats Accredited to Congo," *Les Dépêches de Brazzaville*, March 14, 2016.

[29] Jean-Paul Pigasse, "Is Europe On the Threshold of a Major Crisis?" *Les Dépêches de Brazzaville*, March 7, 2016.

projects and "laid the first stone" for several new projects.[30] From the middle panel of Figure 8.4, *Les Dépêches* covered this extensively. In the two weeks before the campaign – February 22 through March 4 – *Les Dépêches* published between two and three articles per day that featured Sassou Nguesso's infrastructure projects. Meanwhile, *Les Dépêches* presented his victory as genuinely uncertain. Voting, after all, had not yet occurred. On March 1, *Les Dépêches* ran a striking editorial about Sassou Nguesso's working trip: "This tour will provide, *if he is re-elected*, very concrete ideas about the policies to be pursued during the next term."[31,32] *Les Dépêches* used the same phrase in a February 22 editorial, after Sassou Nguesso announced his candidacy:

We have no advice for those who seek the votes of Congolese citizens, but facing a candidate who has demonstrated over several decades his capacity for action, just one attitude is possible: the formulation of precise policy proposals that will permit our country to accelerate its long march to emergence.

Now an official candidate, the president of the Republic has clearly indicated that the youth, *if he is elected*,[33] will figure at the heart of his next five year term. In so doing, he has taken a major step ahead of his competitors.[34]

On March 15, four days before the campaign ended, *Les Dépêches* observed that the crowds at Sassou Nguesso's campaign events may not reflect his actual popularity:[35]

To conclude that [Sassou Nguesso] will win on Sunday, in the first round of the election, is something we are not yet ready to do. But what seems certain is that Congolese citizens, far from losing interest in public affairs, intend to choose their leaders based on the ideas they advocate. The vote on March 20 will indicate whether the attention manifested by the population towards candidate Denis Sassou Nguesso was a simple reflection of curiosity, or reveals a renewed interest in public governance.[36]

The crowds referenced in the March 15 editorial constitute the third component of *Les Dépêches*'s Sassou Nguesso coverage. To cultivate

---

[30] Rominique Nerplat Makaya, "Denis Sassou Nguesso Lays the First Stone," *Les Dépêches de Brazzaville*, February 29, 2016.
[31] Italics added.
[32] "Journey," *Les Dépêches de Brazzaville*, March 1, 2016.
[33] Italics added.
[34] "Continuity," *Les Dépêches de Brazzaville*, February 22, 2016.
[35] Note that the Congolese constitution stipulates a two-round presidential election. If a candidate receives a majority of the first-round vote share, he or she is automatically elected. Otherwise, the election proceeds to a second round featuring the top two vote winners.
[36] "Popularity," *Les Dépêches de Brazzaville*, March 15, 2016.

the appearance of neutrality, *Les Dépêches* focused on creating a narrative of popular support. Once the campaign started, coverage of Sassou Nguesso's infrastructure projects gave way to coverage of his campaign rallies and civil society endorsements, which could be defended as legitimately newsworthy. Figure 8.4 illustrates how carefully this narrative was orchestrated. Coverage of crowd sizes and endorsements steadily increased until, during the final week of the campaign, it constituted a substantial share of Sassou Nguesso coverage. This had the effect of suggesting a groundswell of support, which a March 14 article made explicit. These endorsements routinely referenced Sassou Nguesso's infrastructure campaign:

"You promised electricity in Ngo several years ago and you kept your word, as our locality is now electrified, but we lack clean water," said local campaign director Auguste Gongarad Nkoua. The candidate's response: "The feasibility studies for the Ngo water supply project have already been completed and we will make it a reality."[37]

On March 16, *Les Dépêches* covered a new book that advocated for Sassou Nguesso's reelection. Again, the article was notable for what it conceded:

We wrote this book because we believe many of our compatriots fail to appreciate the work he has achieved. We acknowledge, of course, that he has had shortcomings during his long career. But this cannot justify the fact that a part of public opinion has become almost blind – or pretends to be – to his many achievements.[38]

These excerpts generally feature two components: recognition of what Sassou Nguesso has accomplished and of what remains. Our computational techniques enable us to measure whether this was indeed systematic in *Les Dépêches*'s coverage of Sassou Nguesso's electoral campaign. To do so, we took the total number of words from the twenty surrounding each Sassou Nguesso identifier that appear in the sentiment dictionaries we introduced in Chapter 3. We then estimated models of the form

$$Y_t = \alpha + \beta_1 \left(\text{Week } 1_t \right) + \beta_2 \left(\text{Week } 2_t \right) + \beta_3 \left(\text{Week } 3_t \right)$$
$$+ \beta_4 \left(\text{Week } 4_t \right) + \kappa W_t + \epsilon \tag{8.2}$$

---

[37] Gankama N'Siah, "In Djambala, Denis Sassou Nguesso Assured of Winning in the First Round," *Les Dépêches de Brazzaville*, March 14, 2016.

[38] Josiane Mambou Loukoula, "Advocating in Favor of Denis Sassou Nguesso," *Les Dépêches de Brazzaville*, March 16, 2016.

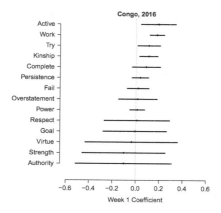

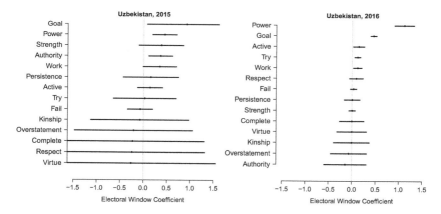

Figure 8.5 How regime coverage shifted during election seasons in Congo and Uzbekistan

where *t* indexes day, *Week 1ₜ* assumes value 1 during the final week of the election campaign, *Week 2ₜ* assumes value 1 during the penultimate week of the campaign, and the vector *Wₜ* gives day-level covariates. The results appear in the top of Figure 8.5. *Les Dépêches*'s coverage of Sassou Nguesso shifted precisely as our theory predicts and the excerpts above suggest. During the final week of the election campaign, Sassou Nguesso was presented as active, as working on the country's behalf, and as someone who enjoys kinship with his compatriots.

Only after fostering the impression of popular support did *Les Dépêches* undertake its final phase: predicting Sassou Nguesso's victory in round one, thus preparing citizens to accept it. From the middle panel of Figure 8.4, this began on March 17, the penultimate day of the campaign, after *Les Dépêches* had spent the preceding week covering Sassou Nguesso's crowds and endorsements. The March 18 front page announced this:

Candidate Denis Sassou Nguesso returned to Brazzaville yesterday through the suburbs of Kintélé, where a jubilant crowd of supporters was waiting to accompany him to Place Saint-Denis, in front of his private residence. There, a large podium had been installed, where the cream of Congolese music, from both sides of the river, put on a concert that closed this lively Thursday.[39]

The day before, on March 17, *Les Dépêches* announced that the real contest was for second place, since Sassou Nguesso's victory appeared "quite likely."[40] *Les Dépêches* cast the prediction as obvious to any objective observer.

8.5.3 The "Moderate" Opposition and the "Radical" Opposition

As we discussed in Chapter 5, the Uzbekistan government, notwithstanding its effective ban on opposition parties, finances quasi-opposition parties that routinely tell their supporters to vote for the ruling party rather than themselves. In Russia, the Putin government finances a handful of "moderate" opposition parties that compete alongside the genuine opposition.

Sassou Nguesso does too, and coverage of this moderate opposition constituted the third feature of *Les Dépêches*'s propaganda campaign. In March 2016, Sassou Nguesso's moderate opposition leader of choice was Anguios Engambé. Engambé competed in the 2009 presidential election as well and was then completely unknown to Congolese citizens, which in the subsequent seven years he did nothing to change. His party was founded after his first presidential bid, in March 2010, but postponed its "official launch" until August 2014.[41] Its theme during the official launch: "Political alternance and a pure vision of development in the Republic of Congo." The slogan was careful not to impugn Sassou Nguesso's democratic credentials.[42] Engambé's position on the October

---

[39] "Triumphant Return to Brazzaville for Candidate Denis Sassou Nguesso," *Les Dépêches de Brazzaville*, March 18, 2016.

[40] "The Battle For Second Place Promises to be Tough Within the Opposition," *Les Dépêches de Brazzaville*, March 17, 2016.

[41] "Life of the Parties: The Party for Action of the Republic Calls the Public Authorities to Dialogue," *Les Dépêches de Brazzaville*, June 30, 2014.

[42] "Political Life: The Party for Action of the Republic Announces Its Launch," *Les Dépêches de Brazzaville*, July 16, 2014.

2015 constitutional revision that let Sassou Nguesso compete for a third term in March 2016 was very similar to Sassou Nguesso's: "The PAR seeks a national dialogue at the conclusion of which all parties taking part will agree on a common way forward, which will render Congo immune from socio-political troubles."[43] His electoral platform was also distinctive. Rather than focusing on Congo's economic stagnation, staggering inequality, or obvious democratic shortcomings, Engambé promised to appoint a female prime minister:[44]

I will present to the Congolese people a plan for governance. As president of Congo, I will appoint a woman as prime minister. My chief of staff will also be a woman. I will set up a joint government team: 12 women and 12 men. Because women have competencies also.[45]

Jeune Afrique, a Paris-based newsmagazine, offered him the opportunity to respond criticisms that he was an instrument of Sassou Nguesso: "How do you respond to those who accuse you of being the *candidat du pouvoir?*" Engambé denied it: "I am not running in the presidential election on account of any other politicians."[46]

During the final week, *Les Dépêches* covered Engambé more than all the genuine opposition candidates combined. The bottom panel of Figure 8.4 illustrates this, and reveals a clear temporal pattern. Although the total volume of opposition coverage remained relatively constant throughout the month before election day, relative shares for the genuine opposition and for Engambé were reversed during the final week. Coverage of Engambé was obviously strategic. Between March 4 and March 16, *Les Dépêches* covered Engambé's campaign events, and in increasingly prominent positions. On March 18, the last publication day before the election, *Les Dépêches* ran three articles about Engambé, one of which appeared on the front page: "Anguios Engambé Inclined to Respect the 'True Verdict' of the Ballot Box."[47] *Les Dépêches* allocated Engambé nearly all of page 3, including a lengthy interview:

43 "Message of the President of the Party for Action of the Republic Mâ (PAR): To the Diplomatic Missions in the Republic of Congo," *La Semaine Africaine* December 12, 2014.
44 "Anguios Nganguia Engambé: Me President of Congo, the Prime Minister Will Be a Woman!" *Jeune Afrique*, March 18, 2016.
45 "Anguios Nganguia Engambé: Me President of Congo, the Prime Minister Will Be a Woman!" *Jeune Afrique* March 18, 2016.
46 "Anguios Nganguia Engambé: Me President of Congo, the Prime Minister Will Be a Woman!" *Jeune Afrique*, March 18, 2016.
47 "Anguios Engambé Inclined to Respect the 'True Verdict' of the Ballot Box," *Les Dépêches de Brazzaville*, March 18, 2016.

LDB: Are you concerned that the results of the vote will be fiddled with, as some candidates fear?

ANE: When a match has not yet been played, no one can know its outcome. We, the opposition, have our representatives in the more than 5,300 polling stations, the minutes will be signed by all, the results posted publicly at each voting center, etc. We cannot prejudge anything. What we want is for public institutions to really serve the people, to secure these elections.

LDB: What will you say if a candidate other than you is elected?

ANE: I am a democrat, I respect the result of the polls. If this is the true result, I will bow and congratulate the winner.[48]

Les Dépêches used Engambé to refute the actual opposition's core criticisms.

While *Les Dépêches* presented Engambé as a democrat, it presented the actual opposition as anti-democratic. This association was subtle. From Figure 8.4, roughly 25 percent of opposition coverage associated the opposition with violence or rejecting the results, whereas 75 percent covered policy platforms and campaign events. Anti-democratic associations were also more common at the campaign's beginning than its conclusion, which, again, focused mostly on Engambé. These associations were infrequent but explicit. From a March 7 editorial:

It appears that some supporters of the so-called "radical" opposition, just a few hours from voting, will attempt to prevent the poll from unfolding smoothly. Among the procedures they plan to use to discredit the vote is the sudden and late withdrawal of a number of candidates. This under the pretext that the vote would be badly organized and for the sole purpose of unleashing international media attention that would tarnish the image of the government, would make the results of the vote suspicious, and perhaps even provoke its cancellation.[49]

On March 17, *Les Dépêches* described one opposition leader, André Okombi Salissa, this way:

This activist, known for his courage and determination, is sometimes considered, *rightly or wrongly*, as a leader who may set fires in a country where all hope for peace, after all the politico-military crises that marked its recent past.[50,51]

Les Dépêches's use of "rightly or wrongly" marks its strategy: as acknowledging what "some" say but withholding judgment itself.

---

[48] Thierry Noungou and Guy-Gervais Kitina, "I Am a Democrat, I Will Respect the Results of the Ballot Box, If They Are True," *Les Dépêches de Brazzaville*, March 18, 2016.

[49] "Alert," *Les Dépêches de Brazzaville*, March 7, 2016.

[50] Italics added.

[51] Thierry Noungou, "The Battle for Second Place," *Les Dépêches de Brazzaville*, March 17, 2016.

8.5.4 *Building Credibility in Other Ways*

As *Les Dépêches* sought to make Sassou Nguesso's victory appear legitimate, it sought to present itself as credible. Alongside coverage of Sassou Nguesso's campaign appeared articles about genuine crises. On the January 27 front page, *Les Dépêches* reported that citizens' purchasing power was declining.[52] On March 17, the penultimate publication day before the election, *Les Dépêches* ran this front page headline: "The Price of Local Fish Is Harming Low Income Households." By covering crises, we observed in Chapter 5, propaganda apparatuses can cover efforts to remedy them. The article ended with this:

To cope with the deficit of 40,000 tons of fish per year, Congo, in addition to policy of importation (Senegal, Namibia and Norway), is implementing a project for the development of fisheries and inland aquaculture, jointly financed by the International Fund for Agricultural Development.[53]

On March 10, *Les Dépêches* reported that just 13 percent of Congolese citizens had access to financial institutions, which had "stagnated." *Les Dépêches* then covered Sassou Nguesso's failure to diversify the economy:

Admittedly, some progress has been made in the last ten years, in terms of the rate of banking, which has gradually increased from 3% in 2007 to 13%, but this result falls far short of the government's expectations, aimed at diversifying the national economy, still dependent on oil.[54]

This admission occurred at the campaign's midpoint and appeared on page 4, alongside an article that covered an opposition leader making the same point. On other occasions *Les Dépêches* covered other concerns of Congolese workers, which occasionally implicated the Sassou Nguesso government:

Managers of Congolese Rural Radio denounce "unimaginable" treatment. Convening in a general meeting in Brazzaville, employees of public radio, under the supervision of the Ministry of Agriculture and Livestock, demand, among other things, the resignation of the chief financial officer.[55]

---

[52] "The Minister of Commerce Concerned By the Cost of Living," *Les Dépêches de Brazzaville*, January 27, 2016.

[53] "The Price of Local Fish Is Harming Low Income Households," *Les Dépêches de Brazzaville*, March 17, 2016.

[54] Firmin Oyé, "The Banking Rate Still Stagnant Around 13%," *Les Dépêches de Brazzaville*," March 10, 2016.

[55] Parfait Wilfried Douniama, "Decision-Makers of Congolese Rural Radio Denounce 'Unimaginable' Treatment," *Les Dépêches de Brazzaville*, February 29, 2016.

On two occasions, *Les Dépêches* covered allegations of human rights abuses. On March 8, *Les Dépêches* covered the opposition's claims of "police harassment":

Activists for Jean-Marie Michel Mokoko called on Congolese citizens to be vigilant and to mobilize against these anti-democratic behaviors, all while calling on the population to not give into fear or intimidation.[56]

On March 3, *Les Dépêches* covered a partnership between *L'Observatoire congolais des droits de l'homme* (OCDH), the only domestic human rights organization, and the European Union: "The project fights against arbitrary detention and torture."[57] The article legitimated OCDH, which, a year later, accused the Sassou Nguesso government of "terrorism."[58]

Les Dépêches expanded to Kinshasa in 2009 and, on March 14, six days before the election, to Paris. It covered this expansion on March 14 and March 16. This coverage featured two subtexts. First, *Les Dépêches* was providing a public service to the Paris diaspora:

Why force readers who live far from Congo to read online a newspaper that brings them daily information from their country? Why not take advantage of the modern means of transmission that allow a newspaper to be printed simultaneously in Brazzaville, Paris or Brussels? Yes, why not offer Congolese in the diaspora the opportunity to buy and read this daily, our daily?

Thus will appear, starting today, in Europe, *Les Dépêches du Congo*, which have the same contents as the newspaper that you hold this morning in the hands with a front page that mixes the headlines of our Brazzaville and Kinshasa editions. A "first" in the history of the African press which, until now, was broadcast only in his country of origin and, for us, a new page that turns in the already rich history of your newspaper.[59]

Second, the Paris edition also enabled *Les Dépêches* to implicitly argue that if it could compete on the Parisian market, the quality of its reporting must be high. Accordingly, on March 16:

Amidst all the classic newspapers available to Parisian readers, *Les Dépêches du Congo* has just enriched the landscape. Almost unanimously, kiosk owners welcomed the new newspaper, which provides a perspective from Brazzaville, "the former capital of free France," one of them remarked.

---

56 Jean Jacques Koubemba, "Activists for Jean-Marie Michel Mokoko Denounce 'the Harassment' of Their Candidate," *Les Dépêches de Brazzaville*, March 8, 2016.

57 Jean Jacques Koubemba, "OCDH Launches Project Against Arbitrary Detention," *Les Dépêches de Brazzaville*, March 3, 2016.

58 Observatoire Congolais des Droits de l'Homme (2017).

59 "Opening," *Les Dépêches de Brazzaville*, March 14, 2016.

Leaving *Les Dépêches du Congo* little time to settle in, kiosk owners already appear to have bet on its popularity among Parisian readers, especially those of the diaspora. Whether tourists, businessmen leaving for Congo, Congolese who live far from Congo, their best choice now is to mark the metro stop where they can purchase the newspaper that brings them information from their country every day. To ensure its success, our journalists promise to remain responsive to the expectations of our readers.[60]

Les Dépêches then listed the metro stops at which its Paris edition was available.

8.6 RESERVING ELECTORAL PROPAGANDA FOR AFTER ELECTION DAY: UZBEKISTAN

Where electoral constraints are non-binding, Section 8.4.3 suggested, electoral propaganda campaigns are dramatically different. Again, Uzbekistan makes this clear. Our corpus encompasses two Uzbek presidential elections, the most of any full dictatorship: one on March 29, 2015, which was the last to feature President Islam Karimov, and the second on December 4, 2016, which occurred three months after Karimov's death. In Chapter 7, we documented how the Uzbek propaganda apparatus responded to the succession crisis that Karimov's sudden death induced. Here, we focus on how the propaganda apparatus covered these two election campaigns.

8.6.1 The 2015 Election "Campaign"

The results of Uzbekistan's 2015 election were announced on March 30, one day after voting. President Islam Karimov claimed 90.39 percent of votes cast, with a turnout of 91.08 percent. One foreign journalist called the election "competition-free."[61] Human Rights Watch called it a "sham."[62] Vladimir Putin described Karimov's victory as evidence of his "high authority among his compatriots."[63] The Shanghai Cooperation Organization claimed the election proceeded "openly and democratically."[64] It was tightly choreographed. The three "opposition"

---

[60] Antoine Daniel Kongo, "Warm Parisian Welcome for Les Dépêches du Congo Newspaper," *Les Dépêches de Brazzaville*, March 16, 2016.
[61] Lillis (2015).
[62] Luhn (2015).
[63] Solovyov (2015).
[64] Lillis (2015).

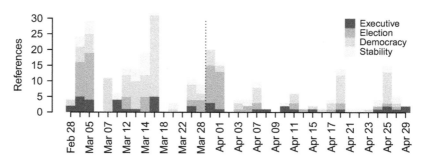

Figure 8.6 Propaganda during Uzbekistan's March 2015 presidential election

candidates were each assigned a platform that focused on the interests of a subset of the population. One was given social protection, another judicial reforms, and still another national values and traditions. None was permitted to criticize Karimov, whose platform featured the issue of broadest concern: economic growth.[65]

Figure 8.6 displays the month before and after the March 29 election. For each day along the x-axis, the y-axis measures the number of times that a series of keywords were referenced: our standard *References: Executive$_{ijt}$* variable, "election," "democracy,"[66] and "stability."[67] The election is marked by the dashed vertical line. For clarity, the x-axis includes only *Narodnoye Slovo*'s publication days.

The results suggest three key observations. First, the Uzbek propaganda apparatus referenced Karimov or his Liberal Democratic Party on just half of all publication days during the month preceding the election, just once on March 26, and not at all on March 28; these dates, respectively, were the penultimate and final publication days before the election. *Narodnoye Slovo* referenced the election just twice on March 26 and four times – all in a single article – on March 28. Before the election, when the election was referenced, references to "democracy" almost always outnumbered references to the election itself. This "electoral coverage" was paired with allusions to "stability," which, as we discuss in Chapter 7, is code for threats of violence. The single article about the election on March 28, the day before voting, focused on local Mahallas, which, as we documented in Chapter 5, are central to the

---

[65] Organization for Security and Cooperation in Europe (2015).
[66] For this, we use the stem "democra," which accommodates both "democracy" and "democratic."
[67] Our stem is "stab," which accommodates both "stable" and "stability."

Uzbek government's surveillance and repressive apparatus. This article made no reference to Islam Karimov.

Mahalla is a unique institution of civil society. ... Today, there are about 9,800 of these self-governing bodies in the country, which successfully perform over 30 functions that were formerly within the competence of local government bodies.

"In Uzbekistan, thorough preparations have been made for the presidential elections," says Ahmad Tarabik (Egypt). "All conditions have been created for voters, they are well aware of the training." ...

International conferences held in the country and abroad have become an important factor in the further improvement of the activities of communities, the wide dissemination of best practices. These include "round tables" and meetings held in the Republic of Korea, the USA, China, Belgium, Great Britain, France and Germany in connection with the presentation of the book "From a strong state to a strong civil society" and the documentary "The Institute of Mahalla in Uzbekistan: Historical Experience and Today." ...

"Within the framework of familiarization with the preparations for an important political event in Uzbekistan – the election of the President of the country – we visited a number of communities," says Zhao Huasheng (China). "They successfully perform a number of significant functions. I would call Mahalla a school of democracy inherent to your people."[68]

Second, *Narodnoye Slovo* covered the election more in its aftermath than in the days before. Coverage was extensive on both March 31 and April 1. On March 31, *Narodnoye Slovo* told citizens "that the election ... was held in full compliance with generally accepted democratic norms."[69] On April 1, it told citizens the same thing: "The election process was held in compliance with the national legislation of Uzbekistan, which is consistent with international standards. ... The people voted primarily for stability and calm."[70] *Narodnoye Slovo* also made reference to the presence of international observers, but primarily to signal to citizens the regime's good standing with the international community rather than the actual credibility of the electoral process. One, a certain Alexander Zinker, the "President of the International Center for the Study of Electoral Systems" in Israel, apparently said this:

I visited a polling station in the rural hinterland, located in a mountainous area, and was amazed at what I saw: a modern school of music and art. This is one

---

[68] "Mahalla Is a Unique Institution of Civil Society," *Narodnoye Slovo*, March 28, 2015.

[69] "On The Way To Strengthening Inter-Parliamentary Relations," *Narodnoye Slovo*, March 31, 2015.

[70] "Uzbekistan Demonstrates Dynamic Development," *Narodnoye Slovo*, April 1, 2015.

example of how you care about young people. A country in which children are loved so much has a great future.[71]

Zinker did not respond to repeated requests for an interview. He is apparently active in the region. He sits on the "International Expert Council" of Kazakhstan's Institute for Analysis, Forecasting and Strategic Initiatives of the Nur Otan Party, which claims to provide "analytical support [for] the Party's activities on long-term political leadership and implementation of the State Course of the President of the Republic of Kazakhstan N. A. Nazarbayev."

The opposition went entirely unmentioned.

8.6.2 *The 2016 Election "Campaign"*

The 2016 presidential election occurred under dramatically different circumstances. Islam Karimov suffered a sudden brain hemorrhage on August 26, his death was announced on September 2, and Shavkat Mirziyoyev was "elected" on December 4. Again, the election was entirely fraudulent, with Mirziyoyev claiming 88.6 percent of the vote and 87.7 percent turnout. The *Economist* announced that Uzbekistan was "cloning Karimov," and "[replacing] one strongman with another."[72] As in 2015, each "opposition" candidate was assigned a platform. The candidate that in 2015 discussed social protections now focused on the disabled; the candidate that in 2015 discussed judicial reforms was now given education; the candidate that earlier discussed national values was assigned national renewal. Again, no one was permitted to criticized Mirziyoyev, whose platform, like Karimov's, focused on economic growth.[73] And again, Vladimir Putin was effusive, calling Mirziyoyev with his "warm congratulations" less than twenty minutes after the results were announced.[74]

Figure 8.7 displays the month before and after the March 29 election. For each day along the *x*-axis, the *y*-axis measures the number of times that *Narodnoye Slovo* referenced the executive or ruling party. For clarity, we include along the *x*-axis only *Narodnoye Slovo*'s publication days. For comparison, in the bottom panel, we reproduce the same figure

---

[71] "Uzbekistan Demonstrates Dynamic Development," *Narodnoye Slovo*, April 1, 2015.
[72] *The Economist* (2016).
[73] Putz (2016).
[74] Grove (2019).

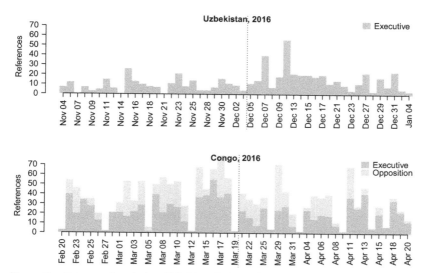

Figure 8.7 Propaganda during Uzbekistan's December 2016 presidential election and Congo's March 2016 presidential election

for Congo's March 2016 election. The results make clear that although *Narodnoye Slovo* allocated substantially more attention to the election than in 2015, its coverage was still dwarfed by that of Congo, which referenced Sassou Nguesso and his PCT four times more often per day. *Les Dépêches*'s references to the executive and the opposition outnumbered *Narodnoye Slovo*'s by seven to one.

Again, *Narodnoye Slovo* covered the election more in its wake than in its run-up. The first post-election spike occurred on December 7, three days after voting and two days after the results were announced. The spike was driven by congratulatory messages to the newly elected Mirziyoyev from ten foreign governments, including Russia and China, many of which were published in their entirety. Alongside those, *Narodnoye Slovo* announced:

the organization of an international competition for the creation of a monument to the great statesman and political figure, the First President of the Republic of Uzbekistan Islam Abduganievich Karimov. The founder of our independent state, the great statesman and political figure, the prominent son of the Uzbek people, the First President of the Republic of Uzbekistan Islam Abduganievich Karimov, having freed our Homeland from the shackles of the totalitarian system, revived the country, which at that time was on the edge of the abyss. In an extremely difficult and unstable situation, in spite of various difficulties and obstacles, in a historically short period, he turned Uzbekistan into a dynamically developing modern democratic state. The first President of the Republic of Uzbekistan, with his many-sided political activities and noble human qualities, left a bright, indelible mark on the centuries-old history of our Motherland. He became famous as an outstanding personality and a major statesman who enjoyed great respect and authority not only in Uzbekistan, but also in the international arena. Taking into account the numerous proposals of compatriots, the will of our people, and the great historical merits of the First President of the Republic of Uzbekistan, the Hero of Uzbekistan Islam Abduganievich Karimov in ensuring the development of the country, it is in our national interests to perpetuate his memory.[75]

Narodnoye Slovo also published the article below, which advertised the special privileges granted by the government to the military in exchange for its loyalty:

About 6,000 servicemen are provided with comfortable housing. Last year alone, the housewarming of 470 families of defenders of the Motherland was granted, and preferential mortgage loans were provided to 465 servicemen of the Tashkent and Eastern military districts for the construction of houses according to standard projects. "It is especially joyful and exciting that we are celebrating housewarming with the family on the eve of the celebration of the Constitution Day," says Major Artem Konstantinov. "My wife and I have become even happier and sincerely grateful to the leadership of the country and the command of the unit for the attention and care for the military. For me personally, it is a great honor to be a defender of the Motherland. Such support lends strength and inspires military service."[76]

On December 9, 2016, *Narodnoye Slovo* published an additional five letters of congratulations from foreign governments, including one ostensibly from the secretary general of the Organization for Security and Cooperation in Europe (OSCE). Although the OSCE declared the election "devoid of genuine competition,"[77] *Narodnoye Slovo* quoted the secretary general as expressing his "highest consideration."[78] On December 10, it published fourteen additional letters of congratulation, including one from Barack Obama and another from the Russian government.[79]

---

[75] "International Competition for the Creation of a Monument to the Great Statesman and Political Figure, the First President of the Republic of Uzbekistan Islam Abduganievich Karimov," *Narodnoye Slovo*, December 7, 2016.

[76] "Housewarming on the Eve of the Holiday," *Narodnoye Slovo*, December 7, 2016.

[77] Organization for Security and Cooperation in Europe (2017).

[78] "Sincere Congratulations to His Excellency Mr. Shavkat Mirziyoyev, President-Elect of the Republic of Uzbekistan," *Narodnoye Slovo*, December 9, 2016.

[79] "Sincere Congratulations to His Excellency Mr. Shavkat Mirziyoyev, President-Elect of the Republic of Uzbekistan," *Narodnoye Slovo*, December 10, 2016.

The implication was clear. However fraudulent the election may have been, the international community overwhelmingly endorsed its outcome. Nothing about *Narodnoye Slovo*'s electoral coverage was intended to persuade citizens of regime merits. Its coverage was designed to force them to accept its outcome.

8.6.3 Measuring Sentiment Shifts

Figures 8.6 and 8.7 make clear that *Narodnoye Slovo*'s propaganda campaign, in both 2015 and 2016, was most intense *after* election day. As in Section 8.5, we used our data to measure how coverage of Islam Karimov, Shavkat Mirziyoyev, and their Liberal Democratic Party shifted in the days immediately surrounding the 2015 and 2016 elections. We estimated models of the form

$$Y_t = \alpha + \beta \left(\text{Election Window}_t\right) + \epsilon \qquad (8.3)$$

where t indexes day and *Election Window$_t$* indicates whether day t occurred within the five days surrounding the 2015 or the 2016 election. The results for the 2015 election appear at the bottom left of Figure 8.5; the results for the 2016 election appear at the bottom right of Figure 8.5. Note that coverage of Karimov around the 2015 election was minimal, and so the standard errors on the estimates in the bottom-left panel are relatively large.

The results are consistent with our theory. During the final week of the Congolese election campaign, *Les Dépêches* presented Sassou Nguesso as active, as working to modernize the Congolese economy, and as having a kinship with his compatriots. In Uzbekistan, Karimov and Mirziyoyev were presented as overwhelmingly powerful.

8.7 SEMANTIC DISTINCTIVENESS DURING ELECTION SEASONS

Finally, we used our measure of semantic distinctiveness to explore the language that the Congolese and Uzbek propaganda apparatuses used during election seasons to describe their respective regimes. We did so in several steps. First, we restricted attention to Congo, and then we extracted the twenty words surrounding each executive reference. Next, we divided this set of words into two groups: words that were used during the March 2016 election season and those that were not. Finally, we computed the distinctive words used to describe Sassou Nguesso and his PCT during the election campaign relative to other times. This

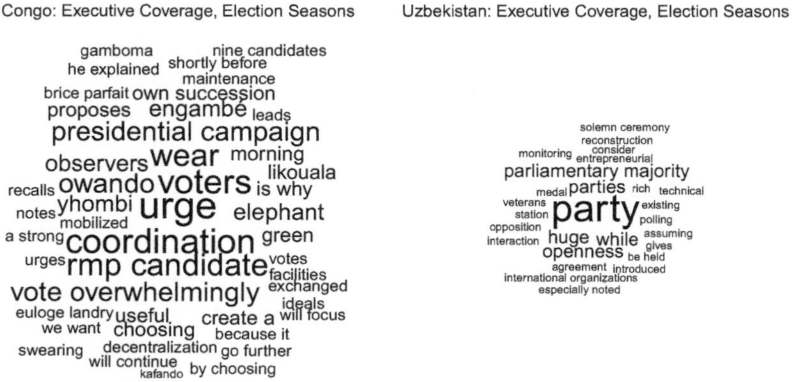

Congo: Executive Coverage, Election Seasons   Uzbekistan: Executive Coverage, Election Seasons

Figure 8.8 Semantic distinctiveness of regime coverage during elections in Congo and Uzbekistan

set of distinctive words appears in the left panel of Figure 8.8. We then did the same for Uzbekistan, which yielded the set of distinctive words in the right panel. These two word clouds illuminate how the propaganda apparatuses reoriented pro-regime propaganda during election seasons.

The results for Congo are striking in three ways. First, Sassou Nguesso's propaganda apparatus covered his election campaign extensively. The term "presidential campaign" is the most obvious indicator, but there are others. During campaign rallies, Sassou Nguesso's aides routinely called on his supporters to "vote overwhelmingly" for him, giving him the legitimacy of a victory in the first round. Sassou Nguesso's electoral platform called for "decentralization" to regional governments, and he held campaign rallies in Likouala, Owando, and Gamboma, each of which appears prominently. The terms "exchanged," "he explained," "proposes," and "create a" each refer to Sassou Nguesso's campaign pitch. Second, Figure 8.8 displays four leaders of other major political parties. Two of these, Jacques Joachim Yhombi-Opango and Euloge Landry Kolélas, endorsed Sassou Nguesso; the term "urge" refers to these endorsements. A third, Anguios Engambé, is the "moderate" opposition candidate financed by Sassou Nguesso. A fourth, Brice Parfait Kolélas, is the elder brother of Euloge Landry Kolélas, and was among Sassou Nguesso's chief opponents. Note that "nine candidates" also appears prominently; there were nine candidates in the election. The final striking aspect is the prominence of Michel Kafando, who visited

Brazzaville on behalf of Francophonie International four days before the election. Kafando offered his ratification:

The clarity that we have received from senior officials and stakeholders gives us a sense for the real situation, much more informed than what we perceive from abroad, a situation that really gives us hope that things will be calm and proceed without problems.[80]

The results for Uzbekistan are striking for different reasons. There are simply fewer words than for Congo, which underscores how seldom *Narodnoye Slovo* covered the candidacies of Karimov and Mirziyoyev. There are none of the references to campaign promises, major endorsements, or opposition rivals that are so common in Congo. And although *Narodnoye Slovo* told citizens that the elections were "monitored" by "international organizations," it said virtually nothing else. Precisely who these observers were went unstated. The terms "veterans" and "medal" reflect *Narodnoye Slovo*'s emphasis on the military's loyalty to the regime.

8.8 CONCLUSION

Where autocrats confront at least somewhat binding electoral constraints, propaganda apparatuses seek credibility to spend it. They can do so at the moment they acquire it, perhaps to persuade citizens to attribute bad news to exogenous shocks that are outside the regime's control. Alternatively, propaganda apparatuses can save credibility for some moment in the future, when the capacity to manipulate citizens' beliefs is most valuable. This chapter made clear that electorally constrained autocrats reserve propaganda campaigns for election seasons, which, as the rate of elite coups decline, increasingly constitute the chief threat to the world's autocrats. In Congo, 40 percent of all propaganda spikes during our four-year sample period were associated with either the constitutional referendum of October 2015 or the presidential election of March 2016. The drawback of recurring and predictable propaganda campaigns is that citizens may discount them. Citizens know, for instance, that autocrats have powerful incentives to manipulate their beliefs during election seasons.

Accordingly, these propaganda campaigns were tightly choreographed. In Congo, this choreography began weeks before election day,

---

[80] Kounga (2016).

when the propaganda apparatus covered Sassou Nguesso's "working tour," essentially an extended commercial for his infrastructure projects. It then moved to cover the credibility of the process: the "independent" electoral commission, the international observers, and even the European Union's reticence, which it cast as an insult to citizens. It covered the opposition extensively, though, as the election approached, quietly shifting attention to the "moderate" opposition candidate who was financed by the regime and who conspicuously avoided impugning the election's credibility. Throughout, the propaganda apparatus continued to cover bad news: the weakness of the banking sector, the government's failure to diversify the economy away from oil, and the high cost of urban living. The propaganda apparatus attempted to thread the needle: to cast Sassou Nguesso's victory as uncertain, but, as the campaign unfolded and citizens made their enthusiasm known, clearly legitimate to the objective observer.

Where autocrats confronted no electoral constraints, we observed a fundamentally different form of choreography. Propaganda spikes occurred immediately prior to election day and were remarkably devoid of persuasive content. In some cases, the volume of electoral coverage after election day was greater than before, when propaganda apparatuses published letters from the international community endorsing the charade that just occurred. Our theory suggests that these endorsements were meant to intimidate, a signal to citizens about the consequences of protest. Whatever the regime's crimes, it is nonetheless esteemed by the international community, and so it is unconstrained by international human rights norms.

This chapter studied the calendar of propaganda in constrained autocracies, where election seasons are most threatening to autocrats. What conditions the calendar of propaganda in the most repressive dictatorships, especially those which refuse to organize national elections? This is the focus of Chapter 9.

9

Memory and Forgetting

9.1 ENFORCED AMNESIA

As the Soviet Union of Vaclav Havel and Milan Kundera recedes into history, a new generation of Chinese luminaries is reminding the world about the struggle of memory against forgetting. In *China Dream*, Ma (2018) introduces readers to Ma Daode, the director of the Propaganda Department's China Dream Bureau. He conceives of a "China Dream Device," which the CCP would implant in citizens' brains to eradicate their memories. As he does, Ma is haunted by his own memories: how, as a child during the Cultural Revolution, he participated in violent mobs and denounced his parents, who then committed suicide. The novel follows Ma's desperate quest to banish his memories before they ruin him. The *South China Morning Post* describes the novel as depicting the "enforced silence and grim memories of the collective Chinese psyche."[1] China's most famous dissident artist, Ai Weiwei, designed the book's cover: a collection of fractured black tree branches against an orange background, meant to evoke "the brutality of autocracy [and] the splintering of the self."[2] Ma is now in exile. His work, which has been banned by the CCP, recalls Havel's (1978, 9) description of Soviet Czechoslovakia: "It falsifies the past. It falsifies the present, and it falsifies the future. ... It pretends to pretend nothing."

Among the central questions about contemporary China is whether the CCP's falsifications have made citizens forget its past crimes: whether, as Kundera might put it, the CCP has won the struggle of memory against forgetting. Many observers believe it has. Army propagandist turned novelist Yan Lianke described "the inherent falsity of life in China":

---

[1] Cormack (2018).
[2] Ma (2018, 179).

Generations of Chinese have been dreamwalking through life, becoming zombies primed to live in accordance with state dictates. Waking up is unimaginable, because living in reality would require one to confront the atrocities of Chinese history. To be Chinese is to live under enforced amnesia, a medicated slumber of propaganda.[3]

In 2013, Yan lamented how little his students seemed to know about the Cultural Revolution and the Tiananmen massacre:

Have today's 20- and 30-year-olds become the amnesic generation? ...I used to assume history and memory would always triumph. ... It now appears the opposite is true. In today's China, amnesia trumps memory. Lies are surpassing the truth. Even memories of events that have only just taken place are being discarded at a dazzling pace.[4]

Lim (2014) entitled her account of the legacy of the Tiananmen massacre *The People's Republic of Amnesia*. This belief has even entered the popular press. In 2014, the *New Republic* quoted a handful of China's youth, reflecting on the Tiananmen massacre:

"A lot of people don't know about this."
"It's like something from a legend."
"I may understand it, but I can hardly feel it."[5]

"There's a sad reality," Edward Steinfeld observed, "that many parts of China have moved on, and to some extent forgotten."[6]

Yan attributes this apparent amnesia to "a medicated slumber of propaganda," which underscores this chapter's key question: What drives the propaganda calendar in the most repressive dictatorships? In Chapter 8, we showed that where electoral constraints are binding, propaganda calendars are driven by election seasons. Whatever credibility propaganda apparatuses acquire is spent to minimize the amount of fraud required for victory and the probability of mass unrest. Yet nearly 2 billion people live under autocracies that refuse to organize national elections, amounting to more than a quarter of the world's population. What drives the propaganda calendars of their governments?

One possibility is that the events that drive protests also drive propaganda campaigns. As we documented in Chapter 8, the Uzbek regime employs propaganda spikes immediately before and after election day, devoid of any persuasive content. It broadcasts its capacity for violence.

---

[3] Fan (2018).
[4] Yan (2013).
[5] Beam (2014).
[6] *Harvard Magazine* (2014).

It publishes expressions of support from the international community. As we documented in Chapter 7, the CCP issues threats of repression around the anniversaries of ethnic separatist movements and other major political events. Yet propaganda spikes at politically sensitive moments entail a drawback. Although propaganda spikes and explicit threats of repression may deter protests, they draw attention to whatever makes the moment sensitive and perhaps give it added salience.

How do the most repressive dictatorships resolve the tension between propaganda strategies that keep historical memories alive and censorship strategies that attempt to foster forgetting? This chapter's central argument is that the response to politically sensitive moments is determined by three forces: whether those moments implicate the regime in historical crimes, whether they have tangible manifestations in the present, and whether forgetting is realistic. The first conditions the value of forgetting to the regime; the second and third condition its plausibility. Empirically, the set of politically sensitive moments in a country is vast, reflecting its historical traumas and cultural touchstones. Therefore, we focus on China, which is an attractive setting for reasons of data availability. The CCP confronts many politically sensitive moments: the quinquennial Party Congress, the annual National People's Congress, and other dates of political and cultural significance. Since seizing power in 1949, the CCP has also inflicted a range of crimes on citizens. It has repressed pro-democracy movements and the separatist campaigns waged by ethnic minorities. These failed efforts are generally associated with specific dates, and so we can probe how different politically sensitive moments generate different propaganda strategies.

The amnesia that Yan Lianke described is more enforced than genuine, for Chinese citizens have long memories for CCP repression. In Carter and Carter (2020a), we show that popular protests are some 20 percent more likely during the anniversaries of failed pro-democracy movements. Their participants employ the language of "rights consciousness," widely regarded as code for democratic resistance. Reflecting their power, these protests are more often repressed by security forces. Pro-democracy anniversaries constitute uniquely powerful focal moments for anti-regime protests.

This makes this chapter's first result especially striking. The CCP propaganda apparatus is conspicuous for pretending these pro-democracy anniversaries do not exist. We find no change in pro-regime propaganda, threats of repression, or any other aspect of coverage. Rather, using data from Hong Kong University's Weiboscope Project, we find that online censorship spikes. Although pro-democracy anniversaries are focal moments for protest, the CCP's interest in purging them from historical memory compels it to forgo propaganda in favor of censorship, an informational strategy that privileges forgetting.[7] Since our propaganda data extend back decades, we can determine whether the CCP's informational strategy around pro-democracy anniversaries ever shifted from one that privileged effusive propaganda and explicit threats to one that privileged forgetting. Across anniversaries, we find, the CCP's strategy of forgetting has been constant over time, save for the year immediately following the original event. By contrast, other politically sensitive moments occasion spikes in pro-regime propaganda and codewords for repression.

There is one exception to this pattern, associated with the pro-democracy anniversary the CCP knows citizens will not forget. On June 4, 1989, after weeks of protest that brought 10 percent of Beijing's population into Tiananmen Square, Deng Xiaoping decided that "two hundred dead could bring 20 years of peace."[8] "Peace" was a euphemism for CCP rule. The death toll ranged from several hundred to several thousand, with Human Rights Watch estimating 2,000.[9] Two decades later and thousands of miles away, the marginalized ethnic Uyghur community in Xinjiang staged a 10,000-person protest, which was violently repressed. Hundreds were killed. Thousands were wounded. The CCP created detention centers that now hold perhaps 30 percent of China's 11 million Uyghurs. This episode is known as the Xinjiang Uprising of 2009. On each anniversary of the Tiananmen massacre, the CCP propaganda apparatus reminds China's urban elite of the Xinjiang Uprising: of Uyghur "terrorism" and the CCP's violent response to it.

Why does the CCP remind the urban elite of repression in Xinjiang on each anniversary of the Tiananmen massacre? Where propaganda serves to dominate, our theory calls attention to fear: to the possibility that the CCP aims to deter in-group protests by signaling its capacity for repression. Scholars increasingly understand that in-group dissenters have a distinctive demographic profile: politically engaged, ethnic Han, and located in major urban areas.[10] To test this, we fielded another survey

---

[7] Fu, Chan, and Chau (2013); Tai and Fu (2020); Zhu and Fu (2021); Chung and Fu (2022).

[8] Cheng (2016).

[9] Human Rights Watch (2010); Buckley (2019).

[10] O'Brien and Li (2005); Chen and Lu (2006); Tang, Woods, and Zhao (2009); Lewis-Beck, Tang, and Martini (2014); Truex (2014); Jiang and Yang (2016); Tang (2016); Pan and Xu (2017); Wright (2018).

experiment, which we timed to coincide with the June 4, 2020, anniversary. To accommodate the possibility of preference falsification, we again employed list experiments. To identify the politically engaged, urban Han elite, we asked respondents a series of demographic questions and measured the nightlight intensity from their IP addresses, which revealed proximity to urban centers.

We find no evidence that Uyghur propaganda content published during the Tiananmen anniversary conditions respondents' feelings about Xi Jinping, the CCP, ethnic Uyghurs, or Chinese nationalism. Rather, Uyghur propaganda content during the Tiananmen anniversary makes the politically engaged, urban Han elite less likely to protest due to fear of repression. Rian Thum, a prominent Uyghur historian, recently expressed shock that the CCP would broadcast repression in Xinjiang: "Officials in Xinjiang are so inured to the horrors they are perpetrating that they often publicize evidence of their crimes."[11] Publicizing the horrors, we argue, is the point.[12]

Perhaps some "memories … are being discarded at a dazzling pace," as Yan feared. But citizens remember the Tiananmen massacre, the CCP knows this, and its internal security interests compel a propaganda strategy that keeps the memory alive. Most broadly, we suggest the CCP's ongoing repression in Xinjiang, in part, has its origins in Beijing: in the CCP's incentives to ensure that the politically engaged, urban Han elite does not again demand change. Whatever its cause, the CCP has instrumentalized it in the *People's Daily*.

This chapter proceeds as follows. Section 9.2 extends our theory to understand how repressive governments set their calendars of propaganda. Section 9.3 probes our theoretical expectations in the context of China. Section 9.4 focuses explicitly on Tiananmen, China's most charged pro-democracy anniversary. Section 9.5 shifts attention to the Xinjiang Uprising of 2009, which, though quickly suppressed by the CCP, helped give rise to ongoing repression against ethnic Uyghurs. Section 9.6 presents the survey experiment.

---

[11] Thum (2020).

[12] The CCP has mounted an aggressive international campaign to justify its policies in Xinjiang. However, in the Online Appendix, we show that there is little evidence that the CCP has sought to censor information about Uyghur repression within China, apart from social media content that criticizes CCP policies in Xinjiang. For more, see Brouwer (2022).

9.2 THEORY

9.2.1 *Focal Moments and Protest in the Absence of Regular Elections*

Scholars have documented a range of politically sensitive moments that may constitute focal moments for collective action in the absence of elections. In China, the list includes obvious dates, like the Tiananmen massacre, and more peripheral events like the 2010 Asian Games; the Qingming cultural festival in April; and even the time a citizen threw a shoe at Fang Binxing, the architect of China's "great firewall," during a university speech in 2011.[13] Repressive governments prepare for them in advance by incarcerating dissidents,[14] amplifying censorship,[15] engineering pro-regime social media campaigns,[16] and coordinating national and provincial propaganda messages.[17]

A propaganda response is analytically different, for it draws attention to the moment in ways that most preemptive repression does not. When a repressive government incarcerates a dissident, few people outside their family are aware. When a social media post is censored, sometimes not even its author is aware. A propaganda response, by contrast, turns the underlying politically sensitive moment into common knowledge. This is why a propaganda response is costly.

9.2.2 *The Power of Pro-Democracy Anniversaries*

How do propaganda apparatuses respond to these politically sensitive moments? Do they employ pro-regime propaganda or threaten citizens with repression? Or do they do nothing, an attempt to scrub the politically sensitive moment from historical memory? Two forces, we argue, condition the propaganda response to politically sensitive moments. The first concerns the value of forgetting. The moments that facilitate collective action are those the regime wants citizens to forget. The second factor conditions the plausibility of forgetting. Politically sensitive moments can

---

[13] Perry (1999, 2001, 2002); Wasserstrom (2009); King, Pan, and Roberts (2013); Roberts and Stewart (2016); Roberts (2018, 201–209); King, Pan, and Roberts (2017); Truex (2019).

[14] Truex (2019). For more on China's repressive apparatus generally, see Wang (2014) and Wang and Minzner (2015).

[15] King, Pan, and Roberts (2013).

[16] King, Pan, and Roberts (2017).

[17] Roberts and Stewart (2016).

be forgotten only when they have no contemporary manifestation, save for however citizens attempt to commemorate them, which regimes often attempt to block.

Together, these two forces draw our attention to the anniversaries of failed pro-democracy movements, which have powerful focal properties for collective action. Pro-democracy anniversaries remind citizens that anti-regime sentiment is longstanding and their compatriots mobilized against the regime in the past. These anniversaries are temporally precise. Committed activists may organize protests on these anniversaries to remind citizens of the regime's violent past and previous opposition to it. For all these reasons, the anniversaries of China's failed pro-democracy movements experience nearly 30 percent more protests than the typical day. The odds that a protest emerges are between 27 percent and 38 percent greater, and the probability of a two standard deviation protest spike doubles.[18]

Protests on pro-democracy anniversaries are stridently anti-regime and routinely call for democracy. We know this because the China Labour Bulletin (CLB) maintains an image repository from all known protests between 2014 through 2019. For each protest, these images feature banners, signs, manifestos, tweets, and various other content. We scraped all 38,078 protest images and then used tesseract, an optical character recognition program, to extract the words these images contain. The result is a corpus of words, by protest, that participants used to describe demands and grievances. To understand whether protests around pro-democracy anniversaries express different demands and grievances than others, we used our measure of semantic distinctiveness. We defined corpus A as all protest content during the three days before and after each of the pro-democracy anniversaries in Table 7.3, and the other corpus as all protest content during the rest of the year. The results appear in Figure 9.1. The left panel displays words that are distinctive to pro-democracy anniversaries; the right panel displays words that are distinctive to other protests.[19] Terms that reflect "rights consciousness" appear in bold.

Rights consciousness, O'Brien and Li (2006, 2–3) write, is "a form of popular contention that operates near the boundary of authorized channels, employs the rhetoric and commitments of the powerful to curb the exercise of power, hinges on locating and exploiting divisions

---

[18] Carter and Carter (2020a).

[19] We conducted the analysis in Chinese, but present the results in English.

Pro-Democracy Anniversary Protests   Other Protests

Figure 9.1 Distinctive protest discourse in China

within the state, and relies on mobilizing support from the wider public." Many scholars have argued that rights-conscious discourse is a form of democratic resistance.[20] Protests during pro-democracy anniversaries are far more likely to embrace rights consciousness. The left panel contains words like "citizen," "netizen," "court enforcement," and "right to know." The term "people power teacher" refers to someone who organizes or inspires citizens to demand "people power," which suggests that activists are a crucial force behind anniversary protests, as they are in helping ordinary citizens register grievances without eliciting repression.[21] The left panel features terms that emphasize the extent of popular frustration: "hundreds of employees," "more than 100 employees," and "dozens of workers." It includes emotionally charged words: "helpless," "powerless," and "bad faith." It even includes language that conveys aspirations for change: "new world." To be sure, the left panel also includes language about economic grievances: "salary payroll," "employee complaints," and "workers' wages." But the combination of rights-conscious terms with economic grievances suggests that protests during pro-democracy anniversaries are indeed distinctive: that citizens with political grievances are savvy enough to cloak their claims as economic grievances, which may reduce the likelihood of repression.

The case study evidence illustrates this. On December 4, 2014 – the first official "Constitution Day," ostensibly designed to commemorate the signing of the state constitution in 1982 – several thousand teachers

---

[20] Bernstein and Lü (2003); Goldman (2005); Li (2010); Pei (2010); Wong (2011); Chen (2013).
[21] Fu (2018).

in Yuzhou, Henan, went on strike for back pay and better wages. They demanded the release of the protest organizer from house arrest and protested in front of local government offices. Protesters were explicit: "According to some Western theories, the government was originally raised by the people. It should listen to the people and act for the people. But the result is reversed." Another even referenced the Constitution Day focal moment: "On the first Constitution Day, teachers in Yuzhou City defended their legitimate rights and interests!"[22] On June 4, 2017 – the twenty-seventh anniversary of the Tiananmen massacre – several hundred people paraded in front of Hanzhong City government headquarters in Shaanxi with a large red flag and lodged a petition. The ostensible motivation: the state-owned Lueyang Iron and Steel plant had not paid workers' social insurance. But protesters' language was distinctly rights conscious. They displayed a large banner signed by hundreds of citizens that proclaimed: "The government works for me."

The CCP treats pro-democracy anniversaries as threatening. Focal moment protests are nearly twice as likely to be repressed by security forces.[23] The power of pro-democracy anniversaries has been documented elsewhere. In Cameroon, anglophone citizens treat October 1 as a pro-democracy anniversary, and routinely mobilize against the Yaoundé-based francophone government. In the Soviet Union, Kowalewski (1980, 439) documented how citizens in the Soviet Union used similar anniversaries to coordinate anti-regime protests.

9.2.3 *The Plausibility of Forgetting*

The third factor that conditions the plausibility of historical forgetting is the nature of the politically sensitive moment. Some moments implicate the regime in such egregious human rights violations that, even if they could be purged from the public space, citizens would never forget.

In China, the Tiananmen Square massacre is the obvious pro-democracy anniversary that cannot be forgotten. This massacre defined a generation. Using survey data from Peking University, Desposato, Wang, and Wu (2021) studied Chinese citizens who entered four-year colleges

---

[22] Wickedonna (2014).

[23] Perry (2008, 2010) is less optimistic that rights consciousness reflects aspirations for democracy. Rights consciousness, she argues, is in fact "rules consciousness," insofar as contention employs scripts accepted by the state. In turns, she suggests, it stabilizes the CCP. Our results – in particular, the coincidence of rights consciousness discourse and pro-democracy anniversaries – call this interpretation into question.

in Beijing between 1985 and 1994. They regard individuals who were enrolled in Beijing universities in April 1989 as treated: exposed to the student-led Tiananmen protests. Individuals who enrolled in Beijing universities during fall 1989 or later constitute the control group. Nearly three decades later, the treatment group reported lower levels of trust in government. This effect was strongest for the central government, which ordered the crackdown, and even obtained for provincial and county governments that carried out local crackdowns.

9.2.4 Hypotheses

This discussion suggests two hypotheses. First, the politically sensitive moments most likely to be subjected to a forgetting strategy are those that constitute strong focal points and have no contemporary manifestation. These are the moments the regime has the strongest incentive to purge from collective memory. Since they have no contemporary manifestation, purging them is at least possible. These two factors call our attention to pro-democracy anniversaries.

> **Hypothesis 9.1:** *Repressive governments are more likely to employ a propaganda strategy that privileges forgetting around the anniversaries of failed pro-democracy movements.*

Some politically sensitive moments constitute powerful focal points, have no contemporary manifestation, and implicate the regime in egregious failures. For these, the likelihood of forgetting is so low that the regime is forced to employ a propaganda strategy that discourages collective action. This strategy comes at the cost of perpetuating the memory itself.

> **Hypothesis 9.2:** *Some politically sensitive moments that would otherwise be subjected to a forgetting strategy may implicate governments in ways that are too egregious for citizens to forget. For these, governments employ propaganda to deter protests.*

9.3 THE INFORMATIONAL RESPONSE

9.3.1 Data and Estimation Strategy

To explore the CCP's propaganda calendar, we focused on the *People's Daily* and the *Workers' Daily*, which are regarded as official mouthpieces and were the focus of Chapter 7. We estimated models of the form

$$Y_{nt} = \alpha + \beta_k \left(\text{Anniversary Window}_t^k \right) + \phi X_t + \gamma_n + \gamma_s + \epsilon \qquad (9.1)$$

where n indexes newspaper, s indexes year, and t indexes day. The term γ_n gives a set of newspaper-fixed effects, which accommodate unobserved newspaper-level features. The term γ_s gives year-fixed effects, which accommodate the possibility that the CCP's informational strategy has changed over time, as we documented in Chapter 4. Year-fixed effects also accommodate differences in economic conditions and other unobserved factors that might condition its informational strategy. The vector X_t records protests on day $t - 1$, which may be correlated with anniversary windows and the CCP's subsequent informational strategy.

We consider three propaganda responses, given by Y_{nt}. First, we measured pro-regime propaganda as we have throughout. For each day t, the variable *Positive Coverage: Executive*$_{nt}$ counts the total number of positive less negative words from among the twenty surrounding each reference to the autocrat and ruling party in newspaper n. We also recorded propaganda spikes: when the observed *Positive Coverage: Executive*$_{nt}$ is greater than the sample mean plus one or two standard deviations. Second, we probed whether the CCP censors online content. We drew censorship data from the Weiboscope Project, led by King-wa Fu at Hong Kong University's Journalism and Media Studies Centre. The Weiboscope Project records tweets on Weibo – China's Twitter equivalent – from Chinese microbloggers with over 1,000 followers and regularly revisits them to check for censorship; censored tweets return a "permission denied" webpage. The Project then computes a censorship index, which measures the number of censored tweets on day t divided by the total number of tweets on day t. Between 2016 and 2017, the CCP censored roughly 7 percent of posts per day. In 2017 alone, the CCP censored 20,561 posts spanning 120,000 users. The variable *Censorship*$_t$ gives the Weiboscope Project's censorship index. Finally, we probed propaganda-based threats of repression, as we did in Chapter 7. The variables *Stability*$_{nt}$ and *Harmony*$_{nt}$ count references to "stability" and "harmony," respectively, on each day t in newspaper n.

The explanatory variables of interest are the anniversary windows from Chapter 7: major political events, nationalist anniversaries, the anniversaries of ethnic separatist movements, and the anniversaries of failed pro-democracy movements.

9.3.2 *What Elicits a Propaganda Response: Political Events, Nationalist Anniversaries, and Ethnic Separatist Anniversaries*

The results appear in Table 9.1. Although sensitive, major political events are not associated with the sorts of widespread protests generated by pro-democracy anniversaries. Strikingly, however, the volume of pro-regime propaganda rises by 350 percent, the odds of one standard deviation spikes are 1.5 times greater, and the odds of two standard deviation spikes 1.83 times greater. Propaganda-based threats of repression are more common as well. References to "stability" and "harmony" increase by 525 percent and 540 percent, respectively. Online censorship increases by 16 percent. As we discussed in Chapter 7, propaganda-based threats of repression spike during ethnic separatist anniversaries, though censorship is unchanged, perhaps because most of China's netizens are unsympathetic to separatist movements and so censorship is unnecessary.

Figures 9.2 and 9.3 visualize pro-regime propaganda and propaganda-based threats of repression, respectively and by day, since Xi Jinping claimed power in 2012. The dashed horizontal lines denote the mean plus two standard deviation cutpoints. For each spike, we consulted the *People's Daily* to identify the issue that drove it. For each figure, we identified five categories, which appear in the bottom panels. From Figure 9.2, pro-regime propaganda spikes cluster around a few politically sensitive moments. Over 30 percent were driven by the quinquennial Party Congress, when senior leadership positions are announced. National Day accounted for another 15 percent. The annual National People's Congress, which begins in early March and remains in session through the March 10 Tibetan Rebellion anniversary, accounted for another 10 percent. The CCP Founding, which occurs four days before the Xinjiang Uprising, accounted for 5 percent of spikes. Only one-third of propaganda spikes were not associated with a major political event. From Figure 9.3, major political events and ethnic separatist anniversaries accounted for roughly 80 percent of threat spikes. National Day accounted for 10 percent, and another 10 percent were generated by other events. The analogous figures for the *Worker's Daily* appear in the Online Appendix and are very similar.

Table 9.1 *Focal moments, propaganda, threats, and censorship*

	Dependent variable:					
	Positive coverage OLS (1)	1 SD spike Logit (2)	2 SD spike Logit (3)	"Stability" OLS (4)	"Harmony" OLS (5)	Censorship OLS (6)
Democratic anniversaries	−0.340	−0.231	−0.171	−0.212	−0.142	1.297**
	(0.721)	(0.150)	(0.242)	(0.174)	(0.303)	(0.602)
Political anniversaries	2.902***	0.389***	0.603***	0.850***	0.548	1.644**
	(0.862)	(0.148)	(0.217)	(0.208)	(0.362)	(0.671)
Ethnic separatist anniversaries	0.456	−0.143	−0.369	0.667***	0.979***	0.047
	(0.704)	(0.140)	(0.242)	(0.170)	(0.296)	(0.596)
Nationalist anniversaries	1.806**	0.241*	0.595***	−0.160	0.434	−0.724
	(0.777)	(0.140)	(0.199)	(0.187)	(0.327)	(0.650)
Protests$_{t-1}$	0.202***	−0.002	0.004	0.074***	0.087***	−0.120***
	(0.065)	(0.011)	(0.017)	(0.016)	(0.028)	(0.038)
Constant	0.824	−4.793***	−5.897***	0.162	0.010	7.876***
	(0.844)	(0.580)	(1.001)	(0.204)	(0.355)	(0.392)
Year-fixed effects	✓	✓	✓	✓	✓	✓
Newspaper-fixed effects	✓	✓	✓	✓	✓	NA
Observations	8,495	8,495	8,495	8,495	8,495	685
R^2	0.311			0.496	0.332	0.032

Note: *p < 0.1; **p < 0.05; ***p < 0.01

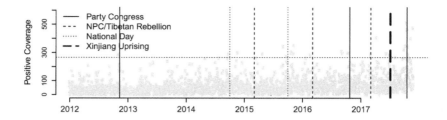

Figure 9.2 Pro-regime propaganda spikes in China

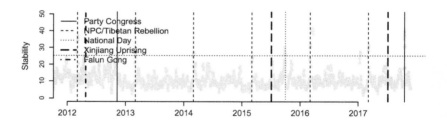

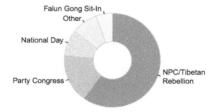

Figure 9.3 Threat spikes in China

9.3.3 *When the Propaganda Apparatus Is Silent:*
Pro-Democracy Anniversaries

The CCP's strategy for pro-democracy anniversaries is different. Although pro-democracy anniversaries are focal moments for protest, the CCP draws no attention to them. Pro-regime coverage actually declines by 41 percent. The odds of a one standard deviation propaganda spike fall by 21 percent. The odds of a two standard deviation spike fall by 16 percent. References to "harmony" and "stability" are unchanged. Figure 9.4 visualizes this. For each anniversary, we indexed the date itself – June 4 for Tiananmen, for example – as day 0, and averaged the levels of pro-regime propaganda, threats, and censorship for the thirty days before and after the anniversary since 2012. The results for

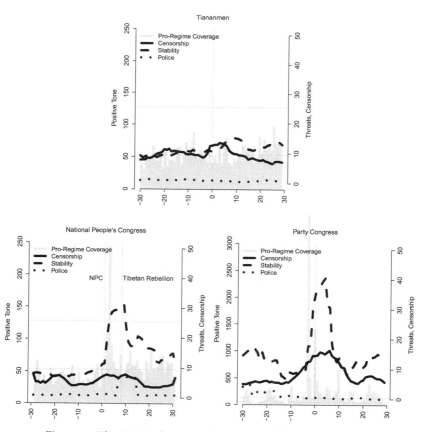

Figure 9.4 The CCP's informational response to different anniversaries

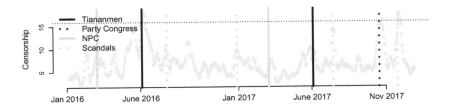

Figure 9.5 Censorship spikes in China

Tiananmen, the most sensitive pro-democracy anniversary, appear in the top panel. For comparison, analogous panels for the National People's Congress and Party Congress appear below. For Tiananmen, the striking feature is how little propaganda changes.

The exception to this is censorship. From Model 6 in Table 9.1, the CCP's baseline daily censorship rate is 7.9 percent of social media posts. During pro-democracy anniversaries, this rises to roughly 9.2 percent, a nearly 20 percent increase. In Chapter 8, we measured the share of propaganda spikes in Sassou Nguesso's *Les Dépêches de Brazzaville* accounted for by the electoral calendar. Figure 9.5 does the same for the CCP's censorship calendar. For each day along the *x*-axis, the *y*-axis gives the rate of censorship. The horizontal line gives the threshold for a censorship spike, defined as the mean plus two standard deviations. Strikingly, the Tiananmen anniversary accounted for half of all censorship spikes in 2016 and 2017.[24]

These results suggest a clear informational strategy. On the anniversaries of failed pro-democracy movements, the CCP privileges forgetting. The propaganda apparatus appears to do nothing to draw attention to them. Censorship spikes.

---

[24] Another pro-democracy event – the death of Liu Xiaobo on July 13, 2017 – accounted for another 15 percent of censorship spikes in this period.

9.4 THE TIANANMEN MASSACRE AS A FOCAL MOMENT

It is possible, however, that propaganda content changes in more subtle ways, which are discernible to citizens but undetectable by our measures of propaganda and threats. We therefore explored the CCP's informational strategy during the Tiananmen anniversary.

Since seizing power in 1949, the CCP has repressed several major pro-democracy movements led by ethnic Han citizens, which now constitute focal moments for anti-regime protests. The calendar of contentious politics in contemporary China is set largely by pro-democracy movements that folded decades ago.[25] Of these, the Tiananmen Square massacre of 1989 is the most sensitive, when anti-regime protests are acutely threatening and security forces are on high alert.[26] The CCP has sought to purge Tiananmen from historical memory. As the anniversary approaches, the CCP censors seemingly innocuous terms: "that day," "that year," "today," "candle," candle emojis, "black clothes," "blood," "anniversary," and "when spring becomes summer." One string of characters that resembles tanks crushing a protester is also censored: "占占占占人占占占点占占点占占点占占点占占占\"\"占占占." The regime censors "pictogram," which could recall the famous tank man, as well as "eight squared," which equals sixty-four and hence June 4, the date of the massacre. The Shanghai Stock Exchange once dropped 64.89 points, recalling the date of the massacre; the regime blocked the search terms "stock exchange" and "index." On June 4, 2015, some WeChat app users in China were unable to make "red envelope" money transfers with values that contained either 64 or 89.[27]

Since our *People's Daily* data extend back decades, we can explore whether the CCP's informational strategy around pro-democracy anniversaries ever shifted: from one that privileged effusive propaganda and threats to one that aimed for forgetting. Did the massacre's anniversary compel a strategy shift in the years immediately after, but diminish over time? Or have the CCP's efforts to purge the massacre from historical memory remained constant? To answer these questions, we computed the mean rate of pro-regime propaganda between June 1 and June 7 for each year since 1970. We then computed the mean rate of pro-regime propaganda for the rest of each year. We subtracted the latter quantity from the former, which yielded an annual measure of how pro-regime

[25] Carter and Carter (2020*a*).
[26] Desposato, Wang, and Wu (2021).
[27] Henochowicz (2016).

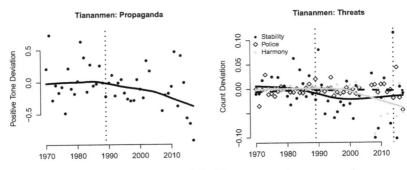

Figure 9.6 Propaganda around the Tiananmen anniversary over time

propaganda changes during the Tiananmen anniversary week. The results appear in the left panel of Figure 9.6, with a lowess smoother overlaid for clarity. Notwithstanding some oscillations, CCP propaganda has called less attention to the Tiananmen anniversary over time. The right panel of Figure 9.6 does the same for several measures of threat codewords: "stability," "harmony," and "police." We observe a spike in "stability" references associated with the first anniversary of the Tiananmen anniversary massacre, which we discussed in Chapter 7: "Stability overrides everything," Deng's front page editorial announced. Strikingly, we also observe a spike in 2013, Xi Jinping's first Tiananmen anniversary in power. Otherwise, the implication is the same.

To probe whether propaganda changes in ways that are discernible to citizens but undetectable by our measures, we used our semantic distinctiveness algorithm. If content around the Tiananmen anniversary is distinctive, this algorithm would detect how. We defined one corpora as all content published between June 1 and June 7 and the other corpora as all content published during the rest of the year.[28] Figure 9.7 displays words that are distinctive to the week surrounding Tiananmen. Distinctive content is mostly random, with three exceptions: "Xinjiang religion," "religious citizen," and "mounted police."[29] These words are

---

[28] We used all years between 2010 and 2017.

[29] "Mounted police" was referenced in one unusual article published on June 5, 2013, about the development of a mounted police force in Shenzhen. It discussed the efficiency of such a force from the taxpayer's perspective and noted that it "arrested suspects of illegal crimes and rescued the masses." It ended with two quotes from a "lawyer at Guangdong Hengtongcheng Law Firm" named *Liu Xiaobo* – who shares a name with China's most famous pro-democracy activist – and who endorsed the force. If read too quickly – or by an uninformed reader – this is tantamount to China's leading democracy activist endorsing the security forces a day after the most sensitive of anniversaries.

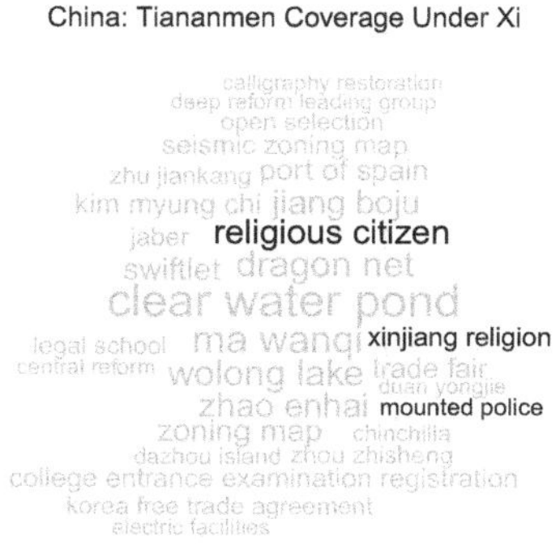

China: Tiananmen Coverage Under Xi

Figure 9.7 Semantic distinctiveness during Tiananmen anniversaries

references to the Uyghur secessionist movement in Xinjiang. To ensure these references did not reflect random chance, we estimated models of the form

$$Y_t = \alpha + \beta \left(\text{Tiananmen Window}_t\right) + \gamma_s + \epsilon \qquad (9.2)$$

where *Tiananmen Window_t* assumes value 1 if day t falls within three days on either side of June 4. Our outcome variables, measured at the day level, include the total number of articles published; the number of articles published that mention "Xinjiang," "Urumqi," or "Uyghur" at least once; and the total number of references to those terms. We included year-fixed effects γ_s to accommodate unobserved differences by year. Since the outcomes are counts, we estimated (9.2) with negative binomial models. The results appear in Table 9.2. Models 1 through 3 focus on the period between 2000 and 2008, before the Xinjiang Uprising of 2009, which we discuss in Section 9.5. Models 4 through 6 focus on the post-Uprising period, spanning 2010 through 2017.

Before the Uprising, Xinjiang was discussed less often during the Tiananmen anniversary. After the Uprising, although the rate of Xinjiang articles remained constant, those that referenced Xinjiang did so much more extensively. On average, Xinjiang is referenced 6.9 times per day. During the Tiananmen anniversary, Xinjiang is referenced 11.9 times per day, or 70 percent more often. In the Online Appendix, we show that this Xinjiang effect obtains only for the Tiananmen anniversary and appears only in the *People's Daily*, which is consumed largely by China's politically engaged urban elite.

Table 9.2 *Tiananmen anniversaries and Xinjiang coverage*

	Dependent variable:					
	Pre-uprising			Post-uprising		
	Total articles (1)	Xinjiang articles (2)	Xinjiang references (3)	Total articles (4)	Xinjiang articles (5)	Xinjiang references (6)
Tiananmen window	−0.067	−0.983**	−1.612***	−0.016	−0.051	0.567***
	(0.075)	(0.392)	(0.484)	(0.019)	(0.125)	(0.195)
Constant	4.613***	−25.287	−24.278	3.888***	0.443***	1.942***
	(0.028)	(9,881.583)	(5,975.763)	(0.008)	(0.049)	(0.077)
Year-fixed effects	✓	✓	✓	✓	✓	✓
Observations	3,287	3,287	3,287	2,890	2,890	2,890

Note: *p < 0.1; **p < 0.05; ***p < 0.01

The CCP's informational strategy during the Tiananmen anniversary is distinctive. Censorship spikes. Pro-regime coverage is less effusive. There are no allusions to social stability or harmony. But articles that reference the secessionist movement in Xinjiang do so at much greater length. To understand the implications of this, we now turn to the Xinjiang Uprising.

9.5 HAN, UYGHUR, AND THE POLITICS OF FEAR

9.5.1 *The Xinjiang Uprising*

Located in far western China, Xinjiang is roughly the size of Britain, France, Germany, and Spain combined. It is home to 22 million citizens, 11 million of whom are ethnic Uyghurs. The Uyghur community has far more in common with China's Central Asian neighbors – Kazakhstan, Kyrgyzstan, Tajikistan, Afghanistan, and Pakistan – than with its Han majority. They are generally Muslim, are of Central Asian descent, and speak a Turkic language. Xinjiang has been home to a handful of separatist movements, including the East Turkestan Islamic Movement, which seeks an independent East Turkestan.

The CCP has long sought to pacify ethnic Uyghurs. In 1949, when Mao annexed Xinjiang, its population was 76 percent Uyghur and 6 percent Han.[30] Xinjiang's population is now 45 percent Uyghur and 42 percent Han. In 2019, Xinjiang had the third-highest net interprovincial immigration flow, just behind the booming provinces of Zhejiang and Guangdong and ahead of the major province-level city, Chongqing. The CCP offers ethnic Han tax incentives to resettle in Xinjiang; a 10,000-yuan annual payment to incentivize Han–Uyghur intermarriage;[31] and 3,000-yuan grants to Uyghur couples who have two children or fewer.[32] For ethnic Uyghurs, these financial incentives are substantial. In 2018, Xinjiang's per capita GDP was just 6,656 yuan. After taking power in 2016, Xinjiang CCP secretary Chen Quanguo – who plagiarized his

---

[30] Hayes (2019).

[31] Chen (2014); Kaiman (2014). Known as the "Uyghur–Han Marriage and Family Incentive Strategy," the plan limited the 10,000-yuan annual payment to five years and only as long as the marriage remained "harmonious." Han–Uyghur married couples also receive housing, education, and healthcare subsidies.

[32] AFP (2015). The plan featured a slogan: "Have fewer children and get rich quick."

doctoral dissertation[33] – amplified repression. He forbade "excessively long beards," veils in public, and traditionally Muslim names like Mohammed and Medina.[34] He required businesses in Uyghur neighborhoods to play two propaganda songs continuously: a children's song about obeying traffic laws and another celebrating the values of communism.[35] He also launched the "Physicals for All" program, which forces Uyghurs to give fingerprint, voice, and face scans, and blood samples for biometric tracking. The CCP then purchased equipment from a Massachusetts company, Thermo Fisher, and teamed with a Yale professor, Kenneth Kidd, to develop methods to distinguish Uyghur DNA markers.[36] As of May 2019, the CCP has detained between 1 and 3 million Uyghurs in facilities the American government calls "concentration camps" but that the CCP calls "vocational training centers" or "boarding schools." Launched in 2014, the program expanded in 2017, when the CCP spent nearly $3 billion on security-related construction and $8.5 billion in total security spending.[37] There are 27 confirmed detention camps and as many as 1,200 in total.[38] In March 2018, an English-language *Xinhua* article cast these policies as part of the global fight against terrorism:

China's fight against terrorism and extremism is an important part of the same battle being waged by the international community. . . .It is in keeping with the purposes and principles of the United Nations to combat terrorism and safeguard basic human rights. In today's world, faced with the severe challenges of terrorism and extremism, no country can shy away from them.[39]

The CCP paired these policies with public murals across Xinjiang. One depicts Uyghurs being crushed by a CCP-branded tractor. Another displays a woman in a burqa alongside a grim reaper, juxtaposed against a happier woman in traditional dress. Other murals discourage children from attending mosques, couples from being married in religious ceremonies, and internet users from downloading jihadist videos.[40]

---

33 Hancock and Liu (2019).
34 Maizland (2019).
35 Schmitz (2017).
36 Wee (2019).
37 Buckley (2018).
38 Maizland (2019).
39 Lu (2019).
40 BBC (2015).

The Xinjiang Uprising occurred in 2009, and its anniversary is now the most important focal moment for ethnic Uyghurs, especially those who favor more autonomy or secession. It was sparked by events at a toy factory in Shaoguan, Guangdong, hundreds of miles away. The CCP had transported some 800 Uyghurs to the toy factory months earlier as part of a resettlement program. One former employee alleged that two Uyghur men raped a Han woman, at which point the factory's 16,000 Han workers rioted. Four hours later, 2 Uyghur men were dead and 120 injured.[41] News of the riot spread to Urumqi, the capital of Xinjiang, with pictures that allegedly showed Han citizens standing over at least 6 dead Uyghurs, arms raised in victory. On July 5, nearly 10,000 Uyghurs protested to demand an investigation.[42] The police intervened; 1,000 Uyghurs fought back; and the CCP paramilitary was called in.[43] According to official estimates, nearly 200 people were killed and 1,700 people were injured, making it the most violent confrontation since Tiananmen. Uyghur groups put the death toll at between 1,000 and 3,000. The CCP imposed a curfew; closed mosques; expanded police patrols; blocked the Internet; and dispatched cars with loudspeakers that blamed the uprising on exiled Uyghur leader Rebiya Kadeer, who was based in the United States.[44] Over 1,000 Uyghurs were detained and nearly thirty death sentences issued.

In the Uprising's aftermath, CCP propaganda cast the Xinjiang Uprising as a Kadeer-engineered terrorist attack and ran footage of Uyghurs attacking Han citizens. Brady (2012a, 175) interprets the propaganda response as a "scare tactic," which "was a reminder to the Chinese public of what would happen if the central government relinquished its stronghold on political power: chaos." Beach (2009) documents how Propaganda Department directives instructed media platforms to "expose the crimes of the East Turkestan movement as much as possible [so] the masses understand the real face of the East Turkestan movement."

The CCP has instrumentalized the Xinjiang Uprising since. We tracked daily references to three words associated with the Uprising: "Xinjiang," "Urumqi," and "Uyghur." In the year before the Uprising, the *People's Daily* referenced these words 2.3 times per day. In the year after, it did so 9.0 times per day, or nearly four times more often. Figure 9.8 probes

---

[41] Wong (2014).
[42] Brady (2012a, 175).
[43] Wong (2009).
[44] Hays (2010).

China: Pre-Uprising Xinjiang Coverage   China: Post-Uprising Xinjiang Coverage

Figure 9.8 Semantic distinctiveness in Uyghur coverage pre- and post-Xinjiang Uprising

how the substance of these references changed. We extracted the ten words on either side of each reference to "Xinjiang," "Urumqi," and "Uyghur," and then divided these concordance segments into two sets: those published in the year before the Shaoguan toy factory riot and those published in the year after. Xinjiang coverage before the Uprising focused on economic policy: "minority cadres" (Uyghur CCP cadres, recruited to make CCP rule more palatable to locals), "China Telecom," "west-east gas transmission," "tacheng highway," and "business administration." It also included "sports news," "victory," and "regular season." Xinjiang coverage in the year after the Uprising was profoundly different. The Uprising was known officially as the "Urumqi incident," and this – not economic policy – dominated the *People's Daily*'s Xinjiang coverage. The propaganda apparatus emphasized the Uprising's brutality. It discussed "serious violent crimes," and the "severe burning" that occurred during it. "Social stability" is among the most distinctive terms, as are the leaders most associated with maintaining order: Hu Jintao, the president, and Zhou Yongkang, the former minister of public security. Xinjiang, readers are reminded, is "inseparable" from China.

9.5.2 *The Calendar of Xinjiang Coverage*

To understand the calendar of Uyghur coverage, we computed mean daily references to "Xinjiang," "Urumqi," and "Uyghur," both before the Xinjiang Uprising of 2009 and after. The results appear in Figure 9.9. The top panels focus on the *People's Daily*. The bottom panels focus

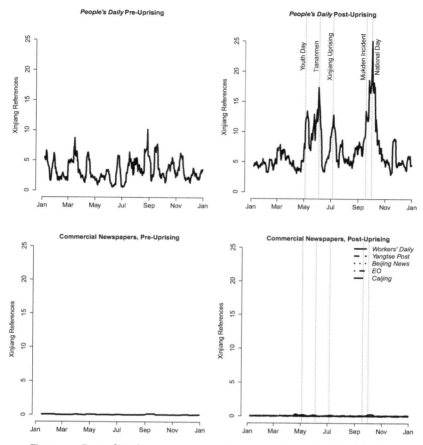

Figure 9.9 Rate of Uyghur coverage over time, pre- and post–Xinjiang Uprising

on the *Workers's Daily, Yangtse Evening Post, Beijing News, Economic Observer,* and *Caijing.*

Before the Uprising, Uyghur coverage in the *People's Daily* was uncommon and random. Since the Uprising, the *People's Daily* has covered Uyghurs at five moments each year. Four of these spikes suggest a propaganda strategy that aims to harden the Han–Uyghur cleavage: the anniversary of the Xinjiang Uprising and three nationalist holidays, when the CCP casts itself as defending the national interest.[45] The final spike

---

[45] The Mukden Incident marks Japan's invasion of China in 1931; National Day marks the founding of the People's Republic of China in 1949; Youth Day marks the birth of modern Chinese nationalism in 1919.

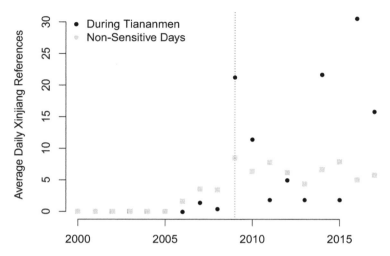

Figure 9.10 Rate of Uyghur coverage during the Tiananmen anniversary over time

is the Tiananmen anniversary, the most sensitive date each year. Among the five Xinjiang spikes, Tiananmen is the obvious outlier, the only pro-democracy anniversary. Since 2009, the *People's Daily* has referenced Xinjiang 7 times a day on average and as many as 25 times a day during spikes. By contrast, other newspapers mention Xinjiang once every three to four days and with no temporal pattern.

Xinjiang discourse is politicized exclusively in official media that targets the regime's central constituents: CCP members and urban elites, who comprise the politically engaged in-group.

Figure 9.10 measures daily average references to Xinjiang terms in the *People's Daily* for each year between 2000 and 2017. The black points record this frequency during Tiananmen focal moments; the gray points do so for other days of the year. Xinjiang, we find, has become more central to CCP propaganda over time, especially during Tiananmen anniversaries.[46]

---

[46] Surprisingly, coverage of Xinjiang was quite high in the 2009 Tiananmen focal moment, a month *before* the uprising occurred. This is consistent with Perry's understanding of 2009 as a "banner year" for anniversaries. The CCP was on high alert, and so this spike may have reflected the regime's efforts to discourage protests by advertising its commitment to territorial integrity and social stability.

9.5.3 *The Content of Uyghur Coverage*

To understand the narratives within these spikes, we coded each Xinjiang article since the 2009 Xinjiang Uprising. Between 2009 and 2017, the *People's Daily* published 90 Xinjiang articles during Tiananmen anniversary windows, defined as the three days before and after the anniversary itself. The *People's Daily* published 560 articles during the other four windows. Outside of these spikes, the *People's Daily* published 100 articles about Xinjiang. We read each article and identified roughly sixty coverage topics. We then recorded each topic's presence in each article.[47] The results appear in Figure 9.11. For each topic along the *x*-axis, the *y*-axis records the share of articles in which the topic appears.

Tiananmen Anniversary: Suppressing Protests The top-left panel displays coverage during the Tiananmen anniversary. The most frequent coverage topic is Islamic terrorism, which appears in more than 10 percent of all Xinjiang Tiananmen coverage. The third most frequent topic is "social stability," which accounts for 9 percent of Xinjiang coverage during the Tiananmen anniversary and is twice as common as otherwise. As we observed in Chapter 7, this term "is broadly understood as a code word for maintaining the stability of the existing regime,"[48] and is associated with Deng Xiaoping's response to the Tiananmen massacre: "Stability overrides everything." Citizens regard allusions to social stability as threatening. We show in Chapter 10 that when these allusions spike, protest declines. The term "rule of law" is similar and appears in 5 percent of Uyghur coverage during the Tiananmen anniversary.

One article from June 7, 2014, underscores how the CCP uses Xinjiang coverage during the Tiananmen anniversary to broadcast its capacity for repression. The article's title was "Xinjiang Corps: Earnestly Fulfilling the Mission of Cultivating and Reclaiming the Frontier, and Doing Utmost to Maintain Social Stability in Xinjiang." It announced that the Xinjiang Party Committee "clearly stated" that the "core task of their work in Xinjiang was to maintain social stability and long-term security." In response to "the current high incidence of violent terrorist activities in Xinjiang," the Party Committee emphasized it would "take a heavy hand, make a heavy punch, fight the enemy first, and resolutely quash the arrogance of violent terrorists." The CCP, the article noted,

---

[47] Topic labels appear in the Online Appendix.
[48] Huang (2015*b*, 426). See also Sandby-Thomas (2011); Chen (2013); Steinhardt (2016); Yue (2012); Benney (2016); Yang (2017); Wang and Minzner (2015).

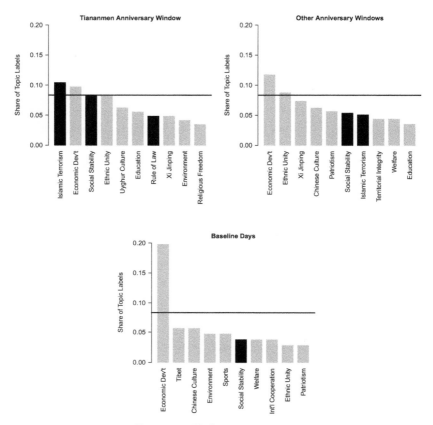

Figure 9.11 Uyghur coverage topics

dispatched over 2.75 million militias to patrol the fifteen prefectures and cities in Xinjiang to "maintain local social stability."

On June 6, 2016, the *People's Daily* covered the threat posed by Uyghur "religious extremism" to the Han majority. The article emphasized the CCP's repressive capacity. The CCP will "resolutely crack down on the 'East Turkistan' terrorist forces" and "learn from the experience of the international community in preventing the infiltration of religious extreme ideas, 'de-extremation,' and combating cyber terrorism."

Xinjiang Uprising and Nationalist Anniversaries: Hardening the Cleavage The top-right panel displays coverage during the three nationalist anniversaries and the Xinjiang Uprising anniversary. Economic development constitutes 12 percent of Xinjiang coverage. The next four topics celebrate the CCP's efforts to advance ethnic Han interests: ethnic unity as a euphemism for Han leadership, Chinese culture as great, patriotism as well-deserved, and Xi Jinping as a steward of all these. CCP propaganda casts Uyghur dissent as threatening. This is why social stability, Islamic terrorism, and territorial integrity are the next most prominent topics.

One article, from May 5, 2014, underscores how the CCP covers the Han–Uyghur cleavage. The article quoted Xi Jinping on the need "to build, develop, and stabilize Xinjiang." "Xinjiang's social stability and long-term stability," Xi proclaimed, "are related to the overall situation of national reform, development and stability, the reunification of the motherland, national unity, national security, and the great rejuvenation of the Chinese nation." The *People's Daily* concluded:

When the frontiers are stable, the interior is safe; when the borders are chaotic, the country is unsafe. Seeking stability, peace, and development are the fundamental interests of the 22 million people of all ethnic groups in Xinjiang and the common will of 1.3 billion people across the country. With social stability and long-term stability as the focus of our work, we can thwart all attempts to divide and destroy, pour the copper and iron walls of frontier security, and build the solid foundation of the Happiness Mansion, making Xinjiang hard-won. We will maintain the results of reform and development, protect the people of all ethnic groups in Xinjiang, and realize the great development and prosperity of Xinjiang.[49]

Baseline Days: Advertising Economic Development Outside of these anniversaries, Xinjiang content in the *People's Daily* mostly focuses on CCP efforts to foster economic growth.[50] Just 4 percent of Uyghur coverage focuses on social stability.

9.6 A SURVEY EXPERIMENT

Why does the CCP recall the Xinjiang Uprising during the most sensitive of China's failed pro-democracy anniversaries, the one most associated

---

[49] Commentator (2017).
[50] The leaked Xinjiang Papers reveal that the regime sees economic development as secondary to social stability. Xi observed that high levels of economic development did not prevent Lithuania, Latvia, and Estonia from leaving the Soviet Union and that development and separatism had been rising simultaneously in Xinjiang. Xi concluded that "economic development does not automatically bring long-term stability, and development issues cannot be used to replace stability issues." (Xi 2014, 7).

with the CCP's crimes against ethnic Han citizens? Why only in the *People's Daily*, which targets Beijing's urban elite?

These are among the most sensitive topics in contemporary China and answering them is difficult. There are several possibilities. The CCP may believe its Han constituents dislike ethnic Uyghurs or value territorial integrity,[51] and hence support repression in Xinjiang. Alternatively, by casting Uyghurs as dangerous to Han interests, the CCP may hope to generate support by casting itself as the guarantor of those interests. The CCP may even hope to build support among party members for future appointments to Xinjiang.

Our theory suggests a darker explanation. By reminding Beijing's urban class of repression in Xinjiang on the anniversary of the Tiananmen massacre, we suspect, the CCP reminds would-be protesters of the consequences of dissent.

9.6.1 Design

To adjudicate among these explanations, we again employed a survey experiment.[52] We partnered with a professional survey company to recruit a sample of over 4,000 Chinese citizens balanced on the most recent census. To maximize verisimilitude, we timed the survey to coincide with the Tiananmen anniversary in June 2020. We first asked respondents a series of demographic questions: their gender, province of residence, ethnicity, age, educational attainment, profession, household income, religion, and party membership status. We also asked questions about political engagement. They were asked to rate their level of interest in domestic politics and international politics, and correctly answer questions about domestic politics and economics. We then probed respondents' cosmopolitanism: whether they speak foreign languages; traveled abroad in 2019; or have good friends who studied, worked, or lived abroad.[53]

Next, respondents were randomly assigned to treatment and control groups. Respondents in the treatment group read an article that was published in the *People's Daily* on June 7, 2014, three days after the anniversary. For reference, the article appears in the Online Appendix. This article is representative of the *People's Daily*'s coverage of Xinjiang

---

[51] Carter, Johnston, and Quek (2018); Johnston and Quek (2018); Johnson (2019).

[52] This survey was granted "exempt" status by our university's IRB.

[53] We drew many demographic questions from Johnston and Quek (2018) and Carter, Johnston, and Quek (2018).

and ethnic Uyghurs during Tiananmen anniversaries. The article's title was "Xinjiang Corps: Earnestly Fulfilling the Mission of Cultivating and Reclaiming the Frontier, and Doing Utmost to Maintain Social Stability in Xinjiang." Readers were told that Che Jun, the secretary of the CCP committee and political commissar of the Xinjiang Production and Construction Corps, described a recent party meeting as "a sharp weapon to unify the thinking and actions of CCP cadres and workers in Xinjiang." The Xinjiang Party Committee "clearly stated" that the "core task of their work in Xinjiang was to maintain social stability and long-term security." In response to "the current high incidence of violent terrorist activities in Xinjiang," the Party Committee emphasized it would "take a heavy hand, make a heavy punch, fight the enemy first, and resolutely quash the arrogance of violent terrorists." The article noted how the Corps had dispatched over 2.75 million militias to patrol the fifteen prefectures and cities in Xinjiang in order to "maintain local social stability." Respondents in the control group did not read an article.[54]

We then asked respondents to rank the most pressing issues facing China. They chose from several options: social stability, legal issues, international security, environmental protection, economic development, corruption, and inequality. We modeled this question on Gallup's surveys of American voters. If the CCP's Xinjiang content during the Tiananmen anniversary aims to make citizens worry about Xinjiang terrorism – against which the CCP can protect them – their responses will reflect that. After, we asked respondents the same direct questions as in Chapter 4: about their support for the CCP and their willingness to protest against it. To gauge respondents' views about ethnic Uyghurs, we asked two additional questions, which appear in Table 9.3. As in Chapter 4, Chinese citizens have powerful incentives to answer these direct questions as they believe the CCP would have them, given its reputation for online surveillance and for repression. To accommodate the possibility of preference falsification, we again asked respondents the same questions in the form of list experiments. To implement the list experiment, within treatment and control groups, we randomized respondents into two groups. One received a set of three non-sensitive items from which they were asked to indicate all that applied to them. The other received the same three non-sensitive items plus one sensitive item, which corresponded to the sensitive direct questions in Table 9.3.

[54] Here we followed Huang (2018).

Table 9.3 *Direct questions*

Ethnic Uyghurs and Xinjiang
I would prefer not to patronize a Uyghur-owned business.
I approve of the government's policies in Xinjiang.

Table 9.4 *List experiments*

I would prefer not to patronize a Uyghur-owned business.
I dislike that seatbelts are required while driving.
It bothers me that professional athletes earn large salaries.
I think insurance companies are dishonest.
I approve of the government's policies in Xinjiang.
Generally speaking, most people cannot be trusted.
We should focus less on the economy and more on the environment.
I like being friends with people who are different than myself.

Respondents were asked to indicate the number of statements that applied to them. This lets respondents express sensitive opinions indirectly, without being explicit. The two additional list experiment prompts appear in Table 9.4.

To avoid design effects, we chose non-sensitive items that were unambiguous and for which respondents were likely to have strong opinions.[55] We also varied the placement of the sensitive item. To avoid ceiling and floor effects, we chose non-sensitive items that were negatively correlated with each other.[56] To accommodate the lack of precision intrinsic to list experiments, we recruited a large sample.[57] To mitigate respondents' concerns about online surveillance, we made the non-sensitive items as non-verifiable as possible. Rather than "I attend a sports match once a week," for instance, we used the more ambiguous "I consider myself a sports fan."[58]

9.6.2 *Potential In-Group Dissenters as the Politically Engaged, Urban Han Elite*

The CCP reserves Xinjiang content during the Tiananmen anniversary for the *People's Daily*, which circulates among China's urban elite. This,

---

[55] Blair and Imai (2012).
[56] Glynn (2013).
[57] Corstange (2009).
[58] Blair and Imai (2012).

we believe, reflects a concern for in-group dissenters, whose protests are most threatening to regime survival. Scholars increasingly understand that these dissenters have a distinctive demographic profile: politically engaged, ethnic Han, and located in major urban areas.[59] They are more supportive of political and economic liberalization,[60] more critical of the central government,[61] and more likely to protest.[62] Wright (2018, 168) puts it succinctly: "Nearly all of those that have participated in political protest activities in the post-Mao period have been urban-based and relatively well educated." Wallace (2014, 5) writes: "[Urbanites] enjoy an advantage in collective action due to their proximity to each other and the seat of government [and so] pose a more immediate threat to regime stability." The CCP has sought to co-opt them throughout the reform era with preferential access to healthcare, education, credit, and capital for start-ups.[63] These are the citizens who are engaged in politics and might join protests that threaten the CCP's survival. These are the citizens who must be made to acquiesce.

The politically engaged, urban Han elite is sensitive to signals of the regime's coercive capacity.[64] Since they often benefit from political connections, they have more to lose from dissent. Since they reside in urban areas with robust security forces, they know the CCP's threats of repression are credible. Since they are politically informed, they are better at interpreting signals that threaten repression. They know more about CCP policies in Xinjiang and hence understand implicit threats of repression.

To identify potential in-group dissenters, we measured the extent to which respondents are members of the politically engaged, urban Han elite. Our index included five subcomponents. To measure political engagement, we asked respondents to rate their level of interest in domestic politics and international politics and to correctly answer questions about domestic politics and economics. To measure in-group status, we asked

---

[59] O'Brien and Li (2005); Chen and Lu (2006); Tang, Woods, and Zhao (2009); Lewis-Beck, Tang, and Martini (2014); Truex (2014); Jiang and Yang (2016); Tang (2016); Pan and Xu (2017); Wright (2018).

[60] Chen and Lu (2006); Tang, Woods, and Zhao (2009); Pan and Xu (2017).

[61] Lewis-Beck, Tang, and Martini (2014); Truex (2014).

[62] O'Brien and Li (2005); Tang (2016).

[63] Dickson (2003), Walder (2004), Guo (2005), Huang (2008), Dickson (2014), Dickson et al. (2016).

[64] Jiang and Yang (2016).

whether respondents were ethnic Han. To measure urbanization, we located respondents' IP addresses within China's 3,000 counties, which are roughly size of U.S. counties. We then computed each county's average nighttime lights in 2019, using high-quality satellite imagery data from the Visible and Infrared Imaging Suite (VIIRS) developed by the Earth Observation Group.[65] Next, we extracted the first principal component of the five outcome variables, which yielded an index of the underlying feature that gave rise to the correlation among them. To facilitate interpretation, we rescaled this measure along the [0, 1] interval. Intuitively, for a set of variables, the first principal component represents the single line that accounts for the largest possible variance among them. This technique has been used to construct indices of racism in the American south and the foreign policy views of American citizens.[66] Here, the first principal component measures how likely it is that a respondent is part of the politically engaged, urban elite.[67]

We defined potential in-group dissenters as those whose index values rank among the top quartile, yielding 866 respondents. The average potential in-group dissenter in our sample is a forty-two-year-old, nonreligious Han man, who is a college graduate; earns around 65,000 RMB a year; lives in a major city; and consumes three news sources a day. He speaks a foreign language and traveled abroad in 2019 but does not have a close friend abroad. In Section 9.6.4, we discuss other ways to identify potential in-group dissenters; in the Online Appendix, we show that the results are substantively unchanged with these alternatives.

9.6.3 Results

The results appear in Figure 9.12. The top two panels show what Xinjiang Tiananmen content does not change. For the statements along the *x*-axes, the *y*-axes present the estimated share of respondents in the treatment and control groups that agree, as well as the estimated difference between those two groups. When the confidence intervals of this estimated difference exclude 0, the treatment effect is statistically significant at the 5 percent level. The top panel shows results for potential in-group dissenters; the middle panel shows results for other citizens.

[65] Elvidge et al. (2021).
[66] Baker (2015); Carter and Carter (2021a).
[67] In the Online Appendix, we report diagnostic statistics that suggest the indicators are correlated.

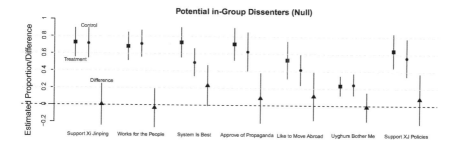

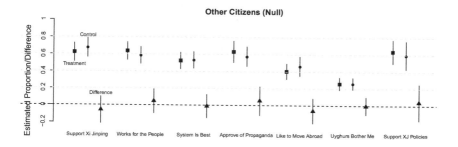

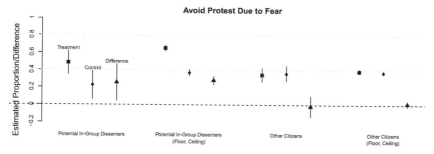

Figure 9.12 Effect of Xinjiang Tiananmen propaganda, list experiments

These panels reveal that Xinjiang Tiananmen propaganda has no effect on support for the CCP. Across treatment status and respondents, the list experiments put support for the CCP at between 50 percent and 70 percent. This is consistent with Robinson and Tannenberg (2019), whose list experiment puts CCP support at roughly 60 percent. To be clear, these constitute upper bounds. Given concerns about online surveillance, these list experiments may not fully mitigate preference falsification. There is no evidence that Uyghur Tiananmen propaganda cues anti-Uyghur racism or compels respondents to support CCP policies in Xinjiang.

The bottom panel of Figure 9.12 reveals what Xinjiang Tiananmen propaganda does change, and for whom. Among potential in-group dissenters, Xinjiang Tiananmen propaganda induces fear. Model 1 presents the results for potential in-group dissenters. Model 2 corrects for floor and ceiling effects. Between 10 percent and 20 percent of respondents in the control group are unwilling to protest due to fear of repression. For the treatment group, this rises to between 50 percent and 70 percent. Models 3 and 4 present the analogous results for other citizens. Xinjiang Tiananmen propaganda has no effect.

These results underscore one of this book's chief arguments. Where electoral constraints are non-binding, propaganda serves to intimidate citizens, not persuade them. This intimidation, the results above suggest, may render anti-regime protests less likely by cueing fear. This possibility was suggested by Young (2018), who, in Robert Mugabe's Zimbabwe, found that cueing fears of past violence rendered citizens less willing to dissent, even without new information about the government's capacity for repression or willingness to employ it. "It may be easier," Young concludes, "for autocrats to influence citizens through the more emotional channels of propaganda, including fear of repression."

9.6.4 *Robustness Checks*

The results in Figure 9.12 are robust to a range of alternative specifications. First, we checked for design effects, which occur when respondents' preferences over non-sensitive items change with the addition of a sensitive item. For Models 1 through 4 in the bottom panel of Figure 9.12, we computed the Bonferroni-corrected p-values, which ranged from 0.397 to 1. This suggests there were no design effects.

Second, we checked for floor and ceiling effects. Floor effects occur when respondents feel negatively about all non-sensitive items and so are deterred from expressing a genuine preference for the sensitive item; ceiling effects occur when respondents feel positively about all non-sensitive items, as well as the sensitive item. To accommodate both, we modeled the likelihood that a respondent is subject to both floor and ceiling effects as a function of observed covariates.[68] The results appear in Models 2 and 4 of Figure 9.12. Table 9.5 presents the estimates for floor and ceiling effects. Across models, we found that no more than 1 percent of respondents misrepresented their true preferences due to ceiling effects

---

[68] Blair and Imai (2012).

Table 9.5 *Ceiling and floor effects*

	Figure 9.12 Bottom panel	
	Model 2	Model 4
Proportion of Liars from Ceiling Effects	0.012	0.003
	(0.001)	(0.001)
Proportion of Liars from Floor Effects	0.070	0.042
	(0.001)	(0.001)

and between 4 percent and 7 percent misrepresented their true preferences due to floor effects. Adjusting Models 1 and 3 for these floor and
ceiling effects improved model fit; the Bayesian Information Criterion
values for Models 2 and 4 are uniformly higher than for Models 1 and 3.
The estimates were substantively unchanged.

In the Online Appendix, we construct our pool of potential in-group
dissenters in three other ways. First, recall that we identified potential
in-group dissenters as those respondents with a PCA index value in the
top quartile, which was 0.85. We re-estimated the list experiments with
cutpoints of 0.8 and 0.9. Second, we defined potential in-group dissenters
as Han citizens living in urban counties with the maximum values of
interest in domestic politics, interest in international politics, and political
knowledge. Third, we defined potential in-group dissenters as ethnic Han
citizens in urban areas who express their opposition to the regime in
direct questioning. We think of these as the committed dissenters among
the urban Han in-group. In each case, Xinjiang Tiananmen propaganda
rendered potential in-group dissenters less willing to protest due to fear
of repression.

Next, we checked for "satisficing" behavior: whether respondents
could have been overcome with the cognitive difficulty of counting items
in response to survey questions.[69] Informed by Kramon and Weghorst
(2012), we asked respondents three non-sensitive questions directly
(whether respondents enjoyed hiking, whether they enjoyed travel, and
whether they preferred urban life to rural life). We later asked respondents these same questions in a list experiment. Kramon and Weghorst
(2012) found a satisficing rate of roughly 40 percent in Kenya; ours

---

[69] Bansak et al. (2018) find that the number of complicated tasks assigned in a survey
experiment does not substantially affect response quality.

was 55 percent. We dropped all satisficers. Again, the results were substantively unchanged.

Finally, we ruled out an alternative explanation for the calendar of Uyghur propaganda that we documented in Section 9.5: The CCP may craft Uyghur propaganda to build support among CCP members for future appointments to Xinjiang.[70] We did so in two steps. First, we exploited the fact that the CCP uses specific language to discuss its efforts to incorporate Xinjiang into the body politic: The most common term is roughly translated as "aid Xinjiang." Second, we replicated the list experiment but with attention restricted to party members. We found no evidence that "aid Xinjiang" coverage spiked during the five in-group/out-group anniversary windows or that the CCP's Uyghur Tiananmen content built support among party members for its policies in Xinjiang. This suggests that the in-group/out-group propaganda strategy we document was not driven by the CCP's efforts to prepare party members for future appointments to Xinjiang.

9.6.5 *The Origins of Uyghur Repression*

Observers have struggled to understand Xi Jinping's brutal campaign of repression against ethnic Uyghurs. Johnson (2019) described it as driven by "Islamophobia," which, he claims, is "rampant in China." These policies, Johnson goes on, are "not only morally wrong but also self-defeating" and hence contrary to the CCP's long-term interests. Victor Shih, a leading scholar of contemporary Chinese politics, agreed, and then attributed the detention centers to a patronage distribution mechanism to compensate CCP loyalists:

What's really galling about what China did is that it was totally unnecessary to lock up all these people. I mean, it's one thing if there is an active insurgency involving, you know, tens of thousands of people. In Xinjiang, there were no active insurgencies; there were isolated terrorist incidents. I don't know why the leadership approved such an unnecessary step.

I think … you have these interest groups within the government – high terrorism officials, officials in Xinjiang – who gain enormously from these very extreme measures, because it costs billions and billions of dollars to build up these camps. Somebody got these contracts. Somebody got rich by operating and building these camps.[71]

---

[70] We thank Victor Shih for this insight.
[71] Chotiner (2019).

This may well be the case. Whatever its origins, this chapter documents how the CCP has instrumentalized its massive campaign of repression in Xinjiang to ensure its security in Beijing. Rural Han citizens will not descend upon Tiananmen to demand the end of the CCP. The politically engaged, urban Han elite may, and may well succeed. By reminding them of ongoing violence against ethnic Uyghurs, the CCP implicitly warns would-be dissenters of its capacity for repression. Most broadly, repression in Xinjiang may have its roots, in part, in the CCP's efforts to secure Beijing. Padro i Miquel (2007) called this the "politics of fear."[72] It is central to the CCP's propaganda strategy.

9.7 CONCLUSION

In the midst of his generally pessimistic 2013 essay in the *New York Times*, Yan Lianke wrote this:

Just as in any kindergarten, there are always a few naughty children who don't like to be told what to do. There are always some people who refuse to be administered amnesia. They are … always spreading their creative wings to fly beyond the boundaries of official memory. Following their conscience, they are willing to fly anywhere, into the past, the present or the future, in order to produce works that can pass our memories onto younger generations.[73]

Some citizens, Yan (2013) suggests, may protest on the anniversaries of failed pro-democracy movements, despite the obvious risks, to remind others neighbors of the CCP's historical crimes. Before these anniversaries, the CCP employs a range of strategies to discourage protests. It incarcerates dissidents, censors online content, and coordinates propaganda content across national and provincial platforms. It does not, however, employ the sort of pro-regime propaganda or "social stability" and "harmony" codewords that are so prevalent during other politically sensitive moments. Doing so would draw attention to the regime's historical crimes, which it wants citizens to forget.

The exception to this is the anniversary of the Tiananmen Square massacre of 1989, when the CCP killed around 2,000 citizens. China's politically engaged, urban Han elite is the most threatening segment of the population: those who once demanded change in Tiananmen and could do so again. For them, in the *People's Daily*, the CCP reserves its

---

[72] Rozenas (2020).

[73] Wang (2019) finds that when Chinese families discuss historical atrocities at home, these memories are passed down to the younger generation.

most threatening message of all on the most sensitive date of the year. During the Tiananmen anniversary, the CCP reminds potential in-group dissenters of its ongoing campaign of repression against ethnic Uyghurs in Xinjiang. Of the 11 million ethnic Uyghurs, as many as 3 million are in detention centers. This content cues fears of repression. Whatever the origins of its ongoing repression in Xinjiang, the CCP has clearly instrumentalized it.

PART IV

Propaganda, Protest, and the Future

IO

Propaganda and Protest

10.1 PROPAGANDA, VOTING, AND COLLECTIVE ACTION

Mass protests increasingly constitute the chief threat to autocratic survival.[1] The world's autocrats employ propaganda explicitly to discourage them. In 2009, one Chinese provincial newspaper, the *Jiangxi Daily*, printed a speech by provincial CCP secretary Su Rong to celebrate its sixtieth anniversary. He cautioned journalists against becoming enamored with freedom of speech in the West, which he described as "fundamentally nonexistent" anyway. The most telling passage:

There must not be any deviation [from the party line] in news and propaganda. This is especially true this year, when many major events are happening in our country. ... News media at various levels have a high degree of political responsibility. They must firmly grasp news and propaganda work in this sensitive period, quickly grasping trends and tendencies and sensitive issues where they are emerging [and work] hard to bring about wholesome and high-spirited mainstream public opinion throughout society.[2]

To prepare for these "major events," the CCP established the 6521 Task Force. It was named for the sixtieth anniversary of the People's Republic, the fiftieth anniversary of the Tibetan Uprising, the twentieth anniversary of the Tiananmen Square massacre, and the tenth anniversary of the Falun Gong crackdown. The first digits of those anniversaries: 6, 5, 2, and 1. The 6521 Task Force was reportedly headed by Xi Jinping, and required provincial and municipal CCP offices to establish their own 6521 Task Forces.

In Chapters 4 through 9, we documented what repressive governments tell their citizens, and we employed survey experiments to measure

---

[1] Marinov and Goemans (2014).
[2] Bandurski (2009).

its cognitive effects. The broader question is whether this matters. Does propaganda discourage protest?

Answering this question is complicated because autocrats employ propaganda strategically, as the preceding chapters make clear. Autocrats do so at specific times, about different topics, and in varying amounts. In this chapter, we identify two forms of selection bias. First, the regimes that employ more propaganda are systematically different from other regimes and in ways that may be correlated with the rate of protest. We refer to this as "unit selection bias." Second, regimes employ propaganda differently at different times, and these moments may be associated with higher or lower levels of protest for reasons unrelated to propaganda. We refer to this as "temporal selection bias." Measuring the effect of propaganda on protest requires accommodating both sources of bias.

Propaganda is also diverse. It encompasses coverage of the regime and opposition, narratives about political and ostensibly non-political content, and threats of repression. In this chapter, we distinguish among three dimensions: pro-regime coverage, non-regime coverage, and threats of repression. We account for unit and temporal selection bias differently across these dimensions. We focus first on the effects of pro-regime and non-regime propaganda. Our identification strategy entails controlling for as many observable features of the strategic environment as possible: whether day t falls during an election season, country j's history of political instability, the rate of internet access, and a range of economic indicators that reflect citizens' living conditions. We control for genuinely positive news in country j by measuring its positive coverage on day t in the world's newspapers of record. We also control for references to country j's political opposition, who may mobilize unrest. To accommodate unit selection bias, we employ country-level fixed effects. In so doing, we ask how changes in the volume of propaganda on day $t - 1$ condition the rate of protest on day t. To ensure our results are robust to arbitrary modeling choices, we employ both our measures of pro-regime propaganda and two cross-country measures of protest.

Next, we focus on the effects of propaganda-based threats of repression. The CCP's calendar of propaganda-based threats, which we uncovered in Chapter 7, suggests a novel identification strategy. We employ an instrumental variables (IV) estimator that leverages two features of China's political geography. First, propaganda in the *Workers' Daily* is set at the national level, but it occasionally responds to local conditions, which are salient in one province but unknown in other provinces. As a result, citizens in one province are occasionally "treated" with propaganda content that is intended for citizens in geographically and culturally distant provinces. Second, because China is ethnically diverse and geographically sprawling, the ethnic separatist anniversaries in Tibet and Xinjiang that drive propaganda-based threats are salient only in those regions and effectively unknown elsewhere. Accordingly, ethnic separatist anniversaries in Tibet and Xinjiang plausibly condition protests in geographically and culturally distant provinces only via propaganda-based threats of repression.

We provide a range of evidence for this exclusion restriction. We conducted a survey – again, balanced on the most recent census – that asked citizens to identify the dates of holidays, anniversaries, and various events. As expected, the dates of ethnic separatist anniversaries are unknown to citizens outside Tibet and Xinjiang, which confirms that they lack political salience in geographically and culturally distant provinces. We show that security forces do not repress protests outside Tibet and Xinjiang during these separatist anniversaries at higher rates than other days, which suggests they are not on high alert. As a final precaution, we excluded not only Tibet and Xinjiang from our analysis but also seven other provinces that are geographically contiguous or contain substantial numbers of co-ethnics and other ethnic minorities. After dropping these nine provinces, our sample nonetheless included 88.5 percent of Chinese citizens.

Across dimensions of propaganda, we found substantively meaningful effects on the rate of protest. By increasing the level of pro-regime propaganda by one standard deviation, autocrats have reduced the odds of protest the following day by between 7 percent and 11 percent. This effect is relatively durable. Drawing on recent models of belief and memory decay,[3] we show that the effect of pro-regime propaganda has a half-life of between two and five days. One month later, very little of the initial effect still persists. This temporal signature is consistent with political messaging in American politics. Likewise, propaganda-based threats of repression have a plausibly causal effect on protest in China. By doubling the number of references to "stability" or "harmony," the CCP's propaganda apparatus halves the number of protests over the subsequent week. These estimates, Conley, Hansen, and Rossi's (2012) sensitivity analysis suggests, are robust to non-trivial violations of the exclusion restriction.

This chapter joins a growing literature that shows propaganda often works. In pre–World War II Germany, state radio increased support for

---

[3] Hill et al. (2013).

the Nazi regime and, in historically anti-Semitic regions, the rate at which Jews were denounced and deported to concentration camps.[4] During the 1994 Rwandan genocide, radio broadcasts increased the Tutsi death toll.[5] During the 1999 Russian parliamentary election, access to independent television decreased support for Vladimir Putin's United Russia.[6] Today, Chinese students exposed to propaganda in an educational setting are less willing to engage in political dissent.[7] Scholars have even documented far-reaching effects of Fox News on American politics: in the 2000 presidential election,[8] in the 2008 presidential election,[9] on local taxes and redistribution programs,[10] and on personal behavior during the COVID-19 pandemic.[11] Propaganda, this chapter shows, has reduced protest across the world's autocracies.[12]

This chapter proceeds as follows. Section 10.2 probes the effect of pro-regime propaganda on popular protest across autocracies. Section 10.3 draws on recent research in American politics to measure the durability of these effects. Section 10.4 documents the effect of propaganda-based threats of repression in China.

10.2 PRO-REGIME PROPAGANDA AND PROTEST

10.2.1 Data and Estimation Strategy

We focus first on the effects of pro-regime and non-regime propaganda. Our baseline estimating equation is

$$Y_{jt} = \alpha + \beta X_{jt} + \psi W_{js} + \gamma_j + \gamma_s + \epsilon \qquad (10.1)$$

where j indexes country; t indexes day, s indexes year; and the vectors X_{jt} and W_{js} give day- and year-level covariates, respectively. To accommodate unobserved characteristics by country, we included country-fixed

---

[4] Adena et al. (2015).

[5] Yanagizawa-Drott (2014).

[6] White, Oates, and McAllister (2005); Enikolopov, Petrova, and Zhuravskaya (2011).

[7] Huang (2015*b*).

[8] DellaVigna and Kaplan (2007).

[9] Martin and Yurukoglu (2017).

[10] Ash and Galletta (2019).

[11] Bursztyn et al. (2020); Jamieson and Albarracin (2020); Simonov et al. (2020).

[12] For more on propaganda in transitional democracies, see McMillan and Zoido (2004); Lawson and McCann (2005); Greene (2011); Boas and Hidalgo (2011), and González and Prem (2018).

effects, given by γ_j. We accommodated unobserved annual characteristics with year-fixed effects, given by γ_s.

The outcome variable Y_{jt} records protests on day t in country j. To ensure the results are robust to alternative specifications, we drew protest data from two sources. First, we used the Armed Conflict Location Event Database (ACLED),[13] which records repression and collective action events throughout Africa, the Middle East, Eastern Europe, Asia, and Latin America by day since 1997. ACLED draws from a wider set of sources than other datasets of collective action, which, for us, is crucial. If measures of repression and collective action were drawn solely from major world publications, they could potentially be confounded by media censorship. If, that is, an autocrat anticipated repressing protesters in advance of some politically sensitive moment,[14] he could preemptively censor foreign media, preventing coverage of the ensuing events. ACLED draws on reports from independent NGOs, local media organizations, and social media. ACLED codes two types of collective action: riots, which are distinguished by violence, and protests, which are generally peaceful. We focused on both. Second, we used the Integrated Crisis Early Warning System (ICEWS) event dataset. ACLED is manually coded; ICEWS is machine coded. Although ICEWS records more events than ACLED – which Raleigh and Kishi (2019) attribute to coding error in the ICEWS algorithm – the two records of protest are tightly correlated.

We specified three explanatory variables. In Chapter 3, we introduced two measures of pro-regime propaganda, *Positive Coverage Standardized: Executive*$_{ijt}$ and *Article Valence: Regime*$_{ijt}$. We estimated variants of equation (10.1) for each. To accommodate the role of narratives, we defined the variable *Article Valence: Non-Regime*$_{ijt}$, which is analogous to *Article Valence: Regime*$_{ijt}$ but focuses exclusively on articles that did not reference government action. Since the estimating equation in (10.1) uses the country-day as the unit of analysis, we used the daily mean of these three measures of propaganda.

Autocrats employ propaganda strategically. Therefore, we confront two forms of selection bias. The first, unit selection bias, refers to the possibility that autocrats who employ more pro-regime propaganda are systematically different than others, and in ways that are correlated with protest. Second, temporal section bias refers to the possibility that autocrats vary the amount of propaganda according to changes in the

---

[13] Raleigh et al. (2010).
[14] Truex (2019).

underlying political environment, and these changes – not pro-regime propaganda – drive protest behavior.

Unit Selection Bias From Chapter 4, we know that pro-regime propaganda is more effusive where electoral constraints are non-binding. If citizens in these autocracies are more or less likely to protest for reasons other than higher levels of pro-regime propaganda, then equation (10.1) will have unit selection bias. To accommodate this possibility, we included country-fixed effects, given by γ_j. That is, we ask how changes in the volume of propaganda over a given time period condition protest on day t.

Temporal Selection Bias: Election Seasons From Chapters 7 through 9, we know that autocrats vary propaganda according to the political calendar. Although we accommodated some of these dynamics with year-level fixed effects, given by γ_s, other dynamics may fluctuate sub-annually. Certain temporal windows could make both propaganda and protest more (or less) common and thus render any observed relationship spurious. We identified four such threats to inference.

The first is elections, which constitute focal moments for protest across autocracies and, from Chapter 8, occasion spikes in pro-regime propaganda. Since both propaganda and protest increase during election seasons, failing to control for the effect of elections could make it appear that pro-regime propaganda actually causes protest. To avoid this possibility, we drew from the National Elections across Democracy and Autocracy (NELDA) dataset,[15] which records the date of every election around the world since 1960. Our field research in Central Africa suggests that the weeks immediately before and after elections are especially sensitive. Campaigning is most intense immediately prior to the election, and results sometimes require a week or two to be finalized and announced. Accordingly, we controlled for whether day t in country j falls within the fifteen days before and after election day. We refer to this thirty-day period as an election season. We also let the effect of propaganda on protest depend on whether day t occurred during an election season. In the Online Appendix, we adjust the size of this election season window to ensure our results are robust to changes.

Temporal Selection Bias: The "Good News" Effect A second potential source of temporal selection bias is the "good news" effect. Propaganda

---

[15] Hyde and Marinov (2012).

Table 10.1 *Our corpus of global newspapers of record*

Al Jazeera English	*AllAfrica.com*	*BBC Monitoring*
International New York Times	*Newsweek*	*Oil and Gas Journal*
Oil Daily	*Petroleum Economist*	*The Standard* (UK)
The Telegraph (UK)	*The Mirror* (UK)	*The Christian Science Monitor*
The Courier Mail (Australia)	*The Daily Mail* (UK)	*The Evening Standard* (UK)
The Globe and Mail (Canada)	*The Washington Post*	*The Toronto Star*
IRIN	*UN News Service*	*USA Today*
Wall Street Journal	*Agence France Presse*	*Associated Press*
CNN	*News Bites – Africa*	*PR Newswire Africa*
United Press International		

apparatuses may provide more positive coverage when there is more genuinely good news: when the unemployment rate falls or when the economic growth rate rises. Citizens are presumably less likely to protest as well. We controlled for a range of economic indicators that reflect living standards: country *j*'s GDP growth rate, unemployment rate, oil supply, and internet penetration rate. Observed annually, however, these indicators are crude. Good news surely emerges by the day or week, the propaganda apparatus reports it objectively, and citizens respond by protesting less. In short, annual economic indicators may be unable to totally account for the sort of good news that mitigates citizens' grievances and renders protests less likely.

To accommodate this, we created the variable *Good News$_{ijt}$* precisely as we did *Article Valence: Regime$_{ijt}$* and *Article Valence: Non-Regime$_{ijt}$*. For each country *j*, we gathered every article that referenced country *j* from the world's news organizations of record. We identified twenty-eight such news sources, which appear in Table 10.1. For each article, we computed the total number of positive less negative words and standardized it by the total number of dictionary hits:

$$\text{Good News}_{ijt} = \frac{\text{Positive Words}_{ijt} - \text{Negative Words}_{ijt}}{\text{Positive Words}_{ijt} + \text{Negative Words}_{ijt}} \quad (10.2)$$

This, we believe, is the most objective measure of "good news" by day that currently exists. Since the unit of analysis in equation (10.1) is the country-day, we defined *Good News$_{it}$* as the daily mean of *Good News$_{ijt}$*.

To assess the measure's plausibility, we estimated several bivariate regressions. The results appear in Table 10.2. From Model 1, our day-level

Table 10.2 *Correlates of* Good News$_{it}$ *in autocracies*

	Dependent variable:			
	Good news$_{it}$			
	(1)	(2)	(3)	(4)
Article valence: Regime$_{it}^{Gov}$	21.008**			
	(9.629)			
Log GDP per capita		204.673***		
		(40.544)		
GDP growth			0.160	
			(1.519)	
Unemployment				−13.856
				(11.560)
Constant	−45.134	−1,438.615***	−40.059	−192.845
	(209.886)	(289.609)	(89.640)	(166.035)
Country-fixed effects	✓	✓	✓	✓
Year-fixed effects	✓	✓	✓	✓
Observations	46,188	195	204	101
R^2	0.429	0.797	0.760	0.858

Note: *p < 0.1; **p < 0.05; ***p < 0.01

measures of *Good News*$_{it}$ and *Article Valence: Regime*$_{ijt}$ are strongly correlated. This is unsurprising, since propaganda apparatuses surely broadcast – and claim credit for – positive developments. At the year level, Models 2 through 4 confirm that *Good News*$_{is}$ is positively correlated with logged GDP per capita and GDP growth, and negatively correlated with unemployment, as expected. These results suggest our day-level measure of *Good News*$_{it}$ reflects good news across autocracies.

Temporal Selection Bias: Histories of Protest and Repression A third potential source of temporal selection bias is political instability. It is possible, for instance, that protests on day $t − 1$ facilitate protests on day t and compel the regime to increase propaganda. Likewise, if the regime employs repression on day $t−1$, citizens may be particularly angry on day t, rendering propaganda more useful. Alternatively, in response to repression on day $t − 1$, citizens may be less inclined to protest on day t, rendering propaganda less critical. The first two sources of bias, if unaccounted for, should bias against an effect of propaganda on protest, whereas the third should bias in favor of it.

We controlled for political instability in several ways. First, we recorded whether day $t − 1$ witnessed a protest or repression event, again using data from ACLED and ICEWS. Second, since these lagged measures of protest and repression may not fully capture prevailing political instability, we also controlled for how many days experienced protest in the preceding three days. We label this variable *Protest History: 3 days$_i$*, and we created a similar variable, *Repression History: 3 days$_i$*, that measures how many days experienced repression over the preceding three days. Finally, to ensure that we fully accommodated any latent political instability that could be associated with both protest and propaganda, we controlled for the number of days that experienced protest in the preceding week and month. We label these variables *Protest History: Week$_i$* and *Protest History: Month$_i$*, respectively, and we created analogous *Repression History: Week$_i$* and *Repression History: Month$_i$* variables similarly. Descriptive statistics for all variables appear in the Online Appendix.

Temporal Selection Bias: The Political Opposition A final potential source of temporal selection bias is coverage of the political opposition. During moments of tension, opposition leaders may intensify efforts to create political change, either by mobilizing constituents or calling international attention to the regime's human rights violations. Consequently, we might observe a negative relationship between pro-regime coverage and protest because references to the opposition – alongside coverage of the government – are driving down our measures pro-regime propaganda and at precisely the moment opposition leaders are mobilizing protests. By failing to control for coverage of the opposition, an estimated negative relationship between our measures pro-regime propaganda and protest might be spurious. From Chapter 3, the variable *References: Opposition$_{it}$* counts references to country *j*'s political opposition on day *t*.

10.2.2 Results

The results appear in Table 10.3. Models 1 through 3 focus on *Positive Coverage Standardized: Executive$_{it}$*. Models 4 through 6 focus on *Article Valence: Regime$_{it}$*. The estimates are consistent across models. The associated odds ratios measure the effect of a unit change in our measures of propaganda on the daily odds of protest. For *Positive Coverage Standardized: Executive$_{it}$*, the odds ratios hover around 0.92. For *Article Valence: Regime$_{it}$*, the odds ratios hover around 0.5. Note that the mean daily value of *Positive Coverage Standardized: Executive$_{it}$* is 0.96 and its standard deviation is 0.93; the mean daily value of *Article Valence:*

Table 10.3 *Propaganda and protest in autocracies*

	(1)	(2)	(3)	(4)	(5)	(6)
	Dependent variable:					
	Protest$_{it}$					
Positive coverage standardized: Executive$_{it-1}$	−0.084** (0.040)	−0.085** (0.043)	−0.064 (0.056)			
Article valence: Regime$_{it-1}$				−0.572** (0.272)	−0.626** (0.297)	−0.656* (0.396)
Article valence: Non-regime$_{it-1}$	−0.354 (0.263)	−0.314 (0.281)	−0.519 (0.370)	−0.292 (0.249)	−0.189 (0.267)	−0.429 (0.359)
Protest$_{it-1}$	0.948*** (0.072)	0.746*** (0.076)	0.632*** (0.091)	0.954*** (0.070)	0.747*** (0.075)	0.662*** (0.089)
Repression$_{it-1}$	0.007 (0.063)	−0.018 (0.068)	0.035 (0.081)	0.010 (0.064)	−0.029 (0.070)	0.035 (0.086)
Protest history: 3 day$_i$		0.169*** (0.052)	0.173*** (0.055)		0.176*** (0.050)	0.167*** (0.053)
Repression history: 3 day$_i$		−0.100 (0.140)	−0.176 (0.186)		−0.118 (0.141)	−0.161 (0.184)
Protest history: 1 week$_i$		0.166*** (0.028)	0.136*** (0.032)		0.170*** (0.027)	0.139*** (0.031)
Repression history: 1 week$_i$		0.079* (0.042)	0.073 (0.053)		0.085** (0.041)	0.068 (0.052)
Election$_{it}$		1.095* (0.652)	2.143* (1.153)		0.929 (0.600)	1.478* (0.846)
Election season$_{it}$		0.375* (0.215)	0.196 (0.279)		−0.250 (0.445)	−0.445 (0.541)
Election season$_{it}$ × Propaganda$_{it-1}$		0.151 (0.222)	−0.025 (0.328)		2.591** (1.288)	2.382 (1.611)
Good news$_{it-1}$		0.0002 (0.0003)	0.0002 (0.0004)		0.0002 (0.0003)	0.0002 (0.0004)
Opposition references$_{it-1}$		−0.046 (0.039)	0.011 (0.058)		−0.095* (0.049)	−0.115 (0.092)
GDP growth			0.687 (96.533)			0.621 (101.587)
Log GDP per capita			−2.145 (3,824.368)			−3.044 (3,781.086)
Unemployment			6.486 (378.007)			6.528 (347.060)
Oil/GDP			0.842 (465.114)			0.440 (459.047)
Government spending/GDP			−2.152 (679.498)			−2.320 (643.706)
Internet censorship			−62.922 (12,701.700)			−49.456 (14,623.520)
Social media censorship			58.969 (12,760.480)			45.317 (14,787.190)
Constant	−3.875*** (1.022)	−4.443*** (1.067)	64.233 (37,819.850)	−3.766*** (1.024)	−4.701*** (1.093)	54.182 (32,388.770)
Country fixed effects	✓	✓	✓	✓	✓	✓
Year fixed effects	✓	✓	✓	✓	✓	✓
Observations	25,909	23,285	9,009	27,416	24,581	9,543

Note: *p < 0.1; **p < 0.05; ***p < 0.01

Regime$_{it}$ is 0.42 and its standard deviation is 0.26. Accordingly, if an autocrat shifts from an average level of pro-regime propaganda on day t to one standard deviation greater, the odds of protest fall by between 7 percent and 11 percent. If an autocrat shifts from an average level of pro-regime propaganda on day t to two standard deviations greater, the odds of protest fall by between 14 percent and 23 percent. These estimated effects are plausible: modest, but non-trivial.

The coefficients for *Article Valence: Non-Regime$_{it}$* are negative across models and, from Models 4 through 6, somewhat smaller than for *Article Valence: Regime$_{it}$*. We treat these results with caution, since *Article Valence: Non-Regime$_{it}$* constitutes a relatively rough measure of propaganda narratives. Still, it suggests that the effect of non-regime content on popular protest is generally weaker and less consistent than the effect of regime content.

We find some evidence that pro-regime propaganda may not discourage protest during election seasons. Across models, the interaction between pro-regime propaganda and *Election Season$_{it}$* is positive, but the total marginal effect – which incorporates the base term for our propaganda measures – is estimated with too little precision to reach statistical significance. There are two explanations for this. First, it may be the case that, during election seasons, pro-regime propaganda has no effect on protest in our sample of countries. Many are poor, their citizens are keen for change, and during election seasons opposition leaders inspire hopes for a better future. As a result, the constraining effects of propaganda may genuinely fail to overcome popular grievances. Alternatively, it may be the case that election seasons are systematically different from other calendar days, and in ways that equation (10.1) does not fully accommodate. Scholars increasingly recognize that elections constitute focal moments for protest, that they are times when collective action problems are easier to overcome. In this sense, we might expect both pro-regime propaganda and protests to emerge simultaneously during election seasons.

We conclude with a note of caution. Though expressed in terms of the marginal effect of a unit increase in pro-regime propaganda on day t, these results do not suggest that more propaganda would further reduce protest. As we noted above, autocrats employ propaganda strategically. They set the amount of propaganda strategically as well. Since, as Goebbels observed, "propaganda becomes ineffective the moment we are aware of it," it may well be the case that additional propaganda would undermine the entire effort. Rather, these results suggest that propaganda, as it has been employed, is associated with less protest across autocracies.

10.2.3 Robustness Checks

We conducted several robustness checks to ensure these results were not sensitive to arbitrary modeling decisions. The results appear in the Online Appendix. We exploited the fact that ACLED records the number of protests in country j on day t. For this, we reestimated equation (10.1) with a negative binomial model. Since protests are relatively rare, we reestimated equation (10.1) with a rare events logit correction. In each case, the results were unchanged.

Protests may be correlated across days. It may be easier, for instance, to sustain a protest once it has emerged than to initiate one in the first place. If so, the outcome variable in equation (10.1) may be serially correlated. We accommodated this in Table 10.3 by controlling for protests on day $t - 1$, as well as the number of days over the preceding week and the preceding month that witnessed a protest. As a robustness check, we employed a Markov transition framework.[16] We restricted attention to country-days where no protests occurred on day $t - 1$ and hence measured the effect of propaganda on the probability that protests emerged on day t. The results were similar to those in Table 10.3.

Readers may be concerned that our data collection process limits the external validity of these statistical results. Since we relied on online archives for data collection, our sample may have been skewed in favor of autocracies with relatively high internet penetration rates. If higher rates of internet access limit the efficacy of propaganda, then these statistical results may well constitute a lower bound. In Chapter 3, we showed that the mean internet penetration rate is slightly higher in our sample of autocracies than the global mean. This difference, however, is entirely driven by the inclusion in our sample of four microstates with particularly high internet access rates: Bahrain, Qatar, Singapore, and the United Arab Emirates. We re-estimated equation (10.1) with these four microstates excluded. The results were unchanged, which suggests that our use of online archives does not threaten external validity.

---

[16] For more on Markov transition models, see Epstein et al. (2005).

10.3 DO THE EFFECTS OF PRO-REGIME PROPAGANDA PERSIST OVER TIME?

10.3.1 Functional Forms

Pro-regime propaganda on day $t-1$, we find, is associated with a meaningful reduction in protest on day t. But are these effects persistent? Does pro-regime propaganda on day $t-1$ continue to discourage protest on day $t+5$ or day $t+10$? To measure persistence, we followed Hill et al. (2013), who studied the effects of political advertisements in two election campaigns in the United States: the 2000 presidential race and a series of state races in 2006. Drawing on an extensive psychology literature that models memory decay for simple facts and words,[17] Hill et al. (2013) identified four decay functions that best characterize the persistence of persuasion effects. They then fit these decay functions to their data and asked which of them best captures "whatever pattern of decay may be present."

Following Hill et al. (2013), we focused on four functional forms, which appear in Table 10.4: the exponential, logarithmic, power, and Weibull. In each, the daily probability of protest entails two effects. The first is the effect of pro-regime propaganda on day $t-1$, which conditions the probability of protest on day $t-1$ through its estimated coefficient, I, which Hill et al. (2013) refer to as an impact parameter. The second is the effect of pro-regime propaganda on the days that preceded $t-1$, which exerts the effect I weighted by the value of the decay function on a given day. The value of the decay function on a given day is determined by the shape parameter δ, which we estimate with maximum likelihood. To

Table 10.4 *Decay functions*

Distribution	Functional form
Exponential	$\text{Protest}_t = I \times \sum_{t=0}^{T} \exp(-\delta \times t) \, \text{Positive Coverage}_{t-1}^{Gov} + X\beta$
Logarithmic	$\text{Protest}_t = \sum_{t=0}^{T} [I - \delta \times \log(t+1)] \times \text{Positive Coverage}_{t-1}^{Gov} + X\beta$
Power	$\text{Protest}_t = I \times \sum_{t=0}^{T} \exp(t+1)^{-\delta} \, \text{Positive Coverage}_{t-1}^{Gov} + X\beta$
Weibull	$\text{Protest}_t = I \times \sum_{t=0}^{T} \exp(-\delta \times t) \, \text{Positive Coverage}_{t-1}^{Gov} + X\beta$

---

[17] Rubin and Wenzel (1996).

Table 10.5 *Parametric decay estimates*

	Exponential (1)	Weibull (2)	Power (3)	Logarithmic (4)
Impact	−0.398**	−0.493*	−0.684**	−0.422***
	(0.218)	(0.322)	(0.352)	(0.172)
Decay	0.094*	0.663**	0.728***	−0.113**
	(0.069)	(0.378)	(0.300)	(0.068)
Control variables	✓	✓	✓	✓
Country-fixed effects	✓	✓	✓	✓
Year-fixed effects	✓	✓	✓	✓
Observations	7,299	7,299	7,299	7,299

Note: *p < 0.1; **p < 0.05; ***p < 0.01

be conservative, we let pro-regime propaganda as temporally distant as thirty days preceding day t condition the probability of protest on day t. The vector X gives covariates from the baseline model and country fixed effects. We estimated a variant of Model 5 in Table 10.3.

10.3.2 Results

Table 10.5 presents results for the two key parameters – the impact parameter I and the decay parameter δ – for each functional form. Figure 10.1 presents the associated survival rates, which display the percent of propaganda impact from each lagged day (two to thirty-one) that survives at day $t = 0$. Importantly, the impact parameter estimates I are similar to the baseline results in Models 4 through 6 of Table 10.3. The effects of pro-regime propaganda, we find, are indeed persistent, much like campaign advertisements in democracies. Across decay functions, the half-life of pro-regime propaganda is between two and five days. One month later, very little of the initial effect persists.

10.4 PROPAGANDA-BASED THREATS OF REPRESSION AND PROTEST

10.4.1 Data and Estimation Strategy

Next, we probed the effects of propaganda-based threats of repression. In Section 10.2, we confronted the possibility of selection bias – both unit and temporal – by controlling for as many features of the strategic

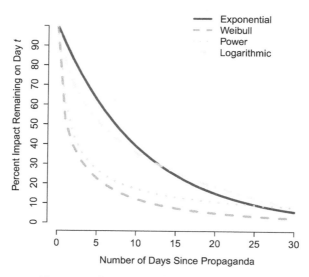

Figure 10.1 Decay rates of pro-regime propaganda

environment as possible. Here, we confront the possibility of selection bias by employing a novel instrumental variables (IV) estimation strategy.

In Chapter 7, we showed that the Chinese government routinely threatens citizens on the anniversaries of ethnic separatist movements. We treat these results as a model of the treatment assignment mechanism: of how the CCP chooses when to threaten citizens. We use this treatment assignment mechanism as the foundation for IV estimates. The key idea is that *Workers' Daily* content is set at the national level, but occasionally it responds to conditions that are salient in one province but not in others. As a result, provinces that are geographically and socially distant from each other are occasionally "treated" with propaganda content directed at the other province's readership. This identification strategy requires identifying events that generate protests in province i, inducing the CCP to issue propaganda-based threats to citizens in province i but which are effectively unknown in some geographically and culturally distant province j.

The ethnic separatist anniversaries from Chapter 7 provide such an instrument. They are highly salient in Tibet and Xinjiang, but, because of China's ethnic diversity, sprawling geography, and low out-migration rates from Tibet and Xinjiang, are essentially unknown in Han China. This lets us exploit profoundly salient events in Tibet and Xinjiang to probe whether the propaganda-based threats induced by those events decrease protests by Chinese citizens elsewhere. The second stage of the IV model is

$$Y_t^{Han} = \alpha_P + \beta_P \left(\widehat{\text{Threat}_t}\right) + \phi_P X_t + \psi_P W_s + \gamma_{Ps} + \epsilon_P \qquad (10.3)$$

where t indexes day, s indexes year, and Y_t^{Han} is a daily measure of protests across Han China. Put differently, we estimated an intent-to-treat IV model in which the ethnic separatist window is the instrument and protest in Han-dominated provinces is the outcome. The endogenous regressor $\widehat{Threat_t}$ is the propaganda-based threat level predicted by the first stage:

$$\text{Threat}_t = \alpha_T + \beta_T \left(\text{Separatist Anniversary Window}_t\right)$$
$$+ \phi_T X_t + \psi_T W_s + \gamma_{Ts} + \epsilon_T \qquad (10.4)$$

In both models, vector X_t includes day-level covariates: whether day t falls within the other anniversary windows from Chapter 7 and the number of nationwide protests on day $t-1$. The vector W_s includes year-level covariates observed at the national level: logged GRP, logged population, rural population share, sex ratio, and urban unemployment. The parameter γ_s gives year-fixed effects. The endogenous regressors are our word count measures of threats – references to "stability" and "harmony" by day – which are continuous and non-negative. Our outcome measure of nationwide protests is also continuous and non-negative. We employed two-stage least squares.

To measure protests, we employed data from Manfred Elfstrom and the China Labour Bulletin (CLB), a Hong Kong NGO that advocates for labor rights. Drawing on international, domestic, and social media, they maintain a geocoded dataset of all known strikes and protests. Elfstrom's dataset covers 2006 through 2012; the CLB dataset covers 2011 through 2016. Their coding rules and sources are essentially identical; in the Online Appendix, we show that the two datasets are virtually identical in 2011 and 2012, when they overlap. To maximize coverage, therefore, we merged the two datasets.[18] The variable *Protests_t* records the number of protests in province i on day t. For 2006 through 2010, we used Elfstrom's data; for 2011 through 2016, we used CLB data.

---

[18] Elfstrom (2019) details the coding procedures.

These datasets are especially appealing for two reasons. First, they complement the *Workers' Daily*. The *Workers' Daily* targets urban labor, whose strikes and protests are the focus of these two datasets. Second, the datasets are very similar to records of protest derived from social media. Göbel and Steinhardt (2019) found that between 2013 and 2016, some 97 percent of the protests recorded by the CLB also appear in Wickedonna, a blog that represents their gold standard source for protests since 2013. This "extreme overlap," as Göbel and Steinhardt (2019, 8) put it, gives us confidence in the Elfstrom and CLB datasets.

The Online Appendix explores these datasets more extensively. We present empirical distributions for the number of protests each day and the number of protests over the course of the coming week. The mean values for the two distributions are 2.9 and 20.2, respectively. We use both protest measures as outcome variables in the statistical models below. The Online Appendix also includes descriptive statistics for protests by province and over time. There is some evidence that, at the province level, protests are correlated with economic output, which may reflect higher levels of social media use or urbanization rates. Likewise, there is some evidence that protests have increased over time. These patterns may reflect reporting bias. To accommodate unobserved differences in the data-generating process, we employed year-fixed effects for intertemporal variation and province-fixed effects for geographic variation.

Figure 10.2 visualizes the life cycle of protest in China. For each day along the *x*-axis, the *y*-axis records the total number of nationwide protests between 2006 and 2016. The dashed horizontal lines indicate daily protest levels equal to the mean plus one and two standard

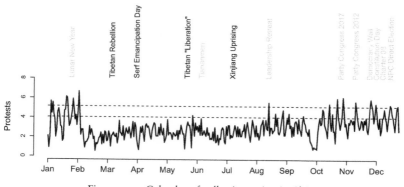

Figure 10.2 Calendar of collective action in China

deviations. As we discussed in Chapters 7 and 9, protests cluster around politically sensitive moments, when citizens are engaged and aware of shared discontent.

10.4.2 *The Exclusion Restriction*

To be a valid instrument, anniversaries of ethnic separatist movements in Tibet and Xinjiang must condition protests elsewhere only through their effects on propaganda-based threats. This exclusion restriction would be violated if the CCP deploys security forces in provinces other than Tibet and Xinjiang during ethnic separatist anniversaries, and these security forces reduce protest rates. We ruled out this possibility in four ways.

Dropping Provinces Ethnic separatist anniversaries elicit widespread repression in Tibet and Xinjiang. Shortly before the fiftieth anniversary of the Tibetan Rebellion, Zhang Qingli, the CCP chief in Tibet, said this to local police:

We must keep a watchful eye, and with clenched fists, constantly be on the alert. We must resolutely and directly strike at criminal elements who dare to stir up incidents. We must foil the separatist schemes of the Dalai clique.[19]

During these anniversaries, the CCP regularly imposes region-wide security alerts, organizes military parades, and bans foreign travel in Tibet and Xinjiang. In 2013, one Xinjiang party member told reporters that "during each anniversary, he had to patrol the neighborhood or visit residents for a whole month to ensure stability."[20] Accordingly, we excluded Tibet and Xinjiang from our analysis.

We also excluded the four provinces that border Tibet and Xinjiang: Qinghai, Gansu, Sichuan, and Yunnan. These neighboring provinces may have Tibetan and Uyghur communities along the Tibet and Xinjiang borders. There is substantial evidence that regional security apparatuses in these neighboring provinces treat the ethnic separatist anniversaries as sensitive. In 2017, the CCP blocked the Internet in the ten Sichuan counties that neighbor Tibet in the weeks around the Tibetan Rebellion anniversary.[21]

---

[19] FlorCruz (2009).
[20] Choi and Zuo (2013).
[21] Finney (2017).

Figure 10.3 Where the CCP is most likely to deploy additional security forces

We dropped three other provinces from the sample as well. Ningxia contains the Hui ethnic group, China's second largest Muslim population. While the Hui are ethnically, linguistically, and culturally distinct from Uyghurs and do not have separatist aims, they may be sympathetic to Uyghur grievances. Inner Mongolia is home to several minority communities, which may be more sympathetic to Uyghur grievances than ethnic Han citizens. Separatist anniversaries may have special significance in Beijing, but for different reasons. Anecdotal reports suggest that anti-terrorism precautions in Beijing were heightened after the 2009 Uyghur bombing in Urumqi, Xinjiang's capital.[22] Uyghur terrorists conducted bombings in Beijing in 2013, and so Beijing residents may be more aware of Uyghur separatism.

In total, we dropped nine provinces where the regime is likely to deploy additional security forces – or place existing security forces on alert – during ethnic separatist anniversaries in Tibet and Xinjiang. Figure 10.3 visualizes our final province sample. Tibet and Xinjiang appear in dark gray; the seven other provinces we excluded appear in medium gray. In 2016, the nine provinces we exclude accounted for 11.5 percent of Chinese citizens. Our sample, in light gray, accounted for 88.5 percent of Chinese citizens.

[22] Yang (2014).

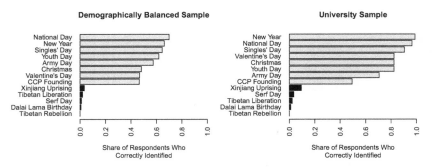

Figure 10.4 Identifying ethnic separatist anniversaries in Tibet and Xinjiang

Are Citizens Aware of Ethnic Separatist Anniversaries? We conducted a survey to confirm that citizens in our final province sample are unaware of ethnic separatist anniversaries from Tibet and Xinjiang. This is important for two reasons. First, if citizens are unaware of these ethnic separatist anniversaries, there is no reason to believe they constitute moments of tension. Likewise, there is no reason to believe the regime places security services on high alert.

The survey was conducted in November 2018 and counted 1,000 respondents. It was fielded over the Internet by a professional survey company in China.[23] Our survey protocol consisted of standard demographic questions, followed by "What is the day of X? (Please respond from memory, do not search on the Internet)," where X represents thirteen political, cultural, and sensitive holidays. Respondents answered in an open-ended text response box.[24] In pre-testing, the survey took native speakers approximately three minutes to complete. To ensure that respondents were not searching for answers online, we dropped all responses that took longer than five minutes to complete. This restriction reduced our sample to 521 respondents. The results appear in the left panel of Figure 10.4. As expected, Chinese citizens accurately identify the dates of major cultural and political holidays, as the top bars demonstrate. Also as expected, they are almost totally unable to identify the

---

[23] This survey was granted "exempt" status by our university's IRB. It was balanced on the most recent census on gender, age, province, and income. Balance statistics appear in the Online Appendix.

[24] The Online Appendix visualizes just how incorrect respondents' guesses were. There is no clustering around the correct anniversary date.

dates of ethnic separatist anniversaries in Tibet and Xinjiang. Put simply, these dates are salient *only* in Tibet and Xinjiang.

Readers may be concerned that respondents were too scared to acknowledge ethnic separatist anniversaries, perhaps because they feared detection by the CCP's online surveillance. Therefore, we recruited a sample of Chinese undergraduates studying abroad at the University of Southern California. This sample consisted of eighty students and was recruited via snowball sampling. Among China's highly educated citizens and far from the government's surveillance apparatus, these students are "most likely cases" for recognizing sensitive anniversaries. These undergraduates recognized major cultural and political holidays with precision. Again, virtually none were able to identify the dates of ethnic secessionist anniversaries in Tibet and Xinjiang. These results suggest that the vast majority of Chinese citizens are unaware of ethnic secessionist anniversaries in Tibet and Xinjiang. They also suggest that the CCP has not drawn attention to these anniversaries by mobilizing its repressive apparatus around them.

Perhaps, however, protest organizers are aware of these ethnic separatist anniversaries and, suspecting the security apparatus might be on high alert, deliberately avoid organizing protests during them. Protest organizers, after all, may be more connected and savvy. In the Online Appendix, we show that there is no "donut pattern" in which protests cluster before and after separatist dates. This suggests that protests are not strategically scheduled by protest organizers to avoid coinciding with ethnic separatist anniversaries.

Is the Security Apparatus on High Alert? Our data let us confirm that the security apparatus is not on high alert in Han China. The Elfstrom and CLB datasets record whether security forces responded to a given protest j by employing repression against participants. If, during ethnic separatist anniversaries that are sensitive in Tibet and Xinjiang, security forces are on high alert *in Han provinces*, they should be more likely to repress protests that emerge. We estimated the model

$$\Pr\left(\text{Repression}_j^{Han} = 1 | \text{Protest}_j^{Han} = 1\right)$$
$$= \alpha_R + \beta_R \left(\text{Separatist Anniversary Window}_j\right)$$
$$+ \phi_R X_j + \psi_R W_s + \gamma_{Rk} + \epsilon_R \qquad (10.5)$$

where j indexes protest, s indexes year, k indexes province, and γ_k gives province-fixed effects. The vector X_j includes recent protests and dichotomous indicators for the anniversaries of failed pro-democracy movements, major political events and anniversaries, and cultural anniversaries. The vector W_s includes annual covariates that may influence repression: logged GRP, logged population, rural population share, sex ratio, and urban unemployment. Descriptive statistics and sources for all variables appear in the Online Appendix. The *Han* superscript indicates that our analysis is limited to provinces in light gray in Figure 10.3, which are dominated by ethnic Han.

The results appear in Table 10.6. Protests during ethnic separatist anniversaries in our final province sample are no more likely to be repressed than those on other days. Rather, the best predictor of whether a protest will be repressed is the number of protests in the preceding week. Put otherwise, in our final province sample, local security apparatuses mobilize in response to past protests, not ethnic separatist anniversaries in Tibet and Xinjiang. There is no evidence that CCP security forces are on high alert during ethnic separatist anniversaries *outside* the nine provinces that we excluded from analysis.

In the Online Appendix, we also control for dissident detentions in the weeks before sensitive anniversaries – a form of preventive repression that might decrease protests by removing their leaders. We measured political detentions with the Congressional-Executive Commission on China's Political Prisoner Database.[25] Our results are robust to controlling for dissident detentions in the seven, fourteen, and thirty days prior to the separatist anniversary.

Are Protests around Ethnic Separatist Anniversaries Different? Finally, we probed whether the protests that emerge during ethnic separatist anniversaries in ethnic Han provinces are different in character than those that occur outside ethnic separatist anniversary windows. If the exclusion restriction holds, we should observe no differences in the character of protests during ethnic separatist anniversaries.

To probe this, we exploited the fact that the CLB maintains an image repository of all protests in its dataset. These images generally feature banners, signs, manifestos, or tweets from a given protest. We scraped all 38,078 protest images and then used `tesseract`, an optical character recognition program, to extract the words that these images contain.

---

[25] We thank Rory Truex for this suggestion.

Table 10.6 *State repression and politically sensitive anniversaries*

	Dependent variable:					
	Repression					
	0 day	1 day	2 day	3 day	4 day	5 day
	(1)	(2)	(3)	(4)	(5)	(6)
Separatist anniversary	−0.516	−0.132	−0.116	−0.111	−0.111	−0.076
	(0.449)	(0.188)	(0.146)	(0.129)	(0.115)	(0.101)
Democratic anniversary	0.048	0.068	0.098	0.061	0.044	0.048
	(0.177)	(0.113)	(0.086)	(0.074)	(0.067)	(0.064)
Political anniversary	−0.112	−0.084	−0.018	0.002	0.002	−0.006
	(0.145)	(0.086)	(0.066)	(0.058)	(0.053)	(0.051)
Cultural anniversary	0.031	0.083	0.085	0.070	0.056	0.010
	(0.163)	(0.088)	(0.069)	(0.060)	(0.054)	(0.051)
Recent protests	0.038	0.037	0.028*	0.023*	0.022**	0.023**
	(0.026)	(0.026)	(0.016)	(0.013)	(0.011)	(0.010)
Log GRP	0.554	0.549	0.550	0.569	0.559	0.551
	(0.367)	(0.368)	(0.367)	(0.368)	(0.367)	(0.367)
Log population	1.347	1.305	1.136	0.892	0.807	0.824
	(2.698)	(2.706)	(2.696)	(2.695)	(2.689)	(2.686)
Rural population share	−6.077**	−6.161**	−6.105**	−6.032**	−6.034**	−5.919**
	(2.426)	(2.423)	(2.425)	(2.427)	(2.428)	(2.431)
Sex ratio	0.014	0.015	0.015	0.015	0.015	0.014
	(0.011)	(0.011)	(0.011)	(0.011)	(0.011)	(0.011)
Urban unemployment rate	0.245*	0.243*	0.243*	0.248*	0.250*	0.247*
	(0.141)	(0.141)	(0.141)	(0.141)	(0.141)	(0.141)
Constant	−16.761	−16.362	−14.954	−13.068	−12.257	−12.281
	(20.770)	(20.828)	(20.747)	(20.730)	(20.688)	(20.661)
Province-fixed effects	✓	✓	✓	✓	✓	✓
Observations	2,793	2,793	2,793	2,793	2,793	2,793

Note: *$p < 0.1$; **$p < 0.05$; ***$p < 0.01$
This analysis excludes dark gray and medium gray provinces from Figure 10.3.
Recent protests records the number of protests in $t − 1:t − N$, for anniversary window length N.

The result was a corpus of words, by protest, that participants used to describe their demands and grievances. We conducted the analysis in Chinese, but present the results in English.

We used our measure of semantic distinctiveness to ascertain whether the language used by protesters during ethnic separatist anniversaries is different than the language employed by protesters during the rest of the year. The results appear in Figure 10.5. The left panel displays words that are distinctive to separatist anniversaries; the right panel displays words that are distinctive to other protests. There are no substantively meaningful differences in the discourse used in protests during separatist

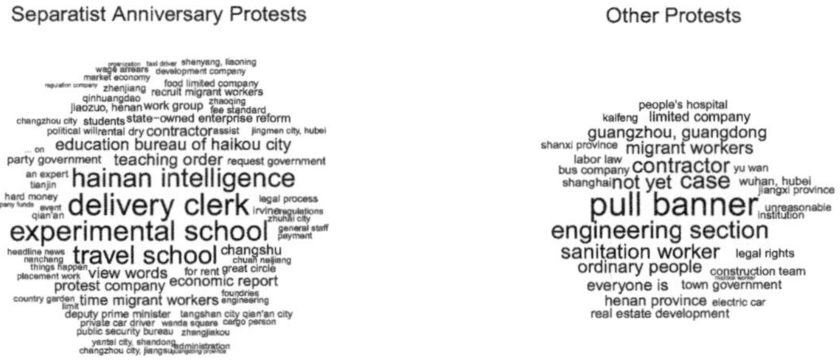

Separatist Anniversary Protests   Other Protests

Figure 10.5 Distinctive protest discourse during ethnic separatist anniversaries

anniversaries compared to protests that occur during other times of the year. The words are random, a feature of the news events that occurred in each period.

10.4.3 Results

All this suggests the plausibility of the exclusion restriction. Virtually no Chinese citizens recognized the dates of ethnic separatist anniversaries. There was no difference in the rate of repression in response to protests during ethnic separatist anniversaries. The protests that did emerge during ethnic separatist anniversaries in ethnic Han provinces were no different in character than those that emerged on other days. As an extra precaution, we focused only on eastern provinces that are ethnically and geographically distant from Xinjiang and Tibet.

The IV estimates appear in Tables 10.7 and 10.8. Models 1 through 3 use the daily number of references to "stability" as the endogenous regressor; Models 4 through 6 use the daily number of references to "harmony." Table 10.7 gives first-stage estimates; Table 10.8 gives second-stage estimates. The models pass standard weak instrument tests at the 1 percent level and Wu-Hausman consistency tests at the 10 percent level. The first stage results are consistent with those in Chapter 7. Ethnic separatist anniversaries are strongly correlated with threats, as are protests on day $t-1$.

The second-stage results suggest that propaganda-based threats reduce the daily rate of protest in provinces that are geographically and culturally distant from Tibet and Xinjiang. The results are visualized in Figure 10.6. When the *Workers' Daily* publishes the mean number of references to "stability" – 8.5 per day – the predicted number of protests over the subsequent week is twenty. At 16 references, or the

Table 10.7 *IV results, first stage*

	"Stability"			"Harmony"		
	(1)	(2)	(3)	(4)	(5)	(6)
Separatist anniversary	2.240***	2.351***	2.196***	2.060***	2.137***	1.864***
	(0.506)	(0.444)	(0.450)	(0.750)	(0.667)	(0.674)
Democratic anniversary			−0.079			−0.041
			(0.438)			(0.656)
Political anniversary			0.487*			1.639***
			(0.289)			(0.433)
Cultural anniversary			−0.687**			−1.099**
			(0.305)			(0.457)
Protests$_{t-1}$		1.872***	1.862***		1.313***	1.306***
		(0.294)	(0.294)		(0.442)	(0.441)
Log GRP			139.199***			−46.170
			(47.716)			(71.508)
Log population			−2,051.149***			−1,094.758
			(769.901)			(1,153.787)
Rural population share			−227.096			−562.187*
			(218.147)			(326.919)
Sex ratio			5,793.777***			−1,482.372
			(1,954.086)			(2,928.428)
Urban unemployment rate			12.935			10.590
			(9.288)			(13.920)
Constant	8.320***	13.884***	16,728.730**	8.750***	12.295***	15,216.800
	(0.140)	(0.361)	(7,185.216)	(0.208)	(0.542)	(10,767.890)
Year-fixed effects		✓	✓		✓	✓
Observations	3,288	3,288	3,288	3,288	3,288	3,288
R^2	0.006	0.236	0.238	0.002	0.214	0.219
F Statistic	19.588***	101.459***	78.857***	7.536***	89.218***	70.728***

Note: *p < 0.1; **p < 0.05; ***p < 0.01
This analysis excludes dark gray and medium gray provinces from Figure 10.3.

mean plus one standard deviation, the predicted number of protests over the subsequent week falls to ten. We estimated slightly larger effects for "harmony."

These effects are substantively meaningful. To halve the number of protests over the course of a subsequent week, CCP propaganda must publish eight additional references to "stability" or "harmony" on day *t*. This represents a doubling of its baseline daily rate of 8.5 "stability" references and 8.9 "harmony" references. We interpret this as reflecting a general linguistic shift toward more threatening content. The CCP issues propaganda-based threats sparingly. When it does, we find, citizens take them seriously.

Table 10.8 *IV results, second stage*

	(1)	(2)	(3)	(4)	(5)	(6)
			Dependent variable:			
			Protests$_{t+1:t+7}$			
Stability	−1.395**	−1.240***	−1.217***			
	(0.581)	(0.378)	(0.404)			
Harmony				−1.520**	−1.361**	−1.429**
				(0.700)	(0.532)	(0.634)
Democratic anniversary			5.276***			5.322***
			(0.868)			(1.157)
Political anniversary			−0.835			0.923
			(0.606)			(1.298)
Cultural anniversary			−2.246***			−2.991***
			(0.702)			(1.145)
Protests$_{t-1}$		5.287***	5.029***		4.776***	4.652***
		(0.900)	(0.930)		(1.013)	(1.117)
Log GRP			563.639***			329.643**
			(109.866)			(129.252)
Log population			−15,079.730***			14,173.780***
			(1,735.217)			(2,154.973)
Rural population share			−5,599.713***			−6,131.160***
			(440.846)			(678.882)
Sex ratio			31,526.400***			22,409.500***
			(4,517.457)			(5,243.749)
Urban unemployment rate			176.910***			176.162***
			(19.074)			(25.395)
Constant	29.263***	18.501***	140,983.300***	30.957***	17.972***	142,608.000***
	(4.945)	(5.347)	(15,750.660)	(6.252)	(6.658)	(21,364.400)
Year-fixed effects		✓	✓		✓	✓
Observations	3,273	3,273	3,273	3,273	3,273	3,273

Note: *p < 0.1; **p < 0.05; ***p < 0.01
This analysis excludes dark gray and medium gray provinces from Figure 10.3.

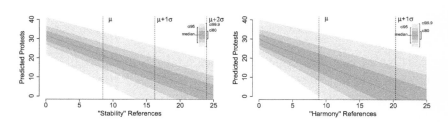

Figure 10.6 Simulated IV results

10.4.4 Robustness Checks

The Online Appendix includes a series of robustness checks. Readers may wonder whether the protest reduction in Han provinces around ethnic separatist anniversaries is generated by Tibetan and Uyghur residents who refrain from protesting because they want to avoid being branded as terrorists. We use China's most recent census data to show that migrants from Tibet and Xinjiang constitute a vanishingly small share of the population in our final province sample. Given so little out-migration from these two regions, we view this potential violation of the exclusion restriction as unlikely and certainly not capable of generating the protest reduction required to invalidate the IV estimates.

The IV estimates in Table 10.8 are robust to different modeling decisions. We varied the size of protest windows for our outcome variable. We focused only on the 2009–2012 period, before a 2013 terrorist attack in Beijing brought national attention to Uyghur separatism. We dropped Guangdong province, which experienced a Han–Uyghur factory brawl in 2009 and a terrorist attack in 2015. We also dropped the winter months, when the Lunar New Year – and associated internal travel – occasions protests by migrant laborers who are owed back pay. In each case, the IV estimates are substantively unchanged.

Finally, although we believe that controlling for political anniversaries absorbs their effects, we nonetheless dropped two separatist anniversaries due to their proximity to political anniversaries. The Tibetan Rebellion anniversary occurs on March 10, just a week after the National People's Congress opens. The Tibetan Liberation occurs on May 23, two weeks before June 4. Our results are robust to excluding these two anniversaries from the instrument.

10.4.5 Sensitivity Analysis

Conley, Hansen, and Rossi's (2012) "plausibly exogenous" method lets us measure how sensitive the IV results are to violations of the exclusion restriction. Consider the following simultaneous equation model:

$$Y = X\beta + Z\gamma + \epsilon \tag{10.6}$$

$$X = Z\lambda + v \tag{10.7}$$

where Y is the outcome, X is the endogenous treatment, β is the treatment parameter of interest, ϵ is the error term, Z is the instrument uncorrelated with ϵ, λ is the first-stage coefficient, and γ measures the extent to which the exclusion restriction is violated.

The standard exclusion restriction is equivalent to the assumption that $\gamma \equiv 0$, such that instrument Z conditions outcome Y only through its effect on X. When $\gamma \neq 0$, the exclusion restriction is subject to some violation. Conley, Hansen, and Rossi's (2012) sensitivity analysis essentially probes the effect of deviations from the dogmatic prior on γ. Put differently, Conley, Hansen, and Rossi (2012) let the exclusion restriction fail by some amount γ, and then determine the γ parameter values that make the IV estimate statistically indistinguishable from zero.[26]

Conley, Hansen, and Rossi (2012) identify two sets of methods for inference about β without assuming γ is exactly 0. The first is the "union of confidence" (UCI) approach, which estimates how large γ can be such that the negative coefficient on propaganda-based threats of repression remains statistically significant. The other approach is Bayesian. It requires that the user specify some prior distribution on γ, and then estimates whether the coefficient of interest remains statistically significant given this prior distribution. This generally produces more precise estimates, but forces the analyst to impose a prior distribution. Since Conley, Hansen, and Rossi's (2012) first approach is more conservative, we employed it. We used Clarke's (2019) `plausexog` module in Stata, and we adapted the R code from Zhu (2016). The results were identical, as expected.

In our case, we are more interested in negative values of γ, since the most likely violations of the exclusion restriction entail negative direct effects of ethnic separatist anniversaries on the rate of protest in Han-dominated provinces. Put differently, the most likely violations of the exclusion restriction – and those that would potentially explain away the IV estimates – are those that would entail negative reductions of the protest rate via ethnic separatist anniversaries, not through the propaganda-based pathway.

The results appear in Table 10.9. The top panel reports the results for the "stability" outcome; Models 1 through 3 correspond to Models 1 through 3 in Table 10.8. The bottom panel reports the results for the "harmony" outcome; Models 1 through 3 correspond to Models 4 through 6 in Table 10.8. Model 3 makes clear that for the IV estimates in the main text to be indistinguishable from zero, it must be that

---

[26] This can also be thought of as decomposing the total effect of Z on Y into an indirect effect through X and a direct effect captured by γ. This indirect effect represents the instrumented (treatment) effect, whereas the direct effect represents the effect of all violations of the exclusion restriction. When the exclusion restriction holds perfectly and $\gamma \equiv 0$, the total effect of Z and Y goes exclusively through X.

Table 10.9 *IV sensitivity analysis*

Threat measure	"Stability"		
Dependent variable	Protests (M1) (1)	Protests (M2) (2)	Protests (M3) (3)
Max γ for significant β	−1.160	−1.890	−1.585
Point estimate β ("stability")	−0.877	−0.438	−0.495
95% Confidence interval	[−1.750, −0.003]	[−0.876, −0.000]	[−0.989, −0.002]
Threat measure	"Harmony"		
Dependent variable	Protests (M4) (1)	Protests (M5) (2)	Protests (M6) (3)
Max γ for significant β	−0.455	−1.513	−0.575
Point estimate β ("harmony")	−1.298	−0.656	−1.122
95% Confidence interval	[−2.596, −0.000]	[−1.312, −0.000]	[−2.243, −0.000]

$\gamma < -1.585$. This γ value implies that violations of the exclusion restriction must be associated with more than $-1.585 \times 7 = -11.095$ fewer protests in Han-dominated provinces per (seven-day) ethnic separatist anniversary window. To put this effect into context, note that the mean number of protests in Han-dominated provinces over a given subsequent week is seventeen, with a third quartile value of twenty-seven protests. This implies that for the effect of propaganda-based threats of repression to be statistically indistinguishable from zero, exclusion restriction violations must reduce the protest rate by an amount that is 110 percent greater than the difference between the mean and third quartile values of the outcome variable. The analogous percentage reduction from Model 1 is 81.2 percent and from Model 2 is 132 percent. The results for "harmony" in the bottom panel are similar, with γ values ranging from −0.455 to −1.513.

At these critical values of γ, the IV-point estimates (β) for "stability" range from −0.438 to −0.877 and for "harmony" range from −0.656 to −1.298. Note that the analogous IV-point estimates from Table 10.8 range from −1.217 to −1.395 and from −1.361 to −1.520. This means that after we subtract the direct effect of ethnic separatist anniversaries on protests from our final province sample, the effects from the main text for "stability" are attenuated by 37 percent to 64 percent. The effects from the main text for "harmony" are somewhat less attenuated: by 14 percent to 51 percent. That is, even after subtracting a potential direct effect of ethnic separatist anniversaries on protests from our final province sample, the effect of propaganda-based threats of repression remains substantively meaningful. This suggests that the effect of propaganda-based threats on protest in Han-dominated provinces is not sensitive to reasonable violations of the exclusion restriction.

10.5 CONCLUSION

It is increasingly clear that propaganda can shape citizens' beliefs in a variety of contexts: Nazi radio broadcasts in pre–World War II Germany, the 1994 Rwandan genocide, and legislative elections in Vladimir Putin's Russia. Partisan media in democracies is similarly potent: in Brazil, Italy, Mexico, and the United States.

It should be no surprise, then, that propaganda has reduced the rate of protest across the world's autocracies as well. The effects of pro-regime propaganda across autocracies, we find, are substantively meaningful and precisely estimated. A one standard deviation increase in pro-regime propaganda has reduced the odds of protest the following day by between 7 percent and 11 percent. The half-life of propaganda in autocracies is between two and five days, strikingly similar to the half-life of campaign advertisements in democracies. Of course, since our identification strategy rests on controlling for as many observed features of the political environment as possible, we treat these results with caution.

The CCP's calendar of propaganda-based threats – which we uncovered in Chapter 7 – offers an opportunity to plausibly measure whether these threats condition citizen behavior. China is ethnically diverse and geographically sprawling, and so the ethnic separatist anniversaries that are profoundly salient in Tibet and Xinjiang are effectively unknown throughout much of the country. This is the premise of our identification strategy. Since propaganda is set at the national level but must occasionally respond to local conditions, citizens in provinces that are geographically and culturally distant from Tibet and Xinjiang are occasionally "treated" with content that is not intended for them. Our IV estimates suggest that by doubling the number of references to "stability" or "harmony," CCP propaganda halves the number of protests during the subsequent week. Conley, Hansen, and Rossi's (2012) sensitivity analysis suggests that these estimates are robust to non-trivial violations of the exclusion restriction.

Propaganda, we find, has a measurable effect on popular protest. These effects are strongest where propaganda is most effusive and most threatening.

I I

Conclusion

Many of the world's autocrats now govern with nominally democratic institutions. They abide national parliaments, organize regular elections, compete against opposition parties, and permit independent newspapers. These institutions are often at least somewhat binding. Where they are, autocrats are constrained: in their use of violence against citizens and fraud to guarantee electoral victory. These constraints ultimately determine how autocrats wage the battle for citizens' minds.

Where autocrats confront at least somewhat binding electoral constraints, they are forced to seek some amount of popular support. They employ propaganda to persuade citizens of regime merits. To be persuasive, propaganda apparatuses must enjoy some credibility. This imperative forces them to concede bad news and policy failures. They must cover devastating fuel crises, vaccine shortages, and persistently high infant mortality rates. We refer to this as honest propaganda, and it is costly. By creating common knowledge among citizens about regime failures, these admissions help citizens coordinate protests and regime insiders organize coups. Where autocrats confront no electoral constraints – where autocrats can fully secure themselves with repression and fraud – propaganda serves not to persuade citizens but to dominate them. Propaganda derives power from its absurdity. By forcing citizens to consume content that everyone knows is false, autocrats make their capacity for repression common knowledge. Put simply, the electoral constraints an autocrat confronts determine the propaganda strategy he employs. As electoral constraints grow more binding, autocrats are forced to persuade citizens rather than dominate them.

These insights help make sense of the range of propaganda that autocrats produce, as we showed in Chapters 4 through 9. We review our key findings in Section 11.2. Our theory treats nominally democratic institutions as constraints that autocrats struggle to loosen and citizens' beliefs as the central battlefield on which the struggle for political change is waged. This framework suggests important questions about autocratic politics in the early twenty-first century. Section 11.3 explores how autocrats attempt to shape citizens' beliefs by weaponizing distinctly modern technologies, not just propaganda and censorship. Section 11.4 discusses how autocrats attempt to loosen the electoral constraints that bind them. Although this book is about propaganda in autocracies, it has implications for politics in democracies, especially as "populist-authoritarian" leaders take power across Europe and North America.[1] Section 11.5 suggests, in particular, that Xi Jinping's propaganda strategy helps us understand the process of democratic erosion underway across the world. Section 11.6 discusses the book's implications for public policy.

11.2 WHAT WE LEARNED

Measuring pro-regime propaganda requires first defining what constitutes the regime. Should a measure of pro-regime propaganda focus only on the autocrat? Or should it encompass the regime more broadly, including government ministers and lower-level appointees, to whom responsibility for policy implementation falls? We accommodated both by measuring pro-regime propaganda in two ways, and the results, we showed in Chapter 4, are the same. Where electoral constraints are nonbinding, propaganda apparatuses cover the regime roughly four times more positively than Fox News covers Republicans. Where electoral constraints are more binding, propaganda apparatuses cover the regime much like Fox News covers Republicans. It is biased, but not so much that it undermines its ability to persuade.[2] To ensure these results were not driven by omitted variable bias or reverse causality, we focused on Gabon and China, for which we have propaganda data that extend back decades. When the Berlin Wall fell and the Third Wave of Democracy

---

[1] The term is from Norris (2017).
[2] DellaVigna and Kaplan (2007); Martin and Yurukoglu (2017); Ash and Galletta (2019); Bursztyn et al. (2020); Jamieson and Albarracin (2020); Simonov et al. (2020).

forced President Omar Bongo to permit democratic reforms, his propaganda strategy changed as our theory predicts. We found no such change in China, where the Third Wave of Democracy forced no such reforms. Despite the dramatic economic and social changes of recent decades, the CCP's flagship propaganda outlet is now more effusive than any point since the Cultural Revolution.

To confirm that pro-regime propaganda in unconstrained autocracies works through our hypothesized theoretical mechanism, in Chapter 4 we presented the first of the book's survey experiments. Many scholars have suggested that CCP propaganda aims to persuade citizens of regime merits, rather than, as we and Huang (2015*b*) contend, intimidate them into submission.[3] Using a list experiment embedded within a nationally representative survey, we show that preference falsification is widespread among Chinese citizens. Questioned directly, citizens were unwilling to criticize the regime. With a list experiment, they were more willing. Chinese citizens, we found, view the CCP's flagship propaganda outlet, the *People's Daily*, as intimidating, not persuasive. The CCP's local, commercialized newspapers cover non-regime topics quite objectively. Their regime content, however, is virtually identical to that of the *People's Daily*, the CCP's flagship newspaper, which is consumed regularly by more than half of all citizens.

The narratives that propaganda apparatuses craft are as important as the language with which they describe the regime. Chapter 5 focused on domestic narratives. Where autocrats confront no electoral constraints, their propaganda apparatuses trumpet their democratic credentials yet omit the stuff of democracy, like electoral campaigns and the opposition. They cover a general, unnamed "opposition" rather than the actual opposition, which would undermine absurd claims of universal support and help citizens coordinate around particular protest leaders. We observed neither of these tactics where autocrats confront electoral constraints, but neither did we observe them denigrate the opposition, since doing so would undermine claims of credibility. Electorally constrained autocrats acknowledge policy failures: fuel crises, vaccine shortages, and persistently high infant mortality rates. They acknowledge that the government has failed to adequately invest in the country's athletes.

---

[3] Brady (2002, 2006, 2008, 2012*b*); Stockmann (2010, 2013); Stockmann and Gallagher (2011); Esarey, Stockmann, and Zhang (2017); Stockmann, Esarey, and Zhang (2018); Roberts (2018); King, Pan, and Roberts (2017).

Our theory suggests two ways that propaganda narratives about international affairs are distinct from narratives about domestic conditions. Each stems from the fact that citizens know less about the former than the latter. First, without common knowledge of the possible, autocrats are unable to employ absurd propaganda, since what constitutes absurdity is unclear. Second, propaganda apparatuses are able to "get away" with more negative coverage without undermining claims to neutrality. As a result, propaganda narratives about international news are relatively similar across autocracies. Chapter 6 documented two common propaganda tactics: comparison sets and selective coverage. The Russian and Chinese propaganda apparatuses are different in many ways, but their coverage of Western democracies is strikingly similar. *Rosiyskaya Gazeta* lets Donald Trump speak for it, as he vindicates longstanding Russian claims: about the slow collapse of the European Union, the prevalence of terrorism in the West, the political allegiances of Crimeans, the misadventures of America's foreign policy, and the flaws of American democracy. The CCP's propaganda apparatus is less fond of Trump, but it covers the same issues, often with sophistication: the corruption of American democracy by monied interests and America's gun violence epidemic, which is partly driven by the outsized influence of the National Rifle Association.

As similar as international news narratives are, Chapter 6 documented important differences in how propaganda apparatuses cover international cooperation. Propaganda apparatuses in constrained autocracies emphasize the regime's pursuit of the national interest: partnering with the international community to advance living conditions or combat terrorism. Where electoral constraints are non-binding, propaganda apparatuses emphasize the regime's immunity from international pressure, either because the regime has powerful foreign backers or, as in China, the regime is so powerful that it is bending the international order to its will.

Our theory treats absurd propaganda as implicitly threatening, a signal of the regime's capacity for violence. This is why, as we showed in Chapter 4, pro-regime propaganda renders Chinese citizens less likely to protest due to fear of repression. Chapter 7 explored the politics of more explicit propaganda-based threats of repression. Though threats remind citizens of the consequences of dissent, they are costly. When propaganda apparatuses seek credibility, threatening violence makes persuading citizens of regime merits more difficult. Threats of repression may also endow certain moments or certain actions with even more significance to citizens. Accordingly, propaganda-based threats are more common where autocrats confront non-binding electoral constraints. In Cameroon, Paul Biya's propaganda apparatus issues far more threatening content in English than French, since he relies on francophone support. Even as Zine El Abidine Ben Ali was losing power in Tunisia, his propaganda apparatus conceded popular frustration and emphasized the government's determination to do better rather than advertise the military's loyalty, training, and technological prowess, all routinely cited during the succession crisis in Uzbekistan.

Where autocrats confront electoral constraints, they seek credibility to persuade citizens of useful fictions. Chapter 8 focused on propaganda campaigns during moments of tension, when credibility is most useful. Propaganda spikes, we found, are overwhelmingly associated with elections. Electoral propaganda in constrained autocracies, moreover, is profoundly different than in unconstrained autocracies. In constrained autocracies, these campaigns begin months before election day and gradually build. They cast the outcome as initially uncertain but, as citizens express different levels of enthusiasm for candidates, ultimately self-evident. Electoral propaganda campaigns are remarkably choreographed. Where electoral constraints are non-binding, the propaganda spike occurs immediately before and after election day, and in some cases the post-election spike is even greater than the pre-election spike. Propaganda spikes aim to threaten, not persuade.

In the absence of regular elections, the chief moments of political tension are anniversaries of failed pro-democracy movements, which often implicate the regime in crimes against citizens. Chapter 9 explored a trade-off. Propaganda spikes intended to threaten citizens – or even explicit threats of repression issued via the propaganda apparatus – may be useful to deter protest, but they call attention to things the regime might prefer citizens forget. To understand how repressive governments resolve this tension between memory and forgetting, we combined our propaganda data with field research in China and censorship data from Hong Kong University's Weiboscope Project. The CCP, we found, goes to extraordinary lengths to scrub the anniversaries of failed pro-democracy movements from public consciousness, and so it reserves propaganda spikes and threats of repression for major political events and the anniversaries of ethnic separatist movements. There is, however, one pro-democracy anniversary that is so powerful that the CCP knows citizens will not forget: the Tiananmen Square massacre of June 4, 1989, when around 2,000 citizens died demanding change. Since the Xinjiang Uprising of 2009, on each anniversary of the Tiananmen massacre, the CCP has used its propaganda apparatus to remind Beijing's urban class of its brutal campaign of repression against ethnic Uyghurs, millions of whom have been incarcerated in detention centers across Xinjiang. The CCP has instrumentalized this repression: to discourage the urban elite from again demanding change. We employed another survey experiment to confirm that these citizens regard references to repression in Xinjiang as profoundly threatening.

Does propaganda discourage the sorts of protests that increasingly constitute the chief threat to autocratic survival? This question was the focus of Chapter 10. Autocrats employ propaganda strategically, and so measuring the effect of propaganda on protest is complicated by two forms of bias. Regimes that employ absurd propaganda are systematically different than those that employ honest propaganda. Moments when propaganda spikes are systematically different than those when it does not. We refer to the first as "unit selection bias" and the second as "temporal selection bias." Drawing on recent research in American politics, we also probed whether the effects of propaganda persist over time. We found that pro-regime propaganda is associated with a substantively meaningful decrease in protest. By increasing the level of pro-regime propaganda by one standard deviation, contemporary autocrats have reduced the odds of protest the following day by between 7 percent and 11 percent. This effect's half-life is between two and five days, a temporal signature strikingly consistent with campaign advertisements in American politics.

Chapter 10 also probed the effects of propaganda-based threats of repression, which again is complicated by the fact that threats are strategic. Repressive governments are more likely to threaten citizens during politically sensitive moments, when frustrations are most likely to coalesce into mass protests, and in response to recent protests. This creates two competing effects on protest: a negative effect due to the threat and a positive effect due to tensions that compelled it. The CCP's calendar of propaganda-based threats, which we documented in Chapter 7, suggests a novel identification strategy. We employed an instrumental variables estimator that leveraged two features of China's political geography. First, propaganda in the *Workers' Daily* is set at the national level, but occasionally it responds to conditions in one province that are unknown in others. As a result, citizens in one province are occasionally "treated" with propaganda content intended for citizens in other provinces. Second, because China is ethnically diverse and geographically sprawling, the ethnic separatist anniversaries in Tibet and Xinjiang that drive propaganda-based threats are salient in those regions but mostly unknown elsewhere. By doubling the number of references to "stability" or "harmony," we found, the CCP halves the number of protests during the subsequent week. These estimates are robust to non-trivial violations of the exclusion restriction.

The electoral constraints an autocrat confronts determine the propaganda strategy he employs. Where electoral constraints are relatively binding, autocrats must concede bad news and policy failures, which confirm citizens' frustrations and enable them to act collectively. Where autocrats can secure themselves with fraud and repression, propaganda serves to dominate, and to make this domination common knowledge.

11.3 SHAPING THE BELIEFS THAT INSPIRE CITIZENS

11.3.1 *From Liberation Technologies to Post-Modern Totalitarianism*

In June 1989, just before the Berlin Wall collapsed, Ronald Reagan spoke at Guildhall, the 700-year-old seat of London government:

> The Goliath of totalitarian control will be brought down by the David of the microchip. ... The biggest of Big Brothers is helpless against communications technology. ... Information is the oxygen of the modern age. ... It seeps through walls topped with barbed wire. It wafts across the electrified, booby-trapped borders. Breezes of electronic beams blow through the Iron Curtain as if it was lace. ... You can't massacre an idea. You cannot run tanks over hope. You cannot riddle a people's yearning with bullets.[4]

Reagan's optimism became conventional wisdom. The first decade of the twenty-first century witnessed a wave of books that celebrated the coming revolutions: *Networks of Outrage and Hope*,[5] *The Digital Origins of Dictatorship and Democracy*,[6] *Here Comes Everybody*,[7] *Tweeting to Power*,[8] and others.[9] In March 2000, Bill Clinton dismissed the CCP's bid for internet censorship, comparing it to "trying to nail Jell-O to the wall."[10] Nicholas Kristof predicted the CCP's imminent collapse:

---

[4] Rule (1989).
[5] Castells (2012).
[6] Howard (2010).
[7] Shirky (2009).
[8] Gainous and Wagner (2013).
[9] For a different view, see Morozov (2012) and Kalathil and Boas (2002).
[10] Allen-Ebrahimian (2016).

The Communist Party's monopoly on information is crumbling, and its monopoly on power will follow. The Internet is chipping away relentlessly at the Party, for even 30,000 censors can't keep up with 120 million Chinese Netizens. With the Internet, China is developing for the first time in 4,000 years of history a powerful independent institution that offers checks and balances on the emperors. ...I don't see how the Communist Party dictatorship can long survive the Internet.[11]

Condoleezza Rice called the Internet "possibly one of the biggest tools for democratization and political freedom that we have ever seen."[12] Mark Pfeifle, then deputy national security advisor to President George W. Bush, credited Twitter with protests that rocked Iran in 2009:

When traditional journalists were forced to leave the country, Twitter became a window for the world to view hope, heroism, and horror. It became the assignment desk, the reporter, and the producer. And, because of this, Twitter and its creators are worthy of being considered for the Nobel Peace Prize.[13]

The Information Age, in short, would make the battle for citizens' minds impossible for autocrats to win. It would enable citizens to uncover regime crimes, share frustrations, organize protests, and topple governments.

A decade after Kristof predicted the CCP's collapse, *Foreign Policy* introduced readers to Lu Wei, the architect of China's internet censorship operation: "The man who nailed Jell-O to the wall." The CCP has not collapsed, and the liberation technologies that Diamond (2010) famously celebrated now underpin "post-modern totalitarianism."[14] Despite the optimism that accompanied the Information Age, autocrats appear to be winning the battle for citizens' minds, in part by exploiting distinctly modern technologies. Understanding how is a critical direction for future research.

11.3.2 *The Power of Propaganda in Cyberspace*

Social media may help citizens organize, but governments have learned to exploit it. The Iranian government used social media to identify and track dissidents during the 2009 uprisings and later to disseminate rumors that snipers were stationed along protest routes and were ordered to shoot. As the Tahrir protests raged in 2011, Hosni Mubarak's government used

---

[11] Kristof (2006).
[12] Soriano (2013).
[13] Pfeifle (2009).
[14] Rod and Weidmann (2015); Diamond (2019b).

Twitter bots to claim that anti-government protests had been canceled. Observers of Chinese politics long suspected that the regime maintains a "50 Cent Party," comprising millions of anonymous citizens who are paid to produce pro-regime content. Using a series of computational techniques and leaked 50 Cent social media posts, King, Pan, and Roberts (2017) find that cyberspace propaganda spikes during politically sensitive moments, much like propaganda in the CCP's flagship platforms, as we showed in Chapter 9. They call this "cheerleading" or "distraction."

Cyberspace propaganda, our theory suggests, is distinct from print propaganda in ways that make it potent. Cyberspace lets propagandists conceal their identities: to conceal the fact that the authors of propaganda are its chief beneficiaries. Where political institutions compel propaganda apparatuses to generate credibility, it is precisely the autocrat's inability to conceal his identity as author that forces him to concede regime failures. The anonymity of cyberspace propaganda makes it potent because it frees the authors of propaganda from the constraints of Bayesian rationality. It enables them to be more forceful in their claims, without the concomitant loss in credibility. Freed from the constraints of Bayesian rationality, propaganda intended to persuade can concede fewer regime failures and trumpet more good news. Cyberspace propaganda is potent in ways that print, radio, and television propaganda is not.

Our theory suggests a different explanation for the 50 Cent Party. We believe it exists to persuade citizens that the regime enjoys genuine support, which makes organizing collective action dangerous. Its anonymity lets the CCP government pair absurdity in official propaganda – which is intended to dominate – with cyberspace propaganda that fosters genuine uncertainty about the CCP's true popular support. Still, it remains unclear which autocrats employ cyberspace propaganda, what explains this variation, and what effects it has on domestic politics.

11.3.3 *Internet Shutdowns*

Kristof's optimism about the Information Age was premised on the Internet's independence from government intrusion. But the Internet, we are learning, is not so independent. Between 2012 and 2014, internet shutdowns numbered roughly 20 per year, and in 2015 rose slightly to 33. In 2016, the number spiked to 75 and in 2017 reached 109.[15] Some of

---

[15] Rydzak (2019a).

these shutdowns have been temporally and geographically sophisticated. During sensitive anniversaries in China, for instance, the CCP routinely blocks internet access in Xinjiang, Tibet, and counties in neighborhood provinces. During Tiananmen anniversaries, it throttles internet speeds nationwide by around 15 percent.

The conditions under which governments block internet access are not well understood, but we believe a theory should incorporate the incentives of politics and the constraints of decentralization. Internet shutdowns are more common in autocracies than democracies, especially in Central Africa.[16] On March 28, 2018, Idriss Déby ordered Chad's two major telecom companies to block social media, an effort to quell protests over constitutional reforms that positioned Déby to rule until 2033.[17] The ban remained in place for sixteen months. Between January 2017 and March 2018, Paul Biya blocked the Internet in parts of Cameroon for roughly 230 days.[18] The ease with which governments block the Internet is partly determined by the regulatory frameworks they confront. In November 2012, Renesys, an internet services firm, estimated a country's vulnerability to internet shutdowns based on how many firms hold "licenses to carry voice and Internet traffic to and from the outside world, and are required by law to mediate access for everyone else."[19] We suspect that internet shutdowns are most likely where governments confront the threat of protest and weak regulatory institutions.

We know little about the effects of internet shutdowns on politics. Do internet shutdowns impede collective action? Do internet shutdowns increase the rate of repression? Are governments increasingly building internet platforms that maximize their control? Counterintuitively, Ogola (2019) suggests that internet shutdowns may "encourage precisely the kind of responses considered subversive by many governments." Similarly, in India, Rydzak (2019b) finds that internet shutdowns have rendered riots more likely, not less. Causality is difficult to establish, however, since governments may block the Internet because they anticipate riots. There is also some evidence that China's internet control regime is emerging as a model for other autocracies.[20] In February 2019,

---

[16] Dahir (2019); Collaboration on International ICT Policy for East and Southern Africa (2019).
[17] Dahir (2018a).
[18] Dahir (2018b).
[19] Garber (2012).
[20] Weber (2017).

Vladimir Putin's government presented a draft law that would require internet service providers to direct data through government-controlled routing points, which the BBC describes as "part of an effort to set up a mass censorship system akin to that seen in China, which tries to scrub out prohibited traffic."[21] This would also let the Putin government block internet access altogether.

11.3.4 Beliefs, Repression, and Surveillance

Sections 11.3.2 and 11.3.3 focused on how autocrats use digital technology to shape citizens' beliefs about other citizens' beliefs. The world's autocrats are also using digital technology to shape citizens' beliefs about the consequences of dissent. For an autocrat, it is arguably more important for citizens to believe dissent will be repressed than for dissent to actually be repressed. Before the Information Age, autocrats could threaten repression by deploying security forces, persuading citizens of an extensive secret police, or creating a network of informants. Each of these, however, is costly. Security forces must be maintained, loyalty must be purchased, and compatriots must be incentivized to inform on each other.

The Information Age is revolutionizing surveillance in ways that let autocrats shape citizens' beliefs about the consequences of dissent. Again, the CCP's surveillance regime has emerged as a model. Launched in 2005, the CCP announced the completion of its "Sky Net" program in 2017, with 176 million surveillance cameras across China and plans for 626 million by 2020, or nearly one camera for every two citizens.[22] The result, according to Qiang (2019), is "the largest video surveillance network in the world." In 2015, the regime described its Beijing surveillance apparatus:

Beijing police have covered every corner of the capital with a video surveillance system, according to the Beijing Public Security Bureau. The complete coverage by the video system … is part of a move to tighten the capital's security. … The number of surveillance cameras on streets across the city has increased 29 percent year-on-year. The video surveillance system has covered 100 percent of the capital, the first time that the system has provided complete coverage.[23]

---

[21] Kleinman (2019).
[22] Russell (2017); Hersey (2017); Qiang (2019).
[23] Cao (2015).

The CCP paired this with massive investments in facial recognition technology and a facial database of every adult citizen.[24] In Xinjiang alone, the regime budgeted more than $1 billion for "security-related investment" in the first quarter of 2017.[25] The CCP also maintains a DNA database that encompasses 54 million citizens and, by 2020, will reportedly reach 100 million.[26]

The conspicuous feature of this surveillance apparatus is how the CCP advertises it. In August 2015, the propaganda apparatus released a map of central Beijing that identified "over 46,000 surveillance cameras."[27] In April 2017, the CCP applied its facial recognition technology to detecting jaywalkers and now notifies offenders via text message. Since text messages are private, they do not create common knowledge about the system's efficacy. Therefore, the regime also displays pictures of offenders in major intersections.[28] In March 2018, the *Worker's Daily* announced that this facial recognition system "can accurately identify people's faces from different angles and lighting conditions, . . . scan China's population in just one second, and . . . scan the world's population" in "two seconds." "Speed does not affect the system's accuracy. Its accuracy rate is up to 99.8 percent even if the person is in motion."[29] Digital surveillance is now central to everyday life. The CCP's facial recognition technology is employed for check-in and security at airports,[30] train stations,[31] and hotels.[32] It is even sometimes used to track toilet paper consumption in public restrooms.[33]

The CCP is exporting surveillance technology abroad. The list of known recipient governments is long: Angola, Bolivia, Cameroon, Congo, Ecuador, Egypt, Ethiopia, Malaysia, Mauritius, Rwanda, Saudi Arabia, Serbia, Tanzania, Uganda, United Arab Emirates, Venezuela, Zambia, and Zimbabwe, and there are surely many others.[34] Again,

---

[24] Chin and Lin (2017).
[25] Feldstein (2019).
[26] Qiang (2019).
[27] Huang (2015c).
[28] Li (2018).
[29] Zhao (2018).
[30] Dai (2018); Yang (2018).
[31] Chen, Jing, and Dai (2018).
[32] Chan (2018a).
[33] Chan (2018b).
[34] Sherman and Morgus (2018); Mozur, Kessel, and Chan (2019), as well as conversations with anonymous senior Western diplomats.

the conspicuous feature of these surveillance technologies is how govern-ments advertise them. In Venezuela, China's ZTE has helped the Chavez and Maduro governments create a national ID card – the "fatherland card" – that records voting behavior, personal finances, and medical histories. Said one technical advisor, who was accused of treason af-ter he objected: "What we saw in China changed everything. … They were looking to have citizen control."[35] On February 17, 2017, one month into the internet shutdown in the anglophone regions, Paul Biya's *Cameroon Tribune* devoted its entire front page to a single headline: "Se-curity Reinforcement: The Video Surveillance Option." It announced a contract between the government and Huawei Technologies that pro-vided for "1,500 cameras in regional capitals and certain strategic points in the country," "2,000 portable listening devices … equipped with cameras," and "the construction of nine command centers." The same month, the Serbian government announced Huawei would install facial and license plate recognition software in 800 locations in Belgrade, part of Huawei's "Safe City Solution."[36]

This book treats autocratic politics as a struggle for citizens' beliefs. In our view, there are no questions more important than those that probe how autocrats attempt to manipulate those beliefs. The novelty of these efforts requires scholars to ask novel questions. Which autocrats em-ploy these sophisticated surveillance devices? Where? Do these devices induce changes in citizen behavior? Do these devices enable autocrats to make other changes to their repressive apparatuses? Xu's (2021) work on the CCP's Golden Shield Project suggests these unprecedented dig-ital surveillance technologies enable autocrats to target repression and hence provide fewer public goods. These are critical directions for future research.

11.4 LOOSENING THE CONSTRAINTS THAT EMPOWER CITIZENS

Our approach to autocratic politics calls attention to how autocrats at-tempt to weaken the constraints that bind them. They do so, in part, by changing the institutional rules. In 2016 alone, five of Africa's au-tocrats either removed term limits or suspended elections altogether.[37]

---

[35] Berwick (2018).

[36] Le Corre and Vuksanovic (2019); Trevisan (2018).

[37] Pierre Nkurunziza of Burundi, Idriss Déby of Chad, Paul Kagame of Rwanda, Denis Sassou Nguesso of Congo, Ali Bongo of Gabon, and Joseph Kabila of the DRC.

Since elections constitute focal moments for protest, Africa's autocrats have also lengthened presidential terms. Another way to weaken electoral constraints is to undercut the external forces that sometimes reinforce them. These efforts are central to modern autocratic politics but poorly understood. Three tactics seem especially salient.

11.4.1 Outward-Facing Propaganda

The world's autocrats have launched a massive propaganda effort to shape the beliefs of citizens in the world's democracies. The Russian government has conducted social media operations in the United States for Donald Trump,[38] in the UK for Brexit,[39] in Germany for Alternative for Germany,[40] and in France for Marine Le Pen.[41] The Russian government operates Sputnik and RT (formerly Russia Today), which, in 2013, became the first news platform to surpass 1 billion views on YouTube.[42] The Saudi government sponsors Al Arabiya; the North Korean government publishes the *Pyongyang Times*; and the CCP government publishes the *China Daily*, which circulates widely in Washington. The CCP also maintains a news network, CGTN, which reaches 30 million American households and "cuts away when wind musses [Xi Jinping's] hair."[43] More insidiously, CGTN presents the CCP's forced labor camps for ethnic Uyghers as "successful vocational training centers," for which Uyghers are "grateful."[44] Turkish president Recep Tayyip Erdogan launched TRT World in 2015. It broadcasts in English twenty-four hours a day from bureaus in Istanbul, Washington, London, and Singapore. Paul Biya and Teodoro Obiang, who have ruled Cameroon and Equatorial Guinea, respectively, for a cumulative seventy-five years, jointly own Africa 24. Denis Sassou Nguesso

---

[38] Bessi and Ferrara (2016); Kollanyi, Howard, and Woolley (2016); Van Herpen (2016); Morgan and Shaffer (2017); Howard et al. (2018); Benkler et al. (2018); Woolley and Guilbeault (2018); Badawy, Ferrara, and Lerman (2018); Stewart, Arif, and Starbird (2018); Linvill et al. (2019); Bastos and Farkas (2019); Woolley and Howard (2018); Golovchenko et al. (2020).

[39] Howard and Kollanyi (2016).

[40] Woolley and Guilbeault (2018).

[41] Ferrara (2020).

[42] Wakabayashi and Confessore (2017).

[43] Mozur (2019). For more on the CCP government's other influence operations, see Diamond and Schell (2019) and Diamond (2019a).

[44] Mozur (2019). For more on the forced labor camps, see Buckley and Ramzy (2018); Samuel (2018); Cumming-Bruce (2018); Duxfield and Burrows (2019).

lured Euronews's Africa subsidiary, Africanews, to Brazzaville by offering them a gleaming skyscraper along the Congo River. Sassou Nguesso also financed *Forbes Afrique*, which circulates among Africa's financial elite.[45] In Latin America, Hugo Chavez launched Telesur in 2005, "a Latin socialist answer to CNN." Though the Venezuelan government is its primary funder, Telesur receives financial support from the governments of Cuba, Nicaragua, Uruguay, and Bolivia.

Inspired by Russia's effort to manipulate elections in Western democracies, observers have studied RT's objectives,[46] content,[47] and impact.[48] Yet outward-facing propaganda apparatuses are apparently common.[49] It remains unclear which autocrats undertake them, why, or when. It is unclear whether they work, although their prevalence suggests so. In 2011, Russian president Vladimir Putin spent $1.4 billion on outward-facing propaganda, more than on programs to curb domestic unemployment.[50] If outward-facing propaganda were not effective, surely Putin would not finance it.

Why do autocrats employ outward-facing propaganda? One possibility is that it aims to improve a country's image abroad. Ioffe (2010) suggests that RT "was conceived as a soft-power tool ... to counter the anti-Russian bias the Kremlin saw in the Western media." This is precisely how RT's founding director described it: "Our goal is still to provide unbiased information about Russia to the rest of the world."[51] Another senior executive put it similarly: "Unfortunately, at the level of mass consciousness in the West, Russia is associated with three words: communism, snow and poverty. We would like to present a more complete picture."[52] Image laundering appears to be a chief objective for Africa's autocrats. In its first issue, in 2011, Denis Sassou Nguesso's *Forbes Afrique* announced that he "has worked tirelessly to bring back hope for 3.5 million compatriots." Africa 24 reliably emphasizes efforts

---

[45] Carter and Carter (2021*a*).

[46] Osborn (2005); Ioffe (2010); Pomerantsev and Weiss (2014); Pomerantsev (2015*a*); Rawnsley (2015); Yablokov (2015); Walker (2015); Van Herpen (2016); Qiu (2017); Ziegler (2017); Carter and Carter (2021*a*).

[47] Nelson, Orttung, and Livshen (2015); Kragh and Asberg (2017); Carter and Carter (2021*a*).

[48] Morgan (2014); Erickson (2017); Mickiewicz (2017); Fock (2018); Carter and Carter (2021*a*).

[49] Brady (2015) focuses on China.

[50] Van Herpen (2016).

[51] Ioffe (2010).

[52] Osborn (2005).

by Paul Biya and Teodoro Obiang to "fight corruption" and foster economic growth, but it covers politics and economics elsewhere with relative objectivity. Brady (2015) treats China's outward-facing propaganda, which routinely fosters the notion of a "Chinese Dream," as an effort to placate concerns about its military expansion.[53] The CCP's outward-facing propaganda may aim to cultivate a constituency for Chinese investment, which may be particularly useful in societies where it is politically contentious, either because Chinese firms have a poor labor record or because they prop up repressive governments. This may explain why, in 2013, an investment arm of the Chinese government purchased 20 percent of South Africa's largest domestic media organization.[54]

Alternatively, outward-facing propaganda may aim to foster disinformation in a foreign target population. In 2015, Russian bots persuaded enough Americans that the Jade Helm military exercises in central Texas were part of Barack Obama's plot to enact martial law that Texas governor Greg Abbott had the State Guard "monitor" them.[55] For Yablokov (2015), disinformation campaigns aim to reshape geopolitics. After the Cold War, when the Russian government was unable to compete with the United States for global dominance, it turned to containment: "the division of the world into the 'majority' of nations led by Russia against the nations of the so-called 'New World Order' led by the US." By casting "Russia as a 'speaker' on behalf of the third-world nations excluded from the US-led 'New World Order'," RT enables the Putin government to exert geopolitical influence beyond its military capacity.[56]

Disinformation campaigns may also attempt to undermine trust in democratic institutions,[57] which might yield several benefits to autocratic governments. If Western voters can be persuaded that democracy is less worthy of promotion, then autocrats may confront less pressure from Western governments to permit democratic reforms. Likewise, negative coverage about a target country's domestic politics could shape opinions in the target country about international engagement: about whether the target country's government should focus more on domestic issues than on democracy promotion. If so, disinformation campaigns

---

[53] For more on the CCP's outward-facing propaganda, see Edney (2014) and Rawnsley (2015).

[54] McKune (2013).

[55] Largey (2018), (Qiu 2017).

[56] This is how Rawnsley (2015) understands RT as well.

[57] Pomerantsev and Weiss (2014); Pomerantsev (2015a); Walker (2015); Ziegler (2017).

may compel citizens in target countries to favor withdrawing from global leadership.[58]

Which governments employ outward-facing propaganda? Why? If outward-facing propaganda aims to persuade foreign citizens of useful fictions, our theory should explain its content. Outward-facing propaganda, our theory suggests, should be premised on honest propaganda and so strive for credibility. There is some evidence of this. The *China Daily*, published in English, routinely broadcasts the country's social ills, putting them on display for the world. Of course, the *China Daily* is propaganda, and so, as our theory predicts, it balances admissions of China's social ills with occasional claims that the "Tiananmen massacre is a myth."[59]

Does outward-facing propaganda work? Many observers are skeptical. In 2014, Nicholas Kristof dismissed RT as "a Russian propaganda arm." He continued: "I don't think it's going to matter very much."[60] In 2017, the *Washington Post* was even sharper: "If Russia Today is Moscow's propaganda arm, it's not very good at its job."[61] Not everyone shares this skepticism. David Remnick, editor of the *New Yorker*, called RT "darkly, nastily brilliant, so much more sophisticated than Soviet propaganda."[62] Policymakers in Eastern Europe, whose interests are most threatened by Russian aggression, are also concerned. In 2014, the Lithuanian minister for foreign affairs said that "Russia Today's propaganda machine is no less destructive than military marching in Crimea."[63] Informative too are the revealed preferences of autocrats themselves. They invest in it.

11.4.2 Foreign Money in Western Democracies

The world's autocrats also attempt to loosen institutional constraints is by purchasing influence in Western capitals. Two influence strategies seem particularly important.

---

[58] Carter and Carter (2021*a*).

[59] Flock (2011).

[60] Morgan (2014).

[61] Erickson (2017). For more skepticism, see Mickiewicz (2017) and Engelhart (2015).

[62] Pomerantsev and Weiss (2014). For a similar argument, see Fock (2018); Erlanger (2017).

[63] Pomerantsev and Weiss (2014).

First, Africa's autocrats have long hired Washington lobbyists to advance their political interests. Denis Sassou Nguesso is especially prolific. By 2000, Congo was the world's most heavily indebted country per capita, due largely to Sassou Nguesso's economic mismanagement in the 1980s. To secure debt relief, Sassou Nguesso had to persuade the IMF and World Bank that, following debt relief and despite all evidence to the contrary, he would direct money to anti-poverty programs that would otherwise have gone to debt service. In 2008, Sassou Nguesso paid nearly $4 million to four lobbying firms. They met with members of Congress, their staffs, and executive branch officials some 1,500 times. They organized a congressional letter-writing campaign to the White House, where Sassou Nguesso pressed his case before George W. Bush. After modest reforms, Sassou Nguesso received debt relief in 2010. The lobbyists also drafted language for a bill, the Stop the Vulture Funds Act, which "would prohibit U.S. citizens from trying to profit from defaulted sovereign debt and bar U.S. courts from acting on cases filed by sovereign debt profiteers."[64] Less pejoratively, the bill would have deprived American citizens of the ability to force Sassou Nguesso to repay his debts in American courts. Sassou Nguesso's lobbyists persuaded Rep. Maxine Waters to sponsor it and met with her staff on more than forty separate occasions and her twice.[65] For Sassou Nguesso, the $4 million bill from 2008 represented just 1 percent of the amount of oil revenue that went missing from the treasury each year in the early 2000s.[66]

Similar lobbying campaigns were employed by Gabonese president Ali Bongo during his 2016 presidential election; by Teodoro Obiang after brutal crackdowns in 2004 and 2009; and by Paul Biya since October 2016, as his government has sought to repress anglophone citizens. The CCP is equally prolific. Hikvision is a state-owned firm that manufactures facial surveillance cameras. After it was banned from U.S. government contracts in summer 2008, it hired four Washington lobbying firms to get the ban lifted.[67] These lobbying campaigns are legal, cheap, and understudied. Which autocrats employ them? When? Do they work? Civil society activists believe so. "Are [Washington lobbyists] enabling

---

[64] Narayanswamy (2009).
[65] Leonnig (2010) and Carter (2018).
[66] Global Witness (2004, 2005, 2007).
[67] The firms are Sidley Austin, the Glover Park Group, Burston-Marteller, and Mercury Public Affairs.

a dictatorship to get away with atrocities?" one Equatoguinean asylee asked rhetorically. "That's exactly why they're hired."[68]

Second, autocrats have sought to purchase influence in Western capitals by investing in electoral campaigns, either with cash or in-kind contributions. This captured the world's attention in 2016, when Donald Trump's surrogates passed polling data to the Russian government, which it used for social media targeting. Putin reportedly helped finance Marine Le Pen's campaign for the French presidency in 2017 and Matteo Salvini's campaign for Italy's European parliamentary election in 2019.[69] Central Africa's autocrats have funded French election campaigns since the 1970s. Former Gabonese president Omar Bongo figured prominently. "Am I of the right, the left, or the center?" Bongo once asked rhetorically. "No, I have friends everywhere."[70] French lawyer Robert Bourgi ferried cash from Central Africa to former French president Jacques Chirac and estimated that Central Africa's autocrats contributed roughly $10 million to Chirac's 2002 election campaign. In 2011, Bourgi was clear about what they received in return: "France would close its eyes to certain abuses of power in Africa."[71] Civil society leaders in Benin and Ghana suspect their presidential candidates now accept money from Central Africa as well.[72] Since these campaigns are surreptitious, there is no reliable data about which governments fund which politicians, when, or to what effect.

11.4.3 *Undermining International Institutions*

Finally, the world's autocrats have sought to undermine international institutions that might constrain them. Africa's autocrats target the African Union (AU). Of the eleven AU chairs since 2009, just three were legitimately elected domestically. The list of AU chairs includes Africa's most repressive autocrats: Muammar Gaddafi, Teodoro Obiang, Robert Mugabe, Idriss Déby, and Paul Kagame, among others. In addition to validating obviously fraudulent elections, the AU is gutting the African Commission on Human and People's Rights (ACHPR), which has proven

---

[68] Quinn (2015).
[69] Gatehouse (2017); Alvarez (2018); Sonne (2018); Tizian and Vergine (2019); Tondo and Giuffrida (2019); Nadeau (2019).
[70] French (1995); Heilbrunn (2014); Carter (2018).
[71] Valdiguié (2001); Carter (2018).
[72] Interview with anonymous civil society leaders in Accra, Ghana, in March 2018.

willing to sanction member governments.[73] In 2016, under Idriss Déby's leadership, Africa's autocrats tried to engineer a coordinated withdrawal from the International Criminal Court, which Africa's democracies rebuffed. By withdrawing collectively, Africa's autocrats hoped, they could conceal that the withdrawal was about avoiding accountability rather than a principled stand against the ICC's alleged racism.[74]

Reflecting the optimism of the early 2000s, Johnston (2008) argued that China would be socialized by international institutions into adopting a more cooperative foreign policy. Instead, the CCP government is refashioning the international order to privilege sovereignty over human rights norms. This effort has two components. First, like its counterparts in Central Africa, the CCP government has moved to gut existing institutions that might prove constraining. Its principal target is the UN Human Rights Council, to which it was elected in 2006, re-elected in 2010, elected again in 2014, and re-elected in 2017.[75] Russia and Saudi Arabia have been crucial partners. Second, the CCP has created new, competing institutions. The Asian Infrastructure Investment Bank and the Belt and Road Initiative rival the IMF and World Bank; the Shanghai Cooperation Organization claims to rival NATO. These institutions prop up member governments, induce them to support Chinese priorities in the UN, and compel multilateral donors to weaken the political conditions they require in exchange for aid.[76]

Since the Berlin Wall collapsed, scholars have sought to understand how the rules-based international order constrained the world's autocrats.[77] Increasingly, autocrats are attempting to undermine it. Which autocrats make sustained efforts to undermine the rules-based international order? When? How do these efforts condition domestic politics?

11.5 ABSURDITY, THE "BIG LIE," AND DEMOCRATIC DECAY

This book is about propaganda in autocracies, but politics in democracies has been implicit throughout. We scaled autocratic propaganda with our Fox News index, which, notwithstanding claims of fairness

---

[73] Kode (2018).

[74] Keppler (2017); Gumede (2018).

[75] Piccone (2018).

[76] Brazys, Elkink, and Kelly (2017); Dreher et al. (2019); Bader (2015); Flores-Macías and Kreps (2013); Dreher, Sturm, and Vreeland (2009).

[77] On the constraining effects of the ICC, see Jo and Simmons (2016) and Dancy and Montal (2017).

and balance, is premised on Fox News's Republican slant. Among our key findings is that in the presence of electoral constraints, propaganda apparatuses cover their regimes roughly as positively as Fox News covers Republicans. Donald Trump also figured prominently in Chapter 6, which documented how Vladimir Putin's propaganda apparatus used his ascension to validate its narrative about the flaws of Western democracy and the decline of the liberal order.

In 2015, Larry Diamond suggested the world was experiencing "a mild but protracted democratic recession," which began around 2006.[78] He located the recession in sub-Saharan Africa and several "strategic swing states" with regional influence. Democratic erosion has spread to the West as well. In Hungary and Poland, democratically elected governments have undermined the judiciary, media, and academic freedom, all while forging a voting bloc that prevents EU sanctions.[79] Norris (2017) refers to France's Marine Le Pen, Netherland's Geert Wilders, Italy's Matteo Salvini, and Germany's AfD as "populist-authoritarian." Each has made substantial electoral gains.[80] These gains have been especially pronounced in Italy, where Salvini's far-right La Lega and Luigi Di Maio's far-left Five Star formed a coalition government in 2018. Salvini quotes Italy's former Fascist dictator Benito Mussolini approvingly, including on the anniversary of his birth: "Many enemies, much honor."[81] Donald Trump has undermined many democratic norms.[82] Anne Applebaum, whose account of the Soviet Gulag won the 2004 Pulitzer Prize and who later chronicled the Iron Curtain's imposition across Eastern Europe,[83] warned in October 2018 that "the worst is yet to come."[84] "Given the right conditions, any society can turn against democracy. Indeed, if history is anything to go by, all societies eventually will."

These leaders share many similarities, among them a proclivity for obvious lies and absurdity. Accordingly, in November 2016, the Oxford English Dictionary named "post-truth" its word of the year. Trump's rhetoric compelled the *Washington Post* fact checker to create a new category, "the Bottomless Pinocchio, ... awarded to politicians

---

[78] Diamond (2015, 144).

[79] Ost (2016); Bustikova and Guasti (2017); Bogaards (2018); Cianetti, Dawson, and Hanley (2018); Krekó and Enyedi (2018); Enyedi (2018).

[80] For more, see Foa and Mounk (2016, 2017); Voeten (2017).

[81] Squires (2018).

[82] Levy (2016); Levitsky and Ziblatt (2018); Frum (2018).

[83] Applebaum (2003, 2012).

[84] Applebaum (2018).

who repeat a false claim so many times that they are ... engaging in campaigns of disinformation."[85] Applebaum (2018) and Snyder (2021) call these absurdities the "big lie." In Hungary, Viktor Orbán's big lie is premised on anti-semitism: George Soros is "plotting to bring down the nation through the deliberate importation of migrants."[86] To block him, among other things, the Orban government effectively shut down Central European University. In Poland, the Law and Justice Party's big lie is the Smolensk conspiracy theory. The plane crash that killed President Lech Kaczyński was orchestrated alternately by the Russian government or the opposition, not a result of poor flight conditions, as the recovered black box revealed.

One explanation for rhetorical strategies premised on "a big lie" is that aspiring autocrats believe their supporters are credulous. Their supporters may be so trusting that they believe anything, even statements that are obviously self-serving. Another explanation is that aspiring autocrats are exploiting a news media that reports "both sides" without explicitly calling out lies. By shifting political discourse to an extreme, these leaders may exploit low-information voters, who update their beliefs by "splitting the difference": by finding a new midpoint between rhetoric from the political left and political right.

Masha Gessen is a Russian American journalist, activist, and outspoken critic of Vladimir Putin and Donald Trump.[87] In 2017, she offered this explanation for Trump's obvious lies:

I think he has a very strong instinct for using lying to assert power. Every time he lies, especially when he lies about something really obvious – like the size of the Inauguration – he's saying "I can say whatever I want, whenever I want to, and there's nothing you can do about it." He has a finely honed sense for power and manipulation.[88]

We agree. But our theory suggests that the appropriate reference for Donald Trump's rhetorical strategy – his obvious lies, which he asks acolytes to repeat and constituents to endorse – is not Vladimir Putin's propaganda strategy, as Gessen suggests, but Xi Jinping's propaganda strategy.

---

[85] Kessler (2018*a*).
[86] Applebaum (2018).
[87] Gessen (2012, 2014).
[88] Clifton (2017).

Democracies increasingly die not because militaries topple them but because democratically elected leaders undermine them.[89] Judiciaries and security forces are packed with loyalists. Electoral rules are changed to enshrine a parliamentary majority. Media freedom is curtailed. Freedom of association is restricted to such a degree that protests are virtually illegal. These power grabs succeed, Svolik (2020) suggests, when voters fail to punish elected leaders for attempting them. This failure is most likely – and hence these power grabs most successful – when societies are polarized. More committed to partisanship than democracy, the aspiring autocrat's voters effectively choose the erosion of democratic institutions over a democratically elected president of another party.

To execute this power grab, the aspiring autocrat must first determine whether his aides and constituents will consent. This is our explanation for Donald Trump's obvious lies and the big lies of Hungary's Viktor Orbán and Poland's Law and Justice Party: By asking his acolytes to lie obviously – and to repeat or defend his obvious lies – the aspiring autocrat lets them signal whether they privilege political power over democracy. By asking his acolytes to incur the stigma of doing so, he forecloses their ability to seek opportunities beyond him, which binds them closer.[90] By asking his voters to choose partisanship over democracy, he tests whether they will penalize him at the ballot box.

Timothy Snyder (2017), an historian of twentieth century Central Europe, wrote in *On Tyranny* that "post-truth is pre-fascism." "To abandon facts is to abandon freedom."[91] We agree, though our theory suggests something more precise. To abandon facts is to determine whether one's allies are willing to privilege power over democracy. The appropriate reference for Donald Trump's rhetorical strategy is Xi Jinping's propaganda strategy.

11.6 BRINGING DOWN THE DICTATOR

Instead of liberating citizens, the Information Age has given autocrats powerful tools to shape citizens' beliefs about the depth of popular

---

[89] Bermeo (2016); Kaufman and Haggard (2018); Levitsky and Ziblatt (2018); Svolik (2020).

[90] Many of Donald Trump's aides, present and former, have been subjected to stigma. Press Secretary Sarah Huckabee Sanders was denied service at a Virginia restaurant. Her predecessor, Sean Spicer, was reportedly unable to find a TV job for "lack of credibility." For more, see Lovelace (2018).

[91] See also Levy (2016).

frustration and the consequences of dissent. How can the international community help citizens topple repressive governments?

Scholars increasingly question whether the world's democracies should attach political conditions to development aid and debt relief. Lust-Okar (2006) put the new conventional wisdom succinctly: "The logic of authoritarian elections should lead us to question the value of pressing for, and applauding, the introduction of elections in authoritarian regimes." We disagree. The world's democracies cannot turn Denis Sassou Nguesso into a democrat. But they can tilt the battlefield on which the struggle for political change is waged. In autocracies, regular elections empower citizens in least two ways. First, they constitute focal moments for collective action when citizens are engaged in politics and aware of their shared discontent. Second, when electoral constraints are at least somewhat binding, autocrats are forced into an information strategy that requires them to concede bad news and policy failures. These concessions are dangerous. By making vaccine shortages and fuel crises common knowledge among citizens, autocrats risk turning frustration into collective action.

To be sure, autocrats attempt to use these institutions to their advantage. But there is a profound difference between choosing nominally democratic institutions and making the best of them. As we documented in Section 11.4, the world's autocrats have sought to undermine nominally democratic institutions. They lengthen presidential terms, abolish term limits, and suspend elections. They undertake sophisticated propaganda campaigns in Western democracies, finance the electoral campaigns of Western politicians, hire lobbyists, and undermine international institutions that espouse human rights norms. Citizens' minds constitute the chief battleground on which the struggle for political change is waged. By insisting on regular elections – and doing whatever it can to make them as binding as possible – the international community can tilt the odds in citizens' favor.

References

Abad-Santos, Alexander. 2013. "China Is Censoring Jokes About Its Propaganda Machine's Penis-Shaped HQ." *The Atlantic* May 3.

Acemoglu, Daron. 2005. "Politics and Economics in Weak and Strong States." *Journal of Monetary Economics* 52(7):1199–1226.

Acemoglu, Daron and James A. Robinson. 2005. *Economic Origins of Dictatorship and Democracy.* New York: Cambridge University Press.

Acemoglu, Daron and James A. Robinson. 2012. *Why Nations Fail: The Origins of Power, Prosperity, and Poverty.* New York: Crown Business.

Acemoglu, Daron and James A. Robinson. 2019. *The Narrow Corridor: States, Societies, and the Fate of Liberty.* New York: Penguin.

Acemoglu, Daron, James A. Robinson and Thierry Verdier. 2004. "Kleptocracy and Divide-and-Rule: A Model of Personal Rule." *Journal of the European Economic Association* 2(2–3):162–192.

Acemoglu, Daron, Simon Johnson, and James A. Robinson. 2001. "Colonial Origins of Comparative Development." *American Economic Review* 91(5):1369–1401.

Achen, Christopher H. and Larry M. Bartels. 2004. "Musical Chairs: Pocketbook Voting and the Limits of Democratic Accountability." Presented at the Annual Meeting of the American Political Science Association.

Adena, Maja, Ruben Enikolopov, Maria Petrova, Veronica Santarosa, and Ekaterina Zhuravskaya. 2015. "Radio and the Rise of the Nazis in Prewar Germany." *Quarterly Journal of Economics* 130(4):1885–1939.

AFP. 2015. "China's Drive to Settle New Wave of Migrants in Restive Xinjiang." *South China Morning Post* May 8.

Aggarwal, Charu C. and ChengXiang Zhai, eds. 2012. *Mining Text Data.* Boston: Springer.

Aidt, Toke S. and Gabriel Leon. 2016. "The Democratic Window of Opportunity: Evidence from Riots in Sub-Saharan Africa." *Journal of Conflict Resolution* 60(4):694–717.

Al Jazeera. 2011. "Gambia's Jammeh wins disputed elections." November 25.

Al Jazeera. 2016. "Cameroon urged to investigate deadly protest dispersal." December 9.

Albaugh, Ericka A. 2011. "An Autocrat's Toolkit: Adaptations and Manipulation in Democratic Cameroon." *Democratization* 18(2):388–414.

Albertus, Michael. 2015. *Autocracy and Redistribution*. New York: Cambridge University Press.

Albertus, Michael, Sofia Fenner, and Dan Slater. 2018. *Coercive Distribution*. New York: Cambridge University Press.

Aldama, Abraham, Mateo Vásquez-Cortés, and Lauren Young. 2019. "Fear and Citizen Coordination Against Dictatorship." *Journal of Theoretical Politics* 31(1):103–235.

Allen-Ebrahimian, Bethany. 2016. "The Man Who Nailed Jello to the Wall." *Foreign Policy* June 29.

Althaus, Scott L., Brittany H. Bramlett, and James G. Gimpel. 2012. "When War Hits Home: The Geography of Military Losses and Support for War in Time and Space." *Journal of Conflict Resolution* 56(3):382–412.

Alvarez, Joshua. 2018. "Marine Le Pen's 'Russiagate' Sounds Awfully Familiar." *Washington Monthly* December 29.

Amat, Consuelo. 2019. "Dissident Resilience to Repression." Stanford University.

Ames, Barry. 1970. "Bases of Support for Mexico's Dominant Party." *American Political Science Review* 64(1):153–167.

Anandarajan, Murugan, Chelsey Hill, and Thomas Nolan. 2019. *Practical Text Analysis: Maximizing the Value of Text Data*. Vol. 2 Boston: Springer.

Anonymous. 2017. "Faking it: The Rwandan GDP Growth Myth." *Review of African Political Economy* July 26.

Anonymous. 2019. "A Straightforward Case of Fake Statistics." *Review of African Political Economy* April 18.

Applebaum, Anne. 2003. *Gulag: A History*. New York: Doubleday.

Applebaum, Anne. 2012. *Iron Curtain: The Crushing of Eastern Europe, 1944–56*. New York: Doubleday.

Applebaum, Anne. 2018. "A Warning From Europe: The Worst Is Yet to Come." *The Atlantic* October 15.

Arceneaux, Kevin, Martin Johnson, René Lindstädt, and Ryan J. Vander Wielen. 2016. "The Influence of News Media on Political Elites: Investigating Strategic Responsiveness in Congress." *American Journal of Political Science* 60(1):5–29.

Arceneaux, Kevin and Rory Truex. 2020. "Does Propaganda Unconsciously Persuade? Testing Implicit Persuasion in the U.S. and Hong Kong." Princeton University.

Arendt, Hannah. 1951. *The Origins of Totalitarianism*. Boston: Schocken Books.

Arezki, Rabah and Markus Bruckner. 2011. "Food Prices and Political Instability." *IMF Working Paper* No. 11/62.

Arriola, Leonardo R. 2009. "Patronage and Political Stability in Africa." *Comparative Political Studies* 42(10):1339–1362.

Ash, Elliott and Sergio Galletta. 2019. "Partisan Media and Fiscal Policy Choices: Evidence from U.S. Cable News Channels." ETH Zurich.

Atabong, Amindeh Blaie. 2017. "Cameroon has shut down the internet in its English-speaking regions." *Quartz Africa* January 23.

Badawy, Adam, Emilio Ferrara, and Kristina Lerman. 2018. "Analyzing the Digital Traces of Political Manipulation: The 2016 Russian Interference Twitter

Campaign." *ASONAM '18: Proceedings of the International Conference on Advances in Social Networks Analysis and Mining* pp. 258–265.

Bader, Julia. 2015. "China, Autocratic Patron? An Empirical Investigation of China as a Factor in Autocratic Survival." *International Studies Quarterly* 59(1):23–33.

Baek, Tae Hyun, Sukki Yoon, and Seeun Kim. 2015. "When Environmental Messages Should Be Assertive: Examining the Moderating Role of Effort Investment." *International Journal of Advertising* 34(1):135–157.

Baker, Andy. 2015. "Race, Paternalism, and Foreign Aid: Evidence from U.S. Public Opinion." *American Political Science Review* 109(1):93–109.

Bakliwal, Akshat, Jennifer Foster, Jennifer van der Puil, Ron O'Brien, Lamia Tounsi, and Mark Hughes. 2013. "Sentiment Analysis of Political Tweets: Towards an Accurate Classifier." *Proceedings of the Workshop on Language in Social Media* 49–58.

Balcells, Laia. 2012. "The Consequences of Victimization on Political Identities: Evidence from Spain." *Politics & Society* 40(3):311–347.

Balcells, Laia, Valeria Palanza, and Elsa Voytas. Forthcoming. "Do Museums Promote Reconciliation? A Field Experiment on Transitional Justice." *Journal of Politics* pp. 1–28.

Bammam, David and Noah A. Smith. 2015. "Open Extraction of Fine-grained Political Statements." *Proceedings of the 2015 Conference on Empirical Methods in Natural Language Processing* 1:76–85.

Bandurski, David. 2009. "Su Rong's Modern Art of Propaganda Spin." China Media Project.

Bandurski, David. 2018. "People's Daily Growls Over Meng Arrest." China Media Project.

Bandurski, David and Martin Hala, eds. 2010. *Investigative Journalism in China: Eight Cases in Chinese Watchdog Journalism*. Hong Kong: University of Hong Kong Press.

Bansak, Kirk, Jens Hainmueller, Daniel J. Hopkins, and Teppei Yamamoto. 2018. "The Number of Choice Tasks and Survey Satisficing in Conjoint Experiments." *Political Analysis* 26(1):112–119.

Barak, Oren. 2007. "'Don't Mention the War?' The Politics of Remembrance and Forgetfulness in Postwar Lebanon." *Middle East Journal* 61(1):49–70.

Barmé, Geremie R. 1998. "Spring Clamor and Autumnal Silence: Cultural Control in China." *Current History* 97:257–262.

Barmé, Geremie R. 1999a. "CCP^{TM} and ADCULT PRC." *China Journal* 41:1–23.

Barmé, Geremie R. 1999b. *In the Red: On Contemporary Chinese Culture*. New York: Columbia University Press.

Bartholow, Bruce D., Brad J. Bushman, and Marc A. Sestir. 2006. "Chronic Violent Video Game Exposure and Desensitization to Violence: Behavioral and Event-Related Brain Potential Data." *Journal of Experimental Social Psychology* 42(4):532–539.

Bastos, Maco and Johan Farkas. 2019. "'Donald Trump Is My President!': The Internet Research Agency Propaganda Machine." *Social Media + Society* 5(3):1–13.

Bates, Robert H. 1983. *Essays on The Political Economy of Rural Africa*. Berkeley: University of California Press.

Baum, Matthew. 2002. "Sex, Lies, and War: How Soft News Brings Foreign Policy to the Inattentive Public." *American Political Science Review* 96(1):91–109.

Baum, Matthew. 2003. *Soft News Goes to War: Public Opinion and American Foreign Policy in the New Media Age*. Princeton: Princeton University Press.

Baumer, Eric, Elisha Elovic, Ying Qin, Francesca Poletta, and Geri Gay. 2015. "Testing and Comparing Computational Approaches for Identifying the Language of Framing in Political News." *Proceedings of the 2015 Conference of the North American Chapter of the Association for Computational Linguistics: Human Language Technologies* 1:1472–1482.

Bautista, María Angélica, Felipe González, Luis R. Martínez, Pablo Munoz, and Mounu Prem. 2021. "The Geography of Repression and Opposition to Autocracy." *American Journal of Political Science* pp. 1–18. https://doi.org/10.1111/ajps.12614

BBC. 2015. "The Colourful Propaganda of Xinjiang." January 12.

BBC. 2016. "Bamenda Protests: Mass Arrests in Cameroon." November 23.

Beach, Sophie. 2009. "Chinese Tweeting about Urumqi." *China Digital Times* July 7.

Beam, Christopher. 2014. "'I think it's already been forgotten': How China's Milennials Talk about Tiananmen Square." *The New Republic* June 3.

Bearce, David H. and Daniel C. Tirone. 2010. "Foreign Aid Effectiveness and Daniel C. Tirone." *Journal of Politics* 72(3):837–851.

Beaulieu, Emily. 2014. *Electoral Protest and Democracy in the Developing World*. New York: Cambridge University Press.

Beaulieu, Emily and Susan D. Hyde. 2009. "In the Shadow of Democracy Promotion: Strategic Manipulation, International Observers, and Election Boycotts." *Comparative Political Studies* 42(3):392–415.

Beber, Bernd, Philip Roessler, and Alexandra Scacco. 2014. "Intergroup Violence and Political Attitudes: Evidence from a Dividing Sudan." *Journal of Politics* 76(3):649–665.

Beeson, Mark. 2009. "Developmental States in East Asia: A Comparison of the Japanese and Chinese Experiences." *Asian Perspective* 33(2):5–39.

Behr, Roy L. and Shanto Iyengar. 1985. "Television News, Real-World Cues, and Changes in the Public Agenda." *Public Opinion Quarterly* 49(1):38–57.

Beissinger, Mark. 2002. *Nationalist Mobilization and the Collapse of the Soviet State*. New York: Cambridge University Press.

Beissinger, Mark. 2007. "Structure and Example in Modular Political Phenomena: The Diffusion of Bulldozer/Rose/Orange/Tulip Revolutions." *Perspectives on Politics* 5(2):259–276.

Belkin, Aaron and Evan Schofer. 2003. "Toward a Structural Understanding of Coup Risk." *Journal of Conflict Resolution* 47(5):594–620.

Bell, Matthew. 2014. "This is a 25th Anniversary China's Leaders Want to Forget." *PRI* May 26.

Bellemare, Marc F. 2015. "Rising Food Prices, Food Price Volatility, and Political Unrest." *American Journal of Agricultural Economics* 97(1):1–21.

Bellin, Eva R. 2004. "The Robustness of Authoritarianism in the Middle East: Exceptionalism in Comparative Perspective." *Comparative Politics* 36(2):139–157.

Benkler, Yochai, Robert Faris, and Hal Roberts. 2018. *Network Propaganda: Manipulation, Disinformation, and Radicalization in American Politics.* New York: Oxford University Press.

Bennett, W. Lance, Regina G. Lawrence, and Steven Livingston. 2006. "None Dare Call It Torture: Indexing and the Limits of Press Independence in the Abu Ghraib Scandal." *Journal of Communication* 56(3):467–485.

"Vladimir Putin's Red Scare? Inside Russia's Resurgent Communist Party." *Newsweek* July 31.

Benney, Jonathan. 2016. "Weiwen at the Grassroots: China's Stability Maintenance Apparatus as a Means of Conflict Resolution." *Journal of Contemporary China* 25(99):389–405.

Benoit, Kenneth, Kohei Watanabe, Haiyan Wang, Paul Nulty, Adam Obeng, Stefan Müller, and Akitaka Matsuo. 2018. "Quanteda: An R Package for the Quantitative Analysis of Textual Data." *Journal of Open Source Software* 3(30):774.

Berger, Helge and Mark Spoerer. 2001. "Economic Crises and the European Revolutions of 1848." *The Journal of Economic History* 61(2):293–326.

Bergsmo, Morten and Ling Yan, eds. 2012. *State Sovereignty and International Criminal Law.* Beijing: Torkel Opsahl Academic Publishers.

Berinsky, Adam J. 2007. "Assuming the Costs of War: Events, Elites, and American Public Support for Military Conflict." *Journal of Politics* 69(4):975–997.

Bermeo, Nancy. 2016. "On Democratic Backsliding." *Journal of Democracy* 27(1):5–19.

Bernard, Philippe. 2008. "Le patrimoine des chefs d'État africains en France." *Le Monde* January 31.

Bernstein, Thomas and Xiaobo Lü. 2003. *Taxation without Representation in Contemporary Rural China.* New York: Cambridge University Press.

Bertoli, Andrew D. 2017. "Nationalism and Conflict: Lessons from International Sports." *International Studies Quarterly* 61(4):835–849.

Berwick, Angus. 2018. "How ZTE helps Venezuela create China-style social control." *Reuters* November 14.

Besley, Timothy J. and Andrea Prat. 2006. "Handcuffs for the Grabbing Hand? Media Capture and Government Accountability." *American Economic Review* 96(3):720–736.

Besley, Timothy J. and Anne C. Case. 1995. "Incumbent Behavior: Vote-Seeking, Tax-Setting, and Yardstick Competition." *American Economic Review* 85(1):25–45.

Besley, Timothy J. and James A. Robinson. 2010. "Quis Custodiet Ipsos Custodes? Civilian Control Over the Military." *Journal of the European Economic Association* 8(2–3):655–663.

Besley, Timothy J. and Robin Burgess. 2002. "The Political Economy of Government Responsiveness: Theory and Evidence from India." *Quarterly Journal of Economics* 117(4):1415–1451.

Besley, Timothy J. and Torsten Persson. 2011. *Pillars of Prosperity: The Political Economics of Development Clusters.* Princeton: Princeton University Press.

Bessi, Alessandro and Emilio Ferrara. 2016. "Social Bots Distort the 2016 U.S. Presidential Election Online Discussion." *First Monday* 21(11).

Bhasin, Tavishi and Jennifer Gandhi. 2013. "Timing and Targeting of State Repression in Authoritarian Elections." *Electoral Studies* 32(4):620–631.

Birney, Mayling. 2007. "Can Local Elections Contribute to Democratic Progress in Authoritarian Regimes? Exploring the Political Ramifications of China's Village Elections." Yale University.

Birney, Mayling, Pierre F. Landry, and J. Yan. 2017. "Vocalizing Dissent in a Repressive Authoritarian Context: The Impact of Modernization and Socio-Economic Shifts in China." London School of Economics and Political Science.

Bishop, Robert. 1989. *Qi Lai! Mobilizing One Billion Chinese: The Chinese Communication System*. Ames: Iowa State University Press.

Blair, Graeme, Alexander Coppock, and Margaret Moor. 2020. "When to Worry about Sensitivity Bias: A Social Reference Theory and Evidence from 30 Years of List Experiments." *American Political Science Review* 114(4):1–19.

Blair, Graeme and Kosuke Imai. 2012. "Statistical Analysis of List Experiments." *Political Analysis* 20(1):47–77.

Blaydes, Lisa. 2011. *Elections and Distributive Politics in Mubarak's Egypt*. New York: Cambridge University Press.

Blaydes, Lisa. 2018. *State of Repression: Iraq under Saddam Hussein*. Princeton: Princeton University Press.

Bleck, Jaimie and Kristin Michelitch. 2017. "Capturing the Airwaves, Capturing the Nation? A Field Experiment on State-Run Media Effects in the Wake of a Coup." *Journal of Politics* 79(3):873–889.

Boas, Taylor C. and F. Daniel Hidalgo. 2011. "Controlling the Airwaves: Incumbency Advantage and Community Radio in Brazil." *American Journal of Political Science* 55(4):869–885.

Bogaards, Matthijs. 2018. "De-Democratization in Hungary: Diffusely Defective Democracy." *Democratization* 25(8):1481–1499.

Bogart, Leo. 1995. *Cool Words, Cold War: A New Look at USIA's Premises for Propaganda*. Washington, D.C.: American University.

Boix, Carles. 2015. *Political Order and Inequality: Their Foundations and Their Consequences for Human Welfare*. New York: Cambridge University Press.

Boix, Carles and Milan Svolik. 2013. "The Foundations of Limited Authoritarian Government: Institutions, Commitment, and Power-Sharing in Dictatorships." *Journal of Politics* 75(2):300–316.

Boydstun, Amber E., Alison Ledgerwood, and Jehan Sparks. 2017. "A Negativity Bias in Reframing Shapes Political Preferences Even in Partisan Contexts." *Social Psychological and Personality Science* 10(1):53–61.

Brady, Anne-Marie. 2002. "Regimenting the Public Mind: The Modernization of Propaganda in the PRC." *International Journal* 57(4):563–578.

Brady, Anne-Marie. 2006. "Guiding Hand: The Role of the Central Propaganda Department in the Current Era." *Westminister Papers in Communication and Culture* 3(1):58–77.

Brady, Anne-Marie. 2008. *Marketing Dictatorship: Propaganda and Thought Work in Contemporary China*. Lanham: Rowman & Littlefield.

Brady, Anne-Marie. 2012*a*. "'We Are All Part of the Same Family': China's Ethnic Propaganda." *Journal of Current Chinese Affairs* 41(4):159–181.

Brady, Anne-Marie. 2015. "China's Foreign Propaganda Machine." *Journal of Democracy* 26(4):51–59.

Brady, Anne-Marie, ed. 2012*b*. *China's Thought Management*. New York: Routledge.

Brady, Anne-Marie and Juntao Wang. 2009. "China's Strengthened New Order and the Role of Propaganda." *Journal of Contemporary China* 18(62):767–788.

Brady, Anne-Marie and Yong He. 2012. "Talking Up the Market: Economic Propaganda in Contemporary China." In *China's Thought Management*, ed. Anne-Marie Brady. New York: Routledge, chapter 2, pp. 36–56.

Brancati, Dawn. 2016. *Democracy Protests: Origins, Features, and Significance*. New York: Cambridge University Press.

Branch, Adam and Zachariah Mampilly. 2015. *Africa Uprising: Popular Protest and Political Change*. London: Zed Books.

Branigan, Tania. 2010. "Ai Weiwei supporters gather for party at condemned studio." *The Guardian* November 7.

Bratton, Michael, Annie Chikwana, and Tulani Sithole. 2005. "Propaganda and Public Opinion in Zimbabwe." *Journal of Contemporary African Studies* 23(1):77–108.

Bratton, Michael and Nicholas van de Walle. 1997. *Democratic Experiments in Africa: Regime Transitions in Comparative Perspective*. New York: Cambridge University Press.

Brazys, Samuel, Johan A. Elkink and Gina Kelly. 2017. "Bad Neighbors? How Co-located Chinese and World Bank Development Projects Impact Local Corruption in Tanzania." *Review of International Organizations* 12(2):227–253.

Brehm, S. S. and J. W. Brehm. 1981. *Psychological Reactance: A Theory of Freedom and Control*. New York: Academic Press.

Breisinger, Clemens, Olivier Ecker, and Jean Francois Trinh Tan. 2015. "Conflict and Food Insecurity: How Do We Break the Links?" In *2014–2015 Global Food Policy Report*, ed. International Food Policy Research Institute. Washington, D.C.: International Food Policy Research Institute, chapter 7, pp. 51–61.

Breslin, Shaun. 2012. "Paradigm(s) Shifting? Responding to China's Response to the Global Financial Crisis." In *The Consequences of the Global Financial Crisis: The Rhetoric of Reform and Regulation*, ed. Wyn Grant and Graham K. Wilson. New York: Oxford University Press, chapter 12, pp. 226–245.

Brewer, John. 1989. *The Sinews of Power: War, Money and the English State, 1688–1783*. Cambridge: Harvard University Press.

Brinkman, Henk-Jan and Cullen S. Hendrix. 2011. "Food Insecurity and Violent Conflict: Causes, Consequences, and Addressing the Challenges." *World Food Programme Occasional Paper* 24.

Brody, Richard A. 1991. *Assessing the President: The Media, Elite Opinion, and Public Support*. Stanford: Stanford University Press.

Brouwer, Joseph. 2022. "Sensitive Words: Top 10 Censored Terms of 2021." *China Digital Times* January 13.

Brown, Kerry. 2017. "Reading Between the Lines: Xi's Epic Speech at the 19th Party Congress." *The Diplomat* October 24.

Brown, Stephen. 2005. "Foreign Aid and Democracy Promotion: Lessons from Africa." *European Journal of Development Research* 17(2):179–198.

Brownlee, Jason. 2007. *Durable Authoritarianism in an Age of Democratization.* New York: Cambridge University Press.

Buchheim, Hans. 1968. *Totalitarian Rule: Its Nature and Characteristics.* Middletown: Wesleyan University.

Buckley, Chris. 2014. "People's Daily Editorial Fanned Flames of 1989 Protest." *The New York Times* April 25.

Buckley, Chris. 2018. "China Is Detaining Muslims in Vast Numbers. The Goal: 'Transformation'." *The New York Times* September 8.

Buckley, Chris. 2019. "30 Years After Tiananmen, a Chinese Military Insider Warns: Never Forget." *The New York Times* May 28.

Buckley, Chris and Amy Qin. 2019. "Xi Praises a Student Protest in China. From 100 Years Ago." *The New York Times* April 29.

Buckley, Chris and Austin Ramzy. 2018. "China's Detention Camps for Muslims Turn to Forced Labor." *The New York Times* December 16.

Bueno de Mesquita, Bruce, Alastair Smith, Randolph M. Siverson, and James D. Morrow. 2003. *The Logic of Political Survival.* Cambridge: Massachusetts Institute of Technology Press.

Bukharbaeva, Galima. 2005. "Testimony before the United States Helsinki Commission." Washington, D.C.: Available at www.csce.gov/sites/helsinkicommission.house.gov/files/GB.pdf.

Bullock, John G. 2011. "Elite Influence on Public Opinion in an Informed Electorate." *American Political Science Review* 105(3):496–515.

Bunce, Valerie and Sharon Wolchik. 2006. "Favorable Conditions and Electoral Revolutions." *Journal of Democracy* 17(4):5–18.

Bunce, Valerie and Sharon Wolchik. 2010. "Defeating Dictators: Electoral Change and Stability in Competitive Authoritarian Regimes." *World Politics* 62(1):43–86.

Bunce, Valerie and Sharon Wolchik. 2011. *Defeating Authoritarian Leaders in Post-Communist Countries.* New York: Cambridge University Press.

Burgoon, Michael, Eusebio Alvaro, Joseph Grandpre, and Michael Voulodakis. 2002. "Revisiting the Theory of Psychological Reactance: Communicating Threats to Attitudinal Freedom." In *The Persuasion Handbook: Developments in Theory and Practice*, ed. James Price Dillard and Michael Pfau. Thousand Oaks: Sage, chapter 12, pp. 259–287.

Bursztyn, Leonardo, Aakaash Rao, Christopher P. Roth, and David H. Yanagizawa-Drott. 2020. "Misinformation During a Pandemic." *NBER Working Paper Series* No. 27417.

Bustikova, Lenka and Petra Guasti. 2017. "The Illiberal Turn or Swerve in Central Europe?" *Politics and Governance* 5(4):166–176.

Cain, Daylian M., George Loewenstein, and Don A. Moore. 2005. "The Dirt on Coming Clean: Perverse Effects of Disclosing Conflicts of Interest." *Journal of Legal Studies* 34(1):1–25.

Cantoni, Davide, Yuyu Chen, David Y. Yang, Noam Yuchtman, and Y. Jane Zhang. 2017. "Curriculum and Ideology." *Journal of Political Economy* 125(2):338–392.

Cao, Yin. 2015. "More 'eyes' fight crime in crowds." *China Daily* October 5.

Card, Dallas, Amber E. Boydston, Justin H. Gross, Philip Resnik, and Noah A. Smith. 2015. "The Media Frames Corpus: Annotations of Frames across Issues." *Proceedings of ACL* .

Card, Dallas, Justin H. Gross, Amber E. Boydston, and Noah A. Smith. 2016. "Analyzing Framing through the Casts of Characters in the News." *Proceedings of the 2016 Conference on Empirical Methods in Natural Language Processing* 1:1410–1420.

Carmack, Roberto J. 2014. "History and Hero-Making: Patriotic Narratives and the Sovietization of Kazakh Front-Line Propaganda, 1941–1945." *Central Asian Survey* 33(1):95–112.

Carnagey, Nicholas L., Craig A. Anderson, and Brad J. Bushman. 2007. "The Effect of Video Game Violence on Physiological Desensitization to Real-Life Violence." *Journal of Experimental Social Psychology* 43(3):489–496.

Carnegie, Allison and Nikolay Marinov. 2017. "Foreign Aid, Human Rights and Democracy Promotion: Evidence from a Natural Experiment." *American Journal of Political Science* 61(3):671–683.

Carothers, Christopher. 2018. "The Surprising Instability of Competitive Authoritarianism." *Journal of Democracy* 29(4):129–135.

Carter, Brett L. 2016a. "Repression and Foreign Aid in Autocracies: Exploiting Debt Relief Negotiations in Post-Cold War Africa." *AidData Working Paper Series* 29.

Carter, Brett L. 2016b. "The Struggle over Term Limits in Africa." *Journal of Democracy* 27(3):36–50.

Carter, Brett L. 2017. "The Trump Card: Denis Sassou Nguesso's embarrassing attempt to ingratiate himself to Donald Trump." *Africa is a Country* January 9.

Carter, Brett L. 2018. "The Rise of Kleptocracy: Autocrats versus Activists in Africa." *Journal of Democracy* 29(1):54–68.

Carter, Brett L. 2022. *Inside Dictatorship: Subverting Democracy in Post-Cold War Africa*. Unpublished Manuscript.

Carter, Brett L. and Mai Hassan. 2021. "Regional Governance in Divided Societies: Evidence from the Republic of Congo and Kenya." *Journal of Politics* 83(1):1–18.

Carter, Erin Baggott and Brett L. Carter. 2020a. "Focal Moments and Protests in Autocracies: How Pro-Democracy Anniversaries Shape Dissent in China." *Journal of Conflict Resolution* 64(10):1796–1827.

Carter, Erin Baggott and Brett L. Carter. 2020b. "Tiananmen's Other Children." *The New York Times* June 4.

Carter, Erin Baggott and Brett L. Carter. 2021a. "Questioning More: RT, America, and the Post-West World." *Security Studies* 30(1):49–78.

Carter, Erin Baggott and Brett L. Carter. 2021b. "When Autocrats Threaten Citizens with Violence: Evidence from China." *British Journal of Political Science* https://doi.org/10.1017/S0007123420000575.

Carter, Erin Baggott, Iain Johnston, and Kai Quek. 2018. "Heterogenous Chinese Nationalism." University of Southern California, Harvard University, and Hong Kong University.

Casper, Brett Allen and Scott A. Tyson. 2014. "Popular Protest and Elite Coordination in a Coup d'état." *Journal of Politics* 76(2):548–564.

Castells, Manuel. 2012. *Networks of Outrage and Hope*. New York: Polity Press.

Central Intelligence Agency. 1986. "Cameroon: Challenges Ahead for Biya." February 3.

Chan, Keith. 2018a. "China's Hotel Facial Recognition Check-ins and AI Smart Rooms are Here to Stay." *South China Morning Post* August 6.

Chan, Tara Francis. 2018b. "22 Eerie Photos Show How China Uses Facial Recognition to Track Its Citizens as They Travel, Shop – and Even Use Toilet Paper." *Business Insider* February 12.

Chang, Tsan-Kuo, Brian Southwell, Hyung-Min Lee and Yejin Hong. 2012. "A Changing World, Unchanging Perspectives: American Newspaper Editors and Enduring Values in Foreign News Reporting." *International Communication Gazette* 74(4):367–384.

Chen, Andrea. 2014. "Uygur-Han Chinese Couples Offered 10,000 yuan a Year to Marry in Xinjiang County." *South China Morning Post* September 2.

Chen, Celia, Meng Jing and Sarah Dai. 2018. "Facial Recognition to Ticketing Apps: How Tech is Helping Ease the Lunar New Year Travel Crush." *South China Morning Post* January 27.

Chen, Jidong and Yiqing Xu. 2015. "Information Manipulation and Reform in Authoritarian Regimes." *Political Science Research and Methods* 5(1):163–178.

Chen, Jie. 2004. *Popular Political Support in Urban China*. Stanford: Stanford University Press.

Chen, Jie. 2013. *A Middle Class without Democracy: Economic Growth and the Prospects for Democratization in China*. Oxford: Oxford University Press.

Chen, Jie and Bruce J. Dickson. 2008. "Allies of the State: Democratic Support and Regime Support Among China's Private Entrepreneurs." *The China Quarterly* 196:780–804.

Chen, Jie and Chunlong Lu. 2006. "Does China's Middle Class Think and Act Democratically? Attitudinal and Behavioral Orientations toward Urban Self-Government." *Journal of Chinese Political Science* 11(2):1–20.

Chen, Jie, Yang Zhong, and Jan William Hillard. 1997. "The Level and Sources of Popular Support for China's Current Political Regime." *Communist and Post-Communist Studies* 30(1):45–64.

Chen, Junhong, ed. 1999. *A Reader on Strengthening and Reforming Political Thought Work* 加强和改进思想政治工作学习读本. 中共中央党校出版社.

Chen, Le, Chi Zhang, and Christo Wilson. 2013. "Tweeting Under Pressure: Analyzing Trending Topics and Evolving Word Choice on Sina Weibo." *Proceedings of the First ACM Conference on Online Social Networks* pp. 89–100.

Chen, Qingqing. 2019. "New Village Loudspeaker Campaign Aims to Spread Ideological Message." *Global Times* January 31.

Chen, Ting and Ji Yeon Hong. 2020. "Rivals Within: Political Factions, Loyalty, and Elite Competition under Authoritarianism." *Political Science Research and Methods* 9(3):599–614.

Chen, Xi. 2012. *Social Protest and Contentious Authoritarianism in China*. New York: Cambridge University Press.

Chen, Xueyi and Tianjian Shi. 2001. "Media Effects on Political Confidence and Trust in the PRC in the Post-Tiananmen Period." *East Asia: An International Quarterly* 19(3):84–118.

Chen, Yuyu and David Y. Yang. 2019. "The Impact of Media Censorship: 1984 or Brave New World?" *American Economic Review* 109(6):2294–2332.

Cheng, Hua and Kishore Gawande. 2017. "State Capacity and China's Economic Performance." *Asian Meeting of Econometric Society Working Paper*.

Cheng, Kris. 2016. "200 Dead Could Bring 20 Years of Peace, Ex-China Leader Deng Said Ahead of Tiananmen Massacre." *Hong Kong Free Post* December 30.

Chenoweth, Erica and Jay Ulfelder. 2015. "Can Structural Conditions Explain the Onset of Non-Violent Uprisings?" *Journal of Conflict Resolution* 61(1):298–324.

Chenoweth, Erica and Maria J. Stephan. 2011. *Why Civil Resistance Works: The Strategic Logic of Nonviolent Conflict*. New York: Columbia University.

Chin, Josh and Liza Lin. 2017. "China's All-Seeing Surveillance State Is Reading Its Citizens' Faces." *The Wall Street Journal* June 26.

China Digital Times. 2019. "River Crab." https://chinadigitaltimes.net/space/River_crab.

ChinaFile. 2013. "Document 9: A ChinaFile Translation." November 8.

China Internet Network Information Center, 中国互联网络信息中心. 2012. "Development of Mobile Internet Usage. 沈: 手机互联网发展的另一个侧面——单一手机上网人群的扩张." .

China News. 2008. "香港文汇报: "二月危机"已经不是危机了." www.chinanews.com/hb/news/2008/12-04/1473209.shtml.

Choi, Chi-Yuk and Mandy Zuo. 2013. "Xinjiang Calm ahead of Anniversary of Deadly Riots." *South China Morning Post* July 5.

Chomsky, Noam and Edward Herman. 1988. *Manufacturing Consent: The Political Economy of the Mass Media*. New York: Pantheon.

Chong, Dennis and James N. Druckman. 2007. "Framing Theory." *Annual Review of Political Science* 10:103–126.

Chotiner, Isaac. 2019. "A Political Economist on How China Sees Trump's Trade War." *The New Yorker* May 22.

Chou, Sophie and Deb Roy. 2017. "Nasty, Brutish, and Short: What Makes Election News Popular on Twitter?" *Proceedings of the Eleventh International AAAI Conference on Web and Social Media* 1:492–495.

Christensen, Darin and Francisco Garfias. 2018. "Can You Hear Me Now? How Communication Technology Affects Protest and Repression." *Quarterly Journal of Political Science* 13(1):89–117.

Chun, Susan. 2008. "Radio Gives Hope to North and South Koreans." *CNN* February 27.

Chung, Regina Wai-man and King wa Fu. 2022. "Tweets and Memories: Chinese Censors Come After Me. Forbidden Voices of the 1989 Tiananmen Square Massacre on Sina Weibo, 2012–2018." *Journal of Contemporary China* 31(134):319–334.

Chwe, Michael. 2001. *Rational Ritual: Culture, Coordination, and Common Knowledge*. Princeton: Princeton University Press.

Cialdini, Robert B. 2006. *Influence: The Psychology of Persuasion, Revised Edition*. New York: Harper Business.

Cianetti, Licia, James Dawson, and Seán Hanley. 2018. "Rethinking 'Democratic Backsliding' in Central and Eastern Europe: Looking Beyond Hungary and Poland." *East European Politics* 24(3):243–256.

Civitello, Linda. 2003. *Cuisine and Culture: A History of Food and People*. New York: Wiley.

Clarke, Damian C. 2019. "PLAUSEXOG: Stata Module to Implement Conley *et al*'s Plausibly Exogenous Bounds." Boston College.

Clee, Mona A. and Robert A. Wicklund. 1980. "Consumer Behavior and Psychological Reactance." *Journal of Consumer Research* 6(4):389–405.

Clifton, Denise. 2017. "Trump and Putin's Strong Connection: Lies." *Mother Jones* October 19.

CNN. 2010. "Ai Weiwei, a Bulldozer and 10,000 River Crabs." November 3.

Cohen, Geoffrey L. 2003. "Party over Policy: The Dominating Impact of Group Influence on Political Beliefs." *Journal of Personality and Social Psychology* 85(5):808–822.

Cohen, Jeffrey E. 1995. "Presidential Rhetoric and the Public Agenda." *American Journal of Political Science* 39(1):87–107.

Cohn, Alain, Jan Engelmann, Ernst Fehr, and Michel André Maréchal. 2015. "Evidence for Countercyclical Risk Aversion: An Experiment with Financial Professionals." *American Economic Review* 105(2):860–885.

Collaboration on International ICT Policy for East and Southern Africa. 2019. "Despots and Disruptions: Five Dimensions of Internet Shutdowns in Africa." https://cipesa.org/?wpfb_dl=283.

Collier, David and Steven Levitsky. 1997. "Democracy with Adjectives: Conceptual Innovation in Comparative Research." *World Politics* 49(3):430–451.

Collier, Paul and Anke Hoeffler. 2007. "Military Spending and the Risks of Coups d'Etat." Oxford University.

Collins, Cath, Katherine Hite, and Alfredo Joignant, eds. 2013. *The Politics of Memory in Chile: From Pinochet to Bachelet*. Boulder: Lynne Rienner Publishers.

Commentator. 2017. "Social Stability and Long-Term Stability is a Starting Point and Focus of Work in Xinjiang 把社会稳定和长治久安作为新疆工作的着眼点和着力点." *People's Daily* May 5.

Conley, Timothy G., Christian B. Hansen, and Peter E. Rossi. 2012. "Plausibly Exogenous." *Review of Economics and Statistics* 94(1):260–272.

Connor, Neil. 2015. "The Cave the Chinese President Called Home." *Telegraph* October 19.

Conover, M., B. Gonçalves, J. Ratkiewicz, A. Flammini, and F. Menczer. 2011. "Predicting the Political Alignment of Twitter Users." *Proceedings of the 2011*

IEEE International Conference on Privacy, Security, Risk, and Trust, and IEEE International Conference on Social Computing 1:192–199.

Cook, Thomas D. and Brian R. Flay. 1978. "The Persistance of Experimentally Induced Attitude Change." *Advances in Experimental Social Psychology* 11:1–57.

Coppedge, Michael, John Gerring, Staffan I. Lindberg, Svend-Erik Skaaning, Jan Teorell, David Altman, Frida Andersson, Michael Bernhard, M. Steven Fish, Adam Glynn, Allen Hicken, Carl Henrik Knutsen, Kyle L. Marquardt, Kelly McMann, Valeriya Mechkova, Pamela Paxton, Daniel Pemstein, Laura Saxer, Brigitte Seim, Rachel Sigman, and Jeffrey Staton. 2022. "Varieties of Democracy (V-Dem) Project." Available at www.v-dem .net/en/.

Cormack, Mike. 2018. "China Dream by Ma Jian is a Scathing Satire of the Absurd Reality Facing a Silenced Nation." *South China Morning Post* November 8.

Corneo, Giacomo. 2006. "Media Capture in a Democracy: The Role of Wealth Concentration." *Journal of Public Economics* 90(1–2):37–58.

Corstange, Daniel. 2009. "Sensitive Questions, Truthful Answers? Modeling the List Experiment with LISTIT." *Political Analysis* 17(1):45–63.

Cotton Campaign. 2017. "Uzbekistan's Forced Labor Problem." Available at www.cottoncampaign.org/uzbekistans-forced-labor-problem.html.

Cox, Gary W. 2009. "Authoritarian Elections and Leadership Succession." Paper Presented at the 2009 Annual Meeting of the American Political Science Association.

Cragin, R. Kim and Sara A. Daly. 2009. *Women as Terrorists: Mothers, Recruiters, and Martyrs.* Santa Barbara: Praeger.

Crassweller, Robert D. 1966. *Trujillo: The Life and Times of a Caribbean Dictator.* New York: MacMillan.

Cumming-Bruce, Nick. 2018. "U.N. Panel Confronts China over Reports That It Holds a Million Uighurs in Camps." *The New York Times* August 10.

Cunningham, Stanley B. 2002. *The Idea of Propaganda: A Reconstruction.* New York: Greenwood Publishing.

Da Silveira, Bernardo S. and Joao M. P. De Mello. 2011. "Campaign Advertising and Election Outcomes: Quasi-natural Experiment Evidence from Gubernatorial Elections in Brazil." *The Review of Economic Studies* 78(2): 590–612.

Dahir, Abdi Latif. 2018a. "Chad Has Blocked Social Messaging Apps and BBC Amid Political and Economic Anxiety." *Quartz* April 8.

Dahir, Abdi Latif. 2018b. "This Documentary Tells the Story of Africa's Longest Internet Shutdown." *Quartz* August 6.

Dahir, Abdi Latif. 2019. "African Strongmen are the Biggest Stumbling Blocks to Internet Access on the Continent." *Quartz* March 20.

Dahl, Robert A. 1971. *Polyarchy: Participation and Opposition.* New Haven: Yale University Press.

Dai, Sarah. 2018. "Beijing's New Zaha Hadid-Designed Airport to Showcase Latest Facial Recognition Technology." *South China Morning Post* July 18.

Dalton, Angela and Victor Asal. 2011. "Is It Ideology or Desperation: Why Do Organizations Deploy Women in Violent Terrorist Attacks?" *Studies in Conflict & Terrorism* 34(10):802–819.

Dancy, Geoff and Florencia Montal. 2017. "Unintended Positive Complementarity: Why International Criminal Court Investigations Increase Domestic Human Rights Prosecutions." *American Journal of International Law* 111(3):689–723.

Dasgupta, Aditya. 2018. "Technological Change and Political Turnover: The Democratizing Effects of the Green Revolution in India." *American Political Science Review* 112(4):918–938.

Davenport, Christian. 2007a. "State Repression and Political Order." *Annual Review of Political Science* 10:1–23.

Davenport, Christian. 2007b. *State Repression and the Domestic Democratic Peace*. New York: Cambridge University Press.

Davenport, Christian. 2007c. "State Repression and the Tyrannical Peace." *Journal of Peace Research* 44(4):485–504.

Davis, Madeline. 2005. "Is Spain Recovering Its Memory? Breaking the *Pacto del Olvido*." *Human Rights Quarterly* 27(3):858–880.

Daxecker, Ursula E. 2012. "The Cost of Exposing Cheating: International Election Monitoring, Fraud, and Post-Election Violence in Africa." *Journal of Peace Research* 49(4):503–516.

de Brito, Alexandra Barahona, Carmen Gonzaléz-Enríquez, and Paloma Aguilar, eds. 2001. *The Politics of Memory: Transitional Justice in Democratizing Societies*. New York: Oxford University Press.

Decalo, Samuel. 1998. *The Stable Minority: Civilian Rule in Africa, 1960–1990*. Gainesville: Florida Academic Press.

De Keersmaecker, Jonas and Arne Roets. 2017. "Fake News: Incorrect, but Hard to Correct. The Role of Cognitive Ability on the Impact of False Information on Social Impressions." *Intelligence* 65:107–110.

de Temmerman, Els. 2006. "Letter from the Editor-in-Chief." *New Vision* November 30.

DellaVigna, Stefano and Ethan Kaplan. 2007. "The Fox News Effect: Media Bias and Voting." *Quarterly Journal of Economics* 122(3):1187–1234.

DeMarzo, Peter M., Dimitri Vayanos, and Jeffrey Zwiebel. 2003. "Persuasion Bias, Social Influence, and Unidimensional Opinions." *Quarterly Journal of Economics* 118(3):909–968.

DeNardo, James. 1985. *Power in Numbers: The Political Strategy of Protest and Rebellion*. Princeton: Princeton University Press.

Deng, Xiaoping. 1993. *Selected Works of Deng Xiaoping, Volume 3*. Beijing: Renmin Chubanshe.

Deng, Yongheng, Randall Morck, Jing Wu, and Bernard Yeung. 2011. "Monetary and Fiscal Stimuli, Ownership Structure, and China's Housing Market." *NBER Working Paper Series* No. 16871.

Desposato, Scott, Gang Wang, and Jason Wu. 2021. "The Long-Term Effect of Mobilization and Repression on Political Trust." *Comparative Political Studies* 54(14):2447–2474.

Diamond, Jared. 1997. *Guns, Germs, and Steel: The Fates of Human Societies.* New York: W.W. Norton.

Diamond, Larry. 2002. "Elections without Democracy: Thinking about Hybrid Regimes." *Journal of Democracy* 13(2):21–35.

Diamond, Larry. 2010. "Liberation Technology." *Journal of Democracy* 21(3):69–83.

Diamond, Larry. 2015. "Facing Up to the Democratic Recession." *Journal of Democracy* 26(1):141–155.

Diamond, Larry. 2019a. *Ill Winds: Saving Democracy from Russian Rage, Chinese Ambition, and American Complacency.* New York: Penguin.

Diamond, Larry. 2019b. "The Road to Digital Unfreedom: The Threat of Postmodern Totalitarianism." *Journal of Democracy* 30(1):20–24.

Diamond, Larry, Juan J. Linz, and Seymour Martin Lipset, eds. 1995. *Politics in Developing Countries: Comparing Experiences with Democracy.* Boulder: Lynne Rienner Publishers.

Diamond, Larry and Orville Schell, eds. 2019. *Chinese Influence & American Interests: Promoting Constructive Vigilance.* Revised edition ed. Stanford: Hoover Institution Press.

Dickson, Bruce J. 2003. *Red Capitalists in China: The Party, Private Entrepreneurs, and Political Change.* New York: Cambridge University Press.

Dickson, Bruce J. 2014. "Who Wants to Be a Communist? Career Incentives and Mobilized Loyalty in Contemporary China." *The China Quarterly* 217:42–68.

Dickson, Bruce J. 2015. *The Dictator's Dilemma: The Chinese Communist Party's Strategy for Survival.* New York: Oxford University Press.

Dickson, Bruce J., Pierre F. Landry, Mingming Shen, and Jie Yan. 2016. "Public Goods and Regime Support in Urban China." *China Quarterly* 228:859–880.

Dietrich, Simone and Joseph Wright. 2015. "Foreign Aid Allocation Tactics and Democratic Change in Africa." *Journal of Politics* 77(1):216–234.

Dincecco, Mark. 2017. *State Capacity and Economic Development.* New York: Cambridge University Press.

Ding, Xiaowen, Bing Liu, and Philip S. Yu. 2008. "A Holistic Lexicon-Based Approach to Opinion Mining." *WSDM '08: Proceedings of the 2008 International Conference on Web Search and Data Mining* 1:231–240.

Djemili, Sarah, Julien Longhi, Claudia Marinica, Dimitris Kotzinos, and Georges-Elia Sarfati. 2014. "What Does Twitter Have to Say about Ideology?" *NLP 4 CMC: Natural Language Processing for Computer-Mediated Communication/Social Media* 1:16–25.

Donald, Stephanie Hemelryk, Michael Keene, and Yin Hong, eds. 2002. *Media in China: Consumption, Content and Crisis.* New York: Routledge.

Donno, Daniela. 2013. "Elections and Democratization in Authoritarian Regimes." *American Journal of Political Science* 57(3):703–716.

Doob, Leonard W. 1935. *Propaganda, Its Psychology and Technique.* New York: Holt.

Doob, Leonard W. 1950. "Goebbels' Principles of Propaganda." *The Public Opinion Quarterly* 14(3):419–442.

Dooley, Michael P., David Folkerts-Landau, and Peter Garber. 2004. "The Revived Bretton Woods System: The Effects of Periphery Intervention and

Reserve Management on Interest Rates & Exchange Rates in Center Countries." *NBER Working Paper Series* No. 10332.

Dragu, Tiberiu and Adam Przeworski. 2019. "Preventive Repression: Two Types of Moral Hazard." *American Political Science Review* 113(1):77–87.

Dreher, Axel, Andreas Fuchs, Roland Hodler, Bradley C. Parks, Paul A. Raschky, and Michael J. Tierney. 2019. "Aid on Demand: African Leaders and the Geography of China's Foreign Assistance." *Journal of Development Economics* 140:44–71.

Dreher, Axel, Jan-Egbert Sturm and James Vreeland. 2009. "Development Aid and International Politics: Does Membership on the UN Security Council Influence World Bank Decisions?" *Journal of Development Economics* 88(1):1–18.

Druckman, James N. and Rose McDermott. 2008. "Emotion and the Framing of Risky Choice." *Political Behavior* 30(3):297–321.

Druckman, James N. and Thomas J. Leeper. 2012. "Is Public Opinion Stable? Resolving the Micro/Macro Disconnect in Studies of Public Opinion." *Daedalus* 141(4):51–68.

Duch, Raymond M. and Randy T. Stevenson. 2008. *The Economic Vote: How Political and Economic Institutions Condition Election Results.* New York: Cambridge University Press.

Dunning, Thad. 2004. "Conditioning the Effects of Aid: Cold War Politics, Donor Credibility, and Democracy in Africa." *International Organization* 58(2):409–423.

Durante, Ruben, Paolo Pinotti, and Andrea Tesei. 2019. "The Political Legacy of Entertainment TV: Evidence from the Rise of Berlusconi." *American Economic Review* 109(7):2497–2530.

Duxfield, Flint and Ian Burrows. 2019. "Uyghur Woman Details Life Inside Chinese 'Re-education Camp' in Xinjiang." *Australian Broadcasting Corporation* January 8.

Easterlin, Richard A. 1995. "Will Raising the Incomes of All Increase the Happiness of All?" *Journal of Economic Behavior & Organization* 27(1):35–47.

Edin, M. 2003. "State Capacity and Local Agent Control in China: CCP Cadre Management from a Township Perspective." *The China Quarterly* 173:35–52.

Edmond, Chris. 2013. "Information Manipulation, Coordination, and Regime Change." *Review of Economic Studies* 80(4):1422–1458.

Edney, Kingsley. 2014. *The Globalization of Chinese Propaganda: International Power and Domestic Political Cohesion.* New York: Palgrave Macmillan.

Egorov, Georgy, Sergei Guriev, and Konstantin Sonin. 2009. "Why Resource-Poor Dictators Allow Freer Media: A Theory and Evidence from Panel Data." *American Political Science Review* 103(4):645–668.

Elfstrom, Manfred. 2019. "Two Steps Forward, One Step Back: Chinese State Reactions to Labour Unrest." *The China Quarterly* 240:855–879.

Ellman, Matthew and Fabrizio Germano. 2009. "What Do the Papers Sell? A Model of Advertising and Media Bias." *Economic Journal* 119(537):680–704.

Ellul, Jacques. 1973. *Propaganda: The Formation of Men's Attitudes.* New York: Vintage.

Elvidge, Christopher D., Mikhail Zhizhin, Tilottama Ghosh, Feng-Chi Hsu, and Jay Taneja. 2021. "Annual Time Series of Global VIIRS Nighttime Lights Derived from Monthly Averages: 2012 to 2019." *Remote Sensing* 13(5):922.

Engelhart, Katie. 2015. "Meet the Colonel in Charge of Countering Russian Propaganda in Lithuania." *Vice News* May 24.

Enikolopov, Ruben, Maria Petrova, and Ekaterina Zhuravskaya. 2011. "Media and Political Persuasion: Evidence from Russia." *American Economic Review* 101(7):3253–3285.

Enos, Ryan, Aaron Russell Kaufman, and Melissa Sands. 2019. "Can Violent Protest Change Local Policy Support? Evidence from the Aftermath of the 1992 Los Angeles Riot." *American Political Science Review* 113(4):1012–1028.

Entman, Robert M. 1993. "Framing: Toward Clarification of a Fractured Paradigm." *Journal of Communication* 43(4):51–58.

Enyedi, Zsolt. 2018. "Democratic Backsliding and Academic Freedom in Hungary." *Perspectives on Politics* 16(4):1067–1074.

Epstein, David, Robert H. Bates, Jack Goldstone, Ida Kristensen, and Sharyn O'Halloran. 2005. "Democratic Transitions." *American Journal of Political Science* 59(3):551–569.

Erickson, Amanda. 2017. "If Russia Today Is Moscow's Propaganda Arm, It's not Very Good at Its Job." *The Washington Post* January 12.

Erlanger, Steven. 2017. "Russia's RT Network: Is It More BBC or K.G.B.?" *The New York Times* March 8.

Esarey, Ashley. 2006. *Speak No Evil: Mass Media Control in Contemporary China*. Washington, D.C.: Freedom House.

Esarey, Ashley, Daniela Stockmann, and Jie Zhang. 2017. "Support for Propaganda: Chinese Perceptions of Public Service Advertising." *Journal of Contemporary China* 26(103):101–117.

Escribà-Folch, Abel. 2013. "Repression, Political Threats, and Survival under Autocracy." *International Political Science Review* 34(5):543–560.

Escribà-Folch, Abel and Joseph Wright. 2015. *Foreign Pressure and the Politics of Autocratic Survival*. New York: Oxford University Press.

Eyster, Erik and Matthew Rabin. 2010. "Naive Herding in Rich-Information Settings." *American Economic Journal: Microeconomics* 2(4):221–243.

Fan, Jiayang. 2018. "Yan Lianke's Forbidden Satires of China." *The New Yorker* October 15.

Fan, Xing. 2001. *Communications and Information in China: Regulatory Issues, Strategic Implications*. Lanham: University Press of America.

Fearon, James D. 2011. "Self-Enforcing Democracy." *Quarterly Journal of Economics* 126(4):1661–1708.

Feldman, Ronen. 2013. "Techniques and Applications for Sentiment Analysis." *Communications of the ACM* 56(4):82–89.

Feldstein, Steven. 2019. "The Road to Digital Unfreedom: How Artificial Intelligence Is Reshaping Repression." *Journal of Democracy* 30(1):40–52.

Ferrara, Emilio. 2020. "Disinformation and Social Bot Operations in the Run up to the 2017 French Presidential Election." *First Monday* 22(8).

Field, Anjalie, Doron Kliger, Shuly Wintner, Jennifer Pan, Dan Jurafsky, and Yulia Tsvetkov. 2018. "Framing and Agenda-Setting in Russian News: A

Computational Analysis of Intricate Political Strategies." *Proceedings of the 2018 Conference on Empirical Methods in Natural Language Processing* 1:3570–3580.

Filipov, David. 2018. "This Russian Presidential Contender Has Zero Chance against Putin: But a Man Can Dream." *The Washington Post* January 6.

Fincher, Leta Hong. 2018. *Betraying Big Brother: The Feminist Awakening in China*. New york: Verso.

Finer, Samuel E. 1976. *The Man on Horseback: The Role of the Military in Politics*. New York: Praeger.

Finney, Richard. 2017. "Internet Blocked in Tibetan Areas of China in Run-up to Sensitive Anniversary." *Radio Free Asia* March 10.

First, Ruth. 1970. *The Barrel of a Gun: Political Power in Africa and the Coup d'état*. London: Penguin.

Fish, Steven M. 2005. *Democracy Derailed in Russia: The Failure of Open Politics*. New York: Cambridge University Press.

Flock, Elizabeth. 2011. "Chinese Newspaper Cites WikiLeaks: 'Tiananmen massacre a myth'." *The Washington Post* July 14.

FlorCruz, Jaime. 2009. "Tensions High on Tibet Anniversary." *CNN* March 10.

Flores-Macías, Gustavo A. and Sarah E. Kreps. 2013. "The Foreign Policy Consequences of Trade: China's Commercial Relations with Africa and Latin America, 1992–2006." *Journal of Politics* 75(2):357–371.

Foa, Roberto Stefan and Yascha Mounk. 2016. "The Danger of Deconsolidation: The Democratic Disconnect." *Journal of Democracy* 27(3):5–17.

Foa, Roberto Stefan and Yascha Mounk. 2017. "The Signs of Deconsolidation." *Journal of Democracy* 28(1):5–15.

Fock, Elizabeth. 2018. "After a Week of Russian Propaganda, I Was Questioning Everything." *PBS News Hour* May 2.

Fortin-Rittberger, Jessica. 2014. "The Role of Infrastructural and Coercive State Capacity in Explaining Different Types of Electoral Fraud." *Democratization* 21(1):95–117.

Fowler, Anthony and Andrew B. Hall. 2018. "Do Shark Attacks Influence Presidential Elections? Reassessing a Prominent Finding on Voter Competence." *Journal of Politics* 80(4):1423–1437.

Fox, Jo. 2012. "Careless Talk: Tensions within British Domestic Propaganda during the Second World War." *Journal of British Studies* 51(4): 936–966.

Francois, Patrick, Ilia Rainer, and Francesco Trebbi. 2014. "The Dictator's Inner Circle." *NBER Working Paper Series* No. 20216.

Frantz, Erica and Andrea Kendall-Taylor. 2014. "A Dictator's Toolkit: Understanding How Co-optation Affects Repression in Autocracaies." *Journal of Peace Research* 51(3):332–346.

Freedom House. 2017. "Uzbekistan: Country Profile." Available at https://freedomhouse.org/report/nations-transit/2017/uzbekistan.

Freeman, Colin. 2011. "Tunisian President Zine el-Abidine Ben Ali and His Family's 'Mafia rule'." *Telegraph* January 11.

French, Howard W. 1995. "Prostitution Trial Upsets France-Gabon Ties." *The New York Times* April 23.

Friedberg, Aaron L. 2017. *The Authoritarian Challenge: China, Russia and the Threat to the Liberal International Order.* Tokyo: The Sasakawa Peace Foundation.

Friedman, George. 2014. "The American Public's Indifference to Foreign Affairs." *Forbes* February 19.

Friedman, Uri. 2012. "8 Crazy Things Americans Believe About Foreign Policy." *Foreign Policy* October 16.

Friedrich, Carl J. and Zbigniew K. Brzezinski. 1956. *Totalitarian Dictatorship and Autocracy.* Cambridge: Harvard University Press.

Frum, David. 2018. "America's Slide Toward Autocracy." *The Atlantic* October 15.

Frye, Timothy, Scott Gehlbach, Kyle L. Marquardt, and Ora John Reuter. 2017. "Is Putin's Popularity Real?" *Post-Soviet Affairs* 33(1):1–15.

Fu, Diana. 2018. *Mobilizing without the Masses: Control and Contention in China.* New York: Cambridge University Press.

Fu, King-wa, Chung-hong Chan, and Michael Chau. 2013. "Assessing Censorship on Microblogs in China: Discriminatory Keyword Analysis and the Real-Name Registration Policy." *IEEE Internet Computing* 17(3):42–50.

Fukuyama, Francis. 2011. *The Origins of Political Order.* New York: Farrar, Straus and Giroux.

Fukuyama, Francis. 2014. *Political Order and Political Decay: From the Industrial Revolution to the Globalization of Democracy.* New York: Farrar, Straus and Giroux.

Gaffey, Conor. 2016. "Cameroon: Arrests in Anglophone Protests at French Language." *Newsweek* November 23.

Gaffey, Conor. 2017. "Understanding Cameroon's Anglophone Protests." *Newsweek* February 13.

Gainous, Jason and Kevin M. Wagner, eds. 2013. *Tweeting to Power: The Social Media Revolution in American Politics.* New York: Oxford University Press.

Galetovic, Alexander and Ricardo Sanhueza. 2000. "Citizens, Autocrats, and Plotters: A Model and New Evidence on Coups d'Etat." *Economics and Politics* 12(2):183–204.

Gallagher, Mary E. and Blake Miller. 2019. "Who Not What: The Logic of China's Information Control Strategy." *The China Quarterly* 248(1):1011–1036.

Gandhi, Jennifer. 2008. *Political Institutions under Dictatorship.* New York: Cambridge University Press.

Gandhi, Jennifer and Adam Przeworski. 2007. "Authoritarian Institutions and the Survival of Autocrats." *Comparative Political Studies* 40(11):1279–1301.

Gandhi, Jennifer and Ellen Lust-Okar. 2009. "Elections under Authoritarianism." *Annual Review of Political Science* 12:403–422.

Gang, Qian. 2013. "Parsing the 'Public Opinion Struggle'." University of Hong Kong.

Gang, Qian. 2014a. "领袖姓名传播强度观察." University of Hong Kong.

Gang, Qian. 2014b. "Observations on the Frequency of Leader Name References 领袖姓名传播强度观察." University of Hong Kong.

Gang, Qian. 2020. "The Politics of Gratitude." University of Hong Kong.

Gang, Qian and David Bandurski. 2011. "China's Emerging Public Sphere: The Impact of Media Commercialization, Professionalism, and the Internet in an Era of Transition." In *Changing Media, Changing China*, ed. Susan L. Shirk. New York: Oxford University Press, chapter 2, pp. 38–76.

Gansu Province Trade Union Federation. 2016. "Notice on Conscientiously Doing the Work of Issuing and Subscribing to the Trade Union Newspapers Such as the *Workers' Daily* and the *Gansu Workers' Daily* in 2017. 关于认真做好2017年度《工人日报》《甘肃工人报》等工会报刊发行订阅工作的通知." November 15.

Garber, Megan. 2012. "These Countries Are At the Greatest Risk of an Internet Blackout." *Quartz* November 30.

García-Ponce, Omar and Benjamin Pasquale. 2015. "How Political Repression Shapes Attitudes Toward the State: Evidence from Zimbabwe." Center for Global Development.

Gardinier, David E. 1997. "Gabon: Limited Reform and Regime Survival." In *Political Reform in Francophone Africa*, ed. John F. Clark and David E. Gardinier. Boulder: Westview Press, chapter 9, pp. 145–161.

Gardinier, David E. 2000. "France and Gabon Since 1993: The Reshaping of a Neo-Colonial Relationship." *Journal of Contemporary African Studies* 18(2):225–242.

Gatehouse, Gabriel. 2017. "Marine Le Pen: Who's Funding France's Far Right?" *BBC Panorama* April 3.

Geddes, Barbara. 1999. "Authoritarian Breakdown: Empirical Test of a Game Theoretic Argument." University of California, Los Angeles.

Geddes, Barbara. 2005. "Why Parties and Elections in Authoritarian Regimes?" Paper presented at the 2005 Annual Meeting of American Political Science Association.

Geddes, Barbara and John Zaller. 1989. "Sources of Popular Support for Authoritarian Regimes." *American Journal of Political Science* 33(2):319–347.

Geddes, Barbara, Joseph Wright and Erica Frantz. 2018. *How Dictatorships Work: Power, Personalization, and Collapse*. New York: Cambridge University Press.

Gehlbach, Scott and Konstantin Sonin. 2014. "Government Control of the Media." *Journal of Public Economics* 118:163–171.

Gehlbach, Scott, Milan Svolik and Konstantin Sonin. 2016. "Formal Models of Nondemocratic Politics." *Annual Review of Political Science* 19:565–584.

Gehlbach, Scott and Philip Keefer. 2011. "Investment without Democracy: Ruling-Party Institutionalization and Credible Commitment in Autocracies." *Journal of Comparative Economics* 39(2):123–139.

Gehrke, Joel. 2018. "Russia: 'We Are in the Post-West World Order'." *Washington Examiner* June 9.

Gelman, Andrew and Jennifer Hill. 2006. *Data Analysis Using Regression and Multilevel/Hierarchical Models*. New York: Cambridge University Press.

Gennaioli, Nicola and Hans-Joachim Voth. 2015. "State Capacity and Military Conflict." *Review of Economic Studies* 82(4):1409–1448.

Gentzkow, Matthew. 2006. "Television and Voter Turnout." *Quarterly Journal of Economics* 121(3):931–972. Stanford University.

Gentzkow, Matthew, Edward L. Glaeser, and Claudia Goldin. 2006. "The Rise of the Fourth Estate: How Newspapers Became Informative and Why It Mattered." In *Corruption and Reform: Lessons from America's Economic History*, ed. Edward L. Glaeser and Claudia Goldin. Chicago: University of Chicago Press, chapter 6, pp. 187–230.

Gentzkow, Matthew and Jesse M. Shapiro. 2006. "Media Bias and Reputation." *Journal of Political Economy* 114(2):280–316.

Gentzkow, Matthew, Jesse M. Shapiro, and Daniel F. Stone. 2014. "Media Bias in the Marketplace: Theory." *NBER Working Paper Series* No. 19880.

Gerber, Alan S., Dean Karlan, and Daniel Bergan. 2009. "Does the Media Matter? A Field Experiment Measuring the Effect of Newspapers on Voting Behavior and Political Opinions." *American Economic Journal: Applied Economics* 1(2):35–52.

Gerber, Alan S., James G. Gimpel, Donald P. Green, and Daron R. Shaw. 2011. "How Large and Long-Lasting Are the Persuasive Effects of Televised Campaign Ads? Results from a Randomized Field Experiment." *American Political Science Review* 105(1):135–150.

Gessen, Masha. 2012. *The Man without a Face: The Unlikely Rise of Vladimir Putin.* New York: Riverhead Books.

Gessen, Masha. 2014. *Words Will Break Cement: The Passion of Pussy Riot.* New York: Riverhead Books.

Gessen, Masha. 2017. *The Future Is History: How Totalitarianism Reclaimed Russia.* New York: Riverhead Books.

Ghazvinian, John. 2007. *Untapped: The Scramble for Africa's Oil.* New York: Harcourt.

Gibson, Clark C., Barak D. Hoffman, and Ryan S. Jablonski. 2015. "Did Aid Promote Democracy in Africa? The Role of Technical Assistance in Africa's Transitions." *World Development* 68:323–335.

Gibson, James L. 2004. "Does Truth Lead to Reconciliation? Testing the Causal Assumptions of the South African Truth and Reconciliation Process." *American Journal of Political Science* 48(2):201–217.

Gleditsch, Kristian S. and Michael D. Ward. 1997. "Double Take: A Reexamination of Democracy and Autocracy in Modern Polities." *Journal of Conflict Resolution* 41(3):361–383.

Gleick, Peter H. 2014. "Water, Drought, Climate Change, and Conflict in Syria." *Weather, Climate, and Society* 6(3):331–340.

Global Witness. 2004. "Time for Transparency: Coming Clean on Oil, Mining, and Gas Revenues." Available at www.globalwitness.org/en/reports/time-transparency/.

Global Witness. 2005. "The Riddle of the Sphynx: Where Has Congo's Oil Money Gone." Available at www.globalwitness.org/en/campaigns/oil-gas-and-mining/riddle-sphynx-where-has-congos-oil-money-gone/.

Global Witness. 2007. "Congo: Is President's Son Paying for Designer Shopping Sprees with Country's Oil Money?" Available at www.globalwitness.org/en/press-releases/republic-congo-presidents-son-paying-designer-shopping-sprees-countrys-oil-money/.

Glynn, Adam N. 2013. "What Can We Learn with Statistical Truth Serum?" *Public Opinion Quarterly* 77(51):159–172.

Göbel, Christian and H. Christoph Steinhardt. 2019. "Better Coverage, Less Bias." University of Vienna.

Godement, François. 2010. "China: Revisiting the Issue of Mercantilism." CEPR Policy Portal.

Gohdes, Anita R. 2020. "Repression Technology: Internet Accessibility and State Violence." *American Journal of Political Science* 64(3):488–503.

Goldman, Merle. 2005. *The Struggle for Political Rights in China*. New York: Cambridge University Press.

Goldstein, Morris and Nicholas R. Lardy. 2005. "China's Role in the Revived Bretton Woods System: A Case of Mistaken Identity." *Peterson Institute for International Economics Working Paper Series* No. WP05-2.

Goldstone, Jack and Charles Tilly. 2009. "Threat (and Opportunity): Popular Action and State Response in the Dynamics of Contentious Action." In *Silence and Voice in the Study of Contentious Politics*, ed. Ronald R. Aminzade, Jack A. Goldstone, Doug McAdam, Elizabeth J. Perry, William H. Sewell, Sidney Tarrow, and Charles Tilly. New York: Cambridge University Press, chapter 7, pp. 179–194.

Golovchenko, Yevgeniy, Cody Buntain, Gregory Eady, Megan A. Brown, and Joshua A. Tucker. 2020. "Cross-Platform State Propaganda: Russian Trolls on Twitter and YouTube during the 2016 U.S. Presidential Election." *The International Journal of Press/Politics* 25(3):357–389.

González, Felipe and Mounu Prem. 2018. "Can Television Bring Down a Dictator? Evidence from Chile's 'No' Campaign." *Journal of Comparative Economics* 46(1):349–361.

Graber, D. A. 2002. *Mass Media and American Politics*. Washington, D.C.: CQ Press.

Granovetter, Mark. 1978. "Threshold Models of Collective Behavior." *American Journal of Sociology* 83(6):1420–1443.

Greene, Kenneth F. 2009. *Why Dominant Parties Lose: Mexico's Democratization in Comparative Perspective*. New York: Cambridge University Press.

Greene, Kenneth F. 2010. "The Political Economy of Single Party Dominance." *Comparative Political Studies* 43(9):1–27.

Greene, Kenneth F. 2011. "Campaign Persuasion and Nascent Partisanship in Mexico's New Democracy." *American Journal of Political Science* 55(2):398–416.

Greene, Stephan and Philip Resnik. 2009. "More Than Words: Syntactic Packaging and Implicit Sentiment." *Proceedings of Human Language Technologies: The 2009 Annual Conference of the North American Chapter of the Association for Computational Linguistics* 1:503–511.

Greenwald, Glenn. 2017. "The Spoils of War: Trump Lavished with Media and Bipartisan Praise for Bombing Syria." *The Intercept* April 7.

Grimmer, Justin and Brandon Stewart. 2013. "Text as Data: The Promise and Pitfalls of Automatic Content Analysis Methods for Political Texts." *Political Analysis* 21(3):267–297.

Groeling, Tim. 2013. "Media Bias by the Numbers: Challenges and Opportunities in the Empirical Study of Partisan News." *Annual Review of Political Science* 16:129–151.

Groeling, Tim and Matthew A. Baum. 2008. "Crossing the Water's Edge: Elite Rhetoric, Media Coverage, and the Rally-Round-the-Flag Phenomenon." *Journal of Politics* 70(4):1065–1085.

Groseclose, T. and J. Milyo. 2005. "A Measure of Media Bias." *Quarterly Journal of Economics* 120(4):1191–1237.

Grossman, Dave and Gloria Degaetano. 1999. *Stop Teaching Our Kids to Kill: A Call to Action against TV, Movie, and Video Game Violence.* New York: Crown.

Grove, Thomas. 2019. "Shavkat Mirziyoyev Wins Uzbekistan Presidential Election." *The Wall Street Journal* December 5.

Guang, Lei, Margaret Roberts, Yiqing Xu, and Jianan Zhao. 2020. "Pandemic Sees Increase in Chinese Support for Regime, Decrease in Views towards the U.S." *UCSD China Data Lab* June 30.

Guangdong Provincial Propaganda Department. 2006. "Internal Propaganda Circular [Neibu Tongxun]."

Guiso, Luigi, Paola Sapienza, and Luigi Zingales. 2013. "Time Varying Risk Aversion." *NBER Working Paper Series* No. 19284.

Gumede, William. 2018. "The International Criminal Court and Accountability in Africa." *Africa at LSE* January 31.

Gunitsky, Seva. 2015. "Corrupting the Cyber-Commons: Social Media as a Tool of Autocratic Stability." *Perspectives on Politics* 13(1):42–54.

Guo, Gang. 2005. "Party Recruitment of College Students in China." *Journal of Contemporary China* 14(43):371–393.

Guriev, Sergei and Daniel Treisman. 2015. "How Modern Dictators Survive: An Informational Theory of the New Authoritarianism." *NBER Working Paper Series* No. 21136.

Guriev, Sergei and Daniel Treisman. 2018. "Informational Autocracy: Theory and Empirics of Modern Authoritarianism." University of California, Los Angeles.

Guriev, Sergei and Daniel Treisman. 2022. *Spin Dictators.* Princeton: Princeton University Press.

Gyimay-Boadi, E. 1999. "Institutionalizing Credible Elections in Ghana." In *The Self-Restraining State: Power and Accountability in New Democracies*, ed. Andreas Schedler, Larry Diamond and Marc F. Plattner. Boulder: Lynne Rienner Publishers, chapter 7, pp. 105–121.

Habyarimana, James, Macartan Humphreys, Daniel Posner, and Jeremy Weinstein. 2007. "Why Does Ethnic Diversity Undermine Public Goods Provision? An Experimental Approach." *American Political Science Review* 101(4):709–725.

Hackett, Claire and Bill Rolston. 2009. "The Burden of Memory: Victims, Storytelling and Resistance in Northern Ireland." *Memory Studies* 2(3):355.

Hadenius, Axel and Jan Teorell. 2007. "Pathways from Authoritarianism." *Journal of Democracy* 18(1):143–157.

Hafner-Burton, Emilie M. 2008. "Sticks and Stones: Naming and Shaming the Human Rights Enforcement Problem." *International Organization* 62(4):689–716.

Haggard, Stephan. 2018. *Developmental States*. New York: Cambridge University Press.

Haggard, Stephan and Robert R. Kaufman. 1997. "The Political Economy of Democratic Transitions." *Comparative Politics* 29(3):263–83.

Hale, Henry E. 2005. "Regime Cycles: Democracy, Autocracy, and Revolution in Post-Soviet Eurasia." *World Politics* 58(1):133–165.

Halverson, Jeffry R., H. L. Goodall Jr. and Steven R. Corman. 2011. *Master Narratives of Islamist Extremism*. New York: Palgrave Macmillan.

Hamilton, James. 2010. "The (many) markets for international news." *Journalism Studies* 11(5):650–666.

Hamilton, James T. 2004. *All the News That's Fit to Sell: How the Market Transforms Information into News*. Princeton: Princeton University Press.

Hancock, Tom and Nicole Liu. 2019. "Top Chinese Officials Plagiarised Doctoral Dissertations." *Financial Times* February 26.

Harvard General Inquirer. 2015. "Positiv and Negativ Semantic Dictionaries." Cambridge: Available at www.mariapinto.es/ciberabstracts/Articulos/Inquirer.htm.

Harvard Magazine. 2014. "Tiananmen Plus Twenty-Five: A Tragedy and Its Aftermath." *Harvard Magazine* July-August.

Hashimova, Umida. 2018. "Uzbekistan Looks to China for Policing Experience." *The Diplomat* September 10.

Hassan, Mai. 2016. "The Strategic Shuffle: Ethnic Geography, the Internal Security Apparatus, and Elections in Kenya." *American Journal of Political Science* 61(2):382–395.

Hassan, Mai O. 2020. *Regime Threats and State Solutions*. New York: Cambridge University Press.

Hassid, Jonathan. 2008. "Controlling the Chinese Media: An Uncertain Business." *Asian Survey* 48(3):414–430.

Hassid, Jonathan. 2011. "Four Models of the Fourth Estate: A Typology of Contemporary Chinese Journalists." *The China Quarterly* 208:13–32.

Hassid, Jonathan. 2016. *China's Unruly Journalists: How Committed Professionals Are Changing the People's Republic*. New York: Routledge.

Havel, Václav. 1978. *The Power of the Powerless*. New York: Vintage Classsics.

Hayes, Andrew F. and Teresa A. Myers. 2009. "Testing the Proximate Casualties Hypothesis: Local Troop Loss, Attention to News, and Support for Military Intervention." *Mass Communication and Society* 12(4): 379–402.

Hayes, Anna. 2019. "Explainer: Who Are the Uyghurs and Why Is the Chinese Government Detaining Them?" *The Conversation* February 14.

Hayes, Danny and Jennifer L. Lawless. 2015. "As Local News Goes, So Goes Citizen Engagement: Media, Knowledge, and Participation in US House Elections." *Journal of Politics* 77(2):447–462.

Hays, Jeffrey. 2010. "Xinjiang Riots in 2009." Available at http://factsanddetails
.com/china/cat5/sub89/item1005.html.

Healy, Andrew J., Neil Malhotra, and Cecilia Hyunjung Mo. 2010. "Irrelevant
Events Affect Voters' Evaluations of Government Performance." *Proceedings
of the National Academy of Sciences* 107(29):12804–12809.

Heilbrunn, John R. 1993. "Social Origins of National Conferences in Benin and
Togo." *Journal of Modern African Studies* 31(2):277–299.

Heilbrunn, John R. 2014. *Oil, Democracy, and Development in Africa.* New
York: Cambridge University Press.

Hendrix, Cullen S. and Stephan Haggard. 2015. "Global Food Prices, Regime
Type, and Urban Unrest in the Developing World." *Journal of Peace Research*
52(2):143–157.

Henochowicz, Anne. 2016. "Five Years of Sensitive Words on June
Fourth." *China Digital Times* pp. http://chinadigitaltimes.net/2016/06/five-
years–sensitive–words–june–fourth/.

Herbst, Jeffrey. 2000. *States and Power in Africa: Comparative Lessons in
Authority and Control.* Princeton: Princeton University Press.

Hersey, Frank. 2017. "China to Have 626 Million Surveillance Cameras within
3 Years." *TechNode* November 22.

Higgins, Andrew and Ivan Nechepurenko. 2020. "Under Siege in Belarus,
Lukashenko Turns to Putin." *The New York Times* August 15.

Hill, Daniel W. and Zachary M. Jones. 2014. "An Empirical Evaluation
of Explanations for State Repression." *American Political Science Review*
108(3):661–687.

Hill, Seth J., James Lo, Lynn Vavreck, and John Zaller. 2013. "How Quickly
We Forget: The Duration of Persuasion Effects from Mass Communication."
Political Communication 30(4):521–547.

Hille, Kathrin. 2008. "Chinese Media Put Positive Spin on Crisis." *Financial
Times* December 8.

Hillman, Ben and Gray Tuttle, eds. 2016. *Ethnic Conflict and Protest in Tibet
and Xinjiang.* New York: Columbia University Press.

Hintze, Otto. 1975. *Historical Essays of Otto Hintze.* New York: Oxford
University Press.

Hobbs, William and Margaret E. Roberts. 2018. "How Sudden Censorship
Can Increase Access to Information." *American Political Science Review*
112(3):621–636.

Höhn, Sabine. 2010. "International Justice and Reconciliation in Namibia: The
ICC Submission and Public Memory." *African Affairs* 109(436):471–488.

Holbrook, R. Andrew and Timothy G. Hill. 2005. "Agenda-Setting and Priming in Prime Time Television: Crime Dramas as Political Cues." *Political
Communication* 22(3):277–295.

Hollyer, James R., B. Peter Rosendorff, and James Raymond Vreeland. 2015.
"Transparency, Protest, and Autocratic Instability." *American Political Science
Review* 109(4):764–784.

Hong, Junhao. 1998. *The Internationalization of Television in China: The
Evolution of Ideology, Society and Media since the Reform.* Westport:
Praeger.

Hopf, Ted. 2002. *Social Construction of Foreign Policy: Identities and Foreign Policies, Moscow, 1955 and 1999*. Ithaca: Cornell University Press.

Howard, Marc Morjé and Philip G. Roessler. 2006. "Liberalizing Electoral Outcomes in Competitive Authoritarian Regimes." *American Journal of Political Science* 50(2):365–381.

Howard, Philip N. 2010. *The Digital Origins of Dictatorship and Democracy: Information Technology and Political Islam*. New York: Oxford University Press.

Howard, Philip N. and Bence Kollanyi. 2016. "Bots, #StrongerIn, and #Brexit: Computational Propaganda during the UK-EU Referendum." Oxford University.

Howard, Philip N., Bharath Ganesh, Dimitra Liotsiou, John Kelly, and Camille François. 2018. "The IRA, Social Media and Political Polarization in the United States, 2012–2018." Oxford University.

Howard, Philip N. and Muzammil M. Hussain. 2011. "Digital Media and the Arab Spring." *Journal of Democracy* 22(3):35–48.

Howard, Philip N. and Muzammil M. Hussain. 2013. *Democracy's Fourth Wave? Digital Media and the Arab Spring*. New York: Oxford University Press.

Huang, Cary and Keith Zhai. 2013. "Xi Jinping Rallies Party for Propaganda War on Internet." *South China Morning Post* September 4.

Huang, Haifeng. 2015a. "International Knowledge and Domestic Evaluations in a Changing Society: The Case of China." *American Political Science Review* 109(3):613–634.

Huang, Haifeng. 2015b. "Propaganda as Signaling." *Comparative Politics* 47(4):419–444.

Huang, Haifeng. 2018. "The Pathology of Hard Propaganda." *Journal of Politics* 80(3):1034–1038.

Huang, Haifeng. 2020. "How Information Bubble Drives the Chinese Public's Views of China's Global Standing and Fuels Grassroots Nationalism." *UCSD China Data Lab* December 16.

Huang, Haifeng and Yao-Yuan Yeh. 2016. "Information from Abroad: Foreign Media, Selective Exposure, and Political Support in China." *British Journal of Political Science* 49(2):611–636.

Huang, Yasheng. 2008. *Capitalism with Chinese Characteristics: Entrepreneurship and the State*. New York: Cambridge University Press.

Huang, Zheping. 2015c. "Absolutely Everywhere in Beijing Is Now Covered by Police Video Surveillance." *Quartz* October 7.

Huddy, Leonie, Nadia Khatib, and Theresa Capelos. 2002. "Trends: Reactions to the Terrorist Attacks of September 11, 2001." *The Public Opinion Quarterly* 66(3):418–450.

Huddy, Leonie, Stanley Feldman, Theresa Capelos, and Colin Provost. 2002. "The Consequences of Terrorism: Disentangling the Effects of Personal and National Threat." *Political Psychology* 23(3):485–509.

Human Rights Watch. 2003. "From House to House: Abuses by Mahalla Committees." Available at www.hrw.org/reports/2003/uzbekistan0903/uzbekistan0903full.pdf.

Human Rights Watch. 2010. "China: End June 1989 Massacre Denial, Free Dissidents." Available at www.hrw.org/news/2010/06/01/china-end-june-1989-massacre-denial-free-dissidents.

Human Rights Watch. 2014. "Rwanda: Repression Across Borders. Attacks and Threats against Rwandan Opponents and Critics Abroad." Available at www.hrw.org/news/2014/01/28/rwanda-repression-across-borders.

Hyde, Susan D. 2011. *The Pseudo-Democrat's Dilemma: Why Election Observation Became an International Norm*. Ithaca: Cornell University.

Hyde, Susan D. and Nikolay Marinov. 2012. "Which Elections Can Be Lost?" *Political Analysis* 20(2):191–201.

Hyde, Susan D. and Nikolay Marinov. 2014. "Does Information Facilitate Self-Enforcing Democracy? The Role of International Election Observation." *International Organization* 68(2):329–359.

Iaccino, Ludovica and Daniele Palumbo. 2016. "Tensions Rise in Cameroon as Teachers Demand 'Respect for Anglo-Saxon Heritage'." *International Business Times* December 7.

Ikenberry, G. John. 2014. "From Hegemony to the Balance of Power: The Rise of China and American Grand Strategy in East Asia." *International Journal of Korean Unification Studies* 23(2):41–63.

Inglehart, Ronald. 1997. *Modernization and Postmodernization: Cultural, Economic, and Political Change in 43 Societies*. Princeton: Princeton University Press.

Inglehart, Ronald and Christian Welzel. 2005. *Modernization, Cultural Change, and Democracy*. New York: Cambridge University Press.

Inglehart, Ronald and Christian Welzel. 2010. "Changing Mass Priorities: The Link between Modernization and Democracy." *Perspectives on Politics* 8(2):551–567.

Ioffe, Julia. 2010. "What Is Russia Today?" *Columbia Journalism Review* September/October.

IREX. 2008. "Media Sustainability Index 2006/2007: Development of Sustainable Independent Media in Africa." Washington, D.C.: Available at http://pdf.usaid.gov/pdf_docs/pnaea448.pdf.

IREX. 2014. "Media Sustainability Index 2012." Washington, D.C.: Available at www.irex.org/sites/default/files/u115/Gambia%202012%20MSI%20Proof.pdf.

Iyengar, Shanto. 1990. "Framing Responsibility for Political Issues." *Political Behavior* 12(1):19–40.

Iyengar, Shanto and Donald R. Kinder. 1987. *News That Matters: Television and American Opinion*. Chicago: University of Chicago Press.

Iyengar, Shanto and Nicholas A. Valentino. 2000. "Who Says What? Source Credibility as a Mediator of Campaign Advertising." In *Elements of Reason: Cognition, Choice, and the Bounds of Rationality*, ed. Arthur Lupia, Mathew D. McCubbins, and Samuel L. Popkin. New York: Cambridge University Press, chapter 6, pp. 108–129.

Iyyer, Mohit, Peter Enns, Jordan Boyd-Graber, and Philip Resnik. 2014. "Political Ideology Detection Using Recursive Neural Networks." *Proceedings of the 52nd Annual Meeting of the Association for Computational Linguistics* 1:1113–1122.

Jahateh, Lamin. 2012. "Controversy of Abdoulaye Wade's Presidential Bid." *Al Jazeera* January 28.

Jamieson, Kathleen Hall and Dolores Albarracin. 2020. "The Relation between Media Consumption and Misinformation at the Outset of the SARS-CoV-2 Pandemic in the US." *The Harvard Kennedy School Misinformation Review* 1:1–22.

Jang, JunHyeok and Haifeng Huang. 2019. "Subnational Elections and Media Freedom in Autocracies: Diffusion of Local Reputation and Regime Survival." Paper presented at the Annual Meeting of the Midwest Political Science Association.

Jaros, Kyle and Jennifer Pan. 2017. "China's Newsmakers: Official Media Coverage and Political Shifts in the Xi Jinping Era." *The China Quarterly* 233:111–136.

Javeline, Debra. 2003. "The Role of Blame in Collective Action: Evidence from Russia." *American Political Science Review* 97(1):107–121.

Jentleson, Bruce W. 1992. "The Pretty Prudent Public: Post Post-Vietnam American Opinion on the Use of Military Force." *International Studies Quarterly* 36(1):49–74.

Jia, Wenshan, Lu Xing, and D. Ray Heisey, eds. 2002. *Chinese Communication Theory and Research: Reflections, New Frontiers, and New Directions.* Westport: Ablex Publishing.

Jiang, Jing. 2012. "Information Extraction from Text." In *Mining Text Data*, ed. Charu C. Aggarwal and ChengXiang Zhai. Boston: Springer, chapter 2, pp. 11–41.

Jiang, Junyan and Dali L. Yang. 2016. "Lying or Believing? Measuring Preference Falsification From a Political Purge in China." *Comparative Political Studies* 49(5):600–634.

Jiao, Guobiao. 2004. "Declaration of the Campaign against The Central Propaganda Department."

Jin, Shuai. 2016. "How Chinese Citizens Respond to Government Propaganda on Economic Inequality." University of Iowa.

Jirik, John. 2004. "China's News Media and the Case of CCTV-9." In *International News in the 21st Century*, ed. Chris Paterson and Annabelle Sreberny. Eastleigh: John Libbey Publishing for University of Luton Press, chapter 7, pp. 127–146.

Jo, Hyeran and Beth Simmons. 2016. "Can the International Criminal Court Deter Atrocity?" *International Organization* 70(3):443–475.

Jo, Hyeran, Mitchell Radtke, and Beth Simmons. 2018. "Assessing the International Criminal Court." In *The Performance of International Courts and Tribunals*, ed. Theresa Squatrito, Oran R. Young, Andreas Follesdal and Geir Ulfstein. New York: Cambridge University Press, chapter 6, pp. 193–233.

Johnson, Eric J. and Amos Tversky. 1983. "Affect, Generalization, and the Perception of Risk." *Journal of Personality and Social Psychology* 45(1):20–31.

Johnson, Ian. 2019. "Islamophobia in China." *ChinaFile* May 14.

Johnson, Kristen, I-Ta Lee, and Dan Goldwasser. 2017. "Ideological Phrase Indicators for Classification of Political Discourse Framing on Twitter." *Proceedings of the Second Workshop on NLP and Computational Social Science* 1:90–99.

Johnston, Alastair Iain. 2008. *Social States: China in International Institutions, 1980–2000.* Princeton: Princeton University Press.

Johnston, Alastair Iain and Kai Quek. 2018. "Can China Back Down? Crisis De-Escalation in the Shadow of Popular Opposition." *International Security* 42(3):7–36.

Johnstone, Sarah and Jeffrey Mazo. 2011. "Global Warming and the Arab Spring." *Survival* 53(2):11–17.

Jones, Zachary M. 2019. "An Analysis of Polity IV and Its Components." Available at http://zmjones.com/polity/.

Jowett, Garth S. and Victoria O'Donnell. 2012. *Propaganda and Persuasion.* London: Sage.

Judah, Ben. 2013. *Fragile Empire: How Russia Fell In and Out of Love with Vladimir Putin.* New Haven: Yale University Press.

Kaiman, Jonathan. 2014. "Chinese Authorities Offer Cash to Promote Interethnic Marriages." *The Guardian* September 2.

Kalathil, Shanthi and Taylor C. Boas. 2002. *Open Networks, Closed Regimes: The Impact of the Internet on Authoritarian Rule.* Washington, D.C.: Carnegie Endowment for International Peace.

Kalyvas, Stathis N. 2006. *The Logic of Violence in Civil War.* New York: Cambridge University Press.

Kamenica, Emir and Matthew Gentzkow. 2011. "Bayesian Persuasion." *American Economic Review* 101(6):2590–2615.

Kapuscinski, Ryszard. 1989. *The Emperor.* New York: Vintage.

Karadeniz, Talha and Erdogan Dogdu. 2018. "Improvement of General Inquirer Features with Quantity Analysis." *2018 IEEE International Conference on Big Data* 1:2228–2231.

Kaufman, Robert R. and Stephan Haggard. 2018. "Democratic Decline in the United States: What Can We Learn from Middle-Income Backsliding?" *Perspectives on Politics* 17(2):1–16.

Kayser, Mark Andreas and Michael Peress. 2012. "Benchmarking across Borders: Electoral Accountability and the Necessity of Comparison." *American Political Science Review* 106(3):661–684.

Kelley, Judith G. 2012. *Monitoring Democracy: When International Election Observation Works, and Why It Often Fails.* Princeton: Princeton University Press.

Kennedy, John James. 2009. "Maintaining Popular Support for the Chinese Communist Party: The Influence of Education and the State-Controlled Media." *Political Studies* 57(3):517–536.

Kent, Lia. 2011. "Local Memory Practices in East Timor: Disrupting Transitional Justice Narratives." *International Journal of Transitional Justice* 5(3):434–455.

Keppler, Elise. 2017. "AU's 'ICC Withdrawal Strategy' Less Than Meets the Eye." New York: Human Rights Watch. Available at www.hrw.org/news/2017/02/01/aus-icc-withdrawal-strategy-less-meets-eye.

Kersting, Erasmus and Christopher Kelly. 2014. "Aid and Democracy Redux." *European Economic Review* 67:125–143.

Kessler, Glenn. 2018a. "Meet the Bottomless Pinocchio, a New Rating for a False Claim Repeated Over and Over Again." *The Washington Post* December 10.

Kessler, Jason. 2017. "Scattertext: A Browser-Based Tool for Visualizing how Corpora Differ." *Proceedings of ACL 2017, System Demonstrations* 1:85–90.

Kessler, Jason. 2018b. "scattertext." Available at https://github.com/JasonKessler/scattertext.

Khan, Saher. 2016. "Cotton Carming in Uzbekistan Is 'Modern Slavery'." *Muftah* May 5.

Kim, Nam Kyu. 2016. "Revisiting Economic Shocks and Coups." *Journal of Conflict Resolution* 60(1):3–31.

Kinetz, Erika. 2018. "China Cancels Christmas: Decorations Pulled Down and Events Cut in at Least Four Cities." *Independent* December 24.

King, Gary, Jennifer Pan, and Margaret E. Roberts. 2013. "How Censorship in China Allows Government Criticism but Silences Collective Expression." *American Political Science Review* 107(2):326–343.

King, Gary, Jennifer Pan, and Margaret E. Roberts. 2017. "How the Chinese Government Fabricates Social Media Posts for Strategic Distraction, Not Engaged Argument." *American Political Science Review* 111(3):484–501.

Kirkpatrick, Jeane. 1981. *Dictatorship and Double Standards: Rationalism and Realism in Politics.* New York: Simon & Schuster.

Kitfield, James. 2018. "The US & China: A Colder Peace or Thucydides' Trap?" *Breaking Defense* December 12.

Kleinman, Zoe. 2019. "Russia Considers 'Unplugging' from Internet." *BBC* February 11.

Knight, Brian and Ana Tribin. 2019. "The Limits of Propaganda: Evidence from Chavez's Venezuela." *Journal of the European Economic Association* 17(2):567–605.

Knutsen, Carl Henrik. 2013. "Democracy, State Capacity, and Economic Growth." *World Development* 43:1–18.

Knutsen, Carl Henrik and Havard Mokliev Nygard. 2015. "Institutional Characteristics and Regime Survival: Why Are Semi-Democracies Less Durable Than Autocracies and Democracies?" *American Journal of Political Science* 59(3):656–670.

Knutsen, Carl Henrik, Havard Mokliev Nygard, and Tore Wig. 2017. "Autocratic Elections: Stabilizing Tool or Force for Change?" *World Politics* 69(1):98–143.

Koch, Natalie. 2012. "Sport and Soft Authoritarian Nation-Building." *Political Geography* 32:42–51.

Kode, Davide. 2018. "African Union Makes Moves to Neutralise Africa's Main Human Rights Body." *Inter Press Service News Agency* October 25.

Kollanyi, Bence, Philip N. Howard, and Samuel C. Woolley. 2016. "Bots and Automation over Twitter during the U.S. Election." Oxford University.

Kounga, Kury. 2016. "Congo Présidentielle 2016: L'OIF souhaite une élection apaisée." *Portail* 242 March 16.

Kowalewski, David. 1980. "The Protest Uses of Symbolic Politics in the USSR." *Journal of Politics* 42(2):439–460.

Kragh, Martin and Sebastian Asberg. 2017. "Russia's Strategy for Influence through Public Diplomacy and Active Measures: The Swedish Case." *Journal of Strategic Studies* 40(6):773–816.

Kramon, Eric and Keith R. Weghorst. 2012. "Measuring Sensitive Attitudes in Developing Countries: Lessons from Implementing the List Experiment." *The Experimental Political Scientist* 3(2):14–24.

Krekó, Péter and Zsolt Enyedi. 2018. "Orbán's Laboratory of Illiberalism." *Journal of Democracy* 28(3):39–51.

Kristof, Nicholas. 2006. "In China It's ******* vs. Netizens." *The New York Times* June 20.

Kronrod, A., A. Grinstein and L. Wathieu. 2012. "Go Green! Should Environmental Messages Be So Assertive?" *Journal of Marketing* 76(1):95–102.

Krosnick, J. A. and D. R. Kinder. 1990. "Altering the Foundations of Support for the President through Priming." *American Political Science Review* 84(2):497–512.

Kuklinski, James H., Michael D. Cobb, and Martin Gilens. 1997. "Racial Attitudes and the 'New South'." *Journal of Politics* 59(2):323–349.

Kuklinski, James H., Paul M. Sniderman, Kathleen Knight, Thomas Piazza, Philip E. Tetlock, Gordon R. Lawrence, and Barbara Mellers. 1997. "Racial Prejudice and Attitudes toward Affirmative Action." *American Journal of Political Science* 41(2):402–419.

Kuran, Timur. 1989. "Sparks and Prairie Fires: A Theory of Unanticipated Political Revolution." *Public Choice* 61(1):41–74.

Kuran, Timur. 1991. "Now Out of Never: The Element of Surprise in the East European Revolution of 1989." *World Politics* 44(1):7–48.

Kuran, Timur. 1997. *Private Truths, Public Lies: The Social Consequences of Preference Falsification.* Cambridge: Harvard University Press.

Kuypers, Jim A. 1997. *Presidential Crisis Rhetoric and the Press in the Post-Cold War World.* Westport: Praeger.

Lamberova, Natalia and Daniel Treisman. 2020. "Confronting Economic Crisis: Putin's Approach." *Democracy and Autocracy* 18(2):24–30.

Laplante, Lisa J. 2007. "The Peruvian Truth Commission's Historical Memory Project: Empowering Truth-Tellers to Confront Truth Deniers." *Journal of Human Rights* 6(4):433–452.

Lardy, Nicholas R. 2012. *Sustaining China's Economic Growth After the Global Financial Crisis.* Washington, D.C.: Peterson Institute for International Economics.

Largey, Matt. 2018. "'Jade Helm' Conspiracy Theories Were Part of Russian Disinformation Campaign, Former CIA Chief Says." *KUT Public Radio* May 3.

Larson, Eric V. 2000. "Putting Theory to Work: Diagnosing Public Opinion on the US Intervention in Bosnia." In *Being Useful: Policy Relevance and International Relations Theory*, ed. M. Nincic and J. Lepgold. Ann Arbor: University of Michigan Press, chapter 7, pp. 174–233.

Lasswell, Harold D. 1927. "The Theory of Political Propaganda." *American Political Science Review* 21(3):627–631.

Lasswell, Harold D. 1938. *Propaganda Technique in the World War*. New York: Peter Smith.

Lawrence, Adria. 2017. "Repression and Activism among the Arab Spring's First Movers: Morocco's (Almost) Revolutionaries." *British Journal of Political Science* 47(3):699–718.

Lawson, Chappell and James A. McCann. 2005. "Television News, Mexico's 2000 Elections and Media Effects in Emerging Democracies." *British Journal of Political Science* 35(1):1–30.

Le Corre, Philippe and Vuk Vuksanovic. 2019. "Serbia: China's Open Door to the Balkans." *The Diplomat* January 1.

Le Floch-Prigent, Loik. 2001. *Affaire Elf, Affaire d'État*. Paris: Cherche Midi.

Le Parisien. 2002. "La justice enquête sur l'ami du président congolais." April 24.

Lee, Chin-chuan, ed. 1990. *Voices of China: The Interplay of Politics and Journalism*. New York: Guilford.

Lee, Chin-chuan, ed. 2000. *Power, Money, and the Media: Communication Patterns and Bureaucratic Control in Cultural China*. Evanston: Northwestern University Press.

Lee, Jaehyon. 2015. "China Is Recreating the American 'Hub-and-Spoke' System in Asia." *The Diplomat* September 11.

Lee, Jong R. 1977. "Rallying around the Flag." *Presidential Studies Quarterly* 7(4):252–256.

Lehoucq, Fabrice E. and Iván Molina. 2002. *Stuffing the Ballot Box: Fraud, Electoral Reform and Democratization in Costa Rica*. New York: Cambridge University Press.

Lei, Xuchuan and Jie Lu. 2016. "Revisiting Political Wariness in China's Public Opinion Surveys: Experimental Evidence on Responses to Politically Sensitive Questions." *Journal of Contemporary China* 26(104):213–232.

Leon, Gabriel. 2014. "Loyalty for Sale? Military Spending and Coups d'Etat." *Public Choice* 159(3/4):363–383.

Leonnig, Carol D. 2010. "Congo Republic's Heavy Use of D.C. Lobbyists Prompts Questions." *The Washington Post* August 25.

Lerner, Jennifer S. and Dacher Keltner. 2000. "Beyond Valence: Toward a Model of Emotion-Specific Influences on Judgment and Choice." *Cognition and Emotion* 14(4):473–493.

Lerner, Jennifer S. and Dacher Keltner. 2001. "Fear, Anger, and Risk." *Journal of Personality and Social Psychology* 81(1):146–159.

Lerner, Jennifer S., Roxana M. Gonzalez, Deborah A. Small, and Baruch Fischhoff. 2003. "Effects of Fear and Anger on Perceived Risk of Terrorism: A National Field Experiment." *Psychological Science* 14(2):144–150.

Levitsky, Steven and Daniel Ziblatt. 2018. *How Democracies Die*. New York: Crown.

Levitsky, Steven and Lucan A. Way. 2002. "The Rise of Competitive Authoritarianism." *Journal of Democracy* 99(3):435–452.

Levitsky, Steven and Lucan A. Way. 2010. *Competitive Authoritarianism: Hybrid Regimes after the Cold War*. New York: Cambridge University Press.

Levy, Jacob T. 2016. "Authoritarianism and Post-Truth Politics." Washington, D.C.: Niskanen Center, November.

Lewis-Beck, Michael S., Wenfang Tang, and Nicholas F. Martini. 2014. "A Chinese Popularity Function: Sources of Government Support." *Political Research Quarterly* 67(1):16–25.

Li, Lianjiang. 2004. "Political Trust in Rural China." *Modern China* 30(2):228–258.

Li, Lianjiang. 2010. "Rights Consciousness and Rules Consciousness in Contemporary China." *China Journal* 64:47–68.

Liñán, Miguel Vázquez. 2009. "Putin's Propaganda Legacy." *Post-Soviet Affairs* 25(2):137–159.

Li Tao. 2018. "Jaywalkers under Surveillance in Shenzhen Soon to Be Punished via Text Messages." *South China Morning Post* March 27.

Li, Xiaojun, Weiyi Shi, and Boliang Zhu. 2018. "The Face of Internet Recruitment: Evaluating the Labor Markets of Online Crowdsourcing Platforms in China." *Research and Politics* 5(1):1–8.

Li, Xiaoping. 2001. "Significant Changes in the Chinese Television Industry and Their Impact in the PRC: An Insider's Perspective." Brookings Institution.

Li, Xiaoping. 2002. "'Focus' (Jiaodian Fangtan) and the Changes in the Chinese Television Industry." *Journal of Contemporary China* 11(30):17–34.

Lichter, Andreas, Max Loëffler, and Sebastian Siegloch. 2021. "The Long-Term Costs of Government Surveillance: Insights from Stasi Spying in East Germany." *Journal of the European Economic Association* 19(2):741–789.

Lillis, Joanna. 2015. "Uzbekistan: Tashkent Voters Back Strongman as He Cruises to Victory." *Eurasianet* March 29.

Lim, Louisa. 2014. *The People's Republic of Amnesia: Tiananmen Revisited*. New York: Oxford University Press.

Lindberg, Staffan I. 2006. *Democracy and Elections in Africa*. Baltimore: Johns Hopkins University Press.

Linvill, Darren, Brandon Boatwright, Will Grant, and Patrick L. Warren. 2019. "'THE RUSSIANS ARE HACKING MY BRAIN!' Investigating Russia's Internet Research Agency Twitter Tactics During the 2016 United States Presidential Campaign." *Computers in Human Behavior* 99:292–300.

Linz, Daniel, Edward Donnerstein, and Steven M. Adams. 1989. "Physiological Desensitization and Judgments about Female Victims of Violence." *Human Communication Research* 15(4):509–522.

Little, Andrew T. 2017. "Propaganda and Credulity." *Games and Economic Behavior* 102:224–232.

Liu, Alan P. L. 1996. *Mass Politics in the People's Republic: State and Society in Contemporary China*. Boulder: Westview Press.

Liu, Bing and Lei Zhang. 2012. "A Survey of Opinion Mining and Sentiment Analysis." In *Mining Text Data*, ed. Charu C. Aggarwal and ChengXiang Zhai. Boston: Springer, chapter 13, pp. 415–463.

Liu, Joyce and Xiqing Wang. 2017. "In Your Face: China's All-Seeing State." *BBC* December 10.

Liuzhou Trade Union Federation, 柳州市总工会. 2016. "Notice on Doing a Good Job in 2017 Trade Union Newspaper and Magazine Subscriptions. 关于做好2017年度工会报刊杂志征订工作的通知.". .

Lohmann, Susanne. 1993. "A Signaling Model of Informative and Manipulative Political Action." *American Political Science Review* 87(2):319–333.

Londregan, John B. and Keith T. Poole. 1990. "Poverty, the Coup Trap, and the Seizure of Executive Power." *World Politics* 42(2):151–183.

Longerich, Peter. 2015. *Goebbels: A Biography*. New York: Random House.

Lorentzen, Peter. 2014. "China's Strategic Censorship." *American Journal of Political Science* 58(2):402–414.

Lorentzen, Peter and Xi Lu. 2018. "Personal Ties, Meritocracy, and China's Anti-Corruption Campaign." University of San Francisco.

Loughran, Tim and Bill McDonald. 2011. "When Is a Liability Not a Liability? Textual Analysis, Dictionaries, and 10-Ks." *Journal of Finance* 66(1):35–65.

Lovelace, Ryan. 2018. "White-Collar Pros Weigh Risks, 'Stigma' of Joining Trump Team." *National Law Journal* March 26.

Lu, Hui. 2019. "China Issues White Paper on Anti-Terrorism, Human Rights Protection in Xinjiang." *Xinhua* March 18.

Luhn, Alec. 2015. "Human Rights Activists' Dismay as Uzbekistan Autocrat Clings to Power." *The Guardian* April 4.

Lupia, A. and M. D. McCubbins. 1998. *The Democratic Dilemma: Can Citizens Learn What They Need to Know?* New York: Cambridge University Press.

Lusher, Adam. 2017. "At Least 10,000 People Died in Tiananmen Square Massacre, Secret British Cable from the Time Alleged." *Independent* December 23.

Lust-Okar, Ellen. 2006. "Elections under Authoritarianism: Preliminary Lessons from Jordan." *Democratization* 13(3):456–471.

Lyall, Jason. 2010. "Are Coethnics More Effective Counterinsurgents? Evidence from the Second Chechen War." *American Political Science Review* 104(1):1–20.

Lynch, Daniel C. 1999. *Media, Politics, and "Thought Work" in Reformed China*. Stanford: Stanford University Press.

Ma, Jian. 2018. *China Dream*. New York: Counterpoint.

MacFarquhar, Roderick. 2011. *The Politics of China: Sixty Years of the People's Republic of China*. New York: Cambridge University Press.

Magaloni, Beatriz. 2006. *Voting for Autocracy: Hegemonic Party Survival and Its Demise in Mexico*. New York: Cambridge University Press.

Magaloni, Beatriz. 2008. "Credible Power-Sharing and the Longevity of Authoritarian Rule." *Comparative Political Studies* 41(4):715–741.

Magaloni, Beatriz. 2010. "The Game of Electoral Fraud and the Ousting of Authoritarian Rule." *American Journal of Political Science* 54(3):751–765.

Magnusson, Bruce and John F. Clark. 2005. "Democratic Survival and Democratic Failure in Africa." *Comparative Studies in Society and History* 47(3):552–582.

Mahood, Samantha and Halim Rane. 2016. "Islamist Narratives in ISIS Recruitment Propaganda." *Journal of International Communication* 23(1):15–35.

Maizland, Lindsay. 2019. "China's Crackdown on Uighers in Xinjiang." Available at www.cfr.org/backgrounder/chinas-repression-uyghurs-xinjiang.

Malka, Ariel and Yphtack Lelkes. 2010. "More Than Ideology: Conservative-Liberal Identity and Receptivity to Political Cues." *Social Justice Research* 23(2–3):156–188.

Manacorda, Marco and Andrea Tesei. 2016. "Liberation Technology: Mobile Phones and Political Mobilization in Africa." *Econometrica* 88(2): 533–567.

Manion, Melanie. 1990. "Reluctant Duelists: The Logic of the 1989 Protests and Massacre." In *Beijing Spring, 1989: Confrontation and Conflict. The Basic Documents*, ed. Michel Oksenberg, Lawrence R. Sullivan, and Marc Lambert. Armonk: M.E. Sharpe, Introduction, pp. xii–xlii.

Manion, Melanie. 2006. "Democracy, Community, Trust: The Impact of Elections in Rural China." *Comparative Political Studies* 39(3):301–324.

Mann, Michael. 1993. *The Sources of Social Power: Volume 2, The Rise of Classes and Nation-States, 1760–1914*. New York: Cambridge University Press.

Manning, Peter. 2011. "Governing Memory: Justice, Reconciliation and Outreach at the Extraordinary Chambers in the Courts of Cambodia." *Memory Studies* 5(2):165–181.

Mao Zedong. 1929. "Problems in Red Army Propaganda [Hongjun Xuanchuan Wenti]." Available at www.lib.szu.edu.cn/szulibhtm/AD_zyjs/BD_dzsk/ML/mzdwx/mx1/022.htm.

Marinov, Nikolay and Hein Goemans. 2014. "Coups and Democracy." *British Journal of Political Science* 44(4):799–825.

Marshall, Monty G. and Keith Jaggers. 2005. *Polity IV Project: Political Regime Characteristics and Regime Transitions, 1800–2004*. Arlington: George Mason University.

Martin, Gregory J. and Ali Yurukoglu. 2017. "Bias in Cable News: Persuasion and Polarization." *American Economic Review* 107(9):2565–2599.

McFaul, Michael. 2002. "The Fourth Wave of Democracy and Dictatorship: Noncooperative Transitions in the Postcommunist World." *World Politics* 54(2):212–244.

McFaul, Michael. 2005. "Transitions from Postcommunism." *Journal of Democracy* 16(3):5–19.

McFaul, Michael. 2007. "Ukraine Imports Democracy: External Influences on the Orange Revolution." *International Security* 32(2):45–83.

McKune, Craig. 2013. "Chinese Companies Scoop Shares in Independent News." *Mail & Guardian* August 15.

McMillan, John and Pablo Zoido. 2004. "How to Subvert Democracy: Montesinos in Peru." *Journal of Economic Perspectives* 18(4):69–92.

Meernik, James. 2015. "The International Criminal Court and the Deterrence of Human Rights Atrocities." *Civil Wars* 17(3):318–339.

Meng, Anne. 2019. "Ruling Parties in Authoritarian Regimes: Rethinking Institutional Strength." *British Journal of Political Science* 51(2):536–540.

Meng, Anne. 2020. *Constraining Dictatorship: From Personalized Rule to Institutionalized Regimes*. New York: Cambridge University Press.

Mengin, Francoise. 2004. *China in the Age of Information*. New York: Palgrave Macmillan.

Miao, Di. 2011. "Between Propaganda and Commercials: Chinese Television Today." In *Changing Media, Changing China*, ed. Susan L. Shirk. New York: Oxford University Press, chapter 4, pp. 91–114.

Mickiewicz, Ellen. 2017. "RT: Influence, Persuasion, and Effects." New York University.

Monroe, Burt L., Michael P. Colaresi, and Kevin M. Quinn. 2008. "Fightin' Words: Lexical Feature Selection and Evaluation for Identifying the Content of Political Conflict." *Political Analysis* 16(4):372–403.

Montefiore, Simon Sebag. 2004. *Stalin: The Court of the Red Tsar*. New York: Alfred A. Knopf.

Morgan, Jonathon and Kris Shaffer. 2017. "Sockpuppets, Secessionists, and Breitbart: How Russia May Have Orchestrated a Massive Social Media Influence Campaign." *Data for Democracy* March 31.

Morgan, Piers. 2014. "New Cold War?" *CNN* March 5.

Morozov, Evgeny. 2012. *The Net Delusion*. New York: PublicAffairs.

Morstatter, Fred, Liang Wu, Uraz Yavanoglu, Stephen R. Corman, and Huan Liu. 2018. "Identifying Framing Bias in Online News." *ACM Transactions on Social Computing* 1(2):1–18.

Moskoff, William. 1992. *Impoverishment and Protest in the Perestroika Years*. Washington, D.C.: The National Council for Soviet and East European Research.

Mozur, Paul. 2019. "Live from America's Capital, a TV Station Run by China's Communist Party." *The New York Times* March 2.

Mozur, Paul, Jonah M. Kessel, and Melissa Chan. 2019. "Made in China, Exported to the World: The Surveillance State." *The New York Times* April 24.

Mueller, J. E. 1973. *War Presidents and Public Opinion*. New York: Wiley.

Mukherjee, Bumba and Ore Koren. 2019. *The Politics of Mass Killing in Autocratic Regimes*. New York: Palgrave Macmillan.

Mullainathan, Sendhil, Joshua Schwartzstein, and Andrei Shleifer. 2008. "Coarse Thinking and Persuasion." *Quarterly Journal of Economics* 123(2): 577–619.

Munck, Gerardo L. 2018. "Modernization Theory as a Case of Failed Knowledge Production." *The Annals of Comparative Democratization* 16(3): 37–41.

Munger, Kevin, Richard Bonneau, John T. Jost, Jonathan Nagler, and Joshua A. Tucker. 2016. "Elites Tweet to Get Feet off the Streets: Measuing Regime Social Media Strategies during Protest." *Political Science Research and Methods* 7(4):815–834.

Musial, Julia. 2017. "'My Muslim Sister, Indeed You Are a Mujahidah.' Narratives in the Propaganda of the Islamic State to Address and Radicalize Western Women." *Journal for Deradicalization* 9:1–62.

Mutegeki, Geoffrey. 2017. "Vision Group Names Building after William Pike." *New Vision* September 23.

Myers, Steven Lee. 2021. "An Alliance of Autocracies? China Wants to Lead a New World Order." *The New York Times* March 29.

Nadeau, Barbie Latza. 2019. "An Italian Expose Documents Moscow Money Allegedly Funding Italy's Far-Right Salvini." *The Daily Beast* February 22.

Nager, Adams. 2016. "Calling Out China's Mercantilism." *International Economy* 30(2):62–64.

Narayanswamy, Anu. 2009. *Corruption Charges Prompt Congo to Lobby Congress*. Washington, D.C.: Sunlight Foundation.

Naughton, Barry. 2009. "China's Emergence from Economic Crisis." *China Leadership Monitor* 29:1–10.

Naughton, Barry. 2016. "Economic Growth from High-Speed to High-Quality." In *The China Reader: Rising Power*, ed. David Shambaugh. New York: Oxford University Press, pp. 104–116.

Naughton, Barry. 2018. *The Chinese Economy: Adaptation and Growth*. Cambridge: Massachusetts Institute of Technology Press.

Neely, Sylvia. 2007. *A Concise History of the French Revolution*. New York: Rowman & Littlefield.

Nelson, Elizabeth, Robert Orttung, and Anthony Livshen. 2015. "Measuring RT's Impact on YouTube." *Russian Analytical Digest* 177:2–9.

New York Times. 2010. "What Chinese Censors Don't Want You to Know." *The New York Times* March 21.

Nguyen, Viet-An, Jordan Boyd-Graber, Philip Resnik, and Kristina Miler. 2015. "Tea Party in the House: A Hierarchical Ideal Point Topic Model and Its Application to Republican Legislators in the 112th Congress." *Proceedings of the 53rd Annual Meeting of the Association for Computational Linguistics and the 7th International Joint Conference on Natural Language Processing* 1:1438–1448.

Nielsen, Richard A. 2013. "Rewarding Human Rights? Selective Aid Sanctions against Repressive States." *International Studies Quarterly* 57(4):791–803.

Nikolskaya, Polina. 2018. "Russian Officials Call for Rare Vote Re-run Over Fraud in Far East." *Reuters* September 19.

Njoroge, John. 2010. "Who Is Taking Over Their Jobs?" *The Independent* May 10.

Nordlinger, Eric A. 1977. *Soldiers in Politics: Military Coups and Governments*. Upper Saddle River: Prentice-Hall.

Norris, Pippa. 2017. "Is Western Democracy Backsliding? Diagnosing the Risks." *HKS Faculty Research Working Paper Series* RWP17-012.

Obama, Barack. 2016. "Remarks of President Barack Obama: State of the Union Address as Delivered." Obama White House Archives.

O'Brien, Kevin J. and Lianjiang Li. 2005. "Popular Contention and Its Impact in Rural China." *Comparative Political Studies* 38(3):235–259.

O'Brien, Kevin and Lianjiang Li. 2006. *Rightful Resistance in Rural China*. New York: Cambridge University Press.

Observatoire Congolais des Droits de l'Homme. 2017. "Congo–Brazzaville: La répression à huit clos se poursuit au Pool et dans le reste du pays." Brazzaville: www.fidh.org/IMG/pdf/note_position_repression-a-huis-clos_12avril2017_final.pdf.

O'Connor, Brendan. 2011. "Be Careful with Dictionary-Based Text Analysis." Available at https://brenocon.com/blog/2011/10/be-careful-with-dictionary-based-text-analysis/.

O'Connor, Brendan, Ramnath Balasubramanyan, Bryan R. Routledge, and Noah A. Smith. 2010. "From Tweets to Polls: Linking Text Sentiment to Public Opinion Time Series." *Proceedings of the Fourth International AAAI Conference on Weblogs and Social Media* 1:122–129.

O'Donnell, Guillermo and Philippe C. Schmitter. 1986. *Transitions from Authoritarian Rule: Tentative Conclusions about Uncertain Democracies.* Baltimore: Johns Hopkins University Press.

Ogola, George. 2019. "Shutting Down the Internet Doesn't Work: But Governments Keep Doing It." *The Conversation* February 19.

Oksenberg, Michel. 2001. "China's Political System: Challenges of the Twenty-First Century." *The China Journal* 45:21–35.

Olson, Mancur. 1977. *The Logic of Collective Action.* Cambridge: Harvard University Press.

Olson, Mancur. 2000. *Power and Prosperity: Outgrowing Communist and Capitalist Dictatorships.* New York: Basic Books.

Opala, Ken. 2013. "William Pike: Why I Left The New Vision." *The Observer* September 3.

Opp, Karl-Dieter and Wolfgang Roehl. 1990. "Repression, Micromoblization, and Political Protest." *Social Forces* 69(2):521–547.

Organization for Security and Cooperation in Europe. 2015. "Limited Election Observation Mission, Republic of Uzbekistan, Presidential Election, 29 March 2015." Vienna: Available at www.osce.org/odihr/elections/uzbekistan/141941.

Organization for Security and Cooperation in Europe. 2017. "Uzbekistan, Early Presidential Election, 4 December 2016: Final Report." Vienna: Available at www.osce.org/office-for-democratic-institutions-and-human-rights/elections/uzbekistan/306451.

Orwell, George. 1949. *1984.* London: Secker & Warburg.

Osborn, Andrew. 2005. "Russia's 'CNN' Wants to Tell It Like It Is." *The Age* August 16.

Ost, David. 2016. "Regime Change in Poland, Carried Out from Within." *The Nation* January 8.

Ostrovsky, Arkady. 2017. *The Invention of Russia: The Rise of Putin and the Age of Fake News.* New York: Penguin.

Ottaway, Marina. 2003. *Democracy Challenged: The Rise of Semi-Authoritarianism.* Washington, D.C.: Carnegie Endowment for International Peace.

Overy, Richard. 2004. *The Dictators: Hitler's Germany, Stalin's Russia.* New York: W.W. Norton.

Padro i Miquel, Gerard. 2007. "The Control of Politicians in Divided Societies: The Politics of Fear." *Review of Economic Studies* 74(4):1259–1274.

Page, Matthew. 2017. "In the War on Boko Haram, Is the U.S. Turning a Blind Eye to Cameroon's Abuses?" *The Washington Post* July 26.

Paletz, D. L. 2002. *The Media in American Politics.* New York: Longman.

Pan, Jennifer and Alexandra A. Siegel. 2020. "How Saudi Crackdowns Fail to Silence Online Dissent." *American Political Science Review* 114(1):109–125.

Pan, Jennifer and Yiqing Xu. 2017. "China's Ideological Spectrum." *Journal of Politics* 80(1):254–273.

Passerini, Luisa, Richard Crownshaw, and Selma Leydesdorff, eds. 2005. *Memory and Totalitarianism*. New York: Routledge.

Passi, Anssi. 1996. *Territories, Boundaries and Consciousness: The Changing Geographies of the Finnish-Russian Border*. New York: J. Wiley & Sons.

Pei, Minxin. 1994. *From Reform to Revolution: The Demise of Communism in China and the Soviet Union*. Cambridge: Harvard University Press.

Pei, Minxin. 2010. "Rights and Resistance: The Changing Context of the Dissident Movement." In *Chinese Society: Change, Conflict and Resistance*, ed. Elizabeth Perry and Mark Selden. 3rd ed. New York: Routledge, chapter 1, pp. 32–56.

Peisakhin, Leonid and Arturas Rozenas. 2018. "Electoral Effects of Biased Media: Russian Television in Ukraine." *American Journal of Political Science* 62(3):535–550.

Pennycook, Gordon, Tyrone D. Cannon, and David G. Rand. 2017. "Prior Exposure Increases Perceived Accuracy of Fake News." *Journal of Experimental Psychology: General* 147(12):1865–1880.

People's Daily. 1990. "Stability Overrides Everything 稳定压倒一切.".

People's Daily. 2020b. "The Leadership of the Chinese Communist Party Is the Most Essential Characteristic of Socialism with Chinese Characteristics 中国共产党领导是中国特色社会主义最本质的特征." July 16.

Pepinsky, Thomas. 2014. "The Institutional Turn in Comparative Authoritarianism." *British Journal of Political Science* 44(3):631–653.

Perry, Elizabeth. 1999. "Chinese Anniversaries in International Perspective." *Harvard Asia Quarterly* Summer:5–9.

Perry, Elizabeth J. 2001. "Challenging the Mandate of Heaven: Popular Protest in Modern China." *Critical Asian Studies* 33(2):163–180.

Perry, Elizabeth J. 2002. *Challenging the Mandate of Heaven: Social Protest and State Power in China*. New York: Routledge.

Perry, Elizabeth J. 2008. "Chinese Conceptions of "Rights": From Mencius to Mao – and Now." *Perspectives on Politics* 6(1):37–50.

Perry, Elizabeth J. 2010. "Popular Protest: Playing by the Rules." In *China Today, China Tomorrow: Domestic Politics, Economy, and Society*, ed. Joseph Fewsmith. New York: Rowman & Littlefield, chapter 1, pp. 11–28.

Pertsev, Andrey. 2018. "The Grudinin Effect: A Populist Shakes Up Russian Politics." Carnegie Moscow Center.

Peslak, Alan R. 2017. "Sentiment Analysis and Opinion Mining: Current State of the Art and Review of Google and Yahoo Search Engines' Privacy Policies." *Journal of Information Systems Applied Research* 10(3):38–46.

Petrova, Maria. 2008. "Inequality and Media Capture." *Journal of Public Economics* 92(1–2):183–212.

Petrova, Maria. 2011. "Newspapers and Parties: How Advertising Revenues Created an Independent Press." *American Political Science Review* 105(4):790–808.

Petrova, Maria. 2012. "Mass Media and Special Interest Groups." *Journal of Economic Behavior and Organization* 84(1):17–38.

Pew Research Center. 2013. "America's Global Image Remains More Positive Than China's: But Many See China Becoming World's Leading Power." Available at www.pewresearch.org/global/2013/07/18/americas-global-image-remains-more-positive-than-chinas/.

Pew Research Center. 2015. "From Brexit to Zika: What Do Americans Know?" Available at www.people-press.org/2017/07/25/from-brexit-to-zika-what-do-americans-know/.

Pfeifle, Mark. 2009. "A Nobel Peace Prize for Twitter?" *Christian Science Monitor* July 6.

Phillips, Tom. 2017. "'A whirlwind of charisma!': China Propaganda Blitz Hails Xi, the Great Statesman." *Guardian* August 31.

Piccone, Ted. 2018. "China's Long Game on Human Rights at the United Nations." Washington, D.C.: Available at www.brookings.edu/research/chinas-long-game-on-human-rights-at-the-united-nations/.

Pilster, Ulrich and Tobias Böhmelt. 2011. "Coup-Proofing and Military Effectiveness in Interstate Wars, 1965–1999." *Conflict Management and Peace Science* 28(4):331–350.

Piotroski, Joseph D., T.J. Wong, and Tianyu Zhang. 2017. "Political Bias in Corporate News: The Role of Conglomeration Reform in China." *Journal of Law and Economics* 60(1):173–207.

Pla, Ferran and Lluís-F. Hurtado. 2014. "Political Tendency Identification in Twitter Using Sentiment Analysis Techniques." *Proceedings of COLING, the 25th International Conference on Computational Linguistics: Technical Papers* pp. 183–192.

Plato. 1864. *Gorgias, literally tr.* Cambridge: Deighton, Bell & Co.

Policzer, Pablo. 2009. *The Rise and Fall of Repression in Chile.* South Bend: University of Notre Dame.

Pollack, Kenneth. 2002. *Arabs at War: Military Effectiveness, 1948–1991.* Lincoln: University of Nebraska Press.

Polumbaum, Judy and Xiong Lei. 2008. *China Ink: The Changing Face of Journalism in China.* New York: Rowman & Littlefield.

Pomerantsev, Peter. 2015a. "The Kremlin's Information War." *Journal of Democracy* 26(4):40–50.

Pomerantsev, Peter. 2015b. *Nothing Is True and Everything Is Possible: The Surreal Heart of the New Russia.* New York: PublicAffairs.

Pomerantsev, Peter and Michael Weiss. 2014. *The Menace of Unreality: How the Kremlin Weaponizes Information, Culture, and Money.* New York: Institute of Modern Russia.

Popp, Elizabeth and Thomas J. Rudolph. 2011. "A Tale of Two Ideologies: Explaining Public Support for Economic Interventions." *Journal of Politics* 73(3):808–820.

Powell, Jonathan M. 2012. "Determinants of the Attempting and Outcome of Coups d'état." *Journal of Conflict Resolution* 56(6):1017–1040.

Prasad, Eswar and Shang-Jin Wei. 2005. "The Chinese Approach to Capital Inflows: Partners and Possible Explanations." *NBER Working Paper Series* No. 11306.

Prat, Andrea. 2015. "Media Capture and Media Power." In *Handbook of Media Economics*, Vol. 1, ed. Simon Anderson, Joel Waldfogel and David Strömberg. Amsterdam: Elsevier, chapter 16, pp. 669–686.

Przeworski, Adam. 1986. "Some Problems in the Study of the Transition to Democracy." In *Transitions from Authoritarian Rule: Comparative Perspectives*, Vol. 3, ed. Guillermo O'Donnell, Philippe C. Schmitter, and Laurence Whitehead. Baltimore: Johns Hopkins University Press chapter 2, pp. 47–63.

Przeworski, Adam. 2006. "Self-Enforcing Democracy." In *The Oxford Handbook of Political Economy*, ed. Barry R. Weingast and Donald A. Wittman. New York: Oxford University Press, pp. 312–328.

Putz, Catherine. 2016. "What to Expect from Uzbekistan's Presidential Election." *The Diplomat* December 2.

Qiang, Xiao. 2019. "The Road to Digital Unfreedom: President Xi's Surveillance State." *Journal of Democracy* 30(1):53–67.

Qin, Bei, David Strömberg, and Yanhui Wu. 2017. "Why Does China Allow Freer Social Media? Protests vs. Surveillance and Propaganda." *Journal of Economic Perspectives* 31(1):117–140.

Qin, Bei, David Strömberg, and Yanhui Wu. 2018. "Media Bias in China." *American Economic Review* 108(9):2442–2476.

Qiu, Linda. 2017. "Fingerprints of Russian Disinformation: From AIDS to Fake News." *The New York Times* December 12.

Quinlivan, James. 1999. "Coup-Proofing: Its Practice and Consequences in the Middle East." *International Security* 24(2):131–165.

Quinn, Erin. 2015. "Who Represents the World's Tyrants and Torturers in Washington? *Slate Magazine*.

Radio Free Europe/Radio Liberty. 2018. "Putin Claims His Election Win Was 'Cleanest' in Russian History." Available at www.rferl.org/a/putin-claims-election-win-cleanest-history-pamfilova-fraud/29141736.html.

Radnitz, Scott. 2010. "The Color of Money: Privatization, Economic Dispersion, and the Post-Soviet 'Revolutions'." *Comparative Politics* 42(2):127–146.

Rahn, Wendy M. 1993. "The Role of Partisan Stereotypes in Information Processing about Political Candidates." *American Journal of Political Science* 37(2):472–496.

Rains, Stephen A. 2013. "The Nature of Psychological Reactance Revisited: A Meta-Analytic Review." *Human Communication Research* 39(1):47–73.

Raleigh, Clionadh, Andrew Linke, Høavard Hegre, and Joakim Karlsen. 2010. "Introducing ACLED-Armed Conflict Location and Event Data." *Journal of Peace Research* 47(5):651–660.

Raleigh, Clionadh and Roudabeh Kishi. 2019. "Comparing Conflict Data: Similarities and Differences across Conflict Datasets." Available at www.acleddata.com/wp-content/uploads/2019/09/ACLED-Comparison_8.2019.pdf.

Rao, Delip, David Yarowsky, Abhishek Shreevats, and Manaswi Gupta. 2010. "Classifying Latent User Attributes in Twitter." *Proceedings of the 2nd*

International Workshop on Search and Mining User-Generated Contents 1:37–44.

Rawnsley, Gary D. 2015. "To Know Us Is to Love Us: Public Diplomacy and International Broadcasting in Contemporary Russia and China." *Politics* 35(3-4):273–286.

Recasens, Marta, Cristian Danescu-Niculescu-Mizil, and Dan Jurafsky. 2013. "Linguistic Models for Analyzing and Detecting Biased Language." *Proceedings of the 51st Annual Meeting of the Association for Computational Linguistics* 1:1650–1659.

Reiter, Dan and Allan C. Stam. 1998. "Democracy, War Initiation, and Victory." *American Political Science Review* 92(2):377–389.

Repnikova, Maria. 2017a. "Media Openings and Political Transitions: *Glasnost* versus *Yulun Jiandu.*" *Problems of Post-Communism* 64(3-4):141–151.

Repnikova, Maria. 2017b. *Media Politics in China: Improvising Power under Authoritarianism.* New York: Cambridge University Press.

Repnikova, Maria. 2018. "Media Politics under Xi: Shifts and Continuities." *SAIS Review of International Affairs* 38(2):55–67.

Repnikova, Maria. 2019. "Thought Work Contested: Ideology and Journalism Education in China." *The China Quarterly* 230:399–419.

Repnikova, Maria and Kecheng Fang. 2019. "Digital Media Experiments in China: 'Revolutionizing' Persuasion under Xi Jinping." *The China Quarterly* 239:679–701.

Reuter, Ora John. 2017. *The Origins of Dominant Parties: Building Authoritarian Institutions in Post-Soviet Russia.* New York: Cambridge University Press.

Reuter, Ora John and David Szakonyi. 2019. "Elite Defection under Autocracy: Evidence from Russia." *American Political Science Review* 113(2):552–568.

Riding, Alan. 1990. "France Ties Aid to Democracy." *The New York Times* June 22.

Ringold, Debra Jones. 2002. "Boomerang Effects in Response to Public Health Interventions: Some Unintended Consequences in the Alcoholic Beverage Market." *Journal of Consumer Policy* 25:27–63.

Roberts, Margaret E. 2018. *Censored: Distraction and Diversion Inside China's Great Firewall.* Princeton: Princeton University Press.

Roberts, Margaret E. and Brandon Stewart. 2016. "Localization and Coordination: How Propaganda and Censorship Converge in Chinese Newspapers." University of California, San Diego.

Robertson, Graeme. 2017. "Political Orientation, Information and Perceptions of Election Fraud: Evidence from Russia." *British Journal of Political Science* 47(3):589–608.

Robinson, Darrel and Marcus Tannenberg. 2019. "Self-Censorship of Regime Support in Authoritarian States: Evidence from List Experiments in China." *Research and Politics* 6(3):1–9.

Rod, Espen Geelmuyden and Nils Weidmann. 2015. "Empowering Activists or Autocrats? The Internet in Authoritarian Regimes." *Journal of Peace Research* 52(3):338–351.

Roessler, Philip G. 2016. *Ethnic Politics and State Power in Africa: The Logic of the Coup-Civil War Trap*. New York: Cambridge University Press.

Rorty, Richard. 1989. *Contingency, Irony, and Solidarity*. New York: Cambridge University Press.

Rosenfeld, Bryn. 2017. "Reevaluating the Middle-Class Protest Paradigm: A Case-Control Study of Democratic Protest Coalitions in Russia." *American Political Science Review* 111(4):637–652.

Rosenfeld, Bryn, Katerina Tertychnaya, and Kohei Watanabe. 2018. "Fridge vs. Television Set: The Economy and Economic Reporting in a Hybrid Regime." Paper presented at the Annual Meeting of the Midwest Political Science Association.

Ross, Michael L. 2001. "Does Oil Hinder Democracy?" *World Politics* 53(3):325–361.

Ross, Michael L. 2012. *The Oil Curse: How Petroleum Wealth Shapes the Development of Nations*. Princeton: Princeton University Press.

Roth, Alan. 2016. "Meet the Woman Who Says She's Going to Fix Russia's Rigged Elections." *The Washington Post* May 14.

Rothstein, Bo. 2015. "The Chinese Paradox of High Growth and Low Quality of Government: The Cadre Organization Meets Max Weber." *Governance* 28(4):533–548.

Rozenas, Arturas. 2020. "A Theory of Demographically Targeted Repression." *Journal of Conflict Resolution* 64(7–8):1254–1278.

Rozenas, Arturas and Denis Stukal. 2018. "How Autocrats Manipulate Economic News: Evidence from Russia's State-Controlled Television." *Journal of Politics* 81(3):982–996.

Rozenas, Arturas, Sebastian Schutte, and Yuri M. Zhukov. 2017. "The Political Legacy of Violence: The Long-Term Impact of Stalin's Repression in Ukraine." *Journal of Politics* 79(4):1147–1161.

Rozenas, Arturas and Yuri M. Zhukov. 2019. "Mass Repression and Political Loyalty: Evidence from Stalin's 'Terror by Hunger'." *American Political Science Review* 113(2):569–583.

Rubin, David C. and Amy Wenzel. 1996. "One Hundred Years of Forgetting." *Psychological Review* 103(4):734–760.

Rule, Sheila. 1989. "Reagan Gets a Red Carpet from British." *The New York Times* June 14.

Russell, Jon. 2017. "China's CCTV Surveillance Network Took Just 7 Minutes to Capture BBC Reporter." *TechCrunch* December 13.

Rydzak, Jan. 2019a. *Disconnected: A Human-Rights Based Approach to Network Disruptions*. Washington, D.C.: Global Network Initiative.

Rydzak, Jan. 2019b. "Of Blackouts and Bandhs: The Strategy and Structure of Disconnected Protest in India." Stanford University.

Salehyan, Idean, Cullen S. Hendrix, Jesse Hamner, Christina Case, Christopher Linebarger, Emily Stull, and Jennifer Williams. 2012. "Social Conflict in Africa: A New Database." *International Interactions* 38(4):503–511.

Samuel, Sigal. 2018. "China Is Treating Islam Like a Mental Illness." *The Atlantic* August 28.

Sandby-Thomas, Peter. 2008. "The Legitimating Logic of Stability: Analysing the CCP's Stability Discourse." University of Nottingham.

Sandby-Thomas, Peter. 2011. *Legitimating the Chinese Communist Party since Tiananmen: A Critical Analysis of the Stability Discourse*. New York: Routledge.

Sassoon, Joseph. 2012. *Saddam Hussein's Ba'th Party: Inside an Authoritarian Regime*. New York: Cambridge University Press.

Schedler, Andreas. 2002. "Elections without Democracy: The Menu of Manipulation." *Journal of Democracy* 99(3):36–50.

Schedler, Andreas. 2009. "Sources of Competition under Electoral Authoritarianism." In *Democratization by Elections: A New Mode of Transition*, ed. Staffan I. Lindberg. Baltimore: Johns Hopkins University Press chapter, pp. 179–201.

Schedler, Andreas. 2010a. "Authoritarianism's Last Line of Defense." *Journal of Democracy* 21(1):69–80.

Schedler, Andreas. 2010b. "Transitions from Electoral Authoritarianism." *CIDE Working Paper Series* No. 222.

Schedler, Andreas, ed. 2006. *Electoral Authoritarianism: The Dynamics of Unfree Competition*. Boulder: Lynne Rienner Publishers.

Schmitz, Rob. 2017. "Wary of Unrest among Uigher Minority, China Locks Down Xinjiang Region." *NPR* September 26.

Schwirtz, Michael and Gaelle Borgia. 2019. "How Russia Meddles Abroad for Profit: Cash, Trolls and a Cult Leader." *The New York Times* November 11.

Scikit-learn Developers. 2018. "Mutliclass and Multilabel Algorithms." Available at https://scikit-learn.org/stable/modules/multiclass.html.

Seeberg, Merete Bech. 2014. "State Capacity and the Paradox of Authoritarian Elections." *Democratization* 21(7):1265–1285.

Seeberg, Merete Bech. 2017. "Electoral Authoritarianism and Economic Control." *International Political Science Review* 39(1):33–48.

Seeberg, Merete Bech. 2018. *State Capacity, Economic Control, and Authoritarian Elections*. New York: Routledge.

Seeberg, Merete Bech. 2020. "How State Capacity Helps Autocrats Win Elections." *British Journal of Political Science* 51(2):541–558.

Service, Robert. 2004. *Stalin: A Biography*. Cambridge: Harvard University Press.

Shadmehr, Mehdi and Dan Bernhardt. 2011. "Collective Action with Uncertain Payoffs: Coordination, Public Signals, and Punishment Dilemmas." *American Political Science Review* 105(4):829–851.

Shadmehr, Mehdi and Dan Bernhardt. 2015. "State Censorship." *American Economic Journal: Microeconomics* 7(2):280–308.

Shambaugh, David. 2007. "China's Propaganda System: Institutions, Processes and Efficacy." *China Journal* 57:25–58.

Shan, Ling and Lu Liu. 2017. "Xin chuanbo shengtai xia Zhongguo chuantong meiti congyezhe de zhuanye shijian diaocha" (A Study on Journalism Practices of Traditional Media in the New Media Ecology)." *Xiandai Chuanbo* 39(10):64–69.

Sharife, Khadija and Mark Anderson. 2019. "The Great Gambia Heist." Washington, D.C.: Available at www.occrp.org/en/greatgambiaheist/.

Shaxson, Nicholas. 2007. *Poisoned Wells: The Dirty Politics of African Oil*. New York: Palgrave Macmillan.

Shen-Bayh, Fiona. 2018. "Strategies of Repression: Judicial and Extrajudicial Methods of Autocratic Survival." *World Politics* 70(3):321–357.

Sherman, Justin and Robert Morgus. 2018. "Authoritarians Are Exporting Surveillance Tech, and with It Their Vision for the Internet." Available at www.cfr.org/blog/authoritarians-are-exporting-surveillance-tech-and-it-their-vision-internet.

Shi, Tianjian. 2000. "Cultural Values and Democracy in Mainland China." *The China Quarterly* 162:540–559.

Shi, Tianjian. 2001. "Cultural Impact on Political Trust: A Comparison of Mainland China and Taiwan." *Comparative Politics* 33(4):401–420.

Shi, Tianjian, Jie Lu, and John Aldrich. 2011. "Bifurcated Images of the U.S. in Urban China and the Impact of Media Environment." *Political Communication* 28(3):357–376.

Shih, Victor. 2008. "Nauseating Displays of Loyalty: Monitoring the Factional Bargain through Ideological Campaigns in China." *Journal of Politics* 70(4):1177–1192.

Shih, Victor. 2020. *Economic Shocks and Authoritarian Stability: Duration, Financial Control, and Institutions*. Ann Arbor: University of Michigan.

Shirk, Susan L. 2008. *China: Fragile Superpower*. New York: Oxford University Press.

Shirk, Susan L. 2011. "Changing Media, Changing China." In *Changing Media, Changing China*, ed. Susan L. Shirk. New York: Oxford University Press, chapter 1, pp. 1–37.

Shirky, Clay. 2009. *Here Comes Everybody: The Power of Organizing without Organizations*. New York: Penguin.

Shue, Vivienne. 2004. "Legitimacy Crisis in China?" In *State and Society in 21st-Century China: Crisis, Contention and Legitimation*, ed. Peter Hays Gries and Stanley Rosen. New York: Routledge, chapter 1, pp. 24–49.

Sides, John and Lynn Vavreck. 2013. *The Gamble: Choice and Chance in the 2012 Election*. Princeton: Princeton University Press.

Siebert, Fredrick S., Theodore B. Peterson, and Wilbur Schramm. 1955. *Four Theories of the Press: The Authoritarian, Libertarian, Social Responsibility, and Soviet Communist Concepts of What the Press Should Be and Do*. Champaign: University of Illinois Press.

Signé, Landry and Remy Smida. 2014. "The Army's Decision to Repress: A Turning Point in Tunisia's Regime Change." Stanford University.

Sim, Yanchuan, Brice D. L. Acree, Justin H. Gross, and Noah A. Smith. 2013. "Measuring Ideological Proportions in Political Speeches." *Proceedings of the 2013 Conference on Empirical Methods in Natural Language Processing* 1:91–101.

Simmons, Beth. 2009. *Mobilizing for Human Rights: International Law in Domestic Politics*. New York: Cambridge University Press.

Simmons, Beth and Allison Danner. 2010. "Credible Commitments and the International Criminal Court." *International Organization* 64(2): 225–256.

Simonov, Andrey and Justin Rao. 2022. "Demand for Online News under Government Control: Evidence from Russia." *Journal of Political Economy* 130(2):259–309.

Simonov, Andrey, Szymon K. Sacher, Jean-Pierre H. Dubé, and Shirsho Biswas. 2020. "The Persuasive Effect of Fox News: Non-Compliance with Social Distancing During the Covid-19 Pandemic." *NBER Working Paper Series* No. 27237.

Simpser, Alberto. 2013. *Why Governments and Parties Manipulate Elections: Theory, Practice, and Implications.* New York: Cambridge University Press.

Simpser, Alberto, Dan Slater, and Jason Wittenberg. 2018. "Dead but Not Gone: Contemporary Legacies of Communism, Imperialism, and Authoritarianism." *Annual Review of Political Science* 21:419–439.

Singh, Naunihal. 2014. *Seizing Power: The Strategic Logic of Military Coups.* Baltimore: Johns Hopkins University Press.

Skocpol, Theda. 1979. *States and Social Revolutions.* New York: Cambridge University Press.

Slater, Dan. 2010. *Ordering Power: Contentious Politics and Authoritarian Leviathans in Southeast Asia.* New York: Cambridge University Press.

Smith, Mary John. 1977. "The Effects of Threats to Attitudinal Freedom as a Function of Message Quality and Initial Receiver Attitude." *Communication Monographs* 44(3):196–206.

Smith, Peter. 2005. *Democracy in Latin America: Political Change in Comparative Perspective.* New York: Oxford University Press.

Smith, Todd Graham. 2014. "Feeding Unrest: Disentangling the Causal Relationship between Food Price Shocks and Sociopolitical Conflict in Urban Africa." *Journal of Peace Research* 51(6):679–695.

Snyder, Timothy. 2017. *On Tyranny: Twenty Lessons from the Twentieth Century.* New York: Tim Duggan Books.

Snyder, Timothy. 2021. "The American Abyss." *The New York Times* January 9.

Soldatov, Andrei and Irina Borogan. 2015. *The Red Web: The Kremlin's War on the Internet.* New York: PublicAffairs.

Solis, Jonathan A. and Philip D. Waggoner. 2020. "Measuring Media Freedom: An IRT Analysis." *British Journal of Political Science* 51(4):1685–1704.

Solovyov, Dmitry. 2015. "Veteran Uzbek Leader Re-elected in Vote OSCE Brands Undemocratic." *Reuters* March 30.

Sonne, Paul. 2018. "A Russian Bank Gave Marine Le Pen's Party a Loan. Then Weird Things Began Happening." *The Washington Post* December 27.

Soriano, Manuel R. Torres. 2013. "Internet as a Driver of Political Change: Cyber-Pessimists and Cyber-Optimists." *Revista del Instituto Español de Estudios Estratégicos* 1:332–352.

South China Morning Post Editorial Board. 2022. "Commitment Remains to Weed out Corruption." *South China Morning Post* .

Spiegel, Peter. 2009. "China's CCTV Network Gets Little Sympathy after Hotel Fire." *Los Angeles Times* February 11.

Spruyt, Hendrik. 1994. *The Sovereign State and Its Competitors*. Princeton: Princeton University Press.

Squires, Nick. 2018. "Italy's Anti-immigration Deputy PM Matteo Salvini under Fire for Citing Mussolini." *Telegraph* July 30.

Stanley, Jason. 2015. *How Propaganda Works*. Princeton: Princeton University Press.

Starr, Paul. 2004. *Paul Starr*. New York: Basic Books.

Steinert-Threlkeld, Zachary C., Delia Mocanu, Alessandro Vespignani, and James Fowler. 2015. "Online Social Networks and Offline Protest." *EPJ Data Science* 4(19):1–9.

Steinhardt, H. Christoph. 2016. "State Behavior and the Intensification of Intellectual Criticism in China: The Social Stability Debate." *Modern China* 42(3):300–336.

Stent, Angela E. 2020. *Russia and China: Axis of Revisionists?* Washington, D.C.: Brookings Institution.

Stern, Rachel E. and Kevin J. O'Brien. 2012. "Politics at the Boundary: Mixed Signals and the Chinese State." *Modern China* 38(2):174–198.

Stern, Steve J. 2010. *Reckoning with Pinochet: The Memory Question in Democratic Chile, 1989–2006*. Durham: Duke University Press.

Sternberg, Troy. 2012. "Chinese Drought, Bread and the Arab Spring." *Applied Geography* 34:519–524.

Stewart, Leo G., Ahmer Arif, and Kate Starbird. 2018. "Examining Trolls and Polarization with a Retweet Network." *Proceedings of WSDM Workshop on Misinformation and Misbehavior Miming on the Web (MIS2)* 1:1–6.

Stewart, Phil. 2019. "China Putting Minority Muslims in 'Concentration Camps,' U.S. Says." *Reuters* May 3.

Stier, Sebastian. 2014. "Democracy, Autocracy and the News: The Impact of Regime Type on Media Freedom." *Democratization* 22(7):1273–1295.

Stockmann, Daniela. 2010. "Who Believes Propaganda? Media Effects during the Anti-Japanese Protests in Beijing." *The China Quarterly* 202: 269–289.

Stockmann, Daniela. 2013. *Media Commercialization and Authoritarian Rule in China*. New York: Cambridge University Press.

Stockmann, Daniela, Ashley Esarey, and Jie Zhang. 2018. "Who Is Afraid of the Chinese State? Evidence Calling into Question Political Fear as an Explanation for Overreporting of Political Trust." *Political Psychology* 39(5):1105–1121.

Stockmann, Daniela and Mary E. Gallagher. 2011. "Remote Control: How the Media Sustain Authoritarian Rule in China." *Comparative Political Studies* 44(4):436–467.

Stone, Philip J., Dexter C. Dunphy, Marshall S. Smith, and Daniel M. Ogilvie. 1966. *The General Inquirer: A Computer Approach to Content Analysis*. Cambridge: Massachusetts Institute of Technology Press.

Strömberg, David. 2004. "Mass Media Competition, Political Competition, and Public Policy." *Review of Economic Studies* 71(1):265–284.

Strömberg, David. 2015. "Media and Politics." *Annual Review of Economics* 7:173–205.

Sudduth, Jun Koga. 2017. "Strategic Logic of Elite Purges in Dictatorships." *Comparative Political Studies* 50(13):1768–1801.

Sundaram, Anjan. 2016. *Bad News: Last Journalists in a Dictatorship*. New York: Doubleday.

Svolik, Milan. 2009. "Power-Sharing and Leadership Dynamics in Authoritarian Regimes." *American Journal of Political Science* 53(2):477–494.

Svolik, Milan. 2020. "When Polarization Trumps Civic Virtue: Partisan Conflict and the Subversion of Democracy by Incumbents." *Quarterly Journal of Political Science* 15(1):3–31.

Svolik, Milan W. 2012. *The Politics of Authoritarian Rule*. New York: Cambridge University Press.

Taboada, Maite, Julian Brooke, Milan Tofiloski, Kimberly Voll, and Manfred Stede. 2011. "Lexicon-Based Methods for Sentiment Analysis." *Computational Linguistics* 37(2):267–307.

Tai, Yun and King-wa Fu. 2020. "Specificity, Conflict, and Focal Point: A Systematic Investigation into Social Media Censorship in China." *Journal of Communication* 70(6):842–867.

Tan, Chenhao, Lillian Lee, and Bo Pang. 2014. "The Effect of Wording on Message Propagation: Topic- and Author-Controlled Natural Experiments on Twitter." *Proceedings of the 52nd Annual Meeting of the Association for Computational Linguistics* 1:175–185.

Tang, M., D. Woods, and J. Zhao. 2009. "The Attitude of Chinese Middle Class towards Democracy." *Journal of Chinese Political Science* 14(1):81–95.

Tang, Wenfang. 2005. *Public Opinion and Political Change in China*. New York: Stanford University Press.

Tang, Wenfang. 2016. *Populist Authoritarianism: Chinese Political Culture and Regime Sustainability*. New York: Oxford University Press.

Tannenberg, Marcus. 2017. "The Autocratic Trust Bias: Politically Sensitive Survey Items and Self-Censorship." *Afrobarometer Working Paper Series* No. 176.

Taylor, Richard. 1998. *Film Propaganda: Soviet Russia and Nazi Germany*. New York: I.B. Tauris.

Tella, Rafael Di and Ignacio Franceschelli. 2011. "Government Advertising and Media Coverage of Corruption Scandals." *American Economic Journal: Applied Economics* 3(4):119–151.

The State Council Information Office of the People's Republic of China. 2021. "The Report on Human Rights Violations in the United States in 2020." Beijing.

The Economist. 2010. "President Paul Kagame under Scrutiny." August 5.

The Economist. 2016. "Uzbekistan Replaces One Strongman with Another." December 10.

Thompson, Jared. 2016. "U.S. Supported Cameroonian Military Unit Accused of Abuse." *Security Assistance Monitor* August 1.

Thomson, Henry. 2022. "The Bureaucratic Politics of Authoritarian Repression: Intra-Agency Reform and Surveillance Capacity in Communist Poland." Arizona State University.

Thomson, Oliver. 1999. *Easily Led: A History of Propaganda*. New York: Sutton.

Thrall, A. Trevor. 2018. "America's Foreign Policy Attention Deficit." *Cato at Liberty* January 19.

Thum, Rian. 2020. "Officials in Xinjiang are so inured to the horrors they are perpetrating that they often publicize evidence of their crimes." Twitter, September 21, https://twitter.com/RianThum/status/1308235439850106880.

Tilly, Charles. 1990. *Coercion, Capital, and European States, AD 990–1992*. New York: Blackwell.

Tizian, Giovanni and Stefano Vergine. 2019. "Quei 3 milioni russi per Matteo Salvini: ecco l'inchiesta che fa tremare la Lega." *L'Espresso* February 21.

Tondo, Lorenzo and Angela Giuffrida. 2019. "Italian MPs Demand Answers over Claims Salvini's League Sought Kremlin Funding." *The Guardian* February 22.

Tong, Jingrong. 2011. *Investigative Journalism in China: Journalism, Power, and Society*. New York: Continuum.

Tong, Jingrong. 2019. "The Taming of Critical Journalism in China." *Journalism Studies* 20(1):79–96.

Trejo, Guillermo. 2014. "The Ballot and the Street: An Electoral Theory of Social Protest in Autocracies." *Perspectives on Politics* 12(2):332–352.

Trevisan, Matteo. 2018. "How Media Freedom in Serbia Is under Attack." *EU Observer* November 2.

Truex, Rory. 2014. "The Returns to Office in a 'Rubber Stamp' Parliament." *American Political Science Review* 108(2):235–251.

Truex, Rory. 2017. "Consultative Authoritarianism and Its Limits." *Comparative Political Studies* 50(3):329–361.

Truex, Rory. 2019. "Focal Points, Dissident Calendars, and Preemptive Repression." *Journal of Conflict Resolution* 63(4):1032–1052.

Tsur, Oren, Dan Calacci, and David Lazer. 2015. "A Frame of Mind: Using Statistical Models for Detection of Framing and Agenda Setting Campaigns." *Proceedings of the 53rd Annual Meeting of the Association for Computational Linguistics and the 7th International Joint Conference on Natural Language Processing* 1(1629–1638).

Tucker, Joshua A. 2007. "Enough! Electoral Fraud, Collective Action Problems, and Post-Communist Colored Revolutions." *Perspectives on Politics* 5(3):535–551.

Tucker, Joshua A., Andrew Guess, Pablo Barberá, Cristian Vaccari, Alexandra Siegel, Sergey Sanovich, Denis Stukal, and Brendan Nyhan. 2018. "Social Media, Political Polarization, and Political Disinformation: A Review of the Scientific Literature." Menlo Park: Available at https://hewlett.org/wp-content/uploads/2018/03/Social-Media-Political-Polarization-and-Political-Disinformation-Literature-Review.pdf.

Tufekci, Zeynep and Christopher Wilson. 2012. "Social Media and the Decision to Participate in Political Protest: Observations from Tahrir Square." *Journal of Communication* 62(2):363–379.

Tullock, Gordon. 1987. *Autocracy*. New York: Springer.

Tullock, Gordon. 2001. "Monarchies: Hereditary and Non-Hereditary." In *The Elgar Companion to Public Choice*, ed. William F. Shughart II and Laura Razzolini. Northampton: Edward Elgar Publishing. Chapter 6, pp. 140–156.

Union Européenne. 2016. "Déclaration du Porte-parole concernant la situation politique en République du Congo." Brussels: Available at www.eeas.europa .eu/archives/delegations/congo/documents/press_corner/2016/19022016_ declaration_situation-politique_congo_fr.pdf.

Valdiguié, Laurent. 2001. "Bourgi: J'ai vu Chirac et Villepin compter les billets." *Le Journal du Dimanche* September 11.

van de Bildt, Joyce. 2015. "The Quest for Legitimacy in Postrevolutionary Egypt: Propaganda and Controlling Narratives." *Journal of the Middle East and Africa* 6(3–4):253–274.

van de Walle, Nicolas. 2001. *African Economies and the Politics of Permanent Crisis, 1979–1999*. New York: Cambridge University Press.

van Ham, Carolien and Staffan I. Lindberg. 2015. "From Sticks to Carrots: Electoral Manipulation in Africa, 1986–2012." *Government and Opposition* 50(3):521–548.

Van Herpen, Marcel H. 2016. *Putin's Propaganda Machine*. New York: Rowman & Littlefield.

Vargas Llosa, Mario. 2000. *The Feast of the Goat: A Novel*. New York: Picador.

Vasher, Nathan. 2015. *Museveni's Power and the Political Economy of Development in Uganda*. Sunnyvale: Lambert Academic Publishing.

Vision Group. 2017. "2016–17 Annual Report: Facing the Challenges Ahead." https://visiongroup.co.ug/wp-content/uploads/2017/11/Annual-Report-2017 .pdf.

Voeten, Erik. 2017. "Are People Really Turning Away from Democracy?" *Journal of Democracy* Online Exchange.

Vosoughi, Soroush and Deb Roy. 2016. "Tweet Acts: A Speech Act Classifier for Twitter." *Proceedings of the Tenth International AAAI Conference on Web and Social Media (ICWSM 2016)* 1:711–714.

Wainer, David. 2019. "China Is Eyeing a Widening Void at the UN Thanks to Trump." *Bloomberg* January 31.

Wakabayashi, Daisuke and Nicholas Confessore. 2017. "Russia's Favored Outlet Is an Online News Giant. YouTube Helped." *The New York Times* October 23.

Walder, Andrew G. 2004. "The Party Elite and China's Trajectory of Change." *China: An International Journal* 2(2):189–209.

Walker, Christopher. 2015. "The New Containment: Undermining Democracy." *World Affairs* 178(1):42–51.

Walker, Shaun and Luke Harding. 2016. "Uzbekistan Plunged into Uncertainty by Death of Dictator Islam Karimov." *Guardian* September 2.

Wallace, Jeremy L. 2014. *Cities and Stability: Urbanization, Redistribution, and Regime Survival in China*. New York: Oxford University Press.

Wang, Haiyan and Colin Sparks. 2019. "Chinese Newspaper Groups in the Digital Era: The Resurgence of the Party Press." *Journal of Communication* 69(1):94–119.

Wang, Tianyi. 2020. "Media, Pulpit, and Populist Persuasion: Evidence from Father Coughlin." *American Economic Review* 111(9):3064–3092.

Wang, Yuhua. 2014. "Empowering the Police: How the Chinese Communist Party Manages Its Coercive Leaders." *The China Quarterly* 219: 625–648.

Wang, Yuhua. 2019. "The Political Legacy of Violence during China's Cultural Revolution." *British Journal of Political Science* 51(2):463–487.

Wang, Yuhua and Carl Minzner. 2015. "The Rise of the Chinese Security State." *The China Quarterly* 222:339–359.

Wang, Zhengxu. 2005. "Before the Emergence of Critical Citizens: Economic Development and Political Trust in China." *International Review of Sociology* 15(1):155–171.

Warren, T. Camber. 2014. "Not by the Sword Alone: Soft Power, Mass Media, and the Production of State Sovereignty." *International Organization* 68(1):111–141.

Wasserstrom, Jeffrey. 2009. "China's Anniversary Tempest." *OpenDemocracy* February 25.

Wasserstrom, Jeffrey N. 2019. "May Fourth, the Day That Changed China." *The New York Times* May 3.

Waxman, Dov. 2011. "Living with Terror, Not Living in Terror: The Impact of Chronic Terrorism on Israeli Society." *Perspectives on Terrorism* 5(5–6):4–26.

Way, Lucan A. 2005. "Kuchma's Failed Authoritarianism." *Journal of Democracy* 16(2):131–145.

Way, Lucan A. 2015. *Pluralism by Default: Weak Autocrats and the Rise of Competitive Politics.* Baltimore: Johns Hopkins University Press.

Weber, Valentin. 2017. "Why China's Internet Censorship Model Will Prevail over Russia's." Available at www.cfr.org/blog/why-chinas-internet-censorship-model-will-prevail-over-russias.

Wedeen, Lisa. 1999. *Ambiguities of Domination: Politics, Rhetoric, and Symbols in Contemporary Syria.* Chicago: University of Chicago Press.

Wee, Sui-Lee. 2019. "China Uses DNA to Track Its People, with the Help of American Expertise." *The New York Times* February 21.

Weeks, Jessica L. 2008. "Autocratic Audience Costs: Regime Type and Signaling Resolve." *International Organization* 62(1):35–64.

Welch, David. 2014. "Introduction." In *Nazi Propaganda: The Power and the Limitations,* ed. David Welch. London: Routledge, chapter 1, pp. 1–9.

Welzel, Christian. 2013. *Freedom Rising: Human Empowerment and the Quest for Emancipation.* New York: Cambridge University Press.

Welzel, Christian and Ronald Inglehart. 2009. "Political Culture, Mass Beliefs, and Value Change." In *Democratization,* ed. Christian W. Haerpfer, Patrick Bernhagen, Ronald F. Inglehart, and Christian Welzel. New York: Oxford University Press, chapter 9, pp. 126–144.

White, Stephen, Sarah Oates, and Ian McAllister. 2005. "Media Effects and Russian Elections." *British Journal of Political Science* 35(2):191–208.

Whitten-Woodring, Jenifer and Douglas A. Van Belle. 2015. "The Correlates of Media Freedom: An Introduction of the Global Media Freedom Dataset." *Political Science Research and Methods* 5(1):179–188.

Wickedonna. 2014. Untitled Description of December 4 Protests, https://wickedonna2.tumblr.com/post/104341050738/2014.

Widner, Jennifer A. 1992. *The Rise of a Party State in Kenya: From Harambee! to Nyayo!* Berkeley: University of California.

Wiebe, Janyce, Theresa Wilson, Rebecca Bruce, Matthew Bell, and Melanie Martin. 2004. "Learning Subjective Language." *Computational Linguistics* 30(3):277–308.

Wilson, Andrew. 2005. *Virtual Politics: Faking Democracy in the Post-Soviet World*. New Haven: Yale University Press.

Wintrobe, Ronald. 1998. *The Political Economy of Dictatorship*. New York: Cambridge University Press.

Woldense, Josef. 2018. "The Ruler's Game of Musical Chairs: Shuffling during the Reign of Ethiopia's Last Emperor." *Social Networks* 52:154–166.

Wong, Edward. 2009. "Riots in Western China Amid Ethnic Tensions." *The New York Times* July 5.

Wong, Edward. 2014. "To Quell Unrest, Beijing Moves to Scatter Uighers across China." *The New York Times* November 6.

Wong, Linda. 2011. "Chinese Migrant Workers: Rights Attainment Deficits, Rights Consciousness and Personal Strategies." *The China Quarterly* 208:870–892.

Woolley, Samuel C. and Douglas Guilbeault. 2018. "United States: Manufacturing Consensus Online." In *Computational Propaganda: Political Parties, Politicians, and Political Manipulation on Social Media*, ed. Samuel C. Woolley and Philip N. Howard. New York: Oxford University Press, chapter 8, pp. 185–211.

Woolley, Samuel C. and Philip N. Howard, eds. 2018. *Computational Propaganda: Political Parties, Politicians, and Political Manipulation on Social Media*. New York: Oxford University Press.

World Health Organization. 2018. "Gambia: Maternal and Newborn Health." African Health Observatory.

Wright, Joseph. 2008. "Do Authoritarian Institutions Constrain? How Legislatures Affect Economic Growth and Investment." *American Journal of Political Science* 52(2):322–343.

Wright, Teresa. 2018. *Popular Protest in China*. New York: Polity Press.

Wu, Guoguang. 2010. "China in 2009: Muddling through Crises." *Asian Survey* 50(1):25–39.

Wu, H. Denis and John Hamilton. 2004. "US Foreign Correspondents Changes and Continuity at the Turn of the Century." *International Communication Gazette* 66(6):517–532.

Wuming District Trade Union Federation (武鸣区总工会). 2018. "Public Announcement [2018] No. 11: Notice of Nanning Wuming District Federation of Trade Unions on Doing a Good Job in the Subscription of the *Workers 'Daily* and *Guangxi Workers' Daily* in 2019. 南武工发〔2018〕11号-南宁市武鸣区总工会关于做好2019年度《工人日报》《广西工人报》征订工作的通知." November 28.

Xi, Jinping. 2014. "Speeches by Comrades Xi Jinping, Li Keqiang and Yu Zhengsheng at the Second Central Xinjiang Work Forum 《习近平、李克强、俞正声同志在第二次中央新疆工作座谈会上的讲话."

The Xinjiang Papers Document No. 2, https://uyghurtribunal.com/wp-content/uploads/2021/11/Transcript-Document-02.pdf.

Xiong, Hui and Jiang Zhang. 2018. "How Local Journalists Interpret and Evaluate Media Convergence: An Empirical Study of Journalists from Four Press Groups in Fujian." *International Communication Gazette* 80(1):87–115.

Xu, Xu. 2021. "To Repress or to Co-opt? Authoritarian Control in the Age of Digital Surveillance." *American Journal of Political Science* 65(2):309–325.

Xue, Melanie Meng. 2019. "Autocratic Rule and Social Capital: Evidence from Imperial China." London School of Economics and Political Science.

Yablokov, Ilya. 2015. "Conspiracy Theories as a Russian Public Diplomacy Tool: The Case of Russia Today (RT)." *Politics* 35(3–4):301–315.

Yan Lianke. 2013. "On China's State-Sponsored Amnesia." *The New York Times* April 1.

Yanagizawa-Drott, David. 2014. "Propaganda and Conflict: Evidence from the Rwandan Genocide." *Quarterly Journal of Economics* 129(4):1947–1994.

Yang, Dali L. 2017. "China's Troubled Quest for Order: Leadership, Organization and the Contradictions of the Stability Maintenance Regime." *Journal of Contemporary China* 26(103):35–53.

Yang, Fan. 2014. "Beijing Steps Up Security Ahead of Urumqi Riot Anniversary." *Radio Free Asia* July 3.

Yang, Yingzhi. 2018. "Shanghai Airport First to Launch Automated Clearance System Using Facial Recognition Technology." *South China Morning Post* October 15.

Yates, Douglas A. 1996. *The Rentier State in Africa: Oil Rent Dependency and Neocolonialism in the Republic of Gabon.* New York: Africa World Press.

Yin, Liangen and Xiaoyan Liu. 2014. "A Gesture of Compliance: Media Convergence in China." *Media, Culture & Society* 36(5):561–577.

Yong, Zhang. 2000. "From Masses to Audience: Changing Media Ideologies and Practices in Reform China." *Journalism Studies* 1(4):617–635.

Young, Crawford. 1994. *The African Colonial State in Comparative Perspective.* New Haven: Yale University Press.

Young, Lauren E. 2018. "The Psychology of State Repression: Fear and Dissent Decisions in Zimbabwe." *American Political Science Review* 113(1):140–155.

Yu, Frederick. 1964. *Mass Persuasion in Communist China.* New York: Praeger.

Yu, Fu-Lai Tony. 2017. "Neo-Mercantilist Policy and China's Rise as a Global Power." *Contemporary Chinese Political Economy and Strategic Relations* 3(3):1043–1073.

Yu, Tinghua. 2021. "Propaganda to Persuade." *Political Science Research and Methods* 9(2):438–444.

Yu, Yongding. 2010. "China's Policy Responses to the Global Financial Crisis." *East Asia Forum* January 24.

Yue, Xie. 2012. "The Political Logic of Weiwen in Contemporary China." *Issues & Studies* 48(3):1–41.

Zajonc, Robert. 1968. "Attitude Effects of Mere Exposure." *Journal of Personality and Social Psychology* 9(2):1–27.

Zajonc, Robert. 1980. "Feeling and Thinking: Preferences Need No Inferences." *American Psychologist* 35(2):151–175.

Zaller, John and Dennis Chiu. 2000. "Government's Little Helper: US Press Coverage of Foreign Policy Crises, 1946–1999." In *Decisionmaking in a Glass House*, ed. Brigitte Lebens Nacos, Robert Y. Shapiro, and Pierangelo Isernia. New York: Rowman & Littlefield, chapter 5, pp. 61–84.

Zaller, John R. 1992. *The Nature and Origins of Mass Opinion*. New York: Cambridge University Press.

Zhang, Juyan and Glen Cameron. 2004. "The Structural Transformation of China's Propaganda: An Ellulian Perspective." *Journal of Communication Management* 8(3):307–322.

Zhao, Yuezhi. 1998. *Media, Market, and Democracy in China: Between the Party Line and the Bottom Line*. Champaign: University of Illinois Press.

Zhao, Yuezhi. 2000a. "From Commercialization to Conglomeration: The Transformation of the Chinese Press within the Orbit of the Party State." *Journal of Communication* 50(2):3–26.

Zhao, Yuezhi. 2000b. "Watchdogs on Party Leashes: Contexts and Implications of Investigative Journalism in Post-Deng China." *Journalism Studies* 1(4):577–597.

Zhao, Yuezhi. 2008. *Communication in China: Political Economy, Power, and Conflict*. Lanham: Rowman & Littlefield.

Zhao Yusha. 2018. "'Sky Net' Tech Fast Enough to Scan Chinese Population in One Second: Report." *Global Times* March 25.

Zhong, Raymond. 2019. "Little Red App: Xi's Thoughts Are (Surprise!) a Hit in China." *The New York Times* February 14.

Zhong, Yang, Jie Chen, and John Scheb. 1998. "Mass Political Culture in Beijing: Findings from Two Public Opinion Surveys." *Asian Survey* 38(8):763–783.

Zhu, Boliang. 2016. "MNCs, Rents, and Corruption: Evidence from China." *American Journal of Political Science* 61(1):84–99.

Zhu, Ying. 2014. *Two Billion Eyes: The Story of China Central Television*. New York: New Press.

Zhu, Yuner and King-wa Fu. 2021. "Speaking up or Staying Silent? Examining the Influences of Censorship and Behavioral Contagion on Opinion (Non-) Expression in China." *Media & Society* 23(12):3634–3655.

Zhukov, Yuri M. and Roya Talibova. 2018. "Stalin's Terror and the Long-Term Political Effects of Mass Repression." *Journal of Peace Research* 55(2):267–283.

Ziegler, Charles E. 2017. "International Dimensions of Electoral Processes: Russia, the USA, and the 2016 Elections." *International Politics* 55(5):557–574.

Index

For EU product safety concerns, contact us at Calle de José Abascal, 56–1°,
28003 Madrid, Spain or eugpsr@cambridge.org.

www.ingramcontent.com/pod-product-compliance
Ingram Content Group UK Ltd.
Pitfield, Milton Keynes, MK11 3LW, UK
UKHW010248140625
459647UK00013BA/1722